Early Childhood Experiences in Language Arts

Early Childhood Educators — Select from these other 1990 Delmar publications for the most current coverage of issues:

The World of Child Development: Conception to Adolescence, by George S. Morrison

Creative Activities for Young Children, 4th Edition, by Mary Mayesky

Creative Resources for the Early Childhood Classroom, by Judy Herr and Yvonne Libby

Math and Science for Young Children, by Rosalind Charlesworth and Karen K. Lind

Infants and Toddlers: Curriculum and Teaching, 2nd Edition, by LaVisa Cam Wilson

Positive Child Guidance, by Darla Miller

A Practical Guide to Solving Preschool Behavior Problems, 2nd Edition, by Eva Essa

Administration of Schools for Young Children, 3rd Edition, by Phillis and Donald Click

Developing and Administering a Child Care Center, 2nd Edition, by Dorothy June Sciarra and Anne G. Dorsey

Developmental Evaluations of Software for Young Children, by Susan W. Haugland and Daniel D. Shade

Early Childhood Experiences in Language Arts

Emerging Literacy

4th Edition

Jeanne M. Machado

Delmar Publishers Inc.®

To my ever-encouraging husband, and Danielle, Romana, Claire, Scott, and Patrick. Each is a uniquely special gift in my life. And to my father who always saw the best in me.

Cover photos: Mark Roberts

Delmar Staff

Editor-in-Chief: Mark W. Huth
Executive Editor: Susan L. Newkirk
Associate Editor: Jay Whitney
Editing Manager: Barbara A. Christie
Production Supervisor: Karen Seebald
Design Coordinator: Susan Mathews

10 9 8 7 6 5 4 3 2 1

Printed in the United States of America
Published simultaneously in Canada
by Nelson Canada
A Division of The Thomson Corporation

Library of Congress Cataloging-in-Publication Data

Machado, Jeanne M.
Early childhood experiences in language arts: emerging literacy /
    Jeanne M. Machado. — 4th ed.
    p.   cm.
    Includes bibliographical references.
    ISBN 0-8273-3504-0 (pbk.). — ISBN 0-8273-3505-9 (instructor's
    guide)
    1. Language arts (Preschool)   I. Title.
LB1140.5.L3M33   1990
372.6 — dc20   89-17023
                                                                   CIP

Contents

SECTION 1 LANGUAGE DEVELOPMENT —
EMERGING LITERACY IN THE YOUNG CHILD

SECTION 2 DEVELOPING LANGUAGE ARTS PROGRAMS

SECTION 3 LISTENING — LITERATE BEGINNINGS

SECTION 4 INTRODUCING LITERATURE

SECTION 5 SPEECH GROWTH — CONVERSATION,
EXPRESSION AND DRAMATIZATION

SECTION 6 WRITING — PRINT AWARENESS AND USE

SECTION 7 READING — A LANGUAGE ART

SECTION 8 SETTINGS PROMOTING LITERACY — HOME AND SCHOOL

NOTICE TO THE READER

Preface

EARLY CHILDHOOD EXPERIENCES IN LANGUAGE ARTS: Emerging Literacy is a state-of-the-art teacher training text designed to help those working in the early childhood education field provide an opportunity-rich program full of interesting, appropriate, and developmental language arts activities. It is both a practical "how-to" manual and collection of resources that includes a large number of classic, tried and true activities.

The first few units present a detailed account of language acquisition, young children's emerging communicative capacities, growth milestones, and age-level characteristics (infancy through preschool) along with suggested professional techniques promoting each child's self-esteem and potential. Because a comprehensive, dynamically planned early childhood language arts curriculum consists of four broad interrelated areas — speaking (oral), listening, writing, and reading, each is fully explored and described in a separate text section. It is hoped that confidence and skill gained by the reader will help to provide young children with an enthusiastic, knowledgeable teacher-companion who enjoys and encourages them in their discovery of the language arts.

Changes in this Fourth Edition emphasize the child's emerging literacy and exposure to language play. Infant and toddler units have been expanded and are intended to increase the reader's understanding of infant and toddler communicational abilities, and the role of adult behavior in promoting language growth. Special attention has been given to ways of providing the child with language-rich environments and enthusiastic, supportive teachers who are dynamic, observant companions offering enjoyable language arts experiences and opportunities. Fine literature and classics appropriate to the child's age level are recommended, as in the previous edition. Additional stories, finger plays, flannel board activities, and dramatizations have been included. As in the previous edition, an integrated instructional approach that highlights the connections between the four language arts areas — speaking, listening, writing, and reading — is emphasized here. A new view of young children's progress in the understanding and use of print in daily life has been added, along with the generally recognized stages of development of writing skills. In an extended discussion of the recent emphasis on early reading instruction, the author advocates dedication to more traditional methods — play and encouraging children's understanding of language — which provide basic skills. The whole-language approach is reviewed. Children's curiosity, and their natural ability to become communicators by continually trying to make sense of their experience, is described, and is intended to give the reader increased confidence in the child's ability to learn. The value of the teacher's attention to the needs of children during classroom discussions and attention to the way that children express ideas is given greater emphasis in this edition.

Each section begins with a special feature that is designed to stimulate discussions as well as invite the students to read the following units. Included are new features entitled "Mother Goose," "Who's that Reader?," *Act One, Millions of Cats,* "Young Children's Acquisition of Offensive Speech," "On Listening to the Language of Children," "What is the Whole

Language Movement and Will It Affect Early Childhood Teachers?," and "Ready...Set...
Role: Parents Role in Early Reading."

An extensive appendix with numerous classroom ideas and activities and lists of additional
resources appear at the end of the text. Traditional learning aids, such as learning objectives,
review questions, and learning activities, have been retained from the previous edition.

ABOUT THE AUTHOR

The author's experience in the early childhood education field has included full-time
assignment as community college instructor and department chairperson. Her duties
included supervision of early childhood education students at two on-campus laboratory
child development centers at San Jose City College and Evergreen Valley College, as well
as child centers in the local community. Her teaching responsibilities encompassed early
childhood education, child development, and parenting courses.

She received her MA from San Jose State University and her vocational community
college life credential with coursework from the University of California at Berkeley. Her
experience includes working as a teacher and director in public early childhood programs, parent cooperative programs, and a self-owned and operated private preschool.
Ms. Machado is an active participant in several professional organizations that relate to the
education and well-being of young children and their families. She is a past president of
CCCECE (California Community College Early Childhood Educators), and Peninsula
Chapter of the California Association for the Education of Young Children. Her authoring
efforts (1984), with Dr. Helen Meyer-Botnarescue of the University of California at
Hayward, produced a new text for student teachers entitled *Early Childhood Practicum Guide*.

Acknowledgments

The author wishes to express her appreciation to the following individuals and agencies.

Nancy Martin, Jayne Musladin, David Palmer, Ann Lane, and Joseph Tardi Associates for the photographs

Theresa and Caryn Macri for appearing in photos for Unit 1

The students at San Jose City College, AA Degree Program in Early Childhood Education

Arbor Hill Day Care Center, Albany, NY

San Jose City College Child Development Center Staff

Marcy Pederson of Magic Moments

Evergreen Valley College Child Development Center personnel, San Jose, CA

James Lick Children's Center, Eastside High School District, San Jose, CA

Lowell Children's Center, San Jose Unified School District, San Jose, CA

Piedmont Hills Preschool, San Jose, CA

Pineview Preschool, Albany, NY

St. Elizabeth's Day Home, San Jose, CA

Sunnymont Nursery School, Cupertino, CA

John Wiley and Sons, Inc. for permission to use figures 3-11 and 13-1 from *Psychology of the Child* by R. I. Watson and H. C. Lindgren, 1973.

K. Romana Machado and Coleen Colbert for research and technical assistance.

Jay Whitney, Barbara Christie, and the staff at Delmar Publishers, Inc.

Fellow colleagues, Cia McClung and Mary Conroy, whose supportive assistance and understanding have been of immeasurable help.

In addition, special appreciation is due the reviewers involved in the development of the Fourth Edition:

Sherri Griffin, Central Methodist College

Sue Miles, Waubonsee Community College

Cindy Leigh, University of Mississippi

To The Student

Since you are a unique, caring individual who has chosen an important career, early childhood teaching, this text is intended to help you discover and share your innate and developing language arts gifts and talents. Create your own activities, author, when possible, your own "quality" literary, oral, and writing opportunities for young children. Share your specialness and those language-arts-related experiences that excite and delight you both now and when you were a child.

In this text, I urge you to become a skilled interactor and conversationalist, "a subtle opportunist," getting the most possible out of each child-adult situation, while also enjoying these daily exchanges yourself.

Collect, select, construct, and practice those appropriate activities you can present with enthusiasm. Your joy in language arts becomes their joy. A file box and/or binder collection of ideas, completed sets, patterns, games, and so on, carefully made and stored for present or future use is suggested. Filling young children's days with developmental, worthwhile experiences will prove a challenge, and your collection of ideas and teaching visual aids will grow and be adapted over the years.

Suggested activities and review sections at the end of units give immediate feedback on your grasp of unit main ideas and techniques. You'll find review-question answers in the back of the book.

In this text, I attempt to help you become increasingly skilled at what you may do well and help you grow in professional competence. Since I'm growing too, I invite your suggestions and comments so that in future revisions I can refine and improve this text's value to students.

You can make a difference in young children's lives. Ideally, this text will help you become the kind of teacher that matters.

Section 1

Language Development

Emerging Literacy in the Young Child

In this section, the child's communicational skills growth is reviewed, giving the reader a background of information highlighting major influences and milestones from infancy through the late preschool period. Teacher techniques are recommended to those working with infants and toddlers. Unit 4 describes growth systems that relate to children's use of language and speech and provides a general overview of concurrent developmental occurrences.

MOTHER GOOSE

They are the beloved heritage of Nobody-Really-Knows how many countries or how many centuries.

Here in America we are likely to lump them all together under a single heading and call them the "Mother Goose" rhymes.

The British refer to them, more accurately, as nursery rhymes — or "melodies" or "songs" or "jingles."

Some, undoubtedly, are rhymes that were created by just plain "folk" — rhymes to be repeated by their children while playing active games, from knee-dandling to skip-rope, from hoop-rolling and ball-bouncing to seesaw and the ride on the rocking-horse.

Akin to these are the counting-out rhymes, like "Eena, Meena, Mina, Mo," whose purpose, even today, is to designate which of a group of children shall be singled out as "It."

Then there are the rhymes that are supposed to help young children learn numbers, letters, and designations — the toe-counting and the feature naming rhymes, to begin at the very beginning.

Other "Mother Goose" rhymes are lullabies, others are prayers, others are drinking and love songs.

Still other "Mother Goose" rhymes are riddles and "catches" and tongue twisters. Still others are charms and incantations, proverbs in verse and weather lore in doggerel. Still others are simple humor — often nonsense humor — pleasantly packaged as a verse, often in the limerick form. And still others are fragments of ballads commemorating actual occurrences of at least local importance.

Finally, there are those rhymes which well may be, as many earnest scholars insist they are "political diatribes, religious philippics, and popular street songs, embodying comedies, tragedies and love episodes of many great historical personages, lavishly interspersed with English and Scotch folklore flung out with dramatic abandon." [1]

[1] William S. Baring-Gould and Ceil Baring Gould, *The Annotated Mother Goose* (New York: Bramhall House, 1962) 11–12.

UNIT 1

Beginnings of Communication

OBJECTIVES

After studying this unit, you should be able to

- describe one theory of human language acquisition.
- identify factors that influence language development.
- discuss the reciprocal behaviors of infants, parents, and caregivers.
- list suggested child-adult play activities for infants 1 to 6 months and infants 6 to 12 months.

Each child is a unique combination of inherited traits and environmental influences. From birth, infants can be described as communicators interested in their surroundings.

Researchers confirm that newborns seem to assimilate information immediately. Technology can now monitor the slightest physical changes in breathing, heartbeat, eye movements, and sucking rhythm and rates. Tronich (1987) suggests that babies begin learning how to carry on conversations quickly and that sucking patterns produce a rhythm that mimics give-and-take dialogues. He notes that infants respond to very specific maternal signals, including tone of voice, looks, and head movements. Babies gesture and make sounds and seem to hold up their ends of conversations. Infants demonstrate an alert state when body activity is suppressed, and energy seems to be channeled into seeing and hearing (Klaus and Klaus, 1985).

"Gaze coupling," witnessed in young infants' eye contacts with their mothers, is seen as one of their first steps in establishing communication (Gleason, 1987). Infants can shut off background noises and pay attention to slight changes in adult voice sounds (Eyler, 1987).

The qualities a child inherits from parents and the events that occur in the child's life help shape the child's language development. In the short four to five years after birth, the child's speech becomes purposeful and adultlike. This growing language skill is a useful tool for satisfying needs and exchanging thoughts, hopes, and dreams with others. As ability grows, the child understands and uses more of the resources of oral and recorded human knowledge, and is well on the way to becoming a literate being.

The natural capacity to categorize, invent, and remember information aids the child's language acquisition. Although unique among the species because of the ability to speak, human beings are not the only ones who can communicate. Birds and animals imitate sounds and signals and are believed to communicate. For instance, chimpanzees exposed to experimental language techniques (American Sign Language, specially equipped machines, and plastic tokens) have surprised researchers with their language abilities. Some have learned to use symbols and follow linguistic rules with a sophistication that rivals that of some two-year-olds (de Villers, 1979). Researchers continue to probe the limits of their capabilities. However, a basic difference between human beings and other species exists. It is nestled separately in the human brain and encompasses a diverse set of talents, including language aptitude, symbol making, and communicational abilities (Ornstein and Sobel, 1987).

The human face becomes the most significantly important communicational factor for the infant, and the facial expressions, which are varied and complex, eventually will be linked to infant body reactions (interior and exterior). Emotional reactions often involve cardiovascular and gastrointestinal systems (Ornstein and Sobel, 1987). Parents and caregivers strive to interpret the infant's state of well-being from reading the infant's face and postures, as infants also search faces in the world around them.

Figure 1-1 identifies a number of signals used by infants and their probable meanings. Response and intentional behavior become apparent as infants age and gain experience:

> The infant, for his part, will respond initially with various pre-programmed proto-social gestures like smiling, intent and interested looking, crying, satisfied sucking or snuggling, soon to be followed by active demanding and attention-seeking patterns in which attempts to attract and solicit caregiver attention rapidly become unmistakable, deliberate and intentional. (Newson, 1979)

Researchers are studying the roles of facial expressions, gestures, and body movements in human social communication. Early smilelike expressions may occur minutes after birth and are apparent in the faces of sleeping babies whose facial expressions seem to constantly change. Totally blind infants have been observed smiling as young as two months of age in response to a voice or tickling (Freedman, 1964).

Speech is much more complex than simple parroting or primitive social functioning. The power of language enables humans to dominate other life forms. The ability to use language creatively secured our survival by giving us a vehicle to both understand and transmit knowledge and to work cooperatively with others (Hoy and Somer, 1974). Language facilitates peaceful solutions between people.

DEFINITIONS

Language, as used in this text, refers to a system of intentional communication through sounds, signs (gestures), or symbols that are understandable to others. The language-development process includes both sending and receiving information. *Input* (receiving) comes before *output* (sending); input is organized mentally by an individual long before there is decipherable output.

Communication is a broader term, defined as giving and receiving information, signals, or messages. A person can communicate with or receive communications from animals, infants, or foreign speakers in a variety of ways. Even a whistling teakettle sends a message that someone can understand. Infants appear to be "in tune," focused on the human voice, hours after birth.

INFANT ACTS	PROBABLE MEANING
Turning head and opening mouth	Feeling hungry
Quivering lips	Adjusting to stimuli
Sucking on hand, fist, thumb	Calming self, feeling overstimulated
Averting eyes	Tuning out awhile
Turning away	Needing to calm down
Yawning	Feeling tired or stressed
Looking wide-eyed	Feeling happy
Cooing	Feeling happy
Appearing dull with unfocused eyes	Feeling overloaded, needing rest
Waving hands	Feeling excited
Moving tongue in and out	Feeling upset or imitating

FIGURE 1-1 Born communicators

FIGURE 1-2 Communications between children in a family start early.

INFLUENCES ON DEVELOPMENT

A child's ability to communicate involves an integration of body parts and systems allowing hearing, understanding, organizing, and using language. Most children accomplish the task quickly and easily, but many factors influence the learning of language (figure 1-2).

Klaus and Klaus (1985) describe an infant's life within the womb, based on ultrasound studies, as "...floating in his private island...after sleeping he opens his eyes, yawns, kicks and rolls to his other side...brings his fingers to his face and sucks his thumb...he can hear his mother's voice...he stops to listen...ever present is the lullaby of his mother's heartbeat...." And immediately after birth, "Hands are stroking and cradling him...He can hear his mother's soothing familiar heartbeat...voices are much clearer and closer...he relaxes...he mouths his fists making small sucking sounds." Current research suggests that babies instinctively turn their heads to face the source of sound and can remember sounds heard in utero. This has promoted mothers talking to, singing to, and reading classic literature and poetry to the unborn. Research has yet to document evidence of the benefits of these activities.

Of all sounds, nothing attracts and holds the attention of infants as well as the human voice — especially the higher-pitched female voice. Rhythmic sounds and continuous, steady tones soothe some infants. A variety of sound-making soothers are now marketed and designed to attach to cribs or are placed within plush stuffed animals. Most emit a staticlike or heartbeat sound or combination of the two. Too much sound in the infant's environment, especially loud, excessive, or high-volume sounds, may have the opposite effect. Excessive household noise can come from television sets, radios, and stereos. Some mothers report that at about age five to eight months their children have an interest in lively, colorful television programs, such as Sesame Street, and seem to watch for reasonably long periods, sitting quietly and focused while doing so. Many have described sensory-overload situations when infants try to turn off sensory input by turning away and somehow blocking that which is at the moment overwhelming, whether the stimuli are mechanical or human.

Although hearing ability is not fully developed at birth, newborns can hear moderately loud sounds, and can distinguish different pitches (Weiser, 1982). Auditory acuity develops swiftly (figure 1-3). Within a few weeks of birth, infants inhibit motor activity in response to strong auditory stimuli or when listening to the human voice. This is seen by some researchers as an indication that infants are "constitutionally geared to orient their whole bodies toward any signal that arouses interest" (Junker, 1979). Researchers have concluded that infants' body responses to human verbalizations are a rudimentary form of speech development.

Sensory-motor development, which involves the use of sense organs and the coordination of motor systems (body muscles and parts), is vital to language acquisition. Sense organs gather information through sight, hearing, smelling, tasting, and touching (figure 1-4). These sense-organ impressions of people, objects, and life encounters are sent to the brain, and each *perception* (impression received through the senses) is recorded and stored, serving as a base for future oral and written language. Sensory-motor tasks are covered in greater depth in Unit 5.

Newborns and infants are no longer viewed as passive, unresponsive "mini" humans. Instead, infants are seen as dynamic individuals, preprogrammed to learn, with functioning sensory capacities, motor abilities, and a wondrous built-in curiosity. Parents and caregivers can be described as guides who open opportunity and act with newborns rather than on them.

AGE	PERCEPTIONS
By 3 months	Differentiates tonal and nontonal sounds
	Differentiates pitch and timbre
	Has auditory fixation to adult's verbalizations
	Looks for source of sound
	Soothed by soft, rhythmical sounds
By 6 months	Differentiates tones of voice
	Differentiates speech sounds
	Likes to "talk" to self
	Coos and gurgles
By 9 months	Associates sound with its source (toy or person)
	Enjoys listening to musical sounds
	Attempts "conversation"
	Babbles
By 12 months	Imitates adult vocalizations
	Responds rhythmically to music
	Knows own name
	Knows name of other persons
	Understands more than verbalizes
	Tries to comply with verbal requests

FIGURE 1-3 Auditory perception during the first 12 months *(From Group Care and Education of Infants and Toddlers by Margaret Weiser, © 1982. C. V. Mosby Co., copyright © 1985 Merrill Publishing Co., Columbus, Ohio. Reprinted by permission.)*

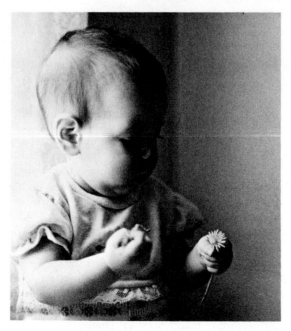

FIGURE 1-4 Look at this exploring concentration.

A child's social and emotional environments play a leading role in both the quality and quantity of beginning language. Brazelton (1979) describes communicative neonatal behaviors that evoke tender feelings in adults:

> When the stimulus is the human voice, the neonate not only searches for the observer's face but, when he finds it, his face and eyes become wide, soft and eager, and he may crane his neck, lifting his chin gently toward the source of the voice. As he does so, his body tension gradually increases, but he is quietly inactive. A nurturing adult feels impelled to respond to these signals by picking the baby up to cuddle him.

Human children have the longest infancy among animals. Our social dependency is crucial to our individual survival and growth (Ornstein and Sobel, 1987). Much learning occurs through contact and interaction with others in family and social settings (figure 1-5). Basic attitudes towards life, self, and other people form early, as life's pleasures and pains are

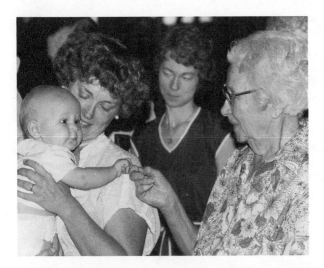

FIGURE 1-5 Positive experiences and interactions are important for language acquisition. *(From* Early Childhood Practicum Guide, *by Machado and Meyer, © 1984 by Delmar Publishers Inc.)*

experienced. The young child depends on parents and other caregivers to provide what is needed for growth and *equilibrium* (a balance achieved when consistent care is given and needs are satisfied). This side of a child's development has been called the *affective sphere*, referring to the affectionate feelings (or lack of them) shaped through experience with others (figure 1-6). As Halliday (1979) observes "at no stage is language an individual matter."

Textbooks often speak indirectly about the infant's need to feel loved...consistently loved...using words like nurturance, closeness, caring, and commitment. The primary goal of parents and caregivers should be handling the infant and satisfying the child's physical needs in a way that leads to mutual love and a bond of trust. This bond, often called *attachment*, is an event of utmost importance to the infant's progress. It is formed through mutual gratification of needs and reciprocal communication influenced by the infant's growing cognitive ability. The two-way nature of the attachment process, referred to also as bonding, is emphasized by Friedrich (1986):

This extremely important emotional interplay, often described as 'bonding,' is a combination of love and play, but it is now seen as something else, a kind of wordless dialogue. The baby not only understands what the mother is communicating,

FIGURE 1-6 Loving care and attention in the early years can influence language development.

or not communicating, but is trying to tell her things, if she will only listen.

The specialness an infant feels for its mother later spreads to include a group of beloved family members, but for awhile it's "mother over all others." If an attachment bond is evident and consistent care continues, the child thrives.

Newborns seem to have an individual preferred level of arousal, *a moderation level*, neither too excited nor too bored. They seek change and stimulation and seem to search out newness. Each human may possess an optimum level of arousal — a state when learning is enhanced and pleasure peaks. Mothers serve as buffers to keep infants at moderate levels of arousal, neither too high nor too low (Kaye, 1979). One can perceive three states during an older infant's waking hours: (1) a state in which everything is all right and life is interesting, (2) a reactive state to something familiar or unfamiliar, when an observer can see an alert "what's that?" or "who's that?" response (figure 1-7), or (3) a crying or agitated state. One can observe a switch from

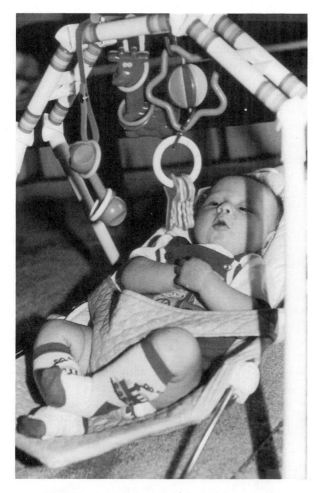

FIGURE 1-7 Look at this infant's alert, focused stare.

The natural curiosity of humans requires discussion here. Curiosity can be defined as a compulsion (drive) to make sense of life's happenings. Exploring, searching, groping, and probing by infants shifts from random to controlled movements as the infant ages. Burton White (1978) speaks about the period starting at about eight months of age as an age when infants possess insatiable appetites for new things — touching, manipulating, and trying to become familiar with everything that attracts them (figure 1-8). Increasing motor skill allows greater possibilities for exploration. Skilled infant caregivers are kept busy trying to provide novelty, variety, and companionship, while monitoring safety. The curiosity of infants seems to wane only when they are tired, hungry, or ill.

Cultural and social forces touch young lives with group attitudes, values, and beliefs. These have a great impact on a child's language development. Some cultures, for instance, expect children to look downward when adults speak, showing respect by this action. Other cultures make extensive use of gestures and signaling. Still others seem to have limited vocabularies. Cultural values and factors can indeed affect language acquisition.

feeling safe or happy to unsafe or unhappy in a matter of seconds. Loud noises can startle the infant and elicit distressed crying. Infants control input and turn away or turn off by moving eyes and head or body and by becoming fussy or falling asleep.

Another important factor that is related to all others is the child's mental maturity or ability to think. The ages, stages, and sequences of increased mental capacity are very closely related to language development. Yet, at times, language skill and intellect seem to be growing independently, with one or the other developing at a faster rate. The relationship of intelligence and language has been a subject of debate for a long time. Most scholars, however, agree these two areas are closely associated.

FIGURE 1-8 Touching and exploring comes naturally.

CURRENT THEORIES OF LANGUAGE EMERGENCE

Many scholars, philosophers, linguists, and researchers have tried to pinpoint exactly how language is learned. Most early childhood educators believe that hearing and imitating are key factors, as well as the child's realization that speech is useful in getting what he or she wants and needs. People in major fields of study — human development, linguistics, sociology, psychology, anthropology, speech-language pathology, and animal study (zoology) — have contributed to current theory. The following are major theoretical positions.

Behaviorist (or Stimulus-Response) Theory

Theorists taking this position emphasize language is only partially learned through imitation. As parents reward, correct, ignore, or punish the young child's communication, they exert considerable influence over both the quantity and quality of language usage and the child's attitudes toward communicating. Under this theory, the reactions of the people in a child's environment have an important effect on a child's language development. In other words, positive, neutral, and/or negative reinforcement plays a key role in the emergence of communicational behaviors.

The child's sounds and sound combinations are thought to be uttered partly as imitation and partly at random or on impulse, without pattern or meaning. The child's utterances may grow, seem to stand still, or become stifled, depending on feedback from others. This theory is attributed to the work of B. F. Skinner, a pioneer researcher in the field of learning theory.

Predetermined Theory

Under this theory, language acquisition is considered innate (a predetermined human capacity). Each new being is believed to possess a mental ability that enables that being to master any language. Chomsky (1968), a linguistic researcher, theorizes that each person has an individual Language Acquisition Device (LAD). Chomsky also theorizes that this device (capacity) has several sets of language system rules (grammar) common to all known languages. As the child lives within a favorable family climate, his or her perceptions spark the device, and the child learns the "mother tongue." Imitation or reinforcement are not ruled out as additional influences.

Chomsky notes two- and three-year-olds can utter understandable, complicated sentences that they have never heard. The child has to possess either remarkable thinking skills to do so or very special skills as a language learner. Chomsky favors the latter explanation. Theorists who support this position note the infant's ability to babble sounds and noises used in languages the child has never heard.

Cognitive-Transactional Theory

Under a third theory, language acquisition develops from basic social and emotional drives. Children are naturally active, curious, and adaptive and are shaped by transactions with the people in their environment. Drives stem from a need for love and care, and the need prompts language acquisition. Children are described as reactors to the human social contact that is so crucial to their survival and well-being. Children's views of the world consist of their mental impressions, built as new life events are fit into existing ones or as categories are created for new events. Language is an integral part of living; consequently, children seek to fit language into some pattern that allows understanding. With enough exposure and with functioning sensory receiving systems, children slowly crack the "code" and eventually become fluent speakers. The works of Jean Piaget, Jerome Bruner, and J. McVicker Hunt have promoted a wide acceptance of this theory by early childhood professionals.

Maturational (Normative) Theory

The writings of Arnold Gesell and his colleagues represent the position that children are primarily a product of genetic inheritance, and environmental influences are secondary. Children are seen as moving from one predictable stage to another with "readiness" the precursor of actual learning. This position was widely accepted in the 1960s when linguists studied children in less than desirable circumstances and discovered consistent patterns of language development. Using this theory as a basis for planning instruction for young children includes (1) identifying predictable stages of growth in language abilities and (2) offering appropriate readiness activities to aid children's graduation to the next higher level.

OTHER THEORIES

There is no all-inclusive theory of language acquisition substantiated by research; rather, there is some truth in each possibility. Many relationships and mysteries are still under study. Current teaching practices involve many different styles and approaches to language arts activities. Some teachers may prefer using techniques in accord with one particular theory. One goal common among educators is the desire to provide instruction that encourages social and emotional development while also offering activities and opportunities in a warm, language-rich, supportive classroom, center, or home. Eveloff (1977) identified three major prerequisites for a child's development and language acquisition. They are (1) thinking ability, (2) a central nervous system allowing sophisticated perception, and (3) loving care. These are all present if children are healthy and in quality day-care and preschool facilities.

This text promotes many challenging activities that go beyond simple rote memorization or passive participation. It offers an enriched program of literary experience that encourages children to think and use their abilities to relate and share their thoughts.

Dr. Maria Montessori, well-known for her work with young children, described a sequence of language development gathered from her observations (figure 1-9). It is offered here to stimulate your observation of young children, and to urge you to be consciously alert to children's emerging abilities.

COMMUNICATIVE BEGINNINGS IN INFANCY

Development of the ability to communicate begins even before the child's birth. Prenatal environment plays an important role, and factors such as the mother's emotional and physical health and nutrition can affect the development and health of the unborn. These factors may also lead to complications later in the child's language-learning capabilities.

Newborns quickly make their needs known. They cry and their parents respond. The parents feed, hold, and keep their children warm and dry. The sounds of parents' footsteps or voices, and their caring touch, often stop the babies' crying. Babies learn to anticipate.

1. Individual sounds.

2. Syllables.

3. Simple words, often doubled syllables like "dada." This is when the child first is said to speak, because the sound he produces communicates an idea.

4. Understanding and saying words that are the names of objects (nouns).

5. Understanding and saying words that refer to qualities of objects named (adjectives).

6. Understanding and saying words that refer to the relationship of objects named.

7. Explosion into language (verbs and the exact form of nouns and adjectives, including prefixes and suffixes).

8. The forms for present, past, and future tenses of verbs, use of the pronoun as a word that "stands in place of" a name.

9. Construction of sentences with mutually dependent parts.

FIGURE 1-9 Montessori sequence of language acquisition (*From* The Discovery of the Child, *by Maria Montessori, translated by M. Joseph Costelloe, Notre Dame, IN: Fides Publishers, 1967.*)

The sense perceptions they receive begin to be connected to stored impressions of the past.

Young infants seem to be "inside" themselves at first, and consciously smile after a period dominated by watching (Johnson, 1987). Lewis and Rosenblum (1974) picture infants as very powerful in shaping relationships with significant caregivers.

An infant can perceive from maternal behavior a willingness to learn from the infant and respond to his or her patterns of behavior and rhythms of hunger. This is accomplished by close observation of infant vocal and body clues, which indicate the child's state of being (Bateson, 1979). At some point, the mother notes her infant's gaze. This usually triggers a type of brief conversation:

...once a pattern of mutual gazing is established, the mother tends to behave in a given way within mutual gaze episodes. This would seem to be the case with proto-conversation: mutual gazing sets the stage for maternal vocalizations which set up the possibility of an unfolding process of learning, probably strengthened by selective attention. (Bateson, 1979)

The infant is a noisemaking person from birth. The child's repertoire includes sucking noises, lip smacking, sneezes, coughs, hiccups, and, of course, different types of cries. As an infant grows, he or she makes vocal noises, such as cooing after feeding. During feeding, slurping and guzzling sounds indicate eagerness and pleasure. Cooing seems to be related to a child's comfort and satisfaction (figure 1-10). During cooing, sounds are relaxed, low-pitched, and gurgly vowel sounds that are made in an open-mouthed way; for example, e (as in see), e (get), a (at), ah, and o, oo, ooo. The infant appears to be in control of this sound making. Discomfort, by comparison, produces consonant sounds, made in a tense manner with lips partly closed.

Parents who attend to infant crying promptly and who feel that crying stems from legitimate needs rather than attempts to control tend to produce contented, trusting infants. Advice for parents of colicky babies consists of holding and carrying the infant more fre-

quently in an effort to soothe. Colic is another human condition not fully understood.

Infants differ in numerous ways from the moment of birth. Freedman's research (1979) concludes that significant ethnic differences and similarities exist in a newborn's reactions to various stimuli. However, in most cases, milestones in language development are reached at about the same age and in a recognizable sequence.

Babies learn quickly that communicating is worthwhile because it results in action on the part of another. Have you ever watched a baby gaze intently into his or her parent's eyes? Somehow, the child knows that this is a form of communication and is avidly looking for clues. If the parent speaks, the baby's entire body seems to respond to the rhythm of the human voice. The reciprocal nature of the interactions aids development. Clarke-Stewart (1981) reported a high degree of relationship between a mother's responsiveness and her child's language competence. In a longitudinal study of infants from 9 to 18 months of age, the more responsive mothers promoted greater language facility and growth.

Infants quickly recognize subtle differences in sounds. A parent's talk and touch increases sound making. Condon and Sanders (1982) observed infants moving their arms and legs in synchrony to the rhythms of human speech. Random noises, tappings, and disconnected vowel sounds didn't produce that behavior.

There's a difference between people in an infant's life. Some talk and touch. Others show delight. Some pause after speaking and seem to wait for a response. The child either "locks on" to the conversationalist, focusing totally, or breaks eye contact and looks away. It's almost as though the infant controls what he or she wants to receive. Of course, hunger, tiredness, and other factors influence this behavior also and may stop the child's interest in being social.

Research continues to uncover response capabilities in both infants and their parents that have previously been overlooked. In one experiment, newborns learned to suck on an artificial nipple hooked to a switch that turned on a brief portion of recorded speech or music. They did not suck as readily when they heard instrumental music as when they heard a human voice (de Villiers, 1982).

The special people in the infant's life adopt observ-

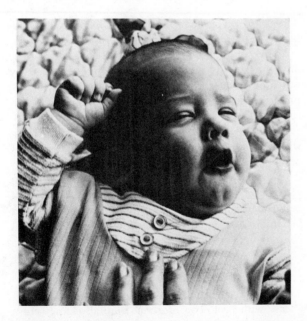

FIGURE 1-10 Cooing is related to a child's comfort level.

able behaviors when "speaking" to the child, just as the child seems to react in special ways to their attention. Mothers sometimes raise their voice pitch to a falsetto, shorten sentences, simplify their syntax, use nonsense sounds, and maintain prolonged eye contact during playful interchanges. Infants display a wide-eyed, playful, and bright-faced attitude toward their mothers and fathers (Brazelton, 1982). A mutual readiness to respond to each other appears built-in to warm relationships. The infant learns that eye contact can hold and maintain attention and that looking away usually terminates both verbal and nonverbal episodes.

CRYING

Crying is an infant's primary method of communication. Cries can be weak or hardy and provide clues to the infant's general health (Lester, 1976). Crying or calling out is the only way an infant or animal has of affecting its situation of need or discomfort (Buchwald, 1984). Infants begin early in life to control the emotional content of their cries. Many parents feel they can recognize different types of crying...sleepy, frightened, hungry, and so on, especially if infant body movements are observed concurrently. Researchers have recently discovered parents do indeed accurately infer the intensity of an infant's emotional state from the sound of the cry itself, even if the baby is not visually observed. Even adults inexperienced with infants seem to possess this ability (Hostetler, 1988).

Child development specialists advise adult alertness and responsiveness to minimize crying. Crying will take place in the best of circumstances, and current research has indicated that there are some positive aspects of crying, including stress reduction, elimination of toxin in tears, and reestablishment of physical and emotional balance (Ornstein and Sobel, 1987). However, although crying may have its benefits, it is not recommended that infants be left to cry, but rather that adults continue to attempt to soothe and satisfy infant's needs.

Lester (1983) describes the direct and indirect effects of an infant's crying:

Crying has direct and indirect effects on the subsequent developmental outcome of the infant. Direct effects are due to the cry as a measure of the integrity of the nervous system; indirect effects

are due to the cry as a determinant of parent-infant interaction, which in turn affects the cognitive and socio-emotional development of the infant.

A baby's crying may cause strong feelings in some adults, including anger, frustration, irritation, guilt, and rejection. Successful attempts at soothing the infant and stopping the crying give both the infant and the caregiver satisfaction, feelings of competence, and a possible sense of pleasure. When out-of-sorts infants cease crying, usually alertness, attentiveness, and visual scanning happen and/or they fall asleep. Infant-parent interaction has been described as "a rhythmic drama," "a reciprocal ballet," and "a finely tuned symphony." All these touch on the beauty and coordination of sound-filled moments between parent and child. Crying is a helpful mechanism promoting maintenance of physical satisfaction and comfort. It releases energy and tension. There is a change in cries as the infant ages:

In the first months, we see a change from crying as a response to physiological demands, to crying as part of the development of affective expression. Toward the end of the first year (seven to nine months), a second biobehavioral shift occurs, characterized by major cognitive and affective changes. (Lester, 1983)

Emotions are expressed frequently in crying as the infant nears his or her first birthday. Fear, frustration, uneasiness with novelty or newness, separation from loved ones, and other strong emotions can provoke crying through childhood and beyond.

Infant care providers in group programs engage in frank staff discussions concerning infant crying. Normal and natural staff feelings concerning crying need open discussion so strategies can be devised in the best interests of both the infants and staff members. Lots of techniques exist to minimize crying and also to monitor the crying levels of individual infants so that health or developmental problems can be spotted quickly.

SMILING AND LAUGHING

Smiling is seen in some babies who are only a few days old. Some smile in their sleep. This type of smiling seems to be tied to inner stimuli. True smiling can occur before six months of age, and it's usually associated with a caretaker's facial, auditory, or motor stimuli. Laughter may occur as early as four months of age, and is thought to be a good predictor of cognitive growth and the child's level of involvement in what the child is doing (Spieker, 1987). Spieker suggests the earlier the baby laughs, the higher the developmental level. In the second half of the first year, infants smile at more complex social and visual items. Laughter at this age may be full of squeals, howls, hoots, giggles, and grins. Incongruity may be noticed by the infant, and laughter follows. If an infant laughs when he or she sees the family dog in the driver's seat with its paws on the wheel, the child may be showing recognition of incongruity — the child has learned something about car drivers.

Responsive mothers promote infant smiling. Ainsworth and Bell (1972) concluded that *responsive mothers* (those who are alert in caring for the infant's needs) had babies who cry less frequently and had a wider range of different modes of communication. These responsive mothers created a balance between showing attention and affording the infant *autonomy* (offering a choice of action within safe bounds) when the infant became mobile. They also provided body contact and involved themselves playfully at times.

BABBLING

Early random sound making is often called *babbling*. Infants the world over babble sounds they've not heard and will not use in their native language. This has been taken to mean that each infant has the potential to master any world language (Jacobson, 1968). Close inspection shows repetitive sounds and "practice sessions" present. Babbling starts at about the fourth to sixth month and continues in some children through the toddler period. However, a peak in babbling is usually reached between 9 and 12 months. Periods before the first words are spoken are marked by a type of babbling that repeats syllables over and over, as in "dadadadadada." This is called *echolalia*. Infants seem to echo themselves and others. Babbling behavior overlaps the one and two (or more) word-making stages ending for some children at about 18 months of age.

Deaf infants also babble and in play sessions will babble for longer periods without hearing either adult sound or their own sounds as long as they can see the adult responding. However, they stop babbling at an earlier age than do hearing children. It is not clearly understood why babbling occurs, either in hearing or nonhearing children, but it is felt that babbling gives the child the opportunity to use and control the mouth, throat, and lung muscles. Possibly, a child's babbling amuses and motivates the child, acting as stimulus that adds variety to the child's existence.

In time, there is an increasing number of articulated (clear, distinct) vowellike, consonantlike, and syllabic sounds. Although babbling includes a wide range of sounds, as children grow older they narrow the range and begin to focus on the familiar, much-heard language of the family. Other sounds are gradually discarded.

There's a point when infant's eyes search and follow sound in their environment, and when the infant can easily turn his or her head toward the speaker. Toys are visually examined and reached for and sometimes talked to (figure 1-11). Almost any feature of environment may promote verbalness.

FIGURE 1-11 This infant is very interested in the toy train.

Physical contact continues to be important. Touching, holding, rocking, and other types of physical contact bring a sense of security and a chance to respond through sound making. The active receiving of perceptions is encouraged by warm, loving parents who share a close relationship. Secure children respond more readily to the world around them. Children who lack social and physical contact, or live in insecure home environments, fall behind in both the number and range of sounds made; differences start showing at about six months of age.

Simple imitation of language sounds begins early. Nonverbal imitated behavior, such as tongue protrusion, also occurs (figure 1-12). Sound imitation becomes syllable imitation, and short words are spoken about the end of the child's first year.

INFANT SIGNALING

During the latter part of the first year, alert caretakers notice hand and body positions that suggest the child is attempting a communication. Infants as young as seven months may bang on a window to get a family cat's attention or reach out, motion, or crawl toward something or someone they want. As time progresses,

Gesture	Meaning
Allows food to run out of mouth	Satisfied or not hungry
Pouts	Displeased
Pushes nipple from mouth with tongue	Satisfied or not hungry
Pushes object away	Does not want it
Reaches out for object	Wants to have it handed to him
Reaches out to person	Wants to be picked up
Smacks lips or ejects tongue	Hungry
Smiles and holds out arms	Wants to be picked up
Sneezes excessively	Wet and cold
Squirms and trembles	Cold
Squirms, wiggles, and cries during dressing or bathing	Resents restriction on activities
Turns head from nipple	Satisfied or not hungry

FIGURE 1-13 Some common gestures of babyhood (*From* Child Development, *by Elizabeth B. Hurlock, 1972. Used with permission of McGraw-Hill Company.*)

more and more infant body signaling takes place (figure 1-13). Signals are used over and over, and a type of sign-language communication emerges. Current research suggests that infants use a "signal and sound system" understood by caretakers. Halliday (1979) believes a "child tongue" develops before "mother tongue." When responded to appropriately, the infant easily progresses to word use and verbal aptitude.

Well-meaning parents may choose not to respond to infant gestures and signals, thinking this will accelerate or force the use of words. The opposite is thought to be true. Alert parents who try to read and receive signals give their infant the message that communication leads to fulfillment of wishes. Successful signaling becomes a form of language — a precursor of verbal signals (words). Sitting down at the child's level at times when the infant is crawling from one piece of furniture to another may facilitate the adult's ability to pick up on signaling. Watching the infant's eyes and the direction the infant's head turns gives clues. Infants about eight months old seem fascinated with the adults sound-making ability. They often turn to look at the adult's lips or want to touch the adult's mouth.

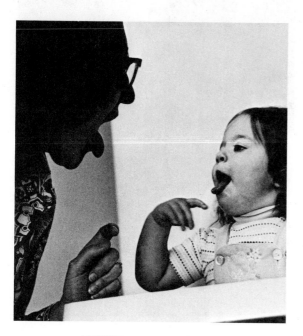

FIGURE 1-12 "I can do that."

UNDERSTANDING

Most babies get some idea of the meaning of a few words at about six to nine months. At about 10 months of age, some infants start to respond to spoken word clues. A game such as "pat-a-cake" may start the baby clapping and "bye-bye" or "peek-a-boo" brings about other imitations of earlier play activities with the parents. The child's language is called passive at this stage, for he or she primarily receives (or is receptive). Speaking attempts will later become active (or expressive). Vocabulary provides a small portal through which adults can gauge a little of what the child knows. There is a point at which children jump the bridge from the nonverbal signals to true language (Angier, 1984).

Older infants communicate with their parents through many nonverbal actions; one common way is by holding up their arms, which most often means, "I want to be picked up." Other actions include facial expression, voice tone, voice volume, posture, and gestures such as "locking in" by pointing fingers and toes at attention-getting people and events.

Although infants at this stage can respond to words, speaking does not automatically follow, because, at this early age, there is much more for infants to understand. Changes in parents' facial expressions, voice tone and volume, and actions and gestures carry feelings and messages important to infants' well-being. Understanding the tone of parents' speech comes before understanding parents' words, and that understanding happens prior to children trying to say words.

FIRST WORDS

Before an understandable, close approximation of a word is uttered, the child's physical organs need to function in a delicate unison, and the child must reach a certain level of mental maturity. The child's respiratory system supplies the necessary energy. As the breath is exhaled, sounds and speech are formed with the upward movement of air. The larynx's vibrating folds produce voice (called *phonation*). The larynx, mouth, and nose influence the child's voice quality (termed *resonation*). A last modification of the breath stream is *articulation* — a final formation done through molding, shaping, stopping, and releasing voiced and nonvoiced sounds that reflect language heard in the child's environment.

Repetition of syllables such as ma, da, and ba in a child's babbling occurs toward the end of the first year. If "mama" or "dada" or a close copy is said, parents show attention and joy. Language, especially in the area of speech development, is a two-way process; reaction is an important feedback to action.

Generally, first words are nouns or proper names of foods, animals, and toys (figure 1-14). The first spoken words usually contain p, b, t, d, m, and n (front of the mouth consonants), which require the least tongue and air control (Beck, 1982). They are shortened versions, such as da for daddy, beh for bed, up for cup. When two-syllable words are attempted, they are often strung together using the same syllable sound, as in dada, beebee. If the second syllable is voiced, the child's reproduction of the sound may come out as dodee for doggy or papee for potty.

At this stage, words tend to be segments of wider happenings in the child's life. A child's word "ba" may represent a favorite often-used toy (such as a ball). As

FIGURE 1-14 The name of a family pet may be among the first words a child learns.

the child grows in experience, any round object seen in the grocery, for instance, will also be recognized and called "ba." This phenomenon has been termed *over-extension*. The child has embraced "everything round," which is a much broader meaning for ball than the adult definition of the word ball.

Lee (1970) describes the child's development from early situation-tied first words to a broader usage:

> All words in the beginning vocabulary are on the same level of abstraction. They are labels of developing categories of experiences.

Following is a list of words frequently understood between 8 and 12 months of age (Parents As Teachers Program Planning and Implementation Guide, 1986): mommy, daddy, bye-bye, baby, shoe, ball, cookie, juice, bottle, no-no, and the child's own name and names of family members.

A child finds that words can open many doors. They help the child get things and cause caretakers to act in many ways. Vocabulary quickly grows from the names of objects to words that refer to actions. This slowly decreases the child's dependence on context (a specific location and situation) for communication and gradually increases the child's reliance on words — the tools of abstract thought. Children learn very quickly that words not only name things and elicit action on another's part, but also convey comments and express individual attitudes and feelings (Beck, 1982).

TODDLER SPEECH

Toddlerhood begins, and the child eagerly names things and seeks names for others. As if playing an enjoyable game, the child echoes and repeats to the best of his or her ability. At times, the words are not recognizable as the same words the parents offered. When interacting with young speakers, an adult must listen closely, watch for nonverbal signs, scan the situation, and use a good deal of guessing to understand the child and respond appropriately. The child's single words accompanied by gestures, motions, and intonations are called *holophrases*. They usually represent a whole idea or sentence.

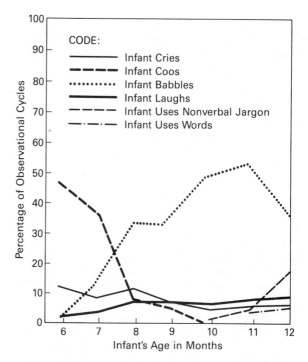

FIGURE 1-15 Infant vocalization to caretaker *(From* Prelinguistic Communication in Infancy, *by Alan Ziajka, Praeger Publishers, CBS Educational and Professional Publishing, 521 Fifth Avenue, NY, NY 10175.)*

While the child is learning to walk, speech, for a short period, may take a back seat to developing motor skill.

> Between 15 to 18 months, while energy is concentrated upon walking, progress in talking may be slow. However, at this time the child may listen more intently to what others say. (Scott, 1968)

The slow-paced learning of new words (figure 1-15) is followed by a period of rapid growth. The child pauses briefly, listening and digesting, gathering forces to embark on the great adventure of becoming a fluent speaker.

IMPLICATIONS FOR INFANT-CENTER STAFF MEMBERS

The importance of understanding the responsive, reciprocal nature of optimum caregiving in group infant centers cannot be underestimated.

Responsive mothers — those who ignore few episodes and respond with little delay — have infants with more variety, subtlety, and clarity of non-crying communication. (Jacobson, 1978)

and

Mothers who vocalize and smile frequently have been found to have infants who vocalize and smile frequently. (Jacobson, 1978)

As Honig (1981) points out "caregivers who boost language are giving the gift of a great power to babies," consequently infants benefit from sensitive, alert, skilled adults. Adult caregivers need to read both non-verbal and vocalized cues, and react appropriately. They need to be attentive and loving. Learning to read each other's signals is basic to the quality of the relationship. Liberal amounts of touching, holding, smiling, and looking promote language as well as the child's overall sense that the world around him or her is both safe and fascinating. Recognizing the child's individuality, reading nonverbal behaviors, and reacting with purposeful actions are all expected of professional infant specialists. The following are suggestions that can be used to promote the infant's sound making and subsequent first spoken words.

During early infancy

- Hold the infant firmly yet gently, and make soft, gentle sounds while moving smoothly and holding the infant close.
- Talk in a pleasant, soothing voice, and use simple language and make frequent eye contact (NAEYC, 1987).
- Make a game out of the infant's smiles, sounds, and movements when the infant is responsive.
- Imitate the infant's babbling, cooing, or other sound making between four and six months of age (playfully echo).
- Whisper in the infant's ear to soothe him or her.
- Be watchful for signs that the infant may need a less stimulating setting and is emitting "escape signals."
- Use the infant's name — "Scott's toes" instead of "Baby's toes."

Especially during late infancy

- Speak clearly.
- Explain what is happening and what will happen next (NAEYC, 1987).
- Encourage the infant to look at you while you speak.
- Don't interrupt vocal play, jargon, or self-communication.
- Engage in word play, rhyme, chants, fun-to-say short expressions.
- Be an animated speaker.
- Try simple finger plays.
- Plan concrete, participatory activities with textures, sights, and sounds.
- Encourage sound making and provide noise making and musical toys.
- Talk about sounds when you hear them — "Knock, knock, there's daddy at the door."
- Remember to pause and wait for the child's response.

Weiser (1982) suggests occasionally using "singing conversations" with infants and also urges change of pitch with expressions like "up comes the spoon." This lays the basis for both speech and later music education. Both recorded and live musical sounds are part of an auditory-rich environment for infants. Tarrow and Lundsteen (1981) have identified goals and additional caregiver activities (figure 1-16).

How does a caregiver go about establishing a dialogue with an infant? First, consider the infant to be communicating from day one and expect many face-to-face opportunities. Newson (1979) provides an example of a caretaker's attempt to establish dialogue:

The child suddenly arrests the ongoing pattern of his play activity in response to a new noise such as a car passing outside. His mother takes her cue from this shift in his attention to mark or 'comment' on his reaction by indicating that she too has noticed the intrusive noise. Perhaps she picks up the child to let him look out of the window and see the car as it disappears down the road. The maintenance of communication in an incident of this kind is only accomplished by the fact that one of the two communicating persons is socially sensitive to the effect of what is happening to the other, moment by moment.

Level	Objective	Activity
Birth to 1 month	1. To develop intimacy and awareness of communication based on personal contact. 2. To introduce the concept or oral communication. 3. To introduce verbal communication. 4. To stimulate interest in the process of talking.	1. Whisper into the child's ear. 2. Coo at the child. 3. Talk to the child. 4. Let the child explore your mouth with his or her hands as you talk.
1 to 3 months	1. To develop oral communication. 2. To develop auditory acuity. 3. To develop the concept that different people sound different. 4. To develop the concept of oral and musical communication of feelings.	1. Imitate the sounds the child makes. 2. Talk to the child in different tones. 3. Encourage others to talk and coo to the child. 4. Sing songs of different moods, rhythms, and tempos.
3 to 6 months	1. To develop the concept of positive use of verbal communication. 2. To stimulate excitement about words. 3. To develop the concept that words and music can be linked. 4. To develop the ability to name things and events.	1. Reward the child with words. 2. Talk expressively to the child. 3. Sing or chant to the child. 4. Describe daily rituals to the child as you carry them out.
6 to 9 months	1. To develop use of words and reinforce intimacy. 2. To develop the concept that things have names. 3. To develop the concept that there is joy in the written word. 4. To develop the concept that language is used to describe.	1. Talk constantly to the child and explain processes such as feeding, bathing, and changing clothes. 2. Name toys for the child as the child plays, foods and utensils as the child eats, and so on. 3. Read aloud to the child, enthusiastically. 4. Describe sounds to the child as they are heard.
9 to 12 months	1. To develop the concept that body parts have names. 2. To reinforce the concept that things have names. 3. To stimulate rhythm and interest in words. 4. To stimulate experimentation with sounds and words.	1. Name parts of the body and encourage the child to point to them. 2. Describe and name things seen on a walk or an automobile trip. 3. Repeat simple songs, rhymes, and finger plays. 4. Respond to sounds the child makes, and encourage the child to imitate sounds.

FIGURE 1-16 Sequential objectives and activities for language development (*From* Activities and Resources for Guiding Young Children's Learning, *by Sara Wynn Lundsteen and Norma Bernstein Tarrow, 1981. Reproduced with permission from McGraw-Hill Book Company.*)

Generally, the types of adults who promote language are those who are alert to the child's achievements, notice them, and enjoy interacting, as well as adults who can offer novelty, assistance, and enthusiasm besides focusing on the child's interests (White, 1985). Language competence at age three is related to maternal (or caregiver) emotional and verbal responsiveness. Play opportunity and play materials also become important at age six months (Elardo, Brady, Caldwell, 1977).

Threats to early language development include:

- hearing loss,
- lack of sharing experiences with caring adults,
- failure of adults to talk frequently to preverbal infants, and
- stifling baby's curiosity (White, 1986).

BABY GAMES AND EXPLORATIONS

Infants almost daily seem to increase the ways they can explore and enjoy verbal-physical games. Many parents and infants develop a set of games of their own (Kaye, 1979). A few favorite infant play pursuits and examples of adult comment follow:

COMMON ACTIVITIES	POSSIBLE ADULT REMARKS
look and watch	"See the kitty."
touch it	"Grandpa's nose."
mouth it	"Eat the cracker."
make a sound	"Ring goes the bell."
pick it up	"A rock, you found a rock."
push it or pull it	"Push the box."
drop it off	"Down goes the block."
empty it, fill it	"Out come the dish towels."
climb it	"Foot goes up."
carry it	"Robert's holding the car."
roll it	"The ball's rolling on the rug."

Since caretakers spend considerable time supervising active infants, it usually takes little effort to supply brief running remarks. Pausing is as important as talking. Co-explorers must give the infant time to send signals and then must issue approving nods or words or reactions. Infants quickly can get the idea that conversation is a two-way process. An infant who is with a caretaker who has primarily a policing orientation that is full of "no-no's" and little else misses tremendous language opportunities.

SOCIAL PLAY

It's obvious that infants six months and older watch, imitate, and attempt physical and verbal contact with other infants and children. There's a strong attraction to other "small people and animals." Most young infants prefer to be in the same room with a favored caretaker. Only as they become mobile and older do they explore adjacent rooms and areas on their own.

CLASSIC LANGUAGE PLAY

The following language and body-action play has brought delight to generations of infants. The most-enjoyed play activities include tickling, bouncing, and lifting with accompanying words and rhymes. Snow et al. (1979) see baby games as especially appropriate to language emergence:

The way mothers talk to babies is well designed to create the feeling of effective communication, and the structure of games and other playful episodes is especially appropriate to that end.

THIS LITTLE PIGGIE

(Recited while holding each toe down to the pinkie.)

This little pig went to market,
This little pig stayed home,
This little pig had roast beef,
This little pig had none,
This little piggie cried, "Wee, wee, wee,
wee!" all the way home.

PAT-A-CAKE

(Recited while helping the child imitate hand-clapping.)

Pat-a-cake, pat-a-cake, baker's man,
Bake me a cake as fast as you can.
Pat it and prick it and mark it with a "B,"
And put it in the oven for baby and me.

SO BIG

Say, *"How big are you?"* and then help the child answer by saying *"So-o-o-o-o big!"* as you raise the child's hands above the child's head. Repeat.

Say *"Ah"* as you slowly bring the child to your face, and then gently say *"Boo!"* Repeat. *"Ah-h-h-h-h . . . Boo!"*

from Pushaw, David R., *Teach Your Child to Talk*, Dantree Press, Inc., N.Y., 1976.

ROUND AND ROUND

(This is a frequently used tickling verse of English mothers.)

Round and round the garden (said slowly while circling the baby's palm)

One step, two steps (walking fingers toward a tickling spot at neck, stomach, or underarms, and said a little faster)

Tickle you there! (Said very fast.)

READING TO INFANTS

Between 6 and 12 months, some infants will sit and look at a picture book with an adult. The child will want to grab pages and test the book in his or her mouth or try to turn pages. The child's head may swivel to look at the adult's mouth. If the child has brought a book to the adult, the child will usually want to sit on the adult's lap as both go through the book. The child gets ever more adept at turning pages as a first birthday nears. The soothing sound of a human voice and close, cuddly physical contact is part of the enjoyment of book-reading settings. Familiar objects in colorful illustration and large faces seem to be particularly fascinating.

Book-reading techniques include reading with average volume and expression, using gesturing or pointing when called for, promoting child imitation, letting the child turn sturdy pages, and making animal or sound noises. Simple, colorful, sturdy-paged books are plentiful, and reading them on a regular basis can become a pleasant activity. A good rule of thumb is to stop before the child's interest wanes. Adults may find that many infants enjoy repeated reading of the same book during the same sitting.

There exists a number of literary classics (although not all experts agree to the same titles) that most children in our culture experience. Many of these involve rhyme, rhythm, touching, motions, or hand gestures.

They have, over time, become polished gems passed on to succeeding generations. Some are shared as songs, and include:

Here We Go Round the Mulberry Bush

One, Two, Buckle My Shoe

Hush-A-Bye Baby

Twinkle, Twinkle, Little Star

Rock-A-Bye Baby

Ba Ba Black Sheep

A few recommended books for babies follow. Many others are in print.

Tafuri, Nancy, *My Friends*, New York: Greenwillow Books, 1987
In a Red House, New York: Greenwillow Books, 1987

Hoban, Tana, *What Is It?* New York: Greenwillow Books, 1974

Ra, Carol F., *Trot Trot to Boston, Play Rhymes for Baby*, New York: Lothrop, Lee, and Shepard Books, 1987

RECORDINGS

Growing numbers of recording tapes, and audiovisuals are being produced for infants. Infants listen and sometimes move their bodies rhythmically. Environmental and animal sound recordings are available. Caretakers find that certain recordings are soothing and promote sleep. Infants are definitely attracted to musical sounds, and researchers are studying whether listening to music during infancy promotes listening abilities and speech production.

EARLY EXPERIENCE WITH WRITING TOOLS

As early as 10 to 12 months, infants will watch intently as someone makes marks on a surface or paper. They will reach and attempt to do the marking themselves. Chalk and thick crayons or crayon "chunks" are recommended for exploring. Large-sized paper (torn apart grocery brown bags) taped at the edges to surfaces and chalkboards work well. These activities require constant, close supervision to prevent infants from biting or chewing writing tools. The child may not realize the writing tool is making marks but may imitate and gleefully move the whole arm. Many feel it's simply not worth the effort to supervise very young children during this activity and rather save this activity until the children are older.

IMPLICATIONS FOR PARENTS

Parents' attitude toward their infant's communicating abilities may influence their progress:

Mothers who believe their babies are potential communicative partners talk to them in ways which serve both to strengthen that belief and to make it come true. (Snow, 1979)

Parenting techniques and home environments of children described as "resilient and capable" by researchers may provide clues to optimum language-promoting factors (Werner and Smith, 1982; Hakuta, 1986). Also, special infant projects that seem to have promoted later school success have provided information in this area as well (Parents As Teachers, 1986). Home factors mentioned from both these sources include:

- Lots of attention by socially responsive caretakers.
- Little or no disruption of bonding attachment between the infant and his or her primary caregiver during the infant's first year.
- Availability of space and objects to explore.
- Good nutrition.
- Active and interactive exchanges and play time.
- Parent knowledge of developmental milestones and the child's emerging skills.
- Parent confidence in infant handling.
- Maintenance of the child's physical robustness.
- Positive attention and touching in play exchange.

Factors bearing little or no relationship to the child's future language competence include parent's age, education, social class, income, native language (other than English), expensive toys and equipment, number of siblings, amount of alternative care, or living in a single-parent family.

Parent (or family) stress and less-than-desirable quality in child-parent interactions seem to hinder children's language development. Since most families face stress, a family's reaction to stress, rather than stress itself, is the determining factor.

It is good practice to talk through the routines of dressing, feeding, and bathing the infant in simple sentences. Also, making statements such as "push the switch on" and "lights off," while these actions are being performed, are recorded in the child's memory. Pausing in conversations for the infant to make his or her own noises, and acknowledging these with a smile or look of recognition, will encourage the infant to continue making sounds.

Fisher (1986) has good advice for parents:

Don't worry about teaching as much as providing a rich and emotionally supportive atmosphere.

The richness to which he refers is a richness of opportunity, rather than expensive toys and surroundings. Parents may get the idea that a parent has to talk constantly, and that early infant "talkers" have parents with more competency in parenting skills. However, current research indicates that parents who spontaneously speak about what the child is interested in and who zoom in and out of the child's play as they go about their daily work are responsive and effective parents. Also, early and late "talkers" usually show little difference in speaking ability by age three. The variation between children with respect to the onset and accomplishment of most human characteristics covers a wide range when considering what is normal and expected.

Summary

Each child grows in language ability in a unique way. The process starts before birth with the development of sensory organs. Parents play an important role in a child's growth and mastery of language.

Perceptions gained through life experiences serve as the base for future learning of words and speech. Babbling, soundmaking, and imitation occur, and first words appear.

A number of related factors influence a child's language acquisition. Most children progress through a series of language ability stages and milestones at about the same ages (figure 1-17) and become adultlike speakers during the preschool period. The way chil-

INFANT'S AGE	STAGES OF LANGUAGE DEVELOPMENT
Before birth	Listens to sounds. Reacts to loud sounds.
At birth	Birth cry is primal, yet individual — vowel-like. Cries to express desires (for food, attention, and so on) or displeasure (pain or discomfort). Makes eating, sucking, and small throaty sounds. Hiccoughs. Crying becomes more rhythmic and resonant during first days. Shows changes in posture — tense, active, or relaxed.
First days	Half cries become vigorous; whole cries begin to take on depth and range. Coughs and sneezes.
1 month	Three to four vowel sounds apparent. Seems to quiet movements and attend to mother's voice. Eating sounds mirror eagerness. Sighs and gasps. Smiles in sleep.
2 to 3 months	Coos and makes pleasurable noises (babbling); and blowing and smacking sounds. Most vowel sounds are present. Open vowel-like babbles may begin. Consonant sounds begin, usually the following — b, d, g, h, l, m, n, p, t. Markedly less crying. Smiles and squeals and may coo for half a minute. Peers into faces. Adults may recognize distinct variations in cries, i.e., cries that signal fear, tiredness, hunger, pain, and so on. Focuses on mother's face and turns head to her voice. May be frightened by loud or unfamiliar noise. May blow bubbles and move tongue in and out.
4 to 5 months	Sound play is frequent. Social smiling more pronounced. Can whine to signal boredom. May laugh. Reacts to tone of voice. Seems to listen and enjoy music. Likes adult vocal play and mimicking. Favorite people seem to induce verbalness. Babbles several sounds in one breath. Body gestures signal state of comfort or discomfort. Attracted to sounds. Approaching 6 months of age, may start to show understanding of words often used in household. Turns head and looks at speaking family members. Consonant sounds more pronounced and frequent.
6 to 8 months	Increased babbling and sound making; repeats syllables; imitates motions and gestures; uses nonverbal signals; vocalizes all vowel sounds; reduplication of utterances; more distinct intonation. Increases understanding of simple words. Enjoys making noise with toys and household objects. Repeats actions to hear sounds again. May blow toy horn. Delights in rhythmic vocal play interchange, especially those that combine touching and speaking. Twists and protrudes tongue, smacks, and watches mother's mouth and lips intently. May look at picture books for short period or watch children's television programs.
9 to 10 months	May make kiss sounds. Increases understanding of words like no-no, mommy, daddy, ball, hat, and shoe. May play pat-a-cake and wave bye-bye. May hand books to adults for sharing. Uses many body signals and gestures. May start jargon-like strings of sounds, grunts, gurgles, and whines. Listens intently to new sounds.
11 to 14 months	Reacts to an increasing number of words. Speaks first word(s) (usually words with one syllable or repeated syllable). Points to named objects or looks toward named word. Makes sounds and noises with whatever is available. Imitates breathing noises, animal noises (like barking dog or cat's meow), or environmental noises (like "boom," or train toot). Pretends to talk on toy telephone. Uses many body signals especially "pick me up" with arms outstretched and "reaching for another's hand," meaning come with me. May understand as many as 40 to 50 words. At close to 15 months, one word has multiple meanings. Jargon-like strings of verbalness continue. The child's direction of looking gives clues to what the child understands, and the child may have a speaking vocabulary of 10 or more words.

FIGURE 1-17 Milestones in developing language behavior

dren learn language is not clearly understood, and so there are a number of differing theories of language acquisition.

Early in life, infants and parents form a reciprocal relationship reacting in special ways to each other. The quality and quantity of parental attention becomes an important factor in language development.

The child progresses from receiving to sending language, which is accompanied by gestures and nonverbal communication. From infancy, the child is an active participant, edging closer to the two-way process required in language usage and verbal communication.

Staff members in infant-care programs can possess interaction skills that offer infants optimum opportunities for speech development.

Student Activities

- Observe three newborns and compare their cries.

- Observe two infants (birth to 12 months). Note situations in which the infants make sounds and how adults (parent or teacher) react to the sound making.

- Describe nonverbal communication that you notice or receive in any situation with a group of people, such as in a classroom, cafeteria, family group, or social group.

- Sit with a young infant facing you. Have a note pad handy. Remain speechless and motionless. Try to determine what moment-to-moment needs the child has, and try to fulfill each need you recognize. Try not to add anything new; just respond to what you feel the child needs. Write a description of the needs observed and your feelings.

- Rate the following adult techniques for quieting and soothing a crying infant on a scale of 1 to 15, with 15 indicating the most common technique, and 1 the least common:
  feeding____, changing____, holding____, swaddling____, massaging____, caressing____, rocking____, giving pacifier____, humming or singing____, using a low "motor-type" noise____, car riding____, pushing in buggy____, lifting to shoulder____, walking the floor____, using a heartbeat-sound plush toy____.
  Can you cite other safe, comforting techniques that might calm a crying infant? Compare your answers with those of a classmate.

- Using the form in figure 1-18, read and review a magazine article or a research article concerning infant language development. Be prepared to briefly review your findings for a fellow student. Make a few statements concerning your reaction to the article's main conclusions.

- Visit an infant-toddler center. Focus on an infant over six months of age. What behaviors can you pinpoint in their caregivers that promote future language?

- Try sharing a colorful, simple book with an 8- to 12-month-old. What did you observe?

Topics:

LANGUAGE DEVELOPMENT, LANGUAGE ACQUISITION, PSYCHOLINGUISTICS, STUDIES IN ANIMAL COMMUNICATION.

Use the *Reader's Guide to Periodical Literature* or another resource guide to locate an article.

Title of article _____

Author(s) _____

Source name _____

Date of publication _____

Number of pages _____

General findings of the research article (number of subjects, ages, procedure, results, or article main points).

SUGGESTED JOURNALS: Child Development, Young Children, Journal of Clinical Psychology, Journal of Personality and Social Psychology, Journal of Marriage and Family, Children, Learning, Journal of Psychology, Journal of Social Psychology, Child Welfare, Exceptional Children, Journal of Speech and Hearing Research, Reading, Journal of Special Education.
MAGAZINES: Parents, Family Circle, Good Housekeeping, Instructor, First Teacher, Early Years.
BOOKS: Readings in Child Development, Readings in Early Childhood Education.

FIGURE 1-18

- Create a new game, rhyme, or movement word play, and test it on an infant 6 to 12 months of age.

- Try the following with a 4- to 12-month-old. Touch the child as you say the words. Report the child's reactions at the next class meeting.

> *Here comes a mouse*
> *Mousie, mousie, mouse*
>
> *With tiny light feet*
> *And a soft pink nose*
> *Tickledy tickle*
> *Wherever he goes*

He runs up your arm
And under your chin
Don't open your mouth
Or the mouse will run in

Mousie, mousie, mouse!

from Watson, Clyde, Catch Me And Kiss Me And Say It Again,
Putnam Publ. Group, 1978.

- Locate three books you feel would be appropriate for older infants, and share them with the class.

Unit Review

A. Write your own theory of language acquisition. (A child learns language...)

B. Finish the following: Caregivers working in group infant-care programs who wish to give infants opportunities to acquire language should carefully monitor their ability to... (list specific techniques).

C. Write definitions for:

phonation	bonding	babbling
resonation	moderation level	articulation
echolalia	infant signing	larynx

D. Discuss and finish the following: "Language is a kind of game infants learn. A game played with precise recognizable rules like...First, I talk; then you talk. To learn the game, it's best to have adults in your life who..."

E. Answer the following questions based on the information in the unit.
1. What are the two basic factors that influence language development?
2. How can parents help the young child develop language?
3. What is one purpose of a child's babbling?
4. Why is language development described as a two-way process?
5. What are the names of the sense organs that receive and transmit messages?
6. What is the name for impressions received through the senses?

F. Select the best answer.
1. Environmental factors that can affect future language development start
   a. at birth.
   b. before birth.
   c. during infancy.
   d. during toddlerhood.
2. The tone of a parent's voice is
   a. understood when a child learns to speak in sentences.
   b. less important than the parent's words.
   c. understood before actual words are understood.
   d. less important than the parent's actions.
3. In acquiring language, the child
   a. learns only through imitation.
   b. is one participant in a two-part process.
   c. learns best when parents ignore the child's unclear sounds.
   d. does not learn anything by imitating.

4. Select the true statement about babbling.
   a. Why babbling occurs is not clearly understood.
   b. Babbling is unimportant.
   c. Babbling predicts how early a child will start talking.
   d. Babbling rarely lasts beyond one year of age.
5. How a child acquires language is
   a. clearly understood.
   b. not important.
   c. only partly understood.
   d. rarely a subject for study.

G. Explain the difference between language and communication.

H. Match the words in Column I with the appropriate meaning or example in Column II.

Column I	**Column II**
1. perception	a. random sound production
2. babbling	b. mama, dada, bye-bye
3. tone	c. the Behaviorist Theory
4. B. F. Skinner	d. close reproduction of alphabet letter sounds
5. imitation	e. zero to four words
6. speaking vocabulary at 12 months	f. language and thought are interrelated
7. nonverbal communication	g. the way words are spoken rather than the meaning of the words
8. deprivation	h. repeating sounds and actions
9. repeated syllables	i. thumb sucking, smiling, crying
10. one of five senses	j. lack of warm, loving care
11. first words	k. impressions sent from sensory organs to brain
12. recognized English language sounds	l. touching
13. authorities agree	m. usually represent objects or people experienced daily

References

Ainsworth, M. D. S., and S. M. Bell. "Mother-Infant Interaction and Development of Competence." ERIC Document, ED 065 180, 1972.

Angier, Natalie. "Medical Clues From Babies' Cries." *Discover* 5.9 (Sept. 1984): 49–51.

Bateson, M. C. "The Epigenesis of Conversational Interaction." *Before Speech*. Ed. M. Bullowa. London: Cambridge UP, 1979.

Beck, M. Susan. *Kidspeak*. New York: New American Library, 1982.

Bee, Helen. *The Developing Child*. New York: Harper and Row, 1981.

Brazelton, T. Berry, in Richard M. Restak's "Newborn Knowledge." *Human Development*, Annual Editions 83/84, Guilford, CT: The Duskin Publishing Group, Inc., 1983. 83–85.

Brazelton, T. Berry. "Evidence of Communication in Neonatal Behavioral Assessment." *Before Speech*. Ed. M. Bullowa. London: Cambridge UP, 1979. 80–96.

Buchwald, Jennifer. "Medical Clues From Babies' Cries." *Discover* 5.9, 1984. 49–51.

Chomsky, Noam. *Language and Mind.* New York: Harcourt, Brace, and World, 1968.

Clark-Stewart, K. A. *Interactions Between Mothers and Their Young Children; Characteristics and Consequences.* Monographs of the Society for Research in Child Development 38 (1973): 6–7.

Condon and Sanders in Richard M. Restak's "Newborn Knowledge." *Human Development,* Annual Editions 83/84, Guilford, CT: The Duskin Publishing Group, Inc., 1983.

Developmentally Appropriate Practice In Early Childhood Programs Serving Children From Birth Through Age 8. Ed. Sue Bredekamp. Washington, D.C.: NAEYC, 1987.

de Villiers, Peter A. and Jill G. de Villiers. *Early Language.* Cambridge: Harvard UP, 1982.

Eden, Alvin N. *Positive Parenting.* New York: New American Library, 1985.

Egolf, D. and S. Chester. *Nonverbal Communication and Disorders of Speech and Language.* Rockville, MD: American Speech-Language-Hearing Assn., 1973.

Elardo, R., R. Bradley, and B. M. Caldwell. "A Longitudinal Study of the Relation of Infants' Home Environments to Language Development at Age Three." *Child Development* 48 (1977): 595–603.

Eveloff, Herbert H. "Some Cognitive and Affective Aspects of Early Language Development." *Child Development Contemporary Perspectives.* Eds. S. Cohen and T. Comiskey. Itasca: F. E. Peacock, 1977. 140–155.

Eyler, Fonda in Jim Kunerth's "Born Communicators." *Orlando Sentinel,* May 18, 1987. 3L.

Fischer, Kurt in Otto Friedrich's "What Do Babies Know?" *Human Development* 85/86, The Duskin Publishing Group, Inc., 1986.

Freedman, Daniel G. "Human Sociobiology." New York: The Free Press, 1979.

Freedman, Daniel G. "Smiling of Blind Infants." *Journal of Child Psychology and Psychiatry* 5.174 (1964): 86–92.

Friedrich, Otto. "What Do Babies Know?" *Human Development* 85/86, Guilford, CT: The Duskin Publishing Group, Inc., 1986.

Gleason, Jean Berko in Jim Kunerth's "Born Communicators." *Orlando Sentinel,* May 18, 1987. 3L.

Hakuta, Kenji. *The Mirror of Language,* New York: Basic Books, 1986.

Halliday, M. A. K. "One Child's Protolanguage." *Before Speech.* Ed. M. Bullowa. London: Cambridge UP, 1979. 171–190.

Honig, Alice Sterling. "What Are The Needs of Infants?" *Young Children,* 36.5. Nov. 1981. 38–41.

Hostetler, A. J. "Why Baby Cries: Data May Shush Skeptics." *The APA Monitor* 19.7, July, 1988. 27–32.

Hoy, J. and I. Somer, eds. *The Language Experience,* New York: Dell, 1974.

Jacobson, Armina Lee. "Infant Day Care: Toward a More Human Environment." *Young Children* 33.5, (July 1978): 31–36.

Jacobson, R. *Child Language,* The Hague: Monton, 1968.

Johnson, Katie. *Doing Words,* Boston: Houghton Mifflin, 1987.

Junker, Karin Stensland. "Communication Starts With Selective Attention." *Before Speech.* Ed. M. Bullowa. London: Cambridge UP, 1979. 307–320.

Kaye, Kenneth. "Thickening Thin Data: The Maternal Role in Developing Communication and Language." *Before Speech.* Ed. M. Bullowa. London: Cambridge UP, 1979. 191–206.

Klaus, Marshall H., and Phyllis H. Klaus. *The Amazing Newborn*, Menlo Park, CA: Addison Wesley, 1985.

Kunerth, Jim. "Born Communicators." *Orlando Sentinel*, May 18, 1987. 3L.

Lee, Laura L. "The Relevance of General Semantics to Development of Sentence Structure in Children's Language." *Communication: General Semantics Perspectives*. Ed. Lee Thayer. New York: Spartan Books, 1970.

Lester, Barry. "There's More to Crying Than Meets The Ear." *Child Care Newsletter*, 2.2 (1983) Johnson and Johnson Co. 4–8.

Lewis, M. and L. A. Rosenblum. *The Effect of The Infant on Its Caregiver*. New York: John Wiley & Sons, 1974.

Meltzoff, Andrew, in Otto Friedrich's "What Do Babies Know?" *Human Development* 85/86, Guilford, CT: The Duskin Publishing Group, Inc., 1986.

Newson, John. "The Growth of Shared Understandings Between Infant and Caregiver." *Before Speech*. Ed. M. Bullowa. London: Cambridge UP, 1979. 207–222.

Ornstein, Robert and David Sobel. *The Healing Brain*. New York: Simon and Schuster, 1987.

Pushaw, David R. *Teach Your Child To Talk*. New York: Dantree Press, 1976.

Scott, Louise Binder. *Learning Time With Language Experiences for Young Children*. New York: McGraw-Hill, 1968.

Snow, Catherine, Akke De Blauw, and Ghislaine Van Roosmalen, "Talking and Playing With Babies." *Before Speech*. Ed. M. Bullowa. London: Cambridge UP, 1979. 269–288.

Spelke, Elizabeth, in Otto Friedrich's "What Do Babies Know?" *Human Development* 85/86, Guilford, CT: The Duskin Publishing Group, Inc., 1986.

Spieker, Susan, "Study Links Tots Smiles," *San Jose Mercury News*, September 13, 1987. 8B.

Stewig, John W. "Teaching Language Arts in Early Childhood." New York: CBS College Publishing, 1982.

Tarrow, Norma Bernstein, and Sara Wynn Lundsteen, *Activities and Resources for Guiding Young Children's Learning*. New York: McGraw-Hill, 1981.

Tronick, Edward, in Jim Kunerth's "Born Communicators." *Orlando Sentinel*, May 18, 1987. 3L.

Watson, Clyde. *Catch Me and Kiss Me and Say It Again*. New York: Philomel Books, 1978.

Weiser, Margaret G. *Group Care and Education of Infants and Toddlers*, St. Louis: The C. V. Mosby Co., 1982.

Werner, E. E. and R. S. Smith. *Vulnerable, But Invincible*. New York: McGraw-Hill, 1982.

White, Burton L. "A Person Is Emerging." *Parents As Teachers Program Planning and Implementation Guide*. Jefferson City, MO: Missouri Dept. of Elem. and Secondary Ed., 1986.

Suggested Readings

Parents As Teachers Program Planning and Implementation Guide. Jefferson City, MO: Missouri Dept. of Elem. and Secondary Ed., 1986.

UNIT 2

The Tasks of the Toddler

BJECTIVES

After studying this unit, you should be able to

- discuss phonology, grammar, and the toddler's understanding of semantics.
- list three characteristics of toddler language.
- identify adult behaviors that aid the toddler's speech development.

If you were amazed at the infant's and one-year-old's ability, wait until you meet the toddler! Toddlerhood marks the beginning of a critical language-growth period. Never again will words enter the vocabulary at the same rate; abilities emerge in giant spurts almost daily. When children stop and focus on things, from specks on the floor to something very large, concentration is total — every sense organ seems to probe for data (figure 2-1). As White (1973) notes, "The one-year-old seems genuinely interested in exploring the world throughout the major portion of his day."

Toddlerhood begins with the onset of *toddling* (walking), a little before or after the child's first birthday. The toddler is perched at the gateway of a great adventure eager to proceed, investigating as the child goes, and attempting to communicate what he or she discovers and experiences. "The bags are packed" with what's been learned in infancy. The child will both monologue and dialogue as he or she ages, always knowing much more than can be verbally expressed.

From a few spoken words, the toddler will move to purposeful speech that gains what is desired, controls others, allows personal comments, and accompanies play. It becomes evident that the toddler realizes the give and take of true conversation, and what it is to be the speaker or the one who listens and reacts — the one

who persuades or is persuaded, the one who questions or is questioned. Toddlers become aware that everything has a name and that playfully trying out new sounds is an enjoyable pursuit. The child's meanings for the few words the child uses at the start of the toddler period may or may not be the same as common public usage (Lay-Dopyera and Dopyera, 1982):

> The task of gradually modifying the private meanings of words to coincide with public meanings continues throughout the life span.

There are four major tasks in learning the rule systems of language that face the toddler. These are (1) understanding *phonology* (the sound system of a language), (2) learning *syntactics* (a system of rules governing word order and combinations that give sense to short utterances and sentences (often referred to as grammar), and (3) learning *semantics* (word meanings), and (4) learning *pragmatics* (varying speech patterns depending on social circumstances and the context of situations). The understanding of these rule systems takes place simultaneously — one area complementing and promoting the other. Rule systems form without direct instruction as toddlers grope to understand the speech of others and as they try to copy what they hear and express themselves.

FIGURE 2-1 "What's this?"

PHONOLOGY

Toddlers learn the phonology of their native language — its phonetic units and its particular and sometimes peculiar sounds. A *phoneme* is the smallest unit of sound that distinguishes one utterance from another — implying a difference in meaning. English has 46 to 50 phonemes, depending on what expert is consulted.

Languages are divided into vowel sounds and consonants. In vowels, the breath stream flows freely from the vocal cords; in consonants, it is blocked and molded in the mouth and throat area by soft tissue, muscle tissue, and bone, with tongue and jaw often working together. The child focuses on those sounds heard most often (figure 2-2). The toddler's speech is full of repetitions and rhythmic speech play. Toddler

FIGURE 2-2 Toddlers spend a lot of time looking and listening.

babbling of this type continues and remains pleasurable during early toddlerhood. Sounds that are combinations of vowels and consonants increase. Sounds that are difficult to form, will continue to be spoken without being close approximations of adult sounds until the child reaches five or six years of age or is even slightly older. Early childhood teachers realize that they will have to listen closely, and watch for nonverbal clues to understand child speech in many instances.

It is a difficult task for the child to make recognizable sounds with mouth, throat, and breath control working in unison. Lenneberg (1971) comments on the difficulties of perfecting motor control of speech-producing muscles, noting that this sophisticated skill comes ahead of many other physical skills.

Speech, which requires infinitely precise and swift movements of tongue and lips, all well-coordinated with laryngeal and respiratory motor systems, is all but fully developed when most other mechanical skills are far below levels of their future accomplishment.

Much of early speech has been called jargon or gibberish. The toddler seems to realize that conversations come in long strings of sound. Rising to the occasion, the child imitates the rhythm of the sound but utters only a few understandable words.

Toddlers hear a word as an adult hears it. Sometimes, they know the proper pronunciation but are unable to reproduce it. The child may say "pway" for play. If the parent says "pway," the child objects, showing confusion and perhaps frustration. Toddler talk, sometimes called baby talk, represents the child's best imitation, given his or her present ability. Adults may be tempted to respond in a playful baby-talk mode because of the perceived "cuteness" of the toddlers speech. This isn't recommended, because it offers immature forms of words rather than correct pronunciations. Play with words can easily be undertaken with adults using simple, clear speech.

Views on adult use of baby talk include the idea that the practice may limit more mature word forms and emphasize dependency. On the other hand, parents may offer simplified, easily-pronounced forms like "bow-wow" for barking poodle. They later quickly switch to adult, harder-to-pronounce forms when the child seems ready. In the beginning, though, most adults automatically modify their speech when speaking with toddlers by using short sentences and stressing key words.

Children progress with language at their individual rates and with varying degrees of clarity. Some children speak relatively clearly from their first tries. Other children, who are also progressing normally, take a longer time before their speech is easily understood. All 50 basic sounds (50 including diphthongs) are perfected by most children by age seven or eight.

Morphology

A *morpheme* is the smallest unit of language standing by itself with recognized meaning. It can be a word or part of a word. Many prefixes (un-, ill-) and suffixes (-s, -ness, -ed, -ing) are morphemes with their own distinct meaning. The study of morphemes is called *morphology.* There are wide individual differences in the rates toddlers utter morphemes (figure 2-3). It is unfortunate if early childhood teachers or parents attempt to

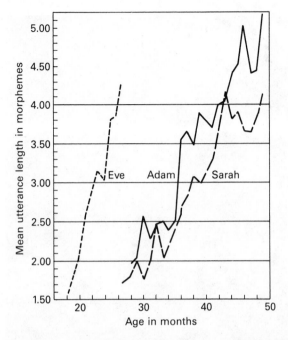

FIGURE 2-3 Individual rates in morpheme usage *(From "The child's grammar from I to III," by R. Brown, C. Cazden, and U. Bellugi-Kilma,* Minnesota Symposium on Child Psychology, *Vol. 2, Ed. John P. Hill, 1969. Reprinted by permission of the University of Minnesota Press.)*

compare the emerging speech of toddlers or equate greater speech usage with higher ability, thus giving the quiet toddler(s) perhaps less of their time.

SYNTACTICS

Languages have word orders and rules, and young children speak in word order and follow the rules of their native tongue. In one language, the subject of a sentence follows the verb; in other languages, it precedes the verb. *Modifiers* (descriptive words) in some languages have *gender* (male and female forms), while in others they do not. Plurals and possessive forms are unique to each language. Young speakers will make mistakes, but adults marvel at the grammar the child does use correctly, having learned the rules without direct instruction. Donoghue (1985) compares children's mastery of phonetics to their mastery of syntax:

In contrast to the gradual mastery of phonology, children use syntax correctly (though incompletely of course) from the very beginning. By age two, and sometimes as early as 18 months, children begin to string together two or more holophrases and have thereby arrived at telegraphic stage.

All telegraphic speech consists of acceptable grammatical sequences which are the precursors of the sentence.

From all the perceptions received and the words spoken to and about the child, the child has noted regularities and has unconsciously formed rules, which are continually revised. Chukovsky (1963) describes this task:

It is frightening to think what an enormous number of grammatical forms are poured over the poor head of the young child. And he, as if it were nothing at all, adjusts to all the chaos, constantly sorting out in rubrics the disorderly elements of words he hears, without noticing as he does this, his gigantic effort. If an adult had to master so many grammatical rules within so short a time, his head would surely burst...In truth, the young child is the hardest mental toiler on our planet. Fortunately, he does not even suspect this.

An understanding of the general rules of grammar develops before an understanding of the exceptions to the rules. Correct grammar forms may change to incorrect forms as the child learns new rules. Slobin (1971) has an interesting example of this phenomena:

In all of the cases which have been studied (and these are children of homes where standard English is spoken, and are usually first-born children) the first past tenses used are the correct forms of irregular verbs — came, broke, went, and so on. Apparently these irregular verbs in the past tense — which are the most frequent past tense forms in adult speech — are learned as separate vocabulary items at a very early age.

Then, as soon as the child learns only one or two regular past tense forms — like helped and walked — he immediately replaces the correct irregular past tense forms with their incorrect over-generalizations from the regular forms. Thus children say "it came off," "it broke," and "he did it" before they say "it comed off," "it breaked," and

"he doed it." Even though the correct forms may have been practiced for several months, they are driven out of the child's speech by the overregularization, and may not return for years.

In later years, during elementary school, the child will formally learn the grammar rules of his or her native language. What the child has accomplished before that time, however, is monumental. The amount of speech that already conforms to the particular syntactical and grammatical rules of language is amazing. The child has done this through careful listening and by mentally reorganizing the common elements in language that have been perceived.

The toddler's growing use of intonation and *inflection* (changes in loudness of voice) adds clarity, as do nonverbal gestures. The child is often insistent that adults listen.

The toddler's system of nonverbal signals, body postures, and motions that he or she used in late infancy has continued and expanded, becoming part of the toddler's communication style. Many signals translated by mothers to strangers, leave strangers bewildered as to how the mother could possibly know what the child wants from what the child and the mother have both observed and heard.

English sentences follow a subject-verb-object sequence. Bruner (1966) notes three fundamental properties of sentences: verb-object, subject-predicate, and modification, and explains their universal use:

There are no human languages whose sentences do not contain rules for these three basic sentential structures, and there are no nonhuman languages that have them.

Learning grammar rules helps the toddler express ideas (Bellugi, 1977). Understanding *syntax* (the arrangement of words to show relationship) helps the child to be understood:

It is our knowledge of the rules of combination — the syntax of the language — that governs how we construct and understand an infinite number of sentences from a finite vocabulary. Syntax gives language its power.

If one listens closely to the older toddler, sometimes self-correction of speech errors takes place. Toddlers talk to themselves and their toys often (figure 2-4). It

FIGURE 2-4 "Beebee"

seems to aid storage and memory. The toddler understands adult sentences because he or she has internalized a set of finite rules or combinations of words.

SEMANTICS

Semantics is the study of meanings. It probes how the sounds of language are related to the real world and life experiences (Clarke-Stewart & Koch, 1983). The toddler absorbs meanings from both verbal and nonverbal communication sent and received. The nonverbal refers to expressive associations of words: rhythm, stress, pitch, gesture, body position, facial change, and so on. Adults perform important functions in the child's labeling and concept formation by giving words meaning in conversations. Adults and teachers seem to unconsciously realize that there are different levels of specificity in naming most objects. One offers dog before spaniel and collie, money before quarter, cookie before chocolate chip. As de Villiers (1982) explains:

So a child will typically learn the word flower before he separates roses from daffodils and tulips and before he can call flowers, trees, and grass plants.

In toddler classrooms, teachers have many opportunities to name objects and happenings as the day unfolds. Using gesturing along with words, (or pointing to pictures in simple picture books and magazines) helps the toddler form a connection between what he or she heard and said. Repeating words with voice stress can be done in a natural way while monitoring whether the child is still interested.

Word meanings are best learned in active, hands-on experiences rather than "repeat-after-me" situations (figure 2-5). Meanings of words are acquired through their connotations, not their denotations (Gonzales-Mena, 1976), that is, in situations that consist of feelings and verbal and nonverbal messages with physical involvement. The word "cold," for instance means little until physically experienced.

For awhile toddlers may use one sound for a number of meanings:

When a baby is first learning to talk, the same sound often serves for several words; for instance, "bah" can mean "bottle," "book," "bath," and "bye." And sometimes babies use one sound to name an object and also to express a more complicated thought, for example, a baby may point to the

FIGURE 2-5 Hands-on experiences aid the learning of new words.

stroller and name it, but later may say the same word and mean, "I want to ride in the stroller." (Sherwin, 1987)

A *concept* is the recognition of one or more distinguishing features of a set of events, persons, or objects (figure 2-6). Some parents help the child discover and point out the differences; others may not. The following passage deals with the concept of thimbles.

A person who espies a thimble is recognizing what he sees, and this certainly entails what he has already learned and not forgotten about what thimbles look like. He has learned enough of the recipe for the looks of thimbles to recognize thimbles when he sees them. (Ryle, 1946)

A toddler may overuse concepts in new situations. Perhaps a bandage on the tip of a brother's finger will be called a thimble. For a short time, all men are daddies; a cow may be called a big dog; and all people in white are feared. As mental maturity and life experiences increase, concepts change; small details and exceptions are noticed. Toddlers underextend words also "by using a word to refer to a smaller category than would adults." An example of this phenomena is the toddler's use of the word "dog" only in reference to the child's pet rather than all dogs encountered.

Concepts, often paired mentally with words, aid categorizing. Concept words may have full, partial, or little depth of meaning. The toddler's level of thought is reflected in speech. When counting to three, the toddler may or may not know what "three" represents. Words are symbols; Huey (1965) explains their importance:

A concept, to be communicable, must be represented by a symbol that is understood by others to carry the same meaning that the child intends. The symbol is usually a word. Symbols are aids to thinking that enable the individual to reflect upon objects or situations which are not actually present.

A toddler's first-hand sensory experiences are very important (figure 2-7). Stored mental perceptions are attached to words. Spitzer (1977) points out that words are only as rich as the experiences and depth of understanding behind them:

Words are the basic elements of language, but they are too often misunderstood. Our society puts tremendous emphasis on the acquisition of a large vocabulary in young children. But few realize that words without experiences are meaningless. They are empty concepts. Language allows humans to communicate meaningfully with others. The more experiences and meaning that backs up words, the more rewarding the communication process will become.

FIGURE 2-6 Focusing on a new object

FIGURE 2-7 Perhaps this toddler is painting with water for the first time.

The activities and experiences found in later units help the early childhood teacher enrich the child's concepts by providing deeper meanings in a wide range of language arts. Every activity for young children — a total school program — gives them a language arts background full of opportunities to explore by handling, tasting, smelling, and touching, as well as by seeing and listening.

PRAGMATICS

The subtleties of our language are many-faceted. *Pragmatics* is the study of how language is used effectively in a social context, or the practical aspect of oral communication. It's the study of "who can say what, in what way, where and when, by what means and to whom" (Hymes, 1971). Language is a tool in questioning, ordering, soothing, ridiculing, and in other social actions. One can request quiet in the form of a question such as "Can't anyone get a peaceful moment around here?" or talk longingly about the candy in a store for the purpose of obtaining it — as in "Oh, they have my favorite kind of chocolate bar!" — without making a direct request.

The language that young children use to express desires, wishes, concerns, and interests becomes a reflection of their social selves (Yawkey, Askov, Cartwright, DuPuis, Fairchild, 1981). When a toddler communicates effectively, the toddler receives feedback from others. Many times, a sense of well-being elicited by positive events help the child shape a feeling of competency and self-esteem. Not yet socially subtle in speech, the toddler has not learned the pragmatically useful or appropriate behaviors of older children. They seem to have one intent, to get messages across by gaining adult attention regardless of who is present and in what situation. The world, from the toddler's perspective, revolves around the toddler and his or her need to communicate.

FIRST WORDS

A toddler's first words usually consist of names of important people or objects the toddler encounters daily. These single words can frequently go further than naming by representing a meaningful idea (a *holophrase*). The task of the adult includes both being responsive and guessing the child's complete thought.

This may sound simple, but many times it's difficult and frustrating. Many factors influence the degree of adult responsiveness and talkativeness, particularly in child-care settings — room arrangements, adult-child ratios, adult job satisfaction, and other emotional and environmental factors. The greatest inhibitor of adults' talking and responding to children seems to be adults' talking to one another. The nature of the work in a group-care program can easily be described as emotion packed, and demanding, besides rewarding and challenging. On the surface, the general public may not see or understand skilled verbal interactions taking place between toddlers and the care providers. What seems to be random, natural playfulness and verbal responsiveness is really very skilled and professionally intentional behavior. The same, of course, is true regarding parent behavior.

Adults sometimes question the practice of responding to toddlers' grunts and "uhs" instead of seeking words first. Many toddlers seem to understand everything said to them and around them but get by and satisfy most of their needs with nonword utterances. The points for adults to consider are that the child is performing and learning a difficult task and that speech will soon follow. The message that responsive adults relay to children when rewarding their early attempts is that the children can be successful communicators and that further attempts at speech will get results.

SYMBOLIC GESTURING

It's old-fashioned to feel that real communication doesn't exist before a child's first words. Researchers have helped us understand that gestures and signs (signals) occur in tandem with early vocalizing (Acredolo and Goodwyn, 1986). Young toddlers can possess a rich repertoire of signals, and female infants tend to rely on or produce them with slightly greater frequency. Signs have been defined by Acredolo and Goodwyn (1986) as nonverbal gestures symbolically representing objects, events, desires, and conditions that are used by toddlers to communicate with those around them. They literally can double a young toddler's vocabulary.

Gesturing significantly increases children's power to obtain what they are after. It enriches their contacts and communicative competence. Adult recognition and attention to toddler signs enhance, rather than impede, language growth.

Acredolo and Goodwyn (1985) studied a child whose parents recognized that their child was interested in communicating and capable of learning nonverbal as well as verbal labels. The parents informally concocted signs on the spot for new events without any reference to a formal sign-language system. Figure 2-8 describes the signs and gives the age the signs appeared in the child's communicative behaviors and the age the child said the word represented by the sign. The list of signs includes the signs the child learned with and without direct parent teaching.

Gestures are integral companions of toddler verbalizations. Adults may have modeled the gestures in their adult-child interactions. Mothers' signals are "read" by toddlers, and a hand held palm up is usually read as "give it to me." Toddlers show their understanding by behaviors. Toddlers can and do invent new ones; consequently, signing isn't simple, imitative behavior. Pointing is probably the most-used gesture of toddlers. Eventually words are preferred, and gesturing remains as an accompaniment of speech. We've all slipped back into a gesturing mode as we search for words in conversation, and hand gestures are used automatically to convey the word(s) that we can't quite express.

SIGNS	DESCRIPTION	AGE OF SIGN ACQUISITION MONTHS	AGE OF WORD ACQUISITION MONTHS
Flower	Sniff, sniff	12.5	20.0
Big	Arms raised	13.0	17.25
Elephant	Finger to nose, lifted	13.5	19.75
Anteater	Tongue in and out	14.0	24.0
Bunny	Torso up and down	14.0	19.75
Cookie monster	Palm to mouth plus smack	14.0	20.75
Monkey	Hands in armpits, up-down	14.25	19.75
Skunk	Wrinkled nose plus sniff	14.5	24.00
Fish	Blow through mouth	14.5	20.0
Slide	Hand waved downward	14.5	17.5
Swing	Torso back and forth	14.5	18.25
Ball	Both hands waved	14.5	15.75
Alligator	Palms together, open-shut	14.75	24.0
Bee	Finger plus thumb waved	14.75	20.00
Butterfly	Hands crossed, fingers waved	14.75	24.0
I dunno	Shrugs shoulders, hands up	15.0	17.25
Hot	Waves hand at midline	15.0	19.0
Hippo	Head back, mouth wide	15.0	24.0
Spider	Index fingers rubbed	15.0	20.0
Bird	Arms out, hands flapping	15.0	18.5
Turtle	Hand around wrist, fist in-out	15.0	20.0
Fire	Waving of hand	15.0	23.0
Night-night	Head down on shoulder	15.0	20.0
X-mas tree	Fists open-closed	16.0	26.0
Mistletoe	Kisses	16.0	27.0
Scissors	Two fingers open-closed	16.0	20.0
Berry	'Raspberry' motion	16.5	20.0
Kiss	Kiss (at a distance)	16.5	21.0
Caterpillar	Index finger wiggled	17.5	23.0

FIGURE 2-8 Symbolic signs, in order of acquisition, produced by case study subject (*from Linda P. Acredolo and Susan Goodwyn, Symbolic Gesturing in Language Development, Human Development, 28, 1985, permission by S. Karger A.G., Basel, Switzerland.*)

FIRST SENTENCES

The shift from one word to a two- (or more) word stage at approximately 18 months is a milestone (figure 2-9). At that time, the toddler has a speaking vocabulary of about 50 words; by 36 months, upwards of 1,000 words.

If one looks closely at two-word utterances, two classes of words become apparent. Braine (1973) termed the smaller group "pivot words." Examples of toddlers' two-word sentences, with pivot words underlined, are shown in figure 2-10. They are used more often than nonpivots but seem to enter the vocabulary more slowly, perhaps because pivot words are stable and fixed in meaning. In analyzing two-word toddler comments, one finds they are both subject-predicate and topic-comment in nature. Frequently stressed syllables in words and word endings are what toddlers first master, filling in other syllables later. At times, toddlers use -um or -ah as place holders for syllables

TWO-WORD SENTENCES	MEANINGS
Dat* car	Nomination
Daddy dare	Location
See kitty	Identification
More cookie	Repetition, recurrence
Milk allgone	Nonexistence
Sit chair	Action — location
No car, no want dat	Negation
Todd shoe, mine toy	Possession, possessor
Big cup	Attribute description
Jin walk, truck go	Agent — action
Kiss you, fix car	Action — direct object
Where ball?	Question

*Underlined words are pivots.

FIGURE 2-10 Pivot words in toddler's two-word sentences

and words and replace these with correct syllables and words as they age.

Understanding grammar rules at this two-word stage is displayed even though many words are missing. Braine (1973) points out the frequency with which toddlers use a simple form and, almost in the same breath, clarify by expansion (by adding another word). The invention of words by toddlers is commonplace. Meers (1976) describes an 18-month-old who had her own private word for "sleep," consistently calling it "ooma." Parents trying to understand their toddler get good at filling in the blanks. They then can confirm the child's statement and can add meaning at a time when the child's interest is focused.

TODDLER-ADULT CONVERSATIONS

Toddlers control attending or turning away in game-like, playlike episodes as do infants. At about one year, they understand many words and begin to display turn-taking in conversation, with "you talk, I answer" episodes.

Toddlers learn that speech deserves attention and that speech is great for getting adult attention. They seem to revel in the joint-endeavor aspect of conversations.

Toddlers are skillful communicators. They converse and correct adult interpretations, gaining pleasure and satisfaction from language exchanges. The following incident shows more than toddler persistence.

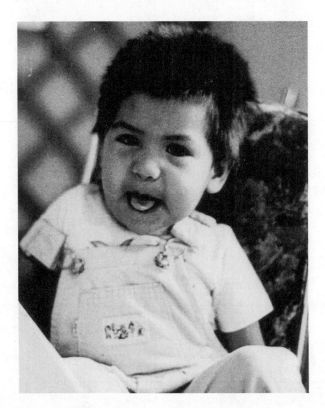

FIGURE 2-9 From phonemes to sentences

A first-time visitor to the home of a 20-month-old toddler is approached by the toddler. The visitor eventually rises out of his chair, accompanies the toddler to the kitchen, gets a glass of water, and hands it to the child. The toddler takes a tiny drink, and returns, satisfied, to the living room. Parents were not involved. Thirst, itself, was unimportant. The pleasure gained by the child seemed to motivate his actions.

For the child to accomplish his ends, the following actions occurred:

Visitor behavior

1. Focuses attention on child.
2. Realizes a "talking" situation is occurring.
3. Listens and maintains a receiver attitude.
4. Corrects own behavior, guesses at child's meaning, and tries new actions.
5. Realizes conversation is over.

Child behavior

1. Stands in front of visitor, searches face to catch eye, makes loud vocalization dropping volume when eye contact made, observes visitor behavior.
2. Repeats first sound (parents understand, visitor doesn't), observes visitor reaction.
3. Grabs visitor's hand, vocalizes loudly, looks in visitor's eyes.
4. Tugs at hand, uses insistent voice tone, gestures toward the kitchen.
5. Pulls visitor to sink, uses new word (visitor doesn't understand), corrects through gestures when visitor reaches for cookie jar.
6. Corrects visitor's guess (milk), gestures towards water, holds out hand.
7. Drinks and hands back glass, smiles, and walks away.

This type of behavior has been called instrumental expression, because vocalization and nonverbal behaviors were used to obtain a certain goal.

The toddler seeks out people willing to listen and learns from each encounter. Adults modify and adapt their speech, based on the abilities they observe in the child. This is done intuitively by use of shorter and less complex comments, and it changes when adults notice increased capacity.

CHARACTERISTICS OF TODDLER LANGUAGE

The speech of young children speaking in two-word, or longer, sentences is termed *telegraphic* and *prosodic*. It is telegraphic because many words are omitted because of the child's limited ability to express and remember large segments of information; the most important parts of the sentence are usually present. "Prosodic" refers to the child's use of voice modulation and word stress with a particular word(s) to give special emphasis and meaning. Donoghue (1985) describes telegraphic speech as follows:

> Their utterances are devoid of function words and resemble messages that adults would send by wire, for instance, "Jimmy truck" could represent "That truck belongs to Jimmy" or "Give me my truck." Meanings will often depend upon context and intonation of the utterance.

NEGATIVES

No discussion of older toddlers' language would be complete without mentioning the use of "no." There seems to be an exasperating time when children say "no" to everything — seemingly testing whether there is a choice. Young children first use "no" to indicate nonexistence (Bloom, 1970). Later it is used to indicate rejection and denial. Even when the child can speak in sentences longer than three words, the "no" often remains the first in a sequence of words. A typical example is "No want go bed." Soon, children insert negatives properly between the subject and the verb into longer utterances, as sentence length increases. Of all speech characteristics, toddlers' use of negatives and their avid energetic demands to be "listened to" stick in the memories of their caretakers.

AIDS TO TODDLER SPEECH DEVELOPMENT

The swift rate of new words entering toddlers' vocabularies indicates that caretakers should begin to become increasingly specific with descriptive terms in their speech. If a truck is blue, a comment like "The blue truck rolled in the mud" is appropriate. If an

FIGURE 2-11 "The red ball is in your hand."

object is on the "bottom" shelf, "top" drawer, or "under" the table, those words can be stressed. A color, number, or special quality can be inserted in simple comments (figure 2-11).

Playing detective to understand toddlers will always be part of adults' conversational style.

Holmes and Morrison (1979) offer adults advice for providing an optimum toddler environment for language stimulation:

- Expose the child to language with speech neither too simple nor too complex, but just slightly above the child's current level.
- Stay in tune with the child's actual abilities.
- Omit unreasonable speech demands, yet encourage attempts.
- Remember positive reinforcement is a more effective tool than negative feedback.
- Accept the child's own formulation of a language concept.
- Channel progress by providing a correct model.
- Make a point of being responsive.
- Follow the child's interest by naming and simple discussion.

Other suggested pointers follow:

- Explain what you are doing as you work. Describe what's happening.

- Show excitement for the child's accomplishments.
- Talk about what the child is doing, wanting, or needing.
- Pause and listen with ears and eyes after you have spoken.
- Encourage toddler imitation of gestures and sounds.
- Imitate the child's sounds.

The following adult behaviors are included in appropriate practices identified by NAEYC (National Association for the Education of Young Children) (1987):

Adults engage in many one-to-one, face-to-face conversations with toddlers. Adults let toddlers initiate language, and wait for a response, even from children whose language is limited. Adults label or name objects, describe events, and reflect feelings to help children learn new words. Adults simplify their language for toddlers who are just beginning to talk (instead of "It's time to wash our hands and have a snack," the adult says, "Let's wash hands. Snacktime!"). Then, as children acquire their own words, adults expand on the toddler's language (for example, TODDLER — "Mary sock." ADULT — "Oh, that's Mary's missing sock, and you found it.").

Tarrow and Lundsteen (1981) suggest some toddler activities for corresponding objectives (figure 2-12). Additional toddler-adult activities promoted by The Parents As Teachers Program Planning and Implementation Guide (1986) include:

- Setting out two or three familiar objects and asking the child to get one.
- Calling attention to interesting things you see, hear, smell, taste, or feel.
- Showing and labeling your facial features and the child's in a mirror.
- Labeling and pointing to objects around a room.
- Labeling verbally items of clothing as the child is dressing and undressing.
- Labeling the people in the toddler's world.

Other toddler-activity ideas are suggested by Sterling (1983) in *Early Childhood Practicum Guide*, Delmar Publishers, pages 277–80.

A toddler movement play follows. Many others are available in teacher sourcebooks that can be obtained at libraries or from school-supply companies.

Take your little hands and go clap, clap, clap
Take your little hands and go clap, clap, clap
Take your little hands and go clap, clap, clap
    Clap, clap, clap your hands.

Take your little foot and go tap, tap, tap
Take your little foot and go tap, tap, tap
Take your little foot and go tap, tap, tap
    Tap, tap, tap your foot.

Take your little eyes and go blink, blink, blink
Take your little eyes and go blink, blink, blink

Take your little eyes and go blink, blink, blink
    Blink, blink, blink your eyes.

Take your little mouth and go buzz, buzz, buzz
Take your little mouth and go buzz, buzz, buzz
Take your little mouth and go buzz, buzz, buzz
    Buzz like a bumblebee.

Take your little hand and wave bye, bye, bye
Take your little hand and wave bye, bye, bye
Take your little hand and wave bye, bye, bye
    Wave your hand bye-bye.

	OBJECTIVES	ACTIVITIES
12 to 18 months	1. To develop the ability to label things and follow directions. 2. To expand vocabulary and lay the foundation for later production of sentences. 3. To reinforce the concept of names and the ability to recognize names and sounds. 4. To encourage verbal communication. 5. To reinforce the concept of labels and increase vocabulary.	1. Line up various objects and, naming one, ask the child to get it. 2. Act out verbs ("sit," "jump," "run," "smile," etc.). 3. Use animal picture books and posters of animals. 4. Let the child talk on a real telephone. 5. Describe things at home or outside, on a walk or an automobile trip.
18 to 24 months	1. To stimulate imitation and verbalization. 2. To improve the ability to name objects. 3. To encourage repetition, sequencing, and rhythm. 4. To develop auditory acuity, passive vocabulary, and the concept of language constancy. 5. To stimulate verbalization, selectivity, and — eventually — descriptive language. 6. To stimulate conversation.	1. Tape-record the child and others familiar to the child, and play the tapes back for the child. 2. On a walk around the home or neighborhood with the child, point out and name familiar objects. 3. Play counting games, sing songs, and tell and retell familiar stories. 4. With the child, listen to the same recording of a story or song over and over. 5. Cut out of magazines and mount on stiff cardboard: pictures of foods, clothing, appliances, etc. Have the child identify them as you show them. Use memorable descriptions: "orange, buttery carrots"; "the shiny blue car." 6. With the child, prepare and eat a make-believe meal.

FIGURE 2-12 Toddler objectives and activities *(Sara Wynn Lundsteen and Norma Bernstein Tarrow,* Activities and Resources for Guiding Young Children's Learning, *1981. Reproduced with permission from McGraw-Hill Book Company.)*

LEARNING FROM MOTHERS

Burton White's projects have influenced many early childhood educators. His writings have highlighted the importance of the environment and mothering behaviors during what's been termed "a critical childhood growth stage" — toddlerhood. White (1973), while observing mothers from all economic levels and watching their children's progress, identified maternal skills that he believed accounted for the competence in the observed children. The competence, ingenuity, and energy of this group of mothers, he felt, was commendable. White felt that mothering can be a vastly underrated occupation.

The following describes some of White's identified mother behaviors:

Mothers talk a great deal to their children, and usually at a level the child can handle. They make them feel as though whatever they are doing is usually interesting. They provide access to many objects and diverse situations. They lead the child to believe that he can expect help and encouragement most, but not all of the time. They demonstrate and explain things to the child, but mostly on the child's instigation rather than their own. They are imaginative, so that they make interesting associations and suggestions to the child when opportunities present themselves. They very skillfully and naturally strengthen the child's intrinsic motivation to learn.

Pflaum (1986), another well-known educator, suggests home language experiences that contribute to language emergence:

The language environment many children experience is one that contains language games during feeding and other caregiving episodes; parental understanding of correct functioning; parental acceptance of utterances; probes to elicit more talk; special baby talk to attract attention and to engage them in talk; parents recast statements to clarify language concepts and offer routines through which to practice. These are the characteristics of the setting in which children learn the vocabulary, syntax (order and structure of word combinations), sounds, and meanings of language.

RECOGNIZING DIFFERENCES IN LANGUAGE GROWTH

Caregivers are better able to identify talented, normal (average), and delayed speakers at about 18 months of age (White, 1973). What causes diversity is too complex to mention here, but some factors can be inferred, and others have been previously mentioned. Mothers' and caregivers' responses to children's verbalness toward the end of the children's first year and into the second year can be a determining factor:

Sooner or later they (mothers or caregivers) become aware of their child's emerging capacity of language acquisition. Some choose to feed the growth of language by going out of their way to talk a great deal to their children. Some provide language input effectively by careful selection of suitable words and phrases and by exploiting the child's interest of the moment. Others provide a great deal of input but with considerably less skill and effectiveness. Other mothers show minimal attention to the language interest of their children or for other reasons provide negligible amounts of language input. (White, 1973)

INTRODUCING TODDLERS TO BOOKS

Toddlers show an interest in simple, colorful books and pictures and enjoy adult closeness and attention (figure 2-13). Pointing and naming can become an enjoyable game. Sturdy pages that are easily turned help the toddler. A scrapbook of favorite objects mounted on cardboard individualize the experience. Clear contact paper and lamination will add life and protection. Since a toddler may move on quickly to investigating other aspects of the environment, adults offering initial experiences with books need to remember that when interest has waned it's time to respect the search for other adventures.

NAEYC (1985) suggests that "adults frequently read to toddlers, individually on laps or in groups of two or three. Adults sing with toddlers, do fingerplays, act out simple stories like "The Three Bears" with children participating actively, or tell stories using a flannelboard or magnetic board, and allow child to manipulate and place figures on the boards."

FIGURE 2-13 Grandmothers can enjoy picture-book reading times as much as toddlers.

Desirable features of toddler appropriate books often include simple uncomplicated storylines, colorful, uncrowded illustrations or photographs, opportunities for the toddler to point and name familiar objects, predictive books (ones allowing the child to guess or predict successfully), strong, short rhymes or repetitive rhythms. "Touch and feel" books are particularly enjoyed; and sturdy, heavy board pages that can be mouthed but not torn are practical. Novelty books that make noise or pop-up books and books with sturdy moving parts capture a toddler's attention. Weiser (1982) lists "reading-related objects" that can be provided for the exploring toddler:

- Catalogs and magazines to look at, touch, finger, mouth, and otherwise investigate.
- Cloth books.
- First books, homemade or center-made on cardboard pages, protected by transparent stick-on coverings.
- Photographs or books containing photographs of

people and objects in the toddler's life. (Include photos of the toddler.)
- Homemade sensory books that call for touching or smelling and that use safe materials.

Techniques for reading books to toddlers are very similar to those used in late infancy. Cozy, undisturbed settings with adults watchful of child interest and disinterest are still important. Label and point to pictures of objects, and expand on the picture a little with whatever comes to mind. If a picture of a cow is encountered, the adult might say, "cow. The cow says 'Moo moo!'." Toddlers enjoy hearing appropriate sound effects. (Parents As Teachers, 1986).

Other book reading techniques are identified by Sherwin (1987):

Sharing books together can be one of the most satisfying experiences you can have with a young child. You don't have to stick to the text or read every word, instead, involve the child in the book by asking questions about the pictures. Your toddler might also enjoy simply turning the book's pages. Knowing when to read is important. It's true that introducing books early can lay the foundation for a lifelong love of books and reading. But pressuring or cajoling a resistant 1-year-old to sit still and listen can have the opposite effect.

David R. Pushaw (1976) offers a bibliography of books for infants and toddlers (figure 2-14). Now is the time to also share the strong rhyming rhythms of Mother Goose and introduce two classics, "Mary Had a Little Lamb" and "Pop Goes the Weasel."

Additional recommended toddler books follow:

Ahlberg, Janet and Allen, *The Baby's Catalogue.* Boston, MA: Little, Brown, 1983. Features objects in a toddler's environment.

Barton, Bryon, *Trucks.* New York: Crowell, 1986. Vivid color, and objects that move.

Brown, Marc, *Hand Rhymes.* New York: E. P. Dutton, 1985

Chorao, Kay, *The Baby's Lap Book*, New York:
E. P. Dutton, 1977
The Baby's Bedtime Book, New York:
E. P. Dutton, 1984
The Baby's Story Book, New York:
E. P. Dutton, 1984

Gretz, Susanna, *Hide and Seek*, New York: Four Winds Press, 1986
Ready for Bed, New York: Four Winds Press, 1986

Keats, Ezra Jack, *Hi Cat*...New York: Macmillan, 1970. Illustrations familiar to inner city children.

Lynn, Sara, *Farm Animals*, New York: Macmillan, 1987

Tafuri, Nancy, *Have You Seen My Duckling?*, New York: Greenwillow, 1984
Where We Sleep, New York: Greenwillow, 1987

Hill, Eric, *Spot Goes to the Farm*, New York: Putnam, 1987

Kunhardt, Dorothy, *Pat the Bunny*, New York: Golden Touch and Feel Books, 1942

Pearson, Susan, *The Baby and the Bear*, New York: Viking, 1987

Price, Mathew and Jean Claverie, *Happy Birthday*, New York: Alfred Knopf Publishers, 1988. Little doors that open to reveal party guests delight toddlers.

Simple Objects, New York: Tuffy Books, Inc., 1987
Show and Tell Me, New York: Tuffy Books, Inc., 1987
Easy Objects, New York: Tuffy Books, Inc., 1987

Pragoff, Fiona, *Alphabet*, New York: Doubleday, 1987
What Color?, New York: Doubleday, 1987
Growing, New York: Doubleday, 1987
How Many?, New York: Doubleday, 1987

Oxenbury, Helen, *Clap Hands*, New York: Macmillan, 1987
All Fall Down, New York: Macmillan, 1987
Tickle, Tickle, New York: Macmillan, 1988
Whose Baby Are You?, New York: Random, 1987

Siler, D. *What Do Babies Do?*, New York: Random, 1985

Read-Aloud Rhymes for the Very Young, Jack Prelutsky, ed., New York: Alfred Knopf Publishers, 1988

Six to Twelve Months

Baby's Book of Animals, James & Jonathan, Inc. Ideal for six-month-old child. Colorful pictures; pages not easily torn.

What the Animals Say, James & Jonathan, Inc. Cloth picture book with brief text; good pictures.

Baby Animals Board Book, illustrated by Gyo Fujikawa, McLoughlin Brothers.

Farm Animals Board Book, illustrated by Irma Wilde, McLoughlin Brothers.

Baby's Mother Goose, illustrated by Alice Schlesinger, McLoughlin Brothers. Colorful pictures; simple, suitable content.

Tall Book of Mother Goose, The, illustrated by Feodor Rojankovsky, Harper and Row. The bold colors of the pictures are attractive to youngsters.

Real Mother Goose, The, illustrated by Blanche Fisher Wright, Rand McNally. Appealing pictures.

One to Two Years

Come Walk With Me; I Look Out My Window; This Is My House; My Toys; Let's Go Shopping; A Trip to the Zoo; designed by Aurelius Battaglia, Playskool Play Books, Playskool Manufacturing Company, Inc.

Baby Farm Animals, by Garth Williams, Golden Press. Just a few words of text — and charming pictures. The pages are made of strong cardboard.

Child's Good Night Book, A, by Margaret Wise Brown, illustrated by Jean Charlot, Addison-Wesley. A thoroughly satisfying book, and one that may be a calming preliminary to going to bed.

Goodnight Moon, by Margaret Wise Brown, illustrated by Clement Hurd, Harper and Row. Part of the fun of this book is locating the mouse in each picture.

FIGURE 2-14 Infant and toddler book list

What can toddlers begin to understand during the reading of picture books? Besides knowing that photographs and illustrations are between the covers of books, the toddler gathers ideas about book pleasure. As the child touches pictured objects, the child may grasp the idea that the objects depicted are representations of familiar objects. The toddler can notice that books are not handled as toys. Near two years of age, the toddler probably still names what's pictured but may understand stories. The toddler may grasp the idea that book characters and events are make believe. If a particular book is reread to a child, the child can know that the particular stories in books don't change, and what's to be read is predictable. Sometimes the toddler finds that he or she can participate in the telling by singing, repeating character lines, and making physical motions to represent actions; for example, "knocking on the door."

BEGINNING LITERACY

During toddlerhood, many children gain general knowledge of books and awareness of print. This can develop into a future interest in alphabet letters and eventually into recognition of a few letters and words. This is viewed as a natural process, which takes place in a literate home or day-care environment (Anbar, 1986). It is possible to establish a positive early bonding between children and book-sharing times — a first step toward literacy. Some toddlers who show no interest in books will, when exposed to books at a later time, find them as interesting as other children. In our get-ahead society, even toddler centers are pressured to provide sit-down instruction. Parents need to understand that a literary interest can be piqued throughout early childhood. The fact that a toddler may not be particularly enamored with books or book-sharing times at a particular stage is not a matter of concern. It may be simply a matter of the child's natural, individual activity level and his or her ability to sit and stay focused in an environment that holds an abundance of features to explore.

TOYS

Certain types of toys have a strong connection to toddlers' emerging language development. Musical toys, dolls and stuffed animals that make noises or talk, and alphabet toys, including magnetic alphabet letters, can be described as language-promoting toys. Noise-making toys or recordings, both audio and visual, capture the toddler's attention. Videos for toddlers are becoming increasingly available. Songs and music are also enjoyed by toddlers and offer another language-inputting opportunity.

ADVICE TO PARENTS OF TODDLERS

Verbally responsive and playful people, and a "toddler-proof" home equipped with objects and toys the toddler can investigate, are positive factors in increasing emerging toddler language. Objects and toys need not be expensive and can be designed and created at home. Social contact outside the home is important also. Toddlers enjoy branching out from the home on excursions with caring adults. Local libraries may offer toddler story hours, and play groups are increasingly popular and sponsored by a wide number of community groups.

Sitting on the floor at times or on a low chair helps adults both send and receive. At this age, toddlers can drive people crazy asking for the names of things and can be insistent and impatient about demands. Words will be learned during real events with concrete (real) objects.

Regularly involving toddlers in educative conversations with educational toys and simple books prompts language growth. Patience and interest — rather than heavy-handed attempts to teach — are best. Getting the most from everyday experiences is a real art that requires an instructive yet relaxed attitude and the ability to talk about what has captured the child's attention. A skilled adult who is with a toddler who is focused on the wrapping paper rather than the birthday present will add comments about the wrapping paper. Or at the zoo, in front of the bear's cage, if the child is staring at a nearby puddle, the adult will discuss the puddle. Providing words and ideas along the child's line of thinking, and having fun while doing so, becomes second nature after a few attempts.

Skilled adults tend to modify their speech according to the child's ability but also add to sentence length and complexity, providing that which is just a little beyond the child's level. Parent talk that sensitively and effectively suggests and instructs primes the child's language growth.

Summary

Language ability grows at its fastest rate of development during the toddler period. Young children accomplish difficult language tasks. They learn their native language sounds (phonetics) and successfully produce an increasing number of sounds. Grammar rules form and reform as the child gets closer to reproducing mature speech patterns. The child listens more carefully, noticing regularities and meanings (semantics) of words and gestures.

Concepts develop, serving as categories that help the child organize life's events. Many concepts are paired with words. Word symbols aid communication and language by allowing the child to speak and to be understood. Parents' conversations and the child's first-hand exploration through sense organs give depth to new words.

Toddlers are active in conversations, speaking and listening, sometimes correcting, trying to get the message across to whoever in the family will listen. Toddlers talk to themselves and their toys in one- and then two- (or more) word sentences. These sentences are barely recognizable at first but gain more and more clarity as children age.

Differences between children's speech output may be noticed, and responsive, sensitive adults are language-promoting companions. Toddler books are enjoyed and plentiful.

Student Activities

- Make a book for toddlers from magazine illustrations or from photographs of common objects familiar to toddlers. Pages should be sturdy. Cut away any distracting backgrounds. If desired, outline objects with a wide tip felt pen and protect pages with clear adhesive plastic or slip into page protectors. (An old binder works well to hold the pages.) Test your book on toddlers, and share your results.

- Form a group of three fellow students. Using the following three statements, explore changing word stress, rhythm, and pitch. Analyze the changed meanings.
  1. What am I doing?
  2. It was his book.
  3. You're a fine person.

- Using only gestures, get the person sitting next to you to give you a tissue or handkerchief or to tell you that one is not available.

- Observe three toddlers (15 to 24 months old). Write down consonant sounds you hear. Record the number of minutes for each observation.

- Using the following scale, rate each of the following statements.

1	2	3	4	5
Strongly Agree	Agree	Can't Decide	Mildly Disagree	Strongly Disagree

  1. Toddlers can be best understood when adults analyze their words instead of their meanings.
  2. Some parents seem to have a knack for talking to young children that they probably don't realize they possess.
  3. The labeling stage is a time when children learn concepts rather than words.

4. Learning language is really simple imitation.
5. The study of semantics could take a lifetime.
6. A toddler who doesn't like books isn't progressing properly.
7. After reading this unit, I won't react to toddler grunts.
8. Parents whose toddlers are speaking many words have purposely taught words to their children.
9. It's a good idea to have a special place in the home where books are enjoyed with a toddler.
10. It's best to give the toddler specific words for things, like pick-ups instead of trucks, or bonnet instead of hat.

Talk about your ratings in a group discussion.

- On a piece of paper, list as many toddler language milestones or accomplishments as you can remember.

Unit Review

A. Match each word in Column I with the phrase it relates to in Column II.

Column I	**Column II**
1. jargon	a. "Allgone cookie."
2. phonology	"Shoe allgone."
3. grammar	b. toddler goes through a naming or labeling stage
4. dis? dat?	c. toddler unconsciously recognizes word order
5. pivot	d. though they are limited in number, many serve a double
6. alphabet	purpose
7. symbol	e. each world language has its own
	f. "Ibbed googa oodle."
	g. a word represents something

B. Write a brief description of experiences that could promote a toddler's learning the word "hat." (Example: Parent points to a picture of a hat in a book, and says "hat.")

C. List five identifying characteristics of the following concepts:

van, rain, needle, giraffe

D. Return to Review Question B. How many of your examples involved the child's sensory exploration of a hat? Why would this aid the child's learning?

E. Why is the toddler period called the prime or critical time for learning language?

F. Write definitions for the following words. Check your definitions with the ones found in the Glossary at the end of the text.

syntax   phonetic   modifier   phoneme   morpheme

G. Select the best answer.
   1. Most children clearly articulate all English letter sounds by age
      a. 7 or 8.   c. 5.
      b. 6.   d. 24 months.

2. Most concept words used correctly by toddlers are
   a. labels and imitative echoing.
   b. fully understood.
   c. used because identifying characteristics have been noticed.
   d. rarely overused.
3. From beginning attempts, children
   a. reverse word order.
   b. use full simple sentences.
   c. use stress, intonation, and inflection in speaking.
   d. are always clearly understood.
4. One should _____ insist that the toddler pronounce "tree" correctly if he or she is saying "twee."
   a. always   c. never
   b. usually   d. tactfully
5. A toddler's one word sentence, "Wawa," may mean:
   a. "I want a drink of water."
   b. The child's dog, Waiter, is present.
   c. The child's father's name is Walter.
   d. Any one or none of the above.

H. What parent behaviors are helpful in the toddler's acquisition of language?

References

Acredolo, Linda P. and Susan W. Goodwyn. "Symbolic Gesturing in Language Development." *Human Development* No. 28, 1986. 53–58.

Anbar, Ada. "Reading Acquisition of Preschool Children Without Systematic Instruction." *Early Childhood Research Quarterly* 1.1 (Mar. 1986): 69–83.

Ainsworth, M. D. S. and S. M. Bell. "Mother-Infant Interaction and Development of Competence," ERIC Document, ED 065 180, 1972.

Angier, Natalie, "Medical Clues From Babies' Cries." *Discover* 5.9 (Sept. 1984): 49–51.

Anglin, J. M. *Word, Object, and Conceptual Development*, New York: Norton, 1977.

Bateson, M. C., "The Epigenesis of Conversational Interaction." *Before Speech*. Ed. M. Bullowa. London: Cambridge UP, 1979. 63–78.

Beck, M. Susan. *Kidspeak*. New York: New American Library, 1982.

Bee, Helen. *The Developing Child*. New York: Harper and Row, 1981.

Bellugi, Ursula. "Learning the Language." *Readings in Psychology Today*. Ed. Robert Schell. New York: Random House, 1977.

Bloom, L. *Language Development: Form and Function in Emerging Grammars*, Cambridge: MIT Press, 1970.

Braine, M. D. S. "The Ontogeny of English Phrase Structures: The First Phase." *Studies of Child Language Development*. Eds. C. A. Ferguson and D. I. Slobin. New York: Holt, Rinehart and Winston, 1973.

Brazelton, T. Berry, in Richard M. Restak's "Newborn Knowledge," *Human Development*, Annual Editions 83/84, Guilford, CT: The Duskin Publishing Group, Inc., 1983. 83–85.

Brazelton, T. Berry. "Evidence of Communication in Neonatal Behavioral Assessment." Ed. M. Bullowa. *Before Speech*. Cambridge: Cambridge UP, 1979. 80-96.

Bruner, Jerome et al. *Studies in Cognitive Growth*. New York: John Wiley & Sons, 1966.

Buchwald, Jennifer. "Medical Clues From Babies' Cries." *Discover*, 1984. 49-51.

Chomsky, Noam. *Language and Mind*. New York: Harcourt, Brace, and World, 1968.

Chukovsky, Kornei. *From Two to Five*. Berkeley: Univ. of California, 1963.

Clark-Stewart, K. A. *Interactions Between Mothers and Their Young Children; Characteristics and Consequences*. Monographs of the Society for Research in Child Development 38 (1973): 6-7.

Condon and Sanders in Richard M. Restak's "Newborn Knowledge," *Human Development*, Annual Editions 83/84, Guilford, CT: The Duskin Publishing Group, Inc., 1983. 83-85.

Developmentally Appropriate Practice In Early Childhood Programs Serving Children From Birth Through Age 8, Ed. Sue Bredekamp. Washington, D.C.: NAEYC, 1987.

de Villiers, Peter A. and Jill G. *Early Language*, Cambridge: Harvard UP, 1979.

Donoghue, Mildren R. *The Child and The English Language Arts*. Dubuque, IA: Wm. C. Brown, 1985.

Eden, Alvin N. *Positive Parenting*. New York: New American Library, 1985.

Egolf, D. and S. Chester. *Nonverbal Communication and Disorders of Speech and Language*, Rockville, MD: American Speech-Language-Hearing Assn., 1973. ASHA, 1973.

Elardo, R., R. Bradley, and B. M. Caldwell, "A Longitudinal Study of the Relation of Infants' Home Environments to Language Development at Age Three." *Child Development* 48 (1977): 595-603.

Eveloff, Herbert H. "Some Cognitive and Affective Aspects of Early Language Development." *Child Development Contemporary Perspectives*. Eds. S. Cohen and T. Comiskey. Itasca: Peacock, 1977. 149-155.

Eyler, Fonda, in Jim Kunerth's "Born Communicators." *Orlando Sentinel*, May 18, 1987, 3L.

Fischer, Kurt, in Otto Friedrich's "What Do Babies Know?" *Human Development* 85/86, Guilford, CT: The Duskin Publishing Group, Inc., 1986.

Freedman, Daniel G. *Human Sociobiology*, New York: The Free Press, 1979.

Freedman, Daniel G. "Smiling of Blind Infants." *Journal of Child Psychology and Psychiatry* 5.174 (1964): 86-92.

Friedrich, Otto. "What Do Babies Know?" *Human Development* 85/86, Guilford, CT: The Duskin Publishing Group, Inc., 1986.

Gleason, Jean Berko, in Jim Kunerth's "Born Communicators." *Orlando Sentinel*, May 18, 1987. 3L.

Gonzalez-Mena, Janet. "English As A Second Language for Preschool Children." *Young Children* 32.1 (1976): 16-21.

Hakuta, Kenji. *The Mirror of Language*. New York: Basic Books, 1986.

Halliday, M. A. K. "One Child's Protolanguage." *Before Speech*. Ed. M. Bullowa. London: Cambridge UP, 1979. 171-190.

Holmes, Deborah L. and Frederick J. Morrison. *The Child*. Monterey: Brooks-Cole, 1979.

Honig, Alice Sterling. "What Are The Needs of Infants?" *Young Children* 36.6, Nov. 1981. 38-41.

Hostetler, A. J., "Why Baby Cries: Data May Shush Skeptics." *The A.P.A. Monitor*, 19.7, July 1988. 27-32.

Hoy, J. and I. Somer, eds. *The Language Experience*. New York: Dell, 1974.

Huey, Francis. "Learning Potential of the Young Child." *Educational Leadership*, 40.6, Nov. 1965.

Hymes, D. "Competence and Performancy in Linguistic Theory." *Language Acquisition: Models and Methods*. Eds. R. Huxley and E. Ingram. New York: Academic Press, 1971.

Jacobson, Armina Lee. "Infant Day Care: Toward a More Human Environment." *Young Children* 33.5 (July 1978): 31–36.

Jacobson, R. *Child Language*. The Hague: Monton, 1968.

Johnson, Katie. *Doing Words*. Boston: Houghton Mifflin, 1987.

Junker, Karin Stensland. "Communication Starts With Selective Attention." *Before Speech*. Ed. M. Bullowa. London: Cambridge UP, 1979. 307–320.

Kaye, Kenneth. "Thickening Thin Data: The Maternal Role in Developing Communication and Language." *Before Speech*. Ed. M. Bullowa. London: Cambridge UP, 1979. 191–206.

Klaus, Marshall H. and Phyllis H. Klaus. *The Amazing Newborn*. Menlo Park, CA: Addison Wesley, 1985.

Kunerth, Jim. "Born Communicators." *Orlando Sentinel*, May 18, 1987. 3L.

Lay-Dopyera, Margaret and John E. Dopyera. *Becoming A Teacher Of Young Children*. Lexington, MA: D. C. Heath and Co., 1982.

Lee, Laura L. "The Relevance of General Semantics to Development of Sentence Structure in Children's Language." *Communication: General Semantics Perspectives*. Ed. Lee Thayer. New York: Spartan Books, 1970.

Lenneberg, Eric H. "The Natural History of Language." *Human Development and Cognitive Processes*. Ed. John Eloit. Toronto: Holt, Rinehart and Winston, 1971.

Lester, Barry. "There's More to Crying Than Meets The Ear." *Child Care Newsletter*, 2.2 (1983): 4–8.

Lewis, M. and L. A. Rosenblum. *The Effect of The Infant on Its Caregiver*. New York: John Wiley & Sons, 1974.

Machado, J. and Helen Meyer-Botnarescue. *Early Childhood Education Practicum Guide*. Albany: Delmar Publishers Inc., 1984.

Meers, Hilda J. *Helping Our Children Talk*, New York: Longman Group, 1976.

Meltzoff, Andrew, in Otto Friedrich's "What Do Babies Know?" *Human Development* 85/86, Guilford, CT: The Duskin Publishing Group, Inc., 1986.

Newson, John. "The Growth of Shared Understandings Between Infant and Caregiver." *Before Speech*. Ed. M. Bullowa. Cambridge: Cambridge UP, 1979. 207–222.

Ornstein, Robert and David Sobel. *The Healing Brain*. New York: Simon and Schuster, 1987.

Parents As Teachers Program Planning and Implementation Guide, Jefferson, MO: Missouri Dept. of Elem. and Secondary Ed., 1986.

Pflaum, Susanna W. *The Development of Language and Literacy in Young Children*. Columbus, OH: Charles E. Merrill Publishing Co., 1986.

Pushaw, David R. *Teach Your Child To Talk*, New York: Dantree Press, 1976.

Ryle, Gilbert. *The Concept of Mind*. London: Hutchinson House, 1949.

Scott, Louise Binder. *Learning Time With Language Experiences for Young Children*. New York: McGraw-Hill, 1968.

Sherwin, Amanda. "Your Baby at 12 Months." *The Beginning Years*, 11.7, Spring, 1987. 27–30.

Slobin, Dan I. *Psycholinguistics*. Glenview, IL: Scott, Foresman, 1971.

Snow, Catherine, Akke De Blauw, and Ghislaine Van Roosmalen. "Talking and Playing With Babies." *Before Speech*. Ed. M. Bullowa. London: Cambridge UP, 1979. 269–288.

Spelke, Elizabeth, in Otto Friedrich's "What Do Babies Know?" *Human Development* 85/86, Guilford, CT: The Duskin Publishing Group, Inc., 1986.

Spieker, Susan, "Study Links Tots Smiles," *San Jose Mercury News*, Sept. 13, 1987. 8B.

Spitzer, Dean R. *Concept Formation and Learning in Early Childhood*. Columbus, OH: Charles E. Merrill, 1977.

Stewig, John W. *Teaching Language Arts in Early Childhood*. New York: CBS College Publishing, 1982.

Tarrow, Norma Bernstein, and Sara Wynn Lundsteen. *Activities and Resources for Guiding Young Children's Learning*. New York: McGraw-Hill, 1981.

Tronick, Edward, in Jim Kunerth's, "Born Communicators," *Orlando Sentinel*, May 18, 1987. 3L.

Watson, Clyde. *Catch Me and Kiss Me and Say It Again*. New York: Philomel Books, 1978.

Weiser, Margaret G. *Group Care and Education of Infants and Toddlers*. St. Louis: C. V. Mosby, 1982.

Werner, E. E. and R. S. Smith. *Vulnerable, But Invincible*, New York: McGraw-Hill, 1982.

White, Burton L. "A Person Is Emerging." *Parents As Teachers Program Planning and Implementation Guide*, Jefferson City, MO: Missouri Dept. of Elem. and Secondary Ed., 1986.

White, Burton. *The First Three Years of Life*, Englewood Cliffs, NJ: Prentice-Hall, 1973.

Yawkey, Thomas D., et al. *Language Arts and The Young Child*, Itasca, IL: F. E. Peacock, 1981.

UNIT 3

Preschool Years

OBJECTIVES

After studying this unit, you should be able to

- identify characteristics of typical preschool speech.
- describe differences in the language of younger and older preschoolers.
- discuss the preschooler's growth of language skill.

The preschool child's speech reflects sensory, physical, and social experiences, as well as thinking ability. Parents and teachers accept temporary limitations, knowing that almost all children will reach adult language levels.

A main concern of teachers is to interact and provide growing opportunities and activities. An understanding of typical preschool speech characteristics can help the teacher do this.

Background experiences with children and child study give a teacher insight into children's language behavior. The beginnings of language, early steps, and factors affecting the infant and toddler's self-expression were covered in Units 1 and 2. This unit pinpoints language use during preschool years. Although speech abilities are emphasized, growth and change in other areas are also covered as they relate to speech.

In addition to the child's home environment, playing with other children is a major factor influencing language development. Finding friends in the child's age group is an important part of attending an early childhood center. In a place where there are fascinating things to explore and talk about, language abilities blossom (figure 3-1).

It is almost impossible to find a child who has all of the speech characteristics of a given age group, but most children possess some of the characteristics that are typical for their age level. There is a wide range within normal age-level behavior, and each child's individuality is an important consideration.

For simplicity's sake, the preschool period is divided into two age groups: early preschoolers (two- to three-year-olds) and older preschoolers (four- to five-year-olds).

FIGURE 3-1 "Lookit, lookit, lookit, caterpillar!"

YOUNG PRESCHOOLERS

Preschoolers communicate needs, desires, and feelings through speech and action. Close observation of a child's nonverbal communication can help uncover true meanings. A raised arm, fierce clutching of playthings, or lying spread-eagle over as many blocks as possible may express more than the child is able to put into words. Stroking a friend's arm, handing a toy to another child who hasn't asked for it but looks at it longingly, and following the teacher around the room, carry other meanings.

One can expect continued fast growth and changing language abilities, and children's understanding of adult statements is surprising. Garvey (1984) discusses the child's third year:

> Talk assumes ever-increasing importance in the child's life from the first verbal exchanges with caregivers, which begin to appear before the second birthday, through the preschool period. With the beginning of formal education, new people and new experience create the need for other uses of talk. Perhaps the most dramatic changes and the most impressive achievements occur during the third year of life.

Squeals, grunts, and screams are often part of play (figure 3-2). Imitating animals, sirens, and environmental noise is common. The child points and pulls to help others understand meanings. Younger preschoolers tend to act as though others can read their thoughts

FIGURE 3-2 Giggles and laughter are abundant during preschool years.

because, in the past, adults anticipated what was needed. A few children may have what seems to be a limited vocabulary at school until they feel at home there.

The words used most often are nouns and short possessives: my, mine, Rick's. Speech focuses on present events, things are observed in newscaster style, and "no" is used liberally. As preschoolers progress in the ability to hold brief conversations, they must keep conversational topics in mind and connect their thoughts with those of others. This is difficult for two-year-olds, and true conversational exchange with playmates is brief if it exists at all. Although their speech is filled with pauses and repetitions in which they attempt to correct themselves, preschoolers are adept at conversational turn taking. Garvey (1984) estimates that talking over the speech of another speaker at this age occurs only about 5% of the time.

Speech may be loud and high-pitched when the child is excited, or barely audible and muffled when the child is embarrassed, sad, or shy. Speech of two- and three-year-olds tends to be uneven in rhythm, with comments issued in spurts rather than in an even flow like the speech of older children.

There seems to be an important step forward in the complexity of content in children's speech at age two. They may begin making comments about cause and effect and sometimes use conjunctions, such as 'cause, 'ah, and 'um, between statements. Pines (1983) describes conversational topics identified in a New York research project that monitored two-year-olds' speech:

> The children talked mostly about their own intentions and feeling, why they wanted or did not want to do certain things, or what they wanted other people to do.

A desire to organize and make sense out of their experiences is often apparent. Colors, counting, and new categories of thought emerge in their speech. There is a tendency for them to live out the action words they speak or hear in the speech of others. An adult who says "We won't run" may motivate a child to run; in contrast, an adult who says "Walk" might be more successful in having the child walk.

The Subdued Two-Year-Old

About 10% of any given group of young children may appear subdued and quiet, having a tendency toward what many might call shyness (Kagan, 1988). These children may possess a natural inclination that tends to inhibit spontaneous speech. Researchers have monitored bodily functions of a group of children identified as "shy" and found muscle tensions, including tensions in the larynx. This possibly may account for the low volume of their speech. Most preschool teachers have worked with children whose speech was difficult to hear. Often, these children seem restrained when faced with unfamiliar situations. Older preschoolers may become more outgoing and talkative or may continue to be less talkative and somewhat subdued when compared with their more boisterous counterparts. Teachers need to respect these children's natural inclinations and tendencies.

Verb Forms

In English, most verbs (regular forms) use -ed to indicate past tense. Unfortunately, many frequently used verbs are irregular, with past-tense forms like came, fell, hit, saw, took, and gave. Since the child begins using often-heard words, early speech contains correct verb forms. With additional exposure to language, the child realizes that past events are described with -ed verb endings. At that point, children tack the -ed on regular verbs as well as on irregular verbs, creating words such as broked, dranked, and other charming past-tense forms. This beautiful logic often brings inner smiles to the adult listeners. Verbs ending with "ing" are used more than before. Even auxiliary verbs are scattered through speech — "Me have," "Daddy did it" (Pflaum, 1974). Words such as wanna, gonna, and hafta seem to be learned as one word, and stick in the child's vocabulary, being used over and over.

A term for children's speech behavior that indicates they've formed a new internal rule about language and are using it is *regularization*. As children filter what they hear, creating their own rule systems, they begin to apply the new rule(s). An expected sequence in formed rules for past-tense verb usage follows:

- Uses irregular tense endings correctly (e.g., ran, came, drank).
- Forms an internal rule when discovering that -ed expresses past events (e.g., danced, called, played).
- Overregularizes. Adds -ed to all regular and irregular verbs that were formerly spoken correctly (e.g., camed, dided, wented, breaked).

- Learns that both regular and irregular verbs express past tense, and uses both.

In using plural noun forms, the following sequence is common:

- Remembers and uses singular forms of nouns correctly (e.g., ball, dog, mouse, bird).
- Uses irregular noun plurals correctly (e.g., men, feet, mice).
- Forms an internal rule that plurals have "s" or "z" ending sounds.
- Applies rule to all nouns (e.g., balls, mens, dogs, feets, birds, mices, or ballsez, dogsez, feetsez).
- Achieves flexible internal rules for plurals, memorizes irregular plural forms, and uses plurals correctly.

Key-Word Sentences

The two-year-old omits many words in sentences, as does the toddler. The remaining words are shortened versions of adult sentences in which only the essentials are present. These words are key words and convey the essence of the message. Without relating utterances to real occurrences, meaning might be lost to the listener. Sentences at this stage are about four words long. Some pronouns and adjectives, such as pretty or big, are used. Very few, if any, prepositions (by, on, with) or articles (a, an, the) are spoken frequently. Some words are run together and are spoken as single units, such as "whadat?" or "eatem," as are the verb forms mentioned earlier. The order of words (syntax) may seem jumbled at times, as in "outside going ball," but basic grammar rules are observed in most cases.

Pronouns are often used incorrectly and are confused, as in "Me all finish milk," and "him Mark's." Concepts of male and female, living things, and objects may be only partly understood, as shown in the following example:

And when a three-year-old says of the ring she cannot find, "Maybe it's hiding!" the listener wonders if she hasn't yet learned that hiding can be done only by an animate object. (Cazden, 1972)

Questions

Wh- questions (where, what, why, who) begin to appear in speech. During the toddler period, rising voice inflection and simple declarative utterances such as "Dolly drink?" are typical. At this stage, questions focus on location, objects, and people, with causation (why), process (how), and time (when). This reflects more mature thinking that probes purposes and intentions in others. Figure 3-3 shows one child's questioning development. Questions are frequent, and the child sometimes asks for an object's function or the causes of certain events. It is as if the child sees that things exist for a purpose that in some way relates to him or her. The answers adults provide stimulate the child's desire to know more.

Vocabularies range between 250 to over 1,000 words (figure 3-4). An average of 50 new words enter the child's vocabulary each month.

Overlapping Concepts and Underextension

Younger preschoolers commonly call all four-footed furry animals "dog," and all large animals "horse." The child has *overextended* and made a logical conclusion because these animals have many of the same features, can be about the same size, and therefore fit the existing word. This phenomenon is seen in the examples given in figure 3-5.

Underextension refers to the child's tendency to call all male adults "daddy" or all dogs by the family dog's name, even though the child can clearly recognize the difference between his or her dad and all other males and his or her dog and other dogs.

Concept development, defined in Unit 2 as the recognition of one or more distinguishing features or characteristics, proceeds by leaps and bounds during preschool years and is essential to meaningful communication. Details, exceptions, and discrepancies are often discussed in four-year-olds' conversations. The younger preschooler can be described as a "looker and doer" who engages in limited discussion of the features of situations. The excitement of exploration and discovery, particularly of something new and novel is readily apparent in preschool classrooms. Children typically crowd around to see, touch, experience, and make comments about objects and events. Teachers notice the all-consuming focusing, the long periods of watching or touching, usually followed by verbalizing and questioning an event or experience.

Running Commentaries

As children play, their actions are sometimes accompanied by running self-commentaries of what they are doing, or what is happening (figure 3-6, page 56). This type of speech is called *private speech* or *egocentric speech* and emerges shortly after the onset of social speech. The production of private speech increases with age, peaking at around age four or five, and gradually diminishes until it disappears at seven or eight (Diaz and Lowe, 1987). It can be described as a kind of verbal thought process, like mentally talking to oneself. It seems to increase in complex play situations as the child problem solves and talks it through.

Brophy (1977) offers reasons for private speech:

Children talk to themselves to give themselves directions for the same reason that they use their fingers in counting; they need sensorimotor activity as a reinforcement or "crutch" because their cognitive schemes are not yet developed well enough to allow them to think silently without such props.

Talking to self and talking to another can occur alternately. Toys, animals, and treasured items still receive a few words. Statements directed to others do not usually need answers. Private speech rarely considers another's point of view. A conversation between young preschoolers may sound like two children talking together about different subjects. Neither child is really listening or reacting to what the other says. When a very young preschooler does wish to talk directly to another child, it is sometimes done through an adult. A child may say, "I want truck," to an adult, even if the other child is standing close by, playing with the truck.

Researchers who have examined self-talk suggest a number of possible developmental reasons and benefits. These include:

- Practicing newly recognized language forms.
- Obtaining pleasure through play with word sounds.
- Exploring vocal capacities.
- Reliving particular significant events.
- Creating dialogue in which the child voices all people's parts, perhaps helping the child later fit into social settings.
- Experimenting with fantasy, thereby accommodating the creative urge.
- Attending objectively to language.
- Facilitating motor behavior in a task or project.

1 Child: Ages	Yes-No Questions	Wh-Questions
Period A (28 mths)	Expressed by intonation only: Sit chair? Ball go?	Limited number of routines: What(s) that? Where NP* go? What NP doing?
Period B (38 mths) More complex sentences being questioned, but no development of question forms themselves, except the appearances, probably as routines, of two negative auxiliaries *don't* and *can't*.	Dat black too? Mom pinch finger? You can't fix it?	What soldier marching? Where my mitten? Why you waking me up?
Period C–F (42–54 mths) Development of auxiliary verbs in the child's entire grammatical system. Inversion of aux. and subject NP in Yes-No, but not in Wh- questions.	Are you going to make it with me? Will you help me? Does the kitty stand up? Can I have a piece of paper? Development of tag questions from *Huh?* to mature form: I have two turn, huh? We're playing, huh? That's funny isn't it? He was scared wasn't he? Mommy, when we saw those girls they were running weren't they?	What I did yesterday? Which way they should go? Why the Christmas Tree? How he can be a doctor? Inversion of aux. and subject NP, first in affirmative questions only: Why are you thirsty? Why can't we find the right one? Later, starting in Period F, negative question also: Why can't they put on their diving suits and swim? Development of complex questions, including indirect Wh-questions: You don't know where you're going. He doesn't know what to do. We don't know who that is.

*NP signifies noun or pronoun substitute.

FIGURE 3-3 Development of question forms (*From* Child Language and Education by *Courtney B. Cazden. Copyright © 1972 by Holt, Rinehart and Winston, CBS College Publishing.*)

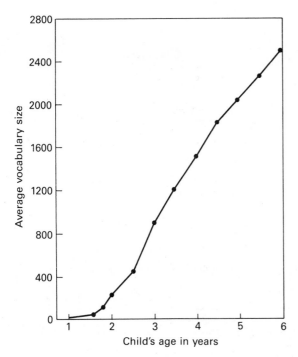

FIGURE 3-4 Growth of vocabulary

Whatever its benefits, self-talk is natural, common behavior. By the age of five, the child's self-talk is observed infrequently. As children approach the age of three, both dialogue and monologue is apparent. Observers of play conversations find it difficult to determine just how much of each is present.

Repetition

Repetition in speech occurs often. Sometimes it happens randomly at play, and at other times it is done with a special purpose. A young child may repeat almost everything said to him or her. Most young preschoolers repeat words or parts of sentences regularly. Honig (1988) suggests that children's growing language skills allow them to create repetitions that rhyme, as in "oogie, woogie, poogie bear," which greatly please them. They quickly imitate words that they like; sometimes, excitement is the cause. Chukovsky (1963) points out that rhyming words or rhyming syllables may promote enjoyable mimicking and that the younger the child, the greater the child's attraction to word repetition that rhymes. Some reasons for repetition are (1) it helps children remember things (just as

Word	Object or Event for Which the Word Was Originally Used	Other Objects or Events to Which the Word Was Later Applied
mooi	moon	cakes, round marks on windows, writing on windows and in books, round shapes in books, tooling on leather book covers, round post-marks, letter *O*
buti	ball	toy, radish, stone spheres at park entrance
sch	sound of train	all moving machines
em	worm	flies, ants, all small insects, heads of timothy grass
fafer	sound of trains	steaming coffee pot, anything that hissed or made a noise
va	white plush dog	muffler, cat, father's fur coat

FIGURE 3-5 Some examples of overextensions in the language of 1- and 2-year-old children *(From "Knowledge, context, and strategy in the acquisition of meaning," by Eve V. Clark. In Gurt 1975: Daniel P. Dato, ed.,* Developmental Psycholinguistics: Theory and Applications. *Copyright 1975 by Georgetown University, Washington, D.C.)*

Situation:	Girls playing with water. (four- and five-year-olds)	
	Commentary	**Characteristic**
Debbie:	"Two of those make one of these." (playing with measuring cups)	Talking to self.
Debbie:	"Two cups or three cups...whoops it went over."	Talks about what happened.
Tifine:	"Stop it or else I'll beat you up." (said to Debbie)	Doesn't respond to another's speech.
Debbie:	"This is heavy." (holding the 2-cup measuring container full of water)	Describes perception.
Christine:	"Is it hot?" (Chris just dropped in)	
Debbie:	"Feel it and see."	Hears another; answers appropriately.
	"It's not hot." (feeling the water)	Child talking to self.
Debbie:	"I'm finished now. Oh this is awfully heavy — I'm going to pour it into the bottle."	Talking about what she is doing.

FIGURE 3-6 Conversation during play activity

adults mentally repeat new telephone numbers), (2) it reduces stress, and (3) it is an enjoyable form of sound making.

Free associations (voiced juggling of sounds and words) occurs at play and at rest and may sound like babbling. Many times, it seems as though, having learned a word, the child must savor it or practice it, over and over.

Lack of Clarity

About one in every four words of the young preschooler is not readily understandable (figure 3-7). This lack of clarity is partially caused by an inability to control mouth, tongue, and breathing and to hear subtle differences and distinctions in speech. Typically, articulation of all English speech sounds is not accomplished until age seven or eight (figure 3-8). Young preschoolers are only 40% to 80% correct in articulation. This lack of intelligibility in children can be partly attributed to the complexity of the task of mastering the sounds. Although children may be right on target in development, their speech may be still hard to understand at times.

The young preschooler may have difficulty with the rate of speech, phrasing, inflection, intensity, syntax, and voice stress. Misarticulation and defective sound

FIGURE 3-7 The younger preschooler can be described as a "watcher" and "doer."

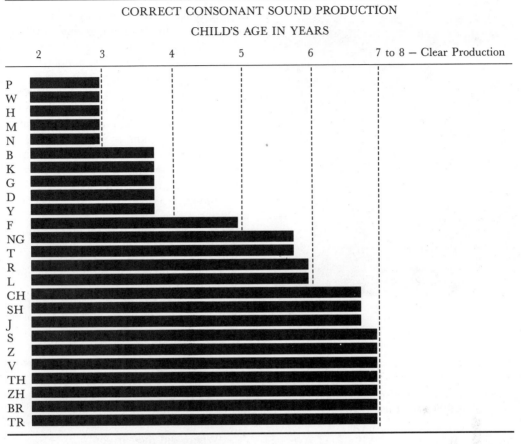

CORRECT CONSONANT SOUND PRODUCTION

CHILD'S AGE IN YEARS

FIGURE 3-8 Correct consonant sound production

making can also contribute to the problem. The child who attempts to form the longest utterances is the one who is hardest to understand. The child who omits sounds is less clear than the one who distorts them. As a rule, expect omissions, substitutions, and distortions in the speech of two- and three-year-olds, for they will be plentiful.

Young children typically omit sounds at the ends of words, saying, for example, "ba" for ball. Middle consonants in longer words are also passed over lightly — "ikeem" for ice cream, or "telfone" for telephone. Even beginning sounds may be omitted, as in "ellow" for yellow.

Substitutions of letter sounds are also common, for example, "aminal," and "pasghetti." Until the new sound is mastered, one consonant may even take the place of another; "wabbit," "wun," and "wain" are frequently heard examples.

Dramatic Play

Short play sequences that involve acting or imitating the behavior of mom or dad begin at home and school (figure 3-9). Speech usually accompanies the reenactments. Although young children at this age play side-by-side, most of this type of play starts as solitary activity. Common play themes mentioned by Caplan and Caplan (1983) include mom on the phone, mom caring for baby, mom or dad cooking. Dolls, toys, and dress-up clothes are usually part of the action and may serve to initiate this type of play. Observers of two- and three-year-olds in classrooms find it hard to determine whether children are engaged in joint planning of play

FIGURE 3-9 Into the oven it goes.

or children are playing in the same area with the same kinds of playthings. Preschools purposely purchase multiple dolls so that many children can feed and rock "their babies" when they see others doing it.

Advice for Parents and Early Childhood Staff Members

Parents sometimes worry about a child who stops, stammers, or stutters when speaking. Calling attention to this speech and making demands on the child cause tension, making the situation worse instead of better. All children hesitate, repeat, stop, and start in speaking — it is typical behavior. Searching for the right word takes time, and thoughts may come faster than words. Adults need to relax and wait. Speech is a complex sending and receiving process. Maintaining patience and optimism and assuming a casual "I'm listening" stance is the best course of action for the adult. Many schools routinely send home informational material to alert parents to age-level speech characteristics.

Attentive interaction with positive feedback is recommended for adults who live or work with two- and three-year-olds. Reacting to the intent of the child's message is more helpful than concentrating on correctness. In other words, focus on what is said rather than the way it is said. A lot of guessing is still necessary to determine what the child is trying to say. The adult's model of speech will override temporary errors as the child hears more and more of it.

Helping the children see details and relationships in what they encounter is useful if done in an unpressured manner. Connecting past events to present events may aid their understanding.

Regular checkups of children's hearing is recommended, because even a moderate hearing loss may affect speech production. Preschoolers are particularly prone to upper respiratory infections and ear problems.

As younger preschoolers get older, adults can expect the following:

- Longer sentences with more words per sentence.
- More specificity.
- More "ing" endings on verbs (figure 3-10).
- Increased correctness in the forms of the verb "to be."
- More auxiliary verbs present.
- More facility with passive-voice verbs, including did and been.
- Changes in negative sentences, from "No want" to "I don't want."
- Changes in question forms, from "Car go?" to "Where did the car go?"

FIGURE 3-10 "Coming out now."

Books for Younger Preschoolers

A wide selection of picture books is available for this age group. Generally, experts suggest books that have:

- Themes, objects, animals or people that are familiar and within their range of life experience.
- Clarity of content, and story line.
- Clear, simple illustrations or photo-illustrations with backgrounds that don't distract from the intended focus.
- Themes concerning everyday tasks and basic human needs.

Most two- and three-year-olds enjoy actively participating in story reading, but they can be very good listeners as well. Participation can include pointing, noisemaking, repeating dialogue, or performing imitative body actions. Books that are repetitive and predictable offer the enjoyment of anticipating what will come next (figure 3-11). For children who are used to being read to at bedtimes, the calming effect of

FIGURE 3-11 Getting familiar with books means a child may "relive" a favorite story over and over.

listening to the human voice becomes very apparent at story-reading times. Unit 9 covers the topic of introducing older children to literature.

OLDER PRESCHOOLERS

Between four and five years of age, most preschoolers approach adultlike speech; their sentences are longer, with almost all words present rather than only key words.

Preschoolers' play is active and vocal, and they copy each other's words and manner of speaking. A word such as "monster," or more colorful words, may swiftly gain interest and spread rapidly from child to child. Remember the joy that both younger and older children exhibited with the phrases: "zip-a-dee-doo-dah," "bibbidi-bobbidi-boo," "scoobi-scoobi-do," "blast off," "fuzzy-wuzzy," and "ooey-gooey"? Every generation of preschoolers seems to have its own favorite sayings, and new ones are constantly appearing.

Social speech and conversations of the older preschooler are heard and interpreted to a greater degree by others of the child's age. The child learns and practices the complexities of social conversation including (1) gaining another's attention by making eye contact, touching, or using words or catchphrases like "Know what?," (2) pausing and listening, (3) correcting himself or herself, (4) maintaining attention by not pausing so as not to let another speaker jump in, (5) taking turns in conversing by developing patience and trying to listen while still holding in mind what he or she wants to say.

Group Play

Joint planning of play activities and active make-believe and role playing takes on a new depth. Adults often see themselves in the play of children (figure 3-12). The four-year-old's main concern seems to be interacting with age mates. Twosomes and groups of play companions are typical in older preschoolers' classrooms and play yards (figure 3-13). As speech blossoms, friendships blossom and disintegrate. Speech is used to discourage and disallow entrance to play groups when running from newcomers is impossible. Speech is found to be effective in hurting feelings, as in statements such as "I don't like you," or "No girls." Children find verbal inventiveness may help them join play or initiate play.

FIGURE 3-12 The child is pretending to read the way the teacher reads.

In group play, pretending is paramount. Make-believe play appears to be at its zenith (Caplan and Caplan, 1983). Many children grow in the ability to (1) verbally suggest new directions and avenues of fantasy, (2) engage in verbal negotiation, (3) compromise,

FIGURE 3-13 "You're my friend, huh?"

(4) argue, and (5) become a group's leader by using the right words. Popular children seem to be those who use speech creatively and become enjoyable companions to others.

Violent statements like "I'm going to shoot you" or "cut you up" are sometimes heard, and these tend to reflect television drama. The reality-fantasy of some play situations may become temporarily blurred, causing some children considerable anxiety.

Older preschoolers talk "in character" as they elaborate their dramatic play. If a scenario calls for mother talking to a baby, preschoolers adopt the appropriate speech of a mother. Imitations of pop singers or cartoon characters are common, and imitations of space pilots are particularly popular.

Four-year-olds seem to boast, brag, and make lots of noise. However, apparently boastful statements like "Look what I did" may just be the child's attempt to show that he or she is capable and to share his or her accomplishments. Although preschoolers enjoy being with their peers, they quickly and easily engage in quarreling and name-calling. Sometimes, they do battle verbally (Caplan and Caplan, 1983). Typically, three- to five-year-olds disagree over possession of objects or territory, and verbal reasons or verbal evidence may help them win arguments. Many conflicts are resolved and lead to continued play. Speech helps them settle their affairs with and without adult help.

As a child develops a sense of humor, giggling becomes part of the noise of play. As Caplan and Caplan (1983) observe, "there's a wonderful silliness." One preschool boy thought it hilarious to go up to a teacher named Alice and say "What's your name, Alice?" and then run off laughing — quite mature humor for a four-year-old! Honig (1988) cites instances in which preschoolers distort and repeat what a caregiver says, making changes in sounds and gleefully chanting the distorted message. She urges teachers who want to cultivate children's ability to understand and appreciate humor to present materials that challenge children's ability to interpret humor.

Relational Words

More and more relational words appear as the child begins to compare, contrast, and revise stored concepts with new happenings. The following teacher-recorded anecdote during a story-telling activity shows how the child attempts to relate previously learned ethics to a new situation:

> During story telling Michael repeated with increasing vigor, "He not berry nice!" at the parts of the story when the wolf says, "I'm going to blow your house down." Michael seemed to be checking with me the correctness of his thinking based on his internalized rules of proper moral conduct. (Busy Bee Preschool)

Beck (1982) describes how concept's mature:

> Just as infants use single-word sentences to name and describe objects, and as the two-year-old combines words to describe the nature of a ball or dolly or truck, and three-year-old children continue to specify and describe, four-year-old children are also creatures of their senses. They are concerned with the smell of a thing, the touch of a thing, the look of a thing and the sound of a thing. What is special about four-year-old children, however, is that their sensual awareness begins to take on conceptual dimensions. They begin to notice function or use and they begin to see it comparatively.

and

> They come to see relationships between several objects and/or several events, and in comparing one to the other, they are learning the principle of categorization.

Space and size relationships and abstract time relationships rarely are expressed with adult precision. Although the words "big" and "little" are common usage with preschoolers, they are overused. Many other comparison words give children trouble, and one hears "biggerer," "big-big-big," and "bestus one" to describe size. Time words elicit smiles from adults as children wrestle with present, past, and future, as in "zillion days" or "tomorrower." Number words are difficult for some children to handle, and expressions like "whole bunches" and "eleventeen" are sometimes heard.

Although four-year-olds are able speakers, many of the "plays on words," double meanings, and connotative language subtleties that are important in adult speech are beyond the children's understanding. Their creative uses of words at times seem metaphoric and poetic and are valiant attempts to put thoughts into words. Half-heard words and partially or fully learned words are blended together and are, at times, wonderfully descriptive.

Speech and Child Behavior

There is tremendous variety in the ways children can modify their voices, and they may speak in a different pitch or rhythm when speaking to different people. They can whine, whisper, change volume, and distort timing and pronunciation (Garvey, 1984).

Some children discover that by increasing volume or changing tone they can affect others' behavior. They find that speech can show anger and be used aggressively to hurt someone.

Preschoolers may mimic the speech of "bad-guy" television characters. Acts of aggression, clothed in the imitated speech and actions of a TV character, can become part of this type of play.

Purposeful echoing or baby talk can irritate or tease. Excessive talking is sometimes used to get one's way, and "talking back" may occur.

Some children find that silence can get as much attention from adults as loud speech. Tattling on another may be simply a way of checking for correctness, or it can be purposeful.

Through trial and error and feedback, the child finds that words can hurt, gain friends or favor, or satisfy a wide range of needs. Because preschoolers are emotion-packed human beings, their statements range from expressions of "you're my buddy" to "you're my enemy" within a matter of minutes.

What may appear to be violent statements may be just role playing or make-believe competition. To some adults, the preschooler speech may appear loud and wild. Speech seems overly nasal and full of moisture that sprays out in some words. A young child may have frequent nasal colds and congestion during this period. Preschoolers tend to stand close to others, and their volume increases when they are intense about their subjects.

Impact Words

Not all speech used by older preschoolers is appreciated by adults. Name-calling and offensive words and phrases may be used by active preschoolers to gain attention and reaction from both adults and children. Children discover that some phrases, sentences, and words cause unusual behavior in others. They actively explore these and usually learn which of these are inappropriate and when they can be used. Children learn that most of this type of talk has "impact value." If certain talk makes people laugh or gives the children some kind of positive rewards, it is used over and over.

Bathroom words seem to be explored and used as put-downs and attention getters. Giggles and uproarious laughter can ensue when these words are used. Adding to the child's enjoyment, new teachers may not know how to handle these situations. The school's policy regarding this matter can be a subject for staff discussion. Generally, newly spoken bathroom talk should be ignored unless it is hurtful, or the child should be told that the place to use the word is in the bathroom. This frequently remedies the behavior, since the child's enjoyment of it is spoiled without an audience. Alternatively, it might suffice to firmly say "That's a word that hurts. His name is Michael." Rubin and Fisher (1982) advise parents that "Since so many preschoolers love using forbidden words, especially when they play together, and since you really can't control everything your child says, there's no way you can stop all toilet talk." What parents and teachers can control is what is said in their presence.

Created Words

Created words such as "turner-overer" for pancake turner, "mudpudders" for rain boots, or "dirt digger" for spade are wonderfully descriptive and crop up occasionally in child speech. Many cite young children's fascination with the functions of objects in their environment as the reason such words are created. As Bettelheim and Zelan (1982) note, children love making up words, including nonsense words and rhymes, and revel in their newly gained abilities to do so.

Myths Concerning Speech and Intelligence

A large and mature vocabulary at this age may tend to lead teachers to think a child has superior intelligence. Making conclusions about children based on language ability at this age has inherent pitfalls considering the many factors which could produce limited or advanced vocabulary particularly when one considers cultural differences, bilingualism, and the child's

access to "language-rich environments". At later ages language usage does seem to be related to school success. Rubin and Fisher (1982) urge teachers to rethink ideas concerning young girls superiority in language abilities "Differences between the sexes (in speaking ability) is small and less significant than was once believed."

Common Speech Patterns

Four-year-olds frequently rhyme words in their play speech, and teachers sometimes join the fun. Older preschoolers engage in self-chatter as do early preschoolers. Older preschoolers continue to make errors in grammar and in the use of the past tense of verbs ("He didn't caught me") and in the use of adjectives ("It's biggerer than yours"), time words ("The next tomorrow"), and negatives ("I didn't did it"). But preschoolers skills are increasing at this stage, and their use of forms of the irregular verb "to be" improve: "I am so," or "Mine are hot and yours are cold." Sentence structure becomes more adultlike, including use of relative clauses and complex and compound sentence forms. Articulation of letter sounds is still developing; about 75% of English letter sounds are made correctly. Omissions of letter sounds ('merca for America) and substitutions (udder for other) are still present.

The older preschooler may have a vocabulary of over 2,000 words. The child is very concerned about the correct names of things and can find the errors in the speech of others. Since the older preschooler is an active explorer, his or her questions still probe the "purposefulness" of objects or actions (as in "Why is the moon in the sky?"). The 4-year-old becomes an active problem solver and tends to explain things through visually noted attributes; for example, "A cow is called that 'cause of its horns." Elkind (1971) describes preschoolers' inability at times to talk about their solutions:

> Although the preschooler can respond to and solve problems posed verbally, he is not able to verbalize his solutions.

The child can transform questions; for example, if asked to carry a message asking mom whether *she's* ready, the child will correctly ask her, "Are *you* ready?"

Most four-year-old children enjoy books, stories, and activities with words. More and more of their time is spent on these pursuits (figure 3-14).

The four-year-old may still stutter and clutter and stop speech when there is stress or excitement. The less-mature speech of a best friend might be copied, and nonverbal expression is always a part of communication. However, most four- and five-year-olds are avid speakers. They are interested in exploring the real world as well as make-believe worlds. Chukovsky (1963) prizes the child's ability to fantasize, and encourages teachers and parents to accept and value it:

> Fantasy is the most valuable attribute of the human mind, and it should be diligently nurtured from earliest childhood, as one nurtures musical sensitivity.

A wide range of individual speech behavior is both normal and possible. Knowing some typical behaviors can help the teacher understand young children. Some younger preschoolers may have the speech characteristics of older preschoolers; while some older preschoolers have the characteristics of younger preschoolers (figure 3-15). Each child is unique in his or her progress and rate of acquiring language skills.

Summary

Knowing typical and common language development characteristics helps the teacher understand that children are unique individuals. Rapid growth of vocabulary and language skills is part of normal

FIGURE 3-14 Enjoying a favorite book

	3 YEARS OLD	4 YEARS OLD	5 YEARS OLD
Average vocabulary	900 words	1500 words	2200 words
Typical sentence length	3–4 words	5–6 words	6+ words
Regular plurals	mastered	mastered	mastered
Irregular plurals	errors common	errors common	errors common
Regular verb tenses	mastered	mastered	mastered
Irregular verb tenses	errors common	errors common	errors common
Conjunctions	uses *and*	adds *but, because*	adds more conjunctions
Questions	uses *who, what*	adds *when, why*	
Pronunciation	mispronounces 40% speech sounds	mispronounces 20% speech sounds	mispronounces 10% speech sounds
Disfluency	common	common	common

FIGURE 3-15 Typical characteristics of language learning in preschoolers (*From* Your Preschooler, *by Richard R. Rubin and John J. Fisher, 1982, Macmillan Publishing Co. Inc., N.Y., p. 50.*)

growth. Errors in the speech of young preschoolers (aged two to three) make verbalizations partly understandable. Key words in the correct order give adults clues to what's intended. Self-talk during the child's play usually describes what the child is doing and may alternate with social comments.

Teachers can use their knowledge of early childhood language development in many ways, such as alerting the staff about a child's need for hearing tests or special help and helping parents who are concerned with their child's speech patterns.

Older preschool children (aged four to five) have almost adultlike speech. They explore words and begin to understand their power. Fantasy play peaks accompanied by speech. Some newly learned speech may be irritating to school staffs and parents, but it can indicate physical, mental, and social growth. Exploring and enjoying books occupies more of the children's time. Exploring the real and make-believe worlds with words becomes children's active pursuit during the early childhood years.

There is no "average" child when it comes to language development; individual differences exist and are treated with acceptance and optimism (figure 3-16).

AGE OF CHILD

2–2½ years
Joins words in sentences of 2 or more words.
Knows name and age.
Has vocabulary of over 3 words.
Understands long spoken sentences and simple commands.
Begins using plurals and past tense.
Changes pitch and/or loudness for specific meaning.
Begins using forms of verb "to be."
Uses a few prepositions.
Uses I, me, and you.
Uses about 25 phonemes.
Articulates about 10 to 12 vowel types and about 12 to 15 consonants.
Points to and names objects in pictures.
Names 5 to 8 body parts.
Enjoys rhythm in words, nursery rhymes, finger plays, and simple stories.
Understands and responds to almost all of adult speech.
Generalizes by calling round objects ball, and so on.

2½–3 years
Negatives, imperatives and commands occur.
Shows variety in question types.
Adds as many as 2 to 3 words to vocabulary daily.
Names items in signs and books.
Uses 3- or 4-word sentences.
Enjoys fun with words.
Follows simple directions.
Points to body parts when asked.
Names many common objects.

Uses an increasing number of nouns, verbs, and pronouns.
Draws lines and circular forms in artwork.
Knows words or lines from books, songs, stories.

3–4 years
Asks why, what, where, how, and when questions.
Loves word play.
Makes closed figures in art.
Begins using auxiliary verbs.
Tells sex and age.
Utters compound sentences with connecting and . . er . . but, and so on.
Engages in imaginary play with dialogue and monologue.
Says full name.
Follows 2- and 3-part requests.
Relates ideas and experiences.
Uses adverbs, adjectives, and prepositions.
Names some colors and is interested in counting.
Looks at books while alone and enjoys reading times.
Talks about relationships.
Memorizes a short song, poem, fingerplay, or story.
Repeats 3 digits and 2 to 3 nonsense syllables if asked.
Uses adjectives and pronouns correctly.
Can copy a recognizable circle or square well if shown a model.

FIGURE 3-16 Developmental language-related milestones at ages 2 through 5

AGE OF CHILD

Can imitate a clapping rhythm.
Starts to talk about the function of objects.
Can find an object in group that's different.
Can find missing parts of wholes.
Can classify using clear, simple distinctions.
Knows names of common shapes.

4–5 years   Has vocabulary of over 1,500 words.
Uses sentences of 5 to 6 (or more) words.
May use impact, shock, and forbidden words.
May use words of violence.
Argues, convinces, and questions correctness.
Shares books with friends.
Acts out story themes or recreates life happenings in play.
Has favorite books.
Likes to dictate words.
Notices signs and print in environment.
Uses etiquette words, such as please, thank you, and so on.

Enjoys different writing tools.
Knows many nursery rhymes and stories.
May add alphabet letters to art work.
Creates and tells long stories.
Can verbally express the highlights of the day.
Knows many colors.
Can repeat a sentence with 6 or more words.
May pretend to read books or may actually read other's nametags.
Holds writing tools in position that allows fine control.
Traces objects with precision.
Classifies according to function.
Asks what words mean.
Is familiar with many literary classics for children.
Knows address and phone number.
Can retell main facts or happenings in stories.
Uses adultlike speech.

FIGURE 3-16 *Continued*

Student Activities

- Observe a two-, three-, four-, and five-year-old for fifteen minute periods. (Omit children's names.) Try to write down what is said and a brief description of the setting and actions. Underline typical characteristics described in this unit. Make comparisons between older and younger preschool children.

- Interview two teachers. Ask if any preschool child within their care seems to have special speech or language problems. Write down the teachers' comments and compare them with typical characteristics mentioned in the unit.

- What rules or restrictions concerning the use of inappropriate speech (name-calling, swearing, and screaming) would you expect to find in a preschool center?

- Write definitions for:

  egocentric speech or private speech
  running commentary
  fantasy
  overextension
  impact words

- Finish the following adding an additional paragraph or page to the discussion: "Hearing in young children needs careful monitoring because...."

Unit Review

A. Associate the following characteristics with the correct age group. Some may seem to fit both categories; choose the most appropriate one. Write the characteristics under the headings Younger Preschooler (two- and three-year-olds) and Older Preschooler (four- and five-year-olds).

75% perfect articulation	nonverbal communication
"Look, I'm jumping."	2,000 to 2,500 word vocabulary
telegram sentences	talking about what one is doing
rhyming and nonsense words	stuttering
name-calling	talking through an adult
repetitions	substitutions
omission of letter sounds	role playing
adultlike speech	planning play with others
bathroom words	arguing

B. Select the correct answers. Many questions have more than one correct response.
   1. The younger preschool child (two to three years old)
      a. may still grunt and scream while communicating.
      b. always replies to what is said to him or her by another child.
      c. articulates many sounds without clarity.
      d. speaks in complete sentences at two years of age.
   2. A truly typical or average child
      a. would have all the characteristics of his or her age.
      b. is almost impossible to find.
      c. is one who speaks better than his or her peers.
      d. sometimes makes up words to fit new situations.
   3. Repetition in the speech of the young child
      a. needs careful watching.
      b. is common for children aged two to five.
      c. can be word play.
      d. happens for a variety of reasons.
   4. Name-calling and swearing
      a. may take place during preschool years.
      b. can gain attention.
      c. shows that children are testing reactions with words.
      d. only happens with poorly behaved children.
   5. A word like "blood" or "ghost"
      a. may spread quickly to many children.
      b. has impact value.
      c. can make people listen.
      d. is rarely used in a preschool group.
   6. Most younger preschoolers
      a. cannot correctly pronounce all consonants.
      b. omit some letter sounds.
      c. have adultlike speech.
      d. will, when older, reach adult-level speech.

7. Stuttering during preschool years
   a. happens often.
   b. should not be drawn to the child's attention.
   c. may happen when a child is excited.
   d. means the child will need professional help to overcome it.
8. "Me wented" is an example of
   a. pronoun difficulty.
   b. a telegram sentence.
   c. verb incorrectness.
   d. the speech of some two- or three-year-olds.
9. Joint planning in play with two or more children is found more often with
   a. two- to three-year-olds.
   b. four- to five-year-olds.
   c. slowly developing children.
   d. male children.
10. Knowing typical speech characteristics is important because teachers
    a. must answer parents questions.
    b. can help individual children.
    c. interact daily with young children.
    d. should be able to recognize normal behavior.
11. Nonverbal communication and gesturing
    a. happens less and less frequently as a child matures.
    b. continues after adolescence.
    c. indicates poor progress if used often.
    d. indicates shyness.
12. One can expect _____ two- and three-year-olds.
    a. hearing unclear speech in most
    b. hearing full sentences in most
    c. hearing incomplete but meaningful sentences in most
    d. books to interest most
    e. incorrect verb use to precede correct verb use in most

References

Beck, M. Susan. *Kidspeak*. New York: New American Library, 1982.

Bettelheim, Bruno and Karen Zelan. *On Learning to Read*, New York: Knopf, 1982.

Brophy, Jere E. *Child Development And Socialization*, Chicago, IL: Science Research Associates, 1977.

Caplan, Theresa and Frank Caplan. *The Early Childhood Years*. G. P. Putnam's Sons, 1983.

Cazden, Courtney B. *Child Language and Education*. New York: Holt, Rinehart and Winston, 1972.

Chukovsky, Kornei. *From Two to Five*. Berkeley: University of California, 1963.

Diaz, Rafael M. and Jean R. Lowe. "The Private Speech Of Young Children At Risk: A Test Of Three Deficit Hypotheses." *Early Childhood Research Quarterly* 2.2 (1987): 27–33.

Donoghue, Mildred R. *The Child And The English Language Arts*. Dubuque, IA: Brown, 1985.

Elkind, David. "Cognition in Infancy and Early Childhood." *Human Development and Cognitive Process*. Ed. John Eliot. New York: Holt, Rinehart and Winston, 1971.

Garvey, Catherine. *Children's Talk*. Cambridge: Harvard UP, 1984.

Honig, Alice Sterling. "Humor Development In Children." *Young Children* 43.4 (May 1988): 60–73.

Kagan, Jerome. "Affect and Cognition." *A.P.A. Monitor* 19.4 (April 1988): 17–26.

Kohlberg, L., J. Yeager, and E. Hjertholm. "Private Speech: Four Studies And A Review Of Theories." *Child Development*, 39.5, Spring, 1968. 40–44.

Linn, Marcia C. *American Educational Research Association Meeting Presentation*. Chicago, IL. 1987.

Pines, Maya. "Can A Rock Walk?" *Psychology Today*, 39.11 (Nov. 1983): 46–50, 52, 54.

Pflaum, S.W. *The Development Of Language And Reading*. Columbus, OH: Charles E. Merrill, 1986.

Rubin, Richard R. and John J. Fisher. *Your Preschooler*. New York: Macmillan, 1982.

Suggested Readings

Charlesworth, Rosalind. *Understanding Child Development*. Albany: Delmar Publishers Inc., 1983. Units 17 and 18.

Feeney, Stephanie, et al. *Who Am I in the Lives of Young Children?* Columbus, OH: Charles E. Merrill, 1983. 205–213.

Hendrick, Joanne. *The Whole Child*. St. Louis: C. V. Mosby, 1984. Chapter 16.

Honig, Alice S. "Language Environments for Young Children." *Young Children* 38.1 (1982). 56–67.

UNIT 4

Growth Systems Affecting Early Language Ability

BJECTIVES

After studying this unit, you should be able to

- describe sequential stages of intellectual development.
- list three perceptual-motor skills that preschool activities might include.
- discuss the importance of a center's ability to meet young children's social and emotional needs.

The child is a total being, and so language growth cannot be isolated from physical, mental, and social-emotional well-being. All body systems need a minimum level of movement (exercise) to keep the body in good working order and to stimulate brain growth. A proper intake of nutritious foods and living conditions that provide emotional security and balance can affect the child's acquisition of language and his or her general health and resistance to disease. A preschool, child center, or day-care center intent on developing language skills focuses on satisfying both physical and emotional needs while also providing intellectual opportunity and challenge by offering a variety of age-appropriate activities.

PHYSICAL GROWTH

Physical development limits or aids capabilities, thereby affecting children's perceptions of themselves, as well as the way they are treated by others. Early childhood teachers are aware of these fundamental physical changes that take place in young children. For

instance, a slightly taller, physically active, strong, and well-coordinated child who can ride a two-wheel bike and drop-kick a football may be admired by his or her peers. These two skills are not usually witnessed during preschool years, but occasionally, a child possesses such physical skills (figure 4-1). A wide range of physical abilities in individual children exists within preschool groups as in all developmental areas.

Preschoolers grow at the rate of two to three inches in height and four to six pounds in weight a year. At about 18 to 24 months, the child's thumb is used in opposition to just one finger. The ability to use tools and drawing markers with a degree of skill emerges. The nutritional quality of the child's diet exerts an influence on both body and neural development. Monitoring nutrient intake, height, weight gain, and emotional well-being can alert parents to possible deficiencies.

Illness during accelerated growth may produce conditions affecting language development if it damages necessary body systems. Hearing loss and vision difficulties impair the child's ability to receive communications and learn his or her native language. A brain

FIGURE 4-1 Riding a two-wheel bike takes balance and coordination, and not many preschoolers accomplish this skill.

FIGURE 4-2 Interesting equipment encourages exploration.

impairment may hinder the child's ability to sort perceptions, slowing progress.

Preschools and day-care programs plan a wide range of motor activities; much of the children's time is devoted to playing with interesting equipment in both indoor and outdoor areas (figure 4-2). The well-known benefits of a healthy mind in a healthy body should be planned for, by incorporating daily physical activities that promote well-exercised and well-coordinated muscles into young children's daily programs.

PERCEPTION

An infant's physical actions are the vehicle of knowledge. Seeing and trying to touch or act upon the environment are the work of infancy. This early physical stage precedes and develops into the child's understanding his or her world, and this makes later verbal labeling and speech possible.

As the child matures, perceptual acuity increases;

finer detail is seen. Most children achieve 20/20 vision (adult optimum) at age 14. At ages two to five vision is in the 20/45 to 20/30 range (Weymouth, 1963). Hearing acuity increases from birth through ages four and five (Weiss & Lillywhite, 1981). At this point, the hearing mechanisms are essentially mature and will not change greatly except through disease or injury.

Young children are noted for their desire to get their hands on what interests them (figure 4-3). If a new child with particularly noticeable hair joins a group, hands and fingers are sure to try to explore its texture. If a teacher wears a soft, fuzzy jacket, the children will stroke it and snuggle into it. Perceptions are gathered with all sense organs. Ornstein and Sobel (1987) believe that the main purpose of receiving, organizing, and interpreting what one encounters perceptually is to achieve constancy — a stable, constant world.

Researchers exploring infant visual preferences have pinpointed a series of changes in attention-drawing features from infancy to age five:

Two months — change from having attention captured by movement and edges of people and objects to active search and explore.

Age 2–5 — change from unsystematic exploring to systematically examining each feature carefully (Gibson, 1969).

Children get better and better at focusing on one aspect of a complex situation: they become selective in

FIGURE 4-3 Children enjoy a variety of toys.

focusing their attention, and they ignore the irrelevant and distracting. Life events that cause tension and anxiety can interfere with their emerging abilities. In complex situations the child does best when perceptual distractions are minimized, allowing deep concentration (Gibson, 1969).

Individual differences have been noted in the way children explore their environment and react to problems. Kagan (1971) has described *conceptual tempo* to contrast the *impulsive* child, who answers quickly and may make mistakes, with the *reflective* child, who spends considerable time examining alternatives. A second difference in perception identifies field independence, and field-dependent styles of perceiving. Field-independent children are those good at ignoring irrelevant context, while field-dependents tend to focus on the total context. See how long it takes you to find the hidden objects in Ahlberg's *Each Peach Pear Plum* illustration in figure 4-4. How would you describe your perceptual style?

Perceptual-Motor Skills

Sensory- (or perceptual-) motor intelligence has been defined by Jewell and Zintz (1986) as a kind of action-knowledge that is not to be confused with the

intelligence involving thinking and logic. The latter grows during preschool years and beyond when children can think about and know without acting out in a physical way.

Piaget, the noted Swiss psychologist and researcher, has greatly affected early childhood educators' interest in perceptual-motor activities. Piaget and others observed that reflective (automatic) movements such as crying, sucking, and grasping in infants became controlled, purposeful body movements as the child grew. He speculated that physical movement served as a base for later mental abilities. His theory (1952) includes stages in the development of human intelligence, which are condensed in the following:

1. *Sensorimotor period* (birth to 18 to 24 months). Reflex actions become coordinated and perfected by physical movement and exploration of real objects and events.
2. *Preoperational period* (18 to 24 months to 7 to 8 years). Mental symbols represent what is experienced; imitation occurs. As the child matures, meanings attached to symbols grow and become detailed and precise, and physical actions combine with mental actions.
3. *Concrete operations period* (7 to 8 years to 11 to 12 years). Child's thinking now is less dependent on physical involvement or immediate perceptual cues that aid classifying, ordering, grouping, numbering, and "inner" and "cross" sub-grouping of concepts.

During the preschool years, the development of motor skills is as important as the development of language skills. The close ties between motor activities and thought processes indicate that the child needs motor activity involving the five sense organs, as well as large-muscle use (figure 4-5). Exactly how much of a child's mental activity is dependent on or promoted by physical activity is unknown. Most educators of young children feel that a definite, strong connection exists.

Motor skill develops in an orderly, predictable, head-to-toe fashion. Head, neck, and upper body muscles are controlled first (large muscles before small muscles), and center of body muscles are coordinated before extremities (fingers and toes). Handedness (left or right) is usually stable by age five or six.

FIGURE 4-4 *(From* Each Peach Pear Plum, *by Janet and Allan Ahlberg. Reprinted by permission of Penguin Books Ltd., London.)*

Montessori's approach (1967) to educating young children is noted for direct manipulation of real objects presented in sequenced form. This led to her design and construction of many tactile (touching) exploring materials for the young child. She explains her motives in the following:

The training and sharpening of the senses has the obvious advantage of enlarging the field of perception and of offering an ever more solid foundation for intellectual growth. The intellect builds up its store of practical ideas through contact with, and exploration of, its environment. Without such concepts the intellect would lack precision in its abstract operations.

Preschools are full of appealing equipment and programs that offer a planned approach to the development of sensory-motor skills. They are seen as integral parts of the curricula. Spitzer (1977) believes that sensory exploration and motor-skill development take place jointly:

Perceptual and motor abilities are almost completely interdependent, particularly in terms of early childhood learning. Actually, when we think of sensory exploration, we must consider motor skills. When we look at an object, we must move our bodies to explore it or manipulate it in some way.

School success in later elementary years may also be influenced by the development of perceptual-motor skill.

There seems to be no clearly accepted or defined separate place within the preschool curriculum for sensory-skill development. Some centers identify a series of sequential activities and label them perceptual or sensory-motor; their main goal is skill development. In other centers, every activity is seen as developing

FIGURE 4-5 Exercising large muscles is an important preschool activity.

- Body coordination (figure 4-6).
- Posture and balance.
- Awareness of spatial relationships.
- Rhythmic body movements.
- The ability to identify objects and surfaces with the eyes closed.
- Awareness of temperatures by touch.
- Ability to trace form outlines with fingers.
- Ability to discriminate color, shapes, similar features, different features, sizes, textures, and sounds.
- Ability to match a wide variety of patterns and symbols.
- Ability to identify parts of figures or objects when a small part of a whole is presented.
- Eye-hand coordination (figure 4-7 and figure 4-8).
- Familiarity with the following terms: same, different, long, longer, longest, small, smaller, smallest, big, little, tall, short, wide, narrow, high, low, above, below, on, in, hard, soft, sweet, salty, sour.
- Ability to identify food by tasting.
- Ability to identify smells of a variety of items.
- Ability to identify common sounds.

FIGURE 4-6 Learning to pump a swing takes hours of practice.

perceptual-motor skill. Commonly, music activities and physical games deal with physical coordination and endurance. Other programs plan for perceptual-motor activities within their language arts curriculum. What remains important is that this type of emphasis be part of every center's program.

This list of objectives designed to refine perceptual-motor skills is drawn from a number of schools' and centers' goal statements:

- Awareness of self in space.
- Awareness of self in relation to objects.
- Flexibility.

FIGURE 4-7 Both coordination and flexibility are needed to master rope climbing.

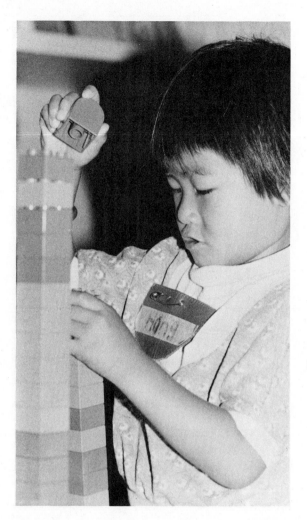

FIGURE 4-8 The child gains skill in eye-hand coordination by fitting pieces together. *(From* Early Childhood Practicum Guide, *by Machado and Meyer.* © *1984 by Delmar Publishers Inc.)*

Activities for
Perceptual-Motor Development

It is difficult to think of one piece of preschool equipment or one activity that does not contain some aspect or component of perceptual-motor development. Figure 4-9 lists perceptual-motor development activities and equipment, gathered from a broad range of early childhood books and sources. It can serve as a beginning.

COGNITIVE DEVELOPMENT

There are two major, opposing views concerning the link between language and thought. One is that language is the foundation of thought and vital to a person's awareness of the world. The second view suggests that language is dependent on thinking; as intelligence grows, language grows, reflecting thoughts. It is difficult to determine which of the two ideas is closer to the truth. White (1987) states that "It's clear that you can't fully separate the topics," and Judy (1980) theorizes that "Language and thinking are hopelessly and happily intertwined. Language provides the major basis for our perception, our cognition, our contacts with the world." Most educators will agree that language and thought are closely associated.

Experiences Dealing With:	Possible Materials and Equipment

Visual Discrimination

long, longer, longest	felt or paper strips; sticks; ribbons
small, smaller, smallest	nested boxes; blocks; buttons; measuring cups
big, little	blocks; jars; buttons; balloons; toys
tall, short	felt figures; stuffed toys
wide, narrow	pieces of cloth and paper; scraps of wood; boxes
high, low	jump rope; small ball; see-saw made from small board with tiny block in middle
above, below	table-shaped piece of felt with box-shaped felt pieces to place above and below box
on, in	with colored stones

Auditory Discrimination

quiet, noisy	two boxes: one containing something that rattles (such as stones or beads) and one containing cloth or paper
bell sounds	bells of varying shapes and sizes for a variety of tones
falling sounds	feather; leaf; stone; block of wood; cotton
shaking sounds	maracas; baby rattle; pebbles inside coffee can
musical sounds	variety of rhythm instruments

Tactile Discrimination

textures	sandpaper; tissue; stone; waxed paper; tree bark; velvet; wool; fur; cotton
outline of shapes	thin wooden circle, square, triangle, rectangle; letters cut from sandpaper
recognition of objects	four different-shaped objects, each tied in end of sock — children guess what each is by feeling it (change objects often)
hard, soft	handkerchief; rock; cotton batting; nail; sponge

Taste Discrimination

identifying food: sweet, salty, sour	small jars: filled with salt, sugar, unsweetened lemonade
trying new foods	variety of vegetables children may not know; samples of fruit juices; honey, molasses, maple syrup

FIGURE 4-9 Perceptual activities *(continues)*

Experiences Dealing With:	Possible Materials and Equipment
Smell Discrimination	
identifying object by smell	cake of soap; vial of perfume; pine sprig; onion; vials of kitchen spices; orange
Kinesthetic Discrimination	
lifting, racing downhill, swinging, throwing, running, jumping, climbing, bending, stretching, twisting, turning, spinning, balancing.	yard and motor play materials

FIGURE 4-9 *Continued*

Classifying Information

Intellect is rooted in each particular child's stored perceptual and sensory-motor experiences. Each child interprets happenings and attempts to connect each to what the child already knows. If it fits, the child understands, and it all falls together. An example of this might be seen if one watches a nine-month-old learn to make noise come out of a toy plastic horn. At first, the child has no knowledge of how the horn works. When he or she first blows into it and it makes a toot, the child blows into it repeatedly (and usually happily). After that, the child knows how to toot the horn. Infants, toddlers, and preschoolers can be thought of as having mental groupings (classes and categories) before they have words for them. The nine-month-old above probably has no word associated with what the child knows about the horn. Each mental grouping is distinguished by a set of distinctive features, and objects yet to be classified are examined for the presence of these features. If the horn-blowing infant reacts by trying to blow into a new toy horn of a similar shape, one can be relatively sure the child is forming a class of "horn" mentally. One can expect that the infant above will try blowing into any horn shape that comes the child's way. Later, a word or language symbol can be attached to a class or category, which makes it possible for the child to communicate about what the class or category means to the child, or how the child feels about it.

Preschool teachers readily see differences between the feelings and meanings expressed by each child. For example, the way that a child reacts when the child meets a new large animal may demonstrate what the child knows and feels about large animals. Another child's reaction might be entirely opposite.

Putting events and experiences into classes and categories is innate — a natural mental process. The mind yearns for order, and knowledge is built within from what is experienced. A child's knowledge is constantly changing, for children are curious and are constantly searching for a variety of experience, fighting to overcome boredom (figure 4-10). A new or novel idea or event may greatly affect a child by adding to or changing all a child knows and feels on a particular subject.

As a child's language ability develops, mental classes, categories, and concepts are represented symbolically by words. Words become an efficient shortcut that eliminates the need to act out by gesturing or signaling to make something known to another. Thoughts can be analyzed and evaluated internally as the child grows older. If there exists a common language system between the child and others, it can be used to reveal the child's unique self.

Piaget's (1955) terms *assimilation* and *accommodation* describe what happens when infants and children experience something new. From the time of conception, each individual unconsciously structures (internally builds and organizes) what is perceived. If a new experience or event is perceived, it is assimilated into what already mentally existed. If it changes or modifies

FIGURE 4-10 Hanging upside down may be a new experience for a child.

those existing structures (ideas or thought patterns), the new is accommodated. In other words, children attend to features that make sense to them, and learning involves adding to what is already known or modifying (changing) what is known. As Spelke (1986) and others point out "children are born with an innate ability to divide their experiences into categories."

Jewell and Zintz (1986) explain the connections between concepts and language:

> A category system of related meaning is formed on the basis of distinguishing criteria, which each child defines. The system constantly expands as new information is encountered. This becomes the cognitive and affective stores, the schemata for operating on the world and making sense of it. Labels are attached to meanings and language emerges.

Different Levels of Maturity

The human brain's cortex contains two differently specialized hemispheres. Each hemisphere appears designed for unique functions, different abilities, and styles of thought, including verbal and spatial thinking. Different brain areas are well defined and possess a rich concentration of certain abilities that are not equal among children (Ornstein and Sobel, 1987). Research indicates that between ages two and four, there is a period when brain-growth spurts increase the child's ability to attain new levels of learning and accept cognitive challenges (Soderman, 1984). Naturally, the brain structures of some children may be developing more slowly than others, which might affect their ability to learn and may cause teachers to compare them unfairly with children of the same age who have developed more quickly. Consequently, teachers need to pay special attention to how they act when comparing children. Competitive, pressurized lessons can create an unhealthy "I'm not good (smart) enough" attitude that can be self-perpetuating.

Preschool children's statements that seem to be "errors in thinking" on the surface can, on deeper analysis, be seen as quite mature and understandable, not just random guesses. When a child says a camel is a horse with a hump, he or she should be given credit for seeing the similarity rather than merely corrected.

The child's fantasy world, which appears and is expressed in speech, should be seen as a giant intellectual leap. Make believe is internal intellectual creation and/or recreation. A preschooler may say he/she is someone else — most often this someone else is a hero of sorts or an admired personage usually from the movies or television or real life. There may be days when the child wishes to assume the name and identity of a friend or animal.

Many children during preschool can readily follow story sequences and identify with book characters. An in-depth discussion of preschoolers and books is found in Unit 9.

Teachers need to realize that there are differences between adult concepts and child concepts. The child's view of the world is usually based on immediate, present happenings and beginning thought processes (figure 4-11). A child's speech is full of many unique misconceptions, conclusions, and errors (as judged by adult standards). These errors arise because of each child's unique way of sorting out experiences — a con-

FIGURE 4-11 There are lots of opportunities for intimate conversations. *(From* Early Childhood Practicum Guide, *by Machado and Meyer.* © *1984 by Delmar Publishers Inc.)*

tinuous process of trying to make sense and order out of daily events. Errors based on just a few happenings may be quite logical conclusions. For example, a child may conclude that "milk comes from the store" or, when looking at an "n," that "that's a baby "m."

Teacher's Role

Teachers who work with infants, toddlers, and preschoolers realize sensory-motor experiences and opportunities with people, toys, and room environments are early intellect-building events. Exploring and experimenting is enhanced by adult provision of materials and equipment. At some point, teachers realize some actions look as though the child thought first and then acted. At about 10 months some infants seem to be majoring in dropping and emptying. They drop things from high-chair trays and watch the objects fall or put things into containers, drawers, or boxes and empty and refill these over and over. One has to smile and think of very young infants as active scientists. The work of Vygotsky (1978) has influenced educators' ideas of how they should verbally interact with young children to increase what children learn from new experiences. When working with two-year-olds and young three-year-olds, teachers notice a good deal of voiced external speech that accompanies play. Vygotsky theorizes that this speech helps the child order and organize thoughts, plan and develop solutions, and come to conclusions. A "zone of proximal development" is what Vygotsky calls the area between what the child can solve alone when faced with problems and experience and what the child can possibly solve or come to know with the help of adults or more experienced, knowing children. When adults name and explain happenings and talk about relationships, this is seen as a stimulant to both language and mental growth. A teacher trying to put into practice Vygotsky's theories would try to talk with children, becoming a catalyst who names, discusses, and prompts the child's exploration and expression of what he or she has discovered or formulated. It also means that adults must know when not to interrupt children's thoughts when they're deeply emerged in play. Dialogue makes much more sense when children seek adult help or when they are companions in activities.

In promoting what children will store (learn and remember), teachers deal with both meaning and feelings. Each intellect building encounter and interaction with children starts with the adult's supportive acceptance and caring. Purposeful teacher dialogue is often part of child-teacher exchanges. It's goal is to advance further discovery or to help put the discovery or experience into words. A teacher listens and observes closely. This listening may expose aspects of the child's thinking, logic, inner concepts, and feelings.

Working with children on a daily basis, teachers strive to understand the logic and correctness behind children's statements. The balance a teacher maintains between gently correcting false impressions and having children discover the misconceptions for themselves is not easy to maintain. Piaget (1952) encourages teachers to concentrate on discovery techniques:

> Each time one prematurely teaches a child something he could have discovered for himself, that child is kept from inventing it and consequently from understanding it completely.

Skillful questioning and sensitive responses from the teacher preserve a child's feelings about expressing worthwhile ideas and makes the child more willing to speak and share. These are some examples:

- "I can see you want to have a turn talking too, Becky, and I want to hear you."
- "Would you tell us, Mark, about the boat you put together this morning?"
- "You thought of a different way to make a hole in

your paper; perhaps your friends would like to hear about it."

- "Did anyone see what happened to Tim's shoe?"
- "I wonder if there's a way for three people to share two pairs of scissors?"

The following is an example of a kindergartner's answers to the question, "What is a grandmother?" Note the concepts that are based on lack of experience and the examples of overgeneralization.

A grandmother is a lady who has no children of her own, so she likes other people's little girls. A grandfather is a man grandmother. He goes for walks with the boys, and they talk about fishing, and tractors and things like that. Grandfathers wear glasses and funny underwear. They can take their teeth off. Grandmas are the only grown-ups who have time.

Huey (1965) lists suggestions for teaching young children that promote use of both cognitive and language abilities:

1. Set the stage for abundant sensory experiences that are varied so as to encourage children to discriminate among these and to make associations.
2. Provide abundant opportunities for self-selected learning activities, especially of the manipulative and experimental types.
3. Provide many opportunities for children to observe work activities of adults so that they will have experiences to think about.
4. Encourage children with toys, other play accessories, conversation, and art materials to symbolize their experiences through play, art, and language.
5. Direct children's attention to learning opportunities they may miss, to opportunities to use their previous associations, and to opportunities for abstracting common elements (e.g., "all blue things").
6. Provide an environment of simple language that helps clothe children's experiences with language while they are absorbing the experiences.
7. Encourage children to use the language that they have to clothe their own experiences in their own language.

FIGURE 4-12 The child is finding out how high he can make his tower.

8. Plan opportunities or experiences that will help children discover new concepts, redefine familiar concepts and differentiate between concepts (figure 4-12).
9. Provide opportunities for vicarious experiences through stories, pictures, and conversations that relate to recent direct experiences.
10. Pace learning opportunities, not too many at one time, for the group and for the individual child, so that clear images are possible, new learnings are reinforced to the point of usefulness, and the hazard of over-stimulation is avoided.

While keeping these suggestions in mind, look at figure 4-13, which illustrates how the preschooler's ability to process information is improving and expanding during this period.

SOCIAL AND EMOTIONAL GROWTH

Interaction with other people is always a major factor in the child's language learning. Children who have positive feelings about themselves — feelings of self-

1. Seeking information. (Focusing)

2. Seeking word labels. (Concept building)

3. Naming, classifying, categorizing, and grouping experiences mentally — objects, ideas, etc. (General to specific; revising concepts)

4. Responding and remembering. (Memorizing and recalling)

5. Comparing and contrasting information. (Abstracting)

6. Making inferences and predicting in general ways. (Predicting)

7. Generalizing. (Inductive thinking)

8. Applying known information to new situations. (Transferring)

9. Making hypotheses (educated guesses) and predicting in specific ways. (Deductive thinking)

FIGURE 4-13 The child's emerging intellectual skills

value and security — speak frequently. New contacts with adults outside the home run smoothly as the child branches out from the home.

Feelings and emotions are part of each human conversation. A child's feelings toward adults are generalized to teachers in early school years. The parent-child bond and its influence on language learning has been described by Douglass (1959):

> The feeling relationships between parents and child appear to be a tremendous factor in the child's learning of language. The child who avoids talking because he fears lack of acceptance, the child whose feelings are not understood, the standards of eating, toilet training, and behaviors which are imposed too soon, and emotional tensions existing in the home, can create surface symptoms produced by a child who attempts to cope with an unsatisfying and hostile world.

During preschool years, children form ideas of self-identity. It becomes difficult for children to believe in themselves — or their language abilities — if self-esteem is constantly undermined. Figure 4-14 suggests teacher behavior and response in communicating with children to promote social growth.

In communication, the teacher:

- cares and is ready to give of self.

- listens intent on understanding.

- adds simple words when the child can't.

- doesn't correct speech when this might break down willingness to speak further.

- is available for help in clarifying ideas or suggesting new play and exploring possibilities.

- senses child interests and guides to new real experiences.

- is available when problems and conflicts happen.

- enjoys time spent in child activities.

- establishes friendships with each child.

- talks positively about each child's individual uniqueness.

- is an enthusiastic and expressive communicator.

- offers friendly support while redirecting undesirable social behavior or stating rules.

- notices and respects each child's work.

FIGURE 4-14 Teacher behaviors helpful to the child's social growth

Erickson's writings (1950) have identified a series of social-emotional developments in the young child.

- (Infants) *Trust vs. Mistrust.* Trust develops from consistent care, which fulfills basic needs (food, warmth, physical contact, and so on), leading to stable and secure feelings rather than anxiousness. A positive view of life forms.

- (Toddlers and two-year-olds) *Autonomy vs. Shame and Doubt.* Children get to know themselves as separate persons. What they control, decisions they can make, and freedom they may have while still being very dependent become apparent. Awareness of inabilities and helplessness is sensed. Behavior may be testing and full of the word "no."

- (Preschoolers) *Initiative vs. Guilt Feelings.* Experimentation and active exploration of new skills and directions occur. There are strong emotions at times in resistance to authority figures and rules, yet children are still dependent on adult approval.

Werner and Smith (1982) have studied what they describe as "resilient children," those who thrive and succeed despite what could be termed "at-risk" childhoods. As children, they displayed positive self-concepts and well-developed identities. As adults, they became socially well-integrated, confident, and autonomous — adults who "worked well, played well, loved well, and expected well."

Social development must not be ignored in planning and conducting language activities or in trying to manage groups. Structure and rules are necessary for group living. An individual child's status in the eyes of the group can be enhanced through the sharing and appreciation of the child's ideas and accomplishments and by providing frequent opportunities for the child to lead or help lead the group in activities, which is almost always a confidence- and status-building experience.

Teachers should be concerned with a child's *social connectedness* — a term defined by Ornstein and Sobel (1987) as characteristic of people with stable, secure lives, supportive families and friends, and close ties to community and accepted as a worthy part of a group and able to weather life's stresses with a sense of individual identity. A teacher is in control of a school's atmosphere and works with the home and community.

Preschoolers begin to learn labels for feelings such as happy, sad, jealous, fearful, and so on. They begin to think of others' feelings (figure 4-15). The conscience is forming and interest in right and wrong is expressed. Teachers who speak of their own feelings as adults set an example and provide a climate in which children's feelings are also accepted and understood (Greenberg, 1969).

Most children explore social actions and reactions. Strong emotions accompany much of children's behavior; their total beings speak. When a child feels left out, life becomes an overwhelming tragedy, while a party invitation may be a time to jump for joy.

The following activities can help children develop a sense of self. These are just a few suggestions; many more are possible.

- Activities using mirrors.
- Activities using children's photographs and home movies.

FIGURE 4-15 "Are you OK?"

- Tracings of the child's outline.
- Touching and naming body parts.
- Making nametags and placing names on belongings, drawings, lockers, and projects.
- Activities using family pictures and discussions about families.
- Activities that identify and discuss feelings.
- Activities concerned with personal opinions.
- Activities that show both similarity to others and individual diversity.
- Activities that build pride or membership in a group.
- Activities that identify favorite pursuits, objects, or individual choices.

Based on research of outstanding and well-developed two- and three-year-olds (24 to 36 months), White (1986) identified social abilities that he feels serve as a strong foundation for future schooling:

- Being able to get and hold the attention of adults in a variety of socially accepted ways.
- Being able to express affection or mild annoyance to adults and peers when appropriate.
- Being able to use adults as resources after determining that a task is too difficult to handle alone.
- Being able to show pride in achievement.
- Being able to lead and follow children of the same age.
- Being able to compete with age mates.

White (1986) goes on to say:

If a three-year-old has acquired this pattern of abilities, we believe she (he) has had a "superior education" during her first years. Furthermore, such a foundation probably goes a long way toward ensuring that a child will enter school well-prepared for future development.

Teachers strive to supply a center atmosphere in which a sense of trust and security thrives. Danoff, Breibart, and Barr (1977) feel this is crucial to each child's opportunity to learn.

Basic to the learning process is children's ability to trust themselves and the adults who teach them. This is totally interactional. Children must trust people in their world, or else they reject all that these people want to teach them. They learn to have faith in those who respect them and accept their feelings. In turn, they learn to trust themselves. In a climate that engenders trust, they want to learn and are able to learn.

Summary

Physical, intellectual, and social-emotional growth is proceeding as is the child's speech. Understanding these growth systems promotes more appropriate teacher techniques and behaviors. Danoff (1976) identifies child characteristics and needs in figure 4-16, and suggests teacher activities.

Perceptual-motor activities are an integral part of many centers' language arts programs. Many educators feel that there is a strong correlation between physical activity during this period and mental growth.

Adults need to react to and sense the correctness of what seem to be errors in children's thinking. Guiding the child's discovery of concepts is an integral part of early childhood teaching.

A child who trusts can learn. Teachers must accept children's feelings and concentrate on establishing bonds between themselves and the children. This encourages growth of abilities. The feeling tone that lies beneath each human contact and conversation creates a setting for learning.

Characteristics	Needs	Suggestions for the Classroom Teacher
Intellectual Are curious: learn best through active involvement through their senses, and through direct experiences with things in the environment.	Opportunities to have sensory experiences — to see, touch, taste, smell and hear things around them. Opportunities to handle materials and make their own discoveries.	Provide firsthand experiences. For example, bring a guinea pig to the classroom and provide enough time and space for a small group of children to sit around and watch and handle the animal. Questions will most likely come from the children. For instance: "What is this?" "Where do guinea pigs come from?" The teacher is there to provide clear and simple explanations as well as to ask questions when necessary.

FIGURE 4-16 Chart of teaching ideas, matching child's needs and intellectual abilities to appropriate activities *(From Open for Children, by Danoff et al., 1976. Used with permission of McGraw-Hill Book Company.)*

Characteristics	Needs	Suggestions for the Classroom Teacher
Are concerned primarily with things that affect them personally.	Opportunities to investigate things that they see around them or experience in their everyday lives. Opportunities to see their names, their photographs, and their work as part of the classroom materials and displays.	Provide activities that enable the children to explore familiar materials like water, soap, and plastic containers. Classroom meetings may include discussions about the children's families and the work their parents do. Snacks can include many foods that the children also eat at home. The children can also make their own snacks — like French toast or pancakes — and can be encouraged to observe and discuss each step in the process. Books can be made about the children's experiences, including names of people they know.
Are concerned primarily with the present.	Opportunities to distinguish between reality and "make-believe."	Stories should be concerned with feelings and experiences that are familiar to the children.
Are increasing their attention span.	Opportunities to have a variety of experiences that are interesting to children.	For younger children, provide many different materials for similar learning experiences. Schedule group activities for relatively short periods of time. Provide games and toys which are open-ended (have more than one way of being played or played with) or which require a relatively short amount of time. Gradually introduce activities that require a longer attention span.
Are developing a sense of time.	Opportunities to recall experiences. Opportunities to plan and organize play.	At snack time the children can be asked what they did earlier in the morning. Classroom discussions on Monday morning should include what the children did over the weekend. The children should be asked to choose where they want to work each day — for example, a child might choose the block area. Block structures can be left intact and added to each day for as long as the children are interested.

FIGURE 4-16 *Continued*

Characteristics	Needs	Suggestions for the Classroom Teacher
Are developing the ability to "symbolize" experiences.	Opportunities to express ideas in a variety of ways. Opportunities to symbolize their experiences through art, language, dramatic play, music, and movement. Opportunities to use materials imaginatively and creatively.	If the children take a trip, they can be encouraged to discuss the experience, and the teacher can write down some of what they say. They can also reproduce some of the sounds they heard with rhythm instruments, or they can make a mural of their visual impressions, or recreate the experience with blocks.
Are developing the ability to deal with complex, abstract ideas.	Opportunities to note similarities and differences between things around them. Opportunities to sort, group, categorize, and classify the things around them.	At a group time, the children can be asked, "Who is wearing pants today?" "Who is not wearing pants?" The children can be asked to compare any two pieces of clothing from the housekeeping area in terms of color, size, or function. A box full of clothes can be sorted in many different ways. For instance, the children can put together all the things that are worn on the head or all the clothes that have stripes.

FIGURE 4-16 *Continued*

Student Activities

- Observe young children (two to four years old) in a public place (restaurant, laundromat, grocery store, park, bus, department store). What do the children seem to notice, and how do they investigate what they notice? Write down those environmental objects, people, and so on, and what features capture children's interest (for example, sound, color, texture).

- With a group of fellow students, pinpoint possible concepts that underlie the following quotes of children that were taken from Chukovsky's *From Two to Five* (Berkeley, CA: University of California Press, 1963).
  a. "Mommie, Mommie, the ship is taking a bath" (e.g., all objects found in water are bathing).
  b. "Can't you see? I'm barefoot all over!"
  c. "Daddy, when you were little, were you a boy or a girl?"
  d. "The stars in the sky are real ones not like the ones we see on holidays."
  e. "Mother, shut off your radio."
  f. "Mommie, please give birth to a baby or a puppy. You know how much I'll love them."
  g. "An ostrich is a giraffe-bird."

- Using the chalkboard or a large piece of newsprint (or shelfpaper) list, with a small group of other students, the teacher behaviors that might develop a sense of trust in children on the first day of school.

- Plan and conduct two activities with preschool children that concentrate on a perceptual-motor skill. Report your successes and failures to the group.

- Describe your reactions to the following statements from children:
  a. "Milk comes from a truck."
  b. "You're ugly!"
  c. "You like her best!"
  d. "He always gets to be first!"
  e. "I don't like Petey." (another child)
  f. "Don't touch me!"
  g. "My dad kills all our bugs."

  What would you say in response to each child?

- With your eyes closed, identify three objects given to you by another person.

- Pair with another student. Each take three personal articles and place them on the table or desk in front of both of you. Try to categorize these articles. How many objects can you put in the same category? Can you find a category that includes all of the items?

Unit Review

A. Give a definition of:

abstract	motor development	conceptual tempo	
concept	assimilation	identity	tactile

B. Write a brief description of Piaget's stages of intellectual development or Erickson's stages of social-emotional development.

C. Choose the category that fits best, and code the following words with the headings (a) perceptual-motor development, (b) social-emotional development, or (c) mental development.

1. trust	6. categorizing	11. security
2. concepts	7. predicting	12. generalizing
3. tasting	8. avoiding people	13. balance
4. self-awareness	9. eye-hand skill	14. conscience
5. self-image	10. body image	15. abstracting

D. Read the teacher behaviors and verbalizations below. Write the numbers of those you feel would help a child develop healthy social-emotional skills.
   1. Recognizing each child by name as he or she enters.
   2. Pointing out (to others) a child's inability to sit still.
   3. Telling a child it's all right to hate you.
   4. Keeping a child's special toy safe.
   5. Encouraging a child's saying "I'm not finished" when another child grabs his or her toy.

6. Saying, "Jerome (child) thinks we should ask the janitor, Mr. Smith, to eat lunch with us."
7. Saying "Hitting makes me angry. It hurts."
8. Planning activities that are either "girls only" or "boys only."
9. Encouraging children who show kindness to others.
10. Allowing a child to make fun of another child without speaking to the first child about it.
11. Changing the rules and rewards often.
12. Ignoring an irritating behavior that seems to be happening more frequently.

E. Discuss children's vision and hearing acuity during preschool years.

F. Why is it important to know young children may have differences in perceiving?

G. Choose the best answer.
1. Most centers agree that perceptual-skill development belongs
   a. somewhere in the program.
   b. in the language arts area.
   c. in the music and physical education area.
   d. to a separate category of activities.
2. The younger the child the more he or she needs
   a. demonstration activities.
   b. to be told about the properties of objects.
   c. sensory experience.
   d. enriching child conversations.
3. Trust usually _____ being able to risk and explore, when considering early childhood school attendance.
   a. follows
   b. combines
   c. is dependent upon
   d. comes before
4. Young children's thinking is focused on
   a. first-hand current happening.
   b. abstract symbols.
   c. pleasing adults for rewards.
   d. the consequences of their behavior.
5. There is a _____ relationship between language and thought.
   a. well-understood
   b. well-researched
   c. clear
   d. cloudy
6. Resilient, able two- and three-year-olds have been described in this unit as children who
   a. don't let others take their toys.
   b. are assertive and smart.
   c. have a strong sense of identity and self-worth.
   d. speak frequently and use "mature" language.

References

Chukovsky, Kornei. *From Two to Five*. Berkeley: University of California, 1963.

Danoff, Judith, Vicki Breitbart, and Elinor Barr. *Open for Children*, New York: McGraw-Hill, 1976.

Douglass, Robert. "Basic Feeling and Speech Defects." *Exceptional Children*, 35.4, (March 1959): 18–23.

Erikson, Erik. *Childhood and Society*. New York: W. W. Norton, 1950.

Gibson, E. J. *Principles of Perceptual Learning and Development*. New York: Appleton-Century-Crofts, 1969.

Greenberg, Herbert M., Dr. *Teaching With Feeling*. New York: Pegasus, 1969.

Huey, J. Francis. "Learning Potential of the Young Child." *Educational Leadership* 23 (Nov. 1965): 36–40.

Jewell, Margaret Greer and Miles V. Zintz. *Learning To Read Naturally*. Dubuque: Kendall/Hunt, 1986.

Judy, Stephen. *The ABC's of Literacy*. Oxford: Oxford UP, 1980.

Kagan, J. *Change and Continuity*. New York: John Wiley & Sons, 1971.

Montessori, Maria. *The Discovery of the Child*. New York: Ballantine, 1967.

Ornstein, Robert and David Sobel. *The Healing Brain*, New York: Simon & Schuster, 1987.

Osborn, Janie Dyson and D. Keith Osborn. *Cognition In Early Childhood*. Athens, Georgia: Education Associates, 1983.

Piaget, Jean. *The Language and Thought of the Child*. London: Rutledge and Kegan Paul, 1952.

Piaget, Jean. *The Language and Thought of the Child*. New York: Meridian, 1955.

Soderman, Anne K. "Schooling All 4-Year Olds: An Idea Full of Romance, Fraught With Pitfalls." *Education Week*, 14 Mar., 1984.

Spelke, Elizabeth, in Otto Friedrick's, "What Do Babies Know?" *Human Development 85/86*, Guilford, CT: The Duskin Publishing Group, Inc., 1986.

Spitzer, Dean R. *Concept Formation and Learning in Early Childhood*, Columbus, OH: Charles E. Merrill, 1977.

Vygotsky, L. S. *Mind in Society*. Cambridge: Harvard UP, 1978.

Weiss, Curtis E., and Herold S. Lillywhite. *Communicative Disorders*, St. Louis: C. V. Mosby, 1981.

Weymouth, F. W. "Visual Acuity of Children." *Vision of Children, A Symposium*. Eds. M. J. Hirsch and R. E. Wick. Philadelphia, 1963.

Werner, E. E. and R. S. Smith. *Vulnerable, But Invincible*. New York: McGraw-Hill, 1982.

White, Burton L. *The First Three Years of Life*. Englewood Cliffs, NJ: Prentice-Hall, 1987.

White, Burton L. "The Learning Experience." *Parents As Teachers Program Planning and Implementation Guide*. Jefferson City, MO: Missouri Dept. of Elem. and Secondary Ed., 1986.

Suggested Reading

Lewis, M. M. *Language, Thought, and Personality*. New York: Basic Books, 1963.

Section 2

Developing Language Arts Programs

Early childhood programs design and implement plans and daily classroom activities to promote children's growth in the four language arts areas: speaking, listening, writing, and reading. Units 5 and 6 explain how goals and objectives are translated in actual activities. Rather than providing one type of program to emulate, the units in this section discuss varying types of programs and describe the usual steps undertaken in program planning. Specific teacher techniques follow a discussion of the teacher's role as a "responsive opportunist" who makes daily attempts to aid children's emerging skills.

WHO'S THAT READER?

Linda Lupton's article (1988) "Who's That Reader?" urges teachers to initiate a guest-celebrity reader program in their classrooms. Using special stationery, she suggests that students dictate an invitation to individuals to read to them. Guests who accept will sit in a specially designated celebrity reader chair. Imagine parents, grandparents, bus drivers, cooks, the sheriff, people from various other vocations and connections to the school sharing a picture book, and contemplate the child benefits.

Lupton writes a teacher's letter of invitation and encloses this with the children's dictated letter:

The enclosed letter was dictated by _____ _____ students in my classroom. I am optimistic that you will read it and accept the invitation to read in Room _____ at _____ School. The objective of this Celebrity Reader Program is to encourage the children to enjoy books through the use of YOU! The excitement of hearing you, a successful adult, read aloud will help to bring books to life and motivate the children to follow your example.

I am hopeful that my class will also learn from you the importance of reading in your career. With your cooperation in this project, I plan to meet my objectives for the Celebrity Reader Program. Please contact me at the school if you are willing to participate. We are anxiously awaiting your reply. [1]

[1] Linda Lupton, "Who's That Reader?" *Instructor* 9:4 (Nov./Dec. 1988): 40–42.

UNIT 5

Achieving Language and Literacy Goals Through Programming

BJECTIVES

After studying this unit, you should be able to

- describe emerging literacy in early childhood.
- discuss programming early childhood language arts activities.
- describe assessment's role in program development.
- write an activity plan for a language art activity.

This text divides language arts into four interrelated areas: listening, speaking, writing (or prewriting), and reading (or prereading). Increasing the child's understanding of how language arts combine and overlap in everyday preschool activities helps to increase language use and literacy. To that end, a unified approach is recommended, one in which the teacher purposefully shows and stresses connections between areas (figure 5-1).

LITERACY GOALS — SKILL AND KNOWLEDGE

Any discussion of literacy begins with a working definition. Hillerich (1976) provides the following:

Literacy is that demonstrated competence in communication skills which enables the individual to function, appropriate to his age, independently of his society and with a potential for movement in society.

Young children usually progress to this level of literacy by developing what Gordon Wells (1981) termed "a knowledge of literacy," which includes oral language skill, and an awareness that written (graphic) marks and words carry meaning. Wells feels that early superficial understandings about picture books and being read to lead to a much deeper understanding of the purpose of reading. Psycholinguistic theory focuses on the unique nature of human language, humans' innate search for order, structure, and meaning (Itzkoff, 1986). Using this theory as a basis, one can see how children will initiate their own first steps toward literacy when exposed to language-rich environments in which positive attitudes develop toward language arts activities.

Itzkoff (1986) describes early awareness of written forms:

Children gradually learn that certain marks — lines, circles, etc. — stand for another set of meanings in the world. The idea is born in the child's mind even while these marks are still "mysterious" that they have a special brand of meaning.

Children's growing awareness and "knowledge of literacy" is evident and can include all language arts areas — reading, writing, speaking, and listening.

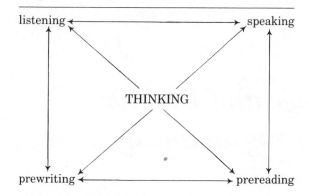

listening ← → speaking

THINKING

prewriting ← → prereading

Listening (receptive language)
One hears speech.
One can listen to another reading orally.
One can listen and write what one hears.

Speaking (oral expressive language)
One can speak to a listener.
One can put speech into written form.
One can read orally.

Writing (prewriting)
One can write what's spoken and heard.
One's writing can be read.
One's writing can be read and spoken.

Reading (reading readiness)
One can read written words.
One can listen to another reading.
One can read speech when it's written.

FIGURE 5-1 Interrelation of early childhood language arts

Becoming literate is an extension and companion of language arts skill. Most children acquire spoken language without sit-down instruction; they all become speakers, although at different rates, unless disease, illness, or trauma interferes. Literacy, on the other hand, isn't attained unconsciously or by all in our society. Literacy requires a shared body of understanding, much of which involves a common exposure to oral and written material and a level of listening, speaking, reading, and writing proficiency. Literacy acquisition involves a commitment of time and mental energy plus opportunity. At the preschool level, this commitment is a teacher's commitment to presenting a program that both promotes language arts skills and furnishes a shared body of understandings appropriate to preschoolers.

Elementary school reading textbooks in the early part of this century were collections of classics. The idea of reading levels was not in vogue but rather the goal was to have every child learn information and skills that were common to the democratic literate public electorate of the time and necessary to the development of a truly educated man or woman. Literacy today is still seen by some as only referring to reading and writing, but many researchers and early childhood educators are concerned with the taproots of literacy, which may be developed during the preschool period.

Great concern over our society's literacy rates by numerous popular writers including Hirsch (1988), Kohl (1982), and Kozol (1985) have caused alarm:

The evidence is clear that our national literacy has been declining not only among disadvantaged children but also among our top students. (Hirsch, 1988)

An estimated 1/3 of the adult population of the U.S., 60 million are felt to be functionally illiterate. (Kozol, 1985)

The largest number of illiterate adults are white, native-born Americans. In proportion to population, however, the figures are higher for blacks and Hispanics than for whites. Sixteen percent of white adults, 44% of blacks, and 56% of Hispanic citizens are functional or marginal illiterates. (Kozol, 1985)

To be considered functionally literate, one must have a knowledge of shared, common information that is neither set down on paper nor explicitly stated in oral communication and that provides the basis for understanding what is heard or read. This idea is well illustrated by a similar phenomenon that occurs when outsiders listen to an in-group whose members have learned a specialized technical vocabulary. For instance, suppose we are having a difficult time understanding a group of computer buffs. We would know they are speaking our language, but we cannot understand the bulk of their conversation. As they chat about bits, bytes, or modems, they do not make any sense to us. We would then consider ourselves functionally illiterate in computer terminology.

Hirsch (1987) feels that learning language arts skills should not be the primary goal of early childhood instruction. He theorizes that skill alone does not guarantee literacy. He feels that preschools should pay attention to *culturally significant information* (information that most beginning reading materials assume that beginning readers know). He points out that different children come to school knowing different things and suggests that "preschool is not too early for starting earnest instruction in literate national culture." The necessary cultural background knowledge one possesses to be considered literate changes over time; the early childhood professional intent on promoting literacy should be aware of this and update the curriculum periodically. The importance of achieving cultural literacy is cited in the following:

> Cultural literacy constitutes the only sure avenue of opportunity for disadvantaged children, the only reliable way of combating the social determinism that now condemns them to remain in the same social and educational condition as their parents. (Hirsch, 1987)

In programming, an integrated language/literacy approach that emphasizes child comprehension is suggested by current research. It is one of the goals of this textbook.

LANGUAGE USE IN ALL CURRICULUM AREAS

Every planned preschool activity uses language in some way. Past experience is basic to all language arts, because a child's success often depends on his or her understanding of what is happening. Language helps children learn, retain, recall, and transmit information (Lerner, 1976). Messages are received through words and nonverbal means. The teacher's speech, behavior, and use of words in planned activities are discussed in Units 6, 13, and 14.

Daily routines, play with peers, and unplanned happenings stimulate language as well as the center's planned program. Teachers use every opportunity to add meanings in a natural, conversational way during the preschool day (figure 5-2). This generally begins with the teacher's personal greeting or affectionate physical contact as the child enters the early childhood center. The "hello" and comments are part of the ritual

FIGURE 5-2 The teacher's conversation often centers on making sense out of preschool happenings.

in preschools that aim to recognize each child's presence each arrival time.

Daily routines are the regular features of a school's program that occur about the same time every day — snacks, toileting, and group activities — in which language is an associate function (figure 5-3).

Group times range from short announcement times to planned child language arts (or other content area) experiences. Instruction may take place with one child, a few, or with a group.

FIGURE 5-3 Snack time is talking time.

LANGUAGE ARTS PROGRAMMING

Preplanned language arts programs develop from identified goals: the knowledge, skills, and attitudes that the school intends to teach. Early childhood teachers also base their goals and teaching techniques on what they feel is best, right, appropriate, and prudent. This, in turn, is connected to views they hold about how, what, when, and where children learn to communicate and use language. The following views about language learning are commonly expressed or implied by staff members involved in planning language arts programs:

- Language permeates all planned and unplanned activities.
- A dynamic, rich-in-opportunity classroom stimulates communication and exchanges of ideas.
- Real experiences are preferred to vicarious ones when practical and possible.
- The reciprocal nature of exploring and discovering together should be promoted by teachers.
- Play provides many opportunities to learn language.
- Teachers' instructional techniques should be skilled and alert to child readiness.
- Stressing relationships between objects, events, and experiences is a useful teaching technique.
- Individual planning, as well as group planning, is desirable.
- Program activities should center on the child's interests.
- Literary classics (preschool level) are an important planned-program component.
- The entire teaching staff should be committed and enthusiastic about their planned program, and understand stated objectives.
- An integrated approach to language arts instruction helps children experience the "connectedness" of language arts areas.

Schools and child centers have given special attention to the last goal in light of recommendations made by The Commission on Reading (1985) in the report entitled "Becoming a Nation of Readers," which emphasizes the need to view all language processes — listening, speaking, reading, and writing — as interrelated and mutually supportive.

Determining Program Effectiveness

Goals pinpointed through staff meetings and solicited parent input can be finalized in written form to serve as a basis for planning. For one child or many, goals are achieved when teachers and staff plan interesting and appropriate activities for daily, weekly, monthly, or longer periods. In addition to the actual program, materials, and classroom equipment and arrangement, teacher techniques and interactions and other resources aid in goal realization (figure 5-4).

FIGURE 5-4 Outdoor equipment can help children with goal realization.

Teacher observation and assessment instruments — teacher-designed and commercial — add extra data that helps in planning programs. In any attempts to gather data, preschool staffs carefully examine which methods or instruments best suit a program planning group's needs and the reliability and suitability of each proposed course of action. Through the use of tests, rating scales, and checklists, teachers gather information that alerts them to levels of development, child interest and abilities, and aids them in finding what Hunt (1961) terms "the match," that is, activities neither too easy nor too difficult. If the activities are "just right," the child experiences inner satisfaction.

Beers and Beers (1980) urge teachers to question using test results during preschool years as a basis for program planning:

> Many standardized tests and testing procedures are of relatively little use with three- to five-year-olds. One important reason for the unreliability of these tests has to do with the nature of children that age. Young children may be restless and fidgety, distracted, and bored when required to sit for any length of time with a task that does not appeal to them: their behavior can differ from hour to hour or from day to day, depending on whether they are hungry, frightened, anxious, or tired.

Early childhood centers often try to determine the center's effectiveness by rating children at both the beginning and ending of a school year. When this is done with young children at the beginning of their first group experience — and possibly their first time away from their home setting — results may not be favorable or accurate. Spodek (1972) points out:

> Administration of tests early in a child's career has certain inherent pitfalls. Many young children are unfamiliar with testing procedures and do not know appropriate response behavior, thus making test results invalid. It may be well to postpone administering tests to young children until they have been in school long enough to have been acculturated to the ways of the school.

And Bredekamp (1988) adds:

> Standardized tests all too often do not tell observant teachers anything that they don't already know about children.

In 1986, NAEYC (National Association for the Education of Young Children) published a position paper concerning the testing of young children that should be mandatory reading for all who work in programs in which testing is done. This position paper is available by writing to NAEYC, 1834 Connecticut Ave. N. W., Washington, D.C. 20009-5786, and requesting the "Position Statement on Standardized Testing of Young Children Three Through Eight Years of Age." An excerpt follows:

> The burden of proof for the validity and reliability of tests is on the test developers and the advocates for their use. The burden of proof for the utility of tests is on administrators or teachers of early childhood programs who make decisions about the use of tests in individual classrooms. Similarly, the burden of responsibility for choosing, administering, scoring, and interpreting a score from a standardized test rests with the early childhood professional and thus demands that professionals be both skilled and responsible. Ensuring that tests meet scientific standards, reflect the most current scientific knowledge, and are used appropriately requires constant vigilance on the part of educators. (NAEYC 1988)

A teacher or assistant teacher (under the supervision of the teacher) may have the responsibility of administering a test to a group of young children. This is usually accomplished by taking each child aside and asking him or her to answer questions or perform tasks. The teacher must have a clear understanding of the test's instruction manual and the necessary training beforehand.

There are many different types of assessments. Figure 5-5 is a developmental checklist for two-and-a-half- to five-year-old children. Some assessments attempt to determine ability and accomplishment in a number of language and communication areas; others may be limited to one language skill.

Teacher Observation

Many child centers encourage teachers to continually observe the language skills of attending children. Each child and group may have different needs, and the center attempts to fulfill needs and offer a language arts program that will be growth producing and enriching. Many different observation methods and

	Present	Date Observed
Two Year Olds Receptive:		
Understands most commonly used nouns and verbs		
Responds to 2-part command		
Enjoys simple story books		
Points to common objects when they are named		
Understands functions of objects, e.g. cup-drink		
Expressive: Verbalizes own actions		
Uses 2–3 word phrases		
Asks what and where questions		
Makes negative statements		
Labels action in pictures		
Approx. 50-word vocabulary (2 yrs.)		
Answers questions		
Speech sounds: Substitutes some consonant sounds, e.g., w for r, d for th		
Articulates all vowels with few deviations		
Three Years Olds Receptive: Understands size and time concepts		
Enjoys being read to		
Understands IF, THEN, and BECAUSE concepts		
Carries out 2–4 related directions		
Responds to or questions		
Expressive: Gives full name		
Knows sex and can state girl or boy		
Uses 3–4 word phrases		
Uses /s/ on nouns to indicate plurals		

FIGURE 5-5 An example of a developmental checklist *(Adapted from* Developmental Checklist, *by E.S.P. Inc., 1983.)*

	Present	Date Observed
Three Year Olds (*Continued*) Expressive:		
Uses /ed/ on verbs to indicate past tense		
Repeats simple songs, fingerplays, etc.		
Speech is 70%–80% intelligible		
Vocabulary of over 500 words		
Four Year Olds Receptive: Follows 3 unrelated commands		
Understands sequencing		
Understands comparatives: big, bigger, biggest		
Expressive: Has mastery of inflection (can change volume and rate)		
Uses 5+ word sentences		
Uses adjectives, adverbs, conjunctions in complex sentences		
Speech about 90%–95% intelligible		
Speech sounds: S, SH, R, CH		
Five Year Olds Receptive: Demonstrates preacademic skills such as following directions and listening		
Expressive: Few differences between child's use of language and adults'		
Can take turns in conversation		
May have some difficulty with noun-verb agreement and irregular past tenses		
Communicates well with family, friends, and strangers		
Speech sounds: Can correctly articulate most simple consonants and many digraphs		

FIGURE 5-5 *Continued*

instruments can be employed. Some may be school-designed; others may be commercially produced.

Observation information is confidential and often useful in program planning. Running accounts of child conversations are difficult to obtain because an adult's presence may affect a child's spontaneity. Also, the child's attention span and mobility make it almost impossible to capture more than a few minutes of speech with preschoolers. Many teachers note a few phrases or speech characteristics on a writing pad they carry with them throughout the day. For many teachers, having time just to observe children is considered a luxury. However, observation is important and can be considered an on-going teacher responsibility in all areas of instruction.

To ensure a language program's quality, plans are changed, updated, and revised based on both the children's progress and staff members' evaluations and observations. Keeping a planned language arts program vital, dynamic, appealing, and appropriate requires continual revision and overhaul of the program.

Individual center and school staff members decide whether identification of children's abilities through testing and assessment will take place. Unfortunately testing emphasizes children's scores rather than the school's ability to offer a program suitable for each attending child. One of the great challenges in teaching is to present what each child needs in a way that turns the child on to additional school and home experiences and activities.

Each center's goals are concerned with (1) attending children's needs (2) parental and community input, and (3) the personalities, training, and experience of staff.

GOAL STATEMENTS

A particular center may have many or few goal statements, which can be both general and specific.

In infant and toddler centers, the following specific objectives might be included in goal statements:

- Making comfort and discomfort sounds.
- Following an object with eyes and reaching for it.
- Smiling and laughing.
- Turning head in a sound's direction.
- Anticipating consequences of a heard sound.
- Recognizing familiar people.

- Picking up small objects.
- Babbling with vowels and consonants.
- Making physical response to words.
- Gesturing in response, as in waving bye-bye.
- Engaging in vocal play.
- Imitating sounds made by others.
- Mimicking nonverbal actions.
- Using jargon suggestive of meaning.
- Using one word sentences.
- Pointing to body parts when requested.
- Pointing to objects to elicit object's name.
- Using telegram speech.
- Using an 8- to 10-word spoken vocabulary.
- Knowing name.

Goal statements for preschoolers two-and-a-half to five years old are usually categorized into the four language arts areas and can include goals dealing with imaginative and creative use of language. *Auditory skill* (listening — receptive language) includes awareness, discrimination, memory, comprehension, and direction following. Possible goal statements follow:

- Listens to stories.
- Is able to retell short parts of stories: plot particulars, main ideas, and character traits.
- Hears rhyme.
- Becomes increasingly understandable, less dependent on context in speech.
- Gives attention to verbal instructions.
- Replies in a relevant fashion to others' remarks.
- Identifies familiar sounds from the environment.
- Describes past listening experience.
- Discriminates sounds.
- Possesses a sense of the rhythm, sequence, and patterns of something heard.
- Evaluates and considers comments or what is heard in a thoughtful manner.

Expressive speaking skills for two-and-a-half to five-year-olds may include the following:

At two-and-a-half
- Uses correct word order most of the time.
- Averages at least 75 words per hour during play.
- Uses two- to three- (or more) word sentences.
- Uses pronouns such as I, me, mine, it, who, and that.
- Uses adjectives and adverbs at times.
- Names common objects and pictures.

- Repeats two or more items from memory.
- Announces intentions before acting.
- Asks questions of adults.

At three
- Gives name.
- Tells simple stories.
- Uses plurals and some prepositions.
- Can describe at least one element of a picture.
- Talks about past and future happenings.
- Uses commands, is critical at times, and makes requests.
- Uses wh- questions and offers answers.

At three-and-a-half
- Uses four- to five- (or more) word sentences.
- Averages over 200 words per hour in play.
- Tells experiences in sequential order at times.
- Recites simple rhymes or finger plays or sings simple songs.

At four
- Speaks in adultlike sentences.
- Repeats nine-word sentences from memory.
- Enjoys and uses nonsense words at times.
- Exaggerates and uses imaginative speech at times.
- Often requests the reasons for things.
- Uses "why."
- Can tell a simple story with picture clues.
- Evaluates own activities in words periodically.

At four-and-a-half
- Uses compound or complex sentences.
- Problem solves in language with peers.
- Creates simple stories.
- Dramatizes simple stories with others.
- Is 85% to 95% fluent in speech.
- Speaks mainly in complete sentences.
- Listens to others, raises questions, and speculates out loud in class.
- Possesses a substantial passive vocabulary.

Prewriting Goals

In the process of literacy development, young children can profit from an understanding of the role of the printed word. The uses of writing, including recording and transmitting information, recording self-authored creations, and providing entertainment, are important to the quality of human life. A knowledge of writing uses may lead to a realization of the value of learning to read. Writing and reading open

each individual to the thoughts, creations, and discoveries, of multitudes of people, living and deceased. This discussion is not intended to promote early printing instruction but rather to point out that there are basic ideas about writing that must be considered when planning a language arts curriculum that promotes literacy (figure 5-6).

There is a strong connection between the child's familiarity with books (and his or her book-reading experiences) and literacy. Illustrations of the reasons for writing and how writing can satisfy everyday needs can be incorporated into any center's goals for promoting literacy growth. Units 17 and 18 cover preschools and written language in greater detail.

Most schools concentrate on exposing children to printed words rather than starting actual writing practice in alphabet letter formation. The following are common child-center activities that involve writing skills:

- Tracing.
- Cutting.
- Using marking tools.
- Dictating words or sentences.
- Contributing to group dictation on charts, experience stories, and so on.

FIGURE 5-6 This child may be signaling an interest in making shapes that look like the letter "e."

- Creating short books with dictated print and illustrations.
- Attempting simple dot-to-dot drawings.
- Making lines and simple shapes.
- Discussing uses of writing in everyday life.

These activities arouse children's curiosity about alphabet letters, numerals, and words, encourage them to make attempts to print their names, and help them gain control in using various writing tools.

Prereading Goals

Reading skills are multiple and complex, and often involve the coordination of other skills and abilities. Some prereading goals that will facilitate later reading skills follow:

- Reads pictures.
- Shows an interest and enjoyment in stories and books.
- Is able to arrange pictures in a sequence that tells a story.
- Finds hidden objects in pictures.
- Guesses at meanings based on context cues.
- Reads own and others' names.
- Predicts events.
- Recognizes letters of own name in other words.
- Senses left-right direction.
- Guesses words to complete sentences.
- Chooses favorite book characters.
- Treats books with care.
- Authors own books through dictation.
- Sees finely detailed differences.
- Recognizes and names alphabet letters at times.
- Shows interest in libraries.
- Shows interest in the sounds of letters.
- Watches or uses puppets to enact simple stories.
- Has background in traditional literature appropriate for age and ability.

Some schools are under considerable pressure to begin teaching reading skills rather than plan a program of activities that fully develops all areas. A carefully planned language arts program provides children with basic experiences that can help make future reading both successful and pleasurable. Reading skill is certainly a key skill in elementary schooling, but no more so than the child's possessing a positive view of his or her own competence, a positive attitude toward reading and books, and a body of general knowledge.

Preschoolers need a wealth of important exploration and discovery activities based on their own choice and agenda.

Nedler (1977), reviewing The Bilingual Early Childhood Program, mentions the following categories of goals that were included in the project:

- Visual training.
- Auditory training.
- Ideas and concepts.
- Syntax of English.
- Building vocabulary.
- Prewriting.
- Exploring and discovering.

Goals That Promote Emerging Literacy

There seems to be some debate over whether "relevant" language arts materials and activities should take precedent over "traditional" ones. Most early childhood educators feel that goal statements should include both when planning programs, and this usually presents no problem. Hirsch (1988) notes that there has been a disappearance of traditional literate culture in the early school curriculum, and others feel early reading skill practice has taken precedence over traditional literature.

Preschool teachers planning and conducting programs that promote language development in young children try to provide a "classic" literary experience, featuring age-level appropriate materials collected from many cultures and eras. Such a curriculum would serve as a basis of human cultural understanding and would include a wide range of oral and listening materials and activities: books, poetry, language games, puppetry, and story telling. Most teachers feel that early exposure to and familiarity with literary classics can help the child understand what might be encountered later in literature, media, or schooling.

At present, a widely circulated list of classics for preschool children has not been available, but a list of these works has existed in the minds and hearts of individual teachers. Mother Goose stories are undisputed classics. Two other classic stories have been identified by Anderson et al. (1985):

Even for beginners, reading should not be thought of simply as a skill subject. It is difficult to imagine, for instance, that kindergartners could be called literate for their age if they did not know *Goldilocks and the Three Bears* or *Peter Rabbit*. For each age there are fables, fairytales, folk tales, classic and modern works of fiction that embody the core of our cultural heritage. (Anderson et al., 1985)

Whether a story, play, rhyme, or song is considered a "classic," however, is usually a matter of judgment by individual teachers.

Jewell and Zintz (1986) have compiled a list of suggestions that can help promote literacy and possibly ease the sometimes burdensome task of learning to read. These activities and provisions can be incorporated into center goals and planning if they aren't already present.

- Read to children that which they cannot read for themselves.
- Read from a variety of materials with a high interest level — stories, poems, and so forth, that are fun.
- Provide a reading environment by having an abundance of reading materials readily available.
- Tape stories and store cassettes for children to use in a listening center.
- Provide flannel boards with appropriate cutouts for children to tell stories to themselves or to others. Teachers should also tell stories.
- Have writing materials readily available.
- Have a scrap or "attic box" filled with a collection of odds and ends for children to sort through, touch, and talk about in whatever way they choose.
- Provide time to engage in all of the above activities (figure 5-7).
- Provide a multitude of hands-on experiences for children to do and to talk about.
- With the emergence of reading behaviors, provide information and help as the child requests.
- Begin to prepare language experience stories by recording child talk about experience in the classroom.
- Provide time for them to read and look at books.
- Continue to share books with the whole group by reading daily. Your own attitude and commitment to reading is a model that demonstrates that reading is an enjoyable, worthwhile activity.

FIGURE 5-7 There are always planned times for child selection of favorite activities.

Professionals should consider reviewing NAEYC's (1986) "identified appropriate practice" when developing goals and planning curriculum. Sections applicable to this discussion follow:

For Three-Year-Olds
- Adults read a story or play music with small groups and allow children to enter and leave the group at will.
- Adults encourage children's developing language by speaking clearly and frequently to individual children and listening to their response. Adults respond quickly and appropriately to children's verbal initiatives. They recognize that talking may be more important than listening for 3-year-olds. Adults patiently answer children's questions (Why? "Howcome?") and recognize that 3-year-olds often ask questions they know the answers to in order to open a discussion or practice giving answers themselves. Adults know that children are rapidly acquiring language, experimenting with verbal sounds, and beginning to use language to solve problems and learn concepts.
- Adults provide many experiences and opportunities to extend children's language and musical abilities. Adults read books to one child or a small group; recite simple poems, nursery rhymes, and finger plays; encourage children to sing songs and listen to record-

ings; facilitate children's play or circle and movement games like London Bridge, Farmer in the Dell, and Ring around the Rosie; provide simple rhythm instruments; listen to stories that children tell or write down stories they dictate; and enjoy 3-year-olds' sense of humor.

For Four- and Five-Year-Olds

- Teachers accept that there is often more than one right answer. Teachers recognize that children learn from self-directed problem solving and experimentation.
- Children are provided many opportunities to see how reading and writing are useful before they are instructed in letter names, sounds, and word identification. Basic skills develop when they are meaningful to children. An abundance of these types of activities is provided to develop language and literacy through meaningful experience: listening to and reading stories and poems; taking field trips; dictating stories; seeing classroom charts and other print in use; participating in dramatic play and other experiences requiring communication; talking informally with other children and adults; and experimenting with writing by drawing, copying, and inventing their own spelling.

LANGUAGE ARTS CURRICULUM

Schools and centers differ widely in curriculum development; however, two basic approaches can be identified. First a unit or thematic approach emerges from identified child interest and teacher-selected areas, such as families, seasons, animals, and so on. Using this approach, some centers use children's books or classic nursery rhymes as their thematic starting topic. Goals are considered, and activities are then outlined and scheduled into time slots. Many teachers feel this type of program approach individualizes instruction by providing many interrelated and, consequently, reinforced learnings while also allowing the child to select activities. The second common instructional approach is to pinpoint traditional preschool subject areas, such as language arts, science, mathematics, art, cooking, and so forth, and then plan how many and what kind of planned activities will take place. This can be done with or without considering a unifying theme. Some teachers feel that this is a more systematic approach to instruction.

In both approaches, the identification of goals has come before curriculum development. Ages of children, staffing ratios, facility resources, and other particulars all have an impact on planning. After planned curriculum activities take place, teachers evaluate whether goals were reached, and modifications and suggestions are noted. Additional or follow-up activities may be planned and scheduled for groups or individual children.

Thematic (Unit) Approach to Language Instruction

Imagine a classroom turned into a pizza parlor or a flower garden. There would be a number of activities going on simultaneously — some for small groups, others for large groups, and some for individuals. Teachers would be involved in activities, and classroom areas might be set up for continuous, or almost continuous, child exploration. Art, singing, number, movement, science-related, health-and-safety-related, and other types of activities would (or could) be preplanned, focusing on the two themes mentioned above. The sensory activities could be included so that children could experience the smells, sounds, sights, tastes, and so on, associated with each theme. Planning language arts instruction using this approach allows teachers to use creativity and imagination. It also requires planning time to gather and set up material that might not be found in the school storeroom or supply area. It is easy to see that there could be many opportunities for children's use of speech, listening, reading, and writing, and the natural connection among these activities might be more apparent to the children. Most teachers feel using a thematic approach is an exciting challenge that is well worth teacher time and effort. They see this approach as one that encourages child-teacher conversations that expand both language usage and knowledge.

The thematic approach, has claimed more advocates since the trend toward whole-language instruction has captured the interest of a growing number of elementary school teachers and early childhood teachers. Many early childhood teachers who work with children who are younger than kindergarten age have used a unit (or thematic) approach to instruction for many years. Whole-language philosophy adds new dimensions to preschool unit instruction. Whole-language teachers believe that when children are immersed in language through reading, writing, being read to, observing, and listening that reading behavior emerges naturally (Ferguson, 1988).

The new dimensions mentioned above include an increased emphasis on language-area relatedness and print use in the daily routine in a preschool. A teacher following a whole-language thematic philosophy might offer a unit on valentines along the lines that follow.

- Discuss valentines.
  "What do you know about valentines?"
- Write children's answers and comments on a wall chart.
- Say "I can read what you told me," and then read it.
- Ask questions or elicit child ideas with:
  "Where can I find a valentine?"
  Talk about valentines you have received.
  "Why would someone send a valentine?"
- Provide each child with a box to use as a mailbox.
  Child chooses sticker to identify box.
  Write child's name on box.
  Place boxes in alphabetical order.
  Number boxes.
- Teacher and children examine envelopes that come to school.
  Point out lines and words across stamp.
  Use word "cancelled."
  Teacher talks about unused stamps.
  Discuss letter carriers. Use pictures of letter carriers to promote conversation.
- Conduct a field trip to the post office.
  Share a book about receiving mail.
  Set up a work center with stamps (any kind), envelopes, writing tools, and lists of names.
- Set up a work area complete with materials used for making valentines.
- Introduce a list of all the names of people in the class.
- Introduce songs about valentines.
- Share a poem about valentines.

A beginning teacher can see from this bare-bones outline that the teacher is identifying possible learning activities associated with the valentine theme. Each teacher or school using a theme or whole-language approach may develop a unit on valentines that has similarities and differences. Many of the differences arise from the teacher's knowledge of what is appropriate for the teacher's particular group of children and the goals that have been identified. On further planning and when presenting this unit to the class, the whole-language teacher would look for opportunities to state and show relationships among language arts areas.

COMMITMENT TO GOALS AND OBJECTIVES

A number of factors determine whether goals are met:

- Enthusiasm and commitment of staff
- Staffing ratios
- Staff ingenuity, resourcefulness
- Methods and techniques used
- Resources available
- General feeling or tone of center
- Examination of sequence (easiest to complex)
- Parental and community support

Effort and staff creativity translate goals into daily activities.

Daily Activity Plans

Recognizing child interests stimulates activity-planning ideas based on what captures and holds the child's attention. Part of the challenge and excitement of teaching is finding ways to be creative in daily activity planning.

Although two staff members work toward the same goal, they may approach the task in a different way. Lesson plans are more frequently used in schools using approaches other than the thematic (unit) approach described above but can also be used for individual teacher-conducted activities within theme planning.

Lesson plans enable teachers to foresee needs — settings, materials, and staffing. The time that children spend waiting can be minimized. Some teachers pinpoint exactly what words and concepts will be emphasized or what questions asked; other teachers prefer a more spontaneous approach.

Some activities in language arts may require teacher practice beforehand. Others may require visual aids or materials that must be gathered in advance. Planning time is time well spent. Preparation reduces teacher tension and results in child activities that run smoothly.

Teachers must strive to be always aware of child safety and comfort. They must also try to maintain a reasonable level of stimulation somewhere between not very interesting or overly exciting activities, so that children are encouraged to process information in a manner that is both pleasurable and efficient. Experienced teachers know when children are interested and are actively participating. Many teachers say this is one of the greatest joys of teaching.

Group size is an important factor in planning. It is easier for teachers to plan for an entire class group, and sometimes staffing demands it. However, many teachers have explored ways to keep children occupied and supervised while working with small groups. Small groups allow greater intimacy, conversational depth, and opportunity for feedback. Research substantiates the idea that both children and adults feel more comfortable sharing their thoughts when in small groups. "Instant replays" with small groups can be planned and coordinated. Beginning preschool teachers may not have seen many small-group activities modeled by other teachers, but this text recommends them.

The three examples on pages 102 through 104 illustrate different types of activity planning (figure 5-8, figure 5-9, and figure 5-10).

Detailed written lesson plans help beginning teachers feel prepared and relaxed (figure 5-11, pages 104–105). After a period of time, teachers internalize lesson-planning components and discontinue detailed written plans, although they continue to use lists and outlines.

Watching the class carefully, keeping a notebook in a handy pocket, and writing down small observations can help a teacher to remember the interests of a young group. A good guide to unearthing new subjects of interest for a particular class is to notice what has already captured the children's attention. What do the children talk about most often? What do they crowd around? Does the activity promote children's interested questions? What has the longest waiting list? Are children eager to explore a particular object with their hands? Who wants to share something discovered or created? For example, if butterflies interest a group, planned butterfly experiences can add depth to the curriculum.

Activities based on teacher enthusiasm for life and growth, skills, talents, hobbies, and pursuits can fit beautifully into language arts goals. Parent and community resources, including borrowed items and field trips increase the vitality of programs.

UNDERSTANDING LOCATIONAL WORDS

Purpose:
The child will, on the first try, correctly place objects "under," "over," "behind," and "in front of" when given verbal directions.

Materials:
Large box (large enough for a child to climb into), cup and plastic man, cloth and bar of soap.

Procedure:
1. Place large box in front of child. Put all objects inside.
2. Ask child to find what is in the box. Say to child, "Tell me about what you find in the box."
3. Pause and let the child talk about objects.
4. Ask, "Can you hide *under* this box?" Encourage the child to do so. "Show me how the plastic man could hide *under* the cup. What can you hide *under* the cloth?"

5. "Put your hand *over* the box. Can you step *over* the cup?" etc.
6. "Let's put everything *in front of* the big box. Now let's hide everything *behind* the box." etc.
7. "You tell me what I should put *under* the cloth. Did I do it? Is it *under?*" Continue in the same manner with over, behind, and in front of.
8. Ask the child to put the objects any way he or she wishes. "Are any *in front of? Behind? Under? Over?* Tell me where you chose to put them."
9. "Is there anything *under* your shoes? What's *over* your chest? Tell me something you see that's *in front of* your eyes. Guess what's *behind* you right now." (Move your hand behind the child.)

FIGURE 5-8 Example 1 — individual activity

VISUAL PERCEPTION

Purpose:

To match identical mittens from an assortment.

Materials:

Picture of three little kittens and 12 pairs of construction paper mittens. All mittens are to be made from the same color paper. Each pair of mittens should be decorated differently. Do not use color or size as the differentiating element. (Trace around a child's hand for size of mittens.)

Procedure:

1. Show children a picture of the three little kittens. Ask, "Do you remember what the three little kittens lost?" (Children answer). "That's right, they lost their mittens. I have some mittens here."

2. Show the children a pair of mittens. "Look at these mittens. How are they the same? What do the mittens have on them? Yes, they each have a flower." Have a child point to both flowers.

3. Show another pair of mittens. "Look! I have another pair of mittens. Are they the same? How are they the same? Yes, these mittens are the same."

4. "Now we're going to play a game. You're just like the three little kittens. Let's start with (child's name)." (Give the child one mitten, and place its mate and one other mitten in the center of the table.) "(child's name), find the mitten that's the same as yours." If the child has difficulty, let him or her put his mitten next to one of the mittens and compare the patterns.

5. Continue the procedure until all children have had several turns. Stress often that the mittens are the same.

6. Separate 5 pairs of mittens into two sets. Place the right-hand mittens in one set and the left-hand mittens in the other. Ask a child to choose a mitten he or she likes from one of the sets and find the matching mitten in the other set. Then say, "(child's name) has two mittens that look the same."

7. Continue the procedure until each child has had a turn. Repeat the activity two or three times, putting out more pairs of mittens each time.

NOTE: At Easter time, the teacher may use eggs for matching patterns. In fall, leaf patterns may be used.

Criterion Activity:

During a play period, ask each child to come with you and play the Mitten Game. Arrange the mittens on the table. "Find a mitten, and then find another one that looks the same." Have the child continue the procedure until he or she has matched all the mittens. The child must match 3 pairs to reach criterion.

Reinforcement:

For extension lessons on the concept of "same" and "not the same," Picture Cards, Set 2, Picture Dominoes can be used.

NOTE: A review of the lesson can help the reader think of similar activities that may be used in future lessons. For example, the gloves and mittens worn to school by the children can also be used as a basis for a lesson. In climates where mittens are not worn, shoes can be used. One of the strengths of the curriculum is its flexibility and adaptability. For example, in one classroom made up of Indian children, the teacher used pairs of feathers, colored beads, and cutouts of tepees (Karnes, 1972).

FIGURE 5-9 Example 2 — group activity

NOTE: This is a portion of a longer description. The words in italics show how the teacher works toward a variety of goals.

This episode is an account of a sequence of planned activities culminating in a cooking experience for four 4-year-old children. Part 1 of the episode details the preparation in the classroom for the purchase of the food and the group's trip to a local store. Part 2 describes the cooking.

The fresh pears at lunch evoked the excited comment "Apples!" from Spanish-speaking Fernando.

"Well, this is a fruit," said Miss Gordon, encouragingly, "but it has another name. Do you remember the apples we had last week?" "They were hard to bite," said Joey.

"And we made applesauce," said Rosina.

"This fruit is called a pear, Fernando; let's taste this pear now. We'll have apples again."

The teacher responds to what is correct in the child's response, valuing his category association. First, she wants to support communication and willingness to experiment with language; later she gives the correct name. The children strengthen the experience by relating it to previous experience in which they were active.

"Mine's soft," said Joey.

"Can we make applesauce again?" begged Rosina.

The teacher replied, "Perhaps we could do what Janice wanted to do. Remember? To take some home to her family?"

"To my mommy, and my grandma, and Danny."

"Not to my baby," said Rosina. "He's too little. Him only drink milk."

FIGURE 5-10 Example 3 — multiple-goal approach *(continues)*

"Tomorrow we'll buy lots of apples," said Miss Gordon.

The teacher is building a sense of continuity by recalling earlier intentions that had been expressed by the children.

She rarely corrects use of pronouns for four-year-olds. She knows the child will learn through greater social maturity and hearing language.

After rest, Miss Gordon asked the children how they could take home their applesauce. "What can we put it in?"

Rosina ran to the house corner and returned with two baby food jars. "I bringed lots," she said. Miss Gordon remembered that Rosina had come to school lugging a bag full of baby food jars, many of which she had put away. "A good idea! And your mommy said she would keep more for us. Let's write a note to tell her we need them tomorrow."

Rosina dictated a note: "I got to bring bunches of jars to school. We are going to make applesauce. I love you, Mommy." And painted her name with a red marker.

The teacher helps children to think ahead to steps in a process.

The use of a tense form, though incorrect, represents learning for the child. The teacher does not correct at this moment, when she is responding to the child's pleasure in solving the practical problem that had been posed. She is strengthening the connection between home and school.

The teacher helps the children learn that writing is a recording of meaning and a way of communicating.

The next day was jar washing and arranging time. Each of the four children put his jars on a tray on which there was a large card with his name.

Janice put on one jar for her mother, one for her grandmother, one for her brother, and after a pause, one for herself.

Rosina changed her mind. "My baby can have a little tiny bit," she said. So she needed a jar for her father, her mother, her baby and herself.

Joey and the teacher figured out that he needed six, and that Fernando needed nine!

The children are actively involved in the steps preparatory to the planned activity — an experience in organization which has personal meaning.

The teacher's plan calls for recognition of one's own name and one-to-one counting of family members.

The teacher turned their attention to a chart near the cooking corner. She had made a recipe chart, pasting colored (magazine) pictures next to the names of the items they would need to make the applesauce and had taped a stick of cinnamon to the chart.

Miss Gordon said, "Let's look at the recipe chart. I have a list so we can remember to buy everything."

The children said, "Apples."

Miss Gordon checked her list.

Then, "Sugar."

The children were silent as they looked at the stick of cinnamon taped to the chart.

Miss Gordon suggested, "Smell it. Have we had it before?"

Joey remembered: "Toast! What we put on toast!"

"Yes," said Miss Gordon, and then gave the word, "cinnamon."

The children are having a dual experience — pictorial representation and formal symbol usage.

The teacher supplies the word after the children have revived their direct experience with the phenomenon (Biber, Shapiro, Wickens, 1977).

FIGURE 5-10 *Continued*

LANGUAGE ACTIVITY PLAN GUIDE

1. Language activity title _____

_____

2. Materials needed _____

_____

_____

3. Location of activity (To be used when plan is developed for a particular classroom or area) _____

_____

4. Number of children _____

5. Language goal or objective _____

_____

FIGURE 5-11 Sample activity plan form

6. Preparation (Necessary teacher preparation, including getting materials or objects, visual aids, etc., ready)

_____

_____

_____

7. Getting started (Introductory and/or motivational statement) _____

_____

_____

8. Show and explore (Include possible teacher questions or statements which promote language ability)

_____

_____

_____

_____

_____

9. Discussion key points (What vocabulary and/or concepts might be included?) _____

_____

_____

_____

_____

_____

_____

_____

10. Apply (Include child practice or application of newly learned knowledge or skill when appropriate)

_____

_____

_____

11. Evaluation: (1) Activity, (2) Teacher, (3) Child participation, (4) Other aspects such as setting, materials, outcomes, etc. _____

_____

_____

_____

_____

_____

_____

FIGURE 5-11 _Continued_

Evaluation

Thinking back over planned activities helps teachers analyze the benefits and possibly leads to additional planning along the same line or with the same theme. Oversights in planning always occur, and activities may develop in unexpected ways. Hindsight is a useful and valuable tool in evaluating activities.

Summary

Preschool professionals are concerned with the literacy of preschoolers and believe attention to beginning literacy should be reflected in the planning of the language arts curriculum. Three factors, skill, a shared body of common knowledge, and attitude promote emerging literacy. Beginning literacy is believed to exist in children who demonstrate beginning competence in language.

Language is part of every preschool activity. This text recommends an integrated approach to early childhood language arts — that is, a program that involves listening, speaking, writing, and reading.

Centers identify language arts goals through a group process. Activities are then planned based on these goals. Daily plans carry out what is intended. Assessment instruments are evaluated, and decisions are made concerning whether these instruments are to be used or not used. Staff observation provides data on children's abilities, interests, and skill levels, as well as additional insights that are useful in activity planning. Every center has a unique set of goals and objectives, so designing child experiences is done in a variety of ways. Since attending children change in any particular school, plans change according to children's needs and interests.

Evaluating a planned activity after it is presented can pinpoint strengths and weaknesses. This also serves as the basis for further activity planning.

Student Activities

- Define literacy in your own words. Share with class.

- List 10 reasons for illiteracy in the United States. Then, list 10 ways preschool centers can help a preschooler's emerging literacy. Ask for a volunteer to make a chart on a large surface that everyone in the classroom can see, listing the reasons for illiteracy that are given by students. Put tallies after ideas so that the class can see what was the most frequently thought of reason. Make a second large listing of the group's ideas concerning how preschools can promote emerging literacy.

- Describe an activity(ies) that might interest young children based on your own personal experience, a talent or skill you possess, a family possession or article, or an interesting field trip. Don't forget clothing you own for special purposes or hobbies or collections or people you know who might share their talents or possessions.

- Form a discussion group with a few fellow students. Take out one item from your pocket or purse. Describe an activity you could use with children to promote the following skills:
  a. Memory (naming or recalling)
  b. Discrimination
  c. Problem solving
  d. Perceptual-motor skill

  Be aware that each activity planned should
  — be interesting and enjoyable.
  — help children feel competent and successful.
  — stimulate children to discover.

– promote sensory exploration.

– include learning by doing.

– promote language by promoting expression of what the child experienced or discovered.

Go on to discuss what activities could be planned that would promote the same four skills (a through d) using a box of paper clips or a doll.

- Design an activity plan form that includes:
  a. Title (What?)
  b. Materials and tools needed (With what?)
  c. An objective (language arts) (Why?)
  d. A preparation section
  e. Setting or location description
  f. Number of children who are to participate at one time
  g. Identification of child skills and abilities necessary for success
  h. A statement that introduces the activity to children
  i. A description of how the activity will proceed (How?)

- Invite teachers to describe their center's language arts curriculum. Try to invite a teacher using the whole-language philosophy to share the teacher's curriculum plans.

- Using any activity plan form, make a written plan for a language development activity. Share your plan with others at the next class meeting. Rate the quality of your participation in the discussion using the following scale, or write a beginning outline for a unit of your own choosing or one you feel is of interest to a group of four-year-old children. Share your unit ideas at the next class meeting.

No Input	Very Little	Contributed About As Much As Classmates	A Fair Amount	Offered Lots of Ideas

- Ask a practicing early childhood teacher to speak about the use of assessment instruments in the language program where the person is employed.

- Ask a school psychologist to describe testing and test construction.

- Look back into your own childhood before age six. What classics, songs, rhymes, language activities were part of your childhood? If you do not remember, answer this alternative question: Which literacy-promoting language activities should not be missed by any child? Be specific, and name poems, books, rhymes, stories, or other literary experiences.

Unit Review

A. Name the four interrelated language arts areas, arranging them in what you feel is their order of appearance in young children.

B. Compare lesson plan Examples 2 and 3 in this unit. How do they differ? In which ways are they similar?

C. Write three language arts goal statements (what you would want children to have the opportunity to experience and learn). These should be statements that would be included in a program where you were (or will be) employed.

D. Select the correct answer. Each item may have more than one correct answer.
1. Assessment instruments can be
   a. a checklist.
   b. a child interest inventory.
   c. counted on to be valid.
   d. teacher made.
2. Compiling and identifying a center's goal statements ideally involves
   a. children's input.
   b. staff.
   c. parents.
   d. interested community members.
3. Early childhood language arts should be offered to children using
   a. an approach that helps children see relationships between areas.
   b. techniques that promote the child's realization that spoken words can be written.
   c. separate times of day to explore reading and writing without combining these skills.
   d. identified goal statements as a basis for activity planning.
4. When goals are identified, a school (or center) could
   a. retain its flexibility in activity planning.
   b. lose its ability to fulfill children's individual needs if the same activity plans are used from year to year.
   c. keep its program "personal" by continually evaluating and updating.
   d. periodically take a close look at goals to see whether staff commitment is strong or weak.
5. Literacy as defined in this unit included
   a. both skills and general knowledge.
   b. the ability to enjoy written language.
   c. the idea that there can be literate preschoolers.
   d. the idea that cultural literacy changes over time.
   e. the idea that reading skill instruction is necessary during preschool years if a child is to become literate.
6. Using commercial assessment instruments
   a. is questionable because reliability varies.
   b. serves as the basis of professional programming.
   c. can mean using teacher-designed assessments is out of the question.
   d. is a group decision.
7. "There is only one correct way to plan and present activities to children." This statement is
   a. true.
   b. false.
   c. partly true because each individual strives to find the one plan that helps planned activities run smoothly and successfully.
   d. incorrect because the plan itself doesn't ensure success or goal realization.

8. Evaluating an activity is
   a. rarely necessary if it is well planned.
   b. admitting that teachers can learn a lot through hindsight.
   c. busywork with little value.
   d. necessary if teachers wish to improve their abilities.
9. Test results are
   a. always valid if a test is standardized.
   b. used primarily to judge children's inherited ability.
   c. used to help teachers plan child growth experiences.
   d. always reliable if the teacher has studied the publisher's instructions.
10. Although language arts goals may be identified, language
    a. is part of every activity.
    b. can be taught through music activities.
    c. of children will grow whether planned activities are offered or not offered.
    d. activities offered daily cannot assure that goals attempted will be attained.

References

Beers, Carol Strickland and James Wheelock Beers. "Early Identification of Learning Disabilities: Facts and Fallacies." *Elementary School Journal* 36.4, Nov. 1980. 30–36.

Becoming a Nation of Readers: The Report of the National Commission on Reading. R. C. Anderson, et. al. (eds.), Washington, DC: National Institute of Education, 1985.

Bettelheim, Bruno and Karen Zelan. *On Learning to Read*, New York: Knopf, 1982.

Biber, Barbara, Edna Shapiro, and David Wickens. *Promoting Cognitive Growth: A Developmental-Interaction Point of View.* Washington, D.C.: National Association for the Education of Young Children, 1977.

Bredekamp, Sue. "Interview with Susan Landers, 'Early Testing: Does It Help Or Hurt?'" *APA Monitor* 19.5 (May 1988): 17–19.

Bredekamp, Sue. *Position Statement on Standardized Testing of Young Children 3 Through 8 Years of Age*, Washington, D.C.: NAEYC, 1987.

Copperman, Paul. *The Literacy Hoax.* New York: William Morrow, 1978.

Developmentally Appropriate Practice in Early Childhood Programs Serving Children From Birth Through Age 8. Ed. Sue Bredekamp. Washington, D.C.: NAEYC, 1987.

Education Product Report, No. 68, EPIE Exchange Institute, 1975. 77.

Elkind, David. "Education of the Very Young: A Call For Clear Thinking." *Today* 6.6 (Jan. 1988): 30–35.

Ferguson, Phyllis. "Whole Language: A Global Approach to Learning." *Instructor* 97.9 (May 1988): 23–28.

Goodman, Kenneth. *What's Whole in Whole Language?* Portsmouth, NH: Heinemann Educational Publishers, 1986.

Hayward, Ruth Ann. "Inside the Whole Language Classroom." *Instructor* 97.9 (Oct. 1988): 15–19.

Judy, Stephen. *The ABC's of Literacy.* Oxford: Oxford UP, 1980.

Hillerich, Robert L. "Toward an Assessable Definition of Literacy." *The English Journal*, 65 (Feb. 1976): 29–31.

Hirsch, E. D., Jr. "Cultural Literacy: Let's Get Specific." *Today* 6.6 (Jan. 1988): 37–39.

Hunt, J. McVicker. *Intelligence and Experience*. New York: The Ronald Press, 1961.

Itzkoff, Seymour. *How We Learn to Read*. New York: Paideia Publishers, 1986.

Jewell, Margaret Greer and Miles V. Zintz. *Learning to Read Naturally*. Dubuque: Kendall/Hunt, 1986.

Karnes, Merle B. *Goal Language Development Program*. Springfield, MA: Milton Bradley, 1972.

Kohl, Herbert. *Basic Skills*, Boston, MA: Little, Brown, 1982.

Kozol, Jonathan. *Illiterate America*. New York: Anchor Press/Doubleday, 1985.

Landers, Susan. "Early Testing: Does It Help Or Hurt?" *APA Monitor*, 19.5 (May 1988): 37–40.

Lerner, J. *Children with Learning Disabilities*, Boston: Houghton Mifflin, 1976.

Nedler, Shari. "A Bilingual Early Childhood Program." *The Preschool in Action*. Eds. Mary Carol Day and Ronald K. Parker. Boston, MA: Allyn and Bacon, 1977.

Spodek, Bernard. *Teaching in the Early Years*. Englewood Cliffs, NJ: Prentice-Hall, 1972.

Taylor, D. *Family Literacy: Young Children Learning to Read and Write*, Exeter, NH: Heinemann Educational Books, 1983.

Wells, Gordon. *Learning Through Interaction: The Study of Language Development*. Cambridge: Cambridge UP, 1981.

UNIT 6

Promoting Language and Literacy

OBJECTIVES

After studying this unit, you should be able to

- list three roles of a teacher in early childhood language education.
- discuss the balances needed in teacher behavior.
- describe ways a teacher can promote language growth.

A good description of a skilled early childhood educator is a "responsive opportunist" who is enthusiastic and enjoys discovery, and who is able to establish and maintain a warm, supportive environment. Ideally, children should join in planned activities eagerly. These activities should end before the child's capacity to focus is exhausted. The child should be able to expect the teacher to listen and respond to the child's communication in a way that respects the child's sense of the importance of the communication.

There are three specific teaching functions that encourage the development of language arts and literacy:

1. The teacher serves as *model* of everyday language use. What is communicated and how it is communicated are important.
2. The teacher is a *provider* of experiences. Many of these events are planned; others happen in the normal course of activities.
3. The teacher is an *interactor*, sharing experiences with the children and encouraging conversation (figure 6-1).

These three functions should be balanced, relative to each child's level and individual needs. The teaching role requires constant decision making: knowing when to supply or withhold information to help self-discov-ery and when to talk or listen. Basically, sensitivity and predictable behavior can make the teacher the child's best ally in the growth of language skills.

The teacher's role as an observer is an on-going responsibility that influences all daily teacher-child exchanges and allows the teacher to decide on courses

FIGURE 6-1 As the teacher interacts in everyday experiences, a smile is a way of showing interest. (*From* Early Childhood Practicum Guide, *by Machado and Meyer,* © *1984 by Delmar Publishers Inc.*)

of action with individual children. Knowing children's interests, present behaviors, and emerging skills helps the teacher perform the three above-mentioned functions, based on group and individual needs.

Observing all elements of a program as well as children's behavior and progress involves watching, listening, and recording. This can be the most difficult part of teaching because of time constraints and supervisory requirements. With so much to supervise and provide, teachers can view observation time as a luxury. In-depth observation is best accomplished when a teacher is relieved of other responsibilities and can focus without distractions. Many teachers who do not have duty-free observation time must observe while on duty, keeping a pocket pad handy to jot down fast notes. Observation often unearths questions regarding children's difficulties, talents, and a wide range of special needs that can then be incorporated into plans and daily exchanges. Hutinger (1978) believes there is value in recording the child's words.

> ...an actual record of what a child does say gives you a lot more information for making curricular decisions than does a test score.

TEACHER AS A MODEL

During the preschool years, a teacher should model speech, speaking in complete sentences in standard English. Teachers model not only speech, but also attitudes and behaviors in listening, writing, and reading. Children watch and listen to the adult's use of grammar, intonation, and sentence patterns and imitate and use the adult as an example. Bernstein's (1972) research suggests that some children use a restricted code rather than an elaborated code. *Restricted code* is defined as speech that contains pronouns rather than nouns, few adverbs and adjectives, a minimum of dependent clauses, and is generally not very informative. In contrast, *elaborated code* is characteristically full of more nouns, adjectives, and adverbs and has a greater variety of syntactic forms, with less taken for granted. Strong teacher (adult) models can promote the child's use of the elaborated code and enhance the child's future school success:

> There clearly are differences in young children's ability to do verbal tasks such as describing pictures so that other people can identify them. This

ability may to some extent correlate with a child's background, but whether it does or not, there is no evidence that once a child uses a particular type of description she or he always uses it, children who seem to be users of a restricted code begin to use an elaborated code if they are given sufficient models of what is expected. (Gleason, 1970)

Adults should use clear, descriptive speech at a speed and pitch easily understood. Articulation should be as precise as possible. Weiss and Lillywhite (1981) describe appropriate models during infancy and toddlerhood. These teacher characteristics are also desirable in teachers of preschoolers.

But being a good model involves more than merely speaking clearly, slowly and appropriately. A good model uses a variety of facial expression and other forms of nonverbal communication; associates talking with love, understanding, affection; provides happy, pleasant experiences associated with talking; demonstrates the importance of clearly spoken words. A good model takes advantage of various timely situations....

and speaking further about infancy:

> A good model imitates what the child says or echoes the sounds the child makes and provides many opportunities for the child to experiment with the vocal mechanism and rewards these early efforts.

Preschool teachers also need to be sure that reward in the form of attention is present in their teaching behavior as they deal with young children's attitudes, skills, and behaviors in language arts activities. Teachers should use language patterns with which they feel comfortable and natural and should analyze their speech, working toward providing the best English model possible. Familiar language patterns reflect each teacher's personality as well as ethnic culture (Weir and Eggleston, 1975). Knowing what kind of model one presents is important, so knowing that there is room for improvement can help a teacher become more professional. Hutinger (1978) suggests:

> Record your own language. Use a tape recorder (or video recorder if available) during the day to record your own language. Play it back after

school. Listen to your questions, to your sentence structure, your pronunciation. Do you use a nonstandard dialect?

Finally, employment prospects and parent attitudes toward nonstandard speech need to be considered along with influences on young children who are learning vocabulary at amazing speeds.

Modeling the correct word or sentence is done by simply supplying it in a relaxed, natural way rather than in a corrective tone. The teacher's example is a strong influence; when a teacher adds courtesy words (please and thank you, for instance), they appear in children's speech.

After hearing corrections modeled, the child will probably not shift to correct grammar or usage immediately. It may take many repetitions by teachers and adults over a period of time. What's important is the teacher's acceptance and recognition of the child's idea within the verbalization and the addition of pertinent comments along the same line.

If adults focus on the way something was said (grammar) rather than the meaning, they miss opportunities to increase awareness and extend child interest. Overt correction often ends teacher-child conversation. Affirming is appropriate; emphasize the child's intended message.

Adults can sometimes develop the habit of talking and listening to themselves rather than to the children; it is hypnotic and can be a deterrent to really hearing the child. If one's mind wanders or if one listens only for the purpose of refuting, agreeing, or jumping to value judgments, it interferes with receiving communication from others. Weiss and Lillywhite (1981) urge teachers to not be afraid of silences and to pause slightly when necessary before answering. They make the following listening suggestions to teachers:

- Work as hard to listen as you do to talk.
- Try to hear the message behind the words.
- Consciously practice good listening.

One teaching technique that promotes language skill is simple modeling of grammar or filling in missing words and completing simple sentences. This is called *expansion*. It almost becomes second nature and automatic after a short period of intentional practice. While using expansion, the teacher can also promote wider depth of meaning or spark interest by contributing or suggesting an idea for further exploration. Additional conversation usually occurs.

Example A

Child: "It's chickun soup."
Teacher: "Yes. I see chicken pieces and something else."
Child: "It's noodles."
Teacher: "Yes, it's different from yesterday's red tomato soup."
Child: "Tastes good. It's 'ellow."
Teacher: "Yellow like the daffodils in the vase." (Pointing.)

Compare Examples B and C.

Example B

Child: "Baby cry."
Adult: "Yes, the baby is crying."

Example C

Child: "Baby cry."
Adult: "You hear the baby crying."
Child: "Uh-huh."
Adult: "Maybe she's hungry and wants some milk."
Child: "Wants bottle."
Adult: "Let's see. I'll put the bottle in her mouth."
Child: "Her hungry."
Adult: "Yes, she's sucking. The milk is going into her mouth. Look it's almost gone."

The teacher is a model for listening as well as speaking (figure 6-2). Words, expressions, pronunciations, and gestures are copied as is listening behavior. A quiet teacher may have a quiet classroom; an enthusiastic, talkative teacher (who also listens) may have a classroom where children talk, listen, and share experiences. The way children feel about themselves is reflected in their behavior. When teachers listen closely, children come to feel that what they say is worthwhile.

Modeling good printscript form (classroom or center manuscript print) will hopefully result after studying Units 18 through 20 of this text. Since children seem to absorb everything in their environment, it is necessary to provide correctly formed alphabet letters and numerals on children's work, charts, bulletin boards, and any displayed classroom print.

FIGURE 6-2 A teacher is a good listener, too.

Teachers' use and care of books are modeled, as well as their attitudes toward story and nonfictional book experiences. Through their observations of teachers' actions, children begin to develop ideas about how books should be handled and stored.

TEACHER AS PROVIDER

As providers, preschool teachers strive to provide experiences that promote literacy. As Kate Briggs (1988) points out:

Our children are our richest natural resource, thus all efforts should be aimed at making certain we have a 100% literate population, starting with our children.

Fortunately, the number of interesting language arts activities one can offer children is almost limitless. Teachers rely on both their own creativity and the many resources available to plan experiences based on identified goals. Early childhood resource books, other teachers, teacher magazines, workshops, and conferences all contribute ideas. A listing of language arts activity ideas and teacher resource books is included in the Appendix.

Gathering activity ideas and storing them in a personal resource file is suggested, since it is almost impossible to remember all the activity ideas one comes upon. An activity file can include new or tried-and-true activity ideas. Developing a usable file starts with identifying initial categories (file headings) and adding more heads as the file grows. Some teachers use large file cards, others use binders or file folders. Whatever the file size, teachers find that files are very worthwhile when it comes to daily, weekly, and monthly planning. Often, files are helpful when ideas on a certain subject or theme are needed or when a child exhibits a special interest.

A large number of activity ideas are presented in following units. Your creativity can produce other ideas. Suggestions for separate file headings (categories) follow.

- Audiovisual Activities
- Bulletin Board Ideas
- Chalkboard Ideas
- Chants
- Charts
- Child Drama Ideas
- Children's Books
- Circle Time Ideas
- Classroom Environment Ideas
    Reading Centers
    Writing Centers
    Listening Centers
- Dramatic Play Stimulators
- Dramatic Play Theme Ideas
- Experience Stories
- Field Trip Ideas
- Flannel Board Ideas
- Finger Plays
- Free and Inexpensive Material Resources
- Language Game Ideas
- Listening Activities
- Listening Center Ideas
- Magazine (Child's) Activities
- Patterns
- Poetry
- Perceptual-Motor Activities
- Printscript Ideas
- Puppets
- Reading Readiness Ideas
- Rebus Stories
- Seasonal Ideas
- Speaking Activities Ideas
- Stories for Storytelling
- Visitor Resources

As a provider of materials, a teacher must realize that every classroom object can become a useful program tool to stimulate language. From the clock on the wall to the door knob, every safe item can be discussed, compared, and explored in some way. Since most school budgets are limited, the early childhood teacher finds ways to use available equipment and materials to their fullest.

Each teacher is a unique resource who can plan activities based on personal interests and abilities. Most teachers are pleasantly surprised to see how avidly their classes respond to the interests of their teachers.

When the teacher shares enthusiasm for out-of-school interests, hobbies, projects, trips, and individual talents, he or she can help to give children an introduction to important knowledge. Almost anything appropriate can be presented at the child's level. Whether the teacher is an opera buff, a scuba diver, a gourmet cook, stamp collector, or violin player, the activity should be shared in any safe form that communicates special interest and love of the activity, and the specific vocabulary and materials relating to the activity should be presented. Enthusiasm is the key to inspired teaching.

Providing for Abundant Play

Abundant opportunities for play are important to the child's language acquisition. Considerable research shows that child's play is in fact more complex than it is commonly believed to be. It provides a rich variety of experiences: communication with other children, verbal rituals, topic development and maintenance, turn taking, intimate speech in friendships, follower-leader conversations, and many other kinds of language exchanges. Peer play helps to develop a wide range of communicative skills (Garvey, 1977). Except where the children's safety is in question, children's natural ability to pretend should be encouraged, and the flow of this kind of play should proceed without the teacher's interference. Children will want to talk to teachers about their play, and the teacher's proper involvement is to show interest and be playful themselves at times.

Some preschool teachers tend to give play a priority above teacher-child conversations (Cazden, 1981):

Many school conversations seemed to be rapidly terminated, not by other demands being made on the teacher, but by her suggestion to the child to start or continue a play activity.

If a child has chosen to engage a teacher in conversation instead of play, or during play, the teacher should be both a willing listener and a competent, skillful conversationalist. Opportunities for play and opportunities to engage both children and adults in extended, warm, and personal conversations should be readily and equally available to the child.

Young children explore constantly. They want to do what they see others doing. Play opportunities usually involve manipulating something. When deeply involved in play, children may seem to be momentarily awe struck in their search for meanings, but soon they will approach adults with questions or comments.

When one observes preschoolers at play, it is obvious that they learn a great deal of language from each other. They may even argue over correct language use. Some observers believe that the majority of language teaching that takes place in the four-year-olds' classroom is child to child teaching.

A resourceful teacher will strive to provide a variety of play by regarding all of a center's area (and furnishings) as a possible place (or object) for safe and appropriate play. Creative use can be made of each foot of floor space.

Providing Accurate and Specific Speech in All Content Areas

Although this text concentrates on teacher-child interactions in the subject field, language arts, other content areas, such as mathematics (numbers), social studies, health and safety, art, music, movement, and so on, will be subjects of teacher-child conversations and discussions. The same teacher techniques that are useful in building children's language competence and vocabulary in language arts are equally useful for other content areas. Every subject area has its own vocabulary and common terms that can overlap other fields of study. For example, the teacher may discuss "applying" paints during an art activity and "applying" an antibacterial on a wound or scratch. If children are focused on the number of muffins on a tray, or whether there are enough scissors to go around, then teacher comments include number words.

Teacher comments should be as accurate, and specific as possible in light of what the teacher feels the children might already know or have experienced.

Purposeful teacher conversation adds a little more information than the children know and reinforces and adds depth to words already in the children's vocabulary. When working with numbers or other subjects, the teacher should use terminology that is appropriate to the subject area but at a level the children will understand. For example, the teacher might say "Let's count the muffins" or "The tool in your hand is a wire whip" or "The metal cylinder attached to the wall is a fire extinguisher. Fire extinguishers have something inside that can be sprayed out to put out fires." In movement or music activities, many descriptive terms can be added to teacher demonstrations and conversations. Terms like hop, jump, and stretch or soft, loud, high, and low are easily understood when the child is in the process of experiencing them.

The teacher prompts children's use of the words that the teacher provides. Sometimes a teacher is careful to define new words immediately after using the new terms. In number activities, number words are used in the presence of a corresponding number of objects. In movement activities, types of movement are discussed with quick demonstrations.

It is important to introduce new terms in a natural conversational tone rather than within the framework of an obvious lesson. Leading a child or groups of children to new discoveries offers the teacher an opportunity to use specific and accurate terms and also makes children feel like partners in the discoveries.

In the theme (unit) approach to instruction, often there is identifiable terminology attached to the theme. Teachers sometimes outline the terms that might be encountered in a particular unit and try to include these specific terms in conversations. A unit on birds could include many terms and specific names that a teacher might need to research.

TEACHER AS INTERACTOR

An *interactor* can be defined as a person who is always interested in what a child is saying or doing (figure 6-3). This person encourages conversation on any subject the child selects. An interactor is never too busy to talk and share interests and concerns. Time is purposely planned for daily conversations with each child. These private, personal, one-on-one encounters build the child's feelings of self-worth and open communica-

FIGURE 6-3 As an interactor, the teacher enjoys participating in an activity that interests the child. *(From Early Childhood Practicum Guide, by Machado and Meyer, © 1984 by Delmar Publishers Inc.)*

tions. Conversations can be initiated with morning greetings such as:

"Alphonse, I've been waiting to talk to you. Tell me about your visit to Chicago?"

or

"How is your puppy feeling today, Andrea?"

or

"Those new blue tennis shoes will be good for running in the yard and for tiptoeing, too."

When a teacher answers a child by showing interest, this rewards the child for speaking. This interest is one type of *positive reinforcement*, defined here as something good that happens to a child after having performed an activity or engaged in a certain behavior. *Negative reinforcement* is the opposite; either something bad happens, or nothing happens. Rewarded actions tend to be repeated. Positive feelings are read internally as an automatic signal to continue to do what we are doing (Ornstein and Sobel, 1987). The child's speech and listening should be given attention and encouragement so that the child will continue to speak and listen. Most often teachers show their attention by listening to, looking at, smiling at, patting, or answering a child, or by acting favorably to what a child has said or done.

Teachers trying to determine their skills as inter-actors can ask themselves the following:

- How often do I respond to child-initiated comments? 100% of the time? 50% of the time?
- Do I keep to the child's topic and include it in my response?
- Do I purposefully prompt the children to see or discover an aspect that they might not have perceived or discovered?
- Are most of my verbalizations directives that sound like commands?
- Am I aware of favorite subjects and interests of individual children and topics that will stimulate talk?
- Are my comments appropriate in light of the children's developmental levels?
- Do children seek me out to share their accomplishments and concerns, or do they turn primarily to other available adults?

The following additional questions are suggested by Mattick (1981).

- Are conversations two-way interactions, or are they monologues on my part?
- Do I encourage the children to engage me in conversation?
- Are my questions open- or close-ended?
- Are my questions thought-inducing or are they merely seeking correct answers?
- Who does most of the talking, the child or I?
- What is the level of specificity in my responses?
- Am I moralizing, telling children how they should be thinking and feeling instead of accepting the way they think or feel?
- Is my language production geared to the children's understanding and at the same time expanding the child's existing language, giving new words for more complex operations?
- Do I finish my sentences, or do I leave the children hanging in midair?
- Do I avoid using pat phrases over and over again?
- Do I involve children in activities that promote, or even necessitate, verbal interactions?
- Is there maximum opportunity for children to converse with each other?
- Do I take action to involve children in verbal communications when there is the opportunity?

- Is verbal interaction related to the real world and, more important, to the child's world?
- Does the interaction take place in the context of mutual trust and respect, a mutual trust and respect based on my genuine friendliness, unconditional acceptance, warmth, empathy, and interest?

Tough (1973) offers teachers interactional techniques to extend conversations;

- Invite children to speak by developing a relationship that encourages talking through being a good listener — smiling, nodding, and saying "mm," "yes," and "really" tell the child to go ahead and you're listening.
- Reflecting back on what the child has said, showing your understanding.
- Using questions that are indirect and give the child the choice of answering or not.
- Letting the child know it's ok not to answer your question such as: "Do you want to tell me about...?", or "If you'd like, I'd like to know how...."
- When the child is eager to talk, use more direct open-ended questions — "What do you see?"

She also suggests that conversations be adult-like, allowing children to make comments, tell about happenings and how they feel, and exchange information. This is possible throughout the preschool day.

A teacher may find it harder to interact verbally with quiet children than with those children who frequently start conversations with the teacher (Monaghan, 1971). The teacher should be aware of this tendency and make a daily effort to converse with all attending children.

Teachers shift to more mature or less mature speech as they converse with children of differing ages and abilities. They try to speak to each according to his or her understanding. They use shorter, less complex utterances and use more gestures and nonverbal signals with infants, toddlers, and speakers of foreign languages. Generally, the ability to understand longer and more complex sentences increases with the child's age.

The teacher who interacts in daily experiences can help to improve the child's ability to see relationships. Although there is current disagreement as to the teacher's ability to promote *cognitive* growth (the act or process of knowing), attention can be focused and help provided by answering and asking questions. Often, a teacher can help children see clear links between material already learned and new material. Words teachers provide are paired with the child's mental images that have come through the senses. Language aids memory because words attached to mental images help the child to retrieve stored information.

Intellectually valuable experiences involve the teacher and parent as active participants in tasks with the child. Adults can label, describe, compare, classify, and question, supporting children's intellectual development (Stevens, 1981). Good examples of this type of interaction follow:

Sara looks at a worm crawling on the ground. Teacher: "It's a worm. It's long and brown, sort of like a stick. See, it's smaller than your finger."

Sonja (24 months old) says something about a circus. Mother: "No, you didn't go to the circus — you went to the parade." Sonja: "I went to the parade." Mother: "What did you see?" Sonja: "Big girls." Mother smiles. "Big girls and what else?" Sonja: "Trumpets." Mother: "Yes, and fire engines. Do you remember the fire engines?" Sonja: "You hold my ears a little bit." Mother smiles. "Yes, I did, just like this," and puts her hands on Sonja's ears. Sonja laughs. (Carew, 1980)

As the teacher interacts by supplying words to fit situations, it should be remembered that often a new word needs to be repeated in a subtle way. It has been said that at least three repetitions of a new word are needed for adults to master the word; young children need more. Teachers often hear the child repeating a new word, trying to become familiar with it. Teacher speech should be purposefully repetitive when a new word is encountered.

There are times when a teacher chooses to supply information in answer to direct child questions. There is no easy way for the child to discover questions like "What's the name of today?" or "Why is that man using that funny stick with a cup on the end?" A precise, age-level answer is necessary, such as "Today is Monday, May 9" and (while demonstrating) "It's a stick, called a plunger. It pushes air and water down the drain and helps open the pipes so that the water in the sink will run out." As a provider of information, the teacher acts as a reference and resource person, providing the infor-

mation a child desires. If the teacher does not wish to answer a question directly, he or she may encourage the child to ask the same question of someone else or help the child find out where the answer is available.

Child: "What's lunch?"
Adult: "Come on, we'll go ask the cook."
                    or
        "I'll have to go and read our posted menu. Come on, let's go see what it says."

A teacher can help the child focus on something of interest. The child's desire to know can be encouraged. Repetition of words and many firsthand activities on the same theme will help the child to form an idea or concept. The child may even touch and try something new with the teacher's encouragement.

The teacher's reaction supplies children with feedback to their actions (figure 6-4). The teacher is responsible for reinforcing the use of a new word and gently ensuring that the children have good attitudes about themselves as speakers.

Every day, the teacher can take advantage of unplanned things that happen to promote language and speech. Landreth (1972) provides an illustration:

While children were sitting in a story group, John noticed that a mobile, hung from the ceiling above, was spinning. "Look," said John pointing, "it's moving!" "How come?" said another child.

FIGURE 6-4 These boys are receiving an answer to a question that interests them.

"Someone must have touched it," said Mary. "Stand up, Mary, and see if you can touch it," added the teacher, standing up and reaching, herself, "I can't reach it either." "Maybe it spins itself," contributed Bill. "No, it can't spin itself," said another child. "Let's see," said the teacher. She got a piece of yarn with a bead tied to the end and held it out in front of the children. It was still. Then she held it near the mobile, which was in a draft of a window. The string swayed gently. "The window, the window is open," suggested the children. "Yes, the wind is coming through the window," said John. "And making it move," said all the children, pleased with their discovery. The teacher held the string so the children could blow at it. "Look, I'm the wind" said one of them. That afternoon, outside, the children were given crepe paper streamers to explore wind direction. They were also read *Gilberto and the Wind*, which tells what happens when wind blows the sail of a boat, the arm of a windmill, the smoke from a chimney, and a child's hat and hair.

Being able to make the most of an unexpected event is a valuable skill. Moving into a situation with skill and helping the child discover something and tell about it is part of promoting word growth.

Stressing Language Connections

The teacher interested in stressing connections between classroom language arts events and activities, as is done in an integrated approach or a whole-language approach, may often purposefully make the following comments.

"I am writing down your ideas."
"This printing I am reading says 'Please Knock.'"
"Do you want me to read what is printed on the wall?"
"I can print that word."
"What does the sign for your parking garage need to say?"
"You seemed to be listening to the story I was reading."
"Yes, 's' is the first alphabet letter in your name."
"You want me to print your name on your work, right?"
"I can read what this small printing on the box says."

Handling Interruptions

Children often interrupt adults during planned activities. When an idea hits, they may not wait to share it. Their interruptions can indicate genuine involvement and interest, or they can reflect a variety of unrelated thoughts and feelings. Teachers usually acknowledge the interruption, accept it, and may calmly remind the interruptor that when one wants to speak during group activities, one should raise one's hand first. A nonverbal technique used to encourage children to raise their hands at group time is to introduce and later (when necessary) flash a picture of an elephant with its trunk raised or a picture of a child with a shell to his or her ear to indicate that hand raising or listening is appropriate at the moment (Casanova, 1989). Interruptions give the teacher an opportunity to make a key decision that affects the flow of the activity. Will the interruption break the flow of what's going on, will it add to the discussion, or is it best discussed at a later time? If the teacher decides to defer a comment, one of the methods suggested below may be employed. Or, the teacher may accept being sidetracked and briefly digress from the main subject, or develop the interruption into a full blown teacher-group discussion, as was the case in the Landreth (1972) example above.

"Megan, I've seen striped cats too."
 (short acknowledgment)

"Megan's cat climbs trees, and the brown horse is standing by a tree."
 (Teacher acknowledges the interruption, but refers statement back to the previous central topic of the group activity.)

"Let's talk about cats climbing trees as soon as we finish."
 (Teacher defers the discussion until later.)

Some teachers feel preschooler's enthusiasm to speak is natural and characteristic. These teachers feel that teaching children to raise their hands during group discussions is best reserved for a later age.

Incorporating the children's ideas and suggestions into group conversations, and giving children credit for their ideas, makes them aware of the importance of their expressed ideas.

"Kimberly's idea was to..."
"Angelo thinks we should..."

"Christal suggests that we..."

"Here's the way Trevor would..."

Using Sequential Approaches to Instruction

Teachers need a clear understanding of how children learn words and concepts. The chart in figure 6-5 includes guidelines for the teacher's words and actions to accompany the child's progress toward new learning.

One approach to teacher interaction during structured, planned, or incidental activities, described by Maria Montessori, is called three-stage interaction. It shows movement from the child's sensory exploration

to showing understanding, and then to verbalizing the understanding. An example follows:

Step 1: Associating sense perception with words.

A cut lemon is introduced and the child is encouraged to taste it. As the child tastes, the adult says, "The lemon tastes sour," pairing the word sour with the sensory experience. Repetition of the verbal pairing strengthens the impression.

Step 2: Probing understanding.

A number of yellow cut fruit are presented. "Find the one that tastes sour," teacher suggests. The child shows by his or her actions his or her understanding or lack of it.

Child Activity	Teacher Actions
• Focuses on an object or activity.	• Name the object, or offer a statement describing the actions or situation. (Supplies words)
• Manipulates and explores the object or situation using touch, taste, smell, sight, sound organs.	• Try to help child connect this object or action to child's past experience through simple conversation. (Builds bridge between old and new)
• Fits this into what he or she already knows. Develops some understanding.	• Help the child see details through simple statements or questions. (Focus on identifying characteristics)
	• Ask "Show me..." or "Give me..." questions that ask for a nonverbal response. (Prompting)
	• Put child's action into words. (Example: "John touched the red ball.") (Modeling)
	• Ask the child for a verbal response. "What is this called?" "What happened when . . . ?" (Prompting)
• Uses a new word or sentence that names, describes, classifies or generalizes a feature or whole part of the object or action.	• Give a response in words indicating the truth factor of the response. "Yes, that's a red ball." or "It has four legs like a horse, but it's called a cow." (Corrective or reinforcing response)
	• Extend one-word answers to full simple sentence if needed. (Modeling)
	• Suggest an exploration of another feature of the object or situation. (Extend interest)
	• Ask a memory or review question. "Tell me about . . ." (Reinforcing and assessing)

FIGURE 6-5 Language learning and teacher interaction

Step 3: Expressing understanding.

A child is presented with a cut lemon and grapefruit and asked, "How do they taste?" If the child is able to describe the fruit as sour, he or she has incorporated the word into his or her vocabulary and has some understanding of the concept.

When using the three-step approach, Montessori (1967) suggests that if a child is uninterested, the adult should stop at that point. If a mistake is made, the adult remains silent. The mistake only indicates the child is not ready to learn — not that he or she is unable to learn.

This verbal approach may seem mechanical and ritualistic to some, yet it points out clearly the sequence in a child's progress from not knowing to knowing.

The following example of a variation of the Montessori three-step approach includes additional steps. In this teaching sequence, the child asks the teacher how to open the tailgate of a dump truck in the sandbox.

TEACHER INTENT	TEACHER STATEMENTS
1. Focus attention.	"Look at this little handle."
2. Create *motivation*, defined as creating a desire to want to do or want to know. (Note that in this situation this isn't necessary because the child is interested.)	"You want the tailgate to open." Pointing.
3. Provide information.	"This handle turns and opens the tailgate." Demonstrating.
4. Promote child attempt or practice.	"Try to turn the handle."
5. Give corrective information or feedback or positive reinforcement.	"The handle needs to turn. Try to push down as you turn it." (Showing.) or "You did it; the tailgate is open."

Steps 1 through 5 above are used in the following situation in which the teacher wants the child to know what is expected in the use of bathroom paper towels.

1. "Here's the towel dispenser. Do you see it?"
2. "You can do this by yourself. You may want to dry your hands after you wash them."
3. Demonstration. "First take one paper towel. Dry your hands. Then the towel goes into this waste basket."
4. "You try it."
5. "That's it. Pull out one towel. Dry your hands. Put the towel in the basket."

"Now you know where the dirty paper towels go. No one will have to pick up your used towel from the floor. You can do it without help now like some of your classmates."

Statements of this kind help the child learn both the task and vocabulary. The ability to provide information that the child needs, without talking too much, is one of the skills required of a really excellent teacher. Some theorists believe that the successful completion of a task is a reward in itself. Others feel an encouraging verbal pat on the back is in order.

The same dump truck scene above could be handled using a discovery approach, instead of a teacher-directed sequence, with the following types of questions. "Did you see anyone else playing with this dump truck? Is there a button to push or a handle to turn that opens the tailgate? What happens if you try to open the tailgate with your hand?"

Prompting in a child-adult conversation intends to encourage the child to express ideas perhaps more precisely and/or specifically. It is used slightly differently with younger preschoolers, as shown in the following examples.

Young preschooler. Child: "Cookie."
Adult: "You want a cookie?"
Child: "Dis cookie."
Adult: "You want this brown cookie."

Older preschooler. Child: "I want that cookie."
Adult: "You want one of these cookies. Which kind, chocolate or sugar?"

Child: "The chocolate one."
Adult: "You wanted the
chocolate cookie."

Can teachers really make a difference in the level and quality of children's language development?

Very significant correlations were found between both the frequency of informative staff talk, the frequency with which the staff answered the children, and the language comprehension scores of the children. (Tizard, 1972)

Interaction does require teachers to "wonder out loud." They express their own curiosity while at the same time noticing each child's quest to find out what makes others tick and what the world is all about.
How can teachers interact skillfully?

- Expand topics in which the child shows interest.
- Add depth to information on topics of interest.
- Answer and clarify child questions.
- Help the child sort out features of events, problems, and experiences, reducing confusion.
- Urge the child to put what's newly learned or discovered into words.
- Cue children into routinely attending to times when the adult and child are learning and discovering together through discussion of daily events.

Dealing With Children's Past Experiences

As an interactor, a teacher encounters a wide range of children's perceptions as to how the children should communicate with adults. A child's family or past child-care arrangements may have taught the child to behave in a certain way. With this in mind, the teacher can almost envision what it means to be a conversationalist in a particular family or societal group. Some families expect children to interrupt; others expect respectful manners. Wild, excited gesturing and weaving body movements are characteristic of some children, while motionless, barely audible whispering is typical of others. Teachers working with newly arrived children from other cultures may see sharp contrasts in communication styles. Some children verbally seek help, while others find this extremely difficult. Some speak their feelings openly; others rarely express their feelings.

Past child-care experiences may have left their mark. A four-year-old child named Perry seemed to give one teacher considerable understanding about how speech can be dramatically affected by past undesirable child-care arrangements (Busy Bee, 1989). The following is that teacher's observation and conclusions.

Perry sat quietly near the preschool's front door, ignoring all play opportunities, and holding his blanket until his mom's return on his first day at school. He only spoke or looked up when teachers tried repeatedly to engage him in conversation. He sat on adults' laps silently when they tried to comfort him, and ate food quickly and then returned to his waiting place near the door. The real Perry emerged a few weeks later as a talkative, socially vigorous child. Our verbal and behavioral interactions concentrated on rebuilding trust with adults and other children; only later was language developing interaction possible.

It can be difficult for a child to engage an adult in conversation as was the case with Perry. As Garvey (1984) notes, "Seeking the availability of a teacher and assuring one's right to her attention and reply often calls for persistence and ingenuity." Perry may have long before given up trying.

THE TEACHER AS A BALANCER

In all roles, the teacher needs to maintain a balance. This means:

- Giving, but withholding when self-discovery is practical and possible.
- Interacting, but not interfering or dominating the child's train of thought or actions.
- Giving support, but not hovering.
- Talking, but not overtalking.
- Listening, but remaining responsive.
- Providing many opportunities for the child to speak.
- Being patient and understanding. As Fields and Lee (1987) point out, "When adults already know an answer, we find it hard to be patient as children go through the process of figuring the answer out for themselves."

To maintain such a balance, the teacher is a model, a provider, and an interactor, matching his or her behavior and speech to the ability of each child. As a model, the teacher's example offers the child a step above — but not too far above — what the child is already able to do. In doing this, the teacher watches and listens while working with individual children, learning as much from the child's misunderstandings or speech mistakes as from correct or appropriate responses and behavior. This does not mean that the motive is always to teach, for the teacher also enjoys just talking with the children (figure 6-6). It does mean that the teacher is ready to make the most of every situation, as teacher and child enjoy learning together.

There's an old story about two preschool boys who discover a worm in the play yard.

First child: "Boy it tickles! Look at him!" (Holding worm in hand.)
Second child: "Let's show it to teacher."
First child: "No way — she'll want us to draw a picture of it and make us print 'worm'!"

A teacher's attitude toward child growth in language should be one of optimism; provide the best learning environment and realize the child will grow and learn new language skills when he or she is ready. Early childhood centers plan for as much growth as possible in language abilities with teachers who model, provide, and interact during activities (figure 6-7).

FIGURE 6-7 "Look at me, teacher!"

Minuchin (1987) identifies what is to be considered in trying to offer a balanced developmentally based curriculum.

- Material to be explored.
- Time and space so a child has choice, free time, and a variety of social experiences.
- Teacher guidance in (1) acquiring knowledge and relating it to the environment, (2) making connections between present experiences and remembered ones, and (3) comparing similarities and differences.
- Teacher questions that raise questions and lead to investigation and answers.

Shapiro and Biber (1972) offer an additional suggestion:

- The provision of many ways to re-express what is felt and what is learned: through blocks, paints, dramatic play, and the creation of stories that can be written down and read back (Shapiro and Biber, 1972).

Summary

Teachers function as models, providers of opportunities for language growth, and interactors. Children copy behaviors and attitudes of both adults and peers. Teacher skills include extending and expanding child conversations. Conversations are a key factor in the child's growing language competence. Extending

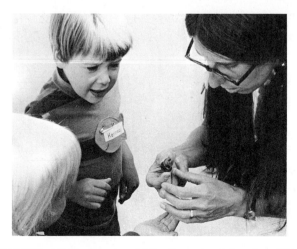

FIGURE 6-6 Sharing the child's discoveries helps the child verbalize.

means adding new information, and expanding means completing a child's statement so that it is grammatically complete.

Words are symbols for objects, ideas, actions, and situations. The teacher can increase the learning of new words and ideas by helping children to recognize

A delicate balance exists in early childhood education. Decisions are made that will affect each child's maximum growth opportunities.

Rewarding the child's actions tends to make those actions happen again. Learning and accomplishing may have its own reward value for the child.

Student Activities

- Observe a teacher interacting with a preschool child. Note the type of teacher speech and behavior that makes the child feel that what he or she says is important.

- Listen intently to three adults. (Take notes.) How would you evaluate them as speech models (good, average, poor)? State the reasons for your decisions.

- Describe what is meant by the following terms:

standard English	image	example
symbol	motivation	cognitive
positive reinforcement	interactor	

- Record a conversation with another classmate. Have the recording analyzed for standard English speech usage.

- Tape record or videotape your interaction with a group of young children for a period of 15 minutes. Analyze your listening, questioning, sentence structure, extending ability, and pronunciation.

- Consider the following slogans. Explain and elaborate their meanings.
  Intent not correctness.
  Your topic not mine.
  The wrong answer is right.
  Logic not mechanics.
  Give them eyes and ears.
  Responsive opportunist here!
  Shh! Here comes the teacher.

- Read the following quote. Discuss its relationship to child language growth.

  The small Zulu also didn't have just one daddy. He had the dadoos, his father's brothers and other male adults who talked to him about hunting, showed him how to make a little bow and arrow and all of this kind of stuff. They spent time with him and they "joyed in his presence," as someone once defined love. So on into adult life there was for both the boys and the girls this abundance of love and affection and attention and tenderness. (Lair, 1985).

- How could the following teachers provide for child awareness and involvement in their special interests: An opera buff, a stamp collector, a gourmet cook, a scuba diver, a cashier, a gardener, a clock collector?
- Fill out the checklist in figure 6-8, and compare your ratings with those of your classmates.

	Agree	Can't Decide	Disagree
1. Every center happening should encourage speech.			
2. It takes considerable time and effort to have personal conversations with each child daily.			
3. Each child is entitled to a personal greeting and goodbye.			
4. "How are you?" is a good opening remark.			
5. A child who bursts out with something to say that has nothing to do with what's presently happening must have something important on his or her mind.			
6. Pausing silently for a few moments after speaking to a shy child is a good idea.			
7. Most new vocabulary words are learned at group times.			
8. Saying "John stepped over the green block" is unnecessary, for the child knows what he has done.			
9. All children have home interests that teachers can discuss with them.			
10. At mealtimes, it's best to remain quiet while children enjoy their food.			
11. If the child talks about a bathroom function, ignore it.			

FIGURE 6-8 Opinion poll *(continues)*

	Agree	Can't Decide	Disagree
12. When Phil says, "Girls can't drive trucks" tell him he's wrong.			
13. Teachers really need to talk more than they listen.			
14. Saying "Tell him you don't like it when he grabs your toy" is poor technique.			
15. I don't think it's possible to use a lot of language building techniques and still speak naturally and comfortably with a child.			
16. Teacher should model a playful attitude at times.			

FIGURE 6-8 *Continued*

Unit Review

A. Name the three basic functions of the early childhood teacher.

B. List five examples of each of the functions you listed for question A.

C. Following is an observation of a teacher and children. After reading it, indicate what you feel was appropriate behavior and inappropriate behavior on the part of the teacher in regard to language development.

Situation: *Teacher is conducting a sharing time with Joey, Mabel, Maria, and Chris.*

Teacher: "It's time for sharing. Please sit down children."

Joey: "I want to share first!"

Teacher: "You'll have your turn. You must learn to wait."

Mabel: "I can't see."

Teacher: "Yes you can."

"Maria, you're sitting quietly and not talking. You may go first."

Maria: "This is a book about Mickey. Mickey clips."

Joey: "What's clips, teacher?"

Teacher: "You're next, Joey."

Joey: "Mickey on T.V. teacher. Tomorrow I went to the fire station. The fireman let me wear his badge, like this."

Chris: "Fireman's truck red. Goes whee-whee."

Teacher: "It's Joey's turn, Chris. Would you wait to talk?

Mabel: "I want to go, now!"

Teacher: "Mabel, you must have your turn to share before you can go."

Mabel: "I see a butterfly on the window."

Teacher: "Later, Mabel. You can go outside later."

D. What two factors should be considered by the teacher in trying to keep the main functions of teaching in balance?

E. Select the correct answers. All have more than one correct reply.
    1. The teacher is a model for
        a. speech.
        b. attitudes.
        c. speech more often than parents may be.
        d. speech only during planned activities.
    2. It is more important for young children to
        a. like to speak than to speak correctly.
        b. participate than sit quietly.
        c. speak than to listen.
        d. have the teacher tell them about something than to explore it themselves.
        e. feel comfortable with a teacher than speak clearly.
    3. Teachers reinforce learning by
        a. using speech to solve problems.
        b. giving attention to the child's use of a new word.
        c. motivating the child's "wanting to know."
        d. linking the old with the new ideas.
    4. When speaking, the teacher should
        a. attempt to use natural language patterns.
        b. speak in full sentences.
        c. make sure each child responds by speaking.
        d. refrain from "overtalking."
    5. Preschool children
        a. are also speech models.
        b. rarely teach others new words.
        c. play and use words in play.
        d. have growing vocabularies only when teachers act appropriately.
    6. Words are
        a. symbols for real happenings.
        b. related to stored images.
        c. learned through the senses.
        d. not labels for concepts.

F. Write a short ending to the following. "A teacher who is not speaking standard English should...."

G. Robert D. Hess and V. C. Shipman have shown that different adults have different styles of communicating with young children. The following is a comparison of two mothers trying to teach the same task to their child.
    First Mother: All right, Susan, this board is the place where we put the little toys; first of all, you're supposed to learn how to place them according to color. Can you do that? The things that are all the same color you put in one section; in the other section you put another group of colors, and in the third section you put the last group of colors. Can you do that? Or would you like to see me do it first?
    Child: I want to do it.

Second Mother (introducing the same task): Now I'll take them all off the board; now you put them all back on the board. What are these?
Child: A truck.
Second Mother: All right, just put them right here; put the other one right here; all right, put the other one there."

From R. D. Hess & V. C. Shipman, "Early Experience and the Socializations of Cognitive Modes in Children." *Child Development*, 1966.

Write a brief comparison of the two mothers, but pretend they are two teachers.

H. Finish the following statement. "Simple expansion of child comments to make full sentences is not as valuable as extending conversations because...."

References

Bartlett, Elsa Jaffe. "Selecting an Early Childhood Language Curriculum." *Language in Early Childhood Education*. Ed. C. B. Cazden. Washington, D.C.: NAEYC, 1981.

Bernstein, B. "A Critique of Concept Compensatory Education." *Functions of Language in the Classroom*. Eds. C. B. Cazden, D. Hymes, and V. P. John. New York: Teachers College Press, 1972.

Briggs, Kate. "Perspective From An Independent Publisher." *CBC Features* 41.3 (May 1988): 2–3.

Busy Bee Children's Center, Teacher Observation, Santa Clara, 1989.

Carew, J. V. "Experience and the Development of Intelligence in Young Children at Home and in Day Care." *Monographs of the Society for Research in Child Development*. 45.187 (1980): 56–78.

Casanova, Ursula. "Putting Research to Work: Changing Minds to Change Behavior." *Instructor* (Jan. 1989): 37–40.

Cazden, C. B. "Language Development and the Preschool Environment." *Language in Early Childhood Education*. Ed. C. B. Cazden. Washington, D.C.: NAEYC, 1981.

Fields, Marjorie V. and Dorris Lee. *Let's Begin Reading Right*, Columbus, OH: Charles E. Merrill, 1987.

Garvey, Catherine. *Play*. Cambridge: Harvard UP, 1977.

Gleason, Jean Berko. "An Experimental Approach to Improving Children's Communicative Ability." *Language in Early Childhood Education*. Ed. C. B. Cazden. Washington, D.C.: NAEYC, 1981.

Hutinger, Patricia L. "Language Development: It's Much More Than A Kit." *Day Care and Early Education*. 5.2 (Spring 1978): 44–47.

Lair, Jess, *I Ain't Much Baby But I'm All I Got*, New York: Fawcett, 1985.

Landreth, Catherine. *Preschool Learning and Teaching*. New York: Harper and Row, 1972.

Mattick, Ilse. "The Teacher's Role in Helping Young Children Develop Language Competence." *Language in Early Childhood Education*. Ed. C. B. Cazden. Washington, D.C.: NAEYC, 1981.

McCandless, Boyd R. *Children*. New York: Holt, Rinehart, and Winston, 1967.

Minuchin, Patricia. "Schools, Families, and the Development of Young Children." *Early Childhood Research Quarterly* 2.3 (Sept. 1987): 245–254.

Monaghan, A. C. "Children's Contacts: Some Preliminary Findings," unpublished term paper, Harvard Graduate School of Education, 1971.

Montessori, Maria. *The Absorbent Mind.* New York: Holt, Rinehart, and Winston, 1967.

Ornstein, Robert and David Sobel. *The Healing Brain.* New York: Simon and Schuster, 1987.

Pellegrini, Anthony and Lee Galda. "Effects of Thematic-Fantasy Play Training on the Development of Children's Story Comprehension." *American Educational Research Journal* 19.3 (1982): 101–116.

Shapiro, E. and B. Biber. "The Education of Young Children." *Teachers College Record* 74 (1972): 83–92.

Stevens, Joseph H., Jr. "Everyday Experiences and Intellectual Development." *Research in Review, Young Children* 36.1 (Nov. 1981): 41–53.

Tizard, B., et al. "Environmental Effects on Language Development: A Study of Young Children in Long-Stay Residential Nurseries." *Child Development*, 43.4 (1972): 337–358.

Tough, J. *Focus on Meaning: Talking to Some Purpose With Young Children.* London: George Allen and Unwin, 1973.

Weir, Mary E., and Pat Eggleston, "Teachers First Words." *Day Care and Early Education*, 21.3 (Nov./Dec. 1975): 37–42.

Weiss, Curtis E., and Herold S. Lillywhite. *Communicative Disorders.* St. Louis: C. V. Mosby, 1981.

Section 3

Listening–Literate Beginnings

Listening precedes speech and is considered basic to growth in other language arts areas. This section alerts students to the types of listening that take place in the early childhood classroom. Children can increase their listening abilities, and teachers can be instrumental in this process. Listening activities are suggested, and teacher techniques described.

ACT ONE

A CITY CHILD'S summer is spent in the street in front of his home, and all through the long summer vacations I sat on the curb and watched the other boys on the block play baseball or prisoner's base or gutter hockey. I was never asked to take part even when one team had a member missing — not out of any special cruelty, but because they took it for granted I would be no good at it. They were right, of course. Yet much of the bitterness and envy and loneliness I suffered in those years could have been borne better if a single wise teacher or a knowledgeable parent had made me understand that there were compensations for the untough and the nonathletic: the world would not always be bounded by the curbstone in front of the house.

It was the custom of the boys to retire to a little stoop that jutted out from the candy store on the corner and that somehow had become theirs through tribal right. No grown-up ever sat there or attempted to. I can no longer remember which boy it was that summer evening who broke the silence with a question; but whoever he was, I nod to him in gratitude now. "What's in those books you're always reading?" he asked idly. "Stories," I answered. "What kind?" asked somebody else without much interest.

They listened to me tell the story with some of the wonder that I had had in reading it. Not one of them left the stoop until I had finished, and I went upstairs that wonderful evening not only a member of the tribe but a figure in my own right among them.

The next night and many nights thereafter, a kind of unspoken ritual took place. As it grew dark, I would take my place in the center of the stoop and, like Scheherezade, begin the evening's tale. I would stop at the most exciting part of a story, and it would have to be continued the following evening. I had to make certain of my new-found power and position, and with a sense of drama that I did not know I possessed I spun out the long summer evenings. Other words of mine have been listened to by larger and more fashionable audiences, but for that tough and grimy one that huddled on the stoop outside the candy store, I have an unreasoning affection that will last forever. [1]

[1] Moss Hart, Catherine Carlisle Hart and Joseph M. Hyman, Trustees, Condensed Version from *Act I* (New York: Random House, 1959). Selection reprinted by permission of Random House, Inc.

UNIT 7

Developing Listening Skills

OBJECTIVES

After studying this unit, you should be able to

- list five types of listening.
- discuss teaching techniques that promote good listening habits.
- demonstrate how to plan an activity that promotes auditory perception.

Auditory perception refers to the process of being aware of sounds and their meanings. The world, with its many sounds, bombards the infant. Although no one formally teaches an infant to listen, certain sounds become familiar and take on meanings from this mass of confusion. The infant has begun to listen.

Listening skill is the first language arts skill learned, and it develops before a child speaks. Many children develop the ability to listen carefully to the speech of others during early childhood; others do not. Since language growth has been described as a receiving process followed by a sending process, a child's listening ability is important to speaking and future reading and writing success (Donoghue, 1985).

Hearing and listening are quite different. Hearing is a process involving nerves and muscles that reach adult efficiency by age four to five. Listening is a learned behavior, a mental process that is concerned with hearing, attending, discriminating, understanding, and remembering. It can be improved with practice. Listening affects social interactions, one's level of functioning, and perhaps one's overall success in life (Weiss and Lillywhite, 1981). Nichols (1948) estimates that we listen to 50% of what we hear and comprehend only 25% of that.

Listening skill can be described as passive and receptive but involves active thinking and interpretation. Lively conversations between adults and young children who feel free to verbalize reactions to life's happenings promote listening and speaking. Children offer more verbal comments in school settings in small, relaxed groups in which comments are accepted and appreciated. Young children sometimes learn that it's best to keep quiet in some classrooms. In other classrooms, every child's opinion counts, and classroom discussions are frequent and animated.

There are usually many opportunities to listen in early childhood centers. Teacher-planned or child-created play is a source of many sounds (figure 7-1). A quality program sharpens a child's listening and offers a variety of experiences. Listening is not left to chance; planned programs develop skills.

TYPES OF LISTENING

Listening occurs in a variety of ways. A person does not always listen for knowledge but may also listen to a sound because it is pleasing to hear. The first time children discover the sounds made by pots and pans, they are fascinated. Preschoolers often make

FIGURE 7-1 Teacher-planned or child-created play is a source of many sounds. *(From Early Childhood Practicum Guide, by Machado and Meyer, © 1984 by Delmar Publishers Inc.)*

their own pleasurable or rhythmic sounds with whatever is available.

The human voice can be interesting, threatening, or monotonous to a child, depending on past experience. Silence also has meaning. Sometimes teachers suspect that a child has a hearing problem, only to find that the child was inattentive for other reasons.

Children may listen but not understand. They may miss sound differences or listen without evaluating what they hear. Listening involves a variety of skills and levels. In order to provide growing opportunities, teachers should be aware of various listening levels, as shown in figure 7-2.

The goal of a good program in early childhood language arts is to guide the young child toward development of these listening levels. Semel (1976) has analyzed the listening process and describes three stages that the child moves through in efficient listening (figure 7-3).

When a sound occurs, it is remembered by thinking about its features: direction, pitch, intensity, newness, and so on.

TODDLER LISTENING EXPERIENCES

Parents and center staff members can engage toddlers in a number of activities to stimulate listening. Body-action play of the old "coo-chee-coo" variety, "this little piggy," and simple rhymes and repetitions are recommended. Connecting noises and sounds with toys and objects and encouraging the child to playfully imitate show the child that joy and sound-making go hand in hand. Rhythmic clapping, tapping, and pan beating in sequence or patterns can be enjoyable. Musical toys and records add variety and listening pleasure. Encouraging children to watch facial expressions as different human sounds are produced and locating environmental sounds together are additional techniques in developing children's listening skills.

Adults exercise care in sound volume, and quality; at all age levels, extra loud, shrill, vibrating, or emergency alert sounds can be frightening.

Purposeful Listening Activities

The intent of purposeful listening practice is to increase the child's ability to follow directions and

Appreciative listening. The child finds pleasure and entertainment in hearing music, poems and stories. It is best to begin with this type of listening because it is passive, but personal for each child.

Purposeful listening. The child follows directions, and gives back responses.

Discriminative listening. The child becomes aware of changes in pitch and loudness. He differentiates sounds in the environment. Eventually, he is able to discriminate the speech sounds.

Creative listening. The child's imagination and emotions are stimulated by his listening experiences. He expresses his thoughts spontaneously and freely through words, or actions, or both.

Critical listening. The child understands, evaluates, makes decisions, and formulates opinions. To encourage this critical listening, the teacher may pose such questions as: "What happens when we all talk at once?" "What if everyone wanted to play in the playhouse at the same time?" The child must think through the responses, decide the most logical solution to the problem, and present a point of view.

FIGURE 7-2 Some of the ways a child listens *(From* Learning Time With Language Experiences, *by Louise B. Scott, New York: McGraw-Hill Book Co., 1968.)*

instructions, perform tasks, or respond appropriately in some fashion. Teachers can use a three-step method to help very young preschoolers gain skill in this type of listening:

1. Tell the children what you are going to tell them.
2. Tell the children.
3. Tell the children what you told them.

Responding to Stimuli	Organizing the Stimuli	Understanding the Meaning
Awareness Focus Figure-Ground Discrimination	Sequencing and Synthesizing Scanning	(Classification; Integration; Monitoring)

←——————— Memory ———————→

Stage 1 — Responding to stimuli: Was there sound? Where was it? Which sound was it? Was there more than one sound? Were the sounds the same?
Stage 2 — Organizing the stimuli: What was the sequence of the sounds? What was the length of time between sounds? Have I heard that sound before? Where have I heard it?
Stage 3 — Understanding the meaning: What do the sounds and words mean?

FIGURE 7-3 Stages of the listening process

Example

1. "I'm going to give you an envelope, and tell you where to take it."
2. "Take the envelope to the cook, Mrs. Corelli, and then come back to our classroom."
3. "You took the envelope to Mrs. Corelli and returned. Thank you."

Purposeful, attentive listening takes concentration. Teachers can perfect a "what I'm going to say next is important" tone and consequently create a desire in children to listen. A statement such as "You might want to know how" or "You can listen closely to find out" or "If you'd like a turn, watch and listen" may also provide the motivation to listen closely.

Planned, purposeful listening activities can include activities that encourage children to listen in order to:

- Do something for themselves.
- Tell another how to do something.
- Carry a message.
- Recall details.
- Put objects in a special order or sequence.
- See how many names or facts they can remember.
- Learn new skills, such as singing new songs or chanting or doing finger plays.

Appreciative Listening Activities

Appreciative listening deals with light listening when enjoyment or pleasure is paramount. A wide variety of recorded and live appreciative listening experiences is possible. Background music can accompany favorite preschool pursuits. Chanting a remembered selection of words gives the children a double treat of hearing voices in unison and feeling part of a group. Some appreciative listening builds moods, touches emotions, and adds another dimension to experience. The world is full of beautiful and not-so-beautiful sounds.

Possible appreciative listening activities include:

- Moving to music.
- Discussing music, rhythms, and sounds.
- Talking about favorite sounds.
- Talking about happy, sad, or funny feelings that sounds produce.
- Tapping, clapping, or moving to music or rhythmic speech.

Critical Listening Activities

Critical listening requires the children's evaluation of what's heard and comprehended. It requires contemplation and reflection, and some preschoolers develop considerable skill in this area and use it frequently. These children seem able to weigh the new against what they already know and feel and are eager to discuss differences. Other children seem rarely to hold any opinion or particular viewpoint and are reticent to share thoughts. Activities that involve critical thinking can be ones in which:

- A problem is discussed and solutions are offered and evaluated.
- A probable outcome or guess is prompted.
- A real or make-believe feature is pinpointed using some criteria.
- Personal preferences or dislikes are discussed.
- Group votes are reviewed, and outcomes are anticipated.
- Errors of some type are discovered or detected.
- Feelings of others are predicted.

TEACHER SKILLS

Good listening habits are especially important in school situations. Instructions from teachers should be clear and simple, with a sequence of what comes first, next, and last. Usually instructions need not be repeated when given clearly and simply. Often, when the attention of the group is required, a signal is used. Any distinctive, easy-to-hear, pleasant sound or visual signal can alert children that it is time to listen. The silent pause before beginning an activity can be used effectively to focus attention on listening.

Teachers also use a short song, finger play, or body-movement activity to stimulate interest and draw the group together (figure 7-4). This helps children focus on what is to follow.

Encouragement and smiles at any time of the day can reward individual listening. Positive, specific statements such as "Michael, you listened to what Janet had to say before you started talking" or "It's quiet, and now we can all hear the beginning of the story" give children feedback on expected listening behavior.

These are sample teacher statements that can promote a group's ability to listen:

At the Beginning

- "When I see everyone's eyes, I'll know you're ready to hear about...."
- "We'll begin when we can all hear the clock ticking."

FIGURE 7-4 A clapping game is used to draw a group together and ready children for listening.

- I'm waiting until everyone can hear before I start. Raise your hand if you can't hear me. Listen." (After starting, if hand goes up — "Michael can't hear. We need to be quiet so Michael can hear about...").
- "It seems everyone is listening; it's time to begin."
- "We take turns speaking. Bill is first, then...."

During Activity

- "Jack had his hand up. Would you like to tell us about your idea?"
- "It's Maria's turn to tell us...."
- "We can hear best when just one person is talking. Louis, you go first, then Cristalee."
- "Bill, it's hard to wait when you want to talk. Gloria is talking now; you can be next." (Later add, "Bill, thank you for waiting for Gloria to finish. Now we will hear what you wanted to tell us.")
- "Everyone wants to tell us about their own pets. Raise your hand — I'll make a waiting list so we can hear everyone." (Make the list quickly and hold it up.) "Isaac, your name is first."

At Activity's End

- "We listened so quietly. We all heard every word of that story."
- "I like the way everyone listened to what their friends said."
- "We listened and found out a lot about...."

Rewarded behavior is usually repeated and becomes a habit. Teachers should consistently notice correct listening behavior and comment favorably about it to the children.

AUDITORY PERCEPTION

Ears respond to sound waves. These sounds go to the brain and become organized in relation to past experience. The same process is used in early childhood and later when the child learns to read. Language development depends on the auditory process.

Educational activities that give practice and help perfect auditory skills usually deal with the following objectives:

- Sustaining attention span.
- Following directions or commands.
- Imitating sounds.

- Identifying and associating sounds.
- Using auditory memory.
- Discriminating between sounds (intensity, pitch, tempo).

The *intensity* of a sound is its degree of force, strength, or energy. *Pitch* is the highness or lowness of sound. *Tempo* is the rate of speed of a sound, in other words, the rhythm of the sound that engages the attention.

Auditory Activities

A wide range of auditory activities can be planned. The following goals often serve as the basis for planning. Simple skills come before more difficult ones:

- Recognizing own name when spoken.
- Repeating two nonsense words, short sayings, chants, poems, finger plays, or any series of words.
- Reporting sounds heard at home.
- Imitating sounds of toys, animals, classroom, rain, sirens, bells.
- Telling whether a sound is near or far, loud or soft, fast or slow, high or low, same or different.
- Identifying people's voices.
- Identifying and repeating rhythms heard.
- Retelling a story, poem, or part of either.
- Trying to perform first one- and then two-part directions.
- Recalling sounds in sequence.
- Coordinating listening skills with body movements in a requested way.
- Enjoying music, stories, poems, and many other language arts, both individually and in groups.

SETTINGS FOR LISTENING

When preparing listening activities, the teacher can plan for success by having activities take place in room areas with a minimum of distracting sounds or objects (figure 7-5). Screens, dividers, and bookcases are helpful. Heating and lighting are checked, and comfortable seating is provided. Decisions concerning the size of a group are important. In general, the younger the children, the smaller the group, and the shorter the length of the activity.

Listening cannot be forced, but experiences can be provided that create a desire to listen (figure 7-6). Some schools offer children the choice of joining a

FIGURE 7-5 Proper placement of a piece of furniture or cabinet can reduce distractions.

FIGURE 7-7 Two children are actively listening; a third seems ready to move on to another activity.

group listening activity or playing quietly nearby. Teachers find that an interesting experience will attract children who are playing nearby (figure 7-7). When activities are enjoyable and successful, the child who was hesitant may look forward to new experiences. A teacher can turn on or turn off attention by ending, changing, or modifying activities when necessary. The

teacher should watch carefully for feedback; this will help to develop active listening in the child. A skillful teacher will complete the learning activity before the group becomes restless. When an activity is planned for which listening is required, it is important to consider that an active preschooler may have to struggle to remain seated for any length of time.

Listening Center

Special listening areas, sometimes called listening posts, can become a part of early childhood classrooms. Enjoying a quiet time by oneself or listening to recorded materials fascinates many children. Headsets plugged in to a jack or terminal help to block out room noise. Partitions cut distractions. Clever listening places where children can settle into become favorite spots, such as:

- large packing boxes lined with soft fabrics and pillows,
- old, soft armchairs, or
- a bunk or loft.

Phonographs, cassette tape recorders, photographs, picture sets, and books offer added dimensions to listening centers. Recordings of the teacher reading a new or favorite story can be available at all times for children's use. These recordings are sometimes called read-alongs, and are also available from commercial sources. Their quality varies widely, so it is recommended that they be reviewed before they are purchased.

FIGURE 7-6 A teacher promotes active speech and tries to motivate listening too. *(From* Early Childhood Practicum Guide, *by Machado and Meyer,* © *1984 by Delmar Publishers Inc.)*

Children can record, with adult help, their own descriptions of special block constructions together with accompanying drawings or photos. "Why I like this book" talks can be made about a special book. Children can record comments about their own pieces of art. A field-trip scrapbook may have a child's commentary with it. Recorded puppet scripts and flannel board stories can be enjoyed while the child moves the characters and listens. The child can explore small plastic animals while listening to a prepared cassette tape story. Possibilities for recorded activities are limited only by preparation time and staff interest.

Children's ages are always a factor in the use of audio-visual equipment. Listening centers need teacher introduction, explanation, and supervision.

Records

Some companies specialize in children's records that improve listening skills. These records involve children in listening for a signal, listening to directions, or listening to sounds. Some records include body-movement activities along with listening skills.

Not all records contain appropriate subject matter for young children. Before purchasing a record for children, the teacher should listen to it. The following criteria may be used to judge a record's worth:

1. Is the subject matter appropriate for young children?
2. Is it clearly presented?
3. Is it interesting to young children?
4. Does it meet the teaching objective?

Many records have been made of children's classics. These can also help to improve children's listening skills.

Tape Recorders

Tape recorders can both fascinate and frighten children. They can be valuable tools for listening activities. Under the teacher's supervision, children can explore and enjoy sounds using tape recorders.

Language Master

A language master is a sturdy, portable piece of equipment. It can record and then play back instantly. Cards are inserted in a left-to-right fashion. Although children need supervision in its use, they can learn how to use it in a short time. This machine has many lis-

tening-activity possibilities. More information about it is given in Unit 22 of this text.

Children's Books with Listening Themes

Using children's books to promote children's listening skill is described in Unit 9. Books with themes concerned with listening are good springboards to discussion about listening skills (figure 7-8).

ARE THERE DIFFERENCES IN CHILDREN'S LISTENING ABILITIES?

Yes, wide differences. As teachers become familiar with the children enrolled in their classes, they may notice that some children display abilities that allow them to note fine differences in sounds. Other children, who are progressing normally, will not acquire these skills until they are older. Many children obviously enjoy a broad range of listening music. Others have no interest. Some can immediately identify rhythms in words, while others seem to have difficulty in doing so.

Borten, Helen. *Do You Hear What I Hear?* New York: Abelard-Schuman, 1960. Describes the pleasures to be found in really listening.

Brown, Margaret Wise. *The Summer Noisy Book.* New York: Harper and Row, 1951. Can be easily made into a "guess-what" sound game.

Glazer, Tom. *On Top of Spaghetti.* New York: Doubleday, 1982. Teacher sings a silly story.

Guilfoile, Elizabeth. *Nobody Listens to Andrew.* Chicago, IL: Follett, 1957. The no-one-ever-listens-to-me idea is humorously handled.

Johnson, LaVerne. *Night Noises.* New York: Parents Magazine Press, 1967. Listening to noises in bed at night.

Showers, Paul. *The Listening Walk.* New York: Thomas Y. Crowell, 1961. Good book to share before adventuring on a group sound walk.

Spier, Peter. *Gobble, Growl, Grunt.* New York: Doubleday, 1971. Lots of variety in animal sounds with brilliant illustrations.

Zolotow, Charlotte. *If You Listen.* New York: Harper and Row, 1980. A touching tale of a child who, missing her father, turns to listening.

FIGURE 7-8 Children's books with listening themes

Some researchers feel that boys have a slight edge in one particular area, listening vocabulary (Brimer, 1969). Theories attempting to explain this difference suggest that boys speak later than girls and consequently depend on discriminative listening for a longer period and gain more skill. Other researchers suggest that mothers respond more frequently to male infant vocalizations, giving males greater vocal input. Chances are that preschool teachers will not notice any significant difference between their male and female students.

Summary

Listening skill is learned behavior. The ability to listen improves with experience and exposure, although young children vary in their ability to listen. Listening ability can be classified by type — appreciative, purposeful, discriminative, creative, and critical.

Planned activities, teacher interaction, and equipment can provide opportunities for children to develop their auditory perception skills.

Listening cannot be forced, but experiences can be provided so that a desire to listen is increased. Signals and attentive teacher encouragement can help to form habits. Settings that limit stimuli and control the size of groups are desirable. When teachers are watchful and act when children seem restless or uninterested during planned activities, listening remains active. One of the responsibilities of the teacher is to plan carefully so that young children consistently want to hear what is being offered.

Student Activities

- With a small group of classmates, discuss some of the ways a home or school environment can make young children "tune out."

- Watch a listening activity in a preschool center, and then answer the following questions.
  a. How did the teacher prepare the children for listening?
  b. What elements of the activity captured interest?
  c. How was child interest held?
  d. Did the teacher have an opportunity to praise listening?
  e. Did children's listening behavior during the activity seem important to the teacher?
  f. Was this the kind of activity that should be repeated? If so why?

- Observe preschoolers in group play. Write down any examples of appreciative, purposeful, discriminative, creative, or critical listening.

- Plan a listening activity. Describe the materials needed, how the activity will start, what is to happen during the activity, and the auditory perception skills that are included in your plan.

- In a paragraph, describe the difference between encouraging a child to listen and trying to force a child to listen.

- Find a source for recorded stories in your community.

- Plan five activities that deal with children's personal preferences.

- Bring one read-along book and recording from a commercial source to class. Check with a library in your area to see whether they are available. With a small group of classmates, develop a rating scale to judge the quality of the read-alongs. Rate and share results with the class.

- Discuss in groups of five to six people the factors that might be present when a preschooler reacts to only about half of the things said to him or her. Share with the total group.

Unit Review

A. Five types of listening have been discussed. After each of the following statements, identify the listening type that best fits the situation.
   1. After hearing an Indian drum on a record, Brett slaps out a rhythm of his own on his thighs while dancing around the room.
   2. During a story of *The Three Little Pigs*, Mickey blurts out "Go get 'em wolfie!" in reference to the wolf's behavior in the story.
   3. Kimmie is following Chris around. Chris is repeating "Swishy, fishy co-co-pop," over and over again; both giggle periodically.
   4. Debbie tells you about the little voice of small Billy Goat Gruff and the big voice of Big Billy Goat Gruff in the story of the *Three Billy Goats Gruff*.
   5. Peter has asked whether he can leave his block tower standing during snacktime instead of putting the blocks away as you requested. He wishes to return and build the tower higher. He then listens for your answer.

B. Name five objectives that could be used in planning listening activities for auditory perception.

C. Select the correct answers. All have more than one correct reply.
   1. Most parents unconsciously teach preschoolers
      a. to develop auditory perception.
      b. attitudes toward listening.
      c. to listen to their teachers.
      d. many words.
   2. A teacher can promote listening by
      a. demanding a listening attitude.
      b. using a signal that alerts children and focuses attention.
      c. encouraging a child.
      d. telling a child he or she is not listening.
   3. Critical listening happens when the
      a. child relates what is new to past experience.
      b. child disagrees with another's statement.
      c. child makes a comment about a word being good or bad.
      d. teacher plans thought-provoking questions, and the child has the maturity needed to answer them.
   4. Children come to early childhood centers with
      a. individual variation in abilities to listen.
      b. habits of listening.
      c. all the abilities and experiences needed to be successful in planned activities.
      d. a desire to listen.

5. Children's ability to follow a series of commands depends on
   a. their auditory memory.
   b. how clearly the commands are stated.
   c. how well their ears transmit the sounds to their brains and how well their brains sort the information.
   d. How well they can imitate the words of the commands.

D. Explain what is meant by intensity, pitch, and tempo.

E. Assume the children are involved in an activity when they are suddenly distracted by a dog barking outside the window. List four things you could say to the children to draw their attention back to the activity.

   If you wished to use their focus on the barking for a spontaneous listening activity, how would you proceed?

References

Allen, Roach and Claryce Allen. *Language Experience Activities*. Boston: Houghton Mifflin, 1982.

Barker, Larry L. *Listening Behavior*. Englewood Cliffs, NJ: Prentice Hall, 1971.

Brimer, M. A. "Sex Difference in Listening Comprehension." *Journal of Research and Development in Education* 9 (1969): 19–25.

Donoghue, Mildred R. *The Child and the English Language Arts*. Dubuque, IA: Brown, 1985.

Hennings, Dorothy Grant. *Communication in Action*. Skokie, IL: Rand McNally, 1978.

Lamberts, Frances, et al. "Listening and Language Activities for Preschool Children." *Language, Speech and Hearing Services in Schools* 31.6 (April 1980): 111–117.

Margolin, Edythe. *Teaching Young Children at School and Home*. New York: Macmillan, 1982. 157–58.

Marten, Milton. "Listening Review." *Classroom-Relevant Research in the Language Arts*. Washington, D.C.: Assoc. for Supv. and Curriculum Development, 1978. 48–60.

Nichols, R. "Factors in Listening Comprehension." *Speech Monographs* 15 (1984): 154–163.

Stewig, John Warren. *Teaching Language Arts in Early Childhood*. New York: Holt, Rinehart and Winston, 1982.

Weiss, Curtis E., and Herold S. Lillywhite. *Communicative Disorders*. St. Louis, MO: Mosby, 1981.

UNIT 8

Listening Activities

OBJECTIVES

After studying this unit, you should be able to

- describe three listening activities, stating the auditory perception skill that is involved in each.
- plan and present a listening activity.
- tell a story that involves purposeful child listening.

Listening activities are used to increase enjoyment, vocabulary, and skill. In this unit, the activities focus on the development of auditory skills through listening and response interactions. Activities that further develop these skills through the use of books and stories are found in later units.

Unit 15 will give you a great deal of encouragement and help you to conduct circle or group activities. If you will be trying out activities in this unit, it is best to skip ahead and read Unit 15 first.

One of your first tasks will be gathering an interested group. Every classroom has some signal that alerts children to a change in activities or a new opportunity. This can range from few notes on a classroom musical instrument to more creative signals. Usually a short invitational, and attention-getting statement will be used to pique children's curiosity such as:

- "Gail has a new game for you in the rug area today."
- "Time to finish what you are doing and join Madelyn in the story-time center with a book about Clifford, the Big Red Dog."
- "Our clapping song begins in two minutes; today, we are going to be jack-in-the-boxes."

In some centers, children are simply requested to finish up what they are doing and join their friends in a particular room area. The enjoyment of already-started finger plays, chants, songs, or movement captures their attention and they are drawn in. This is a great time to recognize all children by name, as in the following: (To the tune of "She'll Be Coming Round the Mountain.")

"Susie is here with us, yes, yes, yes."
(Clap on yes, yes, yes.)

"Larry's here with us, yes, yes, yes."
(Continue until all children are recognized, and ending with the following.)

"We are sitting here together,
We are sitting here together,
We are sitting here together, yes, yes, yes."

Note that the following activities will have to be evaluated for age-level appropriateness and use with a particular group of children. They are provided here as examples of listening activities, but may or may not be appropriate for your teaching situation.

RECOGNIZING VOICES GUESSING GAME

Objective

Practice discriminative listening and auditory memory skills.

Materials

Individual snapshots of school personnel. A tape recording of different school staff members' voices reading sequential paragraphs in a story or describing the work they perform.

Introduction and Activity

Line up snapshots in view of the children after each is identified. "Here are some snapshots of people we know. Now we're going to listen and try to guess who's talking. Raise your hand if you think you know." When a child guesses the voice correctly, have him or her turn the snapshot face down or put it into a box on your lap. Proceed to the next voice.

At the conclusion of the activity, show the photos one by one and name each. A great follow-up is guessing children's voices using the same game format.

BUILD A BURGER

Objective

Practice purposeful listening.

Materials

Cutouts of foods that are added to hamburger buns — onion slices, lettuce, tomato slices, cheese slices, pickles, meat patties, bacon, mayonnaise, mustard, and catsup. Cut out paper buns or make clay bun halves.

Introduction and Activity

Ask the children what kinds of food they like on their hamburgers. After the group discusses the things they like, say "I'm going to show you pictures of some of the things you've said you liked on your hamburger and some things I like. Here are onion slices; Marion said she liked them." Go on to show and name all the cutouts. Select three children to start the activity and have them sit facing the others. One child holds two bun halves, the next holds a flat box lid with all the hamburger parts, and the third child names all the things the first child selected when his or her hamburger is completed. The second child hands the first child the cutouts he or she names and places between the bun halves. At various times, the teacher asks different children in the large group whether the second child has selected the item that the first child has named, or the children can be encouraged to chant "Hamburger, Hamburger, yum, yum, yum. I want that hamburger here on my tongue." After each hamburger is completed and food items are named, second-round children are selected by first-round children.

SOUND CANS

Objective

Match similar sounds by using discriminative listening skills.

Materials

Cans with press-on or screw-off lids. Cards large enough to hold two cans. Outline circles of can bottoms with dark pen. Two circles for each card. Large different color index cards work well. It is best to use cans that are impossible for children to open or to securely tape cans shut. Fill pairs of cans with same materials, such as sand, paper clips, rocks, rice, beans, nuts, and bolts.

Introduction and Activity

This is a solitary activity or one that children can choose to play with others. It can be used in a learning center. An introduction like the following is necessary. "Here are some cans and cards. The way you play this game is to shake one can and then shake all the rest to find the one that sounds the same as the first can. Let's listen to this can." Shake it. "Now I'm going to try to find the can that sounds just like this one when I shake it." Pick up another and ask "Does this sound the same to you?" Shake the first and second can. "No, this sounds different, so I'm going to shake another can." Go on until the mate is found and placed beside the first can on the card.

This activity is a classic one, and many sound sets are found in preschool programs. (Sets are also commercially manufactured.)

"CAN YOU SAY IT AS I DO?"

Objective
Imitate sounds.

Materials
None

Introduction and Activity
The teacher says, "Can you change your voice the way I can?"

"My name is..." (teacher softly whispers his or her name). With changes of voice, speed, and pitch, the teacher illustrates with a loud, low, or high voice, speaking fast or slow, with mouth nearly closed or wide open, when holding nose, and so on.

The teacher then asks for a volunteer who would like to speak in a new or funny way. "Now, let's see if we can change our voices the way Billy does. Do it any way you want, Billy. We'll try to copy you."

The teacher then gives others a turn. This activity may be followed up with a body-action play with voice changes, like the "Mr. Tall and Mr. Small" activity in Unit 15.

WHAT'S CRUNCHY?

Objective
Practice discriminative listening and auditory memory skills.

Materials
Small celery sticks, carrot sticks, cotton balls, miniature marshmallows, uncooked spaghetti.

Introduction and Activity
Put materials in a bag behind your back. Reach in and show a celery stick as you start to sing "Celery is long and green, long and green, long and green" (to the tune of "Mary Had a Little Lamb"). Repeat the first line. "When you eat it, it goes crunch." Pass out a celery stick to each child who wants one, and sing the song again, crunching the celery when you reach the end of the song. Follow up with "What else is crunchy?" Sing the song substituting celery with the child's suggestion. Then introduce the following lyrics, passing out items from your bag to each child:

- "Carrot sticks are long and orange. When you eat them, they go crunch."
- "Cotton balls are soft and white. When you touch them they feel soft."
- "Spaghetti is long and thin. When you break it it goes snap."
- "Marshmallows are small and white. When you squeeze them they pop back."

Variation
Try children's names next, if group is still with you: "Jayne is a girl that's four." Repeat. "When you ask her she says..." (pause, waiting for child to finish sentence; if the child doesn't finish, add "Hello" and try other children).

PARAKEET TALK

Objective
Imitate sounds.

Materials
Popsicle sticks and colored construction paper. Cut out parakeets from colored construction paper and paste them on Popsicle sticks. All forms can be traced and cut from one pattern.

Introduction and Activity
Discuss birds that imitate what people say. Distribute parakeet forms (figure 8-1). Begin with something like, "We can pretend to be parakeets, too."

Teacher: Hi, parakeets!
Children: Hi, parakeets!

Teacher: Pretty bird.
Children: Pretty bird.

Teacher: Now let's hear from Julie, the yellow parakeet. Can the blue parakeet (Mike) say whatever the green parakeet (Sue) says? Let's see."

This activity is a good lead-in to a record with children pretending to be flying. Suggest that the children

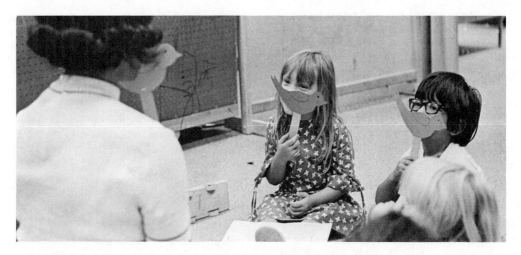

FIGURE 8-1 Parakeet talk

flap their wings through a door to an outdoor area, or take a walk to listen for bird sounds.

"LISTEN, OOPS A MISTAKE!"

Objective

Associate and discriminate among word sounds and objects.

Materials

Four or five common school objects (such as a pencil, crayon, block, toy, cup, and doll) and a low table.

Introduction and Activity

Talk about calling things by the wrong name, being sure to discuss how everyone makes mistakes at times. Begin with something like, "Have you ever called your friend by the wrong name?"

Teacher: When you call your friend by the wrong name, you've made a mistake. Look at the things on the table. I am going to name each of them. (Teacher names them correctly.) All right, now see if you can hear my mistakes. This time I'm going to point to them, too. If you hear a mistake, raise your hand and say, "Oops, a mistake!" Let's say that together once: "Oops, a mistake!" Are you ready? Listen: crayon, ball, doll, cup.

Change objects, and give the children a chance to make mistakes while the others listen (figure 8-2). This activity can later be followed with the story *Moptop* (by Don Freeman, Children's Press), about a long-haired red-headed boy who is mistaken for a mop.

ERRAND GAME

Objective

To follow verbal commands.

Materials

None.

Introduction and Activity

Start a discussion about doing things for parents. Include getting objects from other rooms, from neighbors, and so on. Tell the children you are going to play a game in which each person looks for something another has asked for.

Teacher: "Get me a book, please."
        "Can you find me a leaf, please."

Items to ask for include a rock, a blade of grass, a piece of paper, a block, a doll, a crayon, a toy car, a sweater, a hat, clothes, a hanger, a blanket, and so forth. Send children off one at a time. As they return, talk to each about where he or she found the item.

FIGURE 8-2 "If you hear a mistake, raise your hand."

While the group waits for all members to return, the group can name all the returned items. Put them in a row, ask children to cover their eyes while one is hidden, and then ask the children to guess which item was removed, or chant "We're waiting, we're waiting for . . ." (child's name).

If interest is still high, the teacher can make a request that the items be returned and repeat the game by sending the children for new items.

JACK-IN-THE-BOX

Objective
Discriminate sounds by listening for a signal and responding to it.

Materials
None. (To increase involvement, cardboard boxes may be used. Tops should open easily. Be sure that the children are not afraid to climb inside the box. A back door large enough to climb through works best.)

Introduction and Activity
Recite the following rhyme in a whispered voice until the word "pop" is reached. Using hand motions, hide your thumb in your fist and let it pop up each time the word "pop" is said.

Jack-in-the-box, jack-in-the-box, where can you be?
Hiding inside where I can't see?
If you jump up, you won't scare me.
Pop! Pop! Pop!

Suggest that children squat and pretend to be jack-in-the-boxes. Ask them to listen and jump up only when they hear the word "pop." Try a second verse if the group seems willing.

Jack-in-the-box, jack-in-the-box, you like to play.
Down in the box you won't stay.
There's only one word I have to say.
Pop! Pop! Pop!

PIN-ON SOUND CARDS (ANIMALS AND BIRDS)

Objective
Associate and imitate sounds and use auditory memory.

Materials

Safety pins or masking tape, file cards (3″ × 5″) with pictures of birds and animals (gummed stickers of animals and birds are available in stationery stores and from supply houses). Suggestions: duck, rooster, chick, owl, goose, woodpecker, horse, cow, cat, dog, sheep, lion, mouse, turkey, bee, frog, donkey, seal.

Introduction and Activity

Have a card pinned on your blouse or shirt before the children enter the room. This will start questions. Talk about the sound that the animal pictured on your card makes. Practice it with the children. Ask who would like a card. Have the children come, one at a time, while you pin on the cards (figure 8-3). Talk about the animal and the sound it makes. Imitate each sound with the group. Have one of the children make an animal noise and have the child with the right card stand up and say "That's me, I'm a..." (name of animal). Children usually like to wear the cards the rest of the day and take them home, if possible.

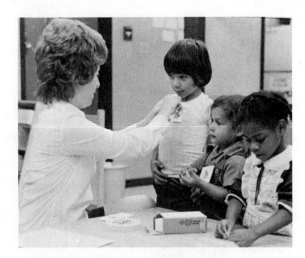

FIGURE 8-3 Pinning on sound cards

GUESS WHAT?

Objective

Identify and discriminate common sounds.

Materials

A bell, hand eggbeater, paper bag to crumple, baby rattle, tambourine, drum, stapler, any other noise-maker; a room divider, screen, table turned on its side, or blanket taped across a doorway. (This activity also works with a prerecorded cassette tape.)

Introduction and Activity

Ask children to guess what you have behind the screen.

Teacher: "Listen; what makes that sound?"

Note that with younger children, it is best to introduce each item with its name first. Ask different children to come behind the screen and make the next noise.

Variation

Clap simple rhythms behind the screen and have children imitate them. Rhythms can be made by using full claps of the hands with light claps and pauses at regular intervals; for example, a loud clap followed by two light ones and a pause repeated over and over.

Ask a child to sit in the "guessing chair" with his or her back to the group. From the group, select a child to say, "Guess my name." If the first child answers correctly, he or she gets a chance to select the next child who is to sit in the guessing chair.

PLAY TELEPHONES

Objective

Focus on listening and responding.

Materials

Paper, blunt toothpicks, string, two small tin cans with both ends removed (check for rough edges).

Introduction and Activity

Cover one end of each tin can with paper. Make a small hole. Insert a long string in the hole. Tie the string around blunt toothpicks. (Paper cups can be substituted for the tin cans.) Make enough sets for the group. Demonstrate how they work.

SOUND STORY

This story contains three sound words. Every time one of the words is mentioned, the children should make the appropriate sound.

Say, "When you hear the word spinach, say 'yum, yum, yum.' When you hear the word dog, bark like a dog. When you hear the word cat, meow like a cat." Then, recite the following story.

Once upon a time, there was a little boy who would not taste SPINACH. Everyone would say, "Marvin, why won't you taste SPINACH?" Marvin would say, "I think SPINACH is yuk!!!" Marvin's DOG Malcolm loved SPINACH. Marvin's CAT Malvina loved SPINACH. If Marvin didn't eat his SPINACH, Malcolm the DOG and Malvina the CAT would fight over who would get the SPINACH. The DOG and CAT would make so much noise fighting over the SPINACH that everyone in the neighborhood would say, "If you don't stop that noise, you will have to move away from here." Marvin loved his house and he didn't want to move away from the neighborhood. Malcolm the DOG loved his house and he didn't want to move away from the neighborhood. Malvina the CAT loved her house and she didn't want to move away from the neighborhood. What could they do?

Let the children tell you the answer. This game is a great deal of fun, and the children never tire of hearing the story. You can make up your own sound stories. You can also add rhythm instruments to make the sounds instead of voices (Weissman, 1979).

LISTENING RIDDLES FOR GUESSING

Animal Riddles

A tail that's skinny and long,
At night he nibbles and gnaws
With teeth sharp and strong.
Beady eyes and tiny paws,
One called Mickey is very nice.
And when there's more than one
We call them _____ .

(MICE)

He has a head to pat.
But he's not a cat.
Sometimes he has a shiny coat.
It's not a hog, it's not a goat.

It's bigger than a frog.
I guess that it's a _____ .

(DOG)

No arms, no hands, no paws,
But it can fly in the sky.
It sings a song
That you have heard.
So now you know
That it's a _____ .

(BIRD)

Sharp claws and soft paws,
Big night eyes, and whiskers, too.
Likes to curl up in your lap,
Or catch a mouse or a rat.
Raise your hand if you know.
Now all together, let's whisper it's name
  very slow. _____ .

(CAT)

Riddle Game

Children take turns calling on others with raised hands.

I'll ask you some riddles.
Answer if you can.
If you think you know,
Please raise your hand.
Don't say it out loud
'Til _____ calls your name.
That's how we'll play
This riddling game.

A beautiful flower we smell with our nose.
It's special name is not pansy but

_____ .

(ROSE)

I shine when you're playing and having fun.
I'm up in the sky and I'm called the

_____ .

(SUN)

If you listen closely you can tell,
I ring and chime because I'm a

_____ .

(BELL)

You've got 10 of me, I suppose,
I'm on your feet and I'm your

_____ .

(TOES)

I'm down on your feet, both one and two
Brown, black, blue, or red, I'm a

_____.

(SHOE)

I sit on the stove and cook what I can
They pour stuff in me, I'm a frying

_____.

(PAN)

It is helpful to have magazine pictures of a rose, the sun, toes, shoes, and a pan, plus a real bell to ring behind you as you speak. These are appropriate for young children who have little experience with rhyming.

Body Parts Riddle

If a bird you want to hear,
You have to listen with your

_____.

(EAR)

If you want to dig in sand,
Hold the shovel in your

_____.

(HAND)

To see an airplane as it flies,
Look up and open up your

_____.

(EYES)

To smell a pansy or a rose,
You sniff its smell with your

_____.

(NOSE)

When you walk across the street
You use two things you call your

_____.

(FEET)

If a beautiful song you've sung,
You used your mouth and your

_____.

(TONGUE)

All these parts you can feel and see
Parts are always with you on your

_____.

(BODY)

Tracing hands or drawing any body part they choose (on a picture with missing hands, feet, and so forth) is a fun follow-up activity for four-and-a-half-year-olds.

LISTEN AND FOLLOW DIRECTIONS — STORIES AND GAMES

Sit-Down — Stand-Up Story

Say to the children, "Let's see if you can stand *up* and sit *down* when I say the words. Listen: Stand *up!* You all are standing. Sit *down!* Good listening; we're ready to start." Then, tell the children the following story.

When I woke *up* this morning, I reached *down* to the floor for my slippers. Then I stood *up* and slipped them on. Next, I went *down*stairs to the kitchen. I opened the refrigerator, picked *up* the milk and sat *down* to drink. When I finished drinking, I tried to stand *up*, but I was stuck in the chair. I pulled and pulled, but I was still sitting.

"Don't sit on the chairs," my dad called from *up*stairs. "I painted them."

"It's too late! I'm sitting *down*," I answered. "Hurry *down* here and help me."

Dad pulled and pulled, but I didn't come *up*.

"I'll go get our neighbor, Mr. Green. Maybe he can pull you *up*," Dad said. Dad and Mr. Green pulled and pulled. "What'll I do?" I said. "The children will be waiting at school for me." Then I got an idea. "Go get the shovel," I said. Well, that worked. They pushed the shovel handle *down* and I came *up*.

You know, I think I'm stuck in this chair, too. Look, I am. _____ (child's name) and _____ (child's name), please help me. Everyone else please sit.

After my story, let's see if just _____ (child's name) and _____ (child's name) can show us with their hands which way is *up*, and which way is *down*.

A good follow-up is to talk about what can be seen in the room that is up above the children's heads and down below their heads, or say this poem together:

When you're up — you're up,
And when you're down — you're down.

But when you're halfway in between,
You're neither up nor down.

Funny Old Hat Game

Gather a bag of old hats (such as discarded paper party hats). Pass the hats out to the children, or let the children choose them.

Say, "We're ready when our hats are on our heads. We're going to put our hats in some funny places and do some funny things. Listen."

Put your hat between your knees.
Put your hat under your arm.
Put your hat over your shoes.
Put your hat under your chin.
Touch the top of your hat.
Sit on your hat.
Stand on your hat.

Encourage the children to choose a place to put the hat, and then say, "Where's the hat? Where's the hat, . . ." (child's name). "Can you see the hat, hat, hat?" (This can be chanted.) "Under the chair, under the chair — I can see the hat, hat, hat."

See If You Can Game

Collect objects from around the classroom (for example, scissors, ruler, eraser, cup, chalk). Put them on the floor on large paper. Say, "I'm not going to say its name. See if you can tell me what object I am talking about. Raise your hand if you know." (Keep giving hints until the children guess.)

"What has two circles for two fingers?" (Scissors)

"It's long and thin with numbers printed on one side." (Ruler)

"What makes pencil marks disappear?" (Eraser)

"You can fill it with milk." (Cup)

"What's white and small and writes on the chalkboard?" (Chalk)

Make up some of your own.

Student Activities

- Choose one of the activities found in a book mentioned in the suggested resource list or one from this unit. Present the activity to a group of preschoolers, modifying the activity to suit the child group if necessary. Then answer the following questions.
  a. Was the activity interesting to the children?
  b. Were they able to perform the auditory perception tasks?
  c. Would you change the activity in any way if you presented it again?

- Find or create five additional listening activities. Provide information regarding the source, name of activity, materials needed, description of activity, and objective. After citing the source, state the title of the book where you found the activity idea. If the idea is original, indicate this by using the word "self." Use a tape recorder in one activity.

- Select a popular children's television program to watch. Study the following questions before watching the program. Answer them after viewing the program.
  a. What is the name of the program, and the time and date of viewing?
  b. Were there attempts to build listening skills? If so, what were they?
  c. Do you have any criticism of the program?
  d. Could teachers of early childhood education use any techniques from the show in their auditory perception activities?

- Practice the listening story in this unit entitled "Sit-down — Stand-up Story," or find another listening story. At the next class meeting, tell the story to a classmate. Share constructive criticism.

Unit Review

A. List three listening activities, stating the objective of each activity and giving a description of the activity.

B. What is a good technique to use if you want a group of four-year-olds to listen at the beginning of a group time?

Reference

Weissman, Jackie. "Sound Story." *Hello Sound.* Mt. Rainier, MD: Gryphon House, 1979.

Resources for Additional Listening Activities

Allen, Roach. *Language Experiences in Early Childhood.* Chicago, IL: Encyclopedia Britanica Educational Corp., 1969.

Beaty, Janice J. *Skills For Preschool Teachers.* Columbus, OH: Charles E. Merrill, 1984. 120.

Cochran, E. V. *Teach and Reach That Child.* Mt. View, CA: Peek Publications, 1971.

Croft, Doreen J. and Robert Hess. *An Activities Handbook for Teachers of Young Children.* Boston: Houghton Mifflin, 1983.

Engel, Rose C. *Language Motivating Experiences for Young Children.* Van Nuys: Educative Toys and Supplies, 1972.

Lundsteen, Sara W. *Children Learn To Communicate.* Englewood Cliffs, NJ: Prentice Hall, 1976.

Mayesky, M., D. Neuman, and R. Wlodkowski. *Creative Activities for Young Children.* Albany: Delmar, 1985.

Rainey, Ernestine W. *Language Development For The Young Child.* Atlanta: Humanics Press, 1978.

Scott, Louise B. *Learning Time with Language Experiences for the Young Children.* St. Louis: Webster Division, McGraw-Hill, 1971.

Yawkey, Thomas D., et al. *Language Arts and the Young Child.* Itasca, IL: F. E. Peacock Publishers, 1981.

Section 4

Introducing Literature

Section 4 will appeal to lovers of picture books and stories. Story telling and other language activities, such as finger plays, chants, and poetry, are plentiful in this section and are accompanied by techniques for teacher presentations. Some of the suggested activities are established teachers' favorites and tried-and-true standbys.

MILLIONS OF CATS

"Cats here, cats there,
Cats and kittens everywhere,
Hundreds of cats,
Thousands of cats,
Millions and billions and trillions of cats."
    (From Wanda Gag's *Millions of Cats*,
    New York: Coward McCann, 1928.)

"*Millions of Cats* began a reputation for the author-illustrator and initiated the picture-book movement in America. Gag's illustrations reflect the clarity of the text. She used her own cats as models. Other details are equally authentic, even the pictures on interior walls. She designed as a whole each two facing pages of the opened book, termed a "double-page spread." Future American illustrators of children's books continued this innovation. English-language lists of recommended books for young children usually include *Millions of Cats.*" [1]

[1]Karen Nelson Hoyle, *Writers For Children*, ed. Jane M. Bingham (New York: Scribner's, 1988) 242.

UNIT 9

Children and Books

OBJECTIVES

After studying this unit, you should be able to

- state three goals for reading books to young children.
- describe criteria for book selection.
- demonstrate suggested techniques for reading a book to a group of children.
- design a classroom library center.

Picture books are an important beginning step on the child's path to literacy, as well as an excellent source of listening activities for the young child. Seeing, touching, and interacting with books is part of a good quality program in early childhood education. Books play an important role in language development.

When they are handled with care, reading experiences at home and at school can create positive attitudes toward literature and help to motivate the child to learn to read. A positive attitude towards literacy is most easily established early in life (Bettelheim and Zelan, 1981). Even older infants and toddlers can enjoy having picture books read to them, as discussed in Units 1 and 2.

Many parents read to their children at home; others do not. A teacher may offer some children their first contact with stories and books (figure 9-1). Teacher and child can share the joy of this very pleasant experience. Jim Trelease (1986) discusses reading to young children and the possible significance to the child and parent:

Next to hugging your child, reading aloud is probably the longest-lasting experience that you can put into your child's life. Reading aloud is important for all the reasons that talking to children is important — to inspire them, to guide

them, to educate them, to bond with them and to communicate your feelings, hopes and fears. You are giving children a piece of your mind and a piece of your time. They're more interested, really, in you than they are in the story — at least in the beginning.

FIGURE 9-1 Children may have their first experiences with picture books at an early childhood center.

Early childhood teachers agree that book-sharing sessions are among their favorite times with children. Teachers introduce each new group of children to favorite books that never seem to lose their magic.

There will be times when young children are rapt with enjoyment during picture-book readings, and at such times the lucky reader will understand the power of literature and realize his or her responsibility as the sharer of a vast treasure. The value of offering thoughtfully selected books in a skilled way will be readily apparent.

What, exactly, do picture books offer young children? They open the door to literacy and create the opportunity to:

- Build positive attitudes about books and reading. Attitude can be the major stumbling block to literacy achievement (Trelease, 1986).
- Explore, re-create, and obtain meaning in human experience. "The book itself has taken over as a partner and is invested with some of the qualities of a human relationship. In this way literature becomes extended dialogue" (Fraiberg, 1987).
- Come in contact with the diversity and complexity of life.
- Feel the texture of other's experiences.
- Look at vulnerability, honesty, and drama in a unique literary form (Hoggart, 1970).
- Experience in well-conveyed literature an art that leaves a lasting radiance (Sebesta and Iverson, 1975).
- Gain a sense of well-being.
- Experience the concise charm of heightened language and form (Lewis, 1976).
- Experience that sense of deepened self — children might call good feelings — that comes from involvement with important human emotions (Lewis, 1976).
- Unearth human truths.
- Nurture and expand imagination (Norton, 1983).
- Understand, value, and appreciate cultural heritage (Norton, 1983).
- Develop language, stimulate thinking, and develop socially (Norton, 1983).
- Gain facts, information, and data (nonfiction).
- Experience visual and aesthetic variety.
- Hear the rhythm and sound qualities of words.
- Gain reading skills.

- Sharpen listening.
- Understand what is acceptable and admirable and what is undesirable or deplorable (Lay-Dopyera and Dopyera, 1982).
- Experience a rich set of perspectives for thinking about their own feelings and behaviors (Lay-Dopyera and Dopyera, 1982).
- Experience vocabulary enrichment (Lay-Dopyera and Dopyera, 1982).

As you read through this unit, other benefits of reading aloud to children will occur to you, and you will clarify your thoughts about the benefits you consider of primary and secondary importance.

Each child gets his or her own meaning from picture-book experiences. Books cannot be used as substitutes for the child's real life experiences, interactions, and discoveries, because these are what help to make books understandable. Books add another dimension and source of information and enjoyment to children's lives.

AGE AND BOOK EXPERIENCES

Careful consideration should be given to selecting books that are appropriate to the child's age. Children under three (and many over this age) enjoy physical closeness, the visual changes of illustrations, and the sound of the human voice reading text. The rhythms and poetry of picture books intrigue them. Beck (1982) points out that very young children's "syntactic dependence" is displayed by their obvious delight in recognized word order. The sounds of language in picture books may be far more important than the meanings conveyed to the very young child. Teachers of two- and three-year-olds may notice this by observing which books chiildren select most often. Four-year-olds are more concerned with content and characterization, in addition to what they previously enjoyed in picture books. Fantasy, realism, human emotions, nonfiction, and books with a variety of other features attract and hold them.

WHERE TO START

This unit contains a list of picture books (page 161) to be considered merely as a starting point. Since the quality of a book is a subjective judgment, your favorites may not appear on this list. There are many other books of quality; each teacher should develop a personal collection. Librarians and bookstore salespeople can offer valuable suggestions and advice. A list of Caldecott Award books is also a good reference for finding appropriate books. The Caldecott medal and honor awards have been presented annually since 1938 by the Children's Service Division of the American Library Association to illustrators of distinguished picture books. Since 1922, the same group has presented medal and honor awards for the year's most distinguished contribution to children's literature published in the United States. Award lists often include literature for all ages of children, so each selection should be examined to determine whether it is suitable for younger children.

QUALITY

Judging quality means reading and viewing a picture book to find out whether it contains something memorable or valuable. For every good book you discover, you may wade through a stack that makes you wonder whether the authors have any experience at all with young children. Remember, appropriate material for a four-year-old may not suit a younger child.

Each book you select may have one or more of the following desirable and valuable features:

- characterization
- color
- an example of human courage, cleverness, or grit
- aesthetic appeal
- a gamelike challenge
- word play
- listening pleasure
- nonsense
- onomatopoeia (the naming of a thing or action by a vocal imitation of the sound associated with it, as in buzz and hiss)
- suspense
- humor or wit
- fantasy
- surprise
- repetition
- hope
- charm
- sensitivity
- modeling of admirable traits
- appealing illustrations

- realistic dialogue
- cultural insight
- action
- predictability

The preceding is only a partial listing. A book can excel in many different ways. An outstanding feature of many good stories is that they can cause the reader to smile with recognition and think "life is like that" or "I've been there myself."

The theme of respect for individual differences in Bill Peet's *Huge Harold*, the gentleness of Uri Shulevitz's *Rain, Rain, Rivers*, or the tenderness of Charlotte Zolotow's *My Grandpa Lew* may fit your criteria of quality. The runaway fantasy of Frank Asch's *Popcorn* and Tomie de Paola's *Strega Nona* might tickle your fancy.

The panoramic scenes of Mitsumasa Anno's *Anno's Counting Book*, the patterns and contrasts in Ezra Jack Keat's *Snowy Day*, or the fun of discovery in Janet and Allan Ahlberg's *Each Peach Pear Plum* might help a book become one of your favorites because of visual appeal.

For humor and wit, you might choose Steven Kellogg's *Can I Keep Him?*, Leah Komaiko's *Annie Bananie*, Robert Kraus's *Leo the Late Bloomer*, James Marshall's *George and Martha*, Mercer Mayer's *What Do You Do With a Kangaroo?*, or a selection of others that may make you laugh. You might never forget the way you trip over your tongue while reading about Jack, Kack, Lack, Mack, Nack, Ouack, Pack, and Quack in Robert McCloskey's *Make Way for Ducklings* or Arlene Mosel's *Tikki-Tikki Tembo*. If you enjoy surprise or an ending with a twist, you might be delighted by Brinton Turkles' *Deep in the Forest* or Jimmy Kennedy's *The Teddy Bears' Picnic*. The sound pleasure in Wanda Gag's *Millions of Cats* or the onomatopoeia in Mabel Brass's *The Little Engine That Could* might make these books memorable.

You might relive your experience of city living in *Tell Me a Mitzi* by Lore Segal. Perhaps discovering the facts through the colorful, precise artwork in Ruth Hellers' *Chicken's Aren't the Only Ones* will attract you to the world of nonfiction. Unforgettable characters like Leo Lionni's Frederick, Don Freeman's Corduroy and Beady Bear, Gene Zion's Harry The Dirty Dog, or Ludwig Bemelman's demure individualist, Madeline, may be counted among your friends as you search for quality. Jewels will stand out, and you will be anxious to share them with children.

You will be looking for fascinating, captivating books. Some captivate by presenting believable characters. "Character-drawing is like a tremendous, complicated conjuring-trick. Appealing to imagination and goodwill, diverting attention by sheer power of technique, the writer persuades us (for the period of reading and sometimes for long afterwards) to accept the identity of certain people who exist between the covers of his book" (Fisher, 1975). Some fascinate to the extent that worries are forgotten, and the child lives in the fantasy world of the story during its reading and beyond (Bettelheim and Zelan, 1981).

You'll want to choose classics so that from the very beginning the child has a chance to appreciate literature. Not everyone will agree with what is a modern-day classic. *Where The Wild Things Are*, by Maurice Sendak, continues to cause arguments among adults about whether it is truly a classic. Martinez (1987) notes that "adults don't like it very much, but nearly all the children really respond to it — Sendak is just on the kids' wavelength."

Illustrations

In many quality picture books, the story stands well by itself. The illustrations simply visualize what's written. In others, illustrations play a dominant role and are an integral part of the entire action (Freeman, 1967). Picture books are defined by Glazer (1986) as "those books that rely on a combination of illustrations and narrative with both being integral to the complete work. Fortunately many picture-book illustrations are created by highly talented individuals. A wide range of artistic styles exists in picture-book illustration, including line drawings, woodcuts, water colors, collage, photography, among others. Poltarnees (1972) describes the true artist as one who is able to enter the realm that his or her work evokes and move as freely there as if it were the kingdom of his birth. As a consequence, the artist can show us things that we would not have seen as mere visitors.

Illustrations help to give words reality. The younger child's picture-book illustrations are usually of familiar objects and lifelike settings, and publishers are careful to emphasize figures rather than backgrounds. In addition to the simple, true-to-life depictions preferred by young preschoolers, illustrations of pure fantasy and illustrations that contain more detail appeal to older preschoolers.

Format

A book's format is defined as its overall and general character, that is, the way it is put together. Decisions concerning format by book publishers and author/illustrators include the size and shape of the cover and interior pages, paper quality, printing colors, typesetting, content of each page, and binding. A book's format can enhance its narrative, appeal, and subsequent enjoyment, or it can confuse, frustrate, and alienate the reader. A book can reflect a thoughtful attempt to create a classic volume of enduring worth and value or represent a sacrifice of quality for the sake of quick profit.

Genre, another way of categorizing books, concentrates on a book's content. Narrative is considered to be poetry or prose. Prose can be further classified as fiction or nonfiction. The category of fiction includes excursions into sheer fantasy as well as more plausible stories about people or situations that could be, could have been, or might be. The latter group is classified as realistic fiction.

GOALS

Because children can gain so much from books, the teacher's way of presenting them is very important. The teacher's goal should be to lead each child to understand that books can be fun and interesting, can hold new experiences, and can be enjoyed alone or in the company of others.

Creating a positive attitude towards reading experiences should be a prime concern. If a child does not enjoy being read to, he or she might avoid all similar situations in the future. Children who enjoy being read to will seek out books (figure 9-2). Frailberg (1987) urges preschool teachers to think of the preschool years as "...a critical period for becoming addicted, the time when urges are felt as irresistible and objects that gratify the urge are also experienced as irresistible. The educator who wishes to capitalize on the addictability of the child at this age must insure early and repeated gratifications from stories told and stories read."

It is the teacher's responsibility to encourage the children's interest (figure 9-3), because not every child in preschool is interested in books or sees them as something to enjoy. Although children cannot be forced to like books, they can acquire positive feelings

FIGURE 9-2 Having a discussion about what has been found in a picture book is a common occurrence.

for them. Part of the positive feelings depends on whether children feel successful and competent during reading time. This, in turn, depends on how skillfully the teacher acts and reacts and how well the book sessions are planned. The key is to draw reluctant children into the story by making story times so attractive and vital that children simply cannot bear to stay away.

FIGURE 9-3 Teachers encourage book exploration. *(From* Early Childhood Practicum Guide, *by Machado and Meyer, © 1984 by Delmar Publishers Inc.)*

An important additional goal in reading books to children is the presentation of knowledge. Books can acquaint the child with new words, ideas, facts, feelings, and happenings. These are experienced in a different form than spoken conversation. In books, sentences are complete; in conversation, they may not be. Stories and illustrations follow a logical sequence in books.

Teachers ought to be concerned with whether the child comprehends what is read. To ensure comprehension, the books must offer significant content, something that relates to the child's everyday experience. Humor and fantasy, for example, are commonplace in favorite picture books. Usually, these books aren't merely frivolous. A closer reading will often reveal that they deal with universal human emotions or imaginations. Comprehension is aided by open discussion. Children should be allowed to ask questions that will help them connect the book's happenings to their own past experiences. The more outgoing and talkative children often clear up misunderstandings of the whole group when books are discussed. Those who work with young children often notice children's innate tendency to try to make sense and derive meaning from the happenings in their lives.

Teachers can show that books may also be used as resources. When a child wants to find out about certain things, teachers can refer to dictionaries, encyclopedias, or books on specialized subjects. The teacher can model the use of books to find facts. When a child asks the teacher a question about some subject of special interest and the teacher says, "I don't know, but I know where we can find out," the teacher can demonstrate how books can be used for finding answers. The teacher tells where to look and follows through by showing the child how the information is found. The joy of discovery is shared, and this opens the door to seeking more answers.

Another goal of the teacher should be to encourage the development of listening skills. During listening times, children's attention can become focused. Many different types of listening — discriminative, appreciative, purposeful, creative, and critical — can all be present in one reading experience.

In contrast, "pressure-cooker" programs, which promise to have four-year-olds reading before kindergarten, often feature drill sessions designed to develop technical reading skills (such as decoding words).

When these drill sessions, which are usually meaningless and boring to young children, are connected to picture-book readings, they could endanger the young child's budding love affair with books. A further discussion of this problem can be found in Unit 21.

Many children pick up reading knowledge and reading skills naturally, as they notice books and become more familiar with their features. They will see regularities and differences in the book's illustrations and text that will aid them in their eventual desire to break the code of reading. An early type of reading has been witnessed by all experienced preschool teachers. Paul Copperman (1982) calls it "imitative reading." He defines this behavior as "reading the story from pictures, sometimes speaking remembered text that precisely follows the book for a page or more." Certain techniques can be used to encourage imitative reading:

- Reading picture books to children daily.
- Planning repeated reading of new and old favorites.
- Reliving enjoyed parts in discussions.
- Being attentive to children's needs to be heard "reading."
- Issuing positive encouragement about your enjoyment of what the children have shared.
- Expecting some creative child deviation from the actual story.
- Suggesting or providing additional ways children could "read" a book (for example, into a tape recorder).
- Viewing the children's activity as emerging literacy and behavior to value as a milestone.

Another goal to consider when planning a program is to encourage children to learn how to care for books and where and how they can be used. Attitudes about books as valuable personal possessions should be instilled during early childhood. A number of emerging behaviors and skills will be noticed as children become fond of books (figure 9-4). Learning to read is a complex skill that is dependent on smaller skills, some of which children develop during story times and by browsing through books on their own.

BOOK SELECTION

Teachers are responsible for selecting quality books that meet the school's stated goals; often teachers are

FIGURE 9-4 A book can be a personal experience.

asked to select new books for the school's collection. Some books may fill the needs completely; others may only partially meet the goals of instruction. The local library offers the opportunity to borrow books that help keep story-telling time fresh and interesting, and children's librarians can be valuable resources.

One child may like a book that another child does not like. Some stories appeal more to one group than to another. Stories that are enjoyed most often become old favorites. Children who know the story often look forward to a familiar part or character.

Professional books and journals abound with ideas concerning the types of books that young children like best. Some writers feel that simple fairy-tale picture books with animal characters who possess life-like characteristics are preferred (Beck, 1982). Others mention that certain children want "true" stories. Most writers agree with Frank Self (1987):

Much of the interest and appeal and therefore success of any book for young children depends on its presentation of basic human tasks, needs, and concerns from their perception and at a level at which they can respond. They do not need books which are condescending, which trivialize their concerns and efforts, and which present easy answers to complex problems. Rather, young children need adults and books, and other materials which support their right to be children, their efforts to meet both their common and their individual needs, and their efforts to create meaning in the world.

Bettelheim (1976) advises that both fairy tales and realism should be offered to young children:

When realistic stories are combined with ample and psychologically correct exposure to fairy tales, then the child receives information which speaks to both parts of his budding personality — the rational and the emotional.

Some beginning teachers worry about book characters such as talking bears and rabbits. Make-believe during preschool years is an ever-increasing play pursuit. Beck (1982) advises:

Children don't mind if bears talk if the message of their speech is something with which they can identify. On the other hand, they will reject stories that seem realistic if the problems the characters face have little to do with their own emotional lives.

The clear-cut story lines in many folk and fairy tales have stood the test of time (Pines, 1983) and are recommended for a beginning teachers' first attempts at reading to preschoolers. Bettelheim and Zelan (1981) feel "good literature has something of meaning to offer any reader of any age, although on different levels of comprehension and appreciation." Each child will interpret and react to each book from an individual point of view, based on his or her unique experience.

Kinds of Books

Children's book publishing is a booming business. Many types of books are available, as illustrated in figure 9-5 (pages 160–161), which lists various categories in the left column. The categories identify the major genre classifications and formats of children's books used in preschool classrooms, but excludes poetry, which is discussed in another unit. Many books do not fit neatly into a single category; some books may fit into two or more categories.

A vast and surprising variety of novelty books are also in print: floating books for bath time; soft, huggable books for bedtime; pocket-sized books; jumbo board and easel books (Scholastic); lift the flap books; movielike flipbooks (Little, Brown & Co.); books that glow in the dark; sing-a-story books (Bantam); potty training books (Barron's); and even books within books.

Criteria for Selection

The following is a series of questions a teacher could use when selecting a child's book.

1. Could I read this book enthusiastically, really enjoying the story?
2. Are the contents of the book appropriate for the children with whom I work?
   a. Can the children relate some parts to their lives and past experience?
   b. Can the children identify with one or more of the characters?

      Look at some children's classics such as Mother Goose. Almost all of the stories have a well-defined character with whom children have something in common. Teachers find that different children identify with different characters — the wolf instead of one of the pigs in "The Three Little Pigs," for example.
   c. Does the book have directly quoted conversation?

      If it does, this can add interest; for example, "Are you my mother?" he said to the cow.
   d. Will the child benefit from attitudes and models found in the book?

   Violence and frightening events are part of some fairy tales and folktales. They should be rejected. Many model behaviors are unsuitable for the young child. Also, consider the following questions when analyzing a book for unfavorable racial stereotypes or sexism:

   - Who are the "doers" and "inactive observers"?
   - Are characters' achievements based on their own initiative, insights, or intelligence?
   - Who performs the brave and important deeds?

- Is value and worth connected to skin color and economic resources?
- Does language or setting ridicule or demean a specific group of individuals?
- Are individuals treated as such rather than as one of a group?
- Are ethnic groups or individuals treated as though everyone in that group has the same human talent, ability, food preference, hair style, taste in clothing or human weakness or characteristic?
- Do illustrations capture natural looking ethnic variations?
- Does this book broaden the cross-cultural element in the multicultural selection of books offered at my school?
- Is the book accurate and authentic in its portrayal of individuals and groups?

3. Was the book written with an understanding of preschool age-level characteristics? See Kathryn Galbraith's *Katie Did!* (Atheneum, 1983).
   a. Is the text too long to sit through? Are there too many words?
   b. Are there enough colorful or action-packed pictures or illustrations to hold attention? See Don Freeman's *Mop Top* (Viking, 1955).
   c. Is the size of the book suitable for easy handling in groups or for individual viewing? See *Anno's Counting Book* by Mitsumasa Anno (Thomas Y. Crowell Co., 1975).
   d. Can the child participate in the story by speaking or making actions? See Esphyr Slobodkina's *Caps for Sale* (William R. Scott, 1947).
   e. Is the fairy tale or folktale too complex, symbolic, and confusing to have meaning? See *East of the Sun and West of the Moon* (Norway) or "Beauty and the Beast" (France) (examples of traditional folktales with inappropriate length, vocabulary, and complexity for the young child).

5. Is the author's style enjoyable?
   a. Is the book written clearly with a vocabulary and sequence the children can understand? See Mercer Mayer's *There's a Nightmare in My Closet* (Dial, 1969). Are memorable words or phrases found in the book? See Wanda Gag's *Millions of Cats* (Coward-McCann, 1928).
   b. Are repetitions of words, actions, rhymes, or story parts used? (Anticipated repetition is part of the young child's enjoyment of stories. Molly Bang's *Ten, Nine, Eight* (Greenwillow, 1983) contains this feature).
   c. Does the story develop and end with a satisfying climax of events? See *Petunia* by Roger Duvoisin (Knopf, 1950).
   d. Are there humorous parts and silly names? The young child's humor is often slapstick in nature (pie-in-the-face, all-fall-down type rather than play on words). The ridiculous and far-fetched often tickle them. See Tomie de Paola's *Pancakes for Breakfast* (Harcourt, Brace, Jovanovich, 1978), a wordless book.

6. Does it have educational value? (Almost all fit this criteria.)
   a. Could you use it to expand knowledge in any special way? See Maureen Roffey's *Home, Sweet Home* (Coward, 1983), which depicts animal living quarters in a delightful way.
   b. Does it offer new vocabulary? Does it increase or broaden understanding? See Masayuki Yabuuchi's *Animals Sleeping* (Philomel, 1983), for an example.

7. Do pictures (illustrations) explain and coordinate well with the text? Examine Leo Lionni's *Swimmy* (Pantheon Books, 1973) and look for this feature or Jane Miller's *Farm Counting Book* (Prentice Hall, 1983).

Some books meet most criteria of the established standards; others meet only a few. The age of attending children makes some criteria more important than others. Schools often select copies of accepted old classics (figure 9-6, page 161). These titles are considered to be part of our cultural heritage, ones that most American preschoolers know and have experienced. Many classics have been handed down through the oral tradition of story telling and can contain archaic words, such as stile and sixpence. Most teachers try to offer the best in children's literature and a wide variety of book types.

BIBLIOTHERAPY

Bibliotherapy, literally translated means book therapy. Teachers, at times, may seek to help children with life problems, questions, fears, and pain. Books, some pro-

TYPES	FEATURES TEACHERS LIKE	FEATURES CHILDREN LIKE
Story books (picture books) • Family and home • Folktales and fables • Fanciful stories • Fairy tales • Animal stories • Others	Shared moments Children enthusiastic and attentive Making characters' voices Introducing human truths and imaginative adventures Sharing favorites Easy for child to identify with small creatures	Imagination and fantasy Identification with characters' humanness Wish and need fulfillment Adventure Excitement Action Self-realization Visual variety Word pleasure
Nonfiction books (informational)	Expanding individual and group interests Developing "reading-to-know" attitudes Finding out together	Facts, discovery of information and ideas Understanding of reality and how things work and function Answers to "why" and "how" New words and new meanings
Wordless books	Promote child speech, creativity, and imagination	Supplying their own words to tell story Discovery of meanings Color, action, and visual variety
Interaction books (books which have active child participation built-in)	Keeping children involved and attentive Builds listening for directions skills	Movement and group feeling Individual creativity and expression Appeal to senses Manipulative features
Concept books (books with central concepts or themes that include specific and reinforcing examples)	Promotes categorization Presents opportunities to know about and develop concepts Many examples	Adds to knowledge Visually presents abstractions
Predictable books (books with repetitions and reinforcement)	Permits successful guessing Build's child's confidence Promotes ideas that books make sense	Opportunity to read along Repetitiveness Builds feelings of competence
Reference books (picture dictionaries, encyclopedias, special subject books)	Opportunity to look up questions with the child Individualized learning	Getting answers Being with teacher Finding a resource that answers their questions
Alphabet and word books (word books have name of object printed near or on top of object)	Supplies letters and word models Paired words and objects Useful for child with avid interest in alphabet letters and words	Discovery of meanings and names of alphabet letters and words
Novelty books (pop-ups, fold-outs, stamp and pasting books, activity books, puzzle books, scratch and sniff books, hidden objects in illustrations, talking books	Adds sense-exploring variety Stimulates creativity Comes in many different sizes and shapes Motor involvement for child	Exploring, touching, moving, feeling, smelling, licking, painting, drawing, coloring, cutting, gluing, acting upon, listening to a mechanical voice, and getting instant feedback

FIGURE 9-5 Categories of children's books

TYPES	FEATURES TEACHERS LIKE	FEATURES CHILDREN LIKE
Paperback books and magazines (Golden Books, Humpty Dumpty Magazine)	Inexpensive Wide variety Many classics available	Children can save own money and choose for themselves
Teacher- and child-made books	Reinforces class learnings Builds understanding of authorship Allows creative expression Records individual, group projects, field trips, parties Promotes child expression of concerns and ideas Builds child's self-esteem	Child sees own name in print Shares ideas with others Self-rewarding
Therapeutic books (books helping children cope with and understand things such as divorce, death, jealousy)	Presents life realistically Offers positive solutions and insights Presents diverse family groups Deals with life's hard-to-deal-with subjects	Helps children discuss real feelings
Seasonal and holiday books	Accompanies child interest May help child understand underlying reasons for celebration	Builds pleasant expectations Adds details
Books and audiovisual combinations (read-alongs)	Adds variety Offers group and individual experiencing opportunities Stimulates interest in books	Projects large illustrations Can be enjoyed individually
Toddler books (durable pages)	Resists wear and tear	Ease in page-turning
Multicultural and cross-cultural books	Increases positive attitudes concerning diversity and similarity Emphasizes the realities in our society	Meeting a variety of people

FIGURE 9-5 *Continued*

A PARTIAL LISTING

Ba, Ba, Black Sheep
Chicken Little
The Crooked Sixpence
Goldilocks and the Three Bears
Here We Go Round the Mulberry Bush
Hey Diddle, Diddle (the Cat and the Fiddle)
Hickory, Dickory, Dock
Humpty Dumpty
Jack and Jill
Jack and the Beanstalk
Jack Be Nimble
Jack Sprat
Little Bo Peep
Little Boy Blue

Little Girl With a Curl
Little Jack Horner
Little Miss Muffet
Little Red Hen
Little Robin Redbreast
London Bridge is Falling Down
Mary Had a Little Lamb
Mary, Mary, Quite Contrary
Old King Cole
Old Mother Hubbard
The Old Woman Who Lived in a Shoe
Peter Piper
Pop Goes the Weasel
Ride a Cock Horse (Banbury Cross)

Rock-A-Bye Baby
Row, Row, Row Your Boat
Silent Night
Simple Simon
Sing a Song of Sixpence
Take Me Out to the Ball Game
The Three Bears
The Three Billy Goats Gruff
The Three Blind Mice
The Three Little Pigs
To Market
Twinkle, Twinkle, Little Star
Ugly Duckling
You Are My Sunshine

FIGURE 9-6 Stories, songs, rhymes, and poems considered classics for preschoolers. Many of the following can be found in picture-book form.

fessionals believe, can help children cope with emotional concerns. At some point during childhood, children may deal with rejection by friends, ambivalence toward a new baby, divorce, grief, or death, along with other strong emotions (Smith and Foat, 1982).

Fairy tales can reveal the existence of strife and calamity in a form that permits children to deal with these situations without trauma (Bettelheim and Zelan, 1981), and these tales can be shared in a reassuring, supportive setting that provides a therapeutic experience. A small sampling of contemporary books considered to be therapeutic in nature follow:

> Dragunwagon, Crescent. *Wind Rose*, New York: Harper and Row, 1976. (birth)
>
> Mayer, Mercer. *There's a Nightmare in My Closet*. New York: The Dial Press, 1968. (fear)
>
> Viorst, Judith. *The Tenth Good Thing About Barney*. New York: Atheneum, 1973. (death of a pet)

A much wider selection of such titles is in print. The following resource books are helpful to preschool teachers looking for books dealing with strong feelings:

> Bernstein, Joanne E. *Books to Help Children Cope With Separation and Loss*. New York: R. R. Bowker, 1977. (A listing of book titles.)
>
> Dreyer, Sharon. *The Book Finder*. Circle Pines, MN: American Guidance Services, Inc., 1980. (Books are listed by their themes; synopsis and author/illustrator information is included.)
>
> Gillis, Ruth J. *Children's Books for Times of Stress*. Bloomington, IN: Indiana University Press, 1978. (An annotated bibliography categorized under headings covering anger, overweight, hospital stays, illness, rivalry, guilt, fear, bravery, hate, rejection, along with other feelings and problem areas.)

Bernstein (1977) urges parents and teachers to use books to open conversations in which children express grief:

> It is from adults that they learn their behavior patterns for the future; whether grieving is normal and permissible or whether it is forbidden and wrong and a source of discomfort. Perhaps the most important aspect of helping young people

cope with loss is the willingness of adult guides to expose their own grief while at the same time encouraging children to express theirs. For the way in which adults handle trauma determines youngsters' abilities to survive, physically and mentally, and they can come forth from crisis strong and ready once again to celebrate life.

READING BOOKS TO YOUNG CHILDREN

Teachers read books in both indoor and outdoor settings, to one child or to many. If a child asks for a story and a teacher is available, the book is shared. Planned reading, called story times, are also part of a quality early childhood program.

Because of the importance of reading to children, teacher techniques need to be carefully planned and evaluated. Most of us have seen well-meaning adults use reading techniques that are questionable and defeat the adult's purpose in reading. Bettelheim and Zelan (1981) emphasize the importance of teaching methods in the following:

> If we wish to induce children to become literate persons, our teaching methods should be in accordance with the richness of the child's spoken vocabulary, his intelligence, his natural curiosity, his eagerness to learn new things, his wish to develop his mind and his comprehension of the world, and his avid desire for the stimulation of his imagination...in short, by making reading an activity of intrinsic interest.

The burden of making reading interesting falls on the teacher. Building positive attitudes takes skill. A step-by-step outline is helpful in conducting group story times.

Step 1.

Think about the age, interests, and special interests of the child group and consider the selection criteria mentioned in this unit. Read the book to yourself enough times to develop a feeling for characters and the story line. Practice dialogue so that it will roll smoothly. In other words, analyze, select, practice, and prepare.

Step 2.

Arrange a setting with the children's and teacher's comfort in mind. The illustrations should be at children's eye level. A setting should provide comfortable seating while the book is being read. Some teachers prefer small chairs for both children and teachers; others prefer rug areas. Avoid traffic paths and noise interruptions by finding a quiet spot in the classroom. Cutting down visual distractions may mean using room dividers, curtains, or furniture arrangements.

Step 3.

Make a motivational introductory statement. The statement should create a desire to listen or encourage listening: "There's a boy in this book who wants to give his mother a birthday present"; "Monkeys can be funny, and they are funny in this book"; "Have you ever wondered where animals go at night to sleep?"; "On the last page of this book is a picture of a friendly monster."

Step 4.

Hold the book to either your left or right side. With your hand in place, make both sides of the page visible. Keep the book at children's eye level.

Step 5.

Begin reading; try to glance at the sentences and turn to meet the children's eyes as often as possible, so your voice goes to the children. Also watch for children's body reactions. Speak clearly with adequate volume, using a rate of speed that enables the children to both look at illustrations and hear what you are reading. Enjoy the story with the children by being enthusiastic. Dramatize and emphasize key parts of the story but not to the degree that the children are watching you and not the book. Change your voice to suit the characters, if you feel comfortable doing so. A good story will hold attention and often stimulate comments or questions.

Step 6.

Answer and discuss questions approvingly. If you feel that interruptions are decreasing the enjoyment for other children, ask a child to wait until the end when you will be glad to discuss it. Then do it. If, on the other hand, most of the group is interested, take the time to discuss an idea. Sometimes, children suck their thumbs or act sleepy during reading times. They seem to connect books with bedtime; many parents read to their children at this time. By watching closely while reading, you will be able to tell whether you still have the attention of the children. You can sometimes draw a child back to the book with a direct question like "Debbie, can you see the cat's tail?" or by increasing your animation or varying voice volume.

Step 7.

You may want to ask a few open-ended discussion questions at the end of the book. Keep them spontaneous and natural — avoid testlike questions. Questions can clear up ideas, encourage use of vocabulary words, and pinpoint parts that were especially enjoyed. You will have to decide whether to read more than one book at one time. It helps to remember how long the group of children can sit before getting restless. Story times should end on an enthusiastic note, with the children looking forward to another story. Some books may end on such a satisfying or thoughtful note that discussion clearly isn't appropriate; a short pause of silence seems more in order. Other times, there may be a barrage of child comments and lively discussion.

Additional Book Reading Tips

- Check to make sure all of the children have a clear view of the book before beginning.
- Watch for combinations of children sitting side by side that may cause either child to be distracted. Rearrange seating before starting.
- Pause a short while to allow children to focus at the start.
- If one child seems to be unable to concentrate, a teacher can quietly suggest an alternative activity to the child. Clear understanding of alternatives or lack of them needs to be established with the entire staff.
- Moving a distracted child closer to the book, or onto a teacher's lap, sometimes works.
- When an outside distraction occurs, recapture attention and make a transitional statement leading back to the story: "We all heard that loud noise. There's a different noise made by the steam

shovel in our story. Listen and you'll hear the steam shovel's noise."

- Personalize books when appropriate: "Have you lost something and not been able to find it?"
- Skip ahead in books, when the book can obviously not maintain interest, by quickly reading pictures and concluding the experience. It's a good idea to have a backup selection close by.
- Children often want to handle a book just read. Plan for this as often as possible. Make a quick waiting list for all who wish to go over the book by themselves.
- Plan reading sessions at relaxed rather than rushed or hectic times of day.
- Handle books gently and carefully.
- Remember it is not so much what you are reading but how you read it (Jaronczyk, 1984).
- Choose material to suit yourself as well as the group. Select a story type that you like. Practice projecting your voice (Jaronczyk, 1984).
- Lower your voice or raise your voice and quicken or slow your pace as appropriate to the text. Lengthen your dramatic pauses, and let your listeners savor the words and ideas (Lay-Dopyera and Dopyera, 1982).
- Periodically point to things in illustrations as the text refers to them, and sweep your fingers under sentences to emphasize the left-to-right pattern of reading (Lay-Dopyera and Dopyera, 1982).

Child Interruptions During Story Time

A slight debate exists as to the degree that child questions and comments during story time mar or enhance the experience for all group members. One position holds that a book should be enjoyed without any loss of flow that diminishes the book's intent and effect. The other position is expressed by Bos (1988): "It's important that we keep conversation going even if we never get to the end of the story." Teachers and schools have arrived at a number of techniques, which follow. It's a good idea to discuss courses of action at a school where you are employed, volunteering, or student teaching.

- Save all comments until the end.
- Answer and accept comments up to the point that you feel the story is being sacrificed.

- Make certain books "taboo" for discussion: "This book is one we won't talk about until the end."

Paraphrasing Stories

Paraphrasing means putting an author's text into one's own words. By tampering with the text, the teacher may interfere with book's intent, message, and style. Many professionals find this objectionable and urge teachers to read stories exactly as they are written, taking no liberties, respecting the author's original text. When a book doesn't hold the interest of its audience, it should be saved for another time and place, perhaps another group. Some teachers feel that maintaining child interest and preserving the child's positive attitude about books supersedes objections to occasional paraphrasing.

Building Participation

Children love to be part of the telling of a story. Good teachers plan for child participation when choosing stories to read. Often books are read for the first time, and then immediately reread, with the teacher promoting as much participation as possible. Some books hold children spellbound and usually take many readings before the teacher feels that it is the right time for active involvement other than listening. Copperman (1982) believes that listening skills are encouraged to develop when "children contribute to read-aloud sessions" and become active, participating listeners. Nonfiction books may not provide as much material for child involvement.

Examining story lines closely can give the teacher ideas for children's active participation. Here is a list of ways to promote child participation and active listening:

1. Invite children to speak a familiar character's dialogue or book sounds. This is easily done in repeated sequences: "I don't care," said Pierre.
2. Pantomime actions: "Let's knock on the door."
3. Use closure: "The cup fell on the..." (floor). When using closure, if children end the statement differently, try saying "It could have fallen on the rug, but the cup in the story fell on the floor.
4. Predict outcomes: "Do you think Hector will open the box?"

5. Ask opinions: "What's your favorite pie?"
6. Recall previous story parts: "What did Mr. Bear say to Petra?"
7. Probe related experiences: "Emil, isn't your dog's name Clifford?"
8. Dramatize enjoyed parts or wholes.

Younger preschoolers, as a rule, find sitting without active motor and/or verbal involvement more demanding than older ones.

Rereading Stories

It never ceases to amaze teachers and parents when preschoolers beg to hear a book read over and over. Beginning teachers take this statement to mean they've done a good job, and even veteran teachers confess it still feels good. Ornstein and Sobel (1987) note that young children enjoy repetition more than older children or adults. A teacher who can read the same book over and over again with believable enthusiasm, as if it were his or her first delighted reading, has admirable technique and dedication. Children often ask to have stories reread because, by knowing what comes next, they feel competent, or they simply want to stretch out what's enjoyable. The decisions that teachers make about fulfilling the request depends on many factors including class schedules and children's desire but lack of capacity to sit through a second reading. It is suggested that books be reread often and that teacher statements such as "I'd like to read it again, but..." are followed by statements such as "After lunch, I'll be under the tree in the yard, if you want to hear the story again."

Using Visuals During Story Times

There are a number of reasons teachers decide to introduce books with objects or other visuals. A chef's hat worn by a teacher certainly gets attention and may motivate a group to hear more about the chef in the picture book. A head of lettuce or horseshoe may clarify some feature of a story. The possibilities are almost limitless. Currently, with the popularity of theme or unit approaches to instruction, a picture book may expand or elaborate a field of study or topic that has already been introduced. If so, some new feature mentioned in a book may be emphasized by using a visual.

When the teacher wears an article of clothing, such as the hat mentioned above, it may help him or her get into character. Since children like to act out story lines or scenes, items that help promote this activity can be introduced at the end of the story. Previewing a picture book may make it easier to find an object or person that could add to the story-telling experience.

AFTER-READING DISCUSSIONS

How soon after a story is read should discussion, which promotes comprehension of stories, take place? It is obvious that a discussion might ruin the afterglow that occurs after certain books are shared. Teachers are understandably reluctant to mar the magic of the moment.

Research suggests that a discussion of the literal meaning of storybook text may foster beginning literacy development (Dickinson & Snow, 1987). Anderson (1988), referring mainly to elementary school reading, states that "there needs to be a strong emphasis on teaching comprehension," and early childhood teachers could at times consider asking what Anderson calls "artful questions" that draw attention to major elements of characterization and plot and the moral or deeper implications of a story, if appropriate. The solution that many teachers favor is to wait until children seem eager to comment, discuss, and perhaps disagree, and only then act as a guide to further comprehension. The opportunity may present itself after repeated readings of favorites or after a first reading. Teachers should take special care to avoid asking testlike questions at the conclusion of book readings, because it discourages open and natural discussion. Unfortunately, many adults have had this kind of questioning in their own elementary schooling, so they automatically and unconsciously copy it.

PICTURE BOOKS AS THE BASIS FOR THEME INSTRUCTION

Early childhood centers are experimenting with using picture books as the basis for theme programming. Under this approach to program planning, instruction branches out from the concepts and vocabulary present in the book. Usually, the meaning of the story is emphasized, and a number of different directions of study and activities that are in some way connected to the book are conducted. Eric Carle's *The Very Hungry Caterpillar* is a favorite theme opener.

The classroom setting can be transformed into the cabbage patch that Peter Rabbit was so fond of exploring. Activities such as counting buttons on jackets, singing songs about rabbits or gardens, field trips to vegetable gardens, and science experiences in vegetable growing are a few examples of associated activities. Memorable experiences connected to classic books can aid literacy development, and an increasing number of preschools are using this approach in language arts programming.

FROM BOOKS TO FLANNEL BOARDS AND BEYOND

Teachers find that a number of books can be made into flannel board stories relatively easily; Unit 12 is devoted to these activities. Five books that are particular favorites have been adapted:

- *The Very Hungry Caterpillar* by Eric Carle
- *The Carrot Seed* by Ruth Kraus
- *Jony and His Drum* by Maggie Duff
- *My Five Senses* by Aliki
- *Brown Bear, Brown Bear, What Do You See?* by William Martin

Books often open the door to additional instruction through activities or games on the same subject or theme. Whole units of instruction on bears, airplanes, families, and many other topics are possible.

Teachers have attempted to advertise particular books in creative ways. Enlarged book characters might be displayed, or displays of the book of the week or book of the day may be placed in a special spot in a classroom. An attending child's mother or father may be a special story-time book reader. Bev Bos (1988), in discussing morning greetings to children, states "Many times I may have a new book in my lap and then share the cover to set the excitement about story time."

LIBRARY SKILLS AND RESOURCES

A visit to the local library is often planned for preschoolers. Librarian-presented story hours often result in the children's awareness of the library as a resource. Selecting and checking out one's choice can be an exciting and important milestone. Most preschools also do their best to encourage this parent-child activity.

Many libraries have well-developed collections and enthusiastic and creative children's librarians who plan a number of activities to promote literacy. Along with books, you may find computers, language-development computer programs, audio and video tape cassettes, records, book and tape combinations, slides, films, children's encyclopedias, foreign language editions, pamphlet collections, puzzles, and other language-related materials and machines.

Finding out more about the authors of children's books can help to provide teachers with added insights and background data. One goal of language arts instruction should be to alert children to the idea that books are created by real people. Most children find a photograph of an author or illustrator interesting, and discussions about authors and authorship can help to encourage children to try their hand at writing books.

Becoming more familiar with authors such as Margaret Wise Brown, often called the "Laureate of the Nursery," helps a reader appreciate the simplicity, directness, humor, and the sense of the importance of life that are found in her writings. The following books give helpful background data on authors:

- Doyle, Brian. *Who's Who in Children's Literature.* New York: Schocken, 1971.
- Hopkins, Lee Bennett. *Books Are By People.* New York: Scholastic Magazine, 1969.

The following resources include autobiographical and biographical sketches:

- *Fourth Book of Junior Authors and Illustrators.* Eds. Doris de Montreville and Elizabeth D. Crawford. New York: Wilson, 1978.
- Hoffman, Miriam, and Eva Samuels. *Authors and Illustrators of Children's Books.* New York: R.R. Bowker Co., 1972.
- *Twentieth-Century Children's Writers.* Ed. D. L. Kirkpatrick. New York: St. Martins Press, 1978.

Some early childhood centers set up author displays, celebrate author/illustrator birthdays, and encourage visiting authors and illustrators. Letters to authors might be written with child input.

A teacher who has done some reading and wants to mention or quote the children's favorite authors might use items like the following that were found in the preceding resources:

- from Steven Kellogg, author/illustrator of *Can I Keep Him?* "I particularly loved (as a child) drawing animals and birds."

  or

  "I made up stories for my younger sisters." (*Fourth Book of Junior Authors and Illustrators*)
- from Mitsumasa Anno, author/illustrator of *Anno's Alphabet*, "The imaginative eye is the source of all the books I have made for children." (*Fourth Book of Junior Authors and Illustrators*)
- from Eric Carle, author/illustrator of *The Very Hungry Caterpillar*, "I remember large sheets of paper, colorful paints and big brushes" (speaking of childhood). (*Authors and Illustrators of Children's Books*)
- from Leo Lionni, author/illustrator of *Little Blue and Little Yellow* "I like to write about birds because I have birds at home: parrots, pigeons, chickens and finches." (*Authors and Illustrators of Children's Books*)

CHILD- AND TEACHER-AUTHORED BOOKS

Books authored by children or their teachers have many values.

- They promote interest in the classroom book collection.
- They help children see connections between spoken and written words.
- The material is based on child and teacher interests.
- They personalize book reading.
- They prompt self-expression.
- They stimulate creativity.
- They build feelings of competence and self-worth.

If a child-authored book is one of the school's books, the book corner becomes a place where the child's accomplishment is exhibited. Teachers can alert the entire group to new book titles as the books arrive and make a point to describe them before they are put on the shelves.

Child-made books require teacher preparation and help. A variety of shapes and sizes (figure 9-7) add interest and motivation. Covers made of wallpaper or contact paper over cardboard are durable. The pages of the books combine child art and child-dictated words, usually on lined printscript paper. Staples, rings, yarn (string), or brads can bind pages together (figure 9-8). Child dictation is taken word for word with no teacher editing.

The following book dictated by a four-year-old illustrates one child's authorship.

The Window

Page 1 Once upon a time the little girl was looking out the window.

Page 2 Child's Art

Page 3 And the flowers were showing.

Page 4 Child's Art

Page 5 And the water was flushing down and she did not know it.

Page 6 Child's Art

Teacher-authored books can share a teacher's creativity and individuality. Favorite themes and enjoyed experiences can be repeatedly relived. Books containing the children's, teachers', staff's, parents', or school pets' names are popular. Photographs of familiar school, neighborhood, or family settings are great conversation stimulators. Field trips and special occasions can be captured in book form.

Vicki's Car Book

What's Round Book

FIGURE 9-7

Bookbinding

1.

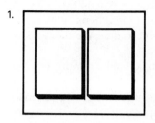

2.

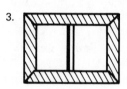

3.

One stitch on outside fold.

4.

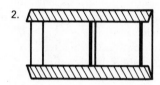

Two stitches on inside fold.

5.

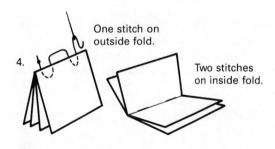

Masking tape with adhesive facing cover boards.

FIGURE 9-8

Lentz and Burris (1985) suggest using what they call caption books with young children. Their caption books carefully place the print in the top left of the page, include photographs that give clues to the print message on the same page, and use short meaningful sentences that repeat on succeeding pages. These writers also suggest teacher-made books that record nature walks, seasonal events, and holiday celebrations. An additional suggestion from Lentz and Burris (1985) involves urging children to illustrate their favorite stories with their own art.

Group authorship is another idea. Books in which every child has contributed one or more pages are enjoyable projects and discoveries.

BOOK AREAS AND CENTERS

Classrooms with inviting book storage areas beckon curious browsers. Books should be at the child's eye level with book front covers in sight (figure 9-9). Book-jacket wall displays and life-size book characters (drawings made by using overhead projectors to increase size then tracing on large sheets of paper) have their own appeal. Comfort and color attract. Softly textured rugs and pillows, comfortable seating, and sprawling spaces prolong time spent in book areas. Low round tables and plump pillows used as seating can also be inviting. Quiet, private spaces that are shielded from outside distractions and sounds and that have good lighting increase the child's ability to stay focused. Hideaways where friends can escape together and experience a book that has captured their attention are ideal (figure 9-10).

Guidelines that outline the rules and responsibilities of book handling should be developed by the school. Rules should be designed to encourage children to return books to shelves, turn pages carefully, and respect the quietness of the area. Well-defined boundaries of library centers help books stay put. Teachers should promote the idea that using the area is a privilege and monitor book centers frequently when younger preschoolers who may have had little past experience with book collections and libraries enter the area.

What kind of collection should a well-stocked classroom library center have? Collections often reflect a school's budget and priorities. The purchase of

FIGURE 9-9 A soft rug, some pillows or chairs, and books at a child's eye level make this an inviting book corner.

FIGURE 9-10 Hiding away with a friend to read.

classroom favorites and classics should be the first priority; after that, a well-rounded collection is recommended that includes a lot of different topics and categories.

Rotating books by removing and storing some books from time to time and providing a different, previously stored set of books will make the area more interesting. Library books supplement the school's collection and may have special, classroom-handling rules. Seasonal and holiday books are provided when possible. Paperbacks round out some collections, and multiple copies are considered for younger preschoolers' classrooms. Constant book repair is necessary in most classrooms because of heavy use.

Teachers should browse in book centers, modeling both interest and enthusiasm when time and supervision duties permit.

Settings

Most classrooms have areas suitable for picture-book reading in groups, besides areas for individual, self-selected browsing and places where children can be in the company of a few others. If these areas are not available, staff members can create them (figure 9-11). The reading or library area should be comfortable and well lit and as far removed from interruptions and distractions as possible. Generally, lighting that comes from behind the children is preferred. Intense, bright light coming from behind the book can make it hard to see. During group readings, one center put a floor lamp in the reading area, and dimmed the overhead lights. This setup worked well to cut distractions and focus the group on the reading. A large, horseshoe-shaped floor pillow can increase child comfort. Many centers use small carpet sample squares for comfort and to outline individual space. A shady spot in the play yard may be a good site for teacher's reading on a warm day.

FIGURE 9-11 One school acquired a giant stuffed bear for children to sit on and lean on while looking at books with friends.

The number of children in groups is an important consideration; as the size of the group increases, intimacy, the child's ease of viewing, and the teacher's ability to be physically close and respond to each child decrease. The ideal group size for story time ranges from 5 to 10 children. Unfortunately, staffing ratios may mandate a much larger group size. Some preschools do "instant replays" — they have many small reading groups in succession, rather than large group reading sessions.

Care and Storage of Books

By setting an example and making clear statements about handling books, the teacher can help children form good book-care habits. However, with time and use, even the sturdiest books will show wear.

Teachers are quick to show their sadness when a favorite book is torn, crayoned, or used as a building block. Some classrooms have signs reading "Books are friends — Handle with Care" or "Books are for looking, talking about, and sharing." Teachers are careful to verbally reward children who turn pages gently and return books to shelves or storage areas.

RESOURCES FOR FINDING READING MATERIALS

Public libraries.

Many libraries have book lists of suggested early childhood editions. Often, seasonal books are together in special displays. Ask the librarian about new books, special services, or resources that include films or slides.

Children's book stores and toy stores.

Many stores carry popular new and older titles. Some stock as many as 15,000 titles.

Teacher supply houses and school supply stores.

Often a wide selection is stocked, sometimes at school discount prices.

Children's book publishers.

Catalogs listing new titles, with summaries of contents, are available for the asking.

Teacher resource books.

These books are good sources for finding titles on specific topics or themes. A few teacher, and parent resources are listed next.

Selections of Children's Books

- *A Guide to Nonsexist Children's Books*, Academy Press Ltd., 176 W. Adams Street, Chicago, IL 60603
- *A Parent's Guide to Children's Reading*, by Nancy Larrick, (Doubleday and Co., Inc., 1975)
- *Books Kids Will Sit For*, by Judy Freeman (Alleyside Press, 1984)
- *Bulletin for the Center for Children's Books*, University of Chicago, 5750 Ellis Avenue, Chicago, IL 60637
- *CBC Features* and *Children's Books: Awards and Prizes*, The Children's Book Council, Inc., 67 Irving Place, New York, NY 10003
- *Children's Books of the Year*, Child Study Child's Book Committee, Bank Street College, 610 W. 112th Street, New York, NY 10025
- *Human Values in Children's Books*, Council on Interracial Books for Children, Inc., 1841 Broadway, New York, NY 10023

- *Multiethnic Books for Young Children*, NAEYC Publication Department, 1834 Connecticut Avenue, N.W., Washington, D.C. 20009
- *Notable Children's Books*, Children's Service Division of the American Library Association, 50 East Huron Street, Chicago, IL 60611
- *The Horn Book Magazine*, 585 Boyleston Street, Boston, MA 02116

Resources for Novice Teacher and Authors

The following provide tips on writing and publishing children's books.

- *Writing Books for Children and Young Adults*, The Children's Book Council, Inc., P.O. Box 706, 76 Irving Place, New York, NY 10003, 1985
- *Publishing Children's Books in America, 1919–1976*, The Children's Book Council, Inc., P.O. Box 706, 76 Irving Place, New York, NY 10003, 1987
- Society of Children's Book Writers, P.O. Box 827, Laguna Beach, CA 92652. (An association of children's book authors holding meetings and conferences.)

Book Clubs

Book clubs offer monthly selections of a wide variety of titles. These clubs usually reward schools with free books and teacher gifts that include posters and teaching visuals. Enough order forms for each child's parent are sent on a monthly basis. This offers parents an easy way to order books for their children by having school personnel send and receive orders.

- Firefly, Scholastic Books Clubs, 2931 E. McCarty Street, P.O. Box 7500, Jefferson City, MO 65102
- Grow-With-Me Book Club, Garden City, NY 11530
- I Can Read Book Club, 1250 Fairwood Avenue, Columbus, OH 43216
- Parent's Magazine Read Aloud and Easy Reading Program, Box 161, Bergenfield, NJ 07621
- Weekly Reader Children's Book Club, 1250 Fairwood Avenue, Columbus, OH 43216
- King Cole Book Club, Simon and Schuster, 1 West Thirty-ninth Street, New York, NY 10018
- Buddy Books, Xerox Paperback Book Clubs, Box 1195, Education Center, Columbus, OH 43216

Children's Periodicals

- *Children's Playmate Magazine*, Children's Better Health Institute, Benjamin Franklin Literary and Medical Society, Inc., Indianapolis, IN 46206

- *Highlights for Children*, 2300 West Fifth Avenue, P.O. Box 269, Columbus, Ohio 43216
- *Humpty Dumpty's Magazine*, Children's Better Health Institute, Benjamin Franklin Literary and Medical Society, Inc., Indianapolis, IN 46206
- *Jack & Jill*, P.O. Box 6567 B, Indianapolis, IN 46206
- *Peanut Butter*, Scholastic Home Periodicals, P.O. Box 1925, Marion, Ohio 43302
- *Sesame Street*, P.O. Box 2895, Boulder, Colo. 80321
- *Young World* (formerly Golden Magazine), P.O. Box 6567 B, Indianapolis, IN 46206
- *Your Big Backyard*, National Wildlife Federation, 1412 Sixteenth Street N.W., Washington, D.C. 20036-2266

A helpful reference book that describes and evaluates nearly 90 children's magazines is *Magazines for Children: A Guide for Parents, Teachers and Librarians* by Selma Richardson, published by the American Library Association.

Book Week

The Children's Book Council has sponsored National Children's Book Week since 1945 (1989 marks its seventieth anniversary) to promote reading and encourage children's enjoyment of books. Mobiles, materials, posters, bookmarks, and book-week kits can be ordered from:

The Children's Book Council, Inc.
67 Irving Place, P.O. Box 706
New York, NY 10276-0706

Book Services to Parents

Preschools that have overnight and weekend book borrowing privileges promote book use and home enjoyment of books. Manila folders or envelopes, preprinted with the center's name, protect books in transit. Book pockets and cards are available at stationery or school-supply stores. This service can operate with minimal teacher supervision. Parents can help their children pull cards on selected titles, if they thoroughly understand the school's system and rules for book borrowing.

Favorite Children's Books

Generally, children's favorites become your favorites. There is really only one way to develop your own list. Preview books and then try them with children. Figure 9-12 provides a list of books that are young children's

Brown, Margaret Wise. *The Dead Bird*. New York: Young Scott Books, 1938 and 1965. Deals tenderly with the death of a bird.

Carle, Eric. *The Very Hungry Caterpillar*. Collins World, 1969. The hungry caterpillar eats through the pictures and emerges as a butterfly on the last page.

Chorao, Kay. *Lester's Overnight*. New York: E. P. Dutton, 1977. Family humor in a child's overnight plans and his teddy bear.

Ets, Marie Hall. *Play With Me*. New York: Viking Press, 1955. A lesson to learn on the nature of animals.

Flack, Marjorie. *Ask Mr. Bear*. New York: Macmillan, 1932. The search for just the right birthday present for a loved one.

Freeman, Don. *Beady Bear*. New York: Viking Press, 1954. Meet Beady and his courage, independence, and frailty.

Freeman, Don. *Corduroy*. New York: Viking Press, 1968. The department store teddy who longs for love.

Gag, Wanda. *Millions of Cats*. New York: Coward-McCann, 1928. Word pleasure and magic — a favorite with both teachers and children.

Guilfoile, Elizabeth. *Nobody Listens to Andrew*. New York: Scholastic Book Services, 1957. An "adults often ignore what children say" theme.

Hazen, Barbara Shook. *The Gorilla Did It*. New York: Atheneum Press, 1974. A mother's patience with a fantasizing child. Humorous.

Hoban, Russell. *A Baby Sister for Frances*. New York: Harper and Row, 1964. Frances, "so human," deals with the new arrival.

Hutchins, Pat. *Good-Night Owl!* New York: Macmillan, 1976. Riddled with repetitive dialogue: a delightful tale of bedtime.

Hutchins, P. *Changes, Changes*. New York: Macmillan, 1971. Illustrations of block constructions tell a wordless story of the infinite changes in forms.

Keats, Ezra Jack. *Peter's Chair*. New York: Harper and Row, 1967. A delightful tale of family life.

Kraus, Robert. *Leo the Late Bloomer*. New York: Dutton, 1973. Wonderful color illustrations and a theme that emphasizes individual development.

Kraus, Ruth. *The Carrot Seed*. New York: Harper and Row, 1945. The stick-to-it-tiveness of a child's faith makes this story charming.

Leonni, L. *Little Blue and Little Yellow*. New York: Astor-Honor, 1949. A classic. Collages of torn paper introduce children to surprising color transformations, blended with a story of friendship.

McCloskey, Robert. *Blueberries for Sal*. New York: Viking Press, 1948. The young of the two species meet.

Mosel, Arlene. *Tiki Tiki Tembo*. New York: Holt, Rinehart, and Winston, 1968. A folktale that tickles the tongue in its telling. Repetitive.

Raskin, Ellen. *Nothing Ever Happens on My Block*. New York: Atheneum Press, 1975. The child discovers a multitude of happenings in illustrations.

Scott, Ann Herbert. *On Mother's Lap*. New York: McGraw-Hill, 1972. There's no place like mother's lap!

Schulevitz, Uri. *Rain Rain Rivers*. New York: Farrar, Straus and Giroux, 1969. Illustrative fine art.

Segal, Lore. *Tell Me A Mitzi*. New York: Farrar, 1970. New York city life.

Slobodkina, Esphyr. *Caps for Sale*. New York: William R. Scott, 1947. A tale of a peddler, some monkeys, and their monkey business. Word play and gentle humor.

Turkle, Brinton. *Deep In The Forest*. New York: Dutton, 1976. Interpretation of "Goldilocks and the Three Bears" in an early American setting.

Viorst, Judith. *The Tenth Good Thing About Barney*. New York: Atheneum, 1971. Loss of family pet and positive remembrances.

Viorst, Judith. *Alexander and the Terrible, Horrible, No Good, Very Bad Day*. New York: Atheneum Press, 1976. Everyone relates to the "everything can go wrong" theme.

Zion, Gene. *Harry The Dirty Dog*. New York: Harper and Row, 1956. Poor lost Harry gets so dirty his family doesn't recognize him.

FIGURE 9-12 Favorite children's books — beginner's book list

favorites. Lay-Dopyera and Dopyera (1982) urge beginning teachers to consider the following:

> You can help children learn the value of reading first by getting "hooked" on books yourself and then by developing your repertoire for sharing that enjoyment with children.

Summary

The teacher has certain goals when reading books to young children:

- Promoting child enjoyment and attitude development.
- Acquainting children with quality literature.

- Presenting knowledge.
- Developing children's listening skills.
- Encouraging emerging literacy (figure 9-13).

A careful selection of books makes it easier to reach these goals and gives reading activities a greater chance for success. Books vary widely in content and format. Teachers who are prepared can interact with enthu-siasm by showing their own enjoyment of language; this helps promote the children's language growth.

Good book-reading technique requires study and practice. Professional interaction is crucial to achieving goals and instilling a love of books.

Settings for group times need to be free of distraction, with optimal comfort and lighting. Book care is expected and modeled by teachers.

YOUNGER PRESCHOOLERS (Ages 2 to 3)

- Able to sit and maintain interest while a quality picture book is skillfully read.
- Able to browse through a book from cover to cover.
- Has a favorite book.
- Points to and talks about objects, people, or features of illustrations when in individual reading sessions.
- Can name one book character.
- Brings a book to adults to read.

- Wants to be present at most book-reading times.
- Brings a book to school to share.
- Discusses or acts out story parts at times.
- Handles book gently.
- Enjoys library trips.
- May point to words or letters.
- Wants name on his or her work.

OLDER PRESCHOOLERS (Age 4 to 5)

- Obviously enjoys story times.
- Asks about words.
- Picks out own nametag.
- Knows beginning letters of a few words.
- Wants his or her ideas and comments written down.
- Has favorite books and book characters.
- Can put book events in sequence.
- Realizes books have beginnings, middles, and endings.
- Understands authoring.
- Explains a number of functions of printed words and signs.
- Asks about the names of letters of his or her own name.
- Can tell a book story from memory.
- Handles and cares for books properly.

- Discusses and shares books with others.
- Finds similar letters in different words.
- Knows spaces exist between words.
- Recognizes a few words.
- Tries to decipher words in books.
- Knows stories in books don't change with rereadings.
- Interested in alphabet games, toys, and activities.
- Tries to copy words or letters from books.
- Knows alphabet letters represent sounds.
- Interested in machines or toys that print words or letters.
- Wants to make his or her own book.
- Knows books have titles and authors.
- Creates own stories.

FIGURE 9-13 Emerging literacy indicators

Student Activities

- Select, prepare and present three books to children. Evaluate your strong points and needed areas of growth.

- Read a children's book to two classmates or to a video camera; take turns evaluating the presentations.

- Form two or more groups for a debate. The topic is "Technical reading-skill development during story times — should it take place?" An example of technical reading-skill development activities would include finding similar alphabet letters, phonics, reading sight words, and so on.

- Interview a local librarian concerning the children's book collection and library services.

- Create a self-authored picture book. Share it with a small group of young children. Share results, outcomes, and your feelings with fellow students.

- Visit the local library. Using the form "Analyzing a Children's Book" (figure 9–14), review five books.

- Develop an annotated book list (10 books) using short descriptions, as follows:
  Zion, Gene. *Harry the Dirty Dog*. New York: Harper and Row Publishers, 1956. About a family dog who gets so dirty his family doesn't recognize him.

- Make a list of five nonfiction books that could be used with preschoolers.

- Present a short oral report about Caldecott and Newberry Medal books.

Name_____ Date_____

Name of Book_____

Author_____

Illustrator_____

Story line

1. What is the book's message?_____

_____

_____

2. Does the theme build the child's self-image or self-esteem? How?_____

_____

_____

3. Are male and female or ethnic groups stereotyped?_____

Illustrations

1. Fantasy? True to Life?_____

2 . Do they add to the book's enjoyment?_____

_____

General Considerations

Could you read this book enthusiastically? Why?
How could you involve children in the book? (besides looking and listening)
How could you "categorize" this book? (i.e., fireman, alphabet book, concept development, emotions, and so on)
On a scale of 1–10 (1 — little value to 10 — of great value to young child) rate this book._____

FIGURE 9-14 Form for analyzing a children's book

- Read the following. React by writing a one page discussion.

  "It is the internal struggle to find out how we feel or who we are that is so central to the idea of reading. More than helping them to read better, more than exposing them to good writing, more than developing their imagination, when we read aloud to children we are helping them to find themselves and to discover some meaning in the scheme of things" (Trelease, 1986).

- Design a preschool classroom library center. Include materials and furnishings and show room features such as windows and doors and adjacent activity areas.

- Describe the most skilled person you've observed reading books to children.

- Review three all-time best sellers: *The Tale of Peter Rabbit* by Beatrix Potter; *The Real Mother Goose* published by Rand McNally; and *Pat the Bunny* by Dorothy Kunhardt. Give reasons for the popularity of these books.

Unit Review

A. Read the following comments by a teacher who is reading to children. Select those comments that you feel would help the child accomplish a goal mentioned in this unit.
  1. "Sit down now and stop talking. It's story time."
  2. "Kathy, can you remember how the mouse got out of the trap?"
  3. "What part of this story made you laugh?"
  4. "John, I can't read any more because you've made Lonnie cry by stepping on her hand. Children, story time is over."
  5. "Children, don't look out the window. Look at the book. Children, the book is more interesting than that storm."
  6. "Donald, big boys don't tear book pages."
  7. "Was the dog striped or spotted? If you can't answer, then you weren't listening."
  8. "Mary, of course you liked the story. Everyone did."
  9. "Tell me, Mario, what was the boy's name in our story? I'm going to sit here until you tell me."
  10. "No, the truck wasn't green, Luci. Children, tell Luci what color the truck was."
  11. "Take your thumb out of your mouth, Debbie; it's story time."
  12. "I like the way you all looked at the book and told me what was in each picture."
  13. "One book is enough. We can't sit here all day, you know."
  14. "Children, we have to finish this book before we can go outside. Sit down."
  15. "That book had lots of colorful pictures."
  16. "Well, now we found out who can help us if we ever lose mama in a store."

B. Answer the following questions:
  1. Why is it important for the teacher to read a child's book before it is read to the children?
  2. How can a teacher help children learn how books are used to find answers?
  3. Why should a teacher watch for the young child's reactions to the story while reading it?

C. Select the best phrases in Column II that apply to items in Column I.

Column I	Column II
1. fairy tales	a. before teacher starts reading to the group
2. first step in planned reading	b. when children show interest in a subject
3. arrange setting with comfort in mind	c. a book with violence
4. stop storytelling to discuss it	d. book may not be appropriate for this age level
5. not appropriate for early childhood level	e. may be too frightening
6. children become restless	f. "Tick-tock," said the clock
7. directly quoted conversation	g. teacher reads the book beforehand
8. "And I'll huff and I'll puff and I'll blow your house down"	h. repetition in "The Three Little Pigs"
9. "So they all had a party with cookies and milk." The End.	i. identification
10. "The rabbit is just like me, I can run real fast."	j. a satisfying climax to a story
11. a book should be read and held	k. in an upright position with the front cover showing
12. books are more inviting when stored this way	l. at children's eye level

D. Describe in step-by-step fashion how you would plan and conduct a group story time.

E. Choose the true statements. Each question may have none or more than one true statement.
1. A book's format
   a. is defined by its content.
   b. includes paper weight.
   c. includes size and shape.
   d. can frustrate children.
2. A teacher's goals when sharing books with children can include
   a. to give information.
   b. to promote literacy.
   c. to build attitudes.
   d. to make them aware of print.
   e. to teach listening behavior.
3. Bibliotherapy refers to books that are
   a. nonfiction.
   b. focused on life's happy moments.
   c. helpful in promoting reading skills.
   d. colorful and well illustrated.
   e. written by people with problems.
4. When it comes to different types of books for young children,
   a. most are suitable.
   b. many contain exceptional art.
   c. the fewer words, the greater the enjoyment.
   d. a wide variety exists.
   e. there are more factual than fantasy books published.

5. When preparing to read a picture book to a group of young children, the following was recommended:
    a. Be prepared to dramatize so that children watch you closely.
    b. Skip over old-fashioned words.
    c. Practice until it easily rolls over your tongue.
    d. The larger the audience the more vivid the experience.
    e. Speak in character dialogue, if it's comfortable for you.

F. What types of resources are available to teachers who want books with specific themes for young children? List.

References

Anderson, Richard. "Putting Reading Research Into Practice." Interview With C. H. Goddard. *Instructor* (Oct. 1988): 31–37.

Beaty, Janice J. *Skills for Preschool Teachers*. Columbus, OH: Charles E. Merrill, 1984. (annotated book list, Chapter 6.)

Beck, M. Susan. *Kidspeak*. New York: New American Library, 1982.

Bernstein, Joanne E. *Books To Help Children Cope With Separation and Loss*. New York: R. R. Bowker, 1977.

Bettelheim, Bruno. *The Uses of Enchantment*. New York: Knopf, 1976. (Adds depth to understanding the relationship of basic human needs and desires to stories and literature.)

Bettelheim, Bruno, and Karen Zelan. *On Learning to Read*, New York: Knopf, 1981.

Bos, Bev. "Working the Magic." 2.6. *Pre-K Today*, Scholastic (Jan. 1988): 21–23.

Bulletin of the Center for Children's Books, Chicago: Chicago UP, 1973. (Critiques and reviews of picture books.)

Child Study Children's Book Committee, *Children's Books of the Year*. New York: Bank Street College. (Offers a listing of selected best books in a given year.)

Commission of Reading, "Becoming a Nation of Readers," Washington, DC: Nat'l Institute of Education, 1985.

Coody, Betty. *Using Literature With Young Children*. Dubuque, IA: Brown, 1983. (Full of practical activity ideas.)

Copperman, Paul. *Taking Books to Heart*. Menlo Park, CA: Addison Wesley, 1982.

Dickinson, David K., and Catherine E. Snow. "Interrelationships Among Prereading And Oral Language in Kindergartners From Two Social Classes." *Early Childhood Research Quarterly* 2.1 (March 1987): 1–25.

Fisher, Margery. *Who's Who In Children's Books*. New York: Holt, Rinehart, and Winston, 1975.

Fraiberg, Selma. *Selected Writings of Selma Fraiberg*, Athens, OH: Ohio State UP, 1987.

Freeman, Ruth S. *Children's Picture Books*. New York: Century House, 1967. (A comprehensive discussion of picture books and their value.)

Gertel-Rutman, Shereen. "Arranging the Library Center," 2.6. *Pre-K Today*, Scholastic (Jan. 1988): 23–24.

Glazer, Joan I. *Literature for Young Children*. Columbus, OH: Charles E. Merrill, 1986.

Greene, Allen, and Madalynne Schoenfeld. *A Multimedia Approach to Children's Literature*. Chicago, IL: American Library Association, 1972. (Helps one find interesting ways to introduce books to young children.)

Hoggart, Richard. Volume II *Speaking to Each Other*. London: Chatto and Windus, 1970. (Add insights concerning the use and benefits of books in young children's lives.)

Huck, Charlotte. *Children's Literature in the Elementary School*. New York: Holt, Rinehart and Winston, 1976.

Jaronczyk, Francine. "The Art of Story Time." *First Teacher* 5.11 (Nov. 1984): 18–24.

Lay-Dopyera, Margaret, and John E. Dopyera. *Becoming a Teacher of Young Children*. Lexington, MA: D. C. Heath, 1982.

Lentz, Kathleen A., and Nancy A. Burris. "How To Make Your Own Books." *Childhood Education* 37.5, Journal of ACEI (Jan/Feb. 1985): 199–202.

Lewis, Claudia. *Writing for Children*. New York: Bank Street College, 1976. (A great aid to teachers interested in authoring picture books. Identifies salient features in quality authorship.)

Martinez, Nancy, and Mark Johnson. "Read Aloud To Give Kids The Picture." *San Jose Mercury News*, Sept. 22, 1987. 4L.

Norton, Donna E. *Through the Eyes of a Child*. Columbus, OH: Charles E. Merrill, 1983. (A classic children's literature course textbook with a section devoted to picture-book features. Lists and recommendations.)

Ornstein, R., and D. Sobel. *The Healing Brain*, New York: Simon and Schuster, 1987.

Pines, Maya. "Can A Rock Walk?" *Psychology Today* 39.11 (Nov. 1983): 46–54.

Poltarnees, Welleran. *All Mirrors Are Magic Mirrors*. New York: *The Green Tiger Press*, 1972 (Illustrations and illustrators are the subject matter.)

Sebesta, Sam Leaton, and William J. Iverson. *Literature for Thursday's Child*. San Francisco, CA: Science Research Assoc., Inc., 1975. (Greater depth and understanding of the therapeutic value of literature.)

Self, Frank. "Choosing For Children Under Three." *CBC Features*, The Children's Book Council, Inc. 41.1 (Jan. 1987): 2–3.

Smith, Charles, and Carolyn Foat. *Once Upon a Mind*, North Central Regional Extension Publication, Kansas State University, 1982. (Using books to help children work out life problems.)

Trelease, Jim. *"Why Reading Aloud Makes Learning Fun."* U.S. News and World Report 17 Mar. 1986: 35–36.

UNIT 10

Story Telling

BJECTIVES

After studying this unit, you should be able to

- describe how story telling can help language growth.
- list teacher techniques in story telling.
- demonstrate the ability to create a story that meets suggested criteria.
- describe promotion of child-created stories.

Story telling is a medium that an early childhood teacher can develop and use to increase a child's enjoyment of language. When good stories are told by a skilled storyteller, the child listens intently; mental images may be formed. Story telling enables teachers to share their life experiences and create and tell stories in an individual way.

Breneman and Breneman (1983) offer the following definition of story telling:

> Story telling is the seemingly easy, spontaneous, intimate sharing of a narrative with one or many persons: the storyteller relates, pictures, imagines, builds what happens, and suggests characters, involving him- or herself and listeners in the total story — all manifested through voice and body.

Early childhood teachers recognize the importance of story telling in a full language arts curriculum. Good stories that are well told have fascinated young listeners since ancient times. Chambers (1970) feels that story telling is a form of expressive art.

The art of story telling remains one of the oldest and most effective art forms. It has survived the printing press, the sound recorder and the camera...The oral story, be it aesthetic or pedagogical, has great value. It seems to be a part of the human personality to use it and want it. The art of the storyteller is an important, valuable ingredient in the lives of children. It has been for thousands of years.

In many cultures, oral stories have passed on the customs, accumulated wisdom, traditions, songs, and legends. Story telling is as old as language itself.

The teacher's face, gestures, words, and voice tell the story when books or pictures are not used. Eye contact is held throughout the story-telling period. The child pictures the story in his or her mind as the plot unfolds.

How could one describe skilled storytellers? Sawyer (1969) describes them as gloriously alive, those who live close to the heart of things and have known solitude and silence and have felt deeply. They have come to know the power of the spoken word. Preschool teachers may know silence only at naptimes, but they indeed live close to the heart of young children's forming character and personality and growing intellect.

STORY TELLING AND LITERACY

The promotion of oral literacy is an important consideration for preschool program planners. Oral literacy involves a shared background and knowledge of orally told stories plus a level of competence. Being able to tell a story well depends on a number of factors, including observation of techniques. Natural storytellers, if they exist, are overshadowed by storytellers who have practiced the art. Some adult job hunters find telling a story is a requested part of their job interview and is used to assess intelligence, communication ability, and literacy.

Preschools are sure to offer picture-book readings, but story telling may be neglected. Some teachers shy away from the activity for a variety of reasons, including not being able to hold their child audience. Young children may be so used to illustration and pictures (books and television) that initial story-telling experiences are foreign to them.

Teachers can increase their skills by observing practiced storytellers, taking classes, or self-study. The best suggestion for skill development is starting by relating short, significant happenings in their daily lives — keeping it lively and working with four-year-olds rather than younger children.

As children observe and listen to teacher's story telling, they notice common elements, including beginnings, middles, and story endings. They discover stories vary little between tellers. They imitate techniques using hand and body gesturing, facial expression, and vocal variation; they speak in character dialogue, and they may even copy dramatic pause. They also may attempt to make their audience laugh or add suspense to their stories.

TELLING STORIES WITHOUT BOOKS

Unit 9 described the merits and use of picture books with young children. Story telling without books has its own unique set of enjoyed language pleasures. Story telling is direct, intimate conversation. Story telling is direct, intimate conversation. Arbuthnot (1953) points out the well-told story's power to hold children spellbound (figure 10-1).

It is the intimate, personal quality of story telling as well as the power of the story itself that accom-

FIGURE 10-1 Children listen intently to a good story.

plishes these minor miracles. Yet in order to work this spell, a story must be learned, remembered, and so delightfully told that it catches and holds the attention of the most inveterate wrigglers.

Teachers observe children's reactions. A quizzical look on a child's face can help the teacher know when to clarify or rephrase for understanding. A teacher's voice can increase the story's drama in parts when children are deeply absorbed.

Many people have noted how quickly and easily ideas and new words are grasped through story telling. This is rarely the prime goal of early childhood teachers but rather an additional benefit. Stories are told to acquaint young children with this enjoyable oral language art. Obvious moralizing or attempts to teach facts by using stories usually turns children away.

Story telling may occur at almost any time during the course of the day, inside or outside. No books or props are necessary. Teachers are free to relate stories in their own words and manner. Children show by their actions what parts of the story are of high interest. The storyteller can increase children's enjoyment by emphasizing these features (figure 10-2).

FIGURE 10-2 An enthusiastic storyteller gets interest and delighted response.

GOALS

A teacher's goal is to become a skilled storyteller so he or she can model story-telling skill while providing another avenue to development of oral competence. Another goal is to acquire a repertoire of stories that offer children a variety of experiences.

The teacher's goals include:

- Increasing children's enjoyment of oral language.
- Making young children familiar with oral story telling.
- Encouraging children's story telling and authorship.
- Increasing children's vocabulary.
- Increasing children's confidence as speakers.
- Increasing children's awareness of story sequence and structure.

Story telling is a wonderful way to promote understanding of audience behaviors, and performer behaviors. Teachers experience rewarding feelings when their technique and story combine to produce audience enjoyment and pleasure. Child storytellers gain tremendous insights into the performing arts, their own abilities, and the power of orally related stories. Most reading experts agree that oral competence enhances ease in learning to read and promotes understanding of what is read.

Thoughtful writers have questioned the wisdom of always exposing children to illustrations at story time.

By not allowing children to develop mental images, they feel we have possibly distracted children from attaining personal meaning (Bettelheim, 1976).

USING PICTURE BOOKS FOR STORY TELLING

At times, a picture book is the source for story telling. The teacher later introduces the book and makes it available in the classroom's book center for individual follow-up. Used this way, story telling motivates interest in books.

There are many picture books, however, that do not lend themselves to story-telling form because illustrations are such an integral part of the experience (figure 10-3). Books that have been successfully used as the basis for story telling can be handled in unique ways. Schimmel (1978) relates her story-telling experiences with *Caps for Sale* by Slobodkina:

I like to make it an audience participation story. I shake my fist at the monkeys, and the audience, with only the slightest encouragement, shakes its fists at the peddler.

She recommends the following for use with young children:

The Fat Cat by Jack Kent, New York: Parents Magazine Press, 1971
The Journey, Mouse Tales by Arnold Lobel, New York: Harper & Row Publishers, 1972
The Old Woman and Her Pig, by Paul Galdone, New York: McGraw Hill Book Company, 1961
The Three Billy Goats Gruff by P. C. Asbjornsen, New York: Harcourt, Brace, Jovanovich, Inc., 1972

Another story suggested for the beginning storyteller is *The Story of Ferdinand* by Munro Leaf (New York: Viking Press, 1936).

SOURCES FOR STORIES

A story idea can be found in collections, anthologies, resource books, children's magazines, films, story records, or from another storyteller. A story idea can also be self-created.

A teacher-created story can fill a void. In any group of young children there are special interests and

FIGURE 10-3 Some picture books cannot be used as sources for oral story telling.

problems. Stories can expand interest and give children more information on a subject. Problems can possibly be solved by the stories and conversations that take place.

New teachers may not yet have confidence in their story-telling abilities, so learning some basic techniques for selecting, creating, and telling stories can help build confidence. This, together with the experience gained by presenting the stories to children, should convince the teacher that story telling is enjoyable for preschoolers and rewarding to the teacher.

SELECTION

The selection of a story is as important as the selection of a book, since stories seem to have individual personalities. Searching for a story that appeals to the teller and can be eagerly shared is well worth the time. A few well-chosen and prepared stories suiting the individual teacher almost insures a successful experience for all. The following selection criteria are commonly used:

Age-level appropriateness.

Is the story told in simple, easily understood words? Is it familiar in light of the child's life experiences? Is it frightening? Can the child profit from traits of the characters?

Plot.

Does the setting create a stage for what is to come? Is there action? Is there something of interest to resolve? Does the story begin with some action or event? Does it build to a climax with some suspense? Does it have a timely, satisfying conclusion? Are characters introduced as they appear?

The stories you'll be searching for will have one central plot; a secondary plot may confuse children. Action-packed stories where one event successfully builds to another holds audience attention.

Style.

Does the story use repetition, rhyme, or silly words? Does it have a surprise ending? Does it include directly quoted conversations or child involvement with speaking or movements? Does the mood help the plot develop?

Values.

Are values and models presented that are appropriate for today's children? Screen for ethnic, cultural, and gender stereotypes.

Memorable characters.

Look for a small number of colorful characters who are distinct entities that are in contrast to the main character and each other. One should be able to identify and recognize character traits.

Sensory and visual images.

The visual and sensory images evoked by stories add interest. "Gingerbread cookies, warm and golden" rather than "cookie" and the "velvet soft fur" rather than "fur" create different mental images. Taste, smell, sight, sound, and tactile descriptions create richness and depth.

Additional selection criteria.

Elements that make stories strong candidates include:

- An economy of words — a polished quality.
- A universal truth.
- Suspense and surprise.

Themes and story structure.

Many well-known and loved stories concern a problem that is insightfully solved by the main character. They begin by introducing a setting, and characters and have a body of events that moves the story forward to a quick, satisfying conclusion. The story line is strong, clear, and logical.

Storyteller enthusiasm.

Is the story well liked by the teller? Does the teller feel comfortable with it? Is it a story the teller will be eager to share?

Finding a story you love may make it easier for the child to enjoy the story you tell:

The easiest door to open for a child, is one that leads to something you love yourself. All good teachers know this. And all good teachers know the ultimate reward: the marvelous moment when the spark you are breathing bursts into a flame that henceforth will burn brightly on its own (Gordon, 1987).

TYPES OF STORIES

Some stories, particularly folktales and fairy tales, have been polished to near perfection through generations of use. Classic tales and folktales may contain dated words and phrases, but these might be important story parts that add to the story's charm. In retelling the story to young children, a brief explanation of these types of terms may be necessary.

Bettelheim (1986) points out that fairy tales may be unique literature. He feels "fairy tales unlike any other forms of literature, direct the child to discover his identity and calling, and they also suggest what experiences are needed to develop his character further." Fairy tales need careful screening before they are told to preschoolers; many contain violence, complicated plots, and unsuitable features.

Fables are simple stories in which animals frequently point out lessons (morals), which are contained in the fable's last line.

Many great stories seem to have opportunities for active child participation and the use of props. Props, such as pictures, costumes and other objects, may spark and hold interest. A cowboy hat worn by the teacher during the telling of a western tale may add to the mood and can later be worn by children in play or during a child's attempt at story telling.

Repetitive phrases or word rhythms are used in all types of stories, and chanting or singing may be necessary in the telling. Most stories have problems to be solved through the ingenuity of the main character. This sequence can be explored in teacher's self-created stories.

Story Ideas

Teachers often begin by telling stories from classic printed sources.

Classic Tales

Goldilocks and the Three Bears
Little Red Riding Hood
The Three Little Pigs
Billy Goats Gruff
The Little Red Hen
The Gingerbread Boy

From Aesop's Fables

The Lion and the Mouse
The Hare and the Tortoise
The Ant and the Grasshopper

Traditional Stories

Hans Christian Anderson, *Ugly Duckling*
Arlene Mosel, *Tiki, Ticki Tembo*
Florence Heide, *Sebastian*
Beatrix Potter, *Peter Rabbit*

PRACTICE AND PREPARATION

When a teacher has selected a story, a few careful readings are in order. Try to determine the story's main message and meaning. Next, look closely at the introduction that describes the setting and characters. Study figure 10-4 and analyze how the selected story fits this pattern. The initial setting often sets up a problem or dilemma. The story can be outlined on a 4″ × 6″ (or larger) cue card to jog your memory during practice sessions (see figure 10-5). Memorizing beginning and ending lines and interior chants or songs is suggested.

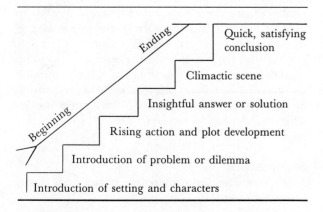

FIGURE 10-4 Common and classic story pattern form.

Intro. "Once upon a time, there were four little rabbits, Flopsy, Mopsy, Cottontail, and Peter. They lived with their mother in a sand-bank, underneath the root of a very big fir tree."

Theme. Mind your mother.

Problem. Peter disobeys and goes into McGregor's garden.

Rising action.
Peter squeezes under garden gate and eats a lot.
McGregor sees him.
McGregor chases him, and he loses a shoe.
Peter gets caught in a gooseberry net and loses his jacket.
Peter hides in the tool shed in a can full of water.
Peter sneezes, almost gets caught, but jumps out a window.
Peter cries and sees cat (another danger).
Peter makes a dash for the gate and gets free.
Gets home without clothes and shoes, goes to sleep, and misses dinner. Mother serves Peter tea.

Ending lines
"But Flopsy, Mopsy, and Cottontail had bread and milk and blackberries for supper. And that's the end of the Tale of Peter Rabbit!"

FIGURE 10-5 Cue and file card example.

Once the story rolls out effortlessly, practice dialogue, pauses, gesturing, and facial expressions. Particular attention should be given to the rising action in the story's body so that one event builds on another until a quick, satisfying conclusion is reached.

Additional Techniques

The following techniques and tips should be kept in mind:

- Guard against sounding mechanical. Tell the story in your own personal way.
- Become familiar with the key ideas. Know the key happenings and their order of appearance in the story.
- Practice before a mirror or with another staff member.
- Enjoy and live the story as you tell it in your own words. Use gestures.
- Maintain eye contact by scanning the group during the telling; watch for children's interest or restlessness.

- Pace the story telling by going faster during exciting or fast-action parts and slower in serious parts.
- Use a clear, firm voice. Try changing voice volume and tone to fit the story; in some parts of the story a whisper may be most effective. Change your voice to fit the characters when they speak.
- Make gestures natural complements of the story (large and descriptive for younger children).
- Involve the children often, especially with repetitions, rhymes or actions, silly words, or appropriate questions, if the story lends itself to this.
- Sit close to the group; make sure all are comfortable before beginning.
- Include children's names and familiar places in the community to clarify meanings or add interest in teacher-created stories.
- Start by telling little personal stories about your family, pets, and daily happenings, if you're a novice; then move on to simple stories with lots of repetition.
- Investigate the cultural backgrounds of children in your care and see if you can find stories that reflect these backgrounds (Leone, 1986).
- Seek out talented storytellers in your community to observe your story telling or to appear as guest storytellers in your classroom.
- Become very familiar with any pronunciations, including proper names and foreign or unfamiliar terms in stories.
- Use dramatic pauses to build suspense, after an exclamation, or to facilitate transitions between story events.
- Try to communicate characters' attitudes and motivations.
- Use a different tone of voice for dialogue only if you feel comfortable doing so.

Even the best storytellers have an occasional flop. If the storyteller senses that the children are restless, the story may be ended very quickly and tried at a later time, using a revised version.

Teacher-created Stories

Many teachers find that they have a talent for creating stories and find that a popular character in one story can have further adventures in the next. Don't forget that "bad guys" in stories are enjoyed as much as "good guys." Having a problem that needs to be resolved serves as the basis for many well known classics.

Whenever a teacher cannot find a story that seems tailor-made for a particular group of children, he or she can create a story. As teachers use their own stories, they tend to cut and add to them based on the reactions of the children. Take care that themes do not always revolve around "mother knows best" episodes, and watch for sexism and stereotypes when creating a story.

Child-created Stories

Encouraging child authorship and child story telling goes hand-in-hand with teacher story telling. It is an excellent way to develop fluency and elaborated language usage (Hough, Nurss, Wood, 1987). One suggestion is to offer activities in which pictures or props are used as motivators (figure 10-6). Children's attempts aren't edited or criticized but simply

FIGURE 10-6 A visiting small animal might promote child story telling.

accepted. Logic should not be questioned, nor should the sequence of events be corrected. Each story is special. If recorded or dictated, the story should be taken verbatim. Some teachers initiate discussions that allow the children to tell what they liked best about a story to alert children to desirable story features. Egg timers may be useful if rambling, long-winded children leave little time for others. Asking for child volunteers to retell stories to other children works in some programs; an announcement may be made that Mark or Susie will be sitting in the storyteller's chair after snack. Teachers tactfully remind children before the volunteer starts his or her story that questions or comments will be saved until the story is over. An adjacent box of story telling props may help a child get in character.

Clipboards can be used to list the stories that are created throughout the day. The creation of stories is given status, and sharing these stories is a daily occurrence. Sharing takes place with the child's permission, and the child chooses whether he or she or the teacher will present the story to the group.

Children's first story-telling attempts often lack sequence, have unclear plots, ramble, and involve long, disconnected events; as children mature and are exposed to stories and books, authorship improves. The goal is not to produce child storytellers but to encourage a love for and positive attitudes toward oral story telling.

SUGGESTED STORIES

The following stories are suggested for the beginning storyteller.

The Little House with No Doors and No Windows and a Star Inside
Author Unknown

(Plan to have an apple, cutting board, and a knife ready for the ending (figure 10-7). A plate full of apple slices is sometimes enjoyed after this story.)

Once there was a little boy who had played almost all day. He had played with all his toys and all the games he knew, and he could not think of anything else to do. So he went to his mother and asked, "Mother, what shall I do now?"

FIGURE 10-7 "This is the little red house with the star inside. Do you see the star?"

His mother said, "I know about a little red house with no doors and no windows and a star inside. You can find it, if you go look for it."

So the little boy went outside and there he met a little girl. He said, "Do you know where there is a little red house with no doors and no windows and a star inside?"

The little girl said, "No, I don't know where there is a little red house with no doors and no windows and a star inside, but you can ask my daddy. He is a farmer and he knows lots of things. He's down by the barn and maybe he can help you."

So the little boy went to the farmer down by the barn and said, "Do you know where there is a little red house with no doors and no windows and a star inside?"

"No," said the farmer, "I don't know, but why don't you ask Grandmother. She is in her house up on the hill. She is very wise and knows many things. Maybe she can help you."

So the little boy went up the hill to Grandmother's and asked, "Do you know where there is a little red house with no doors and no windows and a star inside?" "No," said Grandmother, "I don't know, but you ask the wind, for the wind goes everywhere, and I am sure he can help you."

So the little boy went outside and asked the wind, "Do you know where I can find a little red house with no doors and no windows and a star inside?" And the wind said, "OHHHH! OOOOOOOOOOOO!" And it sounded to the little boy as if the wind said, "Come with me." So the little boy ran after the wind. He ran through the grass and into the orchard and there on the ground he found the little house — the little red house with no doors and no windows and a star inside! He picked it up, and it filled both his hands. He ran home to his mother and said, "Look, Mother! I found the little red house with no doors and no windows, but I cannot see the star!"

So this is what his mother did (teacher cuts apple). "Now I see the star!" said the little boy. (Teacher says to children) "Do you?"

Laughing Stock and Gastly

Sister Carol Bettencourt
(while an ECE student)

There was a family of elephants that lived in the jungle. There were very large mama and papa elephants and smaller baby elephants. They were all the color gray — all except one — his name was Laughing Stock. He got his name because all the other elephants had never seen an elephant the color of Laughing Stock. He was the color orange! Have you ever seen an orange elephant? Poor Laughing Stock; everyone made fun of him because he was so different.

In the same jungle lived a family of giraffes. Oh, they were so tall and so nice looking with their yellow and brown bodies! One day, Laughing Stock was going for a walk when he saw the giraffes eating the leaves right from the top of the trees — those giraffes certainly were tall.

"Hi, giraffes!" said Laughing Stock. "Hi, elephant!" said the giraffes. "Say, elephant," shouted one of the giraffes. "You don't look like an elephant. Your body is the color orange." Then all the giraffes started to laugh. Poor Laughing Stock. One of the giraffes, still laughing loudly, said "You and Gastly would make a fine pair!" "Who's Gastly?" asked the elephant. "I am," said a quiet little voice. Laughing Stock looked around but didn't see anyone except for the giraffes. Then, he saw something move and Laughing Stock looked closely into the green bushes. "Wha wha wha wha you you. . . ?" (Poor Laughing Stock was having a hard time making the words come out.) "You're green! I've I've I've never seen a green giraffe before!" "Neither have we," laughed the other giraffes. "Oh, but I think you're pretty," said Laughing Stock. "You do?" said Gastly. "Thank you, no one ever said that to me before." "You're welcome," smiled Laughing Stock, and right away they became good friends and each one helped the other. And because they were friends, it didn't hurt so much when others laughed at them, because they had someone who liked them just the way they were.

*   *   *   *   *

This story leads well into discussions about colors. Ask the children if they can find something in the room the same color as Laughing Stock or the same color as Gastly. This story also leads into a discussion about likenesses and differences:

- Is your hair the same color as one of your friends?
- Can you think of something that makes you different?

The Pancake Who Ran Away

(a folktale)

Once upon a time there was a mother who had seven hungry children. She made a delicious light and fluffy golden pancake.

"I'm hungry," said one child. "I want some pancake."

Then all the other children said the same thing, and the mother had to cover her ears because they were so loud.

"Hush, Shush!" said the mother. "You can all have some as soon as the pancake is golden brown on both sides."

Now the pancake was listening and did not want to be eaten, so it hopped from the pan and rolled out the door and down the hill.

"Stop, pancake!" called the mother. She and all her children ran after the pancake as fast as they could. The pancake rolled on and on.

When it rolled a long way, it met a man.

"Good morning, pancake," said the man.

"Good morning Mandy-Pandy-Man!" said the pancake.

"Don't roll so fast. Stop and let me eat you," said the man.

"I've run away from the mother and seven hungry children and I'll run away from you Mandy-Pandy-Man." It rolled and rolled down the road until it met a hen clucking and hurrying along.

"Good morning, pancake," said the hen.

"The same to you, Henny-Fenny-Hen."

"Pancake don't roll so fast, stop and let me eat you," said the hen.

"No, no," said the pancake. "I've run away from the mother and the seven hungry children, Mandy-Pandy-Man, and I'll run away from you." And it rolled on and on.

It met a rooster.

"Good morning, pancake," said the rooster.

"The same to you, Rooster-Zooster," said the pancake.

"Stop so I can eat you," said the rooster.

"I've run away from the mother and the seven hungry children, Mandy-Pandy-Man, Henny-Fenny-Hen, and I'll run away from you," said the pancake. And it rolled on and on until it met a duck.

"Good morning, pancake," said the duck.

"The same to you, Quacky Duck," said the pancake.

"Stop so I can eat you," said the duck.

"I've run away from the mother and the seven hungry children, Mandy-Pandy-Man, Henny-Fenny-Hen, Rooster-Zooster, and I'll run away from you," said the pancake. And on and on it rolled until it met a goose.

"Good morning, pancake," said the goose.

"The same to you, Goosey-Loosey," said the pancake.

"Stop so I can eat you," said the goose.

"I've run away from the mother and the seven hungry children, Mandy-Pandy-Man, Henny-Fenny-Hen, Rooster-Zooster, Quacky Duck, and I'll run away

from you." And on and on it rolled until it met a pig at the edge of a dark wood.

"Good morning, pancake," said the pig.

"The same to you Piggy-Wiggy," said the pancake.

"That wood is dark, don't be in such a hurry! We can go through the wood together. It's not safe in there," said the pig.

The pancake thought that was a good idea, so they went along together until they came to a river. The pig was so fat he could float across, but the pancake had no way of crossing.

"Jump on my snout," said the pig, "and I'll carry you across." So the pancake did that. "Oink!" said the pig as he opened his mouth wide and swallowed the pancake in one gulp. And that's how it was... pancakes are for eating, and the pig had his breakfast.

A Lump the Shape of a Hump

Maxwell woke up one bright morning, and saw a brown bird walking on his window sill, and that's not ALL he saw! There was a lump the shape of a hump under the covers at the foot of his bed. Maxwell squeezed against the headboard, folded up his knees, and stared at the lump the shape of a hump. "It's Bellflower the Beagle, my dog," Maxwell thought, but Bellflower bounded into the bedroom and barked at the lump the shape of a hump at the foot of the bed. "It's Tootie, my brother," he thought, but Tootie came into the bedroom and blew his horn, toot-toot at the lump the shape of a hump at the foot of the bed. "Must be Bubbles, my baby sister," Maxwell said to himself, but just then Bubbles crawled into his room. "Maybe it's Toady, my best friend," Maxwell thought, but then he remembered Toady (who was called Toady because he loved to play leapfrog) had gone to visit his grandmother. "What's that lump the shape of a hump?" Maxwell's dad said as he walked into the bedroom. "I think it's my pillow," Maxwell said, but they both saw Maxwell's pillow on the floor. "My teddy?" Maxwell said. "Nope," said Maxwell's dad, "Teddy's sitting over there in the chair."

Just then the lump wiggled. It shook from side to side. Tootie blew his horn. Bellflower barked. Maxwell squeezed against the headboard afraid to move. "There is something strange going on here!" Maxwell's dad said.

Then the lump made a sound like a croak. Maxwell grabbed the covers and pulled and pulled. There was Toady all doubled up ready to play leapfrog, and he was laughing and croaking. "Grandma was sick, so I sneaked into your bed," Toady said. "Let's play leapfrog!" So they did. Maxwell, Tootie, Bellflower, and Toady played leapfrog while Dad and Bubbles watched.

The Fox and the Sack

(traditional)

One day a fox, who was very hungry caught a large yellow and black bumblebee. "That's not big enough for my dinner," he said as he popped it into a sack and tied it with a string. At the first house he came to he asked the farmer's wife, "May I leave my sack here while I go to town?" "Yes," said the woman. "Don't open the sack," cautioned the fox.

As soon as he was gone, the woman began to wonder what was in the sack. "I'll tie it right back up, after I take a peek," she said.

The moment the sack was open the bumblebee flew out and a rooster swallowed it. After a while, the fox came back. He took the sack and knew the bumblebee was gone. So he said with a growl, "Where is my bumblebee?" "I untied the string," she answered, "just to take a little peek, and the bumblebee flew out and the rooster ate him."

"I must have the rooster, then," said the fox. So he caught the rooster and put him in his sack, tied it with string, and went to the next house.

"May I leave my sack here while I go to town?" asked the fox. The woman of the house answered, "Yes." "Don't open the sack," the fox told her as he hurried off.

As soon as he was out of sight, the woman began to wonder what was in the bag. "Just one peek can't do any harm," she said to herself. When she untied the string the rooster flew out, and the pig caught him and ate him. The fox came back, and when he picked up his sack, he knew at once the rooster was gone. "Where is my rooster?" he demanded with a growl. The woman said, "I only wanted a tiny peek. The rooster flew out and my pig ate him." "Then I must have the pig." So he caught the pig, put him in the sack, tied it with string, and left.

Now the fox was hungry and the pig was fat and juicy, but the fox thought, "This is going so well. I started with a bumblebee, and now I have a juicy pig. Maybe at the next house I'll get something bigger and better." So he knocked at the door of the next house. "May I leave my sack while I go to town?" he said to the woman. "Yes," she answered. "Don't open the sack," the fox told her and left.

As soon as the fox was out of sight the woman wondered what was in the sack. "It will do no harm to take a peek," she said untying the string. The pig squealed and jumped out of the sack, and the woman's hungry big bulldog bit it in a flash. The woman tried to get the pig from the dog. She hit it on the head, but she was too late. The dog had already eaten the pig. "What to do?" she thought. "This bulldog is very mean and doesn't obey so he will go in the sack." She put the bulldog, who had been knocked senseless by her broom, into the sack and tied it with string. Then the fox returned. "Where is my sack?" the fox growled. "Right there where you left it," she answered. When he picked it up, it felt heavy, as if the pig was still inside, so without a thank you the fox left. "Good riddance," thought the woman. Now the sack was heavy and there wasn't another house in sight. The fox was hungry and the sack was wiggling. The fox said to himself, "I haven't had anything to eat all day. I'll stop and see how this juicy pig tastes." He put down the sack and carefully untied the string, and reached inside. "Yowl...Ouch," the fox said when the bulldog bit him. "Growl...Grrr...grrr," said the bulldog jumping out of the sack. The fox ran, and the bulldog ran after him. No one knows if the fox was caught by the bulldog, but the fox was never seen again in that farmland.

Participation Stories

Just Like Metoo!

(Children imitate what Metoo does. Metoo does things a little faster each day. Metoo was always late for school. Speedee was always on time.)

Once upon a time, Metoo came to live at Speedee's house. He thought "I'd like to do what Speedee does, but I can't learn everything at one time. Each day I'll do one new thing."

On Monday, when the alarm went off, Metoo jumped out of bed just like Speedee and washed his hands and face at 7:30 in the morning. (Jump up, wash hands and face. Sit down.)

On Tuesday, when the alarm went off, Metoo jumped out of bed and washed his hands and face and brushed his teeth at 7:30 in the morning. (Jump up, wash hands and face, brush teeth. Sit down.)

On Wednesday, when the alarm went off, Metoo jumped out of bed just like Speedee and washed his hands and face, brushed his teeth, and dressed himself at 7:30 in the morning. (Jump up, wash hands and face, brush teeth, dress self, sit down.)

On Thursday, when the alarm went off, Metoo jumped out of bed just like Speedee, washed his hands and face, brushed his teeth, dressed himself, and ate his breakfast at 7:30 in the morning. (Jump up, wash hands and face, brush teeth, dress self, eat breakfast, sit down.)

On Friday, when the alarm went off, Metoo jumped out of bed, just like Speedee, washed his hands and face, brushed his teeth, dressed himself, ate his breakfast, and waved goodbye to Speedee's mother who was on her way to work at 7:30 in the morning. (Very rapidly, jump up, wash hands and face, brush teeth, dress self, eat breakfast, wave goodbye, sit down.) Speedee and Metoo walked to school together. Metoo wasn't late for school!

On Saturday, when the alarm went off, Metoo turned over and shut it off. (Move right arm across body slowly, as if shutting off alarm.) He had heard Speedee say, "This is Saturday. Nobody goes to school on Saturday."

To Grandmother's House

(Before beginning this story, draw the picture in figure 10-8 on the chalkboard or on a large sheet of paper. During the telling let your finger show Clementine's travels.)

One day Clementine's mother said, "I'm making cookies. I need some sugar. Please go to Grandma's house and borrow a cup of sugar." "Yes, Mother, I'll go right away," said Clementine.

Clementine climbed up the first mountain. Climb, climb, climb. (Make climbing motions with arms.) Climb, climb, climb.

When she got to the top of the mountain she slid down. (Make sliding motion with hands.)

At the bottom of the mountain was a wide, wide lake. Clementine jumped in and swam across. Swim, swim, swim. (Make swimming arm motions.)

Clementine climbed the next mountain. Climb, climb, climb. (Make climbing hand motions.) Then she slid down the other side. (Make sliding motions.)

Next, Clementine crossed the bridge. Tromp, tromp, tromp. (Make feet move up and down.) Tromp, tromp, tromp.

Clementine climbed the third mountain. Climb, climb, climb. (motions) Then she slid down the other side. (motions)

Clementine's grandmother was standing next to her house. "Hello, Grandmother, may I have a cup of sugar? My mother's making cookies." "Yes, dear," said Grandmother, and she came out of the house with a little bag.

"Goodbye, Grandmother," Clementine said. Climb, climb, climb. She slid down the other side and crossed the bridge. Tromp, tromp, tromp. She climbed the middle mountain. Climb, climb, climb (motions). Then she slid down the other side (motions). She swam the lake with the bag in her teeth and her head held high. Swim, swim, swim (motions). Next, she climbed

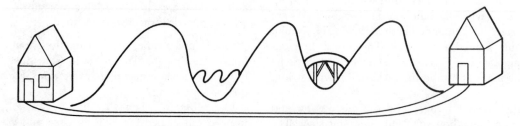

FIGURE 10-8 Clementine's travels

the mountain. Climb, climb, climb (motions). Then she slid down the mountain (motions) to her house.

When she went into the house, she gave her mother the sugar. Her mother said, "This is brown sugar. I wanted white sugar." "I'll go to Grandmother's," said Clementine.

Clementine climbed the first mountain. Climb, climb, climb (motions). She slid down the other side (motions). Then she swam the lake. Swim, swim, swim (motions).

She climbed the second mountain. Climb, climb, climb (motions). She slid down the other side (motions) and crossed the bridge. Tromp, tromp, tromp (motions).

She climbed the third mountain. Climb, climb, climb (motions). Then she slid down the other side (motions).

Grandmother was working in her garden. "Hello, Grandmother," said Clementine. "Two visits in one day. How nice," said Grandmother.

"But I can't stay this time either. Mother needs white sugar instead of brown," said Clementine.

Grandmother went into her house and came out with a little bag.

"You look so tired, Clementine!" said Grandmother.

"I am," said Clementine.

"Take the shortcut home," said Grandmother.

So Clementine did. She walked straight home on the path at the foot of the mountains.

This story can be lengthened by having the mother request additional ingredients and by Clementine taking cookies to Grandmother after they are baked.

He's a Hat, No He's a Boat, No He's Supershirt

Once there was a hat, a sailor's hat, and the hat could talk! "I don't want to be a hat. I want to be a boat." So the hat folded up like this (see figure 10-9 and fold to position 2), and did become a boat sailing in the sea. Everything was going just fine until the boat hit a rock, and the front was torn off (tear off as in number 3). Then a big whale took a bite out of the other end of the boat (tear off as in number 4). A giant wave hit the top of the boat pulling away part of the boat's cabin (5). What was left of the boat drifted to shore. A bird saw it laying there in the sand. "Hey, you don't look like a boat, or a hat! Know what you are? You're a_____SHIRT!" (Then unfold and hold up (6).)

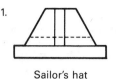

1.

Sailor's hat

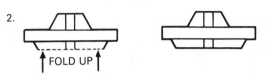

2.

FOLD UP

Folding a hat to look like a boat.

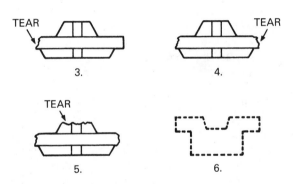

TEAR

3.

TEAR

4.

TEAR

5.

6.

FIGURE 10-9 Tearing parts of the hat to resemble the damaged boat.

What Was Behind the Door?

Dog — "Bow Wow"	Bird — "Peep Peep"
Cat — "Meow"	Lion — "Grrrr"

(Teacher says the following to children: "I need you to help me tell this story! Do you suppose that you can remember all of the sounds that we have talked about? In this story, you can make the animal noises that Granny hears. When the story says, Granny heard a dog, say, 'Bow Wow!' (and so on). Listen carefully."

Granny sat in a big armchair knitting Tommy a sweater. All of a sudden she heard a dog say "_____" (Bow Wow).

"Gracious!" said Granny. "I do believe there's a dog behind the door. Should I have a dog in the house?"

"Oh yes," answered the dog behind the door. "I'm a good dog. I don't jump on people."

"Very well," said Granny, and she went on knitting the sweater for Tommy. All of a sudden Granny heard a cat say "_____" (Meow).

"Gracious!" said Granny. "I do believe that there is a cat behind the door. Should I have a cat in the house?"

"Oh yes," answered the cat. "I am a good cat. I do not scratch the furniture."

"Very well," said Granny, and she went on knitting Tommy's sweater. All of a sudden Granny heard a bird say "_____" (Peep Peep).

"Gracious!" said Granny. "I do believe that I heard a bird behind the door. Should I have a bird in the house?"

"Oh yes," answered the bird. "I am a good bird. I sing very sweetly."

"Very well," said Granny, and she went right on knitting a sweater for Tommy.

All of a sudden, Granny heard a lion say "_____" (Grrrr).

"Gracious!" said Granny. "I do believe that there is a lion behind the door. This is too much!" Carefully, Granny opened up the door, because she wasn't sure she liked having a lion in the house.

And what do you think she found hiding behind her door? There was Tommy. He had been making those noises after all!

Suggest: "Can you all make the noises Tommy made?"

Dog = Bow Wow
Cat = Meow
Bird = Peep Peep
Lion = Grrrr

"What other animal sounds do you know?" (Additional stories are included in the Appendix.)

Summary

Teachers offer orally told stories to promote literacy and encourage children's language enjoyment and development of oral abilities.

One goal of story telling is achieving a feeling of togetherness and enjoyment through the words of a story. Building listening skills, vocabulary development, and expanding interest are other important goals.

Stories for story telling can be found in printed sources or borrowed from other teachers. A story can also be created by the teacher. By following suggested techniques and criteria, a successful activity for both children and teachers is possible.

Stories are told in the teacher's own words with key events clearly in mind. Watching the children's interest and reactions keeps the teacher aware of how well the experience is accepted. Any skill takes practice; story-telling skills improve with use.

Teachers promote child story telling by encouraging children and recognizing their efforts.

Student Activities

- Create a story. In outline form, write the beginning, middle and ending. Practice telling it to a fellow student. Use your own title or select one of the following:
    The Giant Ice Cream Cone
    Magic Shoes
    The Dog Who Wouldn't Bark
    Billy Found a Dollar
    The Big Birthday Present
    The Mouse Who Chased Cats
    The Police Officer and Mike
    The Fastest Bike
    I've Got a Bug in My Pocket

- Tell a story to a group of children. Write an evaluation of both the story and your skill.
    a. What parts interested the children the most?
    b. What would you change if you told it again?
    c. What techniques were used to hold interest?

- Find an ethnic story that could be told to young children. Cite your source and be ready to share the story with fellow classmates.

- Design an evaluation (rating form) to assess a storyteller's skill.

- Invite a librarian or experienced teacher who tells stories during story hours to share favorite stories with the class.

- Tell a story and have it recorded on videotape. Play it back. Look for strong points and areas for growth in skill.

- Listen to a commercial story-telling record. List the techniques used to hold children's interest.

- Create a story in which the children's names for a particular class are woven into the story. Share with children, and share children's reactions with your fellow students.

- List important reasons for teacher story telling.

- Discuss how you would provide for child story telling in your classroom.

- Using the cue card example (figure 10-5), tell a fellow student *The Tale of Peter Rabbit*.

Unit Review

A. Column I lists common preschool characteristics. Select the appropriate story-telling technique or criteria from Column II that matches each item in Column I.

Column I	**Column II**
1. likes to move frequently	a. selects stories without cruel monsters or vivid descriptions of accidents
2. has had experiences at home, school, and in community	b. "Ducky-Ducky and Be-Bop-Boo went to the park to meet Moo-moo the cow"
3. has fear of large animals and bodily harm	c. stories contain familiar objects and animals
4. likes play with words	d. "What did big bird say to baby bird?"
5. likes to be part of the group	e. "Help Tipper blow out the candle. Pretend my finger is a candle and try to blow it out!"
6. likes to talk	f. "Stand up and reach for the moon like Johnny did. Now close your eyes; is it dark like night? You couldn't reach the moon, but can you find your nose with your eyes closed?"

B. Briefly answer the following questions.
   1. Why should story telling take place often in early childhood centers?
   2. Name three resources for stories.
   3. What are stereotypes?

C. Select the correct answers. Each item has more than one correct answer.
   1. In story telling, the storyteller not only uses words but also uses
      a. the hands.
      b. the face.
      c. the eyes.
      d. gestures.
   2. Recommended techniques used by storytellers are
      a. changing the voice to fit the character.
      b. changing the personality of a character during the story.
      c. stopping without ending a story so that children will listen quietly the next time.
      d. watching children closely and emphasizing the parts they enjoy.
   3. Criteria for story selection includes
      a. believable characters.
      b. a plot with lots of action.
      c. a possible problem to be resolved.
      d. making sure the story is one that can be memorized.
   4. Teachers should not
      a. let children be inattentive during their story.
      b. feel defeated if a story occasionally flops.
      c. put bad guys in stories.
      d. tell the story word for word.
   5. During story-telling time, the
      a. child can form his or her own mental pictures.
      b. teacher can share interesting personal life experiences.
      c. teacher models correct speech.
      d. teacher models creative use of words.

D. Write a paragraph or two describing appropriate teacher reactions to child-created stories.

References

Arbuthnot, May Hill. *The Arbuthnot Anthology*. Glenview, IL: Scott, Foresman, 1953. (A collection of children's literature with many classic stories included.)

Bailey, Carolyn, and Clara Lewis. *For the Children's Hour*. New York: Platt and Munk, 1943. (Suggested activities and stories for group times.)

Baker, A., and E. Greene. *Story Telling: Art and Technique*. New York: Bowker, 1982.

Bettelheim, Bruno. *The Uses of Enchantment*. New York: Knopf, 1976.

Breneman, Lucille N., and Bren Breneman. *Once Upon a Time*. Chicago, IL: Nelson-Hall, 1983.

Chambers, Dewey W. *Story Telling and Creative Drama*. Dubuque, IA: Brown, 1970. (Helps one develop technique.)

Gordon, Arthur. *A Touch of Wonder*. Old Tappan, NJ: Revell, 1984.

Hough, Ruth A., Joanne R. Nurss, and Dolores Wood. "Tell Me a Story." *Young Children* 43.1 (Nov. 1987): 71–75.

Leone, Anne H. "Story Telling." *First Teacher* 7.5 (May 1986): 41–46.

Moore, Vadine. *Preschool Story Hour*. Metuchen, NJ: Scarecrow Press, 1972. (Lots of ideas for story-telling times.)

National Catalog of Story Telling Resources, NAPPS (National Society for Preservation and Protection of Story Telling), National Story Telling Resource Center, P.O. Box 112, Jonesborough, Tennessee 37659.

Pellowski, Anne. *The World of Story Telling*. New York: Bowker, 1977.

Sawyer, Dorothy. *The Way of the Storyteller*. New York: Viking, 1969. (One of the best known and studied references on story-telling technique.)

Schimmel, Nancy. *Just Enough to Make a Story*. Berkeley: Sister's Choice Press, 1978. (A practical guide for beginners; includes stories.)

Shedlock, Marie. *The Art of Story Telling*. New York: Appleton, 1951.

Tooze, Ruth. *Story Telling*. Englewood Cliffs, NJ: Prentice-Hall, 1959. (A classic reference in story telling, ever popular and helpful to one who desires to be an outstanding storyteller.)

UNIT 11

Poetry

OBJECTIVES

After studying this unit, you should be able to

- discuss poetry elements.
- demonstrate the ability to present a poem.
- create a poem with features that appeal to young children.

Children's poetry is an enjoyable vehicle for developing listening skills. Activities that involve poetry hold many opportunities to promote language and literacy by associating pleasure with words. Poetry has a condensed quality that makes every word important. It prompts imagery through its sensory descriptions and can introduce enchanting tales. Nonsense verse appeals to the preschoolers' appreciation for slapstick.

Appropriate children's poetry is plentiful and varied. In addition to fast action and mood building, there is the joy of the rhythm of the words in many poems. Some rhythms in classic rhymes are so strong that they can motivate children to move their bodies or clap. The nursery rhymes "Jack and Jill" and "Twinkle, Twinkle, Little Star," and "The Little Turtle" (Lindsay, 1920) are good examples. Norton (1983) notes that "Rhythm encourages children to join in orally, experiment with language, and move to the rhythmical sounds." Some poems appeal to the emotions; others to the intellect (figure 11-1).

A preschool child with beginning literacy might be described as a child familiar with Mother Goose rhymes and other contemporary and classic poems, and one who knows rhyming words sound alike.

LEARNING OPPORTUNITIES

Poetry provides an opportunity for a child to learn new words, ideas, and attitudes and to experience life

FIGURE 11-1 Some poetry brings laughter.

through the eyes of the poet. To remember how many days there are in a month, many people still recite a simple poem learned as a child. If you are asked to say the alphabet, the classic ABC song of childhood may come to mind.

Poetry has form and order. It is dependable and also easy to learn. Simple rhymes are picked up quickly, as most parents have seen from their children's ability to remember television commercials. Children in early childhood centers enjoy the accomplishment of memorizing short verses. They may ask to share the poems they have learned with the teacher, just as they ask to sing songs they know that are often poems set to music.

The teacher should provide encouragement, attention, and positive comments to the child who responds to poetry. As with picture-book reading, story telling, and other language activities, the goal of the teacher in regard to poetry is to offer children pleasure and enjoyment of the language arts, while expanding the children's knowledge and interest.

Poetry, then, is used for a variety of reasons, including:

- Familiarizing and exposing children to classic and contemporary poetry that is considered to be part of our literary heritage.
- Training children to experience the pleasure of hearing sounds.
- Providing enjoyment through the use of poems with silly words and humor.
- Stimulating children's imaginations.
- Increasing vocabulary and knowledge.
- Building self-worth and self-confidence.
- Encouraging an understanding of rhyming.

SELECTION

Poetry introduces children to characters with fun-to-say names such as:

Jonathan Bing by Beatrice Curtis Brown

Mrs. Peck Pigeon by Eleanor Farjeon

Godfrey Gordon Gustavos Gore by William Rands

The characters can live in familiar and far-fetched settings:

Under the toadstool, from "The Elf and the Dormouse" by Oliver Herford

Straight to the animal store, from "The Animal Store" by Rachel Field

In a little crooked house, from Mother Goose

And they have various adventures and difficulties:

"The kids are ten feet tall," from "Grown-Up-Down Town" by Bobbi Katz

"Christopher Robin had wheezles and sneezles," from "Sneezles" by A. A. Milne

"Listen, my children, this must be stopped," from "The Grasshoppers" by Dorothy Aldis

Teachers select poetry that they can present eagerly and that they feel children will like. Delight in words is a natural outcome when the poem suits the audience. Teachers look for poems of quality and merit. Donoghue (1985) suggests that three elements exist in good poetry: *distinguished diction, carefully chosen words and phrases* with rich sensory and associated meanings, and *significant content.* Much of classic poetry has a song quality and a melody of its own. Norton (1983) suggests that teachers should examine a poem's subject matter, because in addition to delighting children, poetry can say something to them, titillate them, recall happy occasions or events, or encourage them to explore.

What is a poem? A poem can be defined as a verbal composition having the suggestive power to engage the feelings and imagination. This is accomplished typically through the highly structured patterning and movement of sound, rhythm, and meaning.

Types of Poetry

Types of poetry are described as follows:

Lyric. Melodic, descriptive poetry that often has a song quality.

Narrative. Poetry that tells a story or describes an event or happening.

Limerick. A poem with five lines of verse set in a specific rhyming pattern that is usually humorous.

Free verse. Poetry that does not rhyme.

Nonsense. Poetry that is often ridiculous and whimsical.

POETRY ELEMENTS

A particular poem's rhythm is influenced by sounds, stress, pitch, and accented and unaccented syllables. Manipulation of one or all of these features creates a particular idea, feeling, or message. Some rhythms are regular; others are not. The enjoyable quality of the Mother Goose rhymes stems from their strong rhythm and cadence. In poetry, authors use rhythm to emphasize words or phrases, consequently capturing children's immediate attention. Exciting, dramatic rhythms and relaxed, soothing rhythms can be included in the same poem. Poetry's rhythm is capable of making children feel that they are actively participating rather than merely listening.

Children's literature is full of rhyming words and rhyming names. Poetic rhyme can occur within sentences or at line endings. Children often rhyme on their own, spontaneously, during play. Nonsense rhymes have given joy to generations of children; sayings like stomper-chomper, icky-sticky, and Dan, Dan elephant man, can spread immediately among children.

Alliteration (defined as the occurrence of two or more words having the same initial sounds, assonance, or vowel sounds) is often used in poetry. All types of repetition are characteristic of children's poetry.

Visual images are stimulated by the poet's use of sensory words and figurative language (nonliteral meanings). A poet may provide a new way of looking at things by comparing previously unconnected objects or events. *Similes* (direct comparisons between two things that have something in common but are essentially different) or *metaphors* (implied comparisons between two things that have something in common but are essentially different) are often found in poetry. Giving human characteristics and emotions to inanimate objects and animals (*personification*) is also commonplace, and talking dishes, trains, birds, bears, and pancakes are plentiful in children's poems.

The format of printed poetry (type size and style, page layout, punctuation, and capitalization) has been used to heighten enjoyment and highlight the subject matter. One can find poems printed in the shape of a tree or in one-word, long, narrow columns.

TEACHER TECHNIQUES

If a poem is read or recited in conversational manner, rather than in a sing-song fashion, the rhyme is subtle and enjoyable. Sing-song reading and recitation may become tiresome and difficult to understand.

Most teachers know that reciting from memory requires practice, so the poems they memorize are a few favorites. However, memorization can create a mechanical quality, as the teacher focuses on remembering rather than enjoyment. Often, poetry is shared through teacher readings from lap cards. A poem should be read smoothly without uncalled for hesitation. This means the teacher has to prepare by reading the poem enough times for it to roll off the tongue with ease, savoring the words in the telling.

The enjoyment of poetry, like other types of literature, can be increased by an enthusiastic adult (Norton, 1983). Glazer (1986) suggests a careful reading of poetry because of poetry's compactness, making every word count.

When encouraging children to join in and speak favorite poetry lines, sensitive handling is in order. A teacher can suggest, "Let's say it together" or "Join me in saying this poem if you like." A child should not be singled out or asked to recite without volunteering. Some gregarious children will want to share poems that they've learned. A number of repetitions of a favorite verse may be needed before it is totally remembered. Children usually start with a few words or phrases.

Poetry charts hanging on a chart stand next to the teacher are a helpful device for capturing attention and freeing a teacher's eyes to meet those of the children. When reading from a chart, quickly glance at a line and then turn so that the words are transmitted to the children (figure 11-2).

Young children sometimes create their own rhymes. The teacher can jot them down for display or to be taken home by the children. "Amber, pamber, big fat bamber," created by a child, may interest other children, so that the teacher who has recorded it can share it at group time as a rhyme created by a playmate.

Poems dictated by children should be recorded verbatim, with no editing or teacher suggestions. Each creation is regarded as special. Lionni's *Frederick*, a wonderful picture book, helps children understand rhyming. This book's last two lines read:

"But Frederick," they said, "you are a poet!"
Frederick blushed, took a bow, and said shyly,
    "I know it."

Ways to Introduce Children to Poetry

Posting poems in conspicuous places may help to create interest, particularly if pictures or illustrations are placed adjacent to the poems. A poetry tree, made by placing a smooth tree limb in plaster of paris, can have paper leaves with poems on the back that can be selected at group times. A poem of the day (or week) bulletin board has worked well in some classrooms.

Pictures and flannel boards can be used in poetry presentation to interest and help children focus on words (figure 11-3). Other props or costumes that relate to the poem (such as a teddy bear or police officer's

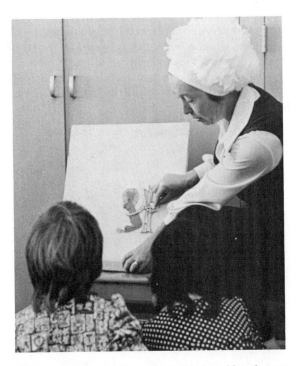

FIGURE 11-3 Poetry can be presented with flannel-board cutouts.

hat) will gain attention. Some of the best collections of poems have no pictures; others have an illustration for each poem.

A poem can be enjoyed indoors or outdoors, or between activities as a fill-in when teacher or children are waiting.

Mounting cut magazine pictures and trying to think up words that rhyme with what's pictured is a rhyming activity many teachers favor. For example, "Here's a cake, let's give it to...."

SOURCES

A fine line divides finger plays, body and movement games, chants, songs, and poems. All can involve rhyme and rhythm. Poetry given later in this unit is primarily the type that children would merely listen to as it is being recited, although some do contain opportunities for child participation.

Many fine picture books contain rhymed verse and can enhance a center's poetry program. Collections, anthologies, and books of children's poetry are avail-

I am a pine tree
growing on a hill.
I can stand so very,
very still. All at
once the wind
begins to blow.
I bend to and fro,
to and fro, to and fro.

FIGURE 11-2 A rhyming chart

able at the public library, book stores, school supply stores, and in children's and teachers' magazines.

Teachers also can create poetry from their own experiences. The following suggestions for creating poems for young children help the teacher-poet by pointing out the special features found in older classics and quality contemporary poetry.

- Include mental images in every line.
- Use strong rhythms that bring out an urge to chant, move, or sing.
- Use frequent rhyming.
- Use action verbs often.
- Make each line an independent thought.
- Change the rhythm.
- Use words that are within the children's level of understanding.
- Use themes and subjects that are familiar to the young child.

Teacher-created poems promote child-created poems.

Many teachers search for ethnic poems that allow them to offer multicultural variety. Jenkins (1973) points out:

No one cultural group has a corner on imagination, creativity, poetic quality, or philosophic outlook. Each has made important contributions to the total culture of the country and the world.

Recalling the poems and verses of one's own childhood may lead a teacher to research poems by a particular poet. Remembering appealing poetry elements may also help a teacher find poetry that may delight today's young child.

The following volumes are recommended:

Brady, L., R. Meirelles, and Nikoghosian, *The Best of Mother Goose*. Hanford: RozaLinda Publications, 1987.

Gander, Father. *Nursery Rhymes*. Santa Barbara: Advocacy Press, 1985.

Read Aloud Rhymes for the Very Young. Ed. by Jack Prelutsky. New York: Knopf, 1988.

Scott, Louise Binder. *Rhymes for Learning Times*. Minneapolis, MN: T. S. Denison & Co. Inc., 1983.

Silverman, Jan. *Some Time to Grow*. Menlo Park, CA: Addison-Wesley, 1988.

The Gingerbread Guide, Glenview: Goodyear Books, 1987.

SUGGESTED POEMS

The poems that follow are examples of the type that appeal to young children.

IF I WERE AN APPLE

If I were an apple
  And grew on a tree,
I think I'd drop down
  On a nice boy like me.

I wouldn't stay there
  Giving nobody joy;
I'd fall down at once
  And say, "Eat me, my boy!"

Old Rhyme

GOOD MORNING

One day I saw a downy duck,
With feathers on his back;
I said, "Good-morning, downy duck."
And he said, "Quack, quack, quack."

One day I saw a timid mouse,
He was so shy and meek;
I said, "Good-morning, timid mouse,"
And he said, "Squeak, squeak, squeak."

One day I saw a scarlet bird,
He woke me from my sleep;
I said, "Good-morning, scarlet bird,"
And he said, "Cheep, cheep, cheep."

Muriel Sipe

ANIMAL CRACKERS

Animal crackers, and cocoa to drink,
That is the finest of suppers, I think;
When I'm grown up and can have what I please
I think I shall always insist upon these.

What do you choose when you're offered a treat?
When Mother says, "What would you like best to eat?"
Is it waffles and syrup, or cinnamon toast?
It's cocoa and animals that I love the most!

The kitchen's the coziest place that I know:
The kettle is singing, the stove is aglow,
And there in the twilight, how jolly to see
The cocoa and animals waiting for me.

Daddy and Mother dine later in state,
With Mary to cook for them, Susan to wait;
But they don't have nearly as much fun as I
Who eat in the kitchen with Nurse standing by:
Having cocoa and animals once more for tea!

ONE STORMY NIGHT

Two little kittens,
  One stormy night
Began to quarrel,
  And then to fight.

One had a mouse,
  The other had none;
And that's the way
  The quarrel begun.

"I'll have that mouse,"
  Said the bigger cat.
"You'll have that mouse?
  We'll see about that!"

"I will have that mouse,"
  Said the eldest son.
"You shan't have the mouse,"
  Said the little one.

The old woman seized
  Her sweeping broom,
And swept both kittens
  Right out of the room.

The ground was covered
  With frost and snow,
And the two little kittens
  Had nowhere to go.

They lay and shivered
  On a mat at the door,
While the old woman
  Was sweeping the floor.

And then they crept in
  As quiet as mice,
All wet with the snow,
  And as cold as ice.

And found it much better
  That stormy night,
To lie by the fire,
  Than to quarrel and fight.

Traditional

WHAT IS RED?

Red is a sunset
Blazy and bright.
Red is feeling brave
With all your might.
Red is a sunburn
Spot on your nose.
Sometimes red
Is a red, red rose
Red squiggles out
When you cut your hand.
Red is a brick and
A rubber band.
Red is a hotness
You get inside
When you're embarrassed
And want to hide.

COUNTING

Today I'll remember forever and ever
Because I can count to ten;
It isn't an accident any more either,
I've done it over and over again.

I used to leave out five and three
And sometimes eight and four.
And once in a while I'd mix up nine
Or seven and two, but not any more.

I count my fingers on one hand first,
And this little pig is one,
And when old thumb goes off to market
That's five, and one of my hands is done.

So then I open my other hand
And start in counting again
From pick up sticks to big fat hen,
Five six seven eight eleven nine ten!

From *Windy Morning*, ©1953 by Harry Behn; renewed 1981 by Alice
Behn Goebel, Pamela Behn Adam, Prescott Behn, and Peter Behn.
Reprinted by permission of Harcourt Brace Jovanovich, Inc.

THE ANIMAL STORE

If I had a hundred dollars to spend,
   Or maybe a little more,
I'd hurry as fast as my legs would go
   Straight to the animal store.

I wouldn't say, "How much for this or that?"
   "What kind of dog is he?"
I'd buy as many as rolled an eye,
   Or wagged a tail at me!

I'd take the hound with the drooping ears
   That sits by himself alone,
Cockers and Cairns and wobbly pups
   For to be my very own.

I might buy a parrot all red and green,
   And the monkey I saw before,
If I had a hundred dollars to spend,
   Or maybe a little more.

Rachel Field

From *Taxis and Toadstools* by Rachel Field, ©1926 by Doubleday and
Company. Reprinted by permission of the publisher.

I HAVEN'T LEARNED TO WHISTLE

I haven't learned to whistle
I've tried —
But if there's anything like a whistle in me
It stops
Inside

Dad whistles,
My brother whistles
And almost everyone I know.

I've tried to put my lips together with wrinkles,
To push my tongue against my teeth
And make a whistle
Come
Out
Slow —

But what happens is nothing but a feeble gasping
Sound
Like a sort of sickly bird.

(Everybody says they never heard
A whistle like that
And to tell the truth
Neither did I.)

But Dad says, tonight, when he comes home,
He'll show me again how
To put my lips together with wrinkles,
To push my tongue against my teeth,
To blow my breath out and really make a whistle.

And I'll try!

Myra Cohn Livingston

Myra Cohn Livingston, "I Haven't Learned to Whistle" from *O Sliver
of Liver*. Text ©1979 by Myra Cohn Livingston. Reprinted with the
permission of Atheneum Publishers.

FEET

There are things
Feet know
That hands never will:
The exciting
Pounding feel
Of running down a hill;

The soft cool
Prickliness
When feet are bare
Walking in
The summer grass
To most anywhere.

Or dabbling in
Water all
Slip-sliddering through toes —
(Nicer than
Through fingers, though why
No one really knows.)

"Toes, tell my
Fingers," I
Said to them one day,
"Why it's such
Fun just to
Wiggle and play."

But toes just
Looked at me
Solemn and still.
Oh, there are things
Feet know
That hands NEVER WILL.

                              Dorothy Aldis

"Feet" by Dorothy Aldis. Reprinted by permission of G. P. Putnam's Sons from *Everything and Anything*, ©1925–1927, Renewed, 1953–1955 by Dorothy Aldis.

MAYTIME MAGIC

A little seed
For me to sow...
A little earth
To make it grow...

A little hole,
A little pat...
A little wish,
And that is that

A little sun,
A little shower...
A little while,
And then — a flower!

                              Mabel Watts

Permission granted by Mabel Watts, 1988.

THE GRASSHOPPERS

High
Up
Over the top
Of feathery grasses the
Grasshoppers hop.
They won't eat their suppers;
They will not obey
Their grasshopper mothers
And fathers, who say:
"Listen, my children,
This must be stopped —
Now is the time your last
Hop should be hopped;
So come eat your suppers
And go to your beds — "
But the little green grasshoppers

Shake their green heads.
"No,
No — "
The naughty ones say,
"All we have time to do
Now is play
If we want supper we'll
Nip at a fly
Or nibble a blueberry
As we go by;
If we feel sleepy we'll
Close our eyes tight
And snoozle away in a
Harebell all night
But not
Now
Now we must hop
And nobody
NOBODY
Can make us stop."

                              Dorothy Aldis

"The Grasshoppers" by Dorothy Aldis. Reprinted by permission of G. P. Putnam's Sons from *All Together* by Dorothy Aldis. Copyright 1925,1926,1927,1928,1934,1939,1952 by Dorothy Aldis.

I BOUGHT ME A ROOSTER

I bought me a rooster and the rooster pleased me.
I fed my rooster on the bayberry tree,
My little rooster goes cock-a-doodle-doo, dee-doodle-dee
doodle dee doodle dee doo!

I bought me a cat and the cat pleased me.
I fed my cat on the bayberry tree,
My little cat goes meow, meow, meow.
My little rooster goes cock-a-doodle-doo, dee-doodle-dee
doodle dee doodle dee doo!

I bought me a dog and the dog pleased me.
I fed my dog on the bayberry tree,
My little dog goes bark, bark, bark.
My little cat goes meow, meow, meow.
My little rooster goes cock-a-doodle-doo, dee-doodle-dee
doodle dee doodle dee doo!

                              Traditional

Note: This is a cumulative poem that takes teacher practice; additional verses include as many animals as you wish.

THE CHICKENS

Said the first little chicken,
  With a queer little squirm,
"I wish I could find
  A fat little worm!"

Said the next little chicken,
  With an odd little shrug:
"I wish I could find
  A fat little bug!"

Said the third little chicken
  With a small sign of grief:
"I wish I could find
  A green little leaf!"

Said the fourth little chicken,
  With a faint little moan:
"I wish I could find
  A wee gravel stone!"

"Now see here!" said the mother,
  From the green garden patch,
"If you want any breakfast,
  Just come here and scratch!"

                    Anonymous

MICE

I think mice
Are rather nice
  Their tails are long,
  Their faces small,
  They haven't any
  Chins at all.
  Their ears are pink,
  Their teeth are white
  They run about
  The house at night.
  They nibble things
  They shouldn't touch
  And no one seems
  To like them much.
But I think mice
Are nice.

                    Rose Fyleman

From *Fifty-One New Nursery Rhymes*, Doubleday & Co.

OVER IN THE MEADOW

Over in the meadow, in the sand in the sun,
Lived an old mother frog and her little froggie one.
"Croak!" said the mother; "I croak," said the one,
So they croaked and were glad in the sand in the sun.

Over in the meadow in a pond so blue
Lived an old mother duck and her little ducks two.
"Quack!" said the mother; "we quack," said the two,
So they quacked and were glad in the pond so blue.

Over in the meadow, in a hole in a tree,
Lived an old mother robin and her little birdies three.
"Chirp!" said the mother; "we chirp," said the three,
So they chirped and were glad in the hole in a tree.

Over in the meadow, on a rock by the shore
Lived an old mother snake and her little snakes four.
"Hiss!" said the mother; "we hiss," said the four,
So they hissed and were glad on a rock by the shore.

Over in the meadow, in a big beehive,
Lived an old mother bee and her little bees five.
"Buzz!" said the mother; "we buzz," said the five,
So they buzzed and were glad in the big beehive.

                    Traditional

LITTLE BOY BLUE

Little Boy Blue,
Come, blow your horn!
The sheep's in the meadow,
The cow's in the corn.
Where's the little boy
That looks after the sheep?
Under the haystack, fast asleep!

                    Mother Goose

THE CAT AND THE FIDDLE

Hey, diddle, diddle!
The cat and the fiddle,
The cow jumped over the moon;
The little dog laughed
To see such sport,
And the dish ran away
With the spoon.

                    Mother Goose

THE LITTLE GIRL WITH A CURL

There was a little girl
Who had a little curl
Right in the middle of her forehead;
When she was good
She was very, very good,
And when she was bad she was horrid.

Mother Goose

The following are poems written by early childhood students who created them to use with young children. These beginning attempts show that most teachers are capable of writing enjoyable and interesting poetry to use for language pleasure.

A SLEEPY PLACE TO BE

Oh, it was a yawning day
That nobody wanted to work or play
And everybody felt the very same way.

There was a duckling who quacked and quacked
He had soft down upon his back.
He was tired of swimming and everything,
So he put his head down under his wing.
And there under the shadowy shade tree
He slept until it was half-past three.

A little old pig gave a big loud squeal
As he ate every scrap of his noonday meal.
And under the shadowy shade tree
He slept as quietly as could be.

A butterfly blue, green and red
Sat with her wings above her head
Up on a branch of the shadowy tree.
Oh, what a sleepy place to be.

Debbie Lauer-Hunter

LITTLE KITTY

Pretty little Kitty
With fur so soft and sweet,
You tiptoe oh so softly
On your tiny little feet.

Fluffy little Kitty
With eyes so big and round,

I never hear you coming,
You hardly make a sound.

Silly little Kitty
Playing with a ball
Listen! Someone's coming!
You scamper down the hall.

Lazy little Kitty
Tiny sleepy head
Curled up, sleeping soundly
In your cozy little bed.

Bari Morgan-Miller

THE PUMPKIN NO ONE WANTED

Out in the pumpkin patch, sad and forlorn,
Sat a funny little pumpkin, shaped like a horn.
He sat and he waited, through the day and the night,
For his own special person, someone just right.

He was thin by his stem,
Fat on the bottom,
Sitting in the corner,
Alone and forgotten.

Along came a Doctor, searching through the vine
Looking for some pumpkins, seven, eight, nine.
She saw the funny pumpkin, sad and forlorn,
She laughed and said, "You are shaped like a horn."

He was thin by his stem,
Fat on the bottom,
Sitting in the corner,
Alone and forgotten.

Along came a teacher, walking down the row,
He came to the pumpkin, laughed and said "No...
For a jack-o-lantern, you won't do at all.
Here you're thin, there you're fat,
you're much too tall."

He was thin by his stem,
Fat on the bottom,
Sitting in the corner,
Alone and forgotten.

Along came a little girl, all by herself.
She wanted a jack-o-lantern to sit on a shelf.
She looked for a pumpkin, round, smooth and fat.
She saw the funny pumpkin and said,
"Not one like that."

He was thin by his stem,
Fat on the bottom,
Sitting in the corner,
Alone and forgotten.

Along came a tall boy, walking all alone,
* Looking for a pumpkin to take to his home.*
He saw the funny pumpkin, shaped like a horn,
* Over in the corner, sad and forlorn.*

He was thin by his stem,
Fat on the bottom,
No longer in the corner,
Alone or forgotten.

Mary Sheridan

Summary

Poems and verses provide an important literary experience, and exposure to classics is something no child should miss. They can be a source of enjoyment and learning for young children. Rhythm, word images, fast action, and rhyme are used to promote listening skill.

Short verses, easily remembered, give children self-confidence with words. Encouragement and attention is offered by the teacher when the child shows interest.

Poems are selected and practiced for enthusiastic, smooth presentations. They can be selected from various sources or can be created by the teacher. Props help children focus on words. Poems are created or selected keeping in mind the features that attract and interest young children.

Student Activities

- Share with the class a poem you learned as a child.

- Select five poems from any source. Be ready to state the reasons you selected them when you bring them to the next class meeting.

- Make a list of 10 picture books that include children's poetry. Cite author, title, publisher, and copyright date.

- Create a poem for young children. Go back and review the features most often found in classic rhymes.

- Present a poem to a group of preschoolers. Evaluate its success in a few sentences.

- Find poetry written in free verse that you feel might be successful with preschool children.

- Form groups of three to six students. Using a large sheet of newsprint tacked (or taped) to the wall and a felt pen, list clever ways to introduce poetry to young children; for example, Poem of the Day. Discuss each group's similar and diverse suggestions.

- Discuss poetry's visual images. Cite examples.

- Find a source of ethnic children's poetry and share it with class members.

- What kind of activity could you plan using the rhyme that follows?

    Bus is comin' down the road, yes it is.
    Bus is comin' down the road, yes it is.
    Bus just turned the corner.
    Now it has come to a stop.
    Hear the doors open and pop.
    Hear the doors open and pop.

Unit Review

A. List a few reasons why poetry is used with young children.

B. Select from Column II the term that matches each item in Column I.

Column I	Column II
1. poetry	a. an action verb
2. rhyme	b. self-confidence
3. beat	c. a rhythmic measure
4. order and form	d. mental pictures
5. images	e. words with like sounds
6. remembered	f. consistent and dependable
7. interest	g. teacher attention
8. goal	h. after practice
9. presentation	i. enjoyment
10. reciting	j. promotes listening skill
11. classics	k. never forced
12. song	l. library
13. props	m. Mother Goose rhymes
14. run	n. musical poem
15. source	o. focus attention

C. List the numbers of the statements that you feel agree with the suggestions mentioned in this unit.
   1. Young children must learn to recite.
   2. Emphasizing the beat of poetry as you read it always increases the enjoyment.
   3. Repeat the poem over and over until a child learns it.
   4. Describe to children the mental pictures created by the poem before reading the poem to the children.
   5. It really isn't too important for young children to memorize the poems they hear.
   6. Memorizing a poem can help a child feel competent.
   7. Most poems are not shared because teachers want children to gain the factual information the poem contains.
   8. Poetry's rhythm comes from its form and order.
   9. Memorizing a poem always causes awkward teacher presentation.
   10. Teachers may try to author some of their own children's poetry.

D. List elements of poetry that can be manipulated to evoke emotion in listeners.

E. Write an example using a line of poetry or free verse for the following: alliteration, personification, simile, and figurative language.

References

Arbuthnot, May H., and Shelton L. Root, Jr. *Time for Poetry*. Glenview, IL: Scott Foresman, 1968.

Brown, Margaret W. *Nibble, Nibble*. Menlo Park, CA: Addison-Wesley, 1959.

Clark, Leonard. *Poetry for the Youngest*. Boston, MA: Horn Book, 1969.

Donoghue, Mildred R. *The Child and the English Language Arts*. Dubuque, IA: Brown, 1985.

Glazer, Joan I. *Literature for Young Children*. Columbus, OH: Charles E. Merrill, 1986.

Hoban, Russell. *Egg Thoughts and Other Frances Songs*. New York: Harper and Row, 1972.

Jenkins, Esther C. "Multi-Ethnic Literature: Promise and Problems," *Elementary English* 31.6 (1973): 17–26.

Katz, Bobbi. *Bedtime Bear's Book of Bedtime Poems*. New York: Random House, 1983.

Lear, Edward. *The Complete Nonsense Book*. New York: Dodd Mead, 1946.

Lindsay, Vachel. *Collected Poems*. New York: Macmillan, 1920.

Lionni, Leo. *Frederick*. New York: Knopf/Pantheon, 1967.

Manson, Beverlie. *Fairy Poems for the Very Young*. New York: Doubleday, 1983.

Milne, A. A. *When We Were Very Young*. New York: Dutton, 1961.

Norton, Donna E. *Through the Eyes of a Child*. Columbus, OH: Charles E. Merrill, 1983.

Poems to Read to the Very Young. Ed. Josette Frank. New York: Random House, 1961.

Watson, Clyde. *Catch Me and Kiss Me and Say It Again*. New York: Philomel Books, 1978.

UNIT 12

Flannel Boards and Activity Sets

BJECTIVES

After studying this unit, you should be able to

- describe flannel boards and types of flannel board activities.
- make and present three flannel board activities.
- describe teacher techniques in flannel board story presentation.

Flannel (or felt) board activities are a rewarding experience for both the child and teacher. Since the attention of young children is easily captured, the teacher finds the use of flannel board activities very popular and effective. Children are highly attentive during this type of activity — straining to see and hear — looking forward to the next piece to be put on the flannel board.

Stories to be used with flannel board activities are selected by the same criteria used for story telling; see Unit 10. In addition to stories, poetry, and songs, other listening and learning activities can be presented with flannel boards.

FLANNEL BOARD CONSTRUCTION

Boards of different sizes, shapes, and designs are used, depending on the needs of the center. They may be freestanding or propped up in the chalkboard tray, on a chair, or on an easel. Boards can be covered on both sides in different colors. Many are made by covering a sheet of heavy cardboard, display board, styrofoam, or wood with a piece of solid-colored flannel or felt yardage (figure 12-1). The material is pulled smooth and held by tacks, tape, glue, or wood staples, depending on the board material. Sometimes an under padding is added. Putting wire mesh or a

sheet of metal between the under padding and the covering material makes pieces with magnets adhere. Since all metal does not attract magnets, the mesh or metal needs testing before purchase.

SIDE VIEWS

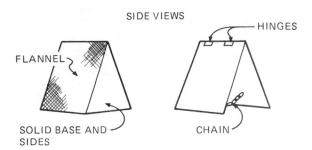

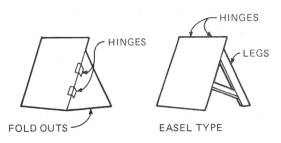

FIGURE 12-1 Free-standing boards

209

Construction:

Obtain a piece of cardboard, of the size you desire for the back of your flannel board, and a large sheet of flannel or heavy wrapping paper. The flannel (or paper) should be several inches wider than the cardboard and about twice as long as the finished chart size. One-inch deep with a back 3 inches high is a good pocket size.

Measure and mark both sides of flannel (paper) at intervals of 3 inches and 1 inch, alternating. Using accordian folds, the first 1-inch section is creased and folded forward over the second 3-inch section, and so on. Pull tight and secure ends.

A pocket chart conveniently holds set pieces in sequence for flannel board stories and can be useful in other child activities with flannel set pieces.

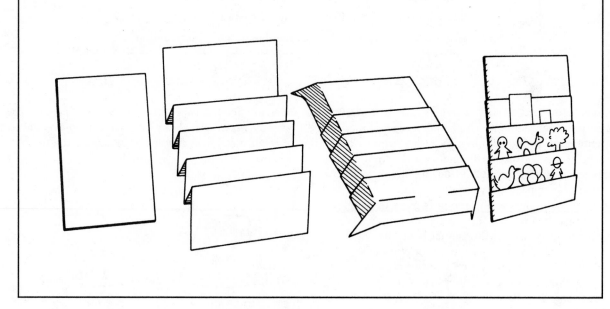

FIGURE 12-2 Pocket chart

Decisions on which materials to use in flannel board construction are often based on the intended use of the flannel board, material cost, and tools or skills needed in construction. Styrofoam is a good choice if having a light-weight board is important; however, wood-based boards are durable.

Making a board that tilts backward at a slight angle is an important consideration for a freestanding flannel board, because pieces applied to a slanted board stick more securely. Stores and companies that sell school supplies have premade boards in various price ranges. Although flannel and felt are popular coverings for boards, other materials also work well. Almost all fuzzy textured material is usable. It is a good idea to press a small piece of felt or pellon to a fabric to see how well it sticks before buying the fabric.

Some boards have pockets in the back so that flannel pieces can be lined up and ready for use (figure 12-2). Some early childhood centers have parts of walls, dividers, and backs of pieces of furniture covered with flannel or felt. A simple homemade freestanding board holder is shown in figure 12-3.

A tabletop flannel board can be made from a cardboard box (see instructions and necessary materials

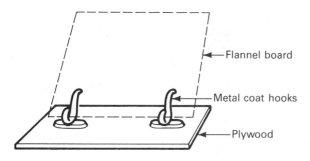

FIGURE 12-3 Two metal coat hooks screwed to a piece of heavy plywood make a good flannel-board holder.

in figure 12-4). One clever idea is using a secondhand attache case. Using a case that opens to a 90° angle, glue a large piece of flannel to the inside of the top lid. When open, the flannel will be in view. The case is used for storing sets, and the handle makes for easy carrying.

Display fabrics to which three-dimensional objects will adhere are available commercially from companies such as Charles Mayer Studios, Inc. (140 E. Market Street, Akron, OH 44308) that produce audiovisuals. Special adhesives and tapes are needed for this type of flannel board.

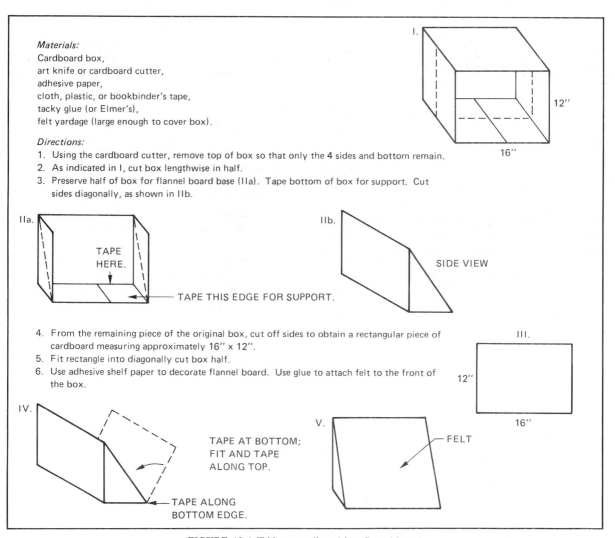

FIGURE 12-4 Tabletop cardboard box flannel board

The size of the flannel board's front surface is important. Consider making or purchasing a board no smaller than 24 by 30 inches. The attache case above could be used for individual child's play or for small groups but may be too small for larger groups. Most centers obtain or construct both a child's flannel board and a staff flannel board.

Activity Sets

Pieces for flannel activity sets can be made in a number of ways and from a number of fabrics and papers. Pellon and felt, because of their low cost and durability, are probably the most popular. Heavy-paper figures with flannel backing also stick well. Commercial tape, sandpaper, fuzzy velour-flocked wallpaper, velcro, and used foamlike laundry softener sheets are other possibilities for backing pieces. Premade flannel board sets are available at school-supply stores and at most teacher conferences. Most communities have at least one teacher who is a small business entrepreneur specializing in making flannel sets for other teachers.

Shapes and figures can be traced from books, magazines, coloring books, self-drawn and created, or borrowed from other sources. Tracing paper is helpful for this purpose. Tracing can be done simply by covering the back of a paper pattern with a heavy layer of pencil lead. Soft art pencils work best. The pattern is then turned over and traced. Another method is cutting the object out, tracing its outline, and then drawing details freehand. Tracing pencils and pens are commercially available and come with directions for use and are found at craft stores. Two suppliers follow: for transfer pencils, W. H. Collins, Inc., Whippany, NJ 07981; for transfer pens, Graphic Techniques, 2531 Neff Road, Dayton, Ohio 45414.

Color can be added to set pieces with felt markers, oil pastels, acrylic or poster paint, embroidery pens, crayons, paints, and colored pencils. Sets take time to make but are well worth the effort. Favorites will be presented over and over again. Pieces can be covered with clear contact paper or can be laminated (fronts only) for durability.

Teachers can be creative with flannel board sets by using:

- layered felt
- wiggly eyes (commercially available at variety stores)
- hand-stitched character clothing
- imitation fur fabric
- liquid glitter
- commercial fluorescent paint or crayons.

Many of the newer copy machines have the ability to enlarge figures or shrink them. Set pieces that are too small are difficult to handle and see. Narrow parts on set pieces should be avoided, because they tend to tear with use. Also, try to preserve the size relationship between characters (such as between a mouse and a human figure) as well as the cultural and ethnic diversity of characters.

Pattern transfer books are plentiful and available from craft and sewing supply stores. Patterns can be ironed on cloth quickly, and it is possible to obtain multiple copies. Publishers of transfer books include Dover Publications, 180 Varick St., New York, NY 10014, and Craftways, 4118 Lakeside Drive, Richmond, CA 94806.

Some schools buy inexpensive picture books and use the illustrations as flannel board set pieces. After the pieces are cut, they are glued to oak tag, and backed with some of the materials mentioned above.

Proper storage and care will preserve pieces and prolong their usefulness. A flat stocking box or large mailing envelope or manila folder is practical for storage. If pieces become bent, a warm iron makes most kinds flat again. Sets can be stored in plastic page protectors used in three-ring binders (available in stationery stores). Large zip-lock plastic household bags, as well as plastic envelopes available at teacher supply stores, can also be used to protect pieces.

PRESENTATION

Like most other listening activities, a semisecluded, comfortable setting should be chosen for presentation. The activity begins with the teacher starting to place pieces on the board in proper sequence as the story or activity unfolds, always focusing on the children's reactions. In this activity, as in many others described in this text, the teacher may be presenting but also watching for reaction. Since pieces are usually added one at a time, they should be kept in an open flat box or manila folder in the teacher's lap, or, better yet, behind the board, stacked in the order they will appear. This is hard to do if the story or activity is not well in mind.

The teacher should periodically check to see whether the set has all its pieces, particularly in large centers where many staff members use the same sets. If pieces are missing or damaged, the teacher or volunteers can make new pieces. New sets are always appreciated by the entire staff and can be developed to meet the needs and interests of a particular group of children.

In order to present activities with ease, the beginner should note these steps:

- Read the story (or activity sequence) and check the pieces to be used.

- Practice until there is a smooth coordination of words and placement of pieces on the board.

- Set up the flannel board.

- Check and prepare pieces in order of their appearance.

- Place pieces out of view, behind the board within easy reach, or in a lap folder.

- Gather children. Make seating adjustments if necessary. Respond to children's needs. Group size should be considered carefully; the smaller the group, the more intimate and conversational the experience. As with other language arts presentations, consider two tellings to reduce group size.

- Introduce the activity with a statement that builds a desire to listen.

- Tell the story (or present the activity), watching for reactions from the children. Create drama and suspense with pauses, speaking in characters' voices, and moving pieces across the board's surface, if the story calls for this. Let your personality guide you.

- Discussion for language development or comprehension is optional. Teachers ask questions or discuss story particulars to elicit children's ideas and comments.

- Keep pieces flat, store them properly, returning sets where other staff members expect them to be.

- Children enjoy doing their retelling with a flannel board and their own activity sets. Most centers construct one set for teachers and another set for child exploration and activity.

In addition to story-telling activities, sets may be used for songs, poetry, numbers, language development, and other activities.

SUGGESTED STORIES AND ACTIVITIES

There are many resources for story ideas. Stories created by teachers can be enjoyed as much as commercial sets and classic stories. Sets can improve listening skills and enhance vocabulary and concept development, often within one activity. The visual shapes or pieces are linked to words and ideas. Occasionally, a child's picture book can be presented as a flannel board activity before the book becomes part of the school's book collection.

An available flannel board placed at children's eye level with an adjacent open box of figures or shapes quickly encourages use and creativity (figure 12-5). Remembered words, lines, and whole stories are relived in children's play. They often go beyond the familiar, devising their own events. Even sturdy felt pieces will need to be ironed flat occasionally and replaced because of frequent and vigorous use by children. As suggested above, children's play with the flannel board often follows a teacher presentation but can also be a free choice activity at other times of the day.

Many centers include flannel boards and sets in their language centers along with alphabet letter cutouts. Teachers can use alphabet letter cutouts in daily activities, and many centers routinely have set pieces, such as a flower shape, labeled with the cut out alphabet letters underneath the shape on the flannel board for viewing. A flannel board with the word "closed" on it may be used to block entrance to a play area or other section of the room.

Set ideas and activity ideas can be obtained from the following sources.

Holiday Kits for Flannelboards, The Sunshine Factory, Box 650, Elizabethville, PA 17023

Community Careers Flannelboard Set, Instructo Corp., can be ordered through The Women's Action Alliance Inc., Dept. C, The Non-Sexist Child Development Project, 370 Lexington Avenue, New York, NY 10017

Magic Moments, P.O. Box 53635, San Jose, CA 95135-0635

Little Folk Felts, 79960 Nassau Place, Indio, CA 92201

FIGURE 12-5 The children are placing pellon story pieces on a board covered with flannel.

The Flannelboard, 3700 South Calvin Drive, West Valley City, UT 84120

The Storytelling Apron, T. S. Denison, Minneapolis, MN 55431

Classics on The Flannelboard, 4305 Windsor Park Drive, San Jose, CA 95136

Life-size Flannelboard, BE BA BO Image Unit, Kaplan School Supply Corp., 1310 Lewisville-Clemmons Road, Lewisville, NC 27023

For additional books and resources see the Reference section at the end of this unit.

The following activities and stories are suggested as a start for the beginning teacher. They may also be used to add variety and ideas for new sets. Patterns for some of the stories can be found in the Appendix. Many of the set pieces found in the appendix will need to be enlarged; if a copy machine with enlargement capability is not available for this purpose, try using an overhead projector. Many urban school districts allow private preschool teachers in their community to use their central office curriculum centers. Additional flannel board stories and patterns may be found in the Appendix.

The Lion and the Mouse

Author Unknown (a classic story)

(See Appendix for patterns.)

Pieces:
lion, sleeping	rope
lion, awake	mouse
tree	two hunters

(On the board, place the sleeping lion next to the tree. Place the mouse near the lion's back, moving it slowly toward the lion while speaking in a soft voice.)

There once was a little mouse who saw a big lion sleeping by a tree. "Oh, it would be fun to climb on top of the lion and slide down his tail," thought the mouse. So — quietly, he tiptoed close to the lion. When he climbed on the lion's back, the fur felt so soft and warm between his toes that he began running up and down the lion's back.

The lion awoke. He felt a tickle upon his back. He opened one eye and saw the little mouse, which he then caught in his paw.

(*Move mouse under lion's paw.*)

"Let me go — please!" said the mouse. "I'm sorry I woke you from your nap. Let me go, and I'll never bother you again. Maybe you and I could be friends — friends help each other, you know."

This made the lion laugh. "A little mouse like you, help me? I'm big, I'm strong, and I'm brave!" Then the lion laughed again, and he let the mouse go.

(*Take the mouse off the board.*)

The mouse ran away, and he didn't see the lion for a long time. But, one day when the mouse was out looking for seeds for dinner, he saw the lion tied to a tree with a rope, and two hunters near him.

(*Remove sleeping lion. Add awake lion, placing it next to tree, with rope on top. Put the two hunters on the other side of the tree.*)

One hunter said, "Well, this rope will hold the lion until we can go get our truck and take him to the zoo." So the hunters walked away.

(*Remove the hunters.*)

The mouse ran up to the lion as soon as the hunters were out of sight. He said, "Hello, lion."

(*Add mouse.*)

The lion answered, "Well, I guess it's your turn to laugh at me tied to this tree."

"I'm not going to laugh," said the mouse, as he quickly started to chew on the rope.

(*Move mouse close to rope.*)

The mouse chewed, and chewed, and chewed. The rope fell apart, and the lion was free.

(*Remove rope.*)

"You are a good friend," said the lion. "Hop on my back and hold on. Let's get away from here before those two hunters come back."

(*Place lion in running position with mouse on lion's back.*)

"OK," said the mouse. "I'd like that."

So you see, sometimes little friends can help big friends. The size of a friend isn't really too important.

Fortunately-Unfortunately

(See Appendix for patterns.)

Pieces:
boy	haystack	shark
plane	pitchfork	tiger
parachute	water	cave
snake	birthday cake	

Once upon a time there was a little boy. Fortunately, he received an invitation to a birthday party. Unfortunately, the party was in Florida, and he was in New York City.

Fortunately, he had a plane. Unfortunately, the plane caught fire. Fortunately, he had a parachute. Unfortunately, the parachute had a hole in it. Fortunately, there was a haystack. Unfortunately, there was a pitchfork in the haystack.

Fortunately, he missed the pitchfork. Unfortunately, he missed the haystack. Fortunately, he landed in the water. Unfortunately, there was a shark in the water.

Fortunately, he could swim, and he swam to the shore. Unfortunately, there were tigers on the land. Fortunately, he could run. Unfortunately, so could the tigers.

Fortunately, he found a cave. Unfortunately, there were snakes in the cave. Fortunately, he found a way out of the cave. Unfortunately, it led him to the middle of a formal ballroom.

Fortunately, there was a party going on. Fortunately, it was for him. And, fortunately, it was his birthday!

Remy Charlip, *What Good Luck, What Bad Luck* (New York: Scholastic Book Services, 1969).

The Pumpkin That Grew

(A Halloween Flannel Board Story/Poem)

(See Appendix for patterns.)

Once there was a pumpkin
And all summer through
It stayed upon a big green vine
and grew, and grew, and grew.

It grew from being small and green
To being orange and bright
And then it said unto itself,
"Now I'm a handsome sight."

And then one day it grew a mouth
A nose and two big eyes;
And so that pumpkin grew into
A Jack O'Lantern wise!

The Seed

Margie Cowsert
(While an ECE student)

(See Appendix for patterns.)

Pieces: small roots   leaves
green shoot   beaver
deer   bird
Mr. Man   large trunk
apples (five or more) large leaves
seed   large roots
small trunk

Once upon a time, there was a seed named Abraham. He didn't know what kind of plant he would be, so he asked Mr. Bird. Mr. Bird didn't know but wanted to eat Abraham. Abraham asked him to wait until after he found out what he would be, and the bird agreed to wait.

Abraham grew small roots and green shoots. He asked Mr. Deer if he knew what he would grow up to be. "Do you know what I'll be when I grow up?" Mr. Deer said, "No," but wanted to eat the tender green shoot. Abraham said, "Please wait." So Mr. Deer decided to wait.

Abraham grew a small trunk and leaves. He was glad he was a tree but still didn't know what kind. He asked Mr. Beaver, "Do you know what I'll be when I grow up?" Mr. Beaver didn't know but wanted to eat Abraham's tender bark. He decided to wait also.

Abraham grew big roots, a big trunk, and more leaves, but still didn't know what kind of tree he was. He asked Mr. Man, "Do you know what I'll be when I grow up?" Mr. Man didn't know, but he wanted to chop down Abraham to make a house. He decided to wait.

Abraham grew apples. Hooray! He knew that he was an apple tree. He told Mr. Bird he could eat him now. Mr. Bird said Abraham was too big, but that he would like one of the apples. Mr. Deer thought the tree was too big, too, but he did want an apple. Mr. Beaver took any apples that fell to the ground home to his

family. Mr. Man loved apples, so he told Abraham Tree that he wouldn't chop him down.

Abraham Apple Tree was so happy to know what he was and that no one was going to eat him or chop him down that he grew lots of apples.

Just Like Daddy

(See Appendix for patterns.)

Pieces: little brown bear   green fish (large)
little brown   green fish (small)
  bear's blue vest   brown mother bear
flower   red boots for little
brown father bear   bear
red boots for   blue vest for
  father bear   father bear
yellow coat for   yellow coat for
  father bear   little bear
purple vest for
  mother bear

When I got up this morning, I yawned a
* big yawn...*
* Just like daddy.*
I washed my face, got dressed, and had a
* big breakfast...*
* Just like daddy.*
And then I put on my yellow coat and blue vest
* and my red boots...*
* Just like daddy.*
And we went fishing — Daddy, Mommy, and me.
On the way, I picked a flower and gave it
* to my mother...*
* Just like daddy.*
When we got to the lake, I put a worm on
* my hook...*
* Just like daddy.*
All day we fished, and I caught a big
* fish...*
* Just like mommy!!!*

The Tree in the Woods

(See Appendix for patterns.)

Pieces: grass   bird's nest
treetop   bird's egg
tree trunk bird
tree limb   wing
tree branch feather

(The flannel board can be used to build the song by placing first the grass and then the treetop, trunk, limb, branch, nest, egg, bird, wing, and feather, as each verse calls for them.)

Now in the woods there was a tree,
The finest tree that you ever did see,
And the green grass grew all around,
*   around, around,*
And the green grass grew all around.

And on that grass there was a trunk,
The finest trunk that you ever did see,
And the trunk was on the tree,
And the tree was in the woods,
And the green grass grew all around,
*   around, around,*
And the green grass grew all around.

And on that trunk there was a limb,
The finest limb that you ever did see,
And the limb was on the trunk,
And the trunk was on the tree,
And the tree was in the woods,
And the green grass grew all around,
*   around, around,*
And the green grass grew all around.

And on that limb there was a branch,
The finest branch that you ever did see,
And the branch was on the limb,
And the limb was on the trunk,
And the trunk was on the tree,
And the tree was in the woods,
And the green grass grew all around,
*   around, around,*
And the green grass grew all around.

And on that branch there was a nest,
The finest nest that you ever did see,
And the nest was on the branch,
And the branch was on the limb,
And the limb was on the trunk,
And the trunk was on the tree,
And the tree was in the woods,
And the green grass grew all around,
*   around, around,*
And the green grass grew all around.

And in that nest there was an egg,
The finest egg that you ever did see,

And the egg was in the nest,
And the nest was on the branch,
And the branch was on the limb,
And the limb was on the trunk,
And the trunk was on the tree,
And the tree was in the woods,
And the green grass grew all around,
*   around, around,*
And the green grass grew all around.

And on that egg there was a bird,
The finest bird that you ever did see,
And the bird was on the egg,
And the egg was in the nest,
And the nest was on the branch,
And the branch was on the limb,
And the limb was on the trunk,
And the trunk was on the tree,
And the tree was in the woods,
And the green grass grew all around,
*   around, around,*
And the green grass grew all around.

And on that bird there was a wing,
The finest wing that you ever did see,
And the wing was on the bird,
And the bird was on the egg,
And the egg was in the nest,
And the nest was on the branch,
And the branch was on the limb,
And the limb was on the trunk,
And the trunk was on the tree,
And the tree was in the woods,
And the green grass grew all around,
*   around, around,*
And the green grass grew all around.

And on that wing there was a feather,
The finest feather that you ever did see,
And the feather was on the wing,
And the wing was on the bird,
And the bird was on the egg,
And the egg was in the nest,
And the nest was on the branch,
And the branch was on the limb,
And the limb was on the trunk,
And the trunk was on the tree,
And the tree was in the woods,
And the green grass grew all around,
*   around, around,*
And the green grass grew all around.

Riddle

Pieces: Triangles of felt in red, blue, yellow, green, purple, orange, brown, black, and white.

Teacher: Riddle, riddle, ree.
      What color do I see?
      _____ (child's name) has it on his/her
      _____ (shirt, pants, and so forth).
      What color can this be?

(When the color is identified the following is said.)

Group: It's _____, _____, _____
      (Example: red, red, red)
      Mary (instead of Mary substitute name of child who named the color) did say.
      Let's see what colors we can find today.

(Teacher puts triangle of same color on flannel board. Child whose name was mentioned is asked whether he or she, or a friend of the child's choice, is going to guess the name of the color. Each child is asked whether he or she wants to guess the color. Activity ends with line of triangles that group names as each triangle is removed.)

One, Two, Buckle My Shoe

Pieces: Numerals 1 through 10   crossed sticks
              shoe   straight sticks
              door   hen

(See Appendix for patterns.)

One, Two,
Buckle my shoe;
Three, four,
Knock at the door;
Five, six,
Pick up sticks;
Seven, eight,
Lay them straight;
Nine, ten,
Big fat hen.

The Three Billy Goats Gruff

Pieces: Big Billy Goat Gruff   stream
              Middle-Sized Billy Goat Gruff   troll
              Small Billy Goat Gruff   grassy hill
              bridge

Once upon a time there lived three billy goat brothers — Big Billy Goat Gruff, Middle-Sized Billy Goat Gruff, and Small Billy Goat Gruff. Their stomachs were empty, and they wanted to eat the soft, tender grass that grew on the hillside across a stream.

To get to the grass, they had to cross on a bridge. Under the bridge, lived an ugly, mean troll with bulging eyes and a long, long nose. The ugly troll liked to eat billy goats!

Small Billy Goat Gruff started to cross the bridge. His hooves made a trip-trop, trip-trop, trip-trop sound.

"Who's that tripping over my bridge?" roared the troll.

"It's only I, Small Billy Goat Gruff, on the way to the green hillside to eat grass," said Small Billy Goat Gruff.

"I'm coming up to eat you!" said the troll. "That would be foolish," said Small Billy Goat Gruff. "My middle-sized brother will be coming this way soon. He's fatter and bigger and would make a fine dinner."

"Be off with you," said the troll.

Small Billy Goat Gruff crossed the bridge and munched the tender blades of grass on the hillside.

Soon Middle-Sized Billy Goat Gruff came across the bridge, trip-trop, trip-trop, trip-trop.

"Who's that tripping over my bridge?" said the troll.

"It is I, Middle-Sized Billy Goat Gruff, on my way to the grassy hillside."

"I'm coming up to eat you!" answered the troll.

"Indeed, that's very foolish, for Big Billy Goat Gruff is right behind me. What a fine dinner he will make for he's much bigger and fatter than I," said Middle-Sized Billy Goat Gruff.

"Be off with you then," the troll said. And Middle-Sized Billy Goat Gruff crossed to eat next to his brother on the grassy hillside.

Soon large, heavy hooves were heard on the bridge, trip-trop, trip-trop, trip-trop. It was Big Billy Goat Gruff.

"Who's that tripping over my bridge?" roared the troll.

"It is I, Big Billy Goat Gruff," answered the Big Billy Goat Gruff in his biggest voice.

"I'm coming up to eat you," said the troll.

"Well come ahead! My two big horns will take care of you!" Big Billy Goat Gruff said, as his head went down, and he ran straight into the troll pushing him into the stream. The troll has not been seen or heard from since that day, and the three Billy Goats Gruff cross the bridge to eat their fill of tender grass every day.

> Snip, Snap, Snout
> This tale's told out.

The Best Home for Me

Author Unknown

Once upon a time, there was a frog. His home was under a great big stone by the side of a river. He thought he had the best home in all the world, but he wasn't quite sure. He thought he would ask and see whether anyone had as nice a home as he.

He sat near his rock wondering who to ask first, and a beautiful bird flew by. "Oh, Mister Bird," he called, "wouldn't you like to have a home like me, under a stone that is cool as can be?"

"It might suit you, but it wouldn't suit me," said the little bird. "I like my nest in a big spreading tree." And away he flew to his nest.

Now the frog was a little bit puzzled, and as he looked down into the clear water of the river, he saw something swimming along.

What was it? Yes, a fish. "Oh, Mr. Fish," called the frog, "wait a moment and talk with me. Wouldn't you like to have a home like me, under a stone that is as cool as can be?"

"It might suit you, but it wouldn't suit me. The seas and the rivers are for fish like me." And away he swam. "Well," thought the frog, "I must ask someone else."

Just then a little bumblebee came flying along to sip the nectar from the flowers that grew by the river's edge. "Oh, Mr. Bumblebee, wouldn't you like to have a home like me, under a stone that is as cool as can be?"

The bumblebee looked at the frog's stone and then answered. "It might suit you, but it wouldn't suit me. A hive is the best place for a bumblebee." And away he flew. The frog watched him fly away to his hive, and then Mr. Frog saw a squirrel who was eating a nut.

"Ho, ho, Mr. Squirrel," he called. "How would you like to have a home like me, under a stone that is as cool as can be?"

"It might suit you, but it wouldn't suit me. I like my home in a hollow tree. That is the home that is best for me." And he winked his little eye and frisked away. The little frog was more puzzled than ever. He thought, "I wonder who does have the nicest home."

Just then he heard the sound of singing, and when he looked up he saw a little girl who had come down to the river's edge to play. "I'm sure that little girl will know who has the best home. I'm going to ask her. "Oh, little girl," he called. "Please tell me something. How would you like to have a home like me, under a stone that is as cool as can be?" And the little girl answered, "It might suit you, but it wouldn't suit me."

> "My mother told me
> That all homes are best;
> For the fishes, the sea;
> For the bird, his nest;
> For the squirrel,
> His home in the hollow tree;
> And for you, your home under a stone
> That is as cool, cool, as can be."

And so the little frog knew that all the homes were best. And he loved his home under the great gray stone where it was cold and damp and dark as can be.

This Old Man

Pieces:

old man	tree
shoe	two clouds (heaven)
door	thumb
sticks	hive
gate	vine
10 bones	hen
dog	numerals 1 through 10

1. This old man, he played one, he played knick-knack on my thumb.
   With a knick-knack paddy-whack, give a dog a bone.
   This old man came rolling home.

2. This old man, he played two, he played knick-knack on my shoe.
   With a knick-knack paddy-whack, give a dog a bone.
   This old man came rolling home.

3. This old man, he played three, he played knick-knack on my tree.
   With a knick-knack paddy-whack, give a dog a bone.
   This old man came rolling home.

4. This old man, he played four, he played knick-knack on my door.

With a knick-knack paddy-whack, give a dog a bone.
This old man came rolling home.

5. This old man, he played five, he played knick-knack on my hive.
With a knick-knack paddy-whack, give a dog a bone.
This old man came rolling home.

6. This old man, he played six, he played knick-knack on my sticks.
With a knick-knack paddy-whack, give a dog a bone.
This old man came rolling home.

7. This old man, he played seven, he played knick-knack up in heaven.
With a knick-knack paddy-whack, give a dog a bone.
This old man came rolling home.

8. This old man, he played eight, he played knick-knack on my gate.
With a knick-knack paddy-whack, give a dog a bone.
This old man came rolling home.

9. This old man, he played nine, he played knick-knack on my vine.

With a knick-knack paddy-whack, give a dog a bone.
This old man came rolling home.

10. This old man, he played ten, he played knick-knack on my hen.
With a knick-knack paddy-whack, give a dog a bone.
This old man came rolling home.

Summary

A flannel board presentation is one of the most popular and successful listening activities for the young child. Stories are told while figures and shapes are moved on the board. The children can learn new ideas and words by seeing the visual model while listening to the story.

Beginning teachers practice presentations with words and pieces until the activity flows smoothly. The children's feedback is noted. Flannel board activities in many other learning areas besides language development take place in early childhood centers.

A wide variety of fabrics are available for both boards and pieces; felt and flannel are the most commonly used materials for boards.

Student Activities

- Visit a center to watch a flannel board presentation, or invite a teacher to present an activity to the class.

- Give a presentation to a small group of classmates. The classmates should make helpful suggestions in written form while watching the presentation, trying to look at the presentations through the eyes of a child.

- Write an original story for the flannel board on ditto masters. Masters can be purchased from a stationery or office supply store. Include patterns for your pieces on ditto masters.

- If videotape equipment is available in your classroom, give a flannel board presentation and evaluate yourself.

- Make three flannel board sets, using any materials desired.

- Visit a school supply store and price commercial flannel boards. Compare costs for constructing a teacher-made flannel board, and report at the next class meeting.

- Make a personal flannel board.

- Research stories and sets with multicultural variety.

- Create set pieces for *The Billy Goats Gruff* or *Best Home For Me.*

Unit Review

A. List the types of materials used in board construction.

B. Name the kinds of materials used to make flannel board pieces.

C. In your opinion, what is the best way to color pieces for flannel boards?

D. Why is the use of visual aids valuable?

E. Place in correct order.
1. Give a flannel board presentation.
2. Set up area with board.
3. Check pieces.
4. Practice.
5. Place pieces in order of appearance.
6. Gather children.
7. Place pieces out of sight.
8. Discuss what happened during the activity with children (optional).
9. Store set by keeping pieces flat.
10. Introduce the set with a motivational statement if you wish.

F. What color flannel (or felt) would you use to cover your own board? Why?

G. Finish the following statements.
1. A board is set up slanting back slightly because _____ .
2. A folding flannel board with handles is a good idea because _____ .
3. If children touch the pieces during a teacher presentation, the teacher should say _____ .
4. The main reason teachers like to store set pieces in a flat position is _____ .
5. One advantage of a flannel board made from a large styrofoam sheet is _____ .
6. One disadvantage of a flannel board made from a large styrofoam sheet is _____ .

Resources

Anderson, Paul. *Storytelling with the Flannel Board*, Book One and Book Two, T. S. Denison and Co., 9601 Newton Avenue S., Minneapolis, MN, 1972. (Useful as a source of additional stories and patterns.)

Kohl, Diane M. *Teaching With The Flannel Board*. Minneapolis, MN: T. S. Denison, 1986.

Pederson, Marcy. *Magic Moments* (self-published brochure). P. O. Box 53635, San Jose, CA 95135-0635, 1984. (A creative young teacher shares her child-participation group time ideas and patterns.)

Peralta, Chris. *Flannel Board Activities for the Bilingual Classroom*. La Arana Publ., 11209 Malat Way, Culver City, CA 90232, 1981. (A collection of Latin-American traditional stories for the flannel board, patterns included.)

Scott, Louise Binder, and J. J. Thompson. *Rhymes for Fingers and Flannel Boards*. Minneapolis, MN: T. S. Denison and Co., Inc., 1984.

Sweeney, Mary, and Jeff Fegan. *Flanneltales*. 310 Sequoia Ave., San Jose, CA 95126. (Classic stories from many cultures. A self-published book.)

Taylor, Frances, and Gloria Vaugh. *The Flannel Board Storybook*. Humanics Learning, P.O. Box 7447, Atlanta, GA 30309, 1980.

Vonk, Idelee. *Storytelling With the Flannel Board*, Book Three. Minneapolis, MN: T. S. Denison and Co., 9601 Newton Avenue S., Minneapolis, MN. (More patterns and activities.)

Wilmes, Liz, and Dick Wilmes. *Felt Board Fun*. Dundee: Building Books, 1987.

Section 5

Speech Growth

Conversation, Expression and Dramatization

Throughout the day in an early child-hood center, children's and teacher's speech and conversation accompany activities. This section focuses on teacher techniques and lively, planned activities that can increase children's talking and expression of ideas. Tips for conducting small-group activities and circle times will interest beginning teachers.

Unit 17, Understanding Differences, provides information on the speech dif-ferences that preschool teachers find in their classrooms. The reader is alerted to alternate courses of action that can be used with children whose speech develop-ment is different from most of the others in the group and is urged to respect diversity while promoting growth of children's language abilities.

YOUNG CHILDREN'S ACQUISITION OF OFFENSIVE SPEECH

When does offensive speech first appear in the speech of young children? How is the acquisition of these spoken words related to other developmental, social, or linguistic processes?

It is reasonable to assume a different set of words is considered offensive to children and to adults. Several reports indicate that common adult obscenities appear in the speech of preschool children. Offensive words are used in the narrative stories that children tell (Sutton-Smith and Abrams, 1978), in spontaneous speech in home settings (Hall, Nagy, and Linn, 1984), and during parent-child "sex" discussions (Berges, et al., 1983). Obscenities also occur as early as two-and-a-half years in metaphoric word play (Stross, 1975), in name-calling episodes (Winslow, 1969), and in children's humor (Wolfenstein, 1954).

It should be noted that initially these words may not be fully realized in a connotative sense and may be used primarily to gain the parents' attention. Parents have reported their interest in childhood obscenity to counselors where concerns about semantic interpretation appear (Harrison and Hinshaw, 1968, Hartmann, 1973, 1975; Mead, 1951).

One precursor of obscenity or name-calling in children is the expression of anger in general. Behaviors such as tantrums, screaming, holding breath, striking, and verbal threats accompany irritating conditions like ill health, loss of sleep or fatigue, bedwetting, constipation, and so forth (Goodenough, 1931). Verbal outbursts occur as early as two years of age in association with such accompanying intrinsic factors. They also appear in relation to other extrinsic activities like bedtime, meals, changing clothes, going to the toilet, and playing with playmates.

(Continues on page 224)

The link to obscenity use in young children probably has its origins in early name-calling and insult rituals that appear in group play settings. These exchanges usually revolve around physical, mental, or social differences between children. Children make up words or descriptors to exacerbate or personalize their comments to the target, which is usually another child.

Anger and name-calling may serve to fill social needs of children, who are establishing the boundaries of proper conduct (in and out of group behavior) or establishing a personal identity. The communication function would be to signal on a child's level the features of physical, mental, and social deviance and put these deviations in concrete terms during conversations.

Offensive words emerge as powerful tools for young children which may be later employed in a variety of emotional and aggressive situations or events. We should determine how children interpret the words they use and why they use the words they do. In doing so, we need to look at parental response to obscenity and how parents reward or punish such events. Additionally, we need to explore how the use of obscenity, parental and peer reaction to it, are related to later personality development. [1]

[1] Dr. Tim Jay, "The Role Of Obscene Speech in Psychology", *Interfaces: Linguistics, Psychology, and Health Therapeutics*, 12.3 (Sept. 1985), 75-91.

UNIT 13

Realizing Speaking Goals

OBJECTIVES

After studying this unit, you should be able to

- state five goals of planned speech activities.
- describe appropriate teacher behavior in daily conversations with children.
- give three examples of questioning techniques.

In a well-planned classroom, a child has many opportunities to speak. While some activities are planned, others just happen. Classroom discussion is paramount; throw away most or all of your ideas about quiet classrooms and instead aim for a dynamic room where discussion reigns. In this type of atmosphere, true literacy emerges. Help children see the uses of speaking in social interactions in their daily lives and tie speech to print and reading activities when possible.

Activities can be divided into two groups: structured and unstructured. *Structured activities* are those that the teacher plans, prepares, and leads. The teacher is, for awhile, at the center of all action — motivating, presenting ideas, giving demonstrations, eliciting child ideas and comments and promoting conversation. *Unstructured activities*, on the other hand, may still be prepared by the teacher, but the children decide the action through self-directed play, and the teacher is cast primarily in the role of cohort, confidant, and interested party. The teacher remains conversational and supportive.

PROGRAM GOALS

Each center contains a unique group of children and adults. A center has its own geography, and its children

come from different segments of society, so the goals and priorities of one program may differ from others. There are, however, some common factors among centers. The following goals are acceptable to most programs. They give the teacher a basis for planning speaking activities and daily conversational exchanges. Each child should be helped to attain:

- Confidence in the ability to use speech with others.
- Enjoyment of speaking experiences in play, conversations, and groups.
- Acceptance of the idea that another's speech may be different.
- A higher level of interest in the meaning of new words.

And each child should be helped to increase his or her skill in:

- Using speech for ideas, feelings, and needs.
- Using speech to solve problems.
- Using speech creatively in play situations.
- Coordinating speech and body actions.
- Waiting for a turn to speak.

The overall goal in the development of speech communication in language arts is to increase each child's

FIGURE 13-1 There should be both a desire and a need to speak.

FIGURE 13-2 A valuable learning experience results from the child's interest in a flower.

ability to use the speech he or she already possesses (figure 13-1), and to help the child move, when ready, toward the use of standard English. Program goals can be realized mainly through (1) the planning of daily activities, (2) daily staff-child and child-child interaction, and (3) the use of equipment and materials.

Skarpness and Carson (1987) note that appropriate child behavior in kindergarten is aided if certain speaking and listening skills have been acquired:

> Children who are encouraged to express themselves, practice their speaking skills, and listen carefully to others are likely to adjust more readily to changing situations within the classroom.

A wide variety of different experiences can provide many learning opportunities. An activity can follow, review, and add depth to a previous one. One has to consider how much practice time is available, as Dumtschin (1988) points out "children need to practice language skills to perfect them, just as they practice walking or riding a bicycle."

The special interests or needs of each child are considered when planning daily programs. Programs then become more valuable and meaningful (figure 13-2).

DAILY CONVERSATIONS

Ginott (1976) advises teachers to treat all children with respect, as though they already are the persons they are capable of becoming. Excellent teachers make their students feel valuable, competent, and worthwhile. These are the attitudes and behaviors every would-be teacher should cultivate in conversation:

- Concern for each child's well-being.
- An unwillingness to interrupt a child's conversation to respond to an adult.
- A willingness to share the small moments of child accomplishment, sometimes even recognizing a child's achievement in a nonverbal way across a busy classroom.
- Consideration of children's verbal comments as worthy contributions and respect for individual opinions.

- Respect of each child's potential.
- Special regard for children as future leaders and discoverers.

Some of the best activities happen when the teacher notices what the child or group is focusing on and uses the opportunity to expand interest, knowledge, and enjoyment. A rainbow, a delivery truck, or any chance happening can become the central topic of active speaking by the children (figure 13-3).

Whether limited or advanced, a child's speech is immediately accepted and welcomed. Teachers carefully guard and protect each child's self-confidence. By waiting patiently and reading nonverbal clues, teachers become understanding listeners (figure 13-4).

Every effort should be made to give a logical response, showing the child that the teacher finds value in the communication. Touching, offering a reassuring arm or hand, and giving one's whole attention to the child often seems to relax him or her and increase speech production.

Children are more willing to speak when the proper classroom atmosphere is maintained:

- The tone of the room is warm and relaxed, and children have choices.
- Speaking is voluntary, not mandatory.
- The speaking group is small.

- The group listens attentively.
- Any speaking attempt is welcomed.
- Effort and accomplishments are recognized.

A teacher's willingness to engage in light-hearted dialogue may make the child more open to talking for the fun of it. When the mood is set for discovery, the teacher becomes active in the quest for answers, carefully guiding children through their exploration and expression (figure 13-5).

Adults who emphasize the reasons for events and who take a questioning, thoughtful, and systematic approach to problems become model explorers. Thinking out loud while sharing activities is a useful device. "I wonder what would happen if you put the block there?" a teacher might ask. In their speech, young children often deal with the reality of what is happening around them; teachers' speech should also be based on this concept.

In reacting to young children's sometimes awkward, fractured, or incorrect speech, adults intuitively provide useful corrective feedback (Lay-Dopyera and Dopyera, 1982). The child's "posta put in" would automatically be accepted and corrected with, "Yes, the blocks go on the shelf." Seasoned teachers listen for content, the ideas behind words, and matter-of-factly model correct usage so smoothly the child isn't made to

FIGURE 13-3 Children speak and listen while they play. *(From Early Childhood Practicum Guide, by Machado and Meyer, © 1984 by Delmar Publishers Inc.)*

FIGURE 13-4 Some activities tend to quiet speech while the child is absorbed in what he or she is doing.

FIGURE 13-5 Teachers hope that children will always feel comfortable asking questions and making comments.

FIGURE 13-6 Many times, conversations increase understandings of word meanings.

feel that his or her speech usage was in any way deficient. The teachers must know how to make alert, sensitive comments that ensure that the children will continue to see the teacher as a responsive, accepting adult.

Halliday (1973) has researched human speech development and classified differing "functions" of human speech. His classifications follow. Teachers observing children will notice the young child's increasing use of speech in social situations.

- *Instrumental* speech satisfies wants and needs.
- *Regulatory* speech helps children control others.
- *Interactional* speech establishes and maintains contact with others.
- *Personal function* speech expresses and asserts individuality.
- *Heuristic function* speech helps children learn and describe.
- *Imaginative function* speech creates images and aids pretending.
- *Representational* speech informs.

All of these speech functions are present in the average preschool classroom.

What are young children fond of talking about? Themselves and what they are doing! They have their own views and opinions about the world around them.

As their social contact increases, they exchange their ideas with other children (figure 13-6). When they become older preschoolers, they typically engage in criticism, commands, requests, threats, and questions and answers (Singer and Revenson, 1979). As a teacher listens to child-to-child conversations, he or she can make out both self-interest speech and speech that indicates social-intellectual involvement. Quite a lot of child conversation reflects the children's active, exploring, questioning minds and their attempts to try, test, manipulate, control, and discover what speech can do for them. Flights of fantasy and make-believe play are also evident.

Certain teacher behaviors and planned programs enhance children's speaking abilities. Are there factors that work counter to the realization of goals? Hough, Nurss, and Goodson (1984) compared everyday interactions in two child centers and found one center they describe as lacking language stimulation. They reported that the children spent most of their time in teacher-directed large-group activities and that most of the children's language behavior was receptive, such as listening to and following teachers' directions. Although teachers provided adequate oral language models, they were not active listeners, did not encourage curiosity, and did not spontaneously expand on children's vocabulary or concepts.

Teachers should try to avoid the following behaviors, because they discourage healthy speech development:

- Inappropriate or irrelevant teacher comments.
- Talking at rather than with children.
- A controlling and commanding mode of interaction.
- Repeating oneself often.
- Criticizing child speech.
- Speaking primarily to other classroom adults.

SUGGESTED INTERACTION GUIDES

A teacher is a speech model for children. The following guides for teachers in daily verbal conversations are based on understanding the level of each child, since preschoolers range in abilities. These guidelines help develop speaking ability when dealing with young nonverbal, or slightly verbal, children.

- Let the child see your face and mouth clearly.
- Bend your knees and talk at the child's eye level.
- Use simple gestures. Show meanings with your hands as well as with your eyes as you talk.
- If possible, let the child touch, feel, smell, taste, and see whatever is interesting as you listen. Talk in simple sentences.
- Watch for nonverbal reactions; the child's face or body actions may show interest, fear, or other emotions (figure 13-7). Supply words to fit the situation: "Here's the ball." "The dog will not hurt you." "Do you want a cracker?"
- Talk to the nonverbal child slowly, stressing key words such as nouns and verbs. Repeat them if the child does not seem to understand.
- If you cannot understand a word, repeat it back to the child in a relaxed way. Say, "Show me, Mary," if the child tries again and you still cannot understand the word.
- Accept a child's attempt to say a word. If a child says "lellow," say, "Yes, the paint is yellow." Articulation will improve with age and good speech modeling.
- Answer *expressive jargon* (groups of sounds without recognizable words) or jabbering with suitable statements such as "You're telling me," or "You don't say." Go along with the child's desire to put words together in a sentence.
- Play games in which the child copies sounds or words; make games fun. Stop before the child loses interest.
- Watch for the child's lead. If he or she is interested in some activity or object, talk about it in simple sentences (figure 13-8), such as, "The kitty feels soft" or "Pet the kitty" or "Bobby's going down the slide."
- Make commands simple: "It's time to go inside." Use gestures with the words: "Put the toys in the box." (Indicate actions as you say the words.)
- Encourage the child's imitations (whether verbal or nonverbal) with a smile or touch or words. Show that the effort is appreciated.
- Pause and wait patiently for the child's response.

The following guidelines help develop speaking ability when dealing with children who speak in one-word phrases or simple sentences.

- Enlarge a child's one-word sentences into meaningful simple sentences, for example, "ball" to "The ball bounces."
- Use naming words to describe objects and actions: "The red ball is round" (figure 13-9). "The dog wants to lick your hand."
- Use conjunctions (and, but, so, also, or), possessives (mine, theirs, ours, Billy's, yours, his, hers), and negatives (is not, will not, do not, isn't, don't, won't, am not).

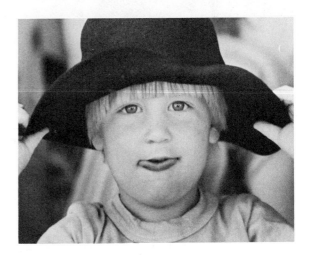

FIGURE 13-7 A face can say a lot to a teacher. *(From* Early Childhood Practicum Guide, *by Machado and Meyer,* © *1984 by Delmar Publishers Inc.)*

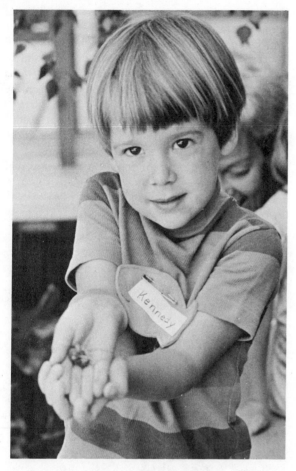

FIGURE 13-8 If the child is interested in some activity or object, talk about it with the child.

- Help the child talk about his or her feelings.
- Use previously learned words with new words: "The black candy is called licorice." "Your dog is a poodle; this dog is a beagle." "It's a kind of hat called a baseball cap."
- Ask simple questions that help the child to find out and discover while his or her interest is high: "Where did you find that round rock?"
- Play labeling games with pictures and objects.
- Correct speech errors such as "wented" or "goed" by matter-of-factly saying the correct word in a sentence: "Yesterday you went to the store." (Omit any corrective tone of voice.) The child may answer by saying it the same as before, but you

have modeled correct usage, and in time it will be copied.
- Accept hesitant speech and stuttering in a patient, interested way. When a child is excited or under stress, ideas may not develop into words properly.
- Wait patiently while a child tries to speak; silently hold eye contact. The thought may get lost, but if you're a good listener, and if you respond with interest to what is said, the child will try again.

When the child speaks in sentences and comes close to mature speech, the teacher should:

- Include appropriate classifications or categories in sentences to help children form concepts: "Dogs and cats are animals."
- Ask questions that help the child pinpoint identifying characteristics (figure 13-10): "Does it have a tail?"
- Ask questions that help the child see what is alike and what is different.
- After modeling a sentence pattern in conversation, ask a simple question so that the child can imitate the proper form while it is still fresh in his or her mind: "I think this lemon tastes sour. How does the lemon taste to you?"
- Help the child keep ideas in order. What happened first? What happened next? What came last?

FIGURE 13-9 "You are talking into the toy telephone."

- State instructions clearly, building from one- to two- or three-part directions: "First wash your hands; then you can choose a cracker."
- Use prepositions in your speech. Say them with gestures: "Put the toy on the shelf. Thank you. The blocks go inside the box." (Use your hand to show position as you speak.)
- Use adjectives (big, little, bright, red, soft, and so forth) and comparatives (more, less, lighter, heavier, shorter, tallest): "Tell me about the rubber doll." "Yes, this pink doll is bigger."
- Ask the child to take simple verbal messages to another staff member: "Tell Mrs. Brown it's time to fix the snack." Alert other staff members to the fact that you are trying to promote verbal memory and self-confidence.
- Help the child discover cause and effect: "Teacher, I'm afraid of bugs." "Why do bugs make you afraid, Billy?"
- Remember that what you say in response to the child helps the child in many ways. Really listen. Answer every child if possible. When children talk at the same time, say "I want to hear each one." "Mary, please say it again." "John, you can tell us next."
- Give ownership to the ideas children contribute: "Yesterday Nancy told us . . . ." "Kate's idea is . . . ."

Dumtschin (1988) mentions a technique in adult-child conversation from the work of Fujiki and Brinton (1984) that is termed *recasting*. This is very similar to expansion and feedback, previously mentioned. Recasting fills in what's missing or gently changes the child's incorrect usage in the adult's answering comment and extends the child's idea. If a child says, "I like apples," for example, the teacher could respond, "Apples taste good, don't they?" or "I like green ones, don't you?"

SETTINGS FOR PREPLANNED SPEAKING ACTIVITIES

Speaking activities occur when children are inside or outside the classroom or when they are on the move. Preplanned activities are more successful when both children and teachers are comfortable and unhurried and when there are no distractions. Peers will be a valuable source of words and meanings.

Close attention should be given to the seating space between children at group times. Lighting and heating in the room must also be considered. Soft textures and rugs add warmth and comfort. A half-circle seating arrangement, with the teacher in the center, provides a good view of both the teacher and what is to be seen.

Ease of viewing depends on eye level and seating arrangement. Whenever possible, the objects children are to look at should be at their eye level. Teachers often sit in child-sized chairs while conducting language arts experiences. Screens, dividers, and bookcases can help to lessen distractions.

QUESTIONING SKILLS

A teacher's questions often prompt children to think. Questions can also help them see details they would otherwise have missed. Sometimes questions help a child form relationships between objects and ideas; they may prompt the child to speak about both feelings and thoughts; they can lead the child to a new interest. Skill in questioning is an important teaching ability.

FIGURE 13-10 "Are there any other shapes that are round like a ball?"

Questions asked by a teacher can often lead children to discovery.

The following example illustrates the teacher's role in stimulating the thought process that emerges from play. The teacher, who has created the climate for learning by supplying and arranging the equipment, sees a child playing with cars on ramps that he has constructed with blocks. She knows that if a car is placed on a slope made with blocks, the speed with which it descends and the distance it goes are affected by the slope and length of the ramp. She asks, "Johnny, did this blue car go faster than the red one?" She also introduces new words to his vocabulary — slant, ramp, slow, faster, above, below, under, tall, smaller than — and uses and elicits this vocabulary in conversation (Danoff et al., 1977).

Teachers need to be sensitive to the anxiety that some children may have. In past experiences, if a child's answers have been overcorrected, or if adults' questions are associated with punishment, teacher's questions can cause children to be silent and tense.

Teachers use "choice" questions at times. It allows them to slip specific, descriptive words into their speech while the child is focused: "Do you want the red paint (pointing) or the blue paint (pointing)?"

Also important in asking questions is the teacher's acceptance of the child's answers. Since each child answers a question based on his or her own experience, children may give very different answers. The following conversation (observed at the San Jose City College Child Development Center) shows how a teacher handled an unexpected answer.

Teacher:	(Conversation has centered around television sets.) "Where could we go to buy a television set?"
Frank:	"Macy's."
Chloe:	"At a pear store."
Wanda:	"The TV store."
Teacher:	"Frank says Macy's sells television sets. Chloe thinks we could buy one at a 'pear' store. Wanda thought at a TV store. Maybe we could go to three places to buy one. Chloe, have you seen television sets at the 'pear' store?"
Chloe:	"The pear store has lots of 'em."
Teacher:	"You've been to a 'pear' store?"
Chloe:	"Our TV broke, and we took it to the 'pear' store."
Teacher:	"The repair shop fixed my broken television set, too. Yes, sets can be for sale at a repair shop."

The teacher's task is to keep the speech and answers coming, encouraging each child's expression of ideas. Sometimes a question can be answered with a question. When a child says, "What does a rabbit eat?" the teacher might say, "How could we find out?" The teacher knows that a real experience is better than a quick answer.

When using questions, the level of difficulty should be recognized. Early childhood teachers can use carefully asked questions to find the child's level of understanding. Teachers try to help each child succeed in activities while offering a challenge at the same time. Even snack time can be a time to learn new language skills.

Open-ended questions are very useful and teachers try to increase their ability to ask them. *Open-ended questions* are defined as questions with many possible answers.

Almy (1975) points out:

Some teachers are so intent on imparting information to children that they forget to assess the ways it may be assimilated. Thus answers to open-ended questions — "Can you tell me about...?" "What do you think about...?" — are often more revealing than answers to questions with a more specific focus. They can be followed by "Tell me more," "How do you explain that?" "Some people think that..." "What do you think?" Learning to ask questions that do not provide children with clues for the expected answer takes both verbal and facial control.

Teachers' questions can be classified into eight main types:

- Recall — asks child to remember information, names, words, and so forth. Recall questions are the type most often asked; teachers ask this type 80% to 90% of the time (figure 13-11). The learning activities section of this unit asks you to conduct an observational study concerning this point. Could it be this type of question was modeled constantly in most teachers' own elementary schooling? Example: What color is this ball?
- Convergent — asks child to compare or contrast

similarities or differences and seek relationships. Example: How are these two toy cars alike?

- Divergent — asks child to predict or theorize. Example: If the boy steps on the marble, what might happen?
- Evaluation — asks child for a personal opinion or judgment or asks child to explore feelings. Example: What would be on your plate if you could have your favorite food?
- Observation — asks child to watch or describe what he or she senses. Example: What's happening to the ant on the window sill?
- Explanation — asks child to state cause and effect, reasons, and/or descriptions. Example: The clay feels different today. What do you think happened to it?
- Action — asks child to move body or perform a physical task. Example: Can you show us how to walk like a duck?
- Open ended — many answers are possible. Example: How do children get from their homes to their school in the morning?

FIGURE 13-11 A teacher asking a recall question might say, "Ben, what's the name of the alphabet letter in your hand?"

The way questions are phrased may produce short or longer answers. Questions using "what" or "where" usually receive one-word or word-phrase answers. Many questions, such as Do you? Did you? Can you? Will you? Have you? Would you? can be answered by yes or no. This type of question fits the level of the very young.

Questions that help a child compare or connect ideas may begin with:

What would happen if . . . ?

Which one is longer?

How are these two alike?

Why did you say these were different?

What happened next?

If it fell off the table, what would happen to it?

Can you guess which one will be first?

Could this ball fit inside this can?

The following are examples of questions that encourage problem solving or stimulate creative thought:

If you had a handful of pennies, what would you buy?

Could you tell me what you are going to do when you're as big as your dad?

Can you think of a way to open this coconut?

How could we find out where this ant lives?

These questions can be answered by the more mature speakers. Through close listening and observation, the teacher can form questions that the child will want to answer.

Summary

Each early childhood educational program is based on goals. Goals state the attitudes and abilities that a center wishes to develop in children. Planned activities and daily teacher-child conversations help the school reach its goals.

Teachers plan for both group and individual needs. They converse skillfully with children of varying degrees of fluency. There are specific teacher techniques that promote children's expression of ideas.

Questions are asked by both children and teachers. By observing, listening, and interacting, teachers are better able to encourage speaking abilities.

Student Activities

- List five speaking area goals in your own order of priority.

- Interview a preschool teacher (or teachers). Ask the question, "If you could do only one thing to help young children's speaking ability, what would that be?"

- Observe a preschool group. What differences do you notice in the children's ability to solve problems with words? Cite specific examples.

- Observe a preschool classroom. Write down the teacher's questions (word for word). Using the eight question types from this unit, tell which recorded questions fit which category. Report your findings to the class. Were more recall questions asked?

- Pair off with another student. Try to find some object (from your pocket or book bag, for example) that might interest a preschool child. Alternate asking each other two recall, two convergent, two divergent, and two evaluation questions about the objects. Then try asking observation, explanation-seeking, or prediction questions. Which questions were easy to formulate? Which were difficult?

Unit Review

A. Explain each of the following terms.
   1. structured activities
   2. possessives
   3. negatives
   4. prepositions
   5. comparatives

B. Answer the following questions related to speaking goals.
   1. How can the goals of a program be met?
   2. When children are interested in an object or event, what should the teacher do in order for the children to learn while they are motivated?
   3. Where should visual material be placed for viewing with a group of children?

C. Select the correct answers. Each item may have more than one correct answer.
   1. When children say "wented,"
      a. correct them.
      b. ignore them.
      c. repeat their message correctly.
      d. have them practice "went."
   2. In daily conversations, the teacher should
      a. answer or respond to nonverbal messages.
      b. pair new word meanings with words the children already know.
      c. listen to children who yell in anger.
      d. patiently accept stuttering and hesitant speech.

3. If a child says "richlotti-gongo" to you,
   a. repeat it back if you can, hoping the child will show you what he or she wants to say.
   b. ignore it and wait until you understand the message.
   c. go along with the statement saying, something like "Really, you don't say."
   d. ask the child to speak more clearly.
4. In using questions with young children,
   a. suit the question to the children.
   b. always give them the answer.
   c. insist that they answer correctly.
   d. answer some of the children's questions with your own questions, when appropriate.
5. Planned activities are based on
   a. goals only.
   b. children's current interests only.
   c. goals and children's interests.
   d. knowledge instead of attitudes.

D. Name three ways a teacher can give children confidence in their speaking abilities.

E. Select the appropriate teacher response to the children's comments.

Child	**Teacher**
1. "Dolly"	a. "Did the door hit you? And then what happened?"
2. "Where do this go?"	
3. "I fell down. The door hit me." (Child is unhurt.)	b. "Yes, they are. They both have four legs."
4. "Horses are big like cows."	c. "They taste good; here's a carrot stick to try."
5. "Dem er goodums."	d. "Where does the block go? The block goes on the top shelf."
6. "That's a mouse, teacher."	e. "You can play with this dolly."
	f. "It has fur like a mouse; it's small like a mouse; but it's called a hamster."

F. From the four question types listed, choose the type that matches questions 1 through 8.

   Recall   Divergent   Convergent   Evaluative

1. What would happen if we left this glass full of ice on the table?
2. If your shoes and socks are the same color, would you please stand up?
3. Who can tell me this puppet's name?
4. If you had a dollar, how would you like to spend it?
5. What do we need to make a birthday cake?
6. Why did the basket fall over?
7. Did the door open by itself?
8. Who has the smallest cup?

G. Write down teacher questions that could lead a child to a discovery and promote the child's verbal expression of the discovery in the following situations.
   1. A bird's nest is found in the yard.
   2. The wheel on a bike squeaks.
   3. A flashlight is taken apart.

H. SITUATION. Formulate appropriate teacher comments in the following (1–3). What might a teacher say in response?
   1. Child is complaining that easel paint drips and doesn't stay where he wants it.
   2. It's clean up time, and Sharie (child) says, "Scott and Keith never put anything away!"
   3. Carter is talking about the way water is disappearing in the sun.

   NOW WORK ON CONVERGENT TYPE QUESTIONS. Formulate a possible teacher question.
   4. Megan noticed a bug on the floor.
   5. Christa says, "Dana has new shoes!"
   6. Ryan brings a toy truck to share at group time.

   PLAN EVALUATION QUESTIONS. In 7, 8, and 9, plan evaluation questions that a teacher might use.
   7. "I don't like peanut butter," Romana says.
   8. "This is my favorite book," Linsay declares.
   9. Teacher is introducing a new toy with plastic boats.

References

Almy, Millie. *The Early Childhood Educator at Work*, New York: McGraw-Hill, 1975.

Danoff, Judith, Vicki Breitbart, and Elinor Barr. *Open for Children*. New York: McGraw-Hill, 1977.

de Villiers, Peter A., and Jill G. de Villiers. *Early Language*. Cambridge: Harvard UP, 1982.

Dumtschin, Joyce Ury. "Recognizing Language Development and Delay in Early Childhood." *Young Children* 43.3 (March 1988): 16–24.

Fujiki, M., and B. Brinton. "Supplementing Language Therapy: Working With The Classroom Teacher." *Language, Speech, and Hearing Services in Schools* 15.2 (1984): 98–109.

Ginott, Hiam. *Teacher and Child*. New York: Macmillan, 1972.

Halliday, Michael. *Explorations In The Functions Of Language*. London: Edward Arnold, 1973.

Hendrick, Joanne. *The Whole Child*. St. Louis: Mosby, 1984.

Hough, R. A., J. R. Nurss, and M. S. Goodson. "Children in Day Care: An Observational Study." *Child Study Journal* 14.1 (1984): 33–41.

Lay-Dopyera, Margaret Z. and John E. Dopyera. *Becoming A Teacher Of Young Children*. Lexington, MA: D. C. Heath, 1982.

Lundsteen, Sara W. *Children Learn to Communicate*. Englewood Cliffs, NJ: Prentice-Hall, 1976.

Mayesky, Mary, et al. *Creative Activities for Young Children*. Albany: Delmar Publishers Inc., 1985.

Singer, Dorothy G., and Tracy A. Revenson. *A Piaget Primer: How a Child Thinks*. New York: Internation, 1979.

Skarpness, Lorie R., and David K. Carson. "Correlates of Kindergarten Adjustment: Temperament and Communicative Competence," *Early Childhood Research Quarterly* 2.4 (Dec. 1987): 215–229.

Stewig, John Warren. *Teaching Language Arts in Early Childhood*. New York: Holt, Rinehart and Winston, 1982.

Yawkey, Thomas, et al. *Language Arts and the Young Child*. Itasca, IL: F. E. Peacock, 1981.

UNIT 14

Speech in Play and Routines

OBJECTIVES

After studying this unit, you should be able to

- describe factors that encourage the development of speaking abilities.
- explain the role of the teacher in dramatic play.
- name activities or describe techniques that promote speaking.

A child center should be full of interesting things for a child to do with other children and teachers (figure 14-1). Speech flows best when a child is able to share his or her ideas frequently.

PLAY

Play stimulates much child-to-child conversation, and some kinds of play promote talking more than others. Quiet activities such as painting or working puzzles may tend to limit speech while the child is deeply absorbed.

Teachers plan opportunities for children to play by themselves and with others in small and large groups. Play with another child or a small group almost always requires children to speak. Toddlers may play near each other in a nonverbal, imitative manner using sounds, squeals, and sometimes screams. Interaction with other children promotes the growth of speaking ability.

Early in life, children act out and repeat the words and actions of others. During preschool years, this is called *dramatic play*, and the staffs in early childhood centers plan and prepare for it. Research suggests that dramatic play has important benefits for children

(Fein, 1981) and holds many learning opportunities. It helps children to:

- Develop conversational skills and the ability to express ideas in words.
- Understand the feelings, roles, or work of others.
- Connect actions with words — actions and words go hand-in-hand in dramatic play.
- Develop vocabulary.
- Develop creativity — children imagine, act, and make things up as play progresses.
- Engage in social interaction with other children (figure 14-2).
- Cope with life, sometimes through acting out troubling situations, thus giving an outlet for emotion (for example, almost every doll in an early childhood center gets a spanking periodically when children play house).
- Assume leadership and group-participant roles.

Griffing (1983) describes dramatic play after observing it closely:

The play was rich in symbolic activity — the transformations of self, objects, and situations into characters, objects, and events that existed in imagination only. The play was cognitively com-

FIGURE 14-1 Some of the children may want to talk about their creations, but right now they are busy working.

plex in its organization, consisting of sequences of related ideas and events rather than isolated pretend behaviors. There was extensive social interaction and verbal communication with children taking roles and carrying them out cooperatively.

Pretending is an enjoyable play activity that helps speech growth. When playing house, the child can start out as the grandfather and end up as the baby or the family dog. Much time and effort is devoted to this type of play in childhood. The child engages in this type of activity often and has the ability to slide easily from the real world into the make-believe world.

Teachers watch dramatic play develop from the simple imitative actions of toddlers and younger preschoolers to the elaborate dramatic play of four-year-olds in which language use blossoms. Teachers support each step along the way by providing the necessary objects and materials that enhance dramatic episodes and by offering assistance. To be effective, teachers must observe and be aware of the adult actions and situations that capture child interest enough to prompt reenactment. One surprised student teacher who dreamed up a shaving activity, complete with mirrors, shaving cream, and bladeless razors, found that the boys rolled up their pants legs and shaved their legs. This points out two interesting items: first the

FIGURE 14-2 Dramatic play promotes social interaction.

wisdom of letting razors, even bladeless ones, become play items, and second, how dramatic play often enlightens teachers. Child safety is always the first criterion used to evaluate whether an activity is appropriate.

Four-year-olds engage vigorously in superhero play. As cowboys and Indians, good guys and bad guys, or monster or ghost enactments captured the imaginations of past generations of American children, new heroes have appeared in television cartoons and movies. Superman, batman, spiderman, robots, and space creatures are very common dramatic play themes for four-year-olds. The children become the chosen power figures in actions and words. Segal (1988) probes the possible reasons for the popularity of this type of play.

Like all forms of pretending, superhero play is the child's way of restructuring his world according to his own rules. By dubbing himself a superman, a four-year-old can instantaneously acquire major powers and awesome strength. This strength represents access to a powerful force that is missing in their adult-controlled everyday lives.

Many teachers feel ambivalent when they witness the violence enacted in some of these play episodes, which can require special handling and supervisory decisions to keep children safe. Most teachers set up times for group dialog about superheroes, so that reality and fantasy come under group discussion. Discussions can also be seen and handled as possible learning opportunities for the entire class or group. Other teachers worry about the perceived lack of child creativity in this type of play, because the same theme and action are generally repeated over and over.

Rich home and school experiences (going places and doing things) serve as building blocks for dramatic play. One would have a difficult time playing "restaurant" or "wedding" if there had been no previous experience with either. Early childhood centers can provide activities and objects that promote dramatic play, such as:

- Field trips (figure 14-3).
- Discussions and readings by visitors and guest speakers.
- Books.
- Discussions based on pictures.
- Films, filmstrips, and slides.
- Kits (boxed sets), equipment, and settings for dramatic play.
- Parent career presentations.

DRAMATIC PLAY SETTINGS

A playhouse area with a child-size stove, refrigerator, table, and chairs encourages dramatic play. An old boat, a service station pump, and a telephone booth are examples of other pieces of equipment that children enjoy using in their play.

Furniture found at early childhood centers can be moved into room arrangements that suggest a bus, a house, a tunnel, or a store. Large cardboard boxes may become a variety of different props with, or without, word labels. Large paper bags, ropes, blankets, and discarded work clothes or dress-up clothing (figure 14-4) also stimulate the child to pretend. Items for dramatic play can be obtained from commercial school supply companies, secondhand stores, flea market sales, garage sales, and other sources.

Dramatic Play Kits

Items that go together and suggest the same type of play can be boxed together, ready for use (Bender, 1971). A shoe-shine kit, complete with cans of natural shoe polish, a soft cloth, a shoe brush, play money, and a newspaper or a magazine, is very popular. Children catch on to the activity quickly. Unfortunately not many have seen a shoe-shine stand, so a teacher demonstration on this kit may be necessary.

Other ideas for kits to be used in dramatic play follow.

Post office. Large index cards, used postcards and letters, stamp pads, stampers, crayons or pencils, stamps (Christmas or wildlife seals), mail boxes (shoe box with slot cut in front and name clearly printed), old shoulder bag purses for mailbags, and men's and women's shirts.

Cleaning set. Several brooms, mops, sponge mops, dust cloths, dust pans, sponges, plastic bottles and spray bottles with water, and paper toweling for windows.

Tea party. Set of cups and saucers, plastic pitchers, napkins, vase, tablecloth, plastic spoons, small empty food packages such as cereal boxes, and clay or plastic cookies or biscuits.

FIGURE 14-3 A trip to the fire station can promote firefighter play.

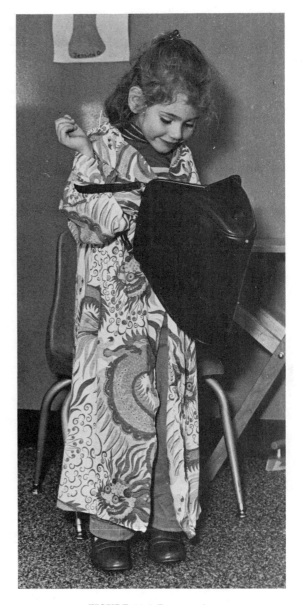

FIGURE 14-4 Dress-up time

Doctor. Stethoscope, bandages, masking tape, red stickers for play wounds, tongue depressors, play thermometer, paper pad and pencil for prescriptions, billing forms for bill, adhesive tape, cotton balls, armband with a red cross on it, bag to carry, paper hospital gowns, and white shirt.

Teacher. Notebooks, pencils, plastic glasses, chalk, bell, chalkboard, flannel board with sets, book about the first day at school.

Santa Claus. Red jacket and hat, beard that ties behind ears, large sack or pillowcase, assorted toys, reindeer horn hats, and flashlight.

Washing babies. Large pieces of toweling to cover the table, several small washable dolls, some sets of toy bathroom furniture, individual plastic pitchers or plastic tubs with soapy water (can be made from plastic bleach bottles), small pieces of toweling, cotton balls, individual talcum cans filled with cornstarch, diapers (smallest size), empty plastic soap bottles, doll clothes, clothesline, and clothespins.

Supermarket. Cash register, play money, paper pads and pencils or crayons, hole punch, paper sacks, empty food cartons, wax fruit, play grocery cart or rolling laundry cart, and purse or wallet.

Hair salon. Plastic brushes, combs, cotton balls, powder, scarves, colored water in nail polish bottles, old hair dryer (no cord or plug), curlers, water spray bottle, hairpins, and mirror.

Service station. Tire pump, pliers, cans, sponges, and bucket, short length of hose and cylinder (for gas pump), hat, squirt bottle, paper towels, paper and pencil, and sign "gas for sale."

Fishing. Hats, bamboo lengths (about three feet) with string and magnet at the end, a basin, and small metal objects such as paper clips for the fish or cutouts for fish shapes with a paper clip attached to each (to attract the magnet).

More kits can be made for the following:

TV repair person	mail carrier
baker	fire fighter
painter	car wash
picnic	pilot
restaurant	circus
wedding	birthday party
police officer	astronaut
construction worker	airport

The ideas for play kits that have been suggested are based on a few of the many themes that are possible (figure 14-5).

Costumes

Costumes and clothing props let a child step into a character quickly (figure 14-6). Strong, sturdy, child-manageable ties and snaps increase self-help. Elastic waistbands slip on and off with ease. Clothing that is cut down to size (so it doesn't drag) can be worn for a longer time. Items that children enjoy are:

- hats of all types (figure 14-7)
- shoes, boots, slippers
- uniforms
- accessories, such as ties, scarves, purses, old jewelry, aprons, badges, key rings
- discarded fur jackets, soft fabrics, and fancy fabric clothing
- wigs
- work clothes

FIGURE 14-5 The most common classroom dramatic play area is the pretend kitchen.

A clever idea for a child-made costume is using a large handled shopping bag. Once the bottom of the bag is cut out, the child can step into it, using the bag handles as shoulder straps. The child can decorate the bag and use it as a play prop.

TEACHER'S ROLE IN DRAMATIC PLAY

Dramatic play is child directed instead of teacher directed. Play ideas come from the child's imagination and experience.

Teachers can motivate dramatic play before they withdraw to remain in the background. They are watchful but don't hover. Sometimes a new play direction is suggested by a teacher to divert the children away from unsafe or violent play. The flow of play preferably is decided by the children. Teachers' close presence and words can stop or change behavior when the situation becomes unsafe or gets out of hand. If things go smoothly, the ideas, words, and dramatic play actions are those of the children.

Periodic suggestions by the teacher and introduction of material may extend and enrich play. Care is taken not to dominate but rather to be available as a friendly resource.

FIGURE 14-6 The center should provide the necessary equipment for dramatic play.

FIGURE 14-7 A bandana has become a prop for dramatic play.

Daily Routines

Periods designed especially for conversation are included in the program of an early childhood center. A gathering or group time at the start of the day is used to encourage individual recognition and speaking. Snack and lunch periods are set up to promote pleasant conversation while eating (figure 14-8). Activities are planned and structured to provide for as much child talk as possible.

Show-and-tell.

One of the most common daily routines is show-and-tell time. It must be noted here that some early child-

hood educators feel that this routine is outdated and prefer to eliminate it from their daily schedules. In contrast, show-and-tell advocates feel that this activity encourages children to talk about their special interests in front of others. The child can bring something from home or share something made or accomplished at school. Here are some helpful hints for conducting show-and-tell.

- Encourage, don't force, children to speak. If they don't want to talk, they can just show what they brought.
- Let the child who is showing something to the group stand or sit near the teacher. A friendly arm around the child's shoulders may help.
- Stimulate the other children to ask the child questions: "Mark, you seem to know more about Gustavos's marbles."
- Limit the time for overly talkative children by using an egg timer.
- Limit the time for the activity so that the children do not become bored.
- Thank each child for his or her participation.
- Try something new such as:
  a. Display all articles and have the group guess who brought them.
  b. Have children swap (if possible) what they have brought so that they can talk about each other's items.

FIGURE 14-8 Pleasant, relaxed conversation can take place at meal times.

c. Bring in a surprise item to share with the children.
d. Make a caption for each item and display it on a table (for example, Betty's Green Rock).
e. Have the child hide the object behind his or her back while describing it to the others. Then the other children can guess what the object is.

Oken-Wright (1988) points out show-and-tell times can be tedious and stressful, but when well-conducted, they can also be:

- An activity for closure (ending activities on a satisfying note) and evaluation and for clarification of feelings,
- A forum for expressive and receptive language development,
- A session for brainstorming, idea catching, and idea expanding,
- An opportunity to reflect and engage in group problem solving,
- A source for curriculum ideas and materials, and
- A window into children's thoughts and feelings.

Show-and-tell items are usually kept out of children's reach to prevent the loss of a valued or favorite toy. The teacher can divide the class into groups and name the days on which each group can bring in items, or the teacher may prefer to allow the children to share whenever they wish. Show-and-tell helps children develop vocabulary, responsibility, and the ability to speak in front of others. When making these goals known to parents, teachers explain that the children have choices in these sharing times, and that items do not have to be brought to school on a daily or regular basis.

The Daily News or Recap Times.

Many centers engage in a daily news or recap group time that focuses on important or interesting events of the day. Teachers and children share news, anecdotes, and happenings in both their home and school life. The teacher can initiate this activity with statements such as the following:

"Keith told me about something new at his house. Would you like to share your news Keith?"

"Aliki and Todd built something today that I've never seen before! Tell us about it Todd, or would you like me to tell your classmates?"

"Scott saw the hampster do something silly this morning. Do you want to talk about what you saw Scott?"

As with all other group times, the teacher must be aware of group reaction and response. On some days, there may be excited response and conversation; on others, there may be little response, and the activity should be kept brief. To give children an opportunity to talk about problems and their solutions, recap times can be partially devoted to children's verbalizing success or lack of it in proposed courses of action and projects.

"Ryan was going to try to make a spaceship today. Ryan do you want to tell us about it?"

"Megan finished making her book today. Would you like to tell us what happened, Megan?"

"Phil wanted to help in the kitchen preparing snack today. Is there anything you want to say about your work?"

Promoting Speech Daily.

The following are suggestions that can promote more child speech in daily programs.

- Have children give verbal messages or directions to other children often: "Petey, please show Flynn our dustpan and hand broom. Tell him how we empty it." (Then follow through by thanking him.)

- Let children describe daily projects: "Danielle, tell us about your rocket ship. I know you worked hard making it. What did you do first?"
- Relate present ideas and happenings to the children's past when possible: "Shane had a new puppy at his house, too. Did your puppy cry at night? What did you do to help it stop? Kathy has a new puppy who cries at night."
- Promote child explanations: "Who can tell us what happens after we finish our lunch?"

- Promote teacher-child conversations where the teacher records children's words on artwork, constructions, or any happenings or project.
- Periodically make pin-on badges (for teachers and interested children) like the ones shown in figure 14-9.
- Play "explaining games" by setting up a group of related items on a table and having the children explain how the items can be used. For example, three groups of items might be (1) a mirror, comb, brush, washcloth, soap, and basin of water;

FIGURE 14-9 Pin-on badges

(2) shoes, white shoe polish, and new shoelaces; and (3) nuts, nutcracker, and two bowls. Encourage child volunteers to explain and demonstrate the use of the items by facing the group from the other side of the table. Other possibilities include items to demonstrate peeling an orange, making a sandwich with two spreads, or making a telephone call.

• Design and create games that encourage children to speak.

GAMES

The following games may promote children's expression of ideas.

Suitcase Game

Teacher: I'm going on a vacation trip. I'm putting suntan oil in my suitcase. What will you put in your suitcase?

Child: A swimming suit.

Child: Candy.

Teacher: (After the group has had an opportunity to contribute.)
Let's see how many items we can remember that people wanted to bring on vacation.

Grocery Store Game

Have a bag handy with lots of grocery items. Pull one out yourself and describe it. Have the children take turns pulling out an item and describing it. Teacher can make a shopping list of items named and explain a shopping list's use.

Letter Game

Provide a large bag of letters. Pull one letter out. Talk about a letter you are going to send to a child in the group. "I'm going to give this pretend letter to Frankie and tell him about my new car," or "I want to send this thank-you card to Janelle because she always helps me when I ask for cleanup helpers. Who would like to pull out a letter from this bag and tell us the person they would like to send it to?"

Guess What's in the Box

Collect small boxes with lids. Put small items inside, such as paper clips, erasers, bottle tops, plastic toys, leaves, flowers, and so forth. Have a child choose a box, guess its contents, open it, and talk about what is in the box.

Describe a Classmate

Choose a child out of the group to stand beside you. Describe or list three of the child's characteristics, for example, red shoes, big smile, one hand in pocket. Ask who would like to choose another classmate and tell three things about that person.

Guessing Picture Messages

Duplicate the drawings shown in figure 14-10 on large newsprint. Help the children translate the messages into words.

FIGURE 14-10 Guessing picture messages *(From* EARLY YEARS *magazine, January 1973. Reprinted with permission of the publishers. Allen Raymond, Inc., Darien, CT 06820.)*

The Mystery Bag

An activity children enjoy in small groups is called the mystery bag. The teacher collects a series of common objects. Turning away from the group, the teacher puts one of the objects in another bag. The game starts when a child reaches (without looking inside) into the second bag and describes the object. It is then pulled out of the bag and discussed: "What can we do with it? Has it a name? It's the same color as what else in the room?" The group should be small, since it is hard for a young child to wait for a turn. Examples of objects that could be used include a rock, comb, orange, pancake turner, feather, plastic cup, sponge, hole punch, flower, toy animal, and whistle.

Parts-of-the-Body Guessing Game

I can see you with my _____ (eyes).
I can smell you with my _____ (nose).
I can chew with my _____ (teeth).
I can hear with my _____ (ears).
I can clap with my _____ (hands).
I walk on my _____ (feet).
I put food in my _____ (mouth).
This is not my nose, it's my _____ (point to ears).
This is not my eye, it's my _____ (point to nose).
This is not my mouth, it's my_____ (point to eye).

LEADING ACTIVITIES

A child can be chosen to lead others in activities if he or she is familiar with the routines and activities. The child can alert the others by saying the right words or calling out the names of the children who need items or who are next for a turn at something. One or more children can be at the front of the group, leading songs or finger plays. (Finger plays will be discussed in the next unit.) Often, children can be chosen as speakers to direct routines with words. Also, teachers can promote speaking by asking one child to tell another child something: "Tell Billy when you want him to pass the wastebasket," or "If you're through, ask Georgette whether she wants a turn."

A watchful teacher uses many ways of encouraging the children to speak. The children tend to speak more if their speech is given attention and if speech helps them achieve their ends. It is helpful during group times to point out that the teacher and the other children want to hear what everyone says and, because of this, children should take turns in speaking.

Summary

When there is a relaxed atmosphere with interested teachers and many activities, more talking takes place. Playing with others helps vocabulary development and language acquisition in settings where children interact in real and make-believe situations.

The teacher's role in dramatic play is to set the stage but remain in the background so that the children can create their own activities. Dramatic play settings and kits are made available, and some are boxed and collected by the teacher.

Part of a teacher's work is to encourage children to share their ideas and give children opportunities to lead speaking activities. Teachers ensure that children are talked with rather than talked at. Teachers plan for conversational group times and conduct games and activities that promote verbal comments.

Student Activities

- Visit a center and record all instances of dramatic play. Note all equipment that seems to promote speaking.

- With a classmate, describe a dramatic play-kit idea on a theme that was not included in this unit. List the items for this theme that you feel would be safe and would promote dramatic play. Share with the class. Vote on one play kit created by classmates in this exercise that you feel would be popular with children. Give the reason(s) for your vote.

- Review dramatic play items commercially produced by looking in school supply catalogs. Report on the cost of three items.

- With some classmates, role-play children playing house. Assign family roles, such as grandmother, mother, father, brother, sister, baby, and family dog. Pretend you are having breakfast or dinner; traveling in the car going on vacation; or in other family situations, such as father or mother telling the family about a raise in pay or a new job. Try a bedtime situation. Did classmates show how the family members cope with life? If not, have the group discuss how young children might do this in the same role-playing situations. Why do you suppose spanking dolls is such a common play enactment in young children?

- Discuss your position concerning show-and-tell time.

- Observe a full morning program in a center. List the activities or routines in which there was active speaking by most of the children.

- Pretend you have acquired a large cardboard packing case, big enough for children to crawl into and stand. In what way would this case enhance dramatic play? In what play situations could the case be used?

- Read and analyze the following from "What's wrong with this Show-and-Tell?" by Oken-Wright (1988):

  > Fifteen four-year-olds are seated in a sprawling group. "Today it's Todd's, Teddy's, Joyce's and Karen's turn," says the teacher. "Todd, did you bring anything for us? You always forget, don't you. You need to start remembering when it's Tuesday, that's your day." When it's her turn, Karen drones on in a monotone for five minutes about a plastic bracelet her mother bought her at the mall. Stevie interrupts many times trying to get the teacher's attention to tell about the frog he caught in the morning. After several warnings, the teacher tells Stevie that he has lost his turn to tell on Wednesday because of his discourteous behavior during Karen's turn today. The teacher says, "This way you don't have too many on any one day and they can talk as long as they like."

- Discuss the following with a group of classmates. "Show-and-tell time is the only time a teacher has to sit back and rest and let the children do the talking. It's a planned time that takes little planning and preparation...it fills program time."

- List and describe teacher group-time skills. Then classify them into the categories "easy for beginning teachers to acquire" or "difficult (takes practice and conscious effort) to acquire." Share with classmates.

Unit Review

A. Define dramatic play.

B. Choose the factors that can help young children develop speaking abilities.
   1. Equipment
   2. Staff members

3. Parents
4. Making a child ask correctly for what he or she wants
5. A relaxed atmosphere
6. Interesting happenings to talk about
7. Lack of play with other children
8. Asking a child if he or she wants to tell something
9. A child's need or desire
10. A teacher's ignoring the child's nonverbal communication
11. Daily speaking routines
12. Teacher attention to speech
13. Teacher rewarding children's speech
14. Planned speaking activities

C. Answer the following questions.
1. What is a dramatic play kit?
2. Name some of the things a teacher does not want to happen during show-and-tell time (for example, one child talking too long).

D. Select the terms that best define the teacher's role in dramatic play.
1. Interactor
2. Background observer
3. Provider of settings
4. Provider of props
5. One who redirects unsafe play
6. Active participant
7. Suggestor of ideas during play
8. Provider of many words
9. Gatherer of dramatic play items

E. Write a short paragraph that finishes the following:

The reasons some teachers do not actively plan programs with children leading activities in front of the child group...

F. In the following description of calling the roll, identify those parts that might make a child feel pressured and tense rather than relaxed. Discuss the attitude of the teacher as well.

"Good morning, children. Everyone say, 'Good Morning, Mrs. Brown.' That's good. Bonnie, you didn't say it. You were playing with your hair ribbon. Say it now, Bonnie.

I'm going to say everyone's name. When I say your name I want you all to say, 'I'm here, Mrs. Brown.' Susie Smith. 'I'm here, Mrs. Brown.' Speak louder, Susie, we can't hear you. Brett Porter. Not 'I'm present,' Brett, say 'I'm here, Mrs. Brown.' David Martinez. Answer please, David. David Martinez. David you must answer when I call your name! Andy Smith. No, Andy, say 'I'm here, Mrs. Brown,' not 'I'm here' and that's all.

I don't know what's the matter with all of you; you did it right yesterday. We're going to stay here until we all do it the right way. Dana Collins. I can't understand what you said, Dana; say it again. Mark Jefferson. Mark, that's very good, you said it the right way. Chris Wong. No, it's not time to talk to Ronnie now; it's time to speak up. What are you supposed to say, children? I give up. You'll never learn. Let's all go outside now and work out all of our wiggles."

References

Beaty, Janice J. *Skills for Preschool Teachers*. Columbus, OH: Charles E. Merrill Publishing, 1984.

Bender, J. "Have You Ever Thought Of A Prop Box?" *Young Children*, 28.3 (Jan. 1971): 47–53.

Croft, Doreen, and Robert Hess. *An Activities Handbook for Teachers of Young Children*. Boston, MA: Houghton Mifflin, 1975.

Fein, G. "Pretend Play: New Perspectives." *Child Development* 30.6 (Dec. 1981): 81–93.

Griffing, Penelope. "Encouraging Dramatic Play In Early Childhood." *Young Children* 38.2 (Jan. 1983): 45–51.

Lorton, Mary. *Workjobs: Activity-Centered Learning for Early Childhood Education*. Menlo Park, CA: Addison-Wesley, 1972.

Oken-Wright, Pamela. "Show-and-Tell Grows Up." *Young Children* 43.2 (Jan. 1988): 52–63.

Segal, Marilyn. "Should Superheroes Be Expelled From Preschool?" *Pre-K Today* 1.8 (Oct. 1987): 37–45.

Tiedt, Sidney, and Iris Tiedt. *Language Arts Activities for the Classroom*. New York: Penguin, 1971.

UNIT 15

Group Times

OBJECTIVES

After studying this unit, you should be able to

- describe circle and group-time speaking activities.
- perform a finger play with children.
- discuss ways to promote child involvement in simple plays, chants, and circle times.

The activities in this unit give children many speaking opportunities. Children involved in the activities have the opportunity to imitate speech, to use creative speech, and to express their own ideas and feelings. However, you should realize that it is difficult to classify activities as listening or speaking activities, because they often overlap.

GROUPS

Circle and group times are chances for children to develop understanding about themselves as group members. They enjoy language together by using familiar songs, favorite finger plays, chants, and a wide variety of activities. Children gain self-confidence, feelings of personal worth, and group spirit (figure 15-1).

School administrators and teachers need to clarify their priorities concerning group times. Since it is difficult to conduct intimate conversations and discussions with large groups, many schools prefer working with small groups of children so that conversations can flourish. But decisions regarding group size may hinge on staffing considerations. Sometimes large groups can be temporarily divided so that there can be "instant replays" of activities for smaller groups.

When presenting new material during group sessions, teachers should allow time to receive and react to children's comments and questions. One pitfall in conducting group activities is the tendency for teachers to remain the center of attention, assuming the role of the great dispenser of knowledge. When this occurs, child feedback is ignored. This is further discussed

FIGURE 15-1 Group time — together time

under the heading entitled "Pitfalls." As Johnson (1987) puts it, "oral language runs a great risk in school of being eliminated or being frowned upon so heavily that children don't feel comfortable. 'Be quiet' is an admonition heard entirely too often in school. Some of the excitement of discovery has to be shouted out. Talk, after all, is the hallmark of humanity."

Language activities add sparkle and liveliness to circle times. The following is a list of words that can be used to describe a successful group experience.

active
  Children's participation includes motor and speech involvement.
enthusiastic
  The teacher's commitment in making a presentation is communicated by the teacher's facial expressions and manner.
prepared
  All necessary materials are at the teacher's fingertips and are used with smooth verbal presentations.
accepting
  The teacher is open to children's ideas and feelings and is appreciative of children's contributions.
appropriate
  The activity suits the particular group.
clear
  The teacher provides purposeful clarification of new concepts.
familiar
  The activity includes previously learned and enjoyed material.
novel
  New ideas and material are presented.
relaxed
  The activity does not pressure or threaten children.
sharing
  All children are invited to take turns in participating in the activity.

CIRCLES

A circle activity (usually, a semicircle seating arrangement) is begun by capturing group attention. A signal or daily routine can be used. To make sure all children are focused, a short silence (pause) adds a feeling of anticipation and expectation.

Occasionally varying the signals keeps one signal from becoming old hat. A visual signal, a xylophone ripple, a tap on a musical triangle, an attention-getting record, a puppet announcing a group activity, or reminder stickers placed on children's hands related to the theme of the activity are a few alternatives.

Opening activities that recognize each child help to build group spirit. Such recognition is a way of communicating to each child that "You're an important person; we're happy to have you with us." The children can then begin group activities on the right note.

Circle Starters

The following activities are circle-time starters, attention getters, socializers, and wiggle reducers.

CIRCLE TIME

> *I've just come in from outside.*
> *I'm tired as can be.*
> *I'll cross my legs*
> *And fold my hands,*
> *I WILL NOT MOVE.*
> *My head won't move.*
> *My toes are still.*
> *I'll put my hands on my chin,*
> *And when it's quiet, we'll begin!*

WIGGLES

> *I'll wiggle my fingers*
> *And wiggle my toes.*
> *I'll wiggle my arms*
> *And wiggle my nose.*
> *And now that all the wiggle's out,*
> *We'll listen to what circle's about.*

HANDSHAKE

(Chant or Sing)

> *Good morning, good morning, good morning to you.*
> *Good morning, good morning, and how do you do?*
> *Shake hands, shake hands with someone near you.*
> *Shake hands, shake hands the other side too.*

SCARECROW

> *Scarecrow, scarecrow, arms up high.*
> *Scarecrow, scarecrow, wink one eye.*
> *Scarecrow, scarecrow, bend your knees.*
> *Scarecrow, scarecrow, flop in the breeze.*

Scarecrow, scarecrow, turn around.
Scarecrow, scarecrow, sit back down.

CLAPPING START

Turn around and face the wall. Clap, Clap, Clap.
Down upon your knees now fall. Clap, Clap, Clap.
Up again and turn around. Clap, Clap, Clap.
Turn around and then sit down. Clap, Clap, Clap.
Not a sound.

WHERE ARE YOUR _____?

Where are your eyes? Show me eyes that see.
Where are your eyes? Shut them quietly.
Where is your nose? A nose that blows.
Where is your nose? Show me your nose and wiggle it so.
Where is your mouth? Open it wide.
Where is your mouth? With teeth inside.
Smile — Smile — Smile.

I LIKE YOU

(Chant or Sing)

I like you. ·
There's no doubt about it.
I like you.
There's no doubt about it.
I am your good friend.
You like me.
There's no doubt about it.
You like me.
There's no doubt about it.
You are my good friend.
There's my friend (child's name), *and my friend*
(child's name)
(Continue around circle.)

THE MORE WE GET TOGETHER

(Chant or Sing)

The more we get together, together, together,
The more we get together, the happier we'll be.
Because (child's name) *friend, is* (child's name
    sitting beside) *friend, and* (repeat child's name)
    is (next child's name) *friend.* (Around the
    circle.)
Yes, the more we get together, the happier we'll be.

(Example: And Colleen is Mark's friend, and Mark is
    Sal's friend.)

OH HERE WE ARE TOGETHER

(Chant or Sing)

Oh here we are together, together, together,
Oh here we are together
At (insert school name) *Preschool*
There's (child's name) *and* (child's name), *and*
    (names of all children).
Oh here we are together to have a good day.

WE'RE WAITING

(Circle Starter)

We're waiting, we're waiting, we're waiting for
    (child's name)
    (Repeat until group is formed.)
We're here, because we're here, because we're here,
    because we're here.
And my name is _____, *and my name*
    is _____ . (Around the circle.)

HELLO

Hello (child's name). *Hello, hello, hello.*
Shake my hand and around we'll go.
Hello (child's name). *Hello, hello, hello.*
Shake my hand and around we'll go.
(Teacher starts; children continue around the
    circle chanting until all are recognized.)

SECRET

I've got something in my pocket
That belongs across my face.
I keep it very close at hand
In a most convenient place.
I know you couldn't guess it
If you guessed a long, long while.
So I'll take it out and put it on
It's a great big friendly SMILE!

TEN FINGERS

I have ten little fingers
And they all belong to me.
I can make them do things.
Would you like to see?
I can shut them up tight
Or open them wide.
I can put them together

Or make them all hide.
I can make them jump high.
I can make them jump low,
I can fold them quietly
And hold them just so.

TO LONDON TOWN

Which is the way to London Town
To see the king in his golden crown?

One foot up and one foot down.
That's the way to London Town.

Which is the way to London Town
To see the queen in her silken gown?

Left! Right! Left! Right! Up and down,
Soon you'll be in London Town!

EVERYBODY DO THIS

Refrain:
Everybody do this, do this, do this.
Everybody do this just like me.

Actions:
   Open and close fists
   Roll fists around
   Touch elbows
   Spider fingers
   Pat head, rub tummy
   Wink
   Wave hand good-bye

(Ask children to create others.)

WHO'S LISTENING?

(To the tune of Kumbaya)

(Child's name) *listening now,*
Kumbaya. (Child's name) *listening now,*
Kumbaya.
(Repeat first line.)
Oh, Oh, Kumbaya.
(Continue around group mentioning all children's names.)

PEASE PORRIDGE GROUP

Pease porridge hot,
(Slap knees, clap hands together, push hands in air towards leader.)
Pease porridge cold,
(Repeat.)
Pease porridge in the pot
(Slap knees, clap hands together, push right hand forward in air, clap, then push left hand in air, clap.)
Nine days old.
(Clap, clap, clap.)
Some like it hot,
(Repeat as above.)
Some like it cold,
Some like it in the pot,
Nine days old.

Circle Activities

A circle group keeps its lively enthusiasm and social enjoyment when well planned. The activities that follow involve both language and coordinated physical movement.

PASSING GAME

Have children arranged in a circle. Pass a small object around the circle. Start by passing it in front of the children, then behind, then overhead, and then under the legs. Directions can be changed on command of the teacher, such as "pass it to your left, pass it to your right," and so on. Ask children for suggestions for other ways to pass the object.

TEDDY BEAR CIRCLE PASS

(Have bear in bag behind leader)

Love somebody, yes, I do.
Love somebody, yes, I do.
Love somebody, yes, I do.
Love somebody, but I won't tell who.
(Shake head sideways.)
Love somebody, yes, I do.
Love somebody, yes, I do.
Love somebody, yes, I do.
Now I'll show (him or her) *to you!*
Here's a hug — Pass it on.

(Group continues to chant as each child hugs
   and hands Teddy to next child. When Teddy
   returns to leader, last verse is repeated,
   ending with the following line.)
Now back in the bag our hugs are through!
(Substituted for last line.)

IF YOU'RE HAPPY AND YOU KNOW IT

If you're happy and you know it, clap your hands.
If you're happy and you know it, clap your hands.
If you're happy and you know it, then your face will
   surely show it.
If you're happy and you know it, clap your hands.

(Additional verses.)
If you're sad and you know it, wipe your eyes.
If you're mad and you know it, pound your fist.
If you're hungry and you know it, rub your stomach.
If you're silly and you know it, go tee-hee.
If you're cold and you know it, rub your arms.
If you're hot and you know it, wipe your brow.
If you're sleepy and you know it, go to sleep . . .
   snore, snore.

BALL ROLLING CIRCLE

The ball will roll across our circle.
Touch toes with your neighbors.
Here comes the ball, Susie. "I roll the ball to Susie."
(Teacher says: "Susie roll the ball across the
   circle and say your friend's name.")
"I roll the ball to _____."

NAME GAME

_____ *wore her* _____ _____,
_____ _____, _____ _____.
(Fill in with clothing particulars like brown
   shoes, red sweater, and so forth.)
(Repeat first line.)
All day at school.
(When the chant gets going, ask children to fill
   in blanks with what a particular child is
   wearing.)

Courtesy of MAGIC MOMENTS

ECHO GAME

Echo me, echo me, echo me do.
Echo my sound and my movement too.
(Teacher) *Meow, meow,* (Teacher pretends to lick
   her arm.)
What am I? Right a cat.
Echo me, echo me, echo me do.
Echo my sound, and my movement too.
Amy, can you be an animal, and make its sound?

Courtesy of MAGIC MOMENTS

OVER THE MOUNTAIN

(To the tune of "The Bear Went
Over the Mountain")

(Child's name) *went over the mountain.*
(Repeat.)
(Repeat.)
To see what he could see.
_____, *what did you see?*
_____ *saw a* (child's answer).
(Repeat.)
(Repeat.)
Pick a friend (child's name).
(Repeat with new child's name.)

Courtesy of MAGIC MOMENTS

THE CARROT SEED WILL GROW

Carrots grow from carrot seeds,
I'll plant this seed and grow one.
I won't be disappointed if my seed doesn't grow.
What makes seeds grow? I don't know!
So I won't be disappointed if my seed doesn't grow.
My brother said "Na, na. It won't come up. Na, na.
   It won't come up.
Na, na. It won't come up. Your carrot won't come up."

(Repeat above, ending with the following.)
Oh, carrots grow from carrot seeds.
I planted one, it grew. I watered it. I pulled the
   weeds.
No matter what he said.
Carrots grow from carrot seeds.

Taking Turns

During circle and other group activities, the following teacher statements are helpful in emphasizing to children the importance of taking turns:

- "It's Monica's turn now."
- "Barry's turn to talk, and everyone's turn to listen."
- "Listen to Bonnie. Bonnie's lips are moving, and ours are resting."
- "Just one person talks at a time."
- "I am guessing that you really want to say something, Jason, but that you are waiting for your turn."

Closing Group Activities

Exciting circles and other group activities sometimes need a quiet, settling close. The following can be used to wind down group activities and prepare excited children for the change to another activity or play.

UP AND DOWN

Up and down,
Up and down,
Clap your hands and turn around.
Up and down,
Up and down,
Clap your hands and sit down.

RAG DOLL

I'm just a limp rag doll.
My arms are limp.
My legs are limp.
My head is limp.
I'm just a limp rag doll.

UP, DOWN, AND REST

Up and down,
Up and down,
Round, round, round,
Up and down.
I stretch, I stretch, I yawn.
I rest and then I start again.
Up and down (and so forth)
(second time — I rest and I rest.)

Transitions

Disbanding a circle or group at an activity's ending calls for a planned approach. You will need to excuse a few at a time, if the group is of any size. When carpet squares are to be picked up and stacked, or small chairs returned to tables, a reminder is in order: "When you hear your name, pick up your rug square, carry it to the stack."

Transitory statements that relate to the just-completed activity work well: "Crawl like Victor the Boa Constrictor to the block center," or "Let the wind blow you slowly to the water table like it blew in the little tree."

TRANSITION POEM

Wiggle both ears.
Touch your nose.
Wiggle your fingers.
Stamp your toes.
Point to your eyes.

Your mouth open wide.
Stick out your tongue.
Put it inside.
Trace your lips.
Go "shh!" Don't speak.
Hands on your neck.
Touch both cheeks.

Shake your hands.
Now let them sleep.
Bend your knees.
Sit on your feet.

Now we finished with this play,
Take your feet and walk away!

Additional Transitions.

A fun way to dismiss the children is to recite the rhyme "Jack be nimble, Jack be quick...," substituting the child's name for "Jack": "(Child's name) be nimble (child's name) be quick (child's name) jump over the candlestick." (Children clap for the child who jumps over a plastic candleholder and unlit candle.)

Courtesy of Thelma Alaniz

Another way to dismiss children is to make a "tickler" from a three-foot long dowel and some yarn.

Say to the children, "Close your eyes. When you feel a tickle on your head, it's time to stand and walk carefully through your classmates to the...."

Courtesy of Dianne Ferry

Some statements that are helpful in moving a group of children in an orderly fashion are listed here. Many identify language concepts and serve a dual purpose.

- "Everyone with brown shoes stand up. Now it's time to...."
- "If your favorite sandwich is peanut butter and jelly (ham, cheese, tuna, and so forth) raise your hand. If your hand is up, please tiptoe to the...."
- "Richie is the engine on a slow, slow train. Richie, chug chug slowly to the...." "Darlene is the coal car on a slow, slow train...." (The last child is, naturally, the caboose.)

Circle-Time Pitfalls

Circle times can fall apart for a number of reasons. An examination of the teacher's goals and planning decisions prior to conducting a circle time may clarify what caused child disinterest or lack of enthusiasm. When circles go poorly, child behavior may be focused away from the circle's theme and action.

Before examining teacher behaviors, other factors should be reviewed, such as the setting, length, and age-level appropriateness of the activity. Then examine whether the children enjoyed, and participated enthusiastically in, the activity and how teacher behavior contributed to this. If the activity was not a success, the activity failed the children rather than vice versa.

A teacher whose goals include child conversation and involvement will not monopolize the activity with a constant up-front presentation. Unfortunately, some beginning teachers seem to possess an overwhelming desire to dispense information, eliminating children's conversation and reactions. When this happens, circle times become passive listening times.

The size of the circle has been discussed in this unit. Dodge (1988) describes the possible reason(s) teachers attempt large-group circle times:

Possible Causes: Teachers are more comfortable with their ability to maintain control when the whole group is involved in the same activity. They want to be sure everyone in the group learns the same concepts and skills. Several teachers said that they do most of their teaching at circle time.

Teachers need to understand that large-group instruction at preschool level may cause group disinterest and restlessness by becoming impersonal.

There seems to be a type of adult who is unable to talk to the child, no matter how important or pertinent the child's comments. It's as if a planned step-by-step circle time must be followed. The teacher has become inflexible, a slave to a plan. One-sided conversations turn everyone off but the speaker.

Waiting a long period for a turn during circle time leads to frustration. Children may tune out for this reason. A simple fact that all experienced teachers know is that active, involved children stay focused.

A teacher who constantly asks questions to maintain child attention may defeat his or her purpose. Some teachers do not understand the difference between asking a question with one right answer (to test a child) and asking questions that encourage thinking. They feel that they are accountable for what children learn, and they believe that they are teaching children concepts like color and number when they ask questions (Dodge, 1988). Most adults remember from past school experiences how it feels when one missed a question. Unskilled teachers may make children afraid to answer or share their ideas.

Hints for Successful Circle Times

Before you conduct your circle:

- Review your goals for circle times periodically.
- Plan for active child participation and involvement.
- Make proposed circle-time duration appropriate to the group's age.
- Practice language games and activities so you can focus on the children.
- Think about group size and settings.
- Remember it's better to stop before enthusiasm wanes.

During a circle time:

- Focus children at the beginning.

- State what you expect early, if necessary:
  "Sit where you can see."
  "My turn to talk, your turn to listen."
- Proceed with enthusiasm.
- Try to enjoy and be unhurried.
- Watch for feedback, and act accordingly.
- Use wind-down activities if the group gets too excited.
- Use wiggle reducers.
- Draw out quiet children's ideas.
- Reduce waiting times.
- Watch the length of time allowed for the activity.
- Think of an orderly transition to the next activity, which may include the children's taking carpet squares to a storage area.
- Remember that your skill increases with experience.

CHANTS AND CHORUSES

Throughout history, rhythmic chants and choruses have been used in group rituals and ceremonies. The individuals in the group gain a group identity as a result of their participation.

Natural enjoyment of rhythmic word patterns can be seen in a child's involvement in group chants. Child and teacher can also playfully take part in call and response during the preschool day. "I made it, I made it," the child says. "I see it, I see it," the teacher answers, picking up the child's rhythm.

This verbal play is common. Sounds in the community and schoolyard can be brought to the children's attention by teachers who notice them and make comments. Weir and Eggleston (1975) point out that:

Urban sounds are sometimes syncopated and rhythmical, such as the fire siren, people walking on side walks, jack hammers or nailing in nails. These are rhythms that children imitate verbally and that adults can point out to children.

Chants and choruses are mimicked, and sound and word patterns that have regularity and predictability are imitated. Choruses usually involve a back and forth conversation (one individual alternating with another) and involve the rise and fall of accented sounds or syllables.

Children need the teacher's examples and directions, such as, "When it's your turn, I'll point to you," or "Let's say it together," before they can perform the patterns on their own. Chants printed on charts with simple illustrations can enhance chanting and chorus times and tie the oral words to written ones.

The chants that follow are some tried-and-true favorites.

THE DUKE OF YORK

Oh, the Duke of York
Had forty thousand men.
They marched up the hill,
And they marched down again.
And when you're up, you're up!
And when you're down, you're down.
And when you're half-way-in-between,
You're neither up nor down.

KNICKERBOCKER KNOCKABOUT

Kickerbocker Knockabout
Sausages and sauerkraut
Run! Run! Run! The hogs are out!
Knickerbocker Knockabout.

AND IT WAS ME!

I looked in my soup, and who did I see?
Something wonderful . . . and it was me.

Additional verses:
I looked in the mirror, and who did I see?
I looked in the puddle . . .
I looked in a window . . .
I looked in the river . . .
I looked in the pond . . .
I looked at a snapshot . . .
I turned off the television . . .

Ending:
When I'm grown up, I'll still be there.
Right in reflections everywhere.
When I'm grown up, how will it be?
A wonderful world with you and me.

IT'S RAINING IT'S POURING

It's raining, it's pouring.
The old man is snoring.

He went to bed and he bumped his head
And he couldn't get up in the morning.
Rain, rain go away — come again some other day.

MISS MARY MACK

Miss Mary Mack, Mack, Mack
All dressed in black, black, black
With silver buttons, buttons, buttons
All down her back, back, back.

She asked her mother, mother, mother
For fifteen cents, cents, cents
To see the elephants, elephants, elephants
Jump the fence, fence, fence.

They jumped so high, high, high
They touched the sky, sky, sky
And never came back, back, back
Till the fourth of July, ly, ly.

July can't walk, walk, walk
July can't talk, talk, talk
July can't eat, eat, eat
With a knife and fork, fork, fork.

She went upstairs, stairs, stairs
To say her prayers, prayers, prayers
She made her bed, bed, bed
She hit her head, head, head
On a piece of corn bread, bread, bread.

Now she's asleep, sleep, sleep
She's snoring deep, deep, deep
No more to play, play, play
Until Friday, day, day
What can I say, say, say
Except hooray, ray, ray!

PANCAKE

Mix a pancake.
Stir a pancake.
Pop it in the pan.
Fry a pancake.
Toss a pancake.
Catch it if you can.

THE BIG CLOCK

Slowly ticks the big clock

Chorus:
Tick-tock, tick-tock
(Repeat twice.)

But the cuckoo clock ticks double quick

Chorus:
Tick-a-tock-a, tick-a-tock-a
Tick-a-tock-a, tick!

LITTLE BROWN RABBIT

Little brown rabbit went hoppity-hop,

All:
Hoppity-hop, hoppity-hop!

Into a garden without any stop,

All:
Hoppity-hop, hoppity-hop!

He ate for his supper a fresh carrot top,

All:
Hoppity-hop, hoppity-hop!

Then home went the rabbit without any stop,

All:
Hoppity-hop, hoppity-hop!

WHO ATE THE COOKIES IN THE COOKIE JAR

All: *Who ate the cookies in the cookie jar?*
All: (Child's or teacher's name) *ate the cookies in the cookie jar.* (Teacher points to different child for each verse.)
Named person: *Who me?*
All: *Yes you.*
Named person: *Couldn't be.*
All: *Then who?*
Named person: (Child or teacher) *ate the cookies in the cookie jar.*
Newly named person: *Who me?* (and so forth).

THE HOUSE THAT JACK BUILT

Chorus: *"the house that Jack built"*

This is malt
That lay in

Chorus: *the house that Jack built.*

This is the rat,
That ate the malt
That lay in

Chorus: *the house that Jack built.*

This is the cat
That chased the rat
That ate the malt
That lay in

Chorus: *the house that Jack built.*

This is the dog
That worried the cat
That chased the rat
That ate the malt
That lay in

Chorus: *the house that Jack built.*

This is the cow with the crumpled horn
That tossed the dog
That worried the cat
That chased the rat
That ate the malt
That lay in

Chorus: *the house that Jack built.*

This is the maiden all forlorn
That milked the cow with the crumpled horn
That tossed the dog
That worried the cat
That chased the rat
That ate the malt
That lay in

Chorus: *the house that Jack built.*

Using Accessories

LITTLE THINGS

(to the tune of "Oh My Darling" or chanted)

Little black things, little black things
Crawling up and down my arm.
I am not afraid of them
For they will do no harm.
(Substitute any color for black.)

Materials Needed.

The following colors of yarn:

red	green	black	pink
orange	blue	brown	gray
yellow	purple	white	

Instructions.

You will need to make a set of eleven colored things for each child. These can be stored easily in zip-lock sandwich bags.

Step 1: For each colored thing, cut five yarn pieces, each measuring eight inches long.

Step 2: Put one yarn piece aside and, keeping the other four together, fold them in half.

Step 3: Using the fifth piece of yarn, tie it around the other four, one inch from the folded ends and knotting it well, to form a "head" and "legs." Fold the knotted ends down to form more legs.

Give each child a bag of "things." Let the children tell you what color to use. While chanting or singing, have the colored thing crawl up and down arms.

Courtesy of MAGIC MOMENTS

FINGER PLAY

Finger play is an enjoyed preschool group (or individual) activity that parents have probably already introduced children to with "peek-a-boo" or "this little piggy went to market." Finger plays use words and actions (usually finger motions) together. Early childhood play frequently goes beyond finger movements and often includes whole body actions (figure 15-2).

When learning a finger play, the child usually practices and joins in the finger movements before learning the words. Words can be learned and retained by doing the play over and over again (figure 15-3).

Finger plays are often done with rhymes. Easy-to-remember rhymes give the children pleasure in listening and a chance to feel good about themselves because (1) they quickly become part of a group having fun and doing the same thing, and (2) they experience a feeling of accomplishment when a rhyme has been learned.

Teachers use finger plays to encourage enjoyment of language, to prepare children for sitting, to keep

FIGURE 15-2 Finger plays use words and actions together.

children active and interested while waiting, and as transitions between activities. Finger plays are also used for special purposes, such as quieting a group or getting toys back on the shelves. They can build vocabulary as well as teach facts and can help a child release pent-up energy.

Teachers should practice a finger play and memorize it beforehand to be sure of a clear and smooth presentation. It should be offered enthusiastically, focusing on enjoyment. As with other activities, the teacher can say, "Try it with me." The child who just watches will join in when ready. Watching comes first, one or two hand movements next, and then repetitions, using words and actions together. Each child learns at his or her own rate of speed.

Suggested Finger Plays

Finger plays can be found in many books for early childhood staff members or can be created by the teacher. The following are recommended because of their popularity with both children and teachers.

FIGURE 15-3 Actions are sometimes learned before words.

HICKORY, DICKORY, DOCK

Hickory, dickory, dock!
(Rest elbow in the palm of your other hand
and swing upraised arm back and forth.)
The mouse ran up the clock;
(Creep fingers up the arm to
the palm of the other hand.)
The clock struck one.
(Clap hands.)
The mouse ran down.
(Creep fingers down to elbow.)
Hickory, dickory, dock!
(Swing arm as before.)

OPEN, SHUT THEM

Open, shut them. Open, shut them.
Give a little clap.
Open, shut them. Open, shut them.
Lay them in your lap.
Creep them, creep them,
Creep them, creep them,
Right up to your chin.
Open wide your little mouth
But do not let them in.
Open, shut them. Open, shut them,
To your shoulder fly
Let them, like the little birds
Flutter to the sky.
Falling, falling, downward falling
Almost to the ground,
Quickly raising all your fingers
Twirl them 'round and 'round and 'round.

CHOO! CHOO!

Choo-o! Choo-o! Choo! Choo!
(Run finger along arm to shoulder slowly.)
This little train goes up the track.
Choo! Choo! Choo! Choo!
(At shoulder turn "train" and head
down arm.)
But this little train comes quickly back
Choo-choo-choo-choo! Choo-choo-choo-choo!
(Repeat last line.)
(Run fingers down arm quickly.)
Whoo-o! Whoo-o! Whoo-o!
(Imitate train whistle.)

FAMILY OF RABBITS

A family of rabbits lived under a tree,
(Close right hand and hide it under left arm.)
A father, a mother, and babies three.
(Hold up thumb, then fingers in succession.)
Sometimes the bunnies would sleep all day,
(Make fist.)
But when night came, they liked to play.
(Wiggle fingers.)
Out of the hole they'd go creep, creep, creep,
(Move fingers in creeping motion.)
While the birds in the trees were all asleep.
(Rest face on hands, place palms together.)
Then the bunnies would scamper about and run
(Wiggle fingers.)
Uphill, downhill! Oh, what fun!
(Wiggle fingers vigorously.)
But when the mother said, "It's time to rest,"
(Hold up index finger.)
Pop! They would hurry
(Clap hands after "Pop.")
Right back to their nest!
(Hide hand under arm.)

FIRE FIGHTERS

Ten little fire fighters, sleeping in a row,
Ding, dong goes the bell, down the pole they go.
Jumping on the engine, oh, oh, oh,
Putting out the fire, shhhhhhhhhhhhhhhhhhhh.
And home again they go
Back to sleep again,
All in a row.

THIS IS THE MOUNTAIN

This is the mountain up so high,
(Form a triangle.)
And this is the moon that sails through the sky.
(Make a circle with thumbs and
index fingers.)
These are the stars that twinkle so bright.
(Make a small circle with thumb and index,
other three fingers moving.)
These are the clouds that pass through the night.
(Make fists.)

This is the window through which I peep,
  (Make a square with thumb and index.)
And here am I, fast asleep.
  (Close eyes.)

CLAP YOUR HANDS

Clap your hands high,
Clap your hands low,
Pat your head lightly,
And down you go.

I'll touch my hair, my lips, my eyes,
I'll sit up straight, and then I'll rise.
I'll touch my ears, my nose, my chin,
Then quietly, sit down again.

BUTTERFLY

Roly-poly caterpillar
Into a corner crept.
Spun around himself a blanket
Then for a long time slept.
A long time passed (Whisper)
Roly-poly caterpillar wakened by and by.
Found himself with beautiful wings
Changed to a butterfly.

SLEEPY TIME

Open wide your little hands,
Now squeeze them very tight.
Shake them, shake them very loose,
With all your might.
Climb them slowly to the sky.
Drop down like gentle rain.
Go to sleep my little hands,
I'll wake you once again.

TWO LITTLE BLACKBIRDS

Two little blackbirds sitting on a hill,
  (Place two forefingers on shoulders
  to represent birds.)
One named Jack,
  (Hold one forefinger out.)
One named Jill
  (Hold other forefinger out.)
Fly away Jack; fly away Jill:
  (Make one hand and then the other
  "fly away.")

Come back Jack; come back Jill.
  (Bring hands back to shoulders
  one at a time.)
Two little blackbirds sitting on a hill.

A FUNNY ONE

'Round the house
'Round the house
  (Put fingers around the face.)
Peep in the window
  (Open eyes wide.)
Listen at the door
  (Cup hand behind ear.)
Knock at the door
  (Knock on head.)
Lift up the latch
  (Push up nose.)
And walk in
  (Stick out tongue and walk fingers in mouth.)
— I caught you!
  (Bite gently down on fingers.)

TWO LITTLE APPLES

Two little apples hanging on a tree,
  (Put hand by eyes.)
Two little apples smiling at me.
  (Smile.)
I shook that tree as hard as I could.
  (Shake tree.)
Down came the apples.
  (Make falling motions.)
Mmmm — they were good.
  (Rub stomach.)

HALLOWEEN

Five little pumpkins sitting on a gate,
  (Hold up five fingers.)
This one says, "My it's getting late."
  (Wiggle index finger.)
This one says, "There are black cats everywhere."
  (Wiggle middle finger.)
This one says, "I don't care."
  (Wiggle ring finger.)
This one says, "It's all for Halloween fun."
  (Wiggle little finger.)
And the other one says, "We better run!"
  (Wiggle thumb.)

Woo, goes the wind
  (Blow.)
Out goes the light!
  (Close eyes.)
And the five little pumpkins run quickly out of sight.
  (Hand runs away.)

BEEHIVE

Here is a beehive.
  (Make fist around other hand.)
Where are the bees?
Hidden away
Where nobody sees.
See them creeping
  (Pull out one finger at a time.)
Out of the hive
1-2-3-4-5! Buzz!
  (Making buzzing sound with hand
  moving in air.)
Here is a beehive.
  (Make fist.)
Where are the bees?
They're buzzing around
  (Buzz around with other hand.)
The flowers and trees.
Soon they'll come home
Back from their fun.
  (Put thumb in first then fingers
  one at a time.)
5-4-3-2-1! Buzz!
  (Make buzzing sound.)

MR. BROWN AND MR. BLACK

This is Mr. Brown (Hold up right thumb, fingers
  outstretched.)
And he lives in this house. (Tuck thumb inside
  fingers.)
And this is Mr. Black (Hold up left thumb,
  fingers outstretched.)
And he lives in this house. (Tuck thumb inside
  fingers.)
Now one day Mr. Brown decided to visit Mr. Black.
So he opened the door (Extend fingers of right
  hand.)
Came out (Hold thumb upright.)
Shut the door. (Close fingers into fist, leaving
  thumb upright.)

*He went up the hill and down the hill and up the hill
  and down the hill* (Move thumb in directions
  indicated.)
Until he came to Mr. Black's house (Hold up left
  fist.)
Knocked on the door (Make knocking motion with
  right fist on left fist.)
No one was home. (Shake head.)
*So he went up the hill and down the hill and up the
  hill and down the hill until he came to his own
  house* (Follow directions with fist.)
Opened the door (Extend fingers out flat.)
Went in (Put thumb in palm.)
Shut the door. (Place fingers over thumb.)
Now one day Mr. Black decided to visit Mr. Brown
  (Repeat sequence, substituting Mr. Black for
  Mr. Brown and using left hand.)
*One day Mr. Brown and Mr. Black decided to visit
  each other.* (Repeat sequence, using both
  hands.)
*They went up the hill and down the hill and up the
  hill and down the hill and they met* (Follow direc-
  tions with both hands.)
And Mr. Brown said, "Hello, Mr. Black!" (Wiggle
  right thumb.)
And Mr. Black said, "Hello, Mr. Brown!" (Wiggle
  left thumb.)
And they shook hands. (Shake hands.)
*Then they went up the hill and down the hill and up
  the hill and down the hill until they came to their
  own houses* (Follow directions with both
  hands.)
Opened the door (Extend fingers.)
Went in (Place thumbs in palms.)
And shut the door. (Close fingers over thumbs.)

PEANUT BUTTER AND JELLY

*First you take the peanuts and you crunch them and
  you crunch them.* (Repeat.)
Peanut butter — jelly! Peanut butter — jelly!
*Then you take the grapes and you squish them and you
  squish them.* (Repeat.)
Peanut butter — jelly! Peanut butter — jelly!
*Then you take the bread and you spread it and you
  spread it.* (Repeat.)
Peanut butter — jelly! Peanut butter — jelly!
*Then you take the sandwich and you eat it and you eat
  it.* (Repeat. Then with your mouth closed hum

the refrain as if you had a mouth full of sandwich.)

Peanut butter — jelly! Peanut butter — jelly!

("Peanut butter" is said in the following fashion: "Pea" (medium pitch) "nut" (low pitch) "but" (medium) "ter" (high pitch with hands above head, fingers shaking to side in vaudeville-type motion). "Jelly" is said in a low, throaty voice, accompanied by hands to opposite side shaking at knee level.)

MR. SNAKE

Mr. Snake, from his hole
Deep in the ground,
Poked out his head
And looked around.
   (From closed right hand, pull thumb out.)
"It's too nice a day
To stay in," he said.
"I think I'll go
For a crawl instead."
So he twitched his tail
   (Jerk right hand back and forth.)
And gave a hiss
And off through the meadow he
Went like this.
   (Make right hand wiggle away.)

FIVE LITTLE ASTRONAUTS

Five little astronauts
   (Hold up fingers on one hand.)
Ready for outer space.
The first one said, "Let's have a race."
The second one said, "The weather's too rough."
The third one said, "Oh, don't be gruff."
The fourth one said, "I'm ready enough."
The fifth one said, "Let's Blast Off!"
10, 9, 8, 7, 6, 5, 4, 3, 2, 1,
   (Start with 10 fingers and pull one down with each number.)
BLAST OFF!!!
   (Clap loudly with "Blast Off!")

MR. TALL AND MR. SMALL

There was once a man
   (Stand on tiptoes.)
Who was tall, tall, tall.
   (Reach up as far as possible.)

He had a friend
Who was small, small, small.
   (Kneel and bend way down.)
The man who was small
Would try to call
To the man who was tall,
   (Cup hands near mouth, look up.)
"Hello, up there!"
   (In high voice.)
The man who was tall
   (Stand on tiptoes.)
At once would call
To the man who was small,
   (Bend from waist.)
"Hello, down there!"
   (Use deep voice.)
Then each tipped his hat
   (Stand straight.)
And made this reply:
"Good-bye, my friend."
   (Tip an imaginary hat; look up, speak in high voice.)
"Good-bye, good-bye."
   (Bow, and speak in low, deep voice.)

Beatrice Wells Carlson, "Mr. Tall and Mr. Small," *Listen and Help Tell the Story* (Nashville, TN: Abingdon Press, 1965)

BODY-ACTION PLAYS

Encourage children to jump in rhythm to this jump-rope chant while doing what the rhyme says. Use this for working out pent-up energy (figure 15-4).

TEDDY BEAR, TEDDY BEAR

Teddy bear, teddy bear, turn around.
Teddy bear, teddy bear, touch the ground.
Teddy bear, teddy bear, show your shoe.
Teddy bear, teddy bear, that will do.
Teddy bear, teddy bear, go upstairs.
   (Alternate hands upwards.)
Teddy bear, teddy bear, say your prayers.
Teddy bear, teddy bear, turn off the light.
Teddy bear, teddy bear, say good night.
   (Lay down and pretend to snore.)

FIGURE 15-4 Body-action play

Touch my armpits and I giggle.
  (Hands under armpits with laugh.)
Head shoulders, knees, and toes.
  (Touch in order.)
That's the way the story goes.
  (Clap.)

MONKEY STAMPS

The monkey stamps, stamps, stamps his feet.
The monkey stamps, stamps, stamps his feet.
Monkey see, monkey do,
The monkey does the same as you.

The monkey claps, claps, claps his hands.
The monkey claps, claps, claps his hands.
Monkey see, monkey do,
The monkey does the same as you.

When you make a funny face, the monkey makes
  a funny face.
When you make a funny face, the monkey makes
  a funny face.
Monkey see, monkey do,
The monkey does the same as you.

When you turn yourself around, the monkey turns
  himself around.
When you turn yourself around, the monkey turns
  himself around.
Monkey see, monkey do,
The monkey does the same as you.

Edith Fowke, *Sally Go Round the Sun: Three Hundred Children's Songs, Rhymes and Games* (Garden City, New York: Doubleday and Company, Inc., 1969)

BEAT ONE HAMMER

My mother told me to tell you
To beat one hammer
  (Pound one fist.)
Like you see me do.
My mother told me to tell you
To beat two hammers
  (Pound two fists.)
Like you see me do.
My mother told me to tell you
To beat three hammers
  (Pound two fists; stamp one foot.)
Like you see me do.

HEAD, SHOULDERS

Head, shoulders, knees, and toes
  (Stand; touch both hands to each part
  in order.)
Head, shoulders, knees, and toes.

Head, shoulders, knees, and toes.
That's the way the story goes.
  (Clap this line.)
This is my head, this is not.
  (Hands on head, then feet.)
These are my shoulders, this is not.
  (Hands on shoulders, then knees.)
Here are my knees; watch them wiggle,
  (Wiggle knees.)

My mother told me to tell you
To beat four hammers
   (Pound two fists; stamp two feet.)
Like you see me do.
My mother told me to tell you
To beat five hammers
   (Add nodding head.)
Like you see me do.
My mother told me to tell you
To beat no hammers
   (Stop!)
Like you see me do.

MY LITTLE THUMBS

My little thumbs keep moving.
My little thumbs keep moving.
My little thumbs keep moving.
   Tra-la tra-la tra-la.
My thumbs and fingers keep moving.
My thumbs and fingers keep moving.
My thumbs and fingers keep moving.
   Tra-la tra-la tra-la.
My thumbs and fingers and hands keep moving.
My thumbs and fingers and hands keep moving.
My thumbs and fingers and hands keep moving.
   Tra-la tra-la tra-la.
My thumbs and fingers and hands and arms keep moving.
My thumbs and fingers and hands and arms keep moving.
My thumbs and fingers and hands and arms keep moving.
   And then I stand right up.
My thumbs and fingers and hands and arms and feet
   keep moving.

My thumbs and fingers and hands and arms and feet
   keep moving.
My thumbs and fingers and hands and arms and feet
   keep moving.
   Tra-la tra-la tra-la.
My thumbs and fingers and hands and arms and feet
   and head keep moving.
My thumbs and fingers and hands and arms and feet
   and head keep moving.
My thumbs and fingers and hands and arms and feet
   and head keep moving.
   Tra-la tra-la tra-la.

Summary

Speaking activities are planned for the young child. Some require simple imitation of words, while others call for the child's creative or expressive response.

Finger plays use words and actions together. They are actively enjoyed by children and build feelings of self-worth. Teachers can memorize finger plays and use them daily.

Circle times instill group spirit and social enjoyment of language. Opening activities capture attention. Chants and choruses add rhythmic word play and often involve physical movement. A smooth transition to other activities takes place when teachers are well prepared.

Teachers evaluate circle times comparing outcomes to goals.

Student Activities

- With a small group of classmates, practice and present a finger play, chant, chorus, or body-action play. Have each student present the activity until it is learned by the others.

- Make a list of at least five books that are resources for finger plays.

- Present a finger play, chant, or chorus to a group of young children.

- List possible reasons that children become disinterested at circle times.

- Find a finger play that is seasonal (generally used at only one time a year). Bring a copy to class.

- Create a finger play, chant, or chorus for young children.
- Observe a circle time and evaluate it. Share it with the class.

Unit Review

A. Finish the following:
  1. A transitional statement at the end of group time is necessary because
     _____.
  2. History shows that chants and choruses were used for _____.
  3. A successful circle time for young children can be described by the following terms: _____.

B. Why are finger plays so popular with young children?

C. Rearrange and place in the best order or sequence.
  1. Child knows words and actions of a finger play.
  2. Teacher knows words and actions of a finger play.
  3. Teacher practices finger play.
  4. Child participates with actions only.
  5. Child watches.
  6. Teacher presents finger play to children.
  7. Teacher evaluates the results of the finger play.
  8. Teacher encourages children to join in actions and words.

D. List five signals or attention getters that a teacher could use at the beginning of a circle time.

E. In what ways should an assistant teacher be helpful when another teacher is leading group language activities?

F. Rate the following teacher statements during planned circles.

      G = Good Technique   P = Poor Technique

  1. "It's my turn to talk."
  2. "Stop wiggling, Jimmy."
  3. "Everyone's listening, it's time to begin."
  4. "When Kate, Tran, and Nancy join us, we'll all be together."
  5. "The first one standing can be the first one to leave the circle."
  6. "We're finished. Let's go."
  7. "Speak up, Gisela. It's time to answer."
  8. "Thuy is doing our new finger play the 'right' way."
  9. "Watch closely, and make your fingers move just like mine."
  10. "I like the way everyone listened to what their friends said and took turns talking today."

References

Allen, Roach Van, and Claryce Allen. *Language Experience Activities*. Boston, MA: Houghton Mifflin, 1976. (Abundant activity ideas)

Church, Ellen Booth. "You Are Special." *Pre-K Today* 1.6 (Aug. 1987): 21–22.

Dodge, Diane Trister. "When Your Program Is Off Track." *Child Care Information Exchange*, 61 (May 1988): 42–48.

Johnson, Katie. *Doing Words*. Boston, MA: Houghton Mifflin, 1987.

Machado, Jeanne, and Helen C. Meyer. *Early Childhood Practicum Guide*. Albany: Delmar, 1984. Unit 5. (Pointers on conducting well-planned and interesting group experiences.)

Rainey, Ernestine W. *Language Development for the Young Child*. Atlanta, GA: Humanics Press, 1978. (Includes suggested group activities.)

Weir, Mary E., and Pat Eggleston. "Teacher's First Words." *Day Care and Early Education* 13.5 (Nov./Dec. 1975): 71–82.

Resources for Fingerplays and Circle Activities

Beckman, Carol, et al. *Channels to Children*, P.O. Box 25834, Colorado Springs, CO 80936. (A wonderful collection of activities based on a theme approach to teaching. Many cross-cultural activities described in last chapter.)

Brashears, D., and Sharron Werlin. *Circle Time Activities (for Young Children)*, 1 Corte Del Rey, Orinda, CA 94563. (A collection of suggested circle-time activities.)

Cochran, E. V. *Teach and Reach That Child*. Palo Alto, CA: Peek Publications, 1975.

Coglin, Mary Lou. *Chants for Children*. Coglin Publ., Box 301, Manilius, NY 13104 (If you enjoy chanting at circle, this will offer you additional chants to try.)

Croft, Doreen J., and Robert Hess. *An Activities Handbook for Teachers of Young Children*. Boston, MA: Houghton Mifflin, 1983.

Crowell, Liz, and Dixie Hibner. *Finger Frolics. First Teacher Inc.*, Box 29, Bridgeport, CT 06602.

Dowell, Ruth L. *Move over Mother Goose*. Pollyanna Productions, Mt. Ranier, MD: Gryphon House Inc., 1987.

Ellis, Mary Jackson. *Fingerplay Approach to Dramatization*. Minneapolis: T. S. Denison, 1978.

Engel, Rose C. *Language Motivating Experiences for Young Children*. Educative Toys and Supplies, 6416 Van Nuys Blvd., Van Nuys, CA 91401. 1971.

Finger Frolics, Mt. Ranier, MD: Gryphon House, 1976.

Finger Plays for Young Children. Scholastic, 2931 East McCarty St., P.O. Box 7502, Jefferson City, MO 65102 (an easel book).

Glazer, Tom. *Eye Winker, Tom Tinker, Chin Chopper: Fifty Musical Fingerplays*, New York: Doubleday, 1973.

Kable, Gratia. *Favorite Finger Plays*, Minneapolis: T. S. Denison, 1979.

Magic Moments, P.O. Box 53635, San Jose, CA 95153–0635. (Activities, patterns, flannel board ideas, drama with props, puppet activities, from .50–$5.00).

Mayesky, Mary et al. *Creative Activities for Young Children*, Albany: Delmar, 1985.

Scott, Louise B. *Learning Time with Language Experiences for Young Children*, Webster Division, New York: McGraw-Hill, 1975.

Wilmes, Liz, and Dick Wilmes. *Everyday Circle Times*. Mt. Ranier: Gryphon House, 1981. (A collection of ideas for exciting group times.)

UNIT 16

Puppetry and Beginning Drama Experiences

BJECTIVES

After studying this unit, you should be able to

- use puppetry in language arts programming.
- describe young children's puppet play.
- list five teaching techniques that offer young children opportunities for simple dramatization.

Puppets provide countless opportunities for children's speech growth. They match and fulfill many of the preschooler's developmental needs, besides being of high interest. Koons (1986) describes the power of puppet play:

Imagine a lifeless puppet lying on a table. Suddenly, a child slips his hand into the puppet and it awakens to a life and personality of its own. Magic happens and the world of make-believe begins. Children love to pretend and puppetry allows them to create their own magic.

When used by a child, puppets can be:

- moved and controlled by the child (figure 16-1)
- a challenge involving coordination of speech and movement
- talked to as an accepting companion
- used individually and in group play
- used to create and fantasize
- used to explore another's personality
- a way to release pent-up emotions
- used to relive and imitate experiences
- seen as an adultlike activity
- used to entertain others
- constructed by children

Many of these uses build and develop children's confidence in their own speaking ability.

There are many ways the *teacher* can use puppetry in language development activities:

When used by a teacher, puppets can:

- motivate
- gain attention and keep it focused
- provide variety in the presentation of ideas and words
- provide a model to imitate
- present stories
- promote child creativity and pretending
- provide a play opportunity that encourages speech and motor-skill coordination
- introduce new information
- promote positive attitudes toward speaking and dramatic activities
- build audience skills
- provide construction activities
- help children express themselves
- build vocabularies
- offer entertaining and enjoyable activities
- provide a wide range of individual personalities through puppets.

FIGURE 16-1 Exploring puppetry

What can puppets offer both children and their teachers? Hunt and Renfro (1982) believe:

For the child, the introduction of puppets can create a fresh and creative learning environment. Young children can generally accept the puppet as a non-threatening, sympathetic friend to whom they can entrust their thoughts and feelings without fear of ridicule or reprimand. This friend is privy to the child's inner world and is able also to communicate with the outer world as an intermediary. It is perhaps here that the teacher finds in puppetry its most valuable asset for contributing to the process of education. A skillful teacher can take advantage of special moments of puppet-inspired communication to tune into the child's thinking and to open up new avenues for learning.

AUDIENCE SKILLS

Audience skills are quickly learned, and teachers encourage them through discussion and modeling. Clapping after performances is recommended. Listening and being a quiet audience is verbally appreciated. Teachers and staff need to decide whether a child in the audience can leave during a performance. Most schools adopt this plan of action, and the child is expected to choose a quiet play activity that does not disturb others.

STIMULATING CHILDREN'S USE OF PUPPETS

Teachers can expand children's experiences with puppets in these ways:

- Present puppet plays and skits.
- Find community resources for puppet presentations: puppeteer groups, children's theater groups, high school and elementary classes, and skilled individuals.
- Introduce each puppet periodically and provide new ones when possible.
- Store puppets invitingly.
- Provide props and puppet theaters (figure 16-2).
- Keep puppets in good repair.

A puppet carried in a teacher's pocket can be useful in a variety of teaching situations, as mentioned previously. Children imitate the teacher's use of puppets, and this leads to creative play.

FIGURE 16-2 Young children enjoy watching a puppet performance.

TEACHER PUPPETRY

Children sit, excited and enthralled, at simple skits and dialogues performed by the teacher. Continually amazed by young children's rapt attention and obvious pleasure, most teachers find puppetry a valuable teaching skill (figure 16-3).

Prerecording puppet dialogue (or attaching puppet speeches inside the puppet stage) helps beginning teacher puppeteers. With practice, performance skills increase and puppet coordination can then become the main teacher task.

FIGURE 16-3 Puppetry is a valuable teaching device. *(From* Early Childhood Practicum Guide, *by Machado and Meyer,* © *1984 by Delmar Publishers Inc.)*

Hunt and Renfro's *Puppetry in Early Childhood Education* (1982) includes many valuable suggestions for increasing teacher puppetry skill, among them developing a puppet voice and personality:

Discover a voice contrasting to your own. Look at the puppet and see what characteristics its physical features suggest. A deep commanding voice, for example, may be appropriate for a large mouth while sleepy eyes may connote a slow, tired voice; many teeth imply a chattering voice while stand-up ears, a snappy voice. Become fully involved with the character and experiment freely; there are many voices never discovered within us, undiscovered simply because our whole range of tones and cadences has never been fully explored. A puppet's personality does not develop immediately; rather it evolves over a span of days, weeks, sometimes months.

and

In developing a puppet personality, it is sometimes easier to pattern a character after a real person than to try to create one that is entirely imaginary. For example, think of a distinct screen or television celebrity, a friend, former teacher, child or even a member of your own family to offer credence to the puppet character. Give the puppet a name.

Naturally, puppet characters in plays or from printed sources already have built-in personalities, but a teacher's daily puppets have no such script and challenge teacher creativity.

Planning and performing simple puppet plays requires time and effort. The plays are selected for suitability and then practiced until the scene-by-scene sequence is firmly in mind. Good preparation helps ensure a smooth performance and adds to children's enjoyment.

Several helpful tips on puppetry follow.

- A dark net peep-hole enables performers to watch audience reactions and helps dialogue pacing.
- Puppets with strong, identifiable personality traits who stay in character are well received. Another way to enhance a puppet's personality is to give it an idiosyncrasy that sets it apart (Hunt and Renfro, 1982).
- Plan your puppet's personality in advance and stick to it. For example, Happy Mabel has the following characteristics: she is always laughing; says "Hot Potatoes!" often; likes to talk about her cat, Christobel; lives on a farm; is an optimist; speaks in a high-pitched voice; lives alone and likes young visitors.
- Use your favorite puppet in at least one activity weekly.

Puppet Activities

Child participation with puppets can be increased when planned puppet activities are performed. The following are a few of the many puppet play activities.

- Invite children to use puppets (with arms) and act out that a puppet is sleepy, hungry, dancing, crying, laughing, whispering, saying "hello" to a friend, climbing a ladder, waving good-bye, and shaking hands. (A large mirror helps children build skill.)
- Ask two volunteers to use puppets and act out a situation in which a mother and child are waking up in the morning. The teacher creates both speaking parts, then prompts two children to

continue on their own. Other situations include a telephone conversation, a child requesting money from a parent to buy an ice cream cone, and a puppet inviting another to a party.

- Urge children to answer the teacher's puppet. For example:

Teacher: "Hi! My name is Mr. Singing Sam. I can sing any song you ask me to sing. Just ask me!"

or

Teacher: "I'm the cook. What shall we have for dinner?"

or

Teacher: "My name is Randy Rabbit. Who are you? Where am I?"

- Record simple puppet directions (such as the following) on a cassette tape recorder and have a large mirror available so that the children can see their actions:
  1. Make your puppet touch his nose.
  2. Have your puppet clap.
  3. Kiss your hand, puppet.
  4. Rub your eyes, puppet.
  5. Reach for the stars, puppet.
  6. Hold your stomach.
  7. Scratch your ear.
  8. Bow low.
  9. Hop.

  Set up this activity in individual, room-divided space (figure 16-4).
- Record simple puppet dramas. After a teacher demonstration, make them available to children on a free-choice basis. Provide a mirror, if possible.

Storage and Theaters

Store puppets in an inviting way, face up, begging for handling; shoe racks, wall pockets, or upright pegs within the child's reach are suggested. An adjacent puppet theater tempts children's use. Old television cabinets (with insides removed and open backs) make durable theaters that the children can climb into. Other theaters can be constructed by the teacher using large packing crates that can be painted and decorated by the children.

Hunt and Renfro (1982) describe what might happen in a puppet corner:

As soon as a child physically picks up a puppet, he wants to make it talk. By giving it a voice, he also

FIGURE 16-4 A paper-bag puppet interests these two children in the housekeeping area.

gives it life. In the puppet corner children will experiment without inhibition using different vocal sounds and character voices. No other form of expression, except creative dramatics, offers such a broad range of opportunities for verbal experimentation.

In most centers, rules are set for using puppets. The puppets should stay in certain designated areas and should be handled with care.

Puppet Plays

Familiar and favorite stories makes good puppet dramas. Many contain simple, repetitive lines that most of the children know from memory. Children will often stray from familiar dialogues in stories, however, adding their own lines, actions, or settings. Older preschoolers speak through puppets easily; younger children may be more interested in manipulating alone or simple imitating.

When children enlarge or change dialogue or a character's personality, their own individuality directs and creates. Schools can wind up with many versions and interpretations of familiar favorites.

Other Puppetry Tips

- Some children are fearful of puppets. They may even think that a puppet has died when they see the puppet limp on the shelf. With reassurance

and additional exposure to teacher puppet use, fear subsides.
- Aggressive puppet play of the "Punch and Judy" type should be redirected. Having puppets punch and hit is common behavior in traditional Punch and Judy shows, and consequently is not presented to young children in school settings. Any modeling of aggressive and violent behavior in puppetry is inappropriate.
- Most public libraries offer puppet shows periodically.
- Parents and volunteers can help construct sturdy classroom puppets.
- Commercial school-supply companies offer well-made, durable puppets and theaters for group use.

PUPPET TYPES

Puppets can be divided into two general categories — those worked with the hands and fingers and those that dangle on strings (figure 16-5). Hand puppets are popular in the preschool because they are so versatile and practical. Teacher-made, child-made, as well as commercially manufactured hand puppets are an essential part of most centers.

Moving arms and pliable faces on puppets increase the possibilities for characterization and action. Rubber, plastic, and papier-mache puppet heads are durable. Cloth faces permit a wider variety of facial expressions.

Papier-Mache Puppet Heads
Materials:

> styrofoam egg or ball (a little smaller than the size you want for the completed head), soft enough to have a holder inserted into it
> neck tube (made from cardboard — about one-and-a-half inches wide and five inches long, rolled into a circle and taped closed, or plastic hair roller)
> bottle (to put the head on while it is being created and to hold it during drying)
> instant papier-mache (from a craft store)
> paints (poster-paint variety)
> spray-gloss coat (optional)
> white glue

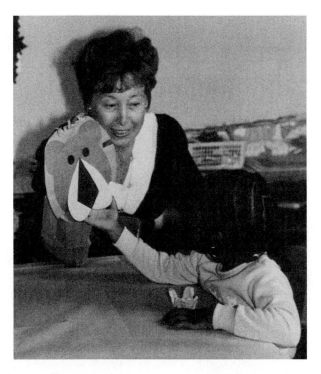

FIGURE 16-5 Paper-bag puppets are hand puppets.

Construction Procedure:

1. Mix instant papier-mache with water (a little at a time) until it is like clay — moist, but not too wet or dry.
2. Place styrofoam egg on neck tube (or roller) securely. Then place egg (or ball) on bottle so that it is steady.
3. Put papier-mache all over head and half way down neck tube. Coating should be about a half inch thick.
4. Begin making the facial features, starting with the cheeks, eyebrows, and chin. Then add eyes, nose, mouth, and ears.
5. When you are satisfied with the head, allow it to dry at least 24 hours in an airy place.
6. When the head is dry, paint the face with poster paint. When that is dry, coat it with spray gloss finish to seal paint.
7. Glue is useful for adding yarn hair, if desired.

Note that children can make this type of puppet if papier-mache is eliminated and felt pens are used to define facial features.

Sock Puppets

Materials:

old sock, felt, sewing machine

Construction Procedure (see figure 16-6):

1. Use an old wool or other thick sock. Turn it inside out and spread it out with the heel on top.
2. Cut around the edge of the toe (about three inches on each side).
3. Fold the mouth material (pink felt) inside the open part of the sock and draw the shape. Cut the mouth piece out and sew into position.
4. Turn the sock right side out and sew on the features.

Paper-Bag Puppets

Materials:

paper bags, scissors, crayons or marking pens, paste, yarn or paper scraps, and paint (if desired)

Construction Procedure:

1. Paper bag puppets are quick and easy. Give each child a small paper sack (no. 6 works well).
2. Show them how the mouth works and let them color or paste features on the sack.
3. You may wish to have them paste a circle on for the face. Paste it on the flap part of the bag and then cut the circle on the flap portion so the mouth can move again.
4. Many children will want to add special features to their paper bag puppets, for example, a tail or ears (figure 16-7).

Stick Puppets

A stick puppet is a picture or object attached to a stick (figure 16-8). It moves when the puppeteer moves the puppet up and down or from side to side, holding the stick.

Materials:

paper, glue, scissors, crayons, popsicle sticks (or tongue depressors or cardboard strips)

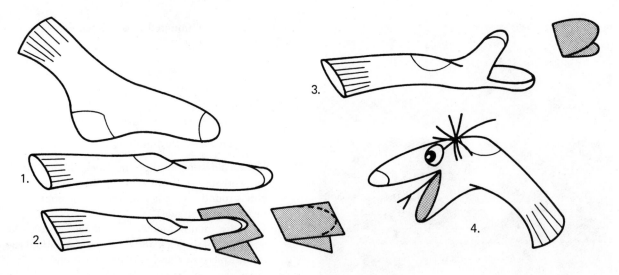

FIGURE 16-6 Sock-puppet construction

Construction Procedure:

1. Characters and scenery can be drawn by children or preoutlined. Depending on the age of the children, the characters and scenery can then be colored or both colored and cut out.
2. Older children may want to create their own figures.

Pop-Ups
Materials:

heavy paper, glue, yarn, stick (tongue depressor or thinner sticks), scissors, plastic, styrofoam or paper cup, felt pens

FIGURE 16-7 Paper-bag puppet

FIGURE 16-8 Stick puppets

Construction Procedure:

1. Cut circle smaller than cup radius. Decorate face.
2. Slit the cup bottom in the center to allow sticks to move up and down.
3. Glue the face to the stick. Glue on yarn hair.
4. Slip puppet in the cup with stick through cup bottom so that the puppet disappears and can pop up.

Large Cloth Hand Puppet
Materials:

fabric, sewing machine, felt scraps, yarn, glue, cardboard sheet (see Appendix for pattern)

Construction Procedure:

1. Sew head darts.
2. With right sides together, sew back and front a quarter of an inch from the edge.
3. Pin mouth at quarters. Ease mouth piece and sew.
4. After the mouth is securely in place, glue cardboard to the inside of the mouth (white glue works fine).
5. If arms are desired, slash at side, insert arm and sew.
6. Decorate as desired (figure 16-9).

Box Puppets
Materials:

one small (individual size) box with both ends intact
one piece of white construction paper, 6″ × 9″
crayons or poster paints and brush
scissors, sharp knife, glue

Construction Procedure (see figure 16-10):

1. Cut box in half as in view 1, with one wide side uncut. Fold over as in view 2.
2. On construction paper, draw the face of a person or an animal. Color or paint features and cut out face.
3. Add yarn for hair, broomstraws for whiskers, and so on, if desired.
4. Cut face along line of mouth and glue to box as in view 4, so that lips come together as in view 5.

Jumping Jacks
Materials:

stiff paper or oak tag, brads, string, hole punch, dowel, glue, curtain pull (optional)

Construction Procedure (see figure 16-11):

1. Design and cut pattern, making arms and legs long enough to secure behind figure. Cut two body pieces.
2. Glue figure to dowel by inserting between front and back.
3. Brads act as joints. Hole punch and add arms, legs, and string.

Frog and Bird Finger Puppets
Materials:

felt fabric, scissors, sewing machine, pattern, elastic ribbon (see Appendix)

Construction Procedure:

Cut and sew pieces, leaving ends open to insert finger.

Additional Puppet Types:

- Wrap-around finger band puppet (see figure 16-12).
- Plastic-bottle-head puppet.
- Dustmop-head puppet.
- Favorite TV character puppet (figure 16-13, page 280).
- Garden glove puppets (different faces can be snapped on or velcro used) (figure 16-14, page 281).
- Suspended toy from stick puppets. (Adding beads to feet give them sound effects.)

TEACHER PUPPET PRESENTATIONS

Many simple stories can be shared with children through teacher puppetry. Figures 16-15 (page 283) and 16-16 (page 284) show ideas for puppet theaters. See the Appendix for additional puppet patterns.

The story on page 280 is an example of a tale that lends itself to a puppet presentation. Teachers can create their own stories that appeal to the interests of the children with whom they work.

FIGURE 16-9 Large, cloth hand puppets

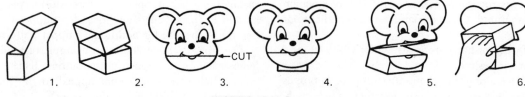

FIGURE 16-10 Box puppet

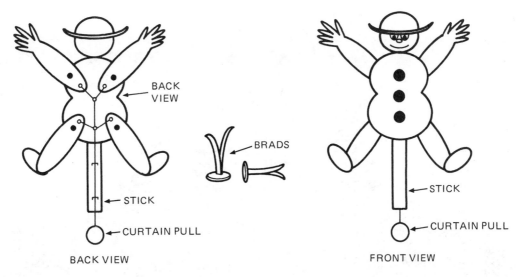

FIGURE 16-11 Jumping jack

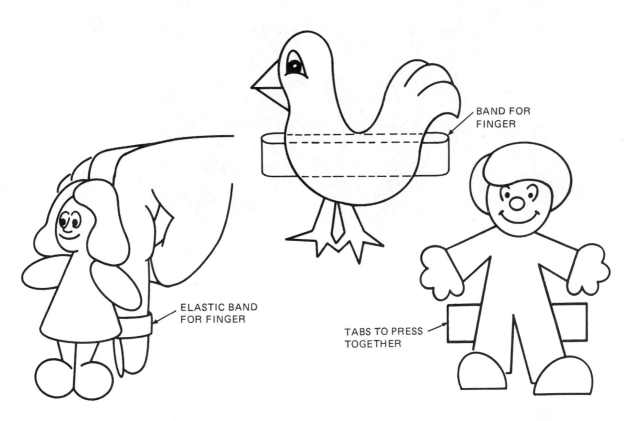

PAPER FINGER PUPPETS (SMALL PATTERN OR TEACHER DRAWING WITH BAND OR TABS FOR FINGER)

FIGURE 16-12 Finger puppets

FIGURE 16-13 Favorite TV character puppet

The Pancake

Narrator:

Once upon a time, an old woman made a pancake. When it was nice and golden brown, it hopped out of the frying pan and began rolling down the road, saying:

Pancake:

Whee! I'm free! Nobody will ever eat me! What a nice day! I'll just roll along till — hey! I wonder what that funny looking round thing is by the river!

Narrator:

He didn't know it, but it was a bridge.

FIGURE 16-14 Garden-glove puppets

Pancake:

I'll bet I can roll over that thing. Watch this! I'll just get a head start back here — (backs up) one... two...three! (As the pancake starts over the bridge, frog comes up and grabs it.)

Pancake:

Let me go! Let me go!

Frog:

I want to eat you! I love pancakes! (Pancake pulls away and rolls out of sight.)

Frog:

Oh, dear...it got away...(Frog down. Bridge down. Pancake rolls in.)

Pancake:

That was a close one! I hope I do not meet any other — (Off stage is heard the sound of barking...)

Pancake:

What's that sound? I do not think I like it...(Dog in, tries to grab pancake.)

Dog:

I want a bite! I love pancakes! (Pancake cries "No! No!" and rolls off.)

Dog:

It got away. Well, better luck next time...(Dog out, pancake rolls in.)

Pancake:

Goodness! Everybody seems to love pancakes, but I do not want to be loved that way! (Off stage is heard the sound of "meow!")

Pancake:

Meow? What kind of animal makes that sound? (Cat in, tries to grab pancake, pancake escapes as before.)

Cat:

Meow? meow, no breakfast now! (Cat out, pancake rolls in panting.)

Pancake:

This is dreadful! Everybody I meet wants to eat me! (Bird flies in.)

Bird:

A pancake! Delicious! I'll just peck a few pieces out of it! (Bird starts to peck at pancake, which rolls away crying, "No! No!" Bird follows, then returns alone.)

Bird:

It's too hot to chase it. Besides, it can roll faster than I can fly. (Bird out. Put bridge up again.)

Narrator:

And all day long the pancake rolled until it finally found itself back at the same bridge. (Pancake rolls in.)

Pancake:

(Wearily) Oh, dear...here I am again, back at the same bridge...I must have been rolling around in circles. And I'm too tired to roll another inch. I must rest. I'll just lie down here next to this round thing over the river...(Pancake lies down flat, or leans against the bridge, if possible. Now puppeteer has two free hands to put on frog and dog. But before they come in, we hear their voices.)

Frog's Voice:

(half-whisper) It's mine!

Dog's Voice:

(half-whisper) No, it's mine. I saw it first!

Frog's Voice:

(same) You did not! I saw it first!

Dog's Voice:

(same) Who cares — I'm going to eat it! (Dog and Frog enter and grab the pancake between them.)

Pancake:

Let me go! Let me go! (Frog and dog tussle, drop pancake out of sight, look after it.)

Frog:

You idiot! You dropped it in the water!

Dog:

You're the idiot! You're the one who dropped it!

Narrator:

And as the pancake disappeared beneath the water, they heard it say, (far away voice) "Nobody will ever catch me..." and nobody ever did. (Sloane, 1942)

Teachers find that play situations that contain a puppet, animal, or other character that is less knowledgeable and mature than the children themselves promote a feeling of bigness in children. The children are then in the position of taking care of and educating another, which often produces considerable child speech and self-esteem. A well-known commercial language development kit (program) cleverly contains a puppet that has no eyes. Children are urged to help this puppet by describing objects and events.

SIMPLE DRAMA

Children often playact familiar events and home situations. This allows them to both try out and work out elements of past experiences that they remember for one reason or another. Their playacting can be an exact imitation or something created by their active imaginations.

Four-year-olds, because of their ability to conceptualize and fantasize, are prime candidates for beginning exposure to this literary form. They pick up both acting skill and audience skill quickly. Three-year-olds enjoy drama presentations and are good audiences. They profit from exposure but can have a difficult time with the acting role. Imitative, pretend play, and pantomime suit their developmental level. Pantomime becomes the foundation on which four-year-olds build their acting skills for created and scripted parts.

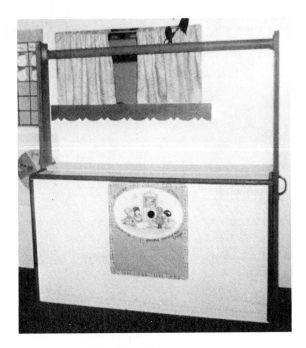

FIGURE 16-15 Puppet stage

In both drama and pantomime, children can act out all the joy, anger, fear, and surprise of favorite characters. This gives children the opportunity to become someone else for a few minutes and to release their frustration and energy in an acceptable way (Perez, 1986).

After young children become familiar with stories, they thoroughly enjoy reenacting or dramatizing the stories. By using both physical motions and verbal comments, children bring words and actions of the stories to life.

Playacting Tips

Children will act out parts from favorite stories as well as scenes from real life. The teacher sets the stage, keeping some points in mind:

- The children must be familiar with the story in order to know what happens first, next, and last.
- Activities in which the children pretend to perform certain actions, to be certain animals, or to copy the actions of another, help prepare them for simple drama.
- Video-taped plays and films are good motivators.
- A first step is to act without words or while listening to a good story or record.
- The teacher can be the narrator, while the children are the actors.
- Children should be encouraged to volunteer for parts.
- Props and settings can be simple. Ask, "What can be used for a bridge?" or a similar question so children can use their creativity.
- Any of the children's imaginative acts should be accepted, whether or not they are a part of the original story. The teacher remains close without directing or interfering (except when necessary).
- Individual and group dramatizations should be appreciated and encouraged. Every child who wishes a turn playing the parts should be accommodated.

Some classic stories that can be used for playacting (drama) include:

- Goldilocks and the Three Bears
- The Three Little Pigs
- The Little Red Hen
- Gingerbread Boy

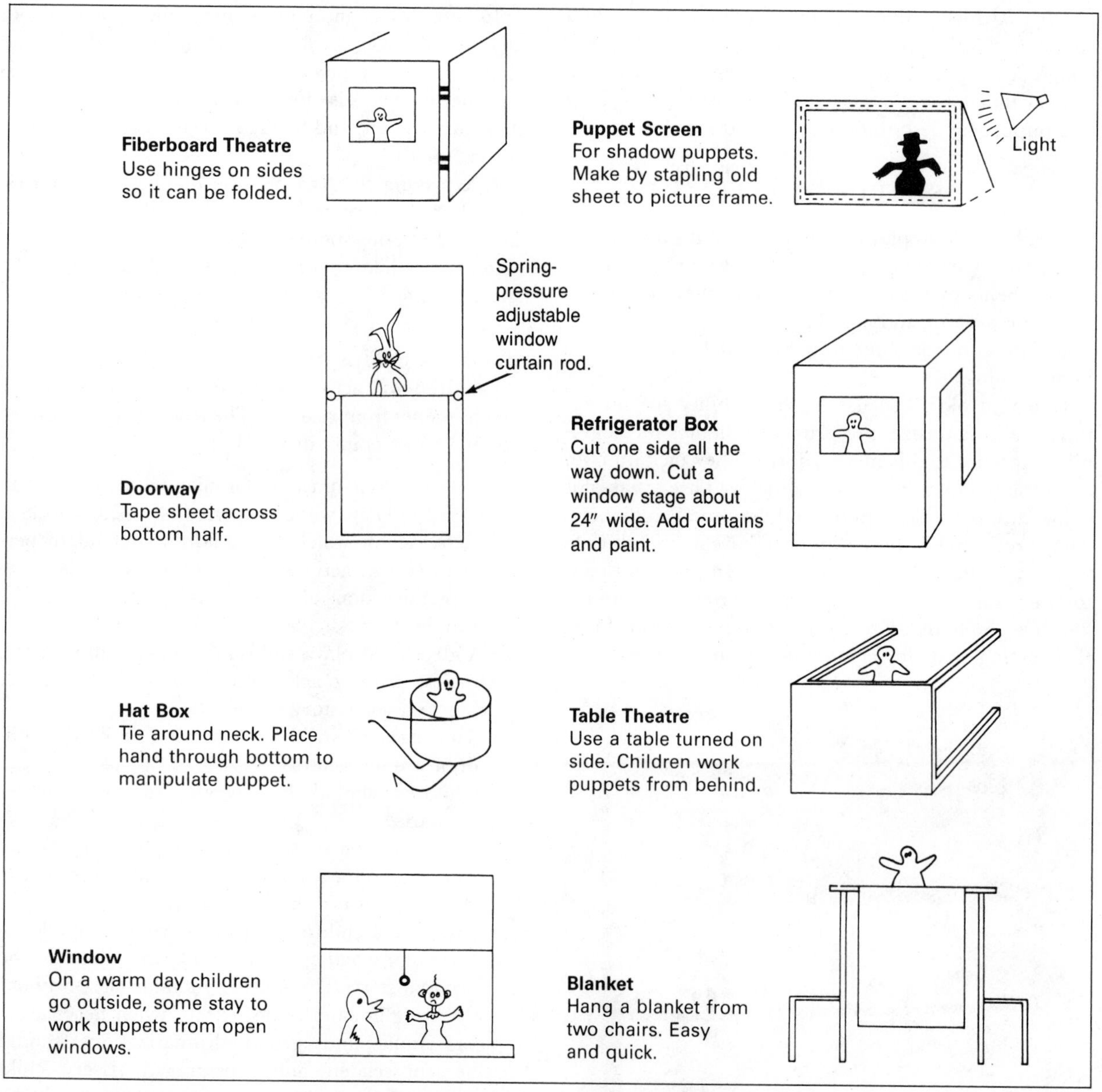

Fiberboard Theatre
Use hinges on sides so it can be folded.

Puppet Screen
For shadow puppets. Make by stapling old sheet to picture frame.

Light

Spring-pressure adjustable window curtain rod.

Doorway
Tape sheet across bottom half.

Refrigerator Box
Cut one side all the way down. Cut a window stage about 24″ wide. Add curtains and paint.

Hat Box
Tie around neck. Place hand through bottom to manipulate puppet.

Table Theatre
Use a table turned on side. Children work puppets from behind.

Window
On a warm day children go outside, some stay to work puppets from open windows.

Blanket
Hang a blanket from two chairs. Easy and quick.

FIGURE 16-16 Ideas for puppet theaters

- Little Red Ridinghood
- Little Miss Muffet

Fast action and simple story lines are best for the young child. Playacting presents many opportunities for children to develop:

- self expression
- use of correct speech
- coordination of actions and words
- creative thinking
- self-confidence
- listening skills
- social interaction

Perez (1986) suggests that children should be reminded that when they act they become someone other than who they really are, for a short time. What other people think and feel is often shown by what they do. By observing other people closely, you become more aware of how others do things and show emotion.

Drama From Picture Books

Bev Bos (1983), a well-known California workshop leader, tells a funny story about children's love of dramatization. Because picture books are frequently enacted at Bev's center, a child who readily identifies with a particular book character often speaks up saying "I want to be the rabbit" long before the picture book reading session is finished.

In enacting stories from books or story-telling sources, the teacher may have to read the book or tell the story over a period of time so it is digested and becomes familiar to the children. A discussion of the story can promote children's expression of opinions about enjoyed parts, the feelings of characters, and what might be similar in their own lives. The teacher can then ask "Who's good at crying and can go "Boo-hoo"? or "Who can act mad and stomp around the floor?" Most child groups have one or more children ready to volunteer. The teacher can play one of the parts.

Many action- and dialog-packed picture books, such as the following, lend themselves to child reenactment:

- *The Funny Thing*, by Wanda Gag
- *Rosie's Walk*, by Pat Hutchins
- *The Gingerbread Boy*, by Paul Galdone
- *One Fine Day*, by Nonny Hogrogian

Stories suggested by Perez (1986) include *The Little Rabbit Who Wanted Red Wings*, by Carolyn Bailey, and stories found in *Let's Pretend It Happened to You*, by Bernice Wells Carlson.

Progressive Skill

Dramatizing a familiar story involves a number of language skills — listening, auditory and visual memory of actions and characters' speech lines, and remembered sequence of events — as well as audience skills. Simple pantomime or imitation requires less maturity. Activities that use actions alone are good as a first step toward building children's playacting skills. Children have imitated others' actions since infancy, and as always, the joy of being able to do what they see others do brings a feeling of self-confidence. The children's individuality is preserved if differences in ways of act-

ing out a familiar story are valued in preschool settings.

Among the all-time favorites for pantomime is the following.

THE BEAR HUNT

We're going on a bear hunt
We're going where?
We're going on a bear hunt.
OK, let's go! I'm not afraid!

Look over there!
What do you see?
A big deep river.
Can't go around it.
Can't go under it.
Have to swim across it.
OK, let's go. I'm not afraid!

What's this tall stuff?
What do you see?
Tall, tall grass.
Can't go around it.
Can't go under it.
Got to go through it.
OK, let's go. I'm not afraid!

Hey, look ahead.
What do you see?
A rickety old bridge.
Can't go around it.
Can't go under it.
Got to go across it.
OK, let's go. I'm not afraid!

Now what's this ahead.
It's a tall, tall tree.
Can't go under it.
Can't go over it.
Have to climb it.
OK, let's go. I'm not afraid!

Do you see what I see?
What a giant mountain!
Can't go around it.
Can't go under it.
Got to climb over it.
OK, let's go. I'm not afraid!

Oh, look at that dark cave.
Let's go inside.
It sure is dark in here.
I think I feel something.

I think it's a nose.
And two furry ears.
HELP! It's a bear!!!!!!!!!!!!!!
Let's get out of here...I'm afraid.

(Pretend to climb back over the mountain and down the tree, run across the bridge, swish through the tall grass, swim the river, open the door, run in, slam the door, collapse in a heap.)

Whew...Home at last...I was afraid!

Creative Drama Programs

Starting a language program that includes creative drama requires planning. Props and play materials must be supplied for children to explore. When children see simple plays and pantomimes performed by teachers, other children, and adult groups, they are provided with a model and a stimulus. Some drama activity ideas for the older preschool child include:

- Pantomiming action words and phrases: tiptoe, crawl, riding a horse, using a rolling pin.
- Pantomiming words that mean a physical state: cold, hot, itchy.
- Pantomiming feeling words: happy, sad, hurt, holding a favorite teddy bear lovingly, feeling surprise.
- Acting out imaginary life situations: opening a door with a key, climbing in and out of a car, helping to set the table.
- Acting familiar character parts in well-known stories: "She covered her mouth so the clown couldn't see her laugh." "The rabbit dug a big hole and buried the carrot." "He tiptoed to the window, raised the shade, and opened it."
- Saying familiar lines from known stories: "And he huffed and he puffed, and he blew the house down."
- Playing a character in a short story or song that involves both spoken lines and actions.
- Pantomiming actions of a character in a short, familiar story that the teacher reads (or from a teacher-recorded story tape). There are a vast number of commercially recorded stories available at school-supply stores.

Kranyik (1986) suggests the following pantomimes for young children:

- Drink a glass of water. Oh! It turned into hot soup and burned your mouth!
- Eat a bowl of spaghetti.
- Row a boat.
- Pour your milk from the carton to a glass. Drink it.
- Play the piano, trumpet, drums, guitar.
- Try to open a jar that will not open.
- Touch something soft and furry.
- Chew a piece of bubble gum. It gets bigger, bigger, and bigger. Suddenly it breaks.
- You and your mom are in a supermarket. Suddenly, you can't find her, and you feel scared. You look up and down all the aisles trying to find her. There she is. You see her.

A simple story for pantomiming follows.

Little Indian's Adventures

(Teacher preface: A long, long time ago, native Americans were the only people who lived where we live today. There were no houses then, except the ones the native Americans made. They had to hunt for food almost every day.)

Little Indian (fingers behind head for feathers) *went out to look for a buffalo. He took his bow and arrow. Little Indian walked down a path.* (Slap thigh.) *Suddenly he thought he heard something.* (Put hand behind ear.) *He stopped and looked all around.* (Shade eyes.) *He saw a squirrel. He walked on.* (Slap thigh.) *He saw a hawk fly by.* (Shade eyes.) *He walked on.* (Slap thigh.) *He heard a rustle in the bushes.* (Put hand behind ear.) *Rustle, rustle, rustle.* (Rub palms together.) *Little Indian didn't wait a second. He began to run. He didn't stop until he reached his teepee.* (Form a triangle with hands.)

Costumes and Props

Imagination and inexpensive, easy-to-make costumes are a great performing incentive. Accessories such as hats can be used in a variety of play and drama situations.

Cutout chartboard or cardboard heads and figures held by the child quickly aid his or her ability to step into character (figure 16-17). (Make sure that chartboard is lightweight and hand holes are comfortable.)

FIGURE 16-17 Story character boards

Older children may be able to draw their own patterns, or patterns for figures can be found in children's books and can be enlarged with the use of an opaque projector. These props allow children to put their faces into the spaces cut out of the characters' faces and are useful in child dramatization. Some teachers feel these props are physically awkward and prefer, instead, simple costumes.

Summary

Using puppetry for language development is a widely accepted practice in preschools. There are many puppet types to choose from. The ability to coordinate puppet actions and words takes practice and maturity. Teachers find that the more children watch puppets being used, the more they will use them. Puppets that are stored attractively and upright near puppet theaters encourage children's exploration.

There is a wide range of uses for puppets as instructional devices. Puppets are interesting and capture attention as an enjoyable play activity.

Drama is another step on the road to literacy. Simple child dramatizations of favorite stories begin during preschool years. Language programs provide many playacting opportunities. Props, playacting, and pantomime activities motivate this expressive art. Skills are acquired through increased experiences with drama. Planning by the teacher aids children's acquisition of dramatization abilities.

Student Activities

- Make a puppet described in this unit, or make one of your own choosing.

- Present a simple puppet play with a few classmates.

- Collect 10 easy-to-make costume ideas that promote creative drama. Share your ideas with the class.

- Using a lesson (activity) plan form, describe a simple drama activity for a group of preschoolers.

- Record a puppet drama and enact the drama with the help of classmates.

- Construct a puppet theater.

- Invite a local puppeteer group to share ideas with the class.

- Bring one simple puppet play script or drama script to class.

- Create a short puppet play.

- Find commercial resources for ethnic puppets. Share names of companies and the prices for puppets.

- List community resources that might help young children in your community become more familiar with drama.

Unit Review

A. Write a short paragraph describing the reasons puppets are a part of preschool language arts programs.

B. Rate the following teachers using this scale.

+	?	−
definitely promotes puppet interest and use	unable to determine or can't decide	will probably turn children off

1. Mrs. G. (teacher) pulled a small puppet from her smock pocket. Reaching behind Mark, age three, she talked through the puppet. "Mark Allen Graham? Rupert sees what you're doing, and he doesn't like children who break crayons." Mark returns the crayon to the container.
2. Miss R. (teacher) is introducing a small group of children to an activity involving a poem on a chart. "Well, there's Petey, Sam, Scott, Adam, Renee, and Jonathan," Miss R. begins. The puppet in her hand moves and claps, and the puppet's voice is low pitched and deep. "I came to talk to you about rabbits. Does anyone know what rabbits look like? I live in a pocket, you know. I've heard about rabbits, but I've never seen one."
3. Mr. O. (teacher) has a large packing carton in the middle of the classroom. Two children notice the carton and ask, "What's that for?" Mr. O. tells the two children that he noticed the school puppets do not have a puppet theater. "How could we make one from this box?" he asks the children. "You need a window," one child says. "Yes, that's true. I'll draw one. Stand here, please. I'll need the window the right height." The conversation and the project has drawn a larger group of children.
4. Mr. T. (teacher) has noticed a puppet lying on the ground in the playground. He picks it up, examines it, and puts it in his pocket. During circle time, he says, "Orvil (puppet's name) was on the ground in the yard today. Raise your hand if you know where he should be put after we play with him. Olivia, I

see your hand. Would you please put Orvil in the place in the classroom that's just for him? Thank you, Olivia. What could happen to Orvil, our puppet, if we left him on the floor or ground?" "He'd get stepped on," Thad offers. "That could happen, Thad," said Mr. T. "Can anyone else think of what might happen to Orvil on the ground outside?" Mr. T. continues. "The ants would crawl on him," Jessica comments.

5. Ms. Y. announces to a group of children, "It's talking time. Everyone is going to talk to Bonzo (the puppet dog) and tell him their names." She reaches behind her and pulls Bonzo from a bag. "Willy, come up and take Bonzo," Ms. Y. directs. "Now, Cleo, you come up here, too. Willy, have Bonzo say, 'Woof, woof, I'm Bonzo.' " Willy fiddles with the puppet and still has not slipped it onto his hand. "We need a barking Bonzo. Who would like to come up, put Bonzo on his hand, and bark?" Ms. Y. asks.

C. Select the best answer for each statement.
1. Because puppets are so appealing, teachers
   a. motivate, model, and plan child activities to enhance the children's experiences.
   b. rarely use puppets in a conversational way, because it interrupts children's play.
   c. feel the large expense involved in supplying them is well worth it.
   d. find child language develops best without teacher modeling.
2. Puppets in preschool centers are used
   a. only by children.
   b. most often to present teacher-planned lessons.
   c. by both teachers and children.
   d. only when children ask for them.
3. Creative playacting (dramatization) is probably more appropriate
   a. for younger preschoolers, aged two to three years.
   b. for older preschoolers.
   c. when children are chosen for familiar characters' parts rather than selected from those children who volunteer for parts.
   d. when teachers help children stick to story particulars rather than promoting new lines or actions.
4. Identifying with a familiar story character through puppet use or playacting may give the child
   a. skills useful in getting along with others.
   b. greater insight into others' viewpoints.
   c. speaking skill.
   d. a chance to use creative imagination.
   e. all of the above.
5. If one is looking for a puppet with an expressive and active movement ability, one should use a
   a. plastic-headed puppet.
   b. papier-mache-headed puppet with arms.
   c. cloth-headed puppet with arms.
   d. stick puppet.
   e. all the above are equally active and expressive.

6. "Punch and Judy" types of child's play with puppets is
   a. to be expected and needs teacher attention.
   b. a rare occurrence.
   c. best when teacher's performance sticks to the script.
   d. expected and should be ignored.
   e. a good puppetry modeling experience.

References

Batchelder, Marjorie. *The Puppet Theatre Handbook*. New York: Harper and Row, 1979.

Bos, Bev. San Jose City College Workshop. "Creativity." 1983.

Hastings, Sue, and D. Ruthenberg. *How to Produce Puppet Plays*. New York: Harper and Row, 1975.

Hunt, Tamara, and Nancy Renfro. *Puppetry in Early Childhood Education*. Austin, TX: Renfro Studios, 1982.

Koons, Katherine. "Puppet Plays." *First Teacher* 7.5 (May 1986): 56–64.

Kranyik, Margery A. "Acting Without Words." *First Teacher* 7.5 (May 1986): 65–71.

Perez, Jeannine. "Don't Perform Share!" *First Teacher* 7.5 (May 1986): 50–55.

Roundtree, B., et al. *Creative Teaching With Puppets*. The Learning Line, P.O. Box 1406, University, Alabama 35486, 1981.

Sloane, G. L. *Fun with Folk Tales*. New York: Dutton, 1942.

Resources

Door puppet playhouse. Fabric Farms, 3590 Riverside Drive, Columbus, OH 43221.

Dress-ups for dramatic play. DRESS-UPS, 652 Glenbrook Road, Stamford, CT 06906.

Felt puppets. Pat's Puppets, 121 W. Simmons, Anaheim, CA 92802.

Puppet patterns. Plaid Enterprises, Inc., P.O. Box 7600, Norcross, GA 30091.

UNIT 17

Understanding Differences

OBJECTIVES

After studying this unit, you should be able to

- discuss standard and nonstandard English.
- describe the teacher's role with children who speak a dialect.
- discuss early childhood centers' language programs for bilingual children.
- identify common speech problems.

Preschool teachers encounter a wide range of language differences in young children. Speech is improved when these children keep talking or trying to communicate. Teachers realize that children whose language skills or patterns are different are just as intelligent and capable as those who speak in standard English. Before discussing language differences, it is important to clarify the intent of this book. The purpose here is to help teachers (1) help the children and (2) help in such a way that it won't actually make matters worse. The teacher's sensitivity to and knowledge of a particular cultural group and different language patterns can aid a particular child's growth. Preserving the child's feelings of adequacy and acceptance is the teacher's prime goal; moving the child toward the eventual learning of standard forms is a secondary goal. Meers (1978) clearly states our primary goal:

> . . . to ensure that his idea of himself is positive; of helping the child see himself as a rich source of ideas, as an inventive, resourceful, problem-solving person who can function successfully in personal relationships; at work; in his leisure; as a full member of his community.

STANDARD ENGLISH

Standard English is the language of elementary schools and textbooks. It is the language of the majority of people in the U.S. The child whose speech reflects different past experiences and a cultural (or subcultural) outlook that is different from the majority is found in increasing numbers in preschool programs. By practicing and copying his or her group's way of speaking and becoming aware of his or her group's values, attitudes, food preferences, clothing styles, and so on, the child gains acceptance as a group member. Some theorize that the child's manner of thinking about life's experiences has also been influenced.

Phillips (1987) believes one of the goals of preschool teachers is to offer language instruction that helps all racial and cultural groups have equal access to opportunities for quality lives and power over their own lives. Standard English usage is advantageous, and possibly, as Jespersen (1945) states, a unifying force that brings together cultures within cultures, thereby minimizing class differences.

Dialect, as used here, refers to language patterns that differ from standard American English. Dialects exist in all languages and fall into categories: (1) regional and geographic and (2) social and ethnic, such as black English, Chicano English, and others (Yawkey et al., 1981). Yawkey also notes that professionals and age groups have dialects, sometimes called *jargon.* Teachers are often thought of as using "educationese."

Speakers of a particular dialect form a speech community that reflects the members' life-styles or professional, national, family, or ethnic backgrounds. Certain common features mark the speech of the members, and no two members of a particular community ever speak alike because each person's speech is unique (Donoghue, 1985). The term "dialect" unfortunately can connote to some people less than correct speech. In the U.S. today, the major regional dialect areas are identified as Northern, Southern, South Midland, Gulf Southern, North Midland, and Plains Southern (Conklin and Lourie, 1983). In describing speakers from these areas, many would describe them as having a speech accent. Dialects differ from one another in a number of ways and are fully formed systems. Dillard (1972) estimates that 80% of people in the U.S. with African ancestry use "black" dialect.

Dialects evolve naturally over time and possess an element of regularity and systematic usage. Individuals react to dialects with prestige, acceptance, ambivalence, neutral feelings or rejection, based on value judgments.

Dialect-speaking teachers, aides, and volunteers (working with children and families of the same dialect) offer children a special degree of familiarity and understanding. A standard-English speaking teacher may sound less familiar but affords the child a model for growth in speaking the dominant language of our society, which is important to his or her life opportunities.

Although a dialect (or accent) may be an advantage in one's community, it may be a disadvantage outside of that community. Just as a child who meets another child from a different part of the country with a different accent might say, "You sound funny!" so others may think of dialectic speech as crude or funny. *Accented speech,* for this discussion, is defined as distinctive, typical speech habits of an individual or group of individuals associated with a geographic location or region. One can speak standard English with an accent, where as, a dialectic speaker is a nonstandard-English speaker.

WORKING WITH DIALECT-SPEAKING BLACK CHILDREN

Much has been researched and debated concerning the best educational techniques for use with young black dialect-speaking children, and it has to be recognized that many blacks certainly do not speak a black-English dialect. Some groups argue that the existence of black English still needs verification. Most educators agree black English is in no way deficient but is different, with complex syntactic, phonological, and semantic individuality. Children seem to be able to switch from this dialect to standard English, responding in whichever form is acceptable after adequate exposure to both forms. Having this native dialect may affect some children's ability to read in elementary school, but probably not as much as the teacher's attitude toward socially nonstandard dialects, comprehension of such dialects, the relationship of dialect to social class and to self-esteem, and other factors such as nutrition, availability and interest level of reading materials, and community tolerance for reading (Hartwell, 1980). Joiner's table (figure 17-1) presents significant features of black English.

Rapsberry (1979) suggests two important aspects of working with nonstandard-English-speaking children that early childhood teachers should note: The child is not on that account (dialect speaking) less intelligent, less admirable — or less anything else.

One problem that may impede younger economically disadvantaged black children's learning of standard English may be their motivation:

It is especially difficult to motivate younger disadvantaged black children to learn standard English. Teachers can't point out the vocational, social, or academic advantages. As long as they remain in their segregated social environment (and couple this with their natural immaturity), they will not be motivated (Johnson, 1969).

Decreased speed in adopting standard English may also be based on personal preference; young dialect-

(Joiner, 1979, p. 343)	Examples
1. The use of the verb <u>be</u> to indicate a reality that is recurring or continuous over time.	1. <u>He be working</u> = He is working every-day.
2. The deletion of some form of the verb <u>to be</u>.	2. <u>Cleo sick today</u> = Cleo is sick today.
3. The use of the third person singular verbs without adding the <u>s</u> or <u>z</u> sound.	3. <u>My mama she talk all the time</u> = My mama talks all the time.
4. The use of the <u>f</u> sound for the <u>th</u> sound at the end of a word.	4. <u>mouf</u> = mouth <u>wif</u> = with
5. The use of an additional word to denote plurals rather than adding an <u>s</u> to the noun.	5. <u>Two boy left for home</u> = Two boys left for home or boys left for home.
6. Non-use of <u>s</u> to indicate possessives.	6. <u>Mr. Green truck got smashed</u> = Mr. Green's truck got smashed.
7. The elimination of <u>l</u> or <u>r</u> sounds in words.	7. <u>hep</u> = help <u>doe</u> = door
8. The use of words with different meanings.	8. <u>bad</u> = great/good
9. The lack of emphasis on the use of tense in verbs.	9. <u>They already walk to the store</u> = They already walked to the store.
10. The deletion of final consonants.	10. <u>toll</u> = told <u>fine</u> = find
11. The use of double subjects.	11. <u>George he here now</u> = George is here now.
12. The use of <u>it</u> instead of <u>there</u>.	12. <u>It ain't none left</u> = There isn't any left.

FIGURE 17-1 Some features of black English *(From "Memorandum Opinion and Order: Martin Luther King Junior Elementary School Children et al. v. Ann Arbor School District Board" (473 F. Supp. 1371 (1979)), by C.W. Joiner. Reprinted in* Black English and the Education of Black Children and Youth, *Ed. G. Smitherman. Detroit, Mich.: Wayne State University Center for Black Studies, 1981.)*

speaking children who do realize that standard English is advantageous and evaluate it as better speech may not like advantaged individuals or want to be like them (Johnson, 1969). Contrary to expectations, black-English vernacular of urban areas is becoming increasingly different from standard English. Labov (1985) concludes that black dialects are moving in a separate direction and away from both present day black vernacular and standard American English because of increasing racial segregation and isolation of urban blacks. The grammar of black vernacular, which is very rich and complicated, is developing its own way. Labov feels that as dialects become ever more diverse this may affect young black dialect-speaking children's ability to learn to read.

Lay-Dopyera and Dopyera (1982) emphasize standard English forms should be learned as a language alternative, that is, not to replace but to expand original speech through a new and different language pattern. The goal of standard English instruction is to facilitate the child's ability to fit comfortably in both settings, the native community and the language of the majority.

WORKING WITH DIALECT-SPEAKING FAMILIES

Many centers employ staff members who have dialects that the children can easily understand, so children feel at home. Teachers who speak the children's dialect may be eagerly sought and in short supply. Additional insight into the child's culture and the particular meanings of their words is often an advantage for teachers who have the same dialect as the children. They may be able to react and expand ideas better than a standard-English-speaking teacher.

It is important for teachers to know whether the children are speaking a dialect and to understand dialectic differences. The four most common dialectic differences between standard English and some common dialects occur in verb forms. These differences occur in the following areas.

- subject-verb agreement
- use of the verb "to be"
- use of present tense for past tense
- use of got for have

In some areas where a language other than English is spoken, part of the rules of the second language may blend and combine to form a type of English, different from the standard. Examples of this are (1) English spoken by some Indian children, and (2) English spoken in communities close to the Mexican/American border.

There are differing opinions about the teaching of preferred standard English in early childhood centers. In most centers, however, preserving the child's native dialect while moving slowly toward standard English usage is considered more desirable than immediate, purposeful instruction in standard forms. Joint parent and center discussions can help clarify program goals.

THE TEACHER'S ROLE

Understanding dialectic differences are important to the teacher's understanding of each child. In order to give young children the best model possible, the teacher should speak standard English. On the other hand, many successful teachers have speech accents and also possess other characteristics, abilities, and useful techniques that aid young children's development of language and literacy. It matters very little to children whether the teacher speaks a bit differently from the way they speak. The teacher's attitude, warmth, and acceptance of the dialect and the children themselves is a very important consideration (figure 17-2).

A child may be a very good speaker of his or her particular dialect, or he or she may be just a beginner. Staff members working with the young child should respect the child's natural speech and not try to stop the child from using it. The goal is to promote the child's use of natural speech in his or her native dialect. Since the child's ability to learn new words and new ways is at its peak during early years, standard English can be taught by having many good speaking models available at the center for the child to hear. Interested adults, play activities, other children, and a rich language arts program can provide a setting where children listen and talk freely.

The teacher should know what parts of the center's program are designed to increase the child's use of words. Teachers can show a genuine interest in words in their daily conversations with the children. The teacher can also use the correct forms of standard English in a casual way, using natural conversation. Correcting the children in an obvious way could embarrass them and stop openness and enthusiasm. Careful listening, skillful response, and appropriate questions during conversations help the child learn to put thoughts into words. The child thinks in terms of his or her own dialect first and, in time, expresses words in standard English (figure 17-3).

Preschool teachers must face the idea that children's accents and dialects may affect their attitudes about those children and, consequently, teacher behaviors. A teacher may tend to seek out and communicate with those children whose speech is most similar to the teacher's speech. Extra effort may be necessary to converse and instruct. Staff-parent meetings and additional planning is a must to meet the needs of children with diverse language patterns. Pronunciation guides helping teachers say children's names correctly are gathered from parents at admitting interviews. This is just a small first step.

FIGURE 17-2 Staff attitude can build each child's feelings of self-confidence.

Additional Teacher Tips

A teacher should guard against:

- Correcting children in a way that makes them doubt their own abilities.
- Giving children the idea that they are not trying hard enough to correct or improve their speech.
- Discouraging children's speaking.
- Allowing teasing about individual speech differences.
- Interrupting children who are trying to express an idea.
- Hurrying a child who is speaking.
- Putting children on stage in an anxiety-producing way.

BILINGUALISM

There are two importantly different groups of young bilingual children: (1) those who have heard two languages spoken since infancy, and (2) those who have spoken only one language (other than standard English) before entering school (Bee, 1981). The first are bilingual, the second monolingual. The true bilingual person speaks two or more languages well. Children, just learning, may possess different degrees of proficiency in two or more languages. White (1986) suggests that if more than one language is spoken in

FIGURE 17-3 "Hat."

the home and both languages are spoken well, the baby should be exposed to both from the beginning. Although the child will be a bit slow in learning language, by the fourth or fifth birthday the child will be capable in both.

Bilingual children grasp rather quickly the idea that one object is represented by a different word in each language. Later tests of intelligence and language in elementary school show that these children do just as well as other children. One has to also recognize that speaking more than one language has long-term career advantages in most cases. Bilingual children, however, can be expected to progress in English usage at slower rates initially than monolingual standard-English-speaking children.

Creole-speaking children from select areas of the South or Hawaiian Creole speakers are not dialect speakers; rather, they speak a distinct language that uses a largely English vocabulary. Often these children will continue to use their native language, which maintains their Creole tradition, until their early twenties (Cazden et al., 1981).

A variety of plans and methods to help bilingual children are adopted in most early childhood centers (figure 17-4). Techniques are often researched and studied by individual staff members and are frequently part of a center's in-service education.

Being unable to understand or to be understood may be one of the problems facing the bilingual child. Learning a second language includes a number of difficult tasks. The child must:

- Produce sounds that may not be used in the native language.
- Understand that native speech sounds or words may have different meanings in the new (second) language.
- Learn and select appropriate responses.
- Sort and revise word orders.
- Learn different cultural values and attitudes.
- Control the flow of air while breathing and speaking.

An important technique — admitting and recognizing that a child is a classroom resource when it comes to explaining other ways of naming and describing objects or other ways of satisfying human needs — should be understood by teachers (Clement, 1981).

FIGURE 17-4 A program rich in experiences is planned.

Printed word cards in both languages can be added to the classroom to reinforce this idea.

The preschooler's language capacity helps the child who learns two languages during the early years. In preschool work, it is common to meet children who can quickly switch fluent conversation between two languages.

The preschool years are described as the best time to learn a second language, for language learning ability is at its peak (figure 17-5). As *U.S. News and World Report* (July 1986) points out, the number of American preschoolers who are learning to speak two and three languages is on the rise, because many experts and parents believe that learning foreign tongues stimulates a child's mental development. Research has promoted the idea that bilingual youngsters are more imaginative, better with abstract notions, and more flexible in their thinking than monolingual children. Some educators point out that even if a child after learning two languages well discontinues use of one,

FIGURE 17-5 Language learning ability is at its peak during the preschool years.

the unused language is stored for future reference and makes that language or another easier to learn at a later age (Lambert, 1986). Another advantage in becoming bilingual during the preschool period has been reported by Hakuta (1986) who notes that bilingual children sometimes learn to read more quickly than their monolingual peers. Other researchers have noticed that bilingualism improves many children's self-esteem and strengthens family ties.

The most successful methods for teaching a second language include the same features mentioned in the child's learning of his or her first language — warm, responsive, articulate adults involved with children's everyday firsthand exploration of the environment. A special project was designed to fit the needs of preschoolers in the southwest United States. The curriculum objectives of this well-known bilingual preschool program (called the Bilingual Early Childhood Program) are as follows:

1. Development of the child's sensory perceptual skills.
2. Development of the child's language skills in both English and Spanish.
3. Development of the child's thinking and reasoning abilities.
4. Development of the child's positive self concept (Nedler, 1977).

Arenas (1987) feels that successful programs for bilingual/bicultural children should:

- Provide an environment that reflects the language and culture of the children it serves. This requires that staff members and program resources be representative of the group's racial and cultural mixture.
- Build on the strengths that bilingual/bicultural children bring to a new learning situation. The children have a language, and with it a rich cultural background with values and expectations — a strong base for learning.
- Continue the development of the first language and facilitate the acquisition of a second. Children should be made to feel that the language or dialect that they use is both acceptable and welcome — the fact that they are communicating is most important. Show children the pleasure and necessity of communication in both languages.
- Be aware of the child's home values and expectations; one way of acquiring this information is to involve parents in various aspects of the program.
- Integrate both languages into all areas of the curriculum in an atmosphere of respect and appreciation for cultural diversity. If both languages are part of the regular classroom environment, children will help each other learn both languages. All children will benefit from understanding that there are many ways of speaking and different ways of behaving.

Since many centers deal with children who speak a language other than English, or who speak very little English, a center with bilingual children has many decisions to make. The first concern should be the child's adjustment to school. Every effort should be made to make the child feel at ease. Often, the teacher is also bilingual.

Elementary schools teaching reading have relied on a variety of methods. Two common strategies are used:

1. Delay reading instruction until the child has mastered English, or
2. Teach reading in the child's native language (dialect) and switch to English during a later grade in school.

Preschools that encourage children to use two languages are given suggestions by Flores (1980). (Ms.

Flores focuses on the Spanish-speaking child, but the comments and suggestions could be applied to other language groups.)

- *Let the children hear both languages.* Speak both languages throughout the day so that children feel comfortable with the second language. Children should have plenty of opportunities to hear the second language without having to speak it.
- *Identify the languages being spoken.* When two languages are being used, identify each language to confirm the child's notion that more than one language is being spoken.
- *Acknowledge and encourage a child's attempt to speak a second language.* Children eventually will experiment with the sounds and intonations of a second language. Encourage them and comment on what they are doing: "That sounds a lot like Spanish, Mark." When a child addresses you in gibberish, answer in the language they are imitating and then translate. This gives the child the feeling that talking and being understood in the second language is possible.
- *Let a child hear you speak his or her second language to another child.* For example, read a story in Spanish to a Spanish-speaking child so that an English-speaking child working nearby on a puzzle can overhear.
- *Occasionally, give simple commands to the whole group in one language without translating.* "Let's clean up now."
- *Once you get along well with a child in his or her first language, talk to that child for short periods in the second language.* A child may not understand at first, but by hearing a lot of the second language in a variety of situations, the child will eventually begin to notice, play with, and grasp intonation patterns and sounds.

Teachers faced with a portion of their enrollment speaking another language face unique problems. An interpreter may be necessary, and a concerted effort should be made to understand the family's culture. Consultants and parents are invaluable. Bilingual teachers or aides are required in a number of centers that serve newly arrived populations. Designing room features and planning curriculum activities that wel-

come and show acceptance are important staff tasks.

Gestures aid communication. Pairing words with actions when speaking and naming distinctly helps children understand.

Both teachers and children can be expected to experience some frustration. Touching and nonverbal behaviors are important cues in communication. The teacher will find that his or her speech slows and sentences shorten to one or two words when speaking to the nonEnglish speaking child. Children will rely heavily on gestures as they try to communicate and speak. However, preschoolers' language ability is amazing, and teachers will notice more and more understanding of English, then hesitant naming, followed by beginning phrases. If the teacher tries to learn the child's language, the same sequence is apparent.

CULTURAL DIFFERENCES

Cultural differences in communicating are important for a teacher to understand. For example, when speaking to adults in some cultures, children are expected to lower their eyes to the floor as a sign of respect. A study of cultural differences can help teachers receive accurate messages. Gestures and body language of the cultural groups attending a center may differ widely in meaning.

Cultures are complex and changing, so understanding cultural similarities and differences can be a life's study in itself. *Culture* is defined here as all the activities and achievements of a society that individuals within that society pass from one generation to the next. Technology, institutions, home, school, religious group, language, values, and customs are typical culture-study categories.

Ethnic origin is often a basic ingredient in subcultural groupings. *Subcultural* is defined as other than a dominant culture. Class structure also exists in societies consisting of upper, middle, and lower income groups. Often, patterns of child rearing vary between cultures and classes (Broman, 1978). Families may express attitudes and values peculiar to their class or culture. Attitudes and feelings of an impoverished group, for instance, often include futility, anger, violence, and loss of trust in anyone or anything.

Teachers try to determine the backgrounds of their attending families, noting the individual nature of children's home communities — housing, income, general numbers and types of cultural groups — in an attempt to better understand children and provide language-developing experiences. Their ability to respond and relate to what attending children verbalize is enhanced.

What cultural differences can inhibit child speech? Adult models' lengths of sentences or their inability to modify their speech to child levels, neutral or negative environments, family arrangements that require children to be alone for long periods or in which children are expected to be quiet or cannot gain adult attention, lack of books or early reading experiences are all factors that can affect speech growth. Hall (1982) states that parents are the primary language teachers in the early years and that language competence grows out of familiar situations such as seeking help or establishing joint attention — situations that provide frameworks in which children learn to make their intentions plain and to interpret the intentions of others.

In planning language activities of all types, every effort must be made to make children aware of cross-cultural similarities and explore difference. Young children can be exposed to the idea that people eat, sleep, wear clothing, celebrate, dance, sing, live in groups, speak to one another in common languages, and that they do these things in ways that may be either the same as or different from the ways their families do these things. Planned activities can make comparisons treating diversity with the dignity it deserves. Skin color, hair styles, food preferences, clothing, and music are starting points for study. Modeling friendship and cooperation between cultures and planning activities showing dissimilar individuals and groups living in harmony is a good idea. Stories exist in all languages and in most dialects. Cultural factors can influence a child's narrative or story-telling style, the skills that are foundations for reading.

It is important to plan language arts programs that incorporate different cultural styles of dramatic play, story-telling, and chanting (IBFC Bulletin, 1983). Librarians can help teachers discover picture books and other materials written in dialects or two language translations.

Program goals for children who have had limited opportunities in learning language commonly include:

- Adding enriching experiences.
- Prompting children's logical thinking abilities.
- Reshaping speech patterns slowly while increasing speech usage.
- Making sure that being different never means "less worthy" and that staff members will not give culturally diverse children the idea that there is a preferred way to speak, look, dress, or live.

Each center designs its own activities, giving each child a chance to accomplish new skills. There are many possible program activities. Most program plans emphasize the following:

- Activities that develop sensory skills — visual, auditory, and tactile (touch), as well as discriminatory, relational, and sequential abilities (figure 17-6).
- Activities that facilitate problem solving and concept development — classifying, organizing, and associating.
- Activities that deal with the language arts and vocabulary and comprehension development — listening, speaking, printing words, and using symbolic forms (figure 17-7).

FIGURE 17-6 Preschools try to provide toys, activities, and events that expand the children's experiences.

Bernheim, Marc and Evelyn
    In Africa, A Margaret K. Mc Elderry Book, New York, 1973.
Beskow, Elsa
    Pelle's New Suit, Harper & Row Publishers, New York, 1929.
Binzen, Bill
    First Day in School, Doubleday & Co. Inc., Garden City, NY, 1972.
Calhoun, Mary
    The Hungry Leprechaun, Wm. Morrow & Co., New York, 1962.
Cohen, Miriam
    The New Teacher, The Macmillian Co., New York, 1972.
Ets, Mary Hall
    Gilberto and the Wind, The Viking Press, New York, 1963.
Fraser, Kathleen & Levy, Miriam F.
    Adam's World: San Francisco, Albert Whitman Co., Chicago, 1971.
Freeman, Don
    Corduroy, The Viking Press, New York, 1968.
Greenberg, Polly
    Oh Lord, I Wish I Was A Buzzard, The Macmillian Co., New York, 1968.
Hoff, Syd
    Roberto and the Bull, McGraw-Hill Book Co., New York, 1969.
Keats, Jack Ezra
    Whistle for Willie, Viking Press, New York, 1964.
    Peter's Chair, Harper & Row Publishers, New York, 1967.
    A Letter to Amy, Harper & Row Publishers, New York, 1968.
Otsuka, Yuzo
    Suho and the White Horse (A Legend of Mongolia), Bobbs-Merrill Co. Inc., Indianapolis, 1981.
Politi, Leo
    Pedro, The Angel of Olvera Street, Charles Scribner's Sons, New York, 1946.
    Little Leo, Charles Scribner's Sons, New York, 1964.
    Rosa, Charles Scribner's Sons, New York, 1951.
    Lito the Clown, Charles Scribner's Sons, New York, 1963.
Schick, Eleanor
    City in the Summer, Macmillan Co., Collier-Macmillan Limited, London, 1969.
Scott, Ann Herbert
    On Mother's Lap, McGraw-Hill Book Co., San Francisco, 1972.
Tresselt, Alvin
    It's Time Now, Lothrop, Lee & Shepherd Co., New York, 1969.
Yashima, Mitsu & Taro
    Momo's Kitten, The Viking Press, New York, 1961.

FIGURE 17-7 Books with multicultural themes and illustrations

Programs are developmental, starting with basics and moving toward higher levels. Supporting, rewarding, and giving language feedback, which expands and clarifies what the children say as they play, is the teacher's role. This includes being an alert listener — really hearing what children say, as well as how they say it. Good listeners can answer with logical statements and sincere interest. They can ask the child to tell more and to give details. They can suggest ideas or plans for the child to think about related to what was said. A teacher talks with children in a way that helps them grow in understanding and ability. The teacher's time is divided as equally as possible between the quiet children and the talkative ones.

When working in communities with newly arrived immigrant populations, teachers have to devote considerable time and study to understanding the families and lives of attending children. A strong connection between home and school should exist, with parents playing a role in program planning and as assistants or teachers in classrooms. Parents can help teachers understand the many areas of similarity and diversity that possibly exist. When parent literacy rates are less than desirable, teachers have to proceed carefully with suggestions concerning reading to their children. Wordless books and parent story telling are alternatives.

IDENTIFYING CHILDREN WITH SPECIAL NEEDS

Special language-development preschool centers with expert personnel are available in most communities for children with easily identifiable communication deficiencies such as hearing loss, visual impairment, and obvious speech impairments. Other children in need of special help may not be identified at the preschool level and function within the wide range of children considered to be average or normal for preschool ages. Most programs are reticent to label children as having language learning problems because of their lack of expertise to screen and evaluate children in a truly professional manner. Referral to speech-language pathologists or local or college clinics is suggested to parents when a question exists concerning a particular child's progress. Dumtschin (1988) points out that early childhood teachers are not speech or language pathologists and should therefore not be expected to diagnose language problems or to prescribe therapy. The National Association for Hearing and Speech Action (NAHSA) (1985) divides communication disorders into two main categories:

Hearing disorders. These are characterized by an inability to hear sounds clearly. Such disorders may range from hearing speech sounds faintly, or in a distorted way, to profound deafness. See figure 17-8, a parent resource published by NAHSA (1988).

Speech and language disorders. These affect the way people talk and understand and range from simple sound substitutions to not being able to use speech and language at all.

SPEECH-LANGUAGE DISORDERS

About 11 to 13 million people in the U.S. have some kind of expressive speech disorder, the most frequent problem involving articulation — an estimated 75% (Weiss and Lillywhite, 1981). The rest, approximately 25%, have language, voice, and fluency disorders, or a combination of these. Most articulation problems not caused by physical, sensory, or neurological damage respond to treatment. Nonorganic causes of problems can include:

- lack of stimulation
- lack of need to talk
- poor speech models
- lack of or low reinforcement
- insecurity, anxiety, crisis

Language Delay

Language delay is characterized by a marked slowness in the development of the vocabulary and grammar necessary for expressing and understanding thoughts and ideas (NAHSA, 1985). It may involve both comprehension and the child's expressive language output and quality. A complete study of a child includes first looking for physical causes, particularly hearing loss, and other structural (voice producing) conditions. Neurological limitations come under scrutiny, as do emotional development factors. Home environments and parental communicating styles are examined when a thorough study by speech-language pathologists takes place. Referral to experts is considered if a child falls two years behind his or her peers or when a sudden change in a well progressing child is noticed. Dumtschin (1988) has identified possible noticeable behavior of language-delayed children:

Language-delayed children may display limited vocabularies, use short, simple sentences, and make many grammatical errors. They may have difficulty maintaining a conversation, talk more about the present and less about the future, and have difficulty in understanding others and in making themselves understood.

In addition to strictly linguistic problems, language-delayed children may also have difficulty classifying objects and recognizing similarities and differences. They may spend little time in

FIND YOUR CHILD'S SPEECH AND HEARING AGE

check one		HEARING and UNDERSTANDING	CHILD'S AGE	TALKING	check one	
√ YES	√ NO				√ YES	√ NO
		Does your child hear and understand most speech in the home? Does your child hear and answer when first called? Does your child hear quiet speech? Does everyone who knows your child think he/she hears well (teacher, baby-sitter, grandparent, etc.)?	5 YEARS	Does your child say all sounds correctly except perhaps s and th? Does your child use the same sentence structure as the family? Does your child's voice sound clear, like other children's?		
		Does your child understand conversation easily? Does your child hear you when you call from another room? Does your child hear television or radio at the same loudness level as other members of the family?	2½-4 YEARS	Does your child say most sounds, except perhaps r, l, th, and s? Does your child usually talk easily without repeating syllables or words?		
		Does your child understand differences in meaning ("go–stop"; "the car pushed the truck – the truck pushed the car")? Can your child point to pictures in a book upon hearing them named? Does your child notice sounds (dog barking, telephone ringing, television sound, knocking at door, an so on)?		Does your child use 200-300 words? Does your child use 2-3 word sentences? Does your child ask lots of "why" and "what" questions? Has your child's jargon and repeating disappeared? Does your child like to name things?		
		Can your child follow two requests ("get the ball and put it on the table")?	1½-2 YEARS	Does your child have 10-15 words (by age 2)? Does your child sometimes repeat requests? Does your child ask 1-2 word questions ("where kitty? go bye-bye? more?")? Does your child put 2 words together ("more cookie")?		
		Has your child begun to respond to requests ("come here", "do you want more")?	9 MONTHS-1 YEAR	Does your child say words (8–10 words at age 1½; 2–3 words at age 1)? (Words may not be clear.)		
		Does your child turn or look up when you call? Does your child search or look around when hearing new sounds? Does your child listen to people talking?		Does your child enjoy imitating sounds? Does your child use jargon (babbling that sounds like real speech)? Does your child use voice to get attention?		
		Does your child respond to "no" and her/his name? Does your child notice and look around for the source of new sounds? Does your child turn her/his head toward the side where the sound is coming from?	6 MONTHS	Does your child's babbling sound like the parent's speech, only not clear? Does your child make lots of different sounds?		
		Does your child try to turn toward the speaker? Does your child smile when spoken to? Does your child stop playing and appear to listen to sounds or speech? Does your child seem to recognize mother's voice?	3 MONTHS	Does your child babble? Does your child cry differently for different needs? Does your child repeat the same sounds a lot?		
		Does your child listen to speech? Does your child startle or cry at noises? Does your child awaken at loud sounds?	BIRTH	Does your child coo or gurgle?		
TOTAL					TOTAL	

INSTRUCTIONS: Read each question through your child's age group and check yes or no. Add the total and see below.

ALL YES: GOOD! Your child is developing hearing, speech, and language normally.

1-3 NO: CAUTION! Your child may have delayed hearing, speech, and language development. Look at the "Reminders" section in this brochure.

MORE THAN 3 NO: ACTION! Take your child for professional help. See "Where to Get Help" section.

FIGURE 17-8 Find your child's speech and hearing age. (*From "How Does Your Child Hear and Talk?" Reprinted with permission from the American Speech-Language-Hearing Association.*)

dramatic play with others and may exhibit general difficulties in the classroom, the extent of concern would necessarily differ according to the age of the child.

Other behaviors a teacher might notice include:

- less variety in sentence structure
- simple two- and three-word sentences
- less frequent speech
- plays alone frequently
- participates less adeptly in joint planning with age mates.

Teachers might readily agree with the following description of a language-delayed child: "Speaks markedly less well than other children of the same age and seems to have normal ability in intellectual, motor, sensory, and emotional control areas."

Indication of language delay mentioned by NAHSA (1985) includes a child's not using words by the age of two years, or not being able to speak in short sentences by age three. Another indication would be a child's inability to respond to simple requests, such as "sit down" or "come here," by age two.

Dumtschin (1988) suggests that preschool teachers provide language-rich environments that effectively support language-delayed children and regard the children as active learners, encouraging communicative attempts in an accepting atmosphere, using interaction techniques that are related to the children's focus of attention, and capitalizing on spontaneous language-teaching opportunities.

Articulation

Articulation disorders involve difficulties with the way sounds are formed and strung together, usually characterized by substituting one sound for another, omitting a sound, or distorting a sound.

If consonant sounds are misarticulated, they may occur in the initial (beginning), medial (middle), or ending positions in words (Weiss and Lillywhite, 1981). It's prudent to point out again that normally developing children don't master the articulation of all consonants until age seven or eight.

Most young children (three to five years old) hesitate, repeat, and re-form words as they speak.

Imperfections occur for several reasons: (1) A child does not pay attention as closely as an adult, especially to certain high-frequency consonant sounds; (2) the child may not be able to distinguish some sounds; (3) a child's coordination and control of his or her articulatory mechanisms may not be perfected. For example, he or she may be able to hear the difference between Sue and shoe but cannot pronounce them differently. About 60% of all children with diagnosed articulation problems are boys (Rubin, 1982).

Articulation characteristics of young children include:

- *Substitution.* One sound is substituted for another, as in "wabbit" for rabbit or "thun" for sun.
- *Omission.* The speaker leaves out a sound that should be articulated. He or she says "at" for hat, "ca" for cat, "icky" for sticky, "probly" for probably. The left out sound may be at the beginning, middle, or end of a word.
- *Distortion.* A sound is said inaccurately but is similar to the intended sound.
- *Addition.* The speaker adds a sound, as in "li-it-tle" for little and "muv-va-ver" for mother.
- *Transposition.* The position of sounds in words is switched, as in "hangerber" for hamburger and "aminal" for animal.
- *Lisp.* The s, z, sh, th, ch, and j sounds are distorted. There are from 2 to 10 types of lisps noted by speech experts.

Articulation problems may stem from a physical condition such as a cleft palate or hearing loss, or they can be related to problems in the mouth such as a dental abnormality. Many times, articulation problems occurring without any obvious physical disability may involve the faulty learning of speech sounds.

Some children will require special help and directed training to eliminate all articulation errors, and others seem to mature and correct articulation problems by themselves.

Teacher behavior that aids the situation includes not interrupting or constantly correcting the child and making sure that others don't tease or belittle the child. Modeling misarticulated words correctly is a good course of action. Simply continue your conversation and insert the correctly articulated word in your answering comment.

Voice Disorders

Teachers sometimes notice differences in children's voice quality, which involves pitch, loudness, resonance, and general quality (breathiness, hoarseness, and so on). The intelligibility of a child's speech is determined by how many of the child's words are understandable. One can expect 80% of the child's speech to be understandable at age three.

Stuttering and Cluttering

Stuttering and cluttering are categorized as fluency disorders. Stuttering involves the rhythm of speech and is a complicated many-faceted problem. Speech is characterized by abnormal stoppages with no sound, repetitions, or prolonged sounds and syllables. There may also be unusual facial and body movements associated with efforts to speak (NAHSA, 1983). This problem involves four times as many males as females and can usually be treated. All young children repeat words and phrases, and this increases with anxiety or stress. It is simply typical for the age and is not true stuttering. A teacher should wait patiently for the child to finish expressing himself or herself and should resist the temptation to say "slow down."

The causes for stuttering are felt to be different for different people. Teachers need to listen patiently and carefully to what the child is saying, not how he or she is saying it. A speech-language pathologist is the appropriate person to evaluate and plan improvement activities.

Cluttering is more involved with the rate of speaking and includes errors in articulation, stress, and pausing. Speech seems too fast with syllables and words running together. Listener reaction and good speech modeling are critical aspects in lack of fluency. Bloodstein (1975) suggests that adults who work with young children should:

- Refrain from criticizing, correcting, helping the child speak, or otherwise reacting negatively or calling a speech problem to the child's attention.
- Improve parent-child relationships if possible.
- Eliminate any factors or conditions that increase problems in fluency.
- Strengthen the child's expectation of normal fluency and self-confidence as a speaker.

OTHER CONDITIONS TEACHERS MAY CONSIDER PROBLEMS

Frequent Crying

Occasionally frustrated children will cry or scream to communicate a need. Crying associated with adjustment to a new situation is handled by providing supportive attention and care. Continual crying and screaming to obtain an object or privilege, on the other hand, calls for the following kinds of teacher statements (Osborn, 1983):

> "I don't understand what you want when you scream. Use words so I will know what you want."

> "Sara does not know what you want when you cry Billy. Saying 'Please get off the puzzle piece,' with your words tells her."

This lets the child know what's expected and helps the child see that words solve problems.

Avid Talkers and Shouters

Occasionally children may discover that talking incessantly can get them what they want. In order to quiet children, others give in. This is somewhat different from the common give and take in children's daily conversations or children's growing ability to argue and state their cases.

Language becomes a social tool. A child may find that loudness in speech can intimidate others and will out shout the opposition. It is prudent to have the child's hearing checked.

Questioners

At times, children ask many questions, one right after another. This may be a good device to hold or gain adults' attention: "Why isn't it time for lunch?" or "What makes birds sing?" or "Do worms sleep?" The questions may seem endless to adults. Most of the questions are prompted by the child's natural curiosity. Teachers help children find out as much as possible and strive to fulfill the needs of the individual child. Along the way, there will be many questions that may be difficult or even impossible to answer.

HEARING

A screening of young children's auditory acuity may uncover hearing loss. The earlier the diagnosis, the more effective the treatment. Since young children develop ear infections frequently, schools alert parents when a child's listening behavior seems newly impaired.

Otitis media is a medical term that refers to any inflammation of the middle ear. There are two types of otitis media: (1) a fluid-filled middle ear without infection and (2) an infected middle ear. Many preschoolers have ear infections during preschool years, and many children have clear fluid in the middle ear that goes undetected (NAHSA, 1985). Even though the hearing loss caused by otitis media may be small and temporary, it may have a serious effect on speech and language learning for a preschool child. If undetected hearing distortion or loss lasts for a long period, the child can fall behind. General inattentiveness, wanting to get close to hear, having trouble with directions, irritability, or pulling and rubbing the ear can be signs a teacher should heed. Most infected ears cause considerable pain, and parents are alerted to the need for medical help. However, if the ear is not infected or if the infection does not cause pain, the problem is harder to recognize.

SEEKING HELP

If a child's speech or language lags behind expected development for the child's mental age (mental maturity), school staff members should observe and listen to the child closely to collect additional data. When speech is unusually difficult to understand — rhythmically conspicuous, full of sound distortion, or consistently difficult to hear — this indicates a serious problem. Professional help is available to parents through a number of resources. Most cities have speech and hearing centers and public and private practitioners specializing in speech-language pathology and audiology. Other resources include:

- universities and medical schools
- state departments of education offices
- The American Speech-Language-Hearing Association Directory (found by checking local medical societies)

A center's director can be alerted to observe a child whom the teacher feels may benefit from professional help. It is important to have a referral system in place at a school or center to assist parents in finding appropriate testing and therapy for their children. Directors can establish a relationship with a therapist or agency before a referral is needed. Speech-language pathologists have master's degrees or doctoral degrees in speech-language pathology and, in many states, hold licenses.

LANGUAGE GIFTEDNESS

Each child is unique. A few children speak clearly and use long, complex, adultlike speech at two, three, or four years of age. They express ideas originally and excitedly, enjoying individual and group discussions. Some may read simple primers (or other books) along with classroom word labels. Activities that are commonly used with kindergarten or first-grade children may interest them. Just as there is no stereotypical average child, language-talented children are also unique individuals. They may, however, exhibit many of the following characteristics.

- Attend to tasks in a persistent manner for long periods of time.
- Focus deeply or submerge themselves in what they are doing.
- Speak maturely and use a larger-than-usual vocabulary (Schwartz, 1980).
- Show a searching, exploring curiosity.
- Ask questions that go beyond immediate happenings.
- Demonstrate avid interest in words, alphabet letters, numbers, or writing tools.
- Remember small details of past experiences and compare them with present happenings.
- Read books (or words) by memorizing pictures or words.
- Prefer solitary activities at times (Schwartz, 1980).
- Offer ideas often and easily.
- Rapidly acquire English skills, if bilingual, when exposed to these skills (Bernal, 1978).
- Tell elaborate stories.
- Show a mature sense of humor for age (Kitano, 1982).

- Express feelings and emotions, as in story telling, movement, and visual arts.
- Use rich imagery in informal language (Torrance, 1969).
- Exhibit originality of ideas and persistence in problem solving.
- Retain information.
- Exhibit a high degree of imagination.

Gifted preschoolers may recognize letters early and show an early focus on printed matter. They may be interested in foreign languages and also exhibit correct pronunciation and sentence structure in their native language. Young gifted children may show an advanced vocabulary and may begin reading before they start school, although the significance of early reading as an indicator of giftedness has not been established (Lupkowski and Lupkowski, 1985).

Kitano (1982) recommends planning activities within the regular curriculum that promote gifted children's creative thinking. Suggestions include providing the following opportunities:

- *Fluency opportunities.* Promoting many different responses, for example, "What are all the ways you can think of to...."
- *Flexibility opportunities.* Having the facility to change a mind set or see things in a different light, for example, "If you were a Christmas tree, how would you feel...."
- *Originality opportunities.* For example, "Make something that no one else will think of."
- *Elaboration opportunities.* Embellishing of an idea or adding detail, for example, presenting a doodle or squiggle and asking "What could it be."

Schwartz (1980) notes that teachers can help ward off problems for gifted students and recommends:

- Grouping gifted children with others of high ability or shared interests.
- Arranging situations in which the child's gifts or talents are seen as a group asset.
- Using special assignments and varied projects.

Summary

Teachers work with children who may differ greatly in language development. One of the teacher's roles is to carefully work toward increasing the child's use of words, while providing a model of standard English through activities and daily interaction. Teachers are careful not to give children the impression that their speech is less worthy than that of others.

Program goals should be clearly understood, as should the needs and interests of children who have developed a language that differs from the language of the school. Cultural differences exist, and teachers need to be aware of them in order to understand the young child. The teacher can provide activities that start at the child's present level and help the child to grow, know more, and speak in both standard English and his or her native speech.

Speech differences require observation and study by a center's staff. There are a variety of language behaviors that are considered speech and language disorders. Parents can be alerted to whether their children may need further professional help.

Student Activities

- List and describe dialects found in your community. Give a few sentence examples of each.

- In small groups, discuss what you feel are essential factors to language growth that may be missing in a disadvantaged child's background.

- Interview the director of a center that cares for bilingual and/or disadvantaged young children. Ask what techniques are used to increase a child's language ability. If there is no early childhood center in your community, give examples of goals or techniques used to increase a child's language ability that you have found from research at a library.

- If possible, have a speech therapist or speech-correction specialist speak with the class.

- Develop a list of community resources or agencies that offer services to children with speech or hearing problems.

- Tape record your voice in a five-minute conversation with a friend. Have the recording analyzed for dialect, accent, and standard English usage.

- Consider the following children. Which children would you suggest to the center's director as possibly needing further staff observation and expert assessment and help.
  1. Trinh seems roughly two years behind his age mates in vocabulary.
  2. Rashad turns his head toward speakers frequently.
  3. Barbara rubs one ear constantly.
  4. Doan cups his hand behind his ear when spoken to.
  5. Tisha is three, and one can't understand her words.
  6. Bill says "Why did his folks call him Rocky, when he can't say it? He says his name is Wocky Weed!"
  7. Maria is always stressed and extremely tense when she has to speak.
  8. Ben has a monotonal quality to his voice.
  9. Becky reads difficult books without help.

- Observe three preschool children (one at a time) for a period of 10 minutes each. Write down exactly what each child says. Include a description of gestures and nonverbal communications. Analyze your notes. Are there any examples of common speech errors or dialectic differences?

- Compare two languages. What are the differences? What are the similarities?

- Photocopy the following cards. Cut into separate cards along the lines. Form discussion groups after each group member rates the cards individually. Compare ratings and discuss.

Rating Scale

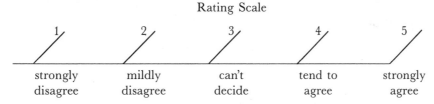

1	2	3	4	5
strongly disagree	mildly disagree	can't decide	tend to agree	strongly agree

---

Certain cultural groups live only a day-to-day existence. Their children tend to be unable to plan ahead or work at a task that has no immediate pleasure or reward. These children should be told that learning and education are important.

The culture of the majority of people and the speaking of standard English is the natural curriculum of the preschool. Children eventually need to compete for jobs; when they do, they need standard-English speech skills.

A dialect usually gives others an idea of the person's background and experience. Some dialects and accents are highly prized. A British accent usually indicates properness and upper-class manners.	If a center has children attending who are bilingual or dialectic speakers, a teacher must be hired who speaks the same language or dialect.
The language of the street is as powerful and complicated as standard English. We all speak two languages — the one we use at home and the one we use at school.	The child who is bilingual is really advantaged now, for schools and preschools provide extra attention and help. The average child with slight difficulties in language is really the most disadvantaged.
Gifted children have many advantages if they attend early childhood centers.	The reason most young children who use little speech in early childhood centers are silent is they don't know how to speak well.
School and preschool staffs who spend much time discussing their programs with parents and community groups are foolish. They already know what is best and right for young children.	Teachers who know they are not speaking standard English should take additional courses to improve their speaking ability.
In an interview for a desirable teaching job, the interviewer noted the teacher's use of non-standard English. The applicant should at that point speak about the advantages of hiring a nonstandard speaker who understands both the speech and culture of attending children.	When working with Spanish-speaking children, teachers should include Spanish names as well as English names for new objects introduced to the children. Celebrations of Mexican holidays should be part of the school's program.
A multicultural program includes activities that give children knowledge of cultural differences. This type of program is necessary only for schools that enroll middle-class children.	Dialectic speaking turns many people off because it usually indicates lack of education. Many view it as inferior, sloppy speech. Actually, it is just as sophisticated as standard English.
Many children could learn a second language easily during preschool years, if preschool teachers planned for it. Some early childhood centers are neglecting this opportunity to teach young children when they have the capacity.	Having the child speak standard English as soon as possible will help him or her be successful in elementary school reading.
Being bilingual is a real advantage in life.	Most differences in cultures are quite understandable if one traces the cultural groups' histories.

Disadvantaged children rarely show language giftedness.	The same preschool activities that help the average child grow in language skill rarely help disadvantaged children.
Speech errors such as substitutions, omissions, and transpositions are not common. Teachers should study and refer these children to experts.	The best thing to do for a child who stutters is to relax and direct the child to repeat what he or she has tried to say.
By the mid 1990s, the majority of children in preschools in the U.S. will be "children of color."	

Unit Review

A. Answer the following questions.
   1. How can a teacher learn about the cultural background of a child?
   2. What should be the teacher's attitude toward children whose speech is different from the teacher's?

B. One of the responsibilities of a teacher is to act as a model to the child for correct forms of speech. Another responsibility is to increase the child's ability to express ideas in words. Quality of responses is more important than just talking. In the following exchanges between teachers and small children, why did the child stop speaking?

   1. *Teacher:* How are you today, Mary?
      Child: Fine.
   2. *Child:* Mrs. Brown, Johnny hit me!
      Teacher: I saw you grab the truck he was playing with. That wasn't nice!
      Child: (Silence)
   3. *Child:* Teacher, I want crayon.
      Teacher: Do you know how to use a crayon?
      Child: Yes.
      Teacher: Tell me how to use a crayon.
      Child: To color.
      Teacher: Say, "To make colored marks on the paper."
      Child: (Silence)
   4. *Child:* I found a bug.
      Teacher: That's nice.
   5. *Child:* Fellow one?
      Teacher: It's yellow, not fellow.
      Child: Fellow one.
      Teacher: You want the yellow one. A fellow is a man, Lindy.
      Child: (Silence)
   6. *Teacher:* Jason, what's your favorite ice cream flavor?
      Child: Huh?

Teacher: What's your favorite ice cream flavor?
Child: Flavorite?
Teacher: Don't you like ice cream?
Child: Yah.
Teacher: What's your favorite ice cream flavor?
Child: (Silence)

C. Define these speech terms.

1. dialect	4. auditory	7. otitis media
2. bilingual	5. cluttering	8. subculture
3. stuttering	6. articulation	9. standard English

D. Listed below are comments made by children. Give an example of the response that a teacher could make in order to encourage more thought and stimulate growth on the part of the child.
1. Child with ball says, "Me play."
2. Child remarks, "I done went to get a red crayun."
3. Child says, "I got this thing."
4. Child says, "I like chitchun choop!"
5. Child asks, "No run in street?"
6. Child exclaims, "I don't wanna play with them childruns."

E. Select the correct answer. Some items have more than one correct answer.
1. Standard English is
   a. the language of textbooks.
   b. often taught slowly to nonstandard speakers.
   c. often different from English spoken in a dialect.
   d. needed for success in any line of work.
2. Early childhood centers try to
   a. teach children standard English during the first days of school.
   b. make sure each child feels secure.
   c. plan activities in which language-different children have an interest.
   d. provide for each child's development of word use in his or her own dialect.
3. Teachers should be careful to guard against
   a. correcting children's speech by drawing attention to errors.
   b. thinking that only standard English is correct and therefore better than English spoken in a dialect.
   c. giving children the idea that they speak differently or "funny."
   d. feeling that children who come from low-income homes are always disadvantaged when compared with children from middle-income homes.
4. Young children with speech errors
   a. rarely outgrow them.
   b. may need special help.
   c. often do not hear as well as adults.
   d. can hear that what they say is different but do not have the ability to say it correctly.
5. Bilingualism in the young child is
   a. always a disadvantage.
   b. sometimes a disadvantage.

      c. a rewarding challenge to the teacher.

      d. a problem when schools make children feel defeated and unaccepted.

6. A disadvantaged child may

      a. also be hyperactive and aggressive.

      b. be more independent and talkative than a middle-class child.

      c. talk a lot but have a smaller vocabulary than the average middle-class child.

      d. need teachers who not only model standard English but also model problem solving with words.

References

Arenas, Soledad. "Bilingual/Bicultural Programs for Preschool Children." *Children Today* (July-Aug. 1978): 37–45.

Bee, Helen. *The Developing Child.* New York: Harper & Row, 1981.

Beers, Carolyn Strickland, and James Wheelock Beers. "Early Identification of Learning Disabilities: Facts and Fallacies." *Elementary School Journal* 46.8 (Nov. 1980): 91–106.

Bernal, E. M. "The Identification of Gifted Chicano Children." *Educational Planning for the Gifted.* Eds. A. Y. Baldwin, G. H. Gear, and L. J. Lucito. Reston: Council For Exceptional Children, 1978.

"Bilingualism: The Accent Is On Youth." U. S. News and World Report, July 1986.

Bloodstein, O. *A Handbook on Stuttering.* Chicago: National Easter Seal Society of Crippled Children and Adults, 1975.

Broman, Betty. *The Early Years,* Chicago: Rand McNally College Publishing, 1978.

Cazden, Courtney B., et al. "Language Development in Day-Care Programs." *Language in Early Childhood Education.* Washington, D.C.: The National Association for the Education of Young Children, 1981. 101–114.

Clement, John. *Promoting Preschool Bilingualism. KEYS to Early Childhood Education* 2.3 (March 1981): 43–51.

Conklin, Nancy F., and Margaret A. Lourie. *A Host Of Tongues.* New York: The Free Press, 1983.

Dee, Rita. *Planning for Ethnic Education: A Handbook for Planned Change.* Chicago, IL: Illinois State Board of Education, Jan. 1980, ERIC ED191 976.

Dillard, J. L. *Black English.* New York: Random House, 1972.

Donoghue, Mildred R. *The Child and the English Language Arts.* Dubuque, IA: William C. Brown, 1985.

Dumtschin, Joyce Ury. "Recognizing Language Development and Delay in Early Childhood." *Young Children* 43.3 (March 1988): 16–24.

Flores, Manna I. *Helping Children Learn a Second Language. KEYS to Early Childhood Education* 1.6 (July 1980): 17–27.

Hakuta, Kenji, in Siewers, Alf, "Parents Accent Two Languages at Home." *San Jose Mercury News,* Feb. 19, 1986. 4L.

Hall, E. *Child Psychology Today.* New York: Random House, 1982.

Hartwell, P. "Dialect Interference in Writing: A Critical View." *Research in the Teaching of English* 14.4 (May 1980): 52–61.

Hendrick, Joanne. *The Whole Child*. St. Louis, MO: Times Mirror/Mosby, 1984.

Jespersen, Otto. *Mankind, Nation, and Individual From a Linguistic Point of View*. Bloomington, IN: Indiana UP, 1945.

Johnson, Kenneth. "Pedagogical Problems of Using Second Language Techniques for Teaching Standard English to Speakers of Nonstandard Negro Dialect." *Linguistic Cultural Differences and American Education*. Eds. Aarons, Gordon, and Stewart, Florida FL. Reporter, 86.10, 1969. 88–96.

Joiner, C. W. "Memorandum Opinion and Order: Martin Luther King Junior Elementary School Children et al v. Ann Arbor School District Board," 473 F. Supp. 1371 (1979). Reprinted in *Black English and the Education of Black Children and Youth*. Ed. G. Smitherman. Detroit: Wayne State University Center for Black Studies, 1981.

Kitano, Margie. "Young Gifted Children: Strategies for Preschool Teachers." *Young Children* 37.4 (May 1982): 29–31.

Klopf, Donald W. "Educating Children for Communication in a Multicultural Society." Paper presented at the Conference on Developing Oral Communication Competence in Children, Sidney, Australia, July 1979, ERIC ED180 026.

Labov, William. Study Report, Washington, DC: National Science Foundation, 1985.

Lambert, Wally in Wells, Stacy, "Bilingualism: The Accent Is On Youth." *U. S. News and World Report* 101.8 (July 1986): 89–92.

Lay-Dopyera, Margaret, and John E. Dopyera, *Becoming a Teacher Of Young Children*, Lexington, MA: D. C. Heath, 1982.

Lupkowski, Ann E., and Elizabeth A. Lupkowski. "Meeting the Needs of Gifted Preschoolers." *Children Today* 33.3 (Mar.-Apr. 1985): 71–84.

"Management Update: Identifying and Referring Children with Speech and Language Disorders." *Pre-K Today* 1.9 (1986): 64–68.

Markham, Lynda R. "De Dog and De Cat — Assisting Speakers of Black English as They Begin to Write." *Young Children* 39.1 (May 1984): 69–75.

Meers, Hilda J. *Helping Our Children Talk*. New York: Longman Group, 1976.

NAHSA (National Association for Hearing and Speech Action, Rockville, MD),
"Answers, Questions About Language," 1983
"Speech and Language Disorders and the Speech-Language Pathologist," 1985
"Otitis Media and Language Development," 1985
"About Stuttering," 1983
"About Articulation Problems," 1985
"Recognizing Communication Disorders," 1985

Nedler, Shari. "A Bilingual Early Childhood Program." *The Preschool in Action*, Eds. Mary Carol Day and Ronald K. Parker. Boston: Allyn and Bacon, 1977.

Osborn, Janie Dyson, and D. Keith Osborn. *Cognition in Early Childhood*. Athens: Education Associates, 1983.

Phillips, Carol Brunson. "Nurturing Diversity for Today's Children and Tomorrow's Leaders." *Young Children* 43.2 (Jan. 1988): 42–47.

Rapsberry, W. *Reading, Writing and Dialect. Young Children* 35.3 (Nov. 1979): 37–46.

Rashid, Hakim M. "Promoting Biculturalism in Young African-American Children." *Young Children* 38.5 (Jan. 1984): 39–47.

Rubin, Richard, and John J. Fisher. *Your Preschooler*. New York: Macmillan, 1982.

Schwartz, Susan. "The Young Gifted Child." *Early Years* 11.5 (Feb. 1980): 55–62.

Torrance, E. *Creativity*. Belmont: Dimensions, 1969.

Weiss, Curtis E., and Herold S. Lillywhite, *Communicative Disorders*. St. Louis, MO: C. V. Mosby, 1981.

White, Burton L. "A Person Is Emerging." *Parents As Teachers Program Planning and Implementation Guide*. Jefferson City, MO: Missouri Dept. of Elem. and Secondary Ed., 1986.

Yawkey, Thomas D., et al. *Language Arts and the Young Child*. Itasca: F. E. Peacock, 1981.

Section 6

Writing

Print Awareness and Use

Young children's emerging awareness and interest in print and printing is examined in this section. Early childhood teachers who are in training are often not sure whether it is appropriate to offer instruction in this language arts area. This section will provide a new perspective and clarify many questions concerning printing and young children. Suggested activities are provided along with print guides for individuals unaware of print-script form.

ON LISTENING TO THE LANGUAGE OF CHILDREN

Grace Smith (1974) has recorded the language of young children. When she was a teacher of three- and four-year-olds at Pacific Oaks College and Children's School in Pasadena, California, she jotted down the following:

Clay is icky gluey
Gooey fooey
Gishy mishy
Stuck
Yuk.

Tie my shoe, I have a flat tire.

Today I found out that ladybugs come in yellow too.

You're older, I'm newer.

How old is a baby when it's born? It is zero old.

I close my eyes. You can't see me.

Maybe you want it, but I want it bad.

I'm not going to get married. I'm going to be a
Boy Scout.

Look at that leaf do a somersault.

I'm the boss of my own face.
I can make my face laugh, and I can make it have
a fit.

When I swing, I close my eyes and I feel higher.

A sister is a friend.
A brother is a friend.
And me is a friend of you.

I didn't find anybody to hold on a hand to.

It's good to have a friend that calls you P.J. if your
name is P.J.

The wind makes the trees go wild.

I can't write, but I can copycat it. [1]

---

[1] Grace Smith, "On Listening to the Language of Children," *Young Children* 27.5, Washington, DC: NAEYC, (March 1974): 22–29.

UNIT 18

Print —
Early Knowledge and Emerging Interest

BJECTIVES

After studying this unit, you should be able to

- discuss the child's development of small hand-muscle control.
- outline the probable sequence of events occurring before a child prints his or her first recognizable alphabet letter.
- describe printscript alphabets.

Two pertinent questions preschool teachers ask themselves concerning print and teaching children to write in printscript are, (1) is it appropriate to offer lessons (activities) that teach print letter recognition and formation at this age? and (2) how is instruction in printscript undertaken? Resolving these questions is made easier by this unit's discussion.

In the past few years, ideas about the child's development of writing (printing) skill has undergone a minor revolution. Older ideas promoted the idea that teaching children to print and read should not be undertaken until children are in kindergarten or first grade. It was felt that at that stage children are mature enough or possess the readiness skills that would make these tasks much easier. Writing and reading skills were thought to be different from listening and speaking skills. Speech was accomplished without direct or formal teaching over a long period, beginning in infancy. Now, however, educators are revising their thoughts. Print awareness and beginning printing skill and reading awareness and beginning reading skills are now viewed as developing at younger ages, simultaneously with children's growing understandings of a number of other symbol systems. The clues have been

there for some time. Early childhood educators have always had children who asked questions and displayed early attempts and interest in printing, reading, number concepts, and representing lifelike objects in drawings (figure 18-1). Fields and Lee (1987) point out that adults expect children to talk before they read but may not have noticed that children are interested in writing before they can read.

Alphabet letters appear in four-year-olds' drawings. Young children go through the motions of reading books, and some have a keen interest in numbers and measurement. This supports the idea that children are attempting to make sense out of what they encounter and are expanding their understandings of symbol systems on a number of fronts. Lesser (1974) reported that as many as half of all children in the U.S., three to five years of age, watch "Sesame Street" regularly. Professional practice promotes teachers' supporting, welcoming, and recognizing child efforts and accepting correct and incorrect child conclusions about printing, just as they accepted and supported incorrect or incomplete speech and welcomed it. Earlier practice may have led some teachers to either ignore or defer supportive guidance in printing, the rationale being that this

FIGURE 18-1 Children's artwork often contains lifelike figures.

instruction would come later in the child's schooling. Teachers today are encouraged to have faith in children's ability to discover and develop their own writing theories and symbol systems, as they did when they taught themselves to speak. This takes place in a print-rich environment with responsive adults.

Writing awareness and beginning writing attempts make more sense to children who have experienced an integrated language arts instructional approach. The areas of speaking, listening, reading, and writing are interrelated. The child's ability to see how these areas fit together is commonly mentioned in school goals. Adults in classrooms communicate with others on a daily basis both orally and in written form. Written communication offers daily opportunities for teachers to point out print's usefulness. Print's necessity can be discussed and shared.

Increased focus on the literacy of children in the U.S. has provided additional impetus for researching early writing and reading relationships. An increasing number of experts believe children establish early ideas about printing (writing) that serve as a basis for early printing attempts. Calkins (1979) suggests that children can begin printing the first day they enter kinder-

garten, and that 90% of all children come to school believing that they can write (figure 18-2). She points out that most children's first drafts concentrate on messages rather than perfection. She advocates children's learning to write in the same way they learned to speak. Generations of children have been asked to learn the letters of the alphabet, sound-symbol correspondences, and a vocabulary of sight words before they learned to write or read. If the same were true of learning to speak, children would be asked to wait until all letter sounds were perfected at age seven or eight before attempting to speak. Throne (1988) suggests that print awareness aids literacy development:

> As children emerge into literacy, they begin to understand that reading is getting meaning from print and become aware of the different functions and uses of written language.

Based on the notion that the child constructs from within, piecing together from life experiences the rules of oral language, educators feel that if children are given time and supportive assistance they can crack the writing and reading code by noticing regularities and

FIGURE 18-2 Many children believe they can write.

incongruencies, thus creating their own unique rules. Children would progress at their own speeds, doing what is important to them and doing what they see others do. Jewell and Zintz (1986) have noticed a number of parallels between learning to read and learning to write. Children appear to teach themselves to write in much the same way that they teach themselves to read (figure 18-3). Without formal instruction, they experiment with and explore the various facets of the writing process. They decorate letters and invent their own symbols — sometimes reverting to their own inventions even after they are well into distinguishing and reproducing different, recognizable alphabet letters. Children expect others to know what they have written, regardless of their coding system.

Natural curiosity leads children to form ideas about print and its use in their lives. Schickedanz (1982) suggests it has often been assumed that children know little or nothing about written language before they receive formal instruction. Evidence indicates, however, that children have extensive knowledge of some aspects of written language.

The concept of writing readiness began with some important figures from the past who influenced the directions that early childhood education has taken (Charlesworth, 1985). It became popular to talk about writing readiness as being that time when an average group of children acquired the capacity, skills, and knowledge to permit the group to accomplish the task. Figure 18-4 compares traditional, readiness, and "natural" instructional approaches with children's writing. It would be difficult finding a center that doesn't use some elements of each of the three approaches in the instructional program.

STAGES IN WRITING DEVELOPMENT

At some point, children learn that written marks have meaning. Just as they sought the names of things, they now seek the names of these marks and, later, the meanings of the marks. Because each child is an individual, this may or may not happen during the preschool years. One child may try to make letters or numbers. Another child may have little interest in or knowledge of written forms. Many children are somewhere between these two examples.

Lay-Dopyera and Dopyera (1982) describe young children's progress in early writing:

> Given the opportunity to observe writing and to experience the functions and values of the reading process, young children will very early become interested in producing "writing" and will gradually give their scribbles more of the appearance of writing — horizontal lines of connected or closely arranged markings. They will move from scribbling to drawing to attempts at copying letters to production of names and other words (but not necessarily read as words.) By age three children are likely to be making good progress in differentiating writing from pictures and by five probably have learned to differentiate letters from letterlike forms that are not letters. They will also likely have figured out some of the conventions of English written language — directionality (from left to right) and the way letters are arranged in groupings with spaces in between to denote separations between words.

Atkins (1984) also discusses events between the ages of three and five:

> Somewhere between three and five years of age, children begin to vary their patterns and move from imitation to creation. They produce a mixture of real letters, mock letters, and innovative

FIGURE 18-3 Look at how this child is concentrating.

Traditional Approach

- providing play materials and free time
- supplying art materials, paper, writing tools, alphabet toys and games, chalkboard
- reading picture books
- planning program that excludes instruction in naming or forming alphabet letters
- incidental and spontaneous teaching about print

Readiness Approach

- providing writing materials and models
- planning program with introduction to tracing, naming alphabet letters, and naming shapes
- reading picture books
- providing a language arts classroom center
- channeling interested children into print and alphabet activities by offering supportive assistance

Natural Approach

- providing writing and reading materials and models
- planning program that emphasizes print in daily life
- promoting dramatic play themes that involve print, such as grocery store, restaurant, newspaper carrier, print shop, and office
- creating a writing center for the classroom
- supplying alphabet toys and models
- answering questions and supporting children's efforts
- making connections between reading and writing and speaking
- reading picture books

FIGURE 18-4 Comparison of instructional approaches in printing

symbols. They write messages which they expect adults to be able to read. These actions signal several new discoveries which the children are making.

- They are attending to the fine features of writing, noting shapes and specific letters.
- They are developing an early concept of sign — the realization that symbols stand for something.
- They are recognizing that there is variation in written language.

Children refine and enlarge these concepts by playing around with writing. They draw, trace, copy, and even invent letter forms of their own.

Print awareness is usually developed in the following sequence:

1. The child notices adults making marks with writing tools.
2. The child notices print in books and on signs.

As Chomsky (1971) notes, "When this time comes, a child seems suddenly to notice all the print in the world around him — street signs, food labels, newspaper headlines, printing on cartons, books, billboards, everything. He tries to read everything, already having a good foundation in translating from pronunciation to print. If help is provided when he asks for it, he makes out wonderfully well. It is a tremendously exciting time for him."

3. The child realizes that certain distinguishable marks make his or her name.

4. The child learns the names of some of the marks — usually the first letter of his or her name. As Jewell and Zintz (1986) point out, while building a sizable store of words recognized on sight, children will begin to make finer and finer distinctions about print by using more and more visual cues. They begin to pay attention to individual letters, particularly the first ones in words.

The usual sequence in the child's imitation of written forms follows.

1. The child's scribbles are more like print than artwork or pure exploration.
2. Linear scribbles are generally horizontal with possible repeated forms. Children's knowledge of linear directionality may have been displayed in play in which they lined up alphabet blocks, cut out letters and pasted them in a row, or put magnetic board letters in left to right rows.
3. Individual shapes are created, usually closed shapes displaying purposeful lines.
4. Letterlike forms are created.
5. Recognizable alphabet letters are printed and may be mirror images or turned on sides, upside down, or in upright position.
6. Words or groupings of alphabet letters with spaces between are formed.
7. Invented spelling appears that may include pictured items along with alphabet letters (figure 18-5).
8. Correctly spelled words with spaces separating words are produced.

Atkins (1984) describes early writing as totally egocentric. Self-expression, fun, and play are the real objects, writing only the medium. It will remain this way, she feels, for most children until near the end of first grade.

The invented spelling stage casts teachers in the role of detectives trying to ascertain meanings that the child may perceive as obvious. Words appear that may look like a foreign language — dg for dog, and jragin for dragon (Vukelich and Golden, 1984). Invented spelling serves as an important stage in the process of deciphering the sound-symbol system of written language (Fields and Lee, 1987). It is felt that at this point phonics becomes important to children. Early on, the child selects letters in his or her inventive spelling that have some relationship to how the word is pronounced. Large items like elephants may be written in huge letters, and the names of letters may represent words (u for you) or parts of words. Atkins (1984) defines young writers' invented spelling as using personal logic rather than or in conjunction with standard spelling. Atkins points out that the child's strategy of using a name of a letter has a frustrating side:

> There are only 26 letters in the alphabet but almost twice that many phonemes or sound units. What do children do when they encounter a sound for which there is no ready letter-name match? They use a system of spelling logic based primarily on what they hear but also influenced by subconscious knowledge of the general rules of language usage and of how sounds are formed in the mouth when spoken.

GOALS OF INSTRUCTION

Providing experiences that match a child's interests and abilities is the goal of many centers. Most schools plan activities with alphabet letters for those children who ask questions or seem ready and then proceed if the child is still interested (figure 18-6). Others work with children on an individual basis. Yet others believe

Random

The child writes (prints) letter groups that are randomly selected from alphabet letters he or she has learned, for example, mlo for cat (the word the child wishes to write).

Consonant Inclusion

The child prints letter groups or words that contain consonants sounding like or near the spoken word, for example, kt for cat, fn for phone, iscm for ice cream.

Alphabet Combinations

The child uses both consonants and vowels in printed words, for example, kat or cat for cat. The child may mix phonetic approaches and alphabet names in spelling, for example, ce for kitty, or I luv u for I love you.

FIGURE 18-5 Possible levels in young children's invented spellings

FIGURE 18-6 This is an early attempt to create symbols. Notice the child's awkward grasp on the brush.

in providing a print-rich environment where the child will progress naturally with supportive adults who also model an interest in print, and point out uses of print in daily activities. It is possible to combine these approaches.

As with other language abilities, goals include stimulating further interest and exploration. This should be done in such a way that the child is not confused by instruction that is too advanced or boring.

As stated previously, an important goal concerning print awareness is relating writing to other language arts areas. It is almost impossible to not do so. Teachers are encouraged to consciously mention connections so children will understand how writing fits in the whole of communicating.

A teacher's goal would include the ability to print every lowercase and uppercase alphabet letter in excellent form, offering children the best model possible.

COORDINATION

Children's muscle control follows a timetable of its own. Control of a particular muscle depends on many factors — diet, exercise, inherited ability, and motivation, to name a few. A baby can control his or her neck and arms long before his or her legs. A child's muscle control grows in a head-to-toe fashion. Muscles closer to the center of the body can be controlled long before those of the hands and fingers. Large-muscle control comes before small-muscle control. Think of a toddler walking; the toddler's legs seem to swing from his or her hips. Just as each child starts walking and develops muscle control at different ages, so too does each child develop fine motor control, which influences his or her ability to control a writing tool (figure 18-7).

COGNITIVE DEVELOPMENT

Realization that there are written symbols is a first step in writing. The discovery that written language is simply spoken language, ideas, or communication is another step. Mental growth, which allows a child to see similarities and differences in written symbols, comes before the ability to write. The child recognizes that a written mark is a shape made by the placement of lines.

Donoghue (1985) lists seven prerequisite skill areas for handwriting:

- small-muscle development and coordination
- eye-hand coordination

FIGURE 18-7 Chalk may be one of the first writing tools experienced.

- ability to hold writing tools properly
- ability to form basic strokes (circles and straight lines)
- letter perception
- orientation to printed language, which includes a desire to write and communicate, including the child's enjoyment of writing his or her own name.
- left to right understanding.

The last three skills deal with the child's cognitive development. Schickedanz (1986) points out that learning to write involves much more than just forming alphabet letters:

> Learning to write also involves knowing (1) how writing and speech relate, (2) how form and style vary depending on the situation, and (3) how a reader will react to what we have written. All of these skills depend on sophisticated and complex thinking, much of which may be beyond preschoolers' abilities. Nevertheless, the beginnings of these skills can be found in preschool children.

DRAWING EXPERIENCE

A young child scribbles if given paper and a marking tool. As the child grows, the scribbles are controlled into lines that he or she places where desired (figure 18-8). Gradually, the child begins to draw circles, then a face, later a full figure, and so on (figure 18-9). Children draw their own symbols representing what they see around them. The length of time it takes this process to develop differs with each child.

A profound connection exists between experience and ability in drawing and interest in and ability to write (Balaban, 1980). Drawings and paintings not only communicate children's thinking (when they reach the level of drawing that is representative of the environment), but also often display early attempts to create symbols. Some of these symbols may be recognized by adults, but others seem to be unique and represent the world in the child's own way. Children often want to talk about their work and create stories to accompany graphics (Kane, 1982).

Since alphabet letters are more abstract than representative drawing, some educators suggest that drawing precedes writing. Brittain's research (1973) found that children who were making closed forms and recognizable letters in their drawings made closed forms and recognizable letters if they attempted writing (figure 18-10). Durkin (1969) identifies a characteristic that was common to almost all children in her research study who read early and continued to hold

FIGURE 18-8 Children start writing by scribbling and, when older, draw symbols of the world around them.

FIGURE 18-9 An elaborate, detailed human figure — the work of a 4½-year-old

FIGURE 18-10 A closed figure drawing with a child-printed name

their lead in reading achievement: The children were described by their parents as "pencil-and-paper kids," whose starting point of curiosity about written language was an interest in scribbling and drawing.

WRITING AND EXPOSURE TO BOOKS

Probably the most common experience that promotes a child's interest in print is hearing and seeing picture books read over and over. Throne (1988) points out that "children begin to understand the conventions of print and how stories work by using familiar and significant texts." Memorized story lines lead to children's questions about print on book pages. Once a word is recognized in print, copying that word onto another paper or manipulating magnetic alphabet letters to form the word is a natural outgrowth. This activity usually leads to parent attention and approval and further attempts. Scribblers, doodlers, drawers, and

pencil-and-paper kids are all labels researchers have used to describe children who have an early interest in writing, and much of what they do has been promoted by seeing print in their favorite books.

Children may begin by thinking a reader looks at pictures to know what a book says. As they gain more experience with books, they begin to realize that it is the print, not the pictures, that a reader reads (Schickedanz, 1986).

Berg (1977) concluded that the acquisition of skills in writing and reading and the development of the attitude that books are enjoyable are not simply academic or technical learning. These skills flourish with a warm physical and emotional base with shared enjoyment and intimacy. Most experts believe considerable support exists for the notion that oral language provides a base for learning to write (Dyson, 1981). The importance of emotionally satisfying adult-child interactions in all areas of language arts can't be underestimated.

PLANNING A PROGRAM FOR PRINT AWARENESS AND PRINTING SKILL

Program planning is often done on an individual basis. If group instruction is planned, it deals with general background information concerning print use during the school day and print use in the home and community.

A great deal of spontaneous and incidental teaching takes place. Teachers capitalize on children's questions concerning mail, packages, signs, and labels. In most preschool settings, print is a natural part of living, and it has many interesting features that children can discover and notice when teachers focus attention on print. Child activities are included in Units 19 and 20.

A discussion is necessary here concerning the practice of asking the child to form alphabet letters and practice letter forms. The danger in planning an individual or group experience of this nature is multiple. One has to consider whether a child has the physical and mental capacity to be successful and whether the child has an interest in doing the exercise or simply trying to please adults.

Early writing instruction is not a new idea. Maria Montessori (1967) (a well-known educator and designer of teaching materials) and numerous other teachers have offered instruction in writing (or printing) to preschoolers. Dr. Montessori encouraged the child's tracing of letter forms using the first two fingers of the hand as a prewriting exercise. She observed that this type of light touching seemed to help youngsters when writing tools were later given to them. Montessori (1967) designed special alphabet letter cutouts as one of a number of prewriting aids. These cutouts were thought to help exercise and develop small muscles while shapes were learned. Montessori suggests the following:

> When a teacher has a child see and touch the letters of the alphabet, three sensations come into play simultaneously: sight, touch, and kinesthetic (muscular) sensation. This is why the image of the graphic symbol is fixed in the mind much more quickly than when it is acquired through sight in ordinary methods.
>
> It should be noted, moreover, that muscular memory is the most tenacious in a small child and is also the readiest; sometimes even he does not recognize a letter when he sees it, but he does when he touches it.

Each center and individual teacher decides whether group printing practice takes place. This text recommends print activity planning that concentrates on awareness of print and its uses in everyday life plus helpful suggestions and encouragement given to individual children who show more than a passing interest. When a child asks for information concerning print or to be shown how to print, he or she is displaying interest and following his or her own curriculum.

ENVIRONMENT AND MATERIALS

Children's access to drawing tools — magic markers, chalk, pencils, crayons, brushes — is important so that children can make their own marks (figure 18-11). It is suggested that teachers create a place where children can comfortably use these tools.

Early childhood educators interested in whole-language approaches to instruction may gather ideas from Hayward's (1988) description of a well-managed and functioning whole-language classroom:

> . . . you immediately become aware of PRINT — printed messages about activities for the day, printed examples of child-written (or dictated) work, lots of printed wall charts and big books, printed labels on equipment, shelves, cupboards, to give information about contents and use.

The following early childhood materials help the child use and gain control of small arm and finger

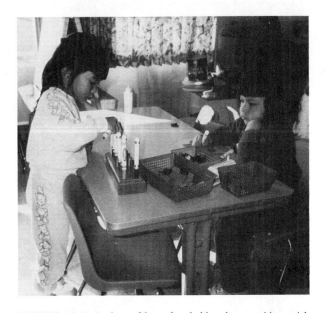

FIGURE 18-11 A clever felt-marker holder that provides quick access and easy return

muscles in preparation for writing (figure 18-12):

- puzzles
- pegboards
- small blocks
- construction toys
- scissors

Most schools plan activities in which the child puts together, arranges, or manipulates small pieces. These are sometimes called tabletop activities and are available for play throughout the day. A teacher can encourage the use of tabletop activities by having the pieces arranged invitingly on tables or resting on adjacent shelves.

Early childhood centers create rooms that are full of symbols, letters, and numbers in clear view of the child. Many toys have circles, squares, triangles, alphabet letters, and other common shapes.

Recommended symbol size for preschool playroom display is at least two to two-and-one-half inches in height or larger. Teachers can add printing to playrooms in the following ways.

Labeling
artwork
name tags
lockers and storage areas (figure 18-13)
belongings

FIGURE 18-12 Scissors in one hand and a writing tool in the other

common objects in the room, such as scissors, paper, crayons, fishbowl, chair, water
school areas, such as block, library or reading center, playhouse, art center, science center
placecards for snacks

Display Areas
magazine pictures with captions
current interest displays, for example, "Rocks we found on our walk"
bulletin boards and wall displays with words
wall alphabet guides (Aa Bb...)
alphabet charts (figure 18-14, page 326)
child's work with explanations, such as "Josh's block tower," or "Penny's clay pancakes"
signs for child activities, such as "store," "hospital," "wet paint," and "Tickets for Sale Here."

Teacher-Made Materials, Games and Toys
brightly colored alphabet letters from felt, cardboard, sandpaper, leather, plastic
games with letters, numbers, or symbols
alphabet cards
games with names and words
greeting cards
hats or badges with words

Writing Centers

Writing centers are planned, teacher-stocked areas where printing is promoted. A writing center can be a separate area of a room or can exist within a language arts center. Child comfort and proper lighting is essential along with minimized distractions. Often dividers or screening are used to cut down outside noise and activity. Supplies and storage areas are provided at children's fingertips so that children can help themselves. Teacher displays or bulletin board areas that motivate printing can be close by. If water-based marking pens are provided, pens with distinct bright colors are preferred (Fields and Lee, 1987).

There should be a variety of paper and writing tools. Printing stamps and printing ink blocks, a hole punch, and brads are desirable. Old forms, catalogs, calendars, and computer paper may be inviting. Scratch paper (one side already used) or lined paper and crayons placed side-by-side invite use. Most local businesses or offices throw away enough scratch paper to supply a preschool center.

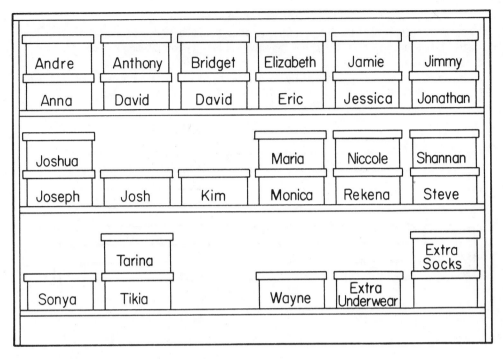

FIGURE 18-13 Large printscript letters are used to label boxes.

Colored or white chalk has an appeal of its own and can be used on paper, chalkboards, or cement. For variety, use oil pastels, which have bright colors, or soft-lead pencils on paper. Most schools install a child-high chalkboard; table chalkboards are made quickly by using chalkboard paint obtained at hardware or paint stores and scrap wood pieces. Easels, unused wall areas, and backs of furniture can be made into chalkboards.

Primary print typewriters capture interest, and some centers have computers and adult computer advisers. Shape books with blank pages and words to copy and trace appeal to some children, as do large rub-on letters or alphabet letter stickers (these can be made by teachers from press-on labels.) Magnetic boards and magnetized letter sets are commonly mentioned as the favorite toy of children interested in alphabet letters and forming words.

Letters, words, and displays are placed for viewing on bulletin boards at children's eye level. Displays in writing centers often motivate and promote print.

FIRST SCHOOL ALPHABETS

Parents may have taught their children to print with all capitals. Early childhood centers help introduce the interested child to the letter forms that are used in the first grades of elementary school.

In kindergarten or first grade, printing is done in printscript, sometimes called manuscript printing (figure 18-15, page 327) or also in a form called D'Nealian print. Centers should obtain guides from a local elementary school, since letter forms can vary from community to community. As in previous text discussions, manuscript and D'Nealian alphabet forms are provided for teachers in this text so that correct forms can be modeled in classrooms when children happen to notice them and individually when children request specific letter or word graphics.

Teachers need to be familiar with printscript (or any other form used locally). It is easier for a child to learn the right way than to be retrained later. All printing

INSTRUCTIONS TO MAKE CHART LINER

Cut a piece of Masonite® 12 inches by 36 inches. Make 7 sawcuts 1½″ apart, beginning and ending 1½″ from either end. Then glue or nail ½″ square pieces of wood 12″ long to each end.

Note: A teacher-made chart liner is a useful device that helps teachers make evenly spaced guidelines on charts that use lines of print. By placing the chart liner over chart paper, quick guidelines are accomplished by inserting a sharp pencil in sawcut slots.

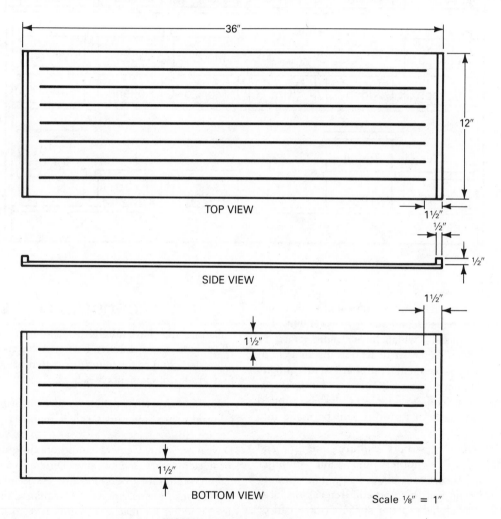

FIGURE 18-14 Making a chart liner

seen by young children in a preschool should be either printscript, using both uppercase (capitals) and lowercase (small letters) or D'Nealian style. Names, bulletin boards, and labels made by teachers should model correct forms. Printscript letters are formed with straight lines, circles, and parts of circles. In figure 18-15, the small arrows and numerals show the direction to follow in forming the letters as well as the sequence of the lines.

The D'Nealian form developed by teacher-principal Donald Neal Thurber, introduced in 1978, has grown in acceptance. Its popularity stems in part from its slant and continuous stroke features, which provide an easy transition to slant and stroke used in cursive writing introduced to children after second grade. Thurber (1986) notes that it takes 58 strokes to print the circle-stick alphabet while only 31 to print D'Nealian. The D'Nealian letter forms are shown in figure 18-16, page 328. They are arranged in groupings of similarly made patterns. Group I is introduced first to learners, and dots indicate where letter forms start. Teachers and parents are encouraged to use voice inflection to establish rhythm and direction during letter-form introduction and practice (figure 18-17, page 329). Further information about this alphabet and teaching suggestions can be obtained from Scott, Foresman, Glenview, IL 60025.

Numbers in printed form are called numerals. Children may have used toys with numerals, such as block sets. Young children will probably hold up fingers to indicate their ages or to tell you they can count. They may start making number symbols before showing an interest in alphabet letters. Numeral forms (figure 18-18, page 330), are also available from elementary schools. The numeral forms in one geographic area may also be slightly different from those of another town, city, or state.

BEGINNING ATTEMPTS

In beginning attempts to write, children commonly grasp writing tools tightly and press down hard enough to tear the paper. With time, the mastery of small muscles, children's tense, unschooled muscles relax and forms and shapes start to resemble alphabet forms and recognizable shapes. Deep concentration and effort is observed. All attempts are recognized and appreciated by early childhood teachers as signs of the children's growing interest and ability.

Lewis and Lewis (1964) developed a listing (figure 18-19, page 330) that arranges alphabet letters in manuscript print from the most difficult for children to manage and form to the easiest.

Summary

The alphabet and printed words are part of preschool life. A center's goals rarely include teaching all attending children to print, but instead attempt to offer a print-rich environment. For the great majority of preschool children attending child centers, sit-down practice of letter forms is developmentally inappropriate. Some preschool children, on the other hand,

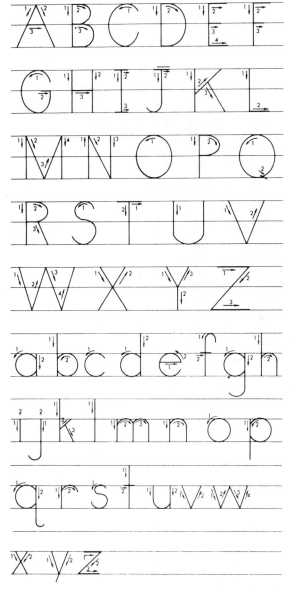

FIGURE 18-15 Printscript alphabet *(Courtesy of the Santa Clara Unified School District, Santa Clara, CA.)*

FIGURE 18-16 D'Nealian print *(From D'Nealian® Handwriting by Donald Neal Thurber. Copyright © 1987 by Scott, Foresman, and Company. Reprinted by permission.*

will attempt repeatedly to form alphabet letters and practice writing them on their own or with the teacher's supportive guidance. Many children will, however, show beginning interest in the uses of print and print in books.

Numerals are also interesting to young children. These symbols appear daily at school, home, and in the neighborhood. Guides for forming numerals and letters of the alphabet can be obtained from local schools. These guides may vary slightly from city to city.

The ability to print depends on the child's:

- muscle control
- skill in recognizing symbols
- ability to note the placement of lines in a symbol

Printscript is used in preschool, kindergarten, and first grade. Letters are formed with lines and circles in uppercase and lowercase symbols.

Children are ready for printing at different ages. They learn alphabet letters at different rates. Printscript is used for labeling, display, and other activities at early childhood centers.

Dear Parents:

The following alphabet is how we present the D'Nealian Manuscript Handwriting program.

Letters are presented in a group of similarly made patterns, starting with Group I. When a child can make 3 of any letter with similar size and shape (although it may not be the perfect finished product), *he or she is at his or her skill level for that lesson.* A suggested audio phraseology of how each letter is formed is also included. The teacher uses voice inflection to help establish rhythm and direction control. A great help is having the child write simple 2-, 3-, or 4-letter words as quickly as new letters are presented; for example, a + d gives *dad* and *add.*

Letters start at the dot.

Group 1 — Around-Down Letters

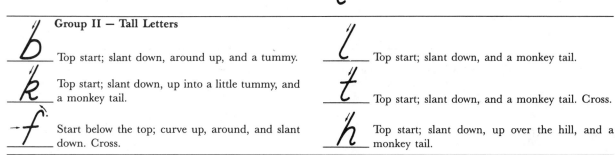

Middle start; around down, close up, down, and a monkey tail.

Middle start; around down, touch, up high, down, and a monkey tail.

Middle start; around, down, and close up.

Start below the middle; curve up, around, down, and a snake tail.

Start below the middle; curve up, around, down, up, and stop.

Middle start; around, down, close up, down under water, and a fishhook.

Start between the middle and bottom; curve up, around, touch, down, up, and stop. Or, curved line up, wrap a *c* around it.

Middle start; around, down, close up, down under water, and a backwards fishhook.

Group II — Tall Letters

Top start; slant down, around up, and a tummy.

Top start; slant down, up into a little tummy, and a monkey tail.

Start below the top; curve up, around, and slant down. Cross.

Top start; slant down, and a monkey tail.

Top start; slant down, and a monkey tail. Cross.

Top start; slant down, up over the hill, and a monkey tail.

Group III

Middle start; slant down and a monkey tail. Add a dot.

Middle start; slant down, up over the hill, up over the hill again, and a monkey tail.

Middle start; slant down, up, and a roof.

Middle start; slant down, around, up, down, and a monkey tail.

Middle start; slant down, around, up, and down, around, up again.

Middle start; slant down, around, up, slant down under water, and a fishhook.

Middle start; slant down, up over the hill, and a monkey tail.

Middle start; slant down under water, up, around, and a tummy.

Middle start; slant down under water and a fishhook. Add a dot.

Middle start; slant down right and slant up right.

Middle start; slant down right and a monkey tail. Cross down left.

Middle start; over right, slant down left, and over right.

FIGURE 18-17 A letter to parents concerning D'Nealian print

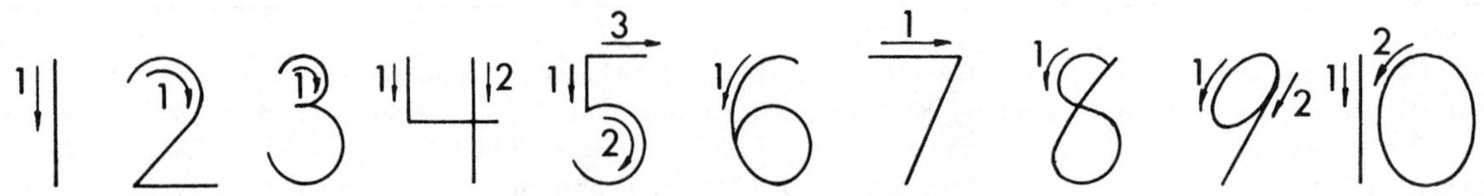

FIGURE 18-18 Printscript numerals *(Courtesy of the Santa Clara Unified School District, Santa Clara, CA.)*

1. q	14. U	27. K	40. F
2. g	15. M	28. W	41. P
3. p	16. S	29. A	42. E
4. y	17. b	30. N	43. X
5. j	18. e	31. C	44. I
6. m	19. r	32. f	45. v
7. k	20. z	33. J	46. i
8. u	21. n	34. w	47. D
9. a	22. s	35. h	48. H
10. G	23. Q	36. T	49. O
11. R	24. B	37. x	50. L
12. d	25. t	38. c	51. o
13. Y	26. Z	39. V	52. l

FIGURE 18-19 Listing of letters from most difficult to easiest to form *(From Elementary English, by Lewis and Lewis, 1964.)*

Student Activities

- Observe a morning program for four-year-olds. Cite as many examples as possible of adults' use of written communication and all child exposure to print.

- Expand the following statement: Practicing alphabet letter formation when a teacher requests it could result in the child's. . . .

- Without turning back to review the printed alphabet guide given in this unit, print the alphabet in both uppercase and lowercase letters.

- Obtain a printscript alphabet from the nearest public school. With a red crayon or pen, circle letters that differ (even slightly) from your attempted alphabet. Print all letters you circled on remaining lines using proper form.

- Observe a preschool program. Notice and list all written forms found in the playroom that are within the children's view. Report the findings to classmates.

- Find some examples of young children's attempts to make letters and numerals in their drawings. What do you notice about the symbols? Are the lines large, small, slanted, or straight? Are capitals or small letters used? What else do you notice?

- Invite a first-grade teacher to speak to the class about methods used to teach print-script in the classroom.

- List all the marking tools you find in a classroom you've chosen to visit.

- What print awareness activities could be added to almost any classroom?

- Interview three practicing preschool teachers and ask how many preschool children within their care have displayed invented spelling.

Unit Review

A. Select the correct answer. Most questions have more than one answer.
  1. Child-care programs
     a. teach all children to print.
     b. try to teach correct printscript form.
     c. all teach the same printscript form.
     d. help children with printing attempts.
  2. Small-muscle control
     a. comes after large-muscle control.
     b. depends on many factors.
     c. is difficult for some preschoolers.
     d. is the only thing involved in learning to print.
  3. If drawings have upside-down alphabet letters, teachers should
     a. immediately begin printing lessons.
     b. know that the child may be interested in activities with printed forms.
     c. quickly tell the child that the letters are upside down.
     d. worry about the child's ability to form the letters perfectly.
  4. A child's readiness to print may depend on his or her
     a. ability to gather information from his or her senses.
     b. knowledge that letters are formed by placing lines.
     c. home and family.
     d. feelings for the teacher.

B. Place the following in the order in which they occur.
  1. a. small-muscle control
     b. large-muscle control
     c. control of fingers
  2. a. child makes letters
     b. child makes scribbles
     c. child makes circles
  3. a. teacher shows child how to make a *Y*
     b. child knows the name of the letter *Y*
     c. child says, "Teacher, make a *Y* on my paper."
  4. a. child tries to write
     b. child sees parent writing
     c. child prints the letter *b*

5. a. child prints letters in artwork
   b. teacher notices and encourages
   c. child knows the names of all the letters in the alphabet

C. Answer the following questions.
   1. What are some possible reasons that children ages two to five years may start to print?
   2. Give examples of preschool equipment that promotes small-muscle and finger control.
   3. What should teachers consider about the printscript form they use?
   4. Why are some preschoolers not interested in letters?
   5. Muscle control is only part of learning to write. Name other factors that affect readiness for written communication.
   6. When a child says, "Is this *M*?" how should one reply?
   7. If a child is not interested in printing, what should be done?
   8. If a child says a *b* is an *f*, what might a teacher say?

References

Atkins, C. "Writing: Doing Something Constructive," *Young Children* 40.6 (Nov. 1984): 31–36.

Balaban, Nancy. "What Do Young Children Teach Themselves?" *Childhood Education* 33.2 (April/May 1980): 56–61.

Berg, Leila. *Reading and Loving.* Henley and Boston: Routledge and Kegan, 1977.

Brittain, W. Lambert. "Analysis of Artistic Behavior in Young Children." Final Report, *ERIC*, *ED* 128 091, Ithaca: Cornell Univ., March 1973.

Caulkins, Lucy McCormick. Speech given at Columbia University, 1979.

Charlesworth, Rosalind. "Readiness — Should We Make Them Ready Or Let Them Bloom?" *Day Care and Early Education* 11.4 (Spring 1985): 53–58.

Chomsky, Carol. "Write Now, Read Later." *Childhood Education* 47.2 (August/September 1971): 42–47.

Durkin, Dolores. *Children Who Read Early.* New York: Teachers College Press, 1969.

Dyson, A. H. "Oral Language: The Rooting System For Learning to Write." *Language Arts* 58.3 (Oct. 1987): 86–92.

Fields, Marjorie V., and Dorris Lee. *Let's Begin Reading Right.* Columbus, OH: Charles E. Merrill, 1987.

Hayward, Ruth Ann. "Inside The Whole Language Classroom." *Instructor* 97.9 (Oct. 1988): 15–19.

Jewell, Margaret Greer, and Miles V. Zintz. *Learning to Read Naturally.* Dubuque: Kendall/Hunt, 1986.

Kane, Frances. "Thinking, Drawing — Writing, Reading." *Childhood Education* 33.5 (May/June 1982): 292–297.

Lay-Dopyera, Margaret, and John E. Dopyera. *Becoming a Teacher of Young Children.* Lexington, MA: D.C. Heath, 1982.

Lesser, G. *Children and Television.* New York: Random House, 1974.

Lewis, E. R., and H. P. Lewis. "Which Manuscript Letters Are Hard For First Graders?" *Elementary English* Dec. 1964.

List, Hindy. "Kids Can Write The Day They Start School." *Early Years* 15.3 (Jan. 1984): 40–51.

Markham, Lynda R. "Assisting Speakers Of Black English As They Begin To Write." *Young Children* 39.5 (May 1984): 81–88.

Montessori, Maria. *The Absorbent Mind.* New York: Holt, Rinehart, and Winston, 1967.

Paul, R. "Invented Spelling in the Kindergarten." *Young Children* 31 (Mar. 1976): 78–85.

Schickedanz, Judith A. *More Than The ABCs.* Washington, DC: NAEYC, 1986.

_____. "The Acquisition of Written Language in Young Children." *Handbook of Research in Early Childhood Education.* Ed. Bernard Spodek. New York: The Free Press, 1982.

Throne, Jeanette. "Becoming A Kindergarten of Readers?" *Young Children* 43.6 (Sept. 1988): 10–16.

Thurber, Donald. "Teaching Handwriting." Glenview, IL: Scott, Foresman, 1988.

Vukelich, C., and J. Golden. "Early Writing: Development and Teaching Strategies." *Young Children* 39.5 (Jan. 1984): 37–45.

UNIT 19

Developing Print Awareness and Skill

OBJECTIVES

After studying this unit, you should be able to

- make the full printscript uppercase and lowercase alphabet.
- list three ways printscript is used daily.
- describe equipment and settings that can be used for printscript development.
- plan print-awareness activities.

There are a number of professional teacher techniques and behaviors that build children's awareness and knowledge of print and printing. To gain insight into why preschool teachers act in certain ways and say certain things to young children examine the following.

- Print sends a message. It is ideas, talk, or communication in written form.
- Print has many uses.
- People can read printed words and understand them.
- Each print mark is called a letter or symbol.
- The alphabet is the name of the customary listing of letters used in the English language. There are 26 alphabet letters.
- Each alphabet letter has a name.
- Each alphabet letter has a different shape.
- Each alphabet letter has a sound. Some have more than one sound.
- Each alphabet letter can be written in uppercase and lowercase.
- All printed words are single letters or combinations of letters.

- Words are read and written from left to right in rows.
- Words in a written message have open spaces between them.
- People can use pictures and marks instead of alphabet letters to send communications.

Most planned activities in this language arts area, and most unplanned child-adult exchanges during the school day, involve one of the above basic understandings. Rules exist in this graphic art as they do in speech. Children form ideas about these rules as they did with oral communication.

Print concerns the use of graphic symbols that represent sounds and sound combinations. Symbols combine and form words and sentences in a prescribed grammatical order. Alphabet letters are spaced and are in uppercase and lowercase form. They are written and read from left to right across a page. Margins exist at beginnings and ends of lines, and lines go from the top to bottom of pages. Punctuation marks end sentences, and indentations separate paragraphs. It is amazing how many rules of printing that interested children discover on their own.

DAILY INTERACTIONS AND TECHNIQUES

The techniques listed in this section are purposeful actions and verbalizations used by teachers in print-script instruction. The teacher uses a natural conversational style rather than a formal teaching tone.

Putting the children's names on their work is the most common daily use of printscript. The teacher asks the children whether they want their names on their work. Many young children feel their creations are their very own and may not want a name added. When a paper is lost because it has no name on it, children see the advantage of printing a name on belongings.

All names are printed in the upper left-hand corner of the paper if possible (figure 19-1). This is done to train the children to look at this spot as a preparation

FIGURE 19-1 Children's names are printed in the upper left-hand corner. How would you describe these teacher-printed children's names?

for reading and writing. Children's comments about their work can be jotted down along the bottom or back of their papers. As Donoghue (1985) points out:

> When pupils verbalize satisfactorily, their oral experiences provide meaningful vocabularies for first writing experiences. They enjoy listening to stories as well as composing and sending written messages. They should have many opportunities to dictate stories, poems, reports, plans, ideas and funny and frightening incidents. When writing for the pupils, the teacher is not only introducing them to writing and reading, but she is also helping to bridge a gap between oral and written language.

The teacher can be prepared to do this by having a dark crayon or felt-tip pen in a handy place or pocket. Dictation is written without major teacher editing or suggestions concerning the way it is said. The teacher can tell the child that the teacher will be writing down the child's ideas and then follow the child's word order as closely as possible. Some teachers prefer to print the statement "Chou dictated these words to Mrs. Brownell on May 2, 1989," before or after the child's message. Most teachers would print the child's "mouses went in hole" as "mice went in the hole," which is minor editing. All teacher printing should be in printscript, using both uppercase and lowercase letters and proper punctuation.

When a child asks a teacher to print, the teacher stands behind the child and works over the child's shoulder (when possible) (figure 19-2). This way the child sees the letters being formed in the correct position. If the teacher faces the child while printing, the child sees the letters upside down. Some teachers say the letter names as they print them.

Letters or names written for the child should be large enough for the child to distinguish the different forms — over one inch high. This may seem large to an adult (figure 19-3).

Some children will attempt printing and ask questions. Each center should clarify its staff responses to ensure that they are in agreement with the center's language arts program goals and to avoid confusion. Phonetic sounds of alphabet letters are preferred in some centers rather than the names of letters. "What's this called?" is answered by "It says m-m-m." Both the letter name and its sound are offered in other centers, a somewhat difficult proposition when letters repre-

FIGURE 19-2 When possible, reach over the child's shoulder to print what the child has requested.

Maryellen Donald

FIGURE 19-3 Letters should be large enough for the child to see easily.

FIGURE 19-4 A teacher can ask an interested child whether he or she would like the teacher to print a particular alphabet letter.

senting more than one sound are encountered. The Appendix includes a phonetic guide to English alphabet letter pronunciation.

Some schools encourage teachers to print examples on lined paper if a child says, "Make an *a*" or "Write my name." Others suggest that teachers blend letter sounds as they print words. Many centers expect teachers to respond to the child's request through conversation and by searching for letters on alphabet charts. This encourages the child to make his or her own copy before the teacher automatically prints it.

Teacher techniques often depend on the circumstances of a particular situation and knowledge of the individual child. What works with one child may not work with the next child (figure 19-4).

One technique common to all centers is supportive assistance and voiced appreciation of children's efforts. As Fields and Lee (1987) suggest, we can rejoice with a young child over approximations of intent in writing, just as we do with a toddler who makes an imprecise attempt to say a new word.

Children may show their printing attempts to the teacher or point out the names of letters they know. A positive statement to the child is appropriate: "Yes, that is an *a*" or "I can see the *a, t,* and *p*" (as the teacher points to each), or "Marie, you did print letters."

With these comments, the teacher encourages and recognizes the child's efforts. Often, the child may have the wrong name or form for a letter. The teacher can react by saying, "It looks like an alphabet letter. Let's go look at our alphabet and see which one" (figure 19-5).

Atkins (1984) describes supportive assistance in the following way:

As they experiment with writing, children need supportive adults. They need adults to provide the

FIGURE 19-5 Letters and words are planned for children's viewing.

tools needed for writing and the time and opportunity to use those tools. They need adults to ensure an atmosphere conducive to exploration and to good feelings about writing. They need adults to accept what is written as worthwhile, and to appreciate the work and effort that goes into learning to write. And, children especially need adults who understand that the errors they make are an important part of the learning process.

The same acceptance and lack of correction on a teacher's part that was suggested with beginning speakers is appropriate for beginning writers. Encourage, welcome, and keep interest in print alive by providing attention. Children have many years ahead to perfect their skill; the most important thing at this early stage is that they are interested in the forms and are supplied with correct models and encouragement.

One technique is to have children who ask for letter forms trace over correct letter models or symbols. This can be done with crayons, felt pens, or other writing tools. To explain the meaning of the word "trace," the teacher gives the child a demonstration.

When reading charts or books to children, a teacher may move his or her hand across the page beneath words. This is done to emphasize the left to right direction in reading and writing and separations between

words. Introducing authors' names periodically helps children realize that they also can create stories, and what they create can be written.

PRINT IN DAILY LIFE

As Fields (1987) has stated, children need to learn what print can do for them in satisfying personal needs. This means something to them; it makes print real. As Throne (1988) notes "children become aware of print by using it for real and meaningful purposes when they dictate and write stories, make signs for the block area, read names on a job chart, write messages, look for EXIT signs, follow recipes, or listen to stories." Children may need teacher assistance in recognizing the usefulness of written messages. Many instances of sending or reading print messages are possible during a school day. Making signs about room areas, using waiting lists, and sending letters or cards to absent children or adults are just a few suggestions.

Since print often protects one's safety, there are many opportunities to discuss and point out words that serve this function. Labels and trademarks on classroom items and printed instructions for using certain items offer opportunities for discussing print.

Print activities include dramatic play with themes that involve print and printing labels for many dramatic play props (figure 19-6). Also, Rich (1985) urges preschool teachers to encourage young children to start personal journals in which the children draw, dictate, and write (if able).

LEFT-HANDED CHILDREN

Left-handedness or right-handedness occurs as the child's nervous system matures. Preschool teachers notice hand preferences when children use writing tools. Some children seem to switch between hands as though hand preference hasn't been established. Most left-handers uses their right hands more often than right-handers use their left hands. Writing surfaces in preschools should accommodate all children. Preschools purchase both right-handed and left-handed scissors.

Teachers should accept hand preference without attempting to change or even point out a natural choice. Seating left-handed children at the ends of

Play Themes

Classroom Post Office

Suggested play items:

Stamps (many come with magazine advertisements), old letters, envelopes, boxes to wrap for mailing, scale, canceling stamp, tape, string, play money, mailbag, mailbox with slots, alphabet strips, writing table, felt pens, counter, postal-employee shirts, posters from post office, stamp-collector sheets, wet sponge, teacher-made chart that lists children by street address and zip codes, box with all children's names on printed individual strips, mailboxes for each child.

Taco Stand

Suggested play items:

Counter for customers, posted charts with prices and taco choices, play money, order pads, labeled baskets with colored paper taco items (including cheese, meat, lettuce, salsa, sour cream, avocado, shredded chicken, and onions), customer tables, trays, bell to ring for service, folded cards with numbers, receipt book for ordered tacos, plastic glasses and pitchers, cash register, napkins, tablecloth, plastic flowers in plastic vase, cook's jacket, waiter/waitress aprons, bus-person suit and cleaning supplies, taped ethnic music, plastic utensils, soft pencils or felt pens, line with clothespins to hang orders, paper plates.

A hamburger stand or pizza parlor are other possibilities.

Grocery Shopping

Suggested items:

Shopping-list paper, bookcase, pencils or felt pens, chart with cut magazine pictures or labels from canned goods or vegetables labeled in print by teacher for children to copy if they desire, empty food cartons and cans, plastic food, shopping cart, purse and wallet, play money, brown bags, cash register on box, dress-up clothes for customers and store clerks.

Letter-Writing Classroom Center
(for writing to relatives and friends)

Print-Awareness Activities

Classroom Newspaper

Make a class newspaper. Print children's dictated news or creative language after sharing a local paper with them. Child drawings on ditto master can be duplicated. Add teacher and parent news, poems, captions, drawings, and so forth. Some children may wish to print their own messages. These may range from scribble to recognizable forms and words.

T-Shirt Autograph Day

Each parent is asked to bring an old T-shirt (any size) to school for T-shirt autograph day. Permanent felt markers are used by children under teacher supervision. (Washable markers can also be used, but teachers must iron or put T-shirts in a clothes dryer for five minutes on a hot setting.) T-shirt forms are necessary, and can be made of cardboard. Material must be stretched over form so marks can be added easily. It is a good idea to have children wear plastic paint aprons to protect clothing from permanent markers. Children are free to autograph shirts in any manner they please. A display of T-shirts with writing usually prompts some children to add letters to their own shirts. Most teachers own or can borrow T-shirts with writing.

Additional print-awareness activities can be found in Unit 20.

FIGURE 19-6 Dramatic play themes and activities that promote print awareness and use

tables when possible during activities or making sure left-handers are not crowded against right-handers is a prudent course of action.

PRACTICING AND PROMOTING PRINT AWARENESS

Printscript should come automatically to the teacher. Practice is in order if one cannot easily and correctly print the entire alphabet in both uppercase and lowercase. Before practicing, obtain a local printscript guide from a neighboring elementary school.

To promote interest in printscript or symbols, a teacher can:

- Make labels for familiar objects.
- Make signs that fit in with child's play:
    John and Jerry's Service Station
    Quiet Please
    Don't Walk on the Grass
    Cookies for Sale
- Create wall displays with words (figure 19-7).
- Make alphabet charts.

FIGURE 19-8 Poetry chart

FIGURE 19-7 Wall displays using print are found in a print-rich classroom.

- Make charts with words (figure 19-8).
- Make alphabet and number games.
- Make word games.
- Print stories of children's experiences, as children tell them (figure 19-9).
- Point out words in the environment.
- Point out symbols in the environment.
- Print children's names on artwork.
- Supply scrap paper and a variety of writing tools.
- Make table chalkboards.

The Picnic

We had lunch
in the park
We sat
on the grass

FIGURE 19-9 An example of an experience chart

- Cut letters in colorful felt, cloth, sandpaper, and tagboard.
- Help children make their own creative or informative books.
- Make clever name tags.
- Make giant alphabet letters.
- Have children dictate captions for their own photographs (figure 19-10).
- Send written messages to children and staff.

Lined Paper

Many companies manufacture lined printing paper for beginners. Some preschoolers acquire the necessary motor control and can use this type of paper. One resource for lined paper is:

Modern Education Corp.
P.O. Box 721
Tulsa, OK 74101

Primary (lined) chart paper is available from:

Union Paper Company
P.O. Box 24164
Oakland, CA 94623

Lines can easily be drawn on a chalkboard by the teacher. This provides a large working surface and an opportunity for children to make large-size letters.

FIGURE 19-10 Displays that pair photographs and labeling words are popular.

Chart Ideas

Printscript can be added to playrooms by posting charts that have been made by the teacher. Charts can be designed to encourage the child's active involvement. Pockets, parts that move, or pieces that can be added or removed add extra interest. Charts made on heavy chart board or cardboard last longer. Clear contact paper can be used to seal the surface. Some ideas for charts include:

- color or number charts
- large clock with movable hands
- chart showing the four seasons

- picture story sequence charts
- calendar
- room task chart ("helpers chart")
- texture chart (for children to feel)
- poetry chart
- recipe chart using step-by-step illustrations
- classification or matching-concepts chart
- birthday charts

- height and weight chart
- alphabet chart
- rebus chart (figure 19-11)

In making a chart, first draw sketches of the way words and pictures could be arranged. With a yardstick, lightly draw on guidelines with a pencil or use a chart liner (figure 18-14, page 326). Then, printscript

FIGURE 19-11 Rebus chart

words with a felt pen or dark crayon. Magazines, old elementary school workbooks, old children's books, and photographs are good sources for picture charts. Brads or paper fasteners can be used for movable parts. Book pockets or heavy envelopes provide a storage place for items to be added later to the chart.

Experience Charts

The purpose of these charts is to have children recognize that spoken words can be put in written form.

Materials:

large paper sheets (newsprint), felt pen or black crayon

Activity:

After an interesting activity, such as a field trip, visit by a special speaker, party, celebration, or cooking experience, the teacher can suggest that a story be written about the experience. A large sheet of paper or chart sheet is hung within the children's view, and the children dictate what happened. The teacher prints on the sheet, helping children sort out what happened first, next, and last.

Figures 19-12 and 19-13 show examples of other word and picture charts.

Homemade chart stands (figure 19-14) can be made by teachers. Commercial chart holders, chart stands, and wing clamps are sold at school supply stores. The alphabet patterns in figure 19-15 (page 344) are useful for teacher-made games, wall displays, and bulletin boards.

Chart Books

A number of books called chart or easel books are in print. These giant books are poster size and easily capture children's attention. The print stands out and can't be missed. Creative teachers have produced their own versions with the help of overhead projectors that enlarge smaller artwork. Chart paper or poster board is used. Two commercial big book titles are *Have You Seen Birds?* and *The New Baby Calf*, both published by Scholastic. Posters with large print are available from The Children's Book Council, Inc., 67 Irving Place, New York, NY 10003.

Jeanette Throne (1988), a kindergarten teacher, points out the benefit of using big books and charts: "...these shared experiences bring the benefits of the bedtime story situation into the classroom because the

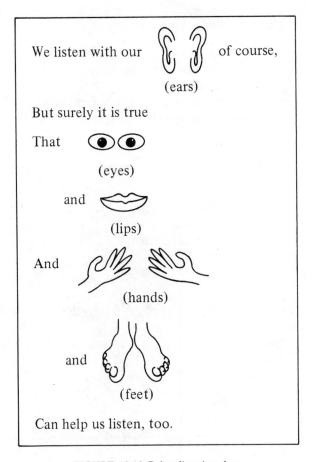

FIGURE 19-12 Rebus listening chart

large, clear print allows the whole class to see the text as we read the story together." Although preschools prefer to use smaller child groups, Throne's comments concerning large, clear print and group sharing appeal to teachers interested in promoting print awareness.

PARENT COMMUNICATION

A conversation with or note to the parents of a child who has asked about or started printing can include the following:

- The teacher has noticed the child's interest in printing alphabet letters, numerals, and/or words.
- The teacher is including a printscript and numeral guide for parents who wish to show their children the letter forms at home.

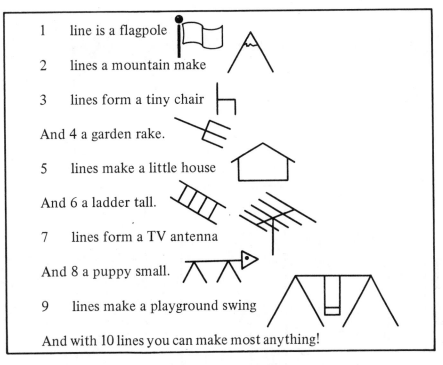

1   line is a flagpole

2   lines a mountain make

3   lines form a tiny chair

And 4 a garden rake.

5   lines make a little house

And 6 a ladder tall.

7   lines form a TV antenna

And 8 a puppy small.

9   lines make a playground swing

And with 10 lines you can make most anything!

FIGURE 19-13 Lines chart

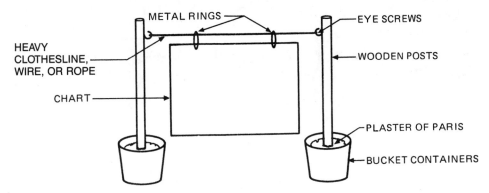

FIGURE 19-14 Homemade chart stand

- The early childhood center encourages printing attempts but does not try to teach printscript to every child. Many children are not interested, and others would find it too difficult at their present developmental level.
- A parent can help by having paper and writing tools for the child at home and by noticing and giving attention to the child when he or she comes to the parent with written letters.
- Children who start printing early often write letters and numerals in their paintings. The printing may be backwards, upside down, or sideways; this is to be expected. (Many parents worry unnecessarily when this is noticed.)

FIGURE 19-15 These letters are about 2 inches high. They are useful patterns for games, wall displays, and bulletin boards. (Note: All of the alphabet letters are not included.)

Centers plan parent meetings for joint discussion of the appropriateness of printing instruction during preschool years. Directors encounter well-meaning but anxious parents who want their children to learn the alphabet and learn to print. Some parents feel that neglecting this area will place their children at a disadvantage. If the center's position is clear, staff members will be able to give articulate answers concerning the center's programming. Most parents are responsive

FIGURE 19-15 *Continued*

when teachers explain to them that the primary goal is to enhance their children's self-concept and that it is pointless to teach children the alphabet if the only purpose served is pleasing adults. The assurance teachers give parents that they will provide both basic experiences and opportunities on an individual basis most often satisfies the parents' need to know that the school cares about each child's progress.

FIGURE 19-15 *Continued*

Summary

Equipment and settings for giving children an opportunity to explore printing are available in a childhood center. Materials are arranged within reach. Printing seen on wall displays and charts helps motivate interest.

Printscript is used in a variety of ways. The most common is in planned activities and labeling artwork. A name or sentence should start in the upper left hand corner and move toward the right.

Teachers need to examine printscript closely and practice so that good models can be supplied. It is also important to encourage children and to recognize their efforts, even if they cannot make correct forms.

Parents should be alerted to children's printing attempts and to the center's policy and practices concerning this language arts skill.

Student Activities

- Use the following checklist to observe a four-year-old or five-year-old child. Interview the child's teacher for items you were unable to determine. (Note: Make sure the teacher knows that this is not a test but an instrument to make you aware of children's emerging abilities.)

Checklist of Print Interest and Understandings

Rate each item as follows.   Y = Most of the time
                             S = Sometimes
                             H = Hasn't attempted as yet
                             U = Unable to determine

The child:

_____ Sits through a book reading and enjoys it.

_____ Asks for a book's rereading.

_____ "Reads" parts or lines of a book to another from memory.

_____ Shows an interest in alphabet letters.

_____ Shows an interest in books or environmental print.

_____ Reads children's name tags or signs.

_____ Puts alphabet letters in artwork.

_____ Knows when words are skipped in favorite books.

_____ Plays with marking tools.

_____ Shares written letters or words with others.

_____ Points to print in the work of others.

_____ Wants name and/or labels on work.

_____ Wants to write own name on work.

_____ Knows that print says something.

_____ Produces a row of symbols.

_____ Attempts to copy symbols, letters, or words.

_____ Reads symbols he or she has written.

_____ Invents spellings.

_____ Discusses a use of print.

_____ Knows print can be read.

_____ Wants his or her talk written down.

_____ Recognizes individual alphabet letters.

_____ Recognizes words that start with the same letter.

_____ Can read some environmental signs.

_____ Follows along in chart activities.

_____ Looks at books while alone.

_____ Has an active interest in something else that then gives a low priority to literary activities.

_____ Which statement best describes this child?

    a. Yet to develop an interest in print.

    b. A possible interest is developing.

    c. Has about the same degree of interest as others his or her age.

    d. Has a fairly strong interest.

    e. Has a continual interest that has led to experimentation and printing attempts.

    f. Is very interested in some other area that takes up his or her time and energy.

    g. Prints almost daily and has invented spellings or spells many words correctly.

- Obtain an order catalog from a preschool supply store or company. Most companies will send the catalogs free of charge. Professional magazines such as *Young Children, Pre-K Today, Instructor, Early Years,* and *Scholastic Teacher* are good sources for finding supply-catalog addresses. Make a list of any pieces of equipment or supply items that could be used to promote printing.

- Watch the children's use of crayons or other writing tools. Take notes. Make observations about the following:

    a. Time spent with marking tools.

    b. Manner used (for example, how do the children hold the crayons?).

    c. Do they have good control of both paper and marking tool?

- Place a pile of paper and two or three felt pens in bright colors on a table. (Pencils are not used often because of safety considerations and the need for sharpening.) Supervise the activity closely — let only two or three children work at a time. Make a waiting list. Then give each interested child a turn. How many of the children tried to make letters? How many said "yes" when you asked them if they wanted you to add their names to their papers?

- Make three sketches of an early childhood chart that uses printscript words. Design a chart that involves child interaction rather than just child attention.

- Design and make one preschool chart.

- Examine three types of felt markers. Look for the words *nontoxic* and *washable.* Report your findings.

Unit Review

A. Answer the following questions.

    1. If a child goes to a teacher to show letters he or she has drawn, how should the teacher react?

    2. If two children are arguing over the name of a letter, how should the teacher handle the situation?

    3. List three ways a teacher can use printscript during the school day.

B. Print the printscript (or D'Nealian, see Unit 18) alphabet in both uppercase and lowercase. Also print the numerals 1 through 10.

C. Referring to figure 19-16, list all of the things the teacher might have done to encourage the children's attempts.

D. Select the correct answer. All have more than one answer.
1. When a child's first name is to be printed on his or her work, it should be
   a. in the center on top.
   b. in the upper right-hand corner.
   c. in the upper left-hand corner.
   d. done with an uppercase first letter and then lowercase letters.
2. The size of the printscript used with young children
   a. doesn't really matter.
   b. should be large enough to see.
   c. can be of any size.
   d. should be at least two inches high.
3. The teacher who does not know how to form printscript letters can
   a. practice.
   b. use an individual style.
   c. get a copy from an elementary school.
   d. write instead.

E. Print your full name and address in printscript.

F. A note to the parents of a child who is interested in learning to print should include what kind of information? State four points that should be included.

G. Describe your handling of the following situations:
1. Mrs. Mason (parent) insists her child must learn to print because her child's friend has learned.
2. Betsy never wants her name written on her artwork.
3. Chris says, "My *a* is better than Sam's, huh, teacher?"

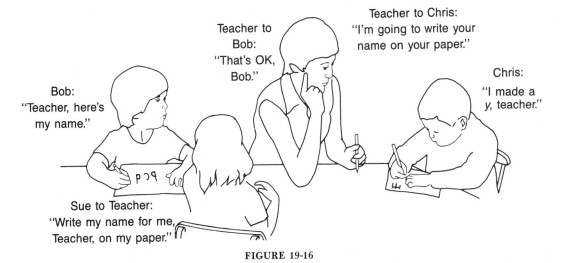

FIGURE 19-16

References

Atkins, C. "Writing: Doing Something Constructive." *Young Children* 40.6 (Nov. 1984): 31–36.

Donoghue, Margaret R. *The Child and The English Language Arts*. Dubuque, IA: William C. Brown, 1985.

Fields, Marjorie V. Conference Presentation, NAEYC Conference, Chicago, 1987.

Fields, Marjorie V., and Dorris Lee. *Let's Begin Reading Right*. Columbus, OH: Charles E. Merrill, 1987.

Littlefield, Patti. "Helping Lefties at Home, School." *Parent Press* 5.10 (Oct. 1984): 5–6.

Montessori, Maria. *The Absorbent Mind*. New York: Holt, Rinehart, and Winston, 1967.

Rich, S. J. "The Writing Suitcase." *Young Children* 40.5 (November 1985): 31–36.

Throne, Jeanette. "Becoming A Kindergarten Of Readers." *Young Children* 43.6 (Sept. 1988): 10–16.

UNIT 20

Activities With Printscript

OBJECTIVES

After studying this unit, you should be able to

- describe a variety of printscript and symbol activities.
- plan and present a printscript activity.

Activities in this unit deal with symbols, letters, and words. The activities range from symbol awareness with symbols such as circles, squares, triangles, and other geometric and common shapes, to those in which the child is exposed to printscript letters and words. Note that the activities in this unit are samples of activity ideas. Teachers should select those that meet the needs of particular children or groups of children in their own classrooms.

Clay-on Patterns

These patterns can be used to enhance small-manipulative-muscle use and tracing skills.

Materials:
clay and contact-covered cardboard sheets with patterns (figure 20-1).

Activity:
Child rolls and forms clay over the cardboard patterns (figure 20-2).

Connecting Dots

The dot patterns for this activity can be made quickly by the teacher on paper or chalkboard and used as a free-play choice (figure 20-3). The purpose of this activity is to enhance small-muscle use and children's skills in forming and recognizing symbols.

Materials:
paper and writing tools (or chalkboard and chalk)

Activity:
Dots are connected to form symbols (figure 20-4).

Sorting Symbols

This activity enhances small-muscle use and the children's skills discriminating symbol differences.

Materials:
paper, writing tool, scissors, paste

Activity:
After the teacher cuts the symbols in squares from sheets, the children are asked to mix them all together and then find the ones that are the same to paste onto another sheet of paper.

Variation:
The teacher can make a cardboard set of symbols that can be sorted by children as a table game (figure 20-5).

FIGURE 20-1 Patterns

FIGURE 20-2 Clay-on patterns activity

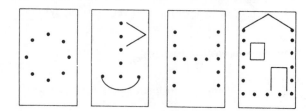

FIGURE 20-3 Connecting-dots activity

FIGURE 20-4 When dots are connected, they form symbols.

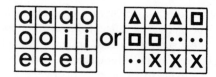

FIGURE 20-5 Symbol cards for sorting game

Aa	Bb	Cc	Dd	Ee	Ff	Gg	Hh	Ii	Jj

FIGURE 20-6 Printscript alphabet line

Alphabet Song

The rhyming song is an easy and fun way for children to recognize letter names.

Materials:
a long printscript alphabet line (figure 20-6).

Song:
ABCDEFG
HIJKLMNOP
QRSTU and V
WX and Y and Z.
Now I've said my ABCs,
Tell me what you think of me.

Activity:
Children sing the song while one child or the teacher touches the corresponding letter on the alphabet line. The teacher can ask the group to sing slowly or quickly, in a whisper or a loud voice, or in a high or low voice.

Gift Wrap

Children are given the opportunity to creatively wrap gifts while learning the usefulness of print.

Materials:
empty boxes, wrapping paper, scissors, decorative stickers, thin-line markers, list that includes the names of all in the class (including teachers), stamps, masking tape, card strips or paper strips

preprinted with "To" and "From," small inexpensive gift items or clay child-made objects

Activity:
Children wrap the gifts in boxes with wrapping paper and dictate messages or try to write names on paper or card strips.

Secret Words

This activity promotes visual discrimination and children's recognition of symbols.

Materials:
white crayon, white paper, water colors, and brush

Activity:
The teacher uses white crayon to write a symbol or word on white paper. The crayon should be heavy. The teacher demonstrates how the symbol appears when water color is painted over the whole paper. The children can guess the shape names.

Sticker Pictures

The children are shown the relationship between objects and words.

Materials:
stickers, paper strips, felt markers

Activity:
The teacher has each child choose a sticker for his or her paper strip. The child names the sticker, and if the child desires, the teacher writes the name of the sticker on back of strip. The children can then decorate the sticker strips.

Label Fun

The children recognize the print word forms for classroom objects.

Materials:
press-on labels (large size), felt marker

Activity:
Each child is given 5 to 10 labels and told to choose 10 items on the child's body or in the room on which he or she will stick word labels. Child is told to stick labels on something which has not been labeled by another. Teacher prints child's dictated word(s).

Alphabet Walk

This is another group activity to promote children's recognition of alphabet letters.

Materials:
large newsprint art paper, felt marker or dark crayon, masking tape

Activity:
The teacher makes giant letters on art paper, one letter per sheet. The children are told that the teacher is going to place giant letters around the room, and the children are going to choose a child to stand by a letter and wait to be told how the chosen child should move to get to the next one. Have four children choose four friends to walk to the letter A, which teacher points out to them. Teacher selects another child to think of a way, besides walking, that the four children can move to the second letter. The teacher can give suggestions like crawling, hopping, tiptoeing, walking like an elephant, and so forth. Children clap for first four, and another four are selected and directed to walk to another letter.

Find Your Shoe

This group activity shows the usefulness of print.

Materials:
press-on labels, marking pen

Activity:
The children are asked to take off their shoes and put them in front of them. The teacher asks what will happen to the shoes if everyone puts the shoes in one pile and the teacher mixes up the pile. The teacher introduces the idea that shoes would be easier to find if the children's names were added to each shoe by putting a press-on label on the inner sole. Labels are given to each child preprinted with the child's name. The child puts the labels on his or her shoes. The shoes go in a pile, which the teacher mixes. Each child describes his or her shoes to a friend and asks the friend to find the shoes. Two or three friends look in the pile for the shoes at a time. The rest chant "Shoes, shoes come in red, white, and blues... Shoes, shoes we will count to 10 and then back to your place and sit again." (Slowly) "1, 2, 3, 4..."

Alphabet Potato Prints

The children recognize letter names.

Materials:

potatoes, sharp knife (for teacher's use), thick paint, paper, flat containers

Activity:

The teacher cuts potato halves into letters or symbols. Some letters need to be reversed for printing. Prints are made by children.

Alphabet Macaroni Prints

This activity promotes shape discrimination and small-muscle activity.

Materials:

alphabet soup macaroni (sand, rice, or salt can also be used), glue and brushes, paper, felt pen

Activity:

Each child traces his or her name or a shape by painting over lines with thinned white glue. The macaroni is then spooned over the glue. When the glue is dry, shake the loose macaroni into a container. The end result will be raised textured letters (figure 20-7). The teacher should demonstrate this process.

ABC "Paste-on" Group
Wall Poster

Small-muscle use and symbol recognition are enhanced.

Materials:

alphabet letters or words cut or torn from magazines or newspapers, large-size poster paper or chart paper

Activity:

A montage effect is created by having children paste letters where they choose on a piece of paper. During a period of one week, the children can return to the work and paste on more letters. At a group time, children are asked to point to three letters or words (or phrases) that they wish the teacher to read.

Alphabet Eaters

Large-muscle use and visual discrimination are enhanced.

Materials:

cards with printscript alphabet letters (small enough to be slipped into animal's mouth), sturdy boxes on which animal heads and alphabet strips are glued (holes are cut in the opposite sides of boxes so children can reach in for cards)

Activity:

A child selects a card and "feeds" it to the animal that has a similar alphabet letter on the strip under its mouth (figure 20-8).

Footprint Alphabet Walk

This promotes large-muscle use and symbol recognition.

Materials:

large cardboard (or cloth) on which 26 footprints have been traced, cardboard footprint cutouts each with a printscript alphabet letter (three sets can be made — lowercase, uppercase, and numerals, if desired), covered with clear contact paper or made from plasticlike material.

Activity:

Children place cutout footprints over footprint of the correct letter (figure 20-9).

Tracers

Tracers can be used over and over again. Waxy crayons or felt markers wipe off with a soft cloth. They can be used to help children recognize and discriminate among symbols and enhance small-muscle coordination.

Materials:

acetate or clear vinyl sheets, cardboard, scissors, strapping or masking tape, paper, felt pen

Construction:

Attach acetate to cardboard, leaving one side open to form a pocket. Make letter or word guide sheets. Simple pictures can also be used (figure 20-10).

FIGURE 20-7 Alphabet macaroni pictures

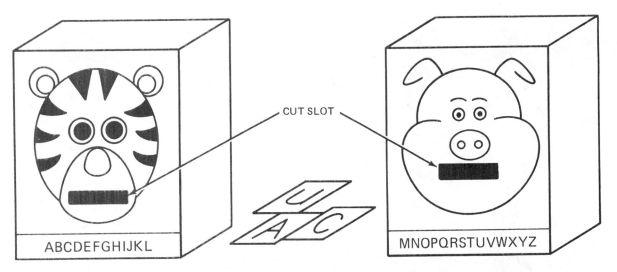

FIGURE 20-8 Alphabet "eaters" and cards

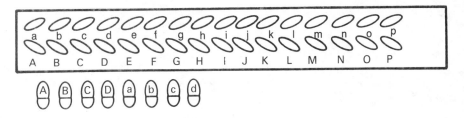

FIGURE 20-9 Footprint alphabet walk

Activity:

A child or the teacher selects a sheet and slips it into the tracer pocket. A wax crayon or marker is used by the child to trace the guide sheet. A soft cloth erases the crayon or marker (figure 20-11).

Alphabet Bingo

This promotes letter recognition and discrimination.

Materials:

cardboard, felt pen, scissors, pencil, ruler, paper, old pack of playing cards, glue, clear contact paper

Construction:

Cardboard is cut to make four or more 8½″ × 11″ sheets (any similar size is also suitable). Each sheet is divided into 9 or 12 sections. An alphabet letter is

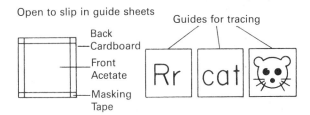

FIGURE 20-10 Tracers

added to each section. Make sure each sheet has a different combination of letters. Cover the sheets with clear contact paper. Turning to the pack of old playing cards, glue paper to the front side of each playing card. Add letters of the alphabet. Cover-

FIGURE 20-11 The child uses a tracer and wax crayon to make a picture.

ing the cards with clear contact paper will make the cards more durable. For markers, cut paper into small pieces; bottle caps or poker chips may also be used.

Activity:

The teacher passes out the sheets to the children. Holding up a playing card (with a letter on it), the teacher asks whether any child has that letter on his or her sheet. If so, the child should cover the letter with a marker. The game is over when every child who wishes completes his or her sheet. At that time, all markers are removed and a new game begins. Many four-year-olds are able to play this game without teacher help after playing it a few times.

His and Hers

This activity can help interested children learn to form print (figure 20-12) (from *Early Years* magazine, 1973).

Materials:

cardboard, paper clips, writing paper, scissors, clear contact paper

Construction:

Cut a 13″ × 15″ piece of cardboard. Place a 9″ × 12″ sheet of writing paper on the cardboard close to the bottom. Just above the top of the paper in the center of the board, cut out a rectangular shape. Put a paper clip through this opening and slip the writing paper under the clip. Print the child's name on a strip of the writing paper, place it above the opening in the cardboard, and cover it with clear contact paper.

Activity:

The children may use these pads to practice writing their names. Make similar practice pads for words, sentences, or paragraphs. (Note: Using clear contact paper on handmade learning devices will make them last longer. It is great for preserving magazine pictures, too.)

Popcorn Names

This promotes small-muscle use and symbol recognition.

Materials:

alphabet letters (drawn by the teacher on 8½″ × 11″ sheets), liquid white glue with brush or stick applicator, popcorn (which can be colored by the teacher

FIGURE 20-12 "His and Hers" activity (*From* Early Years Magazine, *His and Hers Activity, Reprinted with permission of the publishers, Allen Raymond, Inc., Darien, CT, January, 1973.*)

by shaking popcorn in a bag with dry tempera paint) (Note: Use a well ventilated area when working with dry tempera paint.)

Activity:
Children paste the popcorn on lines forming letters (figure 20-13).

Variation:
Colored fish tank rocks, fresh peas, pebbles, seeds, or salt can also be used.

DISPLAYS AND BULLETIN BOARDS

Interesting eye-level wall and bulletin board displays capture the children's attention and promote discussion. Displaying children's work (with children's permission), names, and themes based on their interests increases their feelings of accomplishment and their sense of pride in their classroom. Displays that involve active child participation are suggested. Many can be designed to change on a daily or weekly basis.

Printscript is used on bulletin boards with objects, pictures, or patterns. Book pockets, picture hooks, one-quarter-inch elastic attached to clothespins, and sticky bulletin board strips allow pieces to be added and removed. A helpful teacher resource for bulletin board ideas is Nursery School Bulletin Boards, Fearon-Pitman, 6 Davis Drive, Belmont, CA 94002. (See figures 20-14 and 20-15.)

One bulletin board idea is shown in figure 20-16. The child selects a spot to paste his or her picture (photo) and name. A colored line is drawn between the

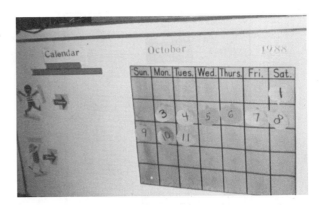

FIGURE **20-14** A wall calendar is used in many preschool programs.

FIGURE **20-15** Notice the variety of displays on the walls, using both words and pictures.

photo and name. Later, colored lines can be drawn connecting friends' pictures.

CHALKBOARD ACTIVITIES

One of the most underutilized instructional items in early childhood centers can be the chalkboard. The following chalkboard activities are suggested to help children's language development.

- *Tracing templates and colored chalk*
  Cut plastic coffee-can lids with a sharp tool into a variety of patterns (figure 20-17). Suspend the

FIGURE **20-13** Popcorn names

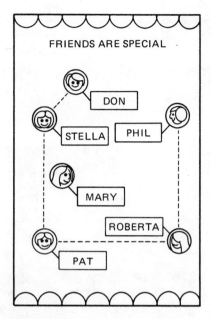

FIGURE 20-16 Bulletin board idea

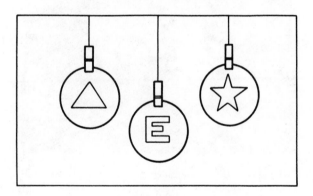

FIGURE 20-17 Coffee-lid blackboard activity

patterns on cord (or elastic with clothespins) over the chalkboard.
- *Pattern games with tracing template*
   Draw figure 20-18 on the chalkboard. Ask the children what shape comes next in the pattern. Then draw figure 20-19 and see whether the children can make a line path from the dog to the doghouse. These activities are very good for developing left-to-right skills needed for reading.

- *Guessing rebus messages* (for older preschoolers)
   The sets of pictures in figure 20-20 are put up on the chalkboard. The teacher asks the children to find the message by guessing the word for each picture. The teacher writes the correct words underneath the pictures.
- *Labeling pictures*
   Tape pictures like the ones in figure 20-21 (page 360) on the board with masking tape. Write identifying names dictated by children underneath each picture.
- *Daily helper identification*
   Make a chart with the children's names printed next to a picture of their jobs for the day (figure 20-22, page 360).
- *Mail us a postcard*
   Children going on trips are urged to have their parents mail postcards back to the school to be read to the group and discussed when the children return. The cards are then added to a classroom postcard display.

Chalk Talk
This motivates children's interest in letter forms.

Materials:
chalk, chalkboard, chalkboard eraser

Activity:
Teacher presents the rhyme and drawings on the chalkboard (figure 20-23, page 360). When the activity ends, ask whether anyone would like a turn at the chalkboard. A "line fence" on the chalkboard between children helps each to know his or her drawing area.

OTHER DRAWING ACTIVITIES

Words on Drawings
In this labeling activity, children select words that can be added to their drawings.

Materials:
felt pen or crayons

Activity:
The teacher asks each child individually whether words can be added to his or her painting, drawing, or illustration. Make sure the child realizes that the teacher is going to write on the drawing. It is a good idea to show the child what has been done to another

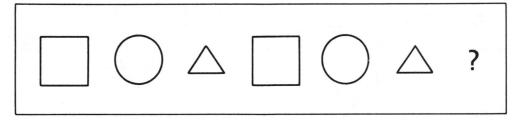

FIGURE 20-18 What comes next in the pattern?

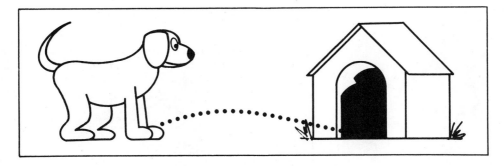

FIGURE 20-19 A left-to-right skill builder

FIGURE 20-20 Rebus messages

child's picture beforehand. Most children will want words added, but some will not. It is best to limit this activity to the children who are making symbols of faces, figures, houses, and so forth, in their work. Younger children might not be able to decide what to have written on their work when asked, "Would you like me to put a word name on something you've drawn in your picture?"

Rebus Stories

Teachers can use drawings or photographs to encourage child participation during story-telling time. At a crucial point in the story, the teacher pauses and holds up a picture, and the children guess the next word in the story. Teachers can name the picture and resume the story if the children haven't guessed the word. Any guess that is a close approximation is accepted; for example, "It is a truck, Josh, a fire truck." The rebus story in figure 20-24 (page 361) can easily be changed to call Fred or Fredricka a fire fighter, if preferred. Many additional teacher-created rebus stories are possible.

FIGURE 20-21 Children help identify the pictures.

COMMERCIAL MATERIALS

A number of school-supply manufacturers provide items that encourage or sustain an interest in alphabet letters. A partial list follows:

- "Desk Tape Manuscript Letter Line" by Instructo
- "Magnetic Alphabet Picture Board" by Child Guidance
- "Alphabet Practice Cards" by Ideal Toy Co.
- "Beaded Tactile-Kinesthetic Manuscript Cards" by Ideal Toy Co.
- "Wooden Alphabet Letters" by Instructo
- "Plastic Display Alphabet Letters" by Planet Greetings

Teachers can sometimes find ideas for homemade games from commercial suppliers' catalogs.

Peggy (Fish Feeder)

John (Waste Basket Passer)

FIGURE 20-22 Daily helper chart

DRAW A FISH

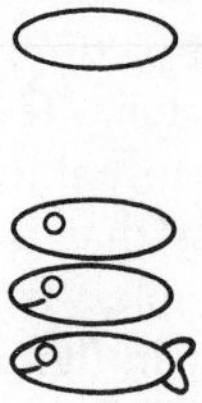

1. *I'll draw an oval*
   Like an egg in the sky.
   What comes next
2. *Why it's a little eye.*
3. *Next comes a mouth*
4. *And a tail to swish*
   Look at that
   I've made a fish!

FIGURE 20-23

FIREMAN FRED

This is Fireman Fred. This is the firehouse. This is Buttons.

[Fireman Fred] works in the [firehouse] on the corner. He and the other [firemen] keep the big [fire truck] polished and ready to go when the fire [bell] clangs. They have a black and white spotted [dog] named Buttons. He rides the [fire truck] when [Fireman Fred] goes to a [fire].

One night [Fireman Fred] and the other [firemen] were playing [checkers] in the [firehouse], and [Buttons] was sleeping. Suddenly the big fire [bell] rang. CLANG! CLANG! CLANG! The [firemen] quickly put on their fire [hats] and rubber [coats] and rubber [boots]. They all jumped on the [fire truck] and off they went. [Buttons] sat on the seat near [Fireman Fred]. WHOOOOO! went the [siren] CLANG! CLANG! CLANG! went the [bell]. BOW WOW WOW! went [Buttons]. When they reached the [fire], smoke was coming out of the [window] of a [house]. The [firemen] put a [ladder] up to the [window]. [Fireman Fred] grabbed a [hose] and climbed the [ladder]. WHOOSH! went the water, and the [fire] was out. [Fireman Fred] came down the [ladder] carrying a little [cat]. He handed it to the [girl] who lived in the [house]. [Buttons] licked the [cat] to be sure it was all right. "It was not a bad [fire]," said [Fireman Fred] to the [mother] and [father] of the [girl]. "You can all go back into the [house]." Then the [firemen] jumped on the [fire truck] and returned to the [firehouse]. They hung up their things neatly. [Fireman Fred] went back to his game of [checkers] and [Buttons] went back to sleep.

FIGURE 20-24 Fireman Fred *(From* Turtle *magazine, © 1988 by Children's Better Health Institute, Benjamin Franklin Literary & Medical Society, Inc. Used by permission of the Children's Better Health Institute, Benjamin Franklin Literary & Medical Society, Inc., Indianapolis, Indiana.)*

Student Activities

- Collect five printscript activity ideas from other resource books or create them yourself. Use the following format:

Title	Activity
Purpose	Construction (if any)
Materials	Variations (if any)

- Create a chalkboard activity.

- Use one of the activities from this unit with a group of children, or with one child, and answer the following questions.
  1. Was it of interest to the child or children?
  2. What was the purpose of the activity?
  3. How were printscript letters or symbols used?
  4. Were the children successful in the activity?

- Make up your own "chalk talk." A rhyme or simple story works well. Try out your creation on young children, and write a description of their reactions.

- Design an early childhood bulletin board. Specify how children will be involved.

- Discuss in a group three or four ways that four- and five-year-olds might discover the following:
  1. Speech can be written down.
  2. Print has meaning.
  3. Print starts at the left of the page.
  4. One reads print from the top to the bottom of a page.
  5. Each alphabet letter is different.

- Create a rebus story.

Unit Review

A. Name common symbols that might be used in designing activities with symbols.

B. What is the purpose of a line fence between children during chalkboard activities?

C. Why involve children in bulletin board displays?

D. List five ideas using printscript and child involvement in a wall display or bulletin board.

E. Describe ways in which bulletin boards and wall displays could be used to increase children's language arts skills.

Section 7

Reading

A Language Art

With elementary school techniques and academic instruction being offered in some preschools, beginning teachers wonder whether the teaching of reading skills should be part of every preschool's program of activities. Section 7 not only answers questions regarding this issue, but also provides an in-depth discussion of reading readiness and current instructional approaches in the teaching of reading.

Unit 22 deals with both teacher-made and commercially produced teaching materials available to enhance children's choice of activities. It provides useful and valuable ideas that can be used to vary both instructional activities and teacher presentations of the language arts.

WHAT IS THE WHOLE-LANGUAGE MOVEMENT, AND WILL IT AFFECT EARLY CHILDHOOD TEACHERS?

There is no simple definition of whole-language teaching. One almost has to pinpoint what it isn't to understand it! It has been called a philosophy (Ferguson, 1988), a movement (Rich, 1985), and an approach (Hayward, 1988). Its advocates have been seen as radical and political (Rich, 1985). It has usually been associated with elementary school teaching, particularly the teaching of reading. Early childhood teachers may see it as a spread of what has existed in early childhood programs for a long time because of its developmentally appropriate, child-centered instructional outlook.

Whole-language elementary school advocates have tossed out much of the commercial basal reading series materials and similar commercially packaged programs that have dominated classrooms in the past. Materials are now sought to fit attending children rather than accomplish someone's (the manufacturer's) identified objectives (Rich, 1985).

Each new whole-language-inspired teacher is struggling to offer a wide variety of classroom reading and writing materials arising from child needs, interests, and experiences. Every effort is made to point out the "utility" of the language arts — that is, what it can do for children and others on a daily basis.

Anyone trying to describe whole-language teaching will encounter its terminology including:

literature based
language rich
integration of language arts
print awareness
literacy developing
child based
theme planning
comprehension centered

A common thread uniting advocates is faith in children's natural ability as learners and a sense of caring for children and childhood (Rich, 1985).

Children are believed to learn to read and write through opportunity and exposure — using language, using writing, thinking about experiences, and reading or being read to (Hayward, 1988). Integration of oral and written language is seen as part of a total curriculum — all that is planned and offered (Goodman, 1986).

Whole-language teachers tend to band together, study together, share ideas, and attend workshops and conferences. The movement is growing rapidly, and teachers are redefining ideas about children's learning as they themselves learn a new way to teach (Rich, 1985).

Will the whole-language movement affect early childhood teachers? Yes, hopefully it will! It may strengthen the resolve to "boot dittos out the door" in those schools that seem to have had materials "filter down from above." It may give teachers additional ammunition to fight academic "bits-and-pieces" teaching, where four-year-olds are led into alphabet, number, or phonics instruction that has no connection to what interests them or is unrelated to some purpose in their daily lives. For this reason, some early childhood educators will stand up and cheer. Whole-language teachers are bound to seem more closely allied to developmentally appropriate instruction.

Hopefully, many early childhood professionals will be interested enough to look and study what's happening in the elementary school, for it may offer new dimensions to their teaching. The whole-language movement shouldn't be shrugged off with an "Oh, we have been doing just that for a long time!"

Ferguson, Phyllis. "Whole Language: A Global Approach to Learning." *Instructor* 97.9 (May 1988): 23–28.

Goodman, Kenneth. *What's Whole In Whole Language*. Portsmouth: Heinemann Educational Publishers, 1986.

Hayward, Ruth Ann. "Inside The Whole Language Classroom." *Instructor* 97.9 (May 1988): 15–19.

Rich, Sharon J. "Restoring Power To Teachers: The Impact of Whole Language." *Language Arts* 62.7 (Nov. 1985): 71–74.

UNIT 21

Reading and Preschoolers

At one time, it was thought that there was an age when all children became ready for reading instruction. That idea has changed to recognize that no two children learn in exactly the same way or at the same age. Some children who are in early childhood centers and kindergartens can read. Some have picked up the skill on their own; others have spent time with an older brother or sister, parents, or others.

Although reading is considered the fourth language art, this unit does not intend to suggest reading instruction for groups of young children or even encourage "sit-down" instruction for those 1% to 5% of children who can read words during preschool years.

READING

The language arts approach and whole-language approach to reading consider reading as one part of the communication process. The language arts are interrelated — not separate, isolated skills. The teacher is responsible for showing the relationship between the various areas of language arts. In other words, the goal is to help children understand that communication is a whole process in which speaking, listening, written symbols, and the reading of those symbols are closely connected (figure 21-1).

In the past, the logical connection between listening, speaking, written words, and reading was overlooked. The subjects were often taught as separate skills, and

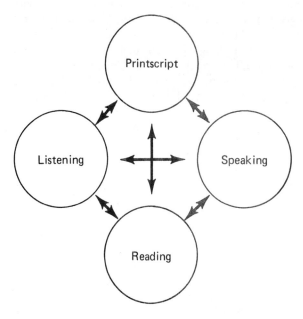

FIGURE 21-1 The four language arts are interrelated and interdependent.

365

the natural connection between each area was not clear to children. In a language arts, whole-language, or natural approach, the connection (the way these areas fit together) is emphasized.

The preschool teacher realizes that certain skills and abilities appear in children before others. Early learning in listening and speaking serve as beginnings for further language and communication. Children's beginning ideas about print, writing, and reading form concurrently, and children may display understanding and skill in all these areas.

Activities with young children can move easily from listening, speaking, seeing, or using printscript to beginning reading attempts: from passive to active participation. It is not uncommon for preschool youngsters to be able to read most of the names of the children in their group after being exposed to the daily use of name tags.

CURRENT THINKING CONCERNING EARLY READING INSTRUCTION

Professional literature currently urges preschool teachers to use an integrated approach to language arts as discussed above. Concerns over national literacy have promoted study and discussion. Most experts recommend a literature-based program for both elementary school and preschool. Ideal classrooms are described as "language rich" or "literacy developing," allowing for a preschool child's discovery of reading. Key ideas presently stress instruction offered in meaningful contexts with children developing strategies to achieve skills they view as useful to them. Lay-Dopyera and Dopyera (1982) point out that young children focus on the meaning of what they hear, including experiences with print in books and elsewhere. Some preschools have focused on reading mechanics (bits and pieces of the reading process), including practicing individual alphabet letter names, sounds, or phoneme sounds. This is felt to be confusing and unwise.

Early childhood professionals want to make sure that their programs of activities offer the best in children's literature, not watered-down versions of classics. There is thought to be both older and contemporary literature and language-related activities that have depth, meaning, and linguistic charm that preschoolers should encounter. Meaning and comprehension are aided by discussion and familiarity and can be guided by sensitive teachers who also monitor the appropriateness of what is offered.

PRESSURE FOR FORMAL READING INSTRUCTION IN PRESCHOOLS

John Rosemond (1988) discusses why he believes young children are having reading skills pushed at them in preschool:

There are two reasons many preschool programs emphasize reading instruction and so many parents knock down the doors to get their children into them. Neither has anything to do with what's best for the children themselves. First, it makes parents proud as peacocks to have a three- and four-year-old offspring who can perform the ABCs and other academic trivia.

Second, a group of preschoolers sitting at a table coloring mimeographed letters and numbers is easier to manage than a group of preschoolers acting like real preschoolers. The issue isn't learning. It's ego and effort, too much of one and not enough of the other.

As Throne (1988) notes, in the last one or two decades, pressures have contributed to the teaching of reading in a more formal, less contextual, less meaningful way. Starting formal academics too early may do more harm than good, Elkind (1988) believes. He points out formal reading instruction in Denmark, where illiteracy rates are very low, is delayed until age seven.

Both Gallagher (1987) and Piaget and Inheldder (1969) fear that concentrating on early reading-skill instruction many reduce time for play and take away symbolic enrichment time. Play provides the interaction of imagery, imitation, and language, which builds a foundation necessary for learning to read.

All of the pressure preschool teachers feel to begin formal reading instruction grates against the belief system of most early childhood educators (Winn, 1981). Many react to the tragedy of finding an increasing number of children in preschools with purple worksheets to complete before they can play (Manning and Manning, 1981). Researchers have yet to find that early reading instruction is advantageous or better than later instruction. Kelly (1985) voices an opinion and observation that many educators feel is valid:

When we make unfair intellectual demands on our children, they'll pay a price. Studies show that children who are pushed to read early may not be such avid readers when they're older — which is when it matters — while their classmates who started slower may read often and spontaneously.

Jewell and Zintz (1986) have a position on the teaching of reading that many early childhood professionals endorse:

There are some four-year-olds interested in mastering print — and they do read. More five-year-olds do, too. Traditionally we have "pushed" reading for six-year-olds, and many have, indeed, learned to read. But there are likely as many seven-year-olds who need to grow into reading more slowly as there are five-year-olds who read early. And a few may not be curious about print until age eight. The school must provide for all children across the range of readiness for reading.

FIGURE 21-2 An interest in books can lead to an interest in printed words.

TEACHER AWARENESS OF CHILD INTEREST AND UNDERSTANDING

Each child will probably hold a totally different view concerning reading (figure 21-2). Possible understandings a preschooler may have include:

- pictures and text have different functions
- print contains the story
- the words the reader says come from the pictures
- stories tend to have some predictable segments and features
- it is possible to write messages
- there are words, and written words are made up of letters
- letters are arranged from left to right
- letters appear in linear fashion to represent the sequence of sounds in spoken words
- spaces delineate word boundaries
- letters come in capitals, in small print, and even in script, but they all have the same significance
- some marks are used to show beginnings and ends of text

The ability to read is present if the child understands and acts appropriately when he or she sees a printed word. In other words, the child must be able to understand the concept that (1) all "things" have a name, (2) the name of the thing can be a written word, (3) the two are interchangeable, and (4) the "word symbols" can be read.

Most teachers have had children "read" to them from a favorite, memorized storybook. Generally, a word from the book will not be recognized out of context and read by the child when seen elsewhere. But this behavior, imitative reading, can be an indication of emerging literacy development.

A child may develop the ability to recognize words because of an interest in printing letters. Another child may pick up the sounds of alphabet letters by listening and finding words that start with the same letter. Books and stories can also lead children into early interest and recognition of words (figure 21-3). Some children have the ability to distinguish one word from another word by sight and can easily remember words.

Early readers are children who have a desire to read. They also have had interactions with others who have answered their questions and stimulated their interest. A few children will read between the ages of four and five, but many will not have the capability or interest to read until a later age. Kelly (1985) estimates that only one to three preschoolers out of a hundred can

FIGURE 21-3 The child's face reveals her feelings toward the book.

read simple books. A teacher should be aware of each child's capabilities. In daily observations and verbal conversations, a child's responses give valuable clues. The wrong answers are as important as the right ones.

The following listing has been identified by Jewell and Zintz (1986) as discernible stages in the child's reading behavior during adult-child reading times:

- listens and looks
- requests repeated readings of favorite books
- corrects adult if a page is skipped
- reads to himself or herself, a doll, or other
- memorizes and reproduces by looking at illustrations (meaning is remembered before exact words)
- supplies words, if adult hesitates, by predicting and/or anticipating events in new books
- identifies specific words
- asks what words say
- repeats phrases and sentences adult reads
- reads most words (adult fills in others)

Unfortunately, few early childhood specialists have been trained to assess reading readiness or teach beginning reading in a manner suited to the developmental level of very young children (Goetz, 1979). Early childhood teachers looking for indicators to identify children who possess "readiness" need to realize that simple recognition of a few sight words is only one area of skill. A more complete listing is outlined by Emery (1975).

The following are Emery's "primary indicators":

- oral vocabulary
- reading curiosity
- auditory discrimination as it relates to clear speech and learning letter sounds
- visual discrimination of letters

Emery's "secondary indicators" include:

- attention
- compliance
- memory as it relates to the general idea of a story
- understanding concepts such as top/bottom, up/down, open/closed, and so forth
- writing in terms of copying straight lines, circles, and so forth
- page turning

In comparing two children, one who knows the alphabet and reads a few words and one who crudely writes his or her own name and makes up barely understandable stories, one may conclude that the first child is bright. However, creativity and logic are important in literacy development, and the second child may be outdistancing the first by progressing at his or her own speed. Literacy at any age is more than merely naming letters or words.

A CLOSER LOOK AT EARLY READERS

Researchers studying both gifted children and early readers notice that parents overwhelmingly report that they have read to their children from birth on or from the time the children learned to sit up. As Strickland (1982) points out, research shows that early readers who learned to read without systematic instruction had one common experience, despite their different backgrounds. They were all introduced to books between the ages of three and five. A study (Anbar, 1986) of activities mentioned by the parents of early readers is shown in figure 21-4. Usually, someone read aloud to those children on a regular basis. And Elkind (1988) notes "a Gallup survey of people who have attained eminence makes it very clear that parents of gifted children did not impose their learning priorities upon their young offspring. They followed the child's lead, emphasizing play and a rich, stimulating environment rather than formal instruction."

Studies of the early reader indicate that the child was usually exposed to a wide variety of reading material and enjoyed watching educational television, spending close to equal time in both pursuits (Schnur, Lowrey, and Brazell, 1985). An interest in print characterizes precocious readers, and their parents are described as responsive — noticing child interests and providing help when asked. Lots of child-centered family activities were part of the early reader's family life-style. These children seemed fascinated and obsessed with the alphabet, and parents reported that they answered questions, read to the child, and engaged in play activities with letters and words but had not set out with a systematic plan to teach reading (Salzer, 1984).

Anbar (1986) in completing a study of early readers has identified possible stages in these children's learning process (figure 21-5).

TYPE OF ACTIVITY	FREQUENCY OF REPORT
Daily readings with pointing at words	6/6
Showing words in magazines	2/6
Teaching names of letters	6/6
Teaching sight vocabulary	5/6
Making rhymes with words	5/6
Playing letter games	6/6
Helping learn sounds of letters	6/6
Helping put words together	6/6
Playing spelling games	6/6
Playing add-a-letter games	1/6
Listening to child read aloud	5/6
Having child read after parent	1/6
Doing alternate reading	2/6
Working on sounding out words	2/6
Providing books on an appropriate level	3/6

FIGURE 21-4 Six parents' reading activities with their children (*From* Early Childhood Research Quarterly 1, *Ablex Publishing Corporation.*)

Stage I	A preliminary period of gaining awareness and general knowledge of books and print (starting any time during the first year)
Stage II	Learning to identify and name the letters and acquiring beginning sight vocabulary (starting around 12–18 months)
Stage III	Learning the sounds of the letters (starting around 20–24 months)
Stage IV	Putting together words (starting around 24–32 months)
Stage V	Active reading from familiar books (starting around 20–30 months)
Stage VI	Sounding out short, unfamiliar words (starting around 32–34 months)
Stage VII	Reading easy, unfamiliar books (around 36 months)
Stage VIII	Reading for enjoyment of content (around 48 months)

FIGURE 21-5 Possible stages in the learning process of early readers (*From* Early Childhood Research Quarterly 1, *Ablex Publishing Corporation.*)

OBJECTIVES

Differences exist in the objectives of instruction between (1) educators who believe in readiness activities and (2) educators who advocate natural self-discovery of reading skills. The first group hopes to facilitate learning and enjoyment of reading. The second group foresees the child's experimentation — creating ideas about reading, based on his or her notions of the use of writing and reading, and attempting to crack the code with supportive assistance. Both groups favor a print-rich classroom, and objectives in many programs are based on a consideration of a blending of the two positions. Both groups also agree that experiences with classic and quality literature and dramatic activity help children's emerging literacy.

Programs that choose to include reading readiness among their instructional goals (objectives) plan activities that promote the following skills and attitudes:

- Recognizing incongruities — the ability to see the inappropriateness of a situation or statement, such as "The mouse swallowed the elephant."
- Recognizing context clues — realizing that pictures on the same page give visual clues to the words.
- Acquiring the ability to listen.
- Building vocabulary through first-hand experiences:
  a. recognizing likenesses and differences (figure 21-6),
  b. identifying through sight and sound,
  c. rhyming,
  d. increasing memory span,
  e. recalling sequence and content, and
  f. following directions.
- Increasing speech output:
  a. developing attitudes of each child's ability and worth, and
  b. increasing imaginative and creative speech.
- Building critical thinking and problem solving with language:
  a. identifying through clues,
  b. classifying, sorting, and organizing,
  c. developing concepts and recognizing relationships
  d. anticipating outcomes, and
  e. seeing cause-and-effect relationships.
- Developing self-confidence — attitudes of competence.

FIGURE 21-6 Magnetic letter play may enable these children to see likenesses and differences.

- Increasing interest and motivation through enjoyment and success in language activities.
- Developing left and right awareness (figure 21-7).
- Developing positive attitudes toward books and skills in book use:
  a. turning pages, and
  b. storing and handling books with care.

FIGURE 21-7 A child may develop spacial awareness through play activities.

SEQUENCE OF READING BEHAVIOR

In the absence of adult intervention that emphasizes another sequence, children generally seem to develop reading and writing abilities as follows:

1. The child develops an awareness of the functions and value of the reading and writing processes prior to becoming interested in acquiring specific knowledge and skills.
2. The child is likely to give greater attention to words and letters that have some personal significance, such as his or her own name or the names of family, pets, and so forth.
3. The child develops both reading and writing skills simultaneously as complementary aspects of the same communication processes, rather than as separate sets of learning. Neugebauer (1981) urges that "the most important issue is the quantity and quality of experiences the child has with print and with adults who help make print 'work.' It is through such interactions with print that the child acquires the information needed to find out what reading is."
4. The child develops an awareness of words as separate entities (as evidenced when he or she dictates words slowly so that the teacher can keep pace in writing them down) before showing awareness or interest in how specific letters represent sounds.
5. The child becomes familiar with the appearance of many of the letters by visually examining them, playing games with them, and so forth, before trying to master their names, the sounds they represent, or their formation.
6. The child becomes aware of the sound similarities between high-interest words (such as significant names) and makes many comparisons between their component parts before showing any persistence in deciphering unfamiliar words by blending together the sounds of individual letters (Lay-Dopyera and Dopyera, 1982).

As stated earlier in this unit, the teacher will probably encounter a few preschool children who have already learned how to read simple words and simple books. Another group of children, usually older four-year-olds, seem quite interested in alphabet letters, words, and writing. Teachers should ask questions about the center's goals for each child.

It is important for teachers to be able to help the child's existing reading abilities and actively plan for future reading skill.

Any teacher of young children over the age of three can anticipate working with some children who already have interest in and abilities for reading and writing. As a teacher you should be aware of various methods used to teach reading. This is no less true for the teachers of three-, four-, and five-year-olds than for teachers of six- and seven-year-olds (Lay-Dopyera and Dopyera, 1977).

READING METHODS

Research studies conducted to try to pinpoint the one best method for teaching children to read have concluded that there is no proven best method. The important factors seem to be the teacher's (1) enthusiasm for the method or technique used, and (2) understanding of the method used. The ideal situation for a child learning to read is a one-to-one child-teacher ratio with the reading activity suited to the child's individual capacity, learning style, and individual interests. This is difficult to fulfill in an early childhood learning center due to the numbers of children per group and the many other duties required of a teacher. Other limitations can include the teacher's amount of training, knowledge of a variety of methods to teach reading, and ability to plan interesting and appropriate activities within a print-rich classroom.

What preschool teachers need to understand is that advocates of many differing methods used to teach reading agree that a rich, strong base in quality children's literature and well-developed oral language and listening skill aid success in whatever reading method is eventually used. Another factor most reading experts will not dispute is that children need experiences that have focused on the meaning of language. Whichever prereading or reading method is used, it is important for children to recognize that "talk" can be written and that "written talk" can be read.

The Natural Approach

Popular approaches to reading include what has been termed "natural reading." The basic premise of this method centers on the idea that a child can learn to read as he or she learned to talk, that is, with adult attention and help with emerging skills. Learning to speak in one's native language is considered a more difficult task than learning to read. In the natural approach, an interest in print (words) leads to invented spelling and reading. Meaning ascends memory and decoding in this method. Huey (1908) anticipated "organic" and natural reading systems by proposing that children learn to read by authoring from their own experiences. He suggested that it was important to expose children to great classic literature as well as child-authored literature (writings) if one wished to promote true literacy.

Educators associated with natural reading include Ashton-Warner (1961), Johnson (1987), and Fields (1987). The well-known work of Allen (1969) has led to a method called the "language-experience approach" and can be thought of as a popular early form of the natural method. Stauffer (1970) points out the specific features of the language-experience approach that he feels make it especially appropriate for young children:

- A base in children's language development and first-hand experiencing.
- Stress on children's interests, experiences, and cognitive and social development.
- Respect for children's need for activity and involvement.
- Requirement for meaningful learning experiences.
- Integration of school and public library resources with classroom reading materials.
- Encouragement of children's creative writing as a meaningful approach to using and practicing reading-writing skills.

Johnson (1987), influenced by the work of Sylvia Ashton-Warner, recommends starting five-year-olds reading through a procedure that elicits children's images. The images are then connected to printed captions. Individual important images merge as meaningful words to be shared with others through sight reading. Slowly, visual discrimination, capitalization, sentence sense, phonetics, and punctuation are accomplished at each child's particular pace.

To many people, the terms natural and organic methods and language-experience and language arts approaches are synonymous and describe the same or similar methods of reading instruction. Durkin (1987) points out that teachers should not mistakenly believe

"natural" readers (early readers included) developed without help to learn. However, Durkin describes parents of natural readers as spending large amounts of time enjoying their children, reading to them, answering their questions about words or anything else, responding to requests to draw a picture or make a letter, initiating and then responding to questions. Chall (1988) adds that "Some people say you don't have to teach phonics, the kids will get it by themselves. But not every child will get it."

Robinson (1983) recommends the language-experience approach to young children's teachers because this method is a very natural way to build on children's expressive and cognitive activities and because of its flexibility and adaptability. She suggests that new teachers collect a large repertoire of activities from the many writers who have contributed to the development of this method. Allen and Allen's *Language Experience Activities* (1982) is a valuable resource. Since no one reading method is superior, teachers should be able to use features of phonic, linguistic, or sight-word recognition that seem useful at any given time (Robinson, 1983). In other words, combine methods.

The language arts approach to reading instruction introduces children to written words through their own interest in play; their enjoyment of speaking; and by listening to language. Often children's first experience with written words comes from their own speech and actions. A sign that says, "John's Block Tower" or "Free Kittens" may be the child's first exposure to reading. The emphasis is on the fact that words are part of daily living.

The increasing acceptance of the natural or organic methods may in part be due to the bulk of criticism that the other methods have received. These criticisms include:

- An overemphasis on skills (decoding, phonics, letter recognition, and so forth).
- Children's lack of a common background in the reading of literary classics.
- Children's lack of focus on comprehending what's read.
- A questioning of reading circles' oral-reading benefits.
- Poor performance of many children in reading.
- The labeling of slow or immature child readers.
- The number of remedial classes necessary.

The Whole-Language Movement

Much enthusiasm for a reading philosophy and approach called "whole language" is apparent in a growing number of elementary school reading teachers. The whole-language approach is very similar to what's termed "natural-language approach" in early childhood books, journals, and professional teacher-training literature. Ferguson (1988) describes whole-language as a philosophy that suggests that children learn language skill by following the natural learning behavior that governs the way they learn to talk. She notes that it is important that writing, listening, reading, and speaking activities grow from a child's experiences and interests. The teacher directs natural curiosity into activities that develop skills.

All sorts of literature (instead of basal readers) are used in whole-language classrooms, including posters, comics, classic literature, quality books, magazines, and newspapers, to mention a few. Poetry, songs, chants, and simple drama activities are among the language activities offered. The whole-language teacher presents opportunities for learning and development by relating activities to a single theme. Spontaneous conversational exchanges are typical and seen as enhancing and extending learning. Teachers using this approach draw attention to connections between speaking, writing, and reading by saying things like "I heard you say boat. This is how you write that. Now let's read it." There are usually no ability-grouped reading circles, and classrooms are described as busy, active, and full of talk.

Whole-language instruction is not without its critics. Criticism usually centers on the teacher's ability to assess each child's reading progress, lack of instruction in phonics, and a possible "fad" factor (Chall, 1988).

Resources for early childhood teachers wishing to know more about whole language follow.

"Teachers Networking: The Whole Language Newsletter"
Richard C. Owen, Publisher
Rockefeller Center, Box 819, New York, NY 10185

"The Whole Idea"
The Wright Group
10949 Technology Place, San Diego, CA 92127

What's Whole In Whole Language, by Kenneth Goodman, Portsmouth: Heinemann Educational Publishers, 1986

Decoding — Phonetic — Reading Approach

Decoding, using a phonetic approach to reading instruction, is based on teaching children the 44 language sounds (*phonemes*), which represent 26 alphabet letters and combinations (*graphemes*). Although phonetic approaches differ widely, most users believe that when children know which sounds are represented by which letters or letter combinations, they can "attack" an unknown word and decode it. Some schools using this approach begin decoding sessions when all sounds have been learned; others expose children to select sounds and offer easily decoded words early. A few phonetic approach systems require teachers to use letter sounds exclusively and later introduce the individual letter names, such as *a, b, c,* and so forth.

Five "word-attack" (or decoding) skills are helpful in the complicated process of learning to read.

1. *Picture clues.* Using an adjacent picture (visual) to guess at a word near it (usually on the same page).
2. *Configuration clues.* Knowing a word because you remember its outline.
3. *Context clues.* Guessing an unknown word by known words that surround it.
4. *Phonetic clues.* Knowing the sound a symbol represents (See Appendix for English alphabet letter pronunciation guide).
5. *Structural clues.* Seeing similar parts of words and knowing what these symbols say and mean.

Proponents of this method may have the following views that were published by a phonetic-approach (method) advocacy group:

We Americans must really hate our children otherwise how can we let them spend six years memorizing words (look-and-say reading system) when they could be decoding words and reading in six months or less with intensive phonics and enjoying good literature by second grade? An intensive phonics program would not require expensive remedial work or expensive books with words limited to those studied at each grade level. The look-and-say system has almost one out of three failing (Reading Reform Foundation, 1987).

Anderson (1985), author of *Becoming a Nation Of Readers*, has urged a sound foundation of phonics instruction in the earliest grades combined with a rich diet of good literature at all levels. This combined approach has been accepted by many kindergarten and elementary school teachers.

Look-Say Method

Many of the children who do read during preschool years have learned words through a "look-and-say" (whole-word) approach. That is, when they see the written letters of their name or a familiar word, they can identify the name or word. They have recognized and memorized that group of symbols. It is felt that children who learn words in this fashion have memorized the shape or configuration of the word. They often confuse words that have similar outlines such as Jane for June or saw for sew. They may not know the alphabet names of the letters or the sounds of each letter. This approach was prevalent in public school reading instruction earlier in this century, and it is still used today. Children who are good at noticing slight differences and who have good memories seem to progress and become successful readers.

TEACHER AND PARENT ATTITUDES

The staff in early childhood centers closely examine the advantages and disadvantages of various methods. Individual plans for individual children are formed, and activities increase children's interest while developing their skills.

Staff members facing "the back-to-academics" push need to be prepared and articulate. If they can discuss the real basics necessary in beginning reading and the benefits of a well-rounded developmental curriculum, which includes physical, social, intellectual, and creative opportunities and plenty of play, they may be able to curb pressure for a more limited academic approach to preschool programs that provide only bits and pieces of reading instruction. The importance of print-rich classrooms and literacy-based curriculum needs to be emphasized.

Most parents understand how critical their children's perception of their own abilities as learners is in determining school success. Parents are aware that early experiences in failing to perform academic tasks beyond children's capacity or developmental level can be detrimental. Most parents listen closely when teachers urge them to analyze the rush in pressuring children to learn to read at age four or five. Many parents want teachers

to encourage natural curiosity, promote searching, questioning minds, and prompt a joy in discovery and problem solving. Parents realize that in teaching reading skills teachers must avoid the risk that children will develop a thorough dislike for the activity. Many can relate to the commercial sell and the trend to hurry children in our increasingly technological society. Thinkers as well as socially integrated and creative people will always be our most precious natural resource. Parents need to know that research in the field of education simply does not support the position that reading should be taught as early as possible.

Many parents did not themselves learn to read until age six or seven. They can remember their early feelings about reading instruction and perhaps how this affected their self-esteem as children. Some can describe the importance of play, physical exercise, and access to people who loved books in their early lives. They can remember the pleasure and challenge of reading. Teachers can emphasize their attempts to acquaint children in their programs with a wide variety of quality literary experiences — experiences that would be sacrificed if instruction in skill and reading mechanics were to dominate language arts programming. Offering a well-rounded, developmentally appropriate language arts program that includes integrated speaking and listening activities, an awareness of print, and exposure to reading through books and a variety of other reading activities provides the experiences that will aid children in their eventual quest to learn to read, because they enjoy it and see its value.

Parents who realize that a broad background in quality books and literary experiences is necessary to be considered literate will want this type of language arts program for their children. Most parents also prize their children's comprehension of both oral and written language, which grows in classrooms where discussion flourishes.

Hillerich (1977) has pointed out nine skills and abilities that serve as a foundation for reading. These can be shared with parents who are intent on the school's teaching reading mechanics and isolated skills.

1. Development of an adequate oral language, including both sentence patterns and vocabulary.
2. Awareness of children's ability to use oral context to anticipate a word.
3. Ability to discriminate minor differences between letter forms.

4. Understanding what is meant by "the beginning" of a spoken word.
5. Experience in classifying spoken words according to beginning sounds.
6. Association of consonant letters with the sounds those letters represent at the beginning of a word.
7. Ability to apply the skill of using oral context along with the consonant sound association for the first letter of a printed word in order to read that word.
8. Familiarity with the patterns of the literary language from having been read to.
9. Experience with certain high-frequency words, enabling instant recognition of these printed words.

Speaking about readiness programs and individual differences, Hillerich (1977) states:

The typical child who has experienced the pre-reading skills program in or before kindergarten will be ready about the end of kindergarten or beginning of first grade to make use of these skills in actual reading. Of course, there will be some children entering first grade who are well beyond this level and others who have not yet mastered the necessary prereading skills, even though they may have been exposed to them.

READING-READINESS ACTIVITIES

Many of the activities found in this text can be considered readiness activities because each involves an area of language arts. The following activities deal with the development of the ability to use picture clues and configuration clues, which are both useful to the beginning reader. Note that the following may be developmentally appropriate for only specific groups or individual children.

Picture-Clue Activities

1. Draw several shapes on a piece of paper. Ask the child for a word label for each. Print the word beneath the picture. Ask the child what he or she wants to do with the paper. (Some will want to cut it, color it, or take it home.)
2. Tell the child that you are going to draw objects on the chalkboard and that the child can guess their names. Record the child's guesses next to each object.

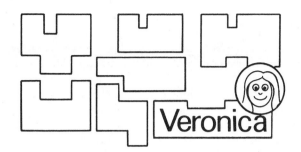

FIGURE 21-8 Name puzzle

Configuration-Clue Activities

1. Use chartboard or newsprint to make a large wall chart called a Name Puzzle. Post it so that the children can see it. Make the configuration outline of each child's and teacher's name.
2. Introduce the activity to interested children by printing your name on a strip of colored construction paper. Outline the name as shown in figure 21-8, and then cut it out. Move to the chart, finding the matching shape. If photos are available, paste these above the shape after pasting the configuration name shape over the matching chart shape.
3. Draw a picture of some simple object (such as a jar, eraser, scissors, classroom toy). Have the child match each drawing with the real object.
4. Trace around objects on the chalkboard. Have the child reach into a bag and feel the object, then guess its name. Write the guess under the chalkboard outline.

THE ROLE OF STORY TIMES AND BOOK-READING EXPERIENCES

Most elementary school teachers who are faced with the responsibility of teaching reading feel that the ease in learning to read is directly related to the amount of time a child has been read to by parents, teachers, and others. Think of the difference in exposure hours between a child who has had a nightly bedtime storybook and one who has not.

Books have a language of their own; conversation is quite different. Books are not just written oral conversation but include descriptions, primarily full sentences, rhythm, dialogue, and much more. Listen to adults as they read books to young children; they adopt special voices and mannerisms and communicate much differently from everyday speech. Through repeated experience, children learn that illustrations usually reflect what a book is saying; this knowledge helps them make educated guesses of both meanings and printed words adjacent to pictures.

Storybook sessions are reading readiness sessions and can greatly affect the child's future with books. If teachers wish to evaluate how well they are doing in making books important to children in their programs, the following set of questions (Cazden, 1981) will help.

- During free-choice periods, how many children go to the library corner and look at books by themselves?
- How many requests to read during the day do adults get from children?
- How many children listen attentively during story time?
- How many books have been borrowed by parents during the week?
- Which books have become special favorites, as shown by signs of extra wear?

Classroom Resource Books for Children

Classroom reference and word books for children interested in words are a valuable resource. Among the many volumes of this type are:

The Macmillan Picture Wordbook, by Kathleen N. Daly
Macmillan Very First Dictionary, Macmillan Publishers
The Rebus Treasury, compiled by Jean Marzollo, Dial Books

BASAL READERS IN ELEMENTARY CLASSROOMS

About 90% of elementary schools use basal readers to teach reading. Basal readers are packaged in sets or series that are used through as many as seven or eight grade levels. Readers (books) are collections of stories, facts, activities, poems, and assignments of increasing difficulty. As the age level for the reader increases, print becomes smaller, illustrations are less frequent, and book length is longer. Teachers must devote considerable study to the teacher manuals accompanying

a series if goals are to be realized. Lesson plans recommend specific activities and procedures, and workbooks are provided to follow and elaborate on readings. Many basal-series packages use a combination of reading approaches, including sight recognition and phonetic decoding.

Durkin (1987) suggests that commercially prepared phonic-instruction workbooks dominate in kindergartens where prereading and reading instruction takes place. Some of this type of instruction has found its way into four-year-olds' classrooms.

Criticism of basal readers abounds. Many worry that the overwhelming use of basal readers in which word usage in early elementary school has been simplified may reduce children's ability to see causal relationships. Bettelheim and Zelan (1981) believe that year after year these texts have become emptier, using fewer words and becoming increasingly repetitive and boring. Additional criticisms include:

- Children's ethnic, geographic, and economic situation and homelife may be extremely different from the experiences depicted in basal books, stories, and illustrations.
- Basal readers are usually the dominant reading materials in the classroom rather than materials of true literary value.
- They may promote learning to read before the child has the necessary understanding (knowledge) to make sense of this prepackaged material.
- They include mind-numbing drills that emphasize letter sounds rather than stories and their meanings.

Honig (1988), a vocal advocate of overhauling basal books, describes them as "bland, boring affairs, stripped of emotion and interest by their emphasis on simple sentence structure and limited vocabulary."

PARENTS' ROLE IN READING READINESS

Parents often want to find ways to help their children succeed in school. Since the ability to read is an important factor in early schooling, parents may seek the advice of the teacher.

Many programs keep parents informed of the school's agenda and goals and the children's progress.

An early childhood center's staff realizes that parents and teachers working together can reinforce what children learn at home and at school.

The following are suggestions for parents who want to help their children's language and reading-skill development. Many are similar to suggestions for teachers in early childhood centers.

- Show an interest in what children have to say. Respond to children, giving clear, descriptive, full statements.
- Arrange for children to have playmates and to meet and talk to people of all ages.
- Make children feel secure. Encourage and accept their opinions and feelings.
- Develop a pleasant voice and offer the best model of speech possible. Shouting and loud voices can create tension.
- Encourage children to listen and to explore by feeling, smelling, seeing, and tasting, when possible.
- Enjoy new experiences. Talk about them as they happen. Each community has interesting places to visit with young children — parks, stores, museums, zoos, buses, and trains are only a few suggestions (figure 21-9).
- Read to children and tell them stories; stop when they lose interest. Try to develop children's enjoyment of books and knowledge of how to care for them. Provide a quiet place for children to enjoy books on their own (figure 21-10).
- Listen to what children are trying to say rather than how they are saying it.
- Have confidence in children's abilities. Patience and encouragement help language skills grow.
- If parents have questions about their children's language skills, they should consult the children's teachers.

Summary

The fourth area of the language arts is reading. Early childhood centers do not offer formal reading instruction because it is developmentally inappropriate. A few preschoolers do have actual reading skill. The majority of preschoolers, however, are only beginning to form ideas about reading.

The goal of the teacher is to blend the language arts skills — listening, speaking, reading, and printscript — into successful experiences. Because the skills are so closely connected, one activity can flow into another activity in a natural way. This gives young children a clearer picture of communication.

Experiences in classic and contemporary, quality literature and other language arts activities provide a background for reading. Abilities, attitudes (figure 21-11), skills, and understanding grow at an individual rate. There are many methods of teaching language arts; each center decides which course of action or activities are best suited for attending children. Children exposed to a rich offering of language opportunities that includes paying attention to the understanding of written and oral materials are judged to have the best chance of becoming successful and lifelong readers.

A teacher's knowledge of reading skills aids in the identification of beginning readers and helps developmental activity planning. Parents and teachers work together to give children the opportunity to gain prereading skill and to keep children's interest alive and personally rewarding.

FIGURE 21-9 A library can become a familiar place to visit.

FIGURE 21-10 Look at this child's deep concentration and focus.

YES NO	1.	Asks to be read to, or asks for story time.
YES NO	2.	Hurries to be near the reader when story time is announced.
YES NO	3.	Comes willingly when story time is announced.
YES NO	4.	Likes to leaf through picture books.
YES NO	5.	Talks aloud (pretends to read or reads) as books are examined.
YES NO	6.	Looks over shoulder at what another child is "reading."
YES NO	7.	Picks books to "read" with some care (after examining more than one).
YES NO	8.	Has memorized some of the words from some books.
YES NO	9.	Has memorized most of the words in some books.
YES NO	10.	"Reads aloud" to others.
YES NO	11.	Usually enjoys hearing stories read aloud.
YES NO	12.	Borrows books from library.
YES NO	13.	Takes books home to read with no urging by teacher or parents.
YES NO	14.	Laughs aloud or smiles when reading funny material.
YES NO	15.	Asks others to listen as he reads something (of interest to him) aloud.
YES NO	16.	Treats books with care.
YES NO	17.	Asks for help locating book on specific topics.
YES NO	18.	Asks for help locating book about particular characters.
YES NO	19.	Gets "lost" in books and ignores activities in the room.

FIGURE 21-11 Checklist of reading attitudes for young children *(Adapted from* A Primer on Teaching Reading, *by George Mason, F. E. Peacock Publishers, Inc., 1981.)*

Student Activities

- Invite a kindergarten teacher and a first-grade teacher to discuss their experiences and knowledge about young children and reading.

- Observe a kindergarten class. List and describe any activities that increase a child's reading readiness or actual reading instruction.

- Make a chart of printscript words (common words such as dog, cat, and highly advertised words such as those naming commercial beverages or cereals; include children's names). Test these words with a group of four-year-olds in a gamelike way. Describe the children's response to your game.

- Find and borrow the Edward Dolch Basic Reading Word List (Dolch, Edward W. *A Manual for Remedial Reading*. Champaign: Garrard, 1939) from a library. Share it with the group. Note the date it was developed.

- Create an activity that includes:
  a. speaking and printscript.
  b. listening and printscript.
  c. printscript and reading.

- In a small group, discuss what you would do and what your limitations would be if you were working with a group of young children and found that two of them were reading a few words.

- Stage a debate. Divide the class into two groups: one presenting the disadvantages in teaching young children to read before first grade and the other presenting the advantages. Do some research at the library. Have each group discuss its position separately. Debaters from each team need to substantiate arguments by citing experts or written sources. Each team gets one point for each substantiation used during the actual debate.

- Have volunteers role-play the following situation.
  A parent states to a teacher: "I know you don't believe in teaching Jonathan (her child) the alphabet, but all the other parents are teaching it to their children. Jonathan is going to be behind. The other children will seem bright to their kindergarten teacher, while Jonathan will seem slow."

Unit Review

A. Discuss the following situations briefly.
   1. A child asks you to listen while he or she reads a favorite book to you.
   2. You have noticed a young child who is able to read all of the printscript in the playroom.
   3. A parent notices his or her child is reading a few words and asks advice as to what to do.

B. How can a teacher include the four language arts in activities?

C. Explain what is meant by:

reading   phonics

readiness   configuration

method   incongruities

D. Select the phrase that best completes each of the following sentences.

1. Between the ages of four and five,
   a. many children learn to read.
   b. a few children learn to read.
   c. children should be given reading instruction.
   d. most children will be ready to read.
2. The language arts are
   a. reading, printscript, and listening.
   b. speaking, reading, and listening.
   c. listening, speaking, writing (print), and reading.
   d. reading readiness, listening, speaking, and alphabet knowledge.
3. Children may begin reading because they
   a. have an interest in alphabet letters.
   b. have an interest in books.
   c. want to see what they say written down.
   d. have an interest in speaking, listening, or writing (printscript).
4. Reading readiness
   a. includes a variety of skills, motives, and attitudes.
   b. can be defined as having an interest in reading.
   c. means at a certain age a child will perfect all the skills needed to read.
   d. means that reading should be taught to most preschoolers.
5. Parents and early childhood teachers work together so that
   a. parents will teach their children to read at home.
   b. teachers can teach reading during preschool years.
   c. what children learn at home and school can be reinforced by both parents and teachers.
   d. children's experiences at home and school will be the same.

E. Describe which of the reading instructional methods reviewed in this unit seems more logical to you and why. Mention the distinguishing features of the method you choose.

References

Allen, Roach V. *Language Experiences in Early Childhood*. Chicago: Encyclopedia Britannica, 1969.

Allen, Roach V., and Claryce Allen. *Language Experience Activities*. Boston: Houghton Mifflin, 1982.

———. *Language Experience in Reading*. Chicago: Encyclopedia Britannica, 1968.

Anbar, Ada. "Natural Reading Acquisition of Preschool Children." Doctoral Dissertation, State University of New York at Buffalo, 1984.

Anbar, Ada. "Reading Acquisition of Preschool Children Without Systematic Instruction." *Early Childhood Research Quarterly* 1.1 (March 1986): 69–83.

Anderson, Richard. "Putting Reading Research Into Practice." Interview with C. H. Goddard. *Instructor* 98.2 (Oct. 1988): 31–37.

Ashton-Warner, S. *Teacher*. New York: Bantam, 1961. (An unforgettable account of a creative teacher who uses children's own dictated words as the basis for reading instruction.)

Atwerger, Bess, Carole Edelsky, and Barbara Flores. "Whole Language: What's New?" *Reading Teacher* 40.2 (Nov. 1987).

Berg, Leila. *Reading And Loving*. London: Henley and Boston, 1977.

Bettelheim, Bruno, and Karen Zelan. *On Learning To Read*. New York: Alfred A. Knopf, 1981.

Cazden, Courtney. *Language in Early Childhood Education*. Washington, DC: NAEYC, 1981.

Chall, Jeanne. "Climbing Out Of The Fourth Grade Slump." Interview with Mary Harbaugh. *Instructor* 97.9 (Oct. 1988): 51–58.

Commission On Reading, *Becoming a Nation Of Readers*. Washington, DC: National Institute of Education, 1985.

Durkin, Dolores. "A Class-Observation Study of Reading Instruction in Kindergarten." *Early Childhood Research Quarterly* 2.3 (Sept. 1987): 275–300.

Durkin, Dolores. *Strategies for Identifying Words*. New York: Allyn and Bacon, 1980.

_____. *Teaching Them To Read*. New York: Allyn and Bacon, 1983.

Elkind, David. "Educating the Very Young: A Call for Clear Thinking." *NEA Today* 6.6 (Jan. 1988): 37–39.

Emery, Robert L. *Reading Fundamentals for Preschoolers and Primary Children*. Columbus, OH: Charles E. Merrill, 1975.

Ferguson, Phyllis. "Whole Language: a Global Approach to Learning." *Instructor* 97.9 (May 1988): 23–28.

Fields, Marjorie. "NAEYC Developmentally Appropriate Guidelines and Beginning Reading Instruction." Conference Presentation. NAEYC, Chicago, 1987.

Fields, Marjorie, and D. Lee. *Let's Begin Reading Right*. Columbus, OH: Charles E. Merrill, 1987.

Gallagher, Jeanette M., and Judith Coche. "Hothousing: The Clinical and Education Concerns Over Pressuring Young Children." *Early Childhood Research Quarterly* 2.3 (Sept. 1987): 203–210.

Goetz, Elizabeth M. "Early Reading." *Young Children* 34.6 (July 1979): 94–99.

Goodman, Kenneth. *What's Whole In Whole Language*. Portsmouth, NH: Heinemann Educational Publishers, 1986.

Goodman, Y. *Emergent Literacy: Writing and Reading*. Norwood, NJ: Ablex, 1986.

Hayward, Ruth Ann. "Inside The Whole Language Classroom." *Instructor* 97.9 (May 1988): 15–19.

Hillerich, Robert L. *Reading Fundamentals for Preschool and Primary Children*. Columbus: Charles E. Merrill, 1977.

Hills, Tynette W. "Children in the Fast Lane: Implications for Early Childhood Policy and Practice." *Early Childhood Research Quarterly* 2.3 (Sept. 1987): 265–274.

Holdaway, Don. *The Foundations of Literacy*. Portsmouth, NH: Heinemann, 1979.

Honig, William, in Watson, Aleta's "Dick And Jane Meet The Classics." *San Jose Mercury News* (Oct. 14, 1988): 4L.

Huey, Edmund Burke. *The Psychology and Pedagogy of Reading*. New York: Macmillan, 1908.

Jewell, Margaret Greer, and Miles V. Zintz. *Learning to Read Naturally*. Dubuque, IA: Kendall/Hunt, 1986.

Johnson, Katie. *Doing Words*. Boston: Houghton Mifflin, 1987.

Kelly, Marguerite. "At 4, Reading Shouldn't Be an Issue." *San Jose Mercury News* (Sept. 4, 1985): 16E.

Lay-Dopyera, Margaret Z., and John E. Dopyera. *Becoming a Teacher of Young Children*. Lexington, MA: D. C. Heath, 1982.

Manning, Maryann, and Gary Manning. "The Schools' Assault on Childhood." In J. McKee (Ed.) *Early Childhood Education 83/84*. Guilford, CT: Dushkin Publishing Group, 1983.

Mason, George E. *A Primer on Teaching Reading*. Itasca, IL: F. E. Peacock, 1981.

Montessori, Maria. *The Discovery of the Child*. New York: Ballantine Books, 1965.

Neugebauer, Bonnie. "The Parents' Role in the Reading Process." *Parent Pages*, Child Care Information Exchange 14.6 (Sept./Oct. 1981): 31–34.

Pflaum, Susanna W. *The Development Of Language and Literacy in Young Children*. Columbus, OH: Charles E. Merrill, 1986.

Piaget, J., and B. Inheldder. *The Psychology of the Child*. New York: Basic Books, 1969.

Reading Reform Foundation, *San Jose Mercury News* (Aug. 17, 1987): 16E.

Robinson, Helen F. *Exploring Teaching in Early Childhood Education*. Boston: Allyn and Bacon, 1983.

Rosemond, John. "The ABCs Can Wait Until School Starts." *San Jose Mercury News* (April 10, 1988): 3L.

Salzer, Richard T. "Early Readers" Conference Presentation, NAEYC Conference, New Orleans, 1985.

_____. "Early Reading and Giftedness — Some Observations and Questions." *Gifted Child Quarterly* 25.3 (May 1984): 112–121.

Schickedanz, J. *More Than The ABCs: The Early Stages of Reading and Writing*. Washington, DC: NAEYC, 1986.

Schnur, James, Mildred A. Lowrey, and Wayne Brazell. "A Profile of the Precocious Reader." Hattiesburg: Univ. of Southern Mississippi, College of Ed. and Psychology, 1984.

Stauffer, R. C. *The Language Experience Approach to The Teaching of Reading*. New York: Harper and Row, 1970.

Stewig, John Warren. *Teaching Language Arts in Early Childhood*. New York: Holt, Rinehart and Winston, 1982.

Strickland, Dorothy, in "The Last Word on the First 'R.'" *New York Daily News* (Dec. 4, 1982): 13F.

Throne, Jeanette. "Becoming a Kindergarten of Readers?" *Young Children* 43.6 (Sept. 1988): 10–16.

Winn, Marie. *Children Without Childhood*. New York: Pantheon, 1981.

UNIT 22

Language-Development Materials

BJECTIVES

After studying this unit, you should be able to

- explain the need for materials in language-development activities.
- assist teachers in the care, storage, and replacement of materials.
- describe early childhood language games.

This text has emphasized the need to provide children with a wide variety of interesting classroom materials, objects, and furnishings. Such materials are important in keeping programs alive, fascinating, and challenging.

Classroom materials and objects promote language skills in many ways.

- They provide the reality behind words and ideas.
- They provide children with opportunities for sensory exploration that increase children's knowledge of relationships and ability to identify the things around them.
- Materials capture attention, motivate play, and build communication skills.
- Familiar and favorite materials can be enjoyed over and over, with the child deciding how much time to devote to them.
- Many materials isolate one language and perceptual skill so that it can be practiced and accomplished.

In language arts centers, related instructional materials are located in one convenient area. Stocking, supervision, and maintenance of materials, furnishings, and equipment is easily accomplished.

LANGUAGE ARTS CENTER

Full of communication-motivating activities, every inch of floor and wall space of a language arts center is used. Small areas are enlarged by building upward with lofts or bunks to solve floor-space problems in crowded centers (figure 22-1). Adding areas that children can climb into is another useful space-opening device.

Language centers have three main functions: (1) they provide looking and listening activities for children, (2) they give children an area for hands-on experiences with communication-developing materials, and (3) they provide a place to store materials. The ideal area has comfortable, soft furnishings with ample work space, proper lighting, and screening to block out other areas of active classrooms. Miller (1987) urges teachers to make centers cozy and inviting with pillows, a covered crib mattress, or a bean bag chair or two. He believes the area can become a place of refuge for the child who needs to get away from the bustle of the group and a nice place for the teacher to spend some time with children individually.

Language arts centers should be quiet places that are separated from the more vigorous activities of the average playroom. Suggested furnishings are listed by category.

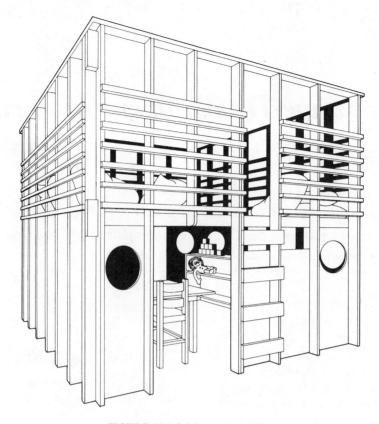

FIGURE 22-1 Solving space problems

General-Use Materials

- one or more child-size tables and a few chairs
- shelving
- dividers or screens
- soft cushioned rocker, easy chair, or couch
- soft pillows
- crawl-into hideaways, lined with carpet or fabric (figure 22-2)
- individual work space or study spots
- audio-visuals and electrical outlets
- book racks that display book covers (figure 22-3, page 386)
- chalkboard
- storage cabinets
- flannel board
- pocket chart
- children's file box (figure 22-4, page 386)
- bulletin board

- carpet, rug, or soft floor covering
- chart stand or wall-mounted wing clamps
- wastebasket

Writing and Prewriting Materials

- paper (scratch, lined, and typing paper in a variety of sizes)
- table
- file or index cards
- paper-storage shelf (figure 22-5, page 386)
- writing tools (crayons, nontoxic washable felt markers, and soft pencils in handy contact-covered containers)
- primary typewriter
- small, sturdy typewriter table or desk
- word boxes
- picture dictionary
- wall-displayed alphabet guides
- cutouts of colorful alphabet letters

FIGURE 22-2 A crawl-into area for quiet language activities

- tabletop chalkboards with chalk
- blank book skeletons
- scissors
- tape
- erasers
- tracing envelopes, patterns, wipe-off cloth
- large, lined chart paper (or newsprint)
- magnet board with alphabet letters

Reading and Prereading Materials

- books (including child-made examples)
- book and audiovisual combinations (read-alongs)
- favorite story-character cutouts
- rebus story charts

Speech Materials

- puppets and puppet theaters
- flannel-board sets
- language games

Audio-Visual Equipment

- record player, headsets, jacks
- story records
- tape recorder (cassette), headsets, jacks (figure 22-6, page 387)
- language master, recording cards (figure 22-7, page 387)
- picture files
- television screen and VCR (video cassette recorder)
- computer and printer

Adults usually supervise use of audiovisual equipment in a language center, and a number of the simpler machines can be operated by children after a brief training period. Tape recorders and headsets require careful introduction by the teacher.

TEACHER'S ROLE

Teachers are congenial, interested companions for the children: sharing books; helping them with proj-

FIGURE 22-3 Book covers can be easily seen when they are displayed on a child-size book rack.

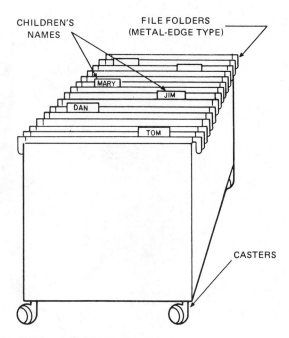

FIGURE 22-4 Children's work file box

ects; recording their dictation; playing and demonstrating language games; making words, word lists, signs or charts (figure 22-8, page 388); and helping children use the center's equipment.

Children direct their own activities. Teachers slip in and out as needed and monitor equipment use. Vigorous or noisy play is diverted to other room areas. Children who have been given clear introductions to a language center's materials, and clear statements concerning expectations in use of the center's furnishings, may need little help. It may be necessary, however, to set rules for the number of children who can use a language center at a given time.

The teacher explains new materials that are to become part of the center's collection. The mate-

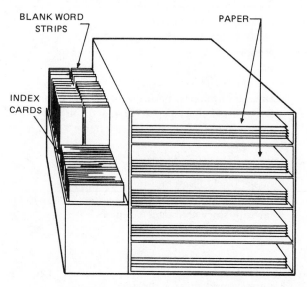

FIGURE 22-5 Tabletop paper holder

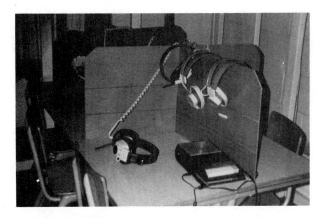

FIGURE 22-6 Individual listening areas can be created.

rials are demonstrated before they are made available to the children.

Posting children's work on the center bulletin board and planning chalkboard activities and printing messages that may catch the children's attention motivates interest in and use of the center. Plants and occasional fresh flowers in vases add a pleasant touch. To help children use equipment, materials, and machines on their own, teachers have become inventive using step-by-step picture charts posted, above or near materials. Color-coded dots make buttons or dials stand out.

Some centers control machine use by giving training sessions in which children obtain "licenses." Children without licenses need to have adult companions.

Preschool teachers may be asked to select films and videos for classroom use. Most of these visuals are based on selected children's literature. Gaffney (1988) offers screening suggestions:

> From my perspective, evaluating literature-based films for children involves a careful consideration of three things; the integrity and level of craft in the film itself; how well the print or print and picture medium was transformed to cinema: and how effectively the film communicates to an audience of children (film stands for both film and video).

Appropriateness and values presented would also be scrutinized.

Another task the teacher may want to undertake is making read-along tape cassettes to accompany a class's favorite books. Ditlow (1988) points out that the popularity of read-alongs cannot be denied, nor can the educational benefits. Children who use read-alongs are learning word recognition as well as some of the more advanced reading skills. For fun and pleasure, the lure of read-alongs makes them one of the best gateways for children into the world of books. Ditlow urges teachers to consider the following when making these classroom aids:

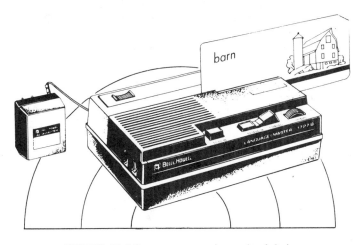

FIGURE 22-7 Language master instructional device

Hurt no living thing:
Ladybug nor butterfly,
Nor moth with dusty wing,
Nor cricket chirping cheerily
Nor grasshopper
    so light of leap,
Nor dancing gnat,
Nor beetle fat,
Nor harmless worms
    that creep.

FIGURE 22-8 Language-center chart

A narrator's pacing is important. It cannot be too fast, or the child trying to follow along will be lost. If it is too slow, the child will become bored. The inflection and tone of the voice are also vital. The narrator cannot be condescending or patronizing; neither should there be an attempt to "act out" the story and run the risk of making the story secondary to the performance.

Besides these factors a teacher needs to estimate audience attention span and use a pleasant page-turning signal.

AUDIOVISUAL EQUIPMENT

Budgets often determine the availability of audiovisual materials in a center. Care of equipment and awareness of operating procedures are important. Special fund-raising projects, rental agreements, borrowing arrangements, or donations have secured audiovisuals for some programs. The machine's instruction manual should be studied for the proper care and maintenance necessary for efficient use.

The following audiovisual equipment enriches a center's language arts program activities.

Camera. Polaroid or standard-type cameras provide photos that are useful in speaking activities, displays, and games.

Slide Projector and Slides. Common home, school, field trip, and community scenes can be discussed, written about (experience stories), or used for storytelling.

Lite-bord (registered trademark). This is a special display board that uses nontoxic erasable crayons for making colorful drawings and words that glow. It is available from Lite-bord Ltd., New Hertford House, 96 St. Albans Rd., Watford Herts, WD 2 4AB, England.

Super 8 Projector and Film Loops. Children enjoy films during group and private showings. Audio tapes can be made for children's or teachers' stories to accompany silent films.

Dukane Projector. Used with or without headsets, this projector provides filmstrip and sound presentations of language arts materials available from commercial suppliers.

Overhead Projectors and Transparencies. Stories with silhouettes or numerous transparency activities can be designed. Small patterns and alphabet letters are enlarged and copied by teachers or children for a variety of uses (figure 22-9). Mac Donald (1989) suggests drawing or placing images on the screen while story telling or reading poetry (for example, using a Humpty Dumpty picture sequence while reciting the rhyme).

Opaque Projector. Pages of picture books can be projected on wall areas to offer a new way to read books. Guessing games are also possible. Picture book characters can become life-size companions.

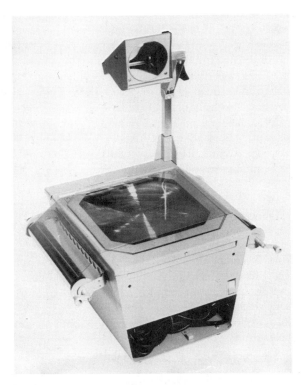

FIGURE 22-9 Audiovisual equipment (overhead projector) *(Photo courtesy of Buhl, Inc.)*

Filmstrip Projector and Filmstrips. Easy operation and low cost make this equipment popular. Teacher-made filmstrips can be created. Newer models have automatic threading and rewind features with both front and rear projection.

16 mm Film Projectors, Films, and Screens. Many films are made for use with preschool children. Often libraries stock films. Programs attached to public school systems have film catalogs listing available titles. Screens are optional, since blank walls can also be used as projection surfaces.

Language Master. This machine instantly records and plays back. Children can easily operate this equipment. Words and sounds are paired. Prepackaged language development programs can be purchased. For additional information contact: Bell and Howell,

Audiovisual Products Division, 2100 McCormick Road, Chicago, IL 60645.

Listening Center Equipment. Headsets accommodating up to eight children at one time adapt to both cassette and record players. Volume control is set on the jack box.

Record Player. Most centers have this piece of equipment. Commercial suppliers of story records are plentiful.

Tape Recorders. This is a popular audiovisual aid that is used frequently in early childhood centers. The tape recorder opens up many activity ideas. Suggestions for language development activities with tape recorders follow:

- •. Record children's comments about their artwork or project. "Tell me about _____" is a good starter. Put the tape and artwork together in the language center, so that it is available for the children's use.
- Let the children record their comments about a group of plastic cars, human figures, animals, and so on, after they arrange them as they wish.
- Have children discuss photographs or magazine pictures.
- Record a child's comments about a piece of fruit that he or she has selected from a basket of mixed fruit.
- Record a "reporter's" account of a recent field trip.
- Gather a group of common items, such as a mirror, comb, brush, toothbrush. Let the child describe how these items are used.
- Record a child's description of peeling an orange or making a sandwich with common spreads and fillings.
- Record a child's comments about his or her block structures. Take a polaroid photo and make both tape and photo available in the listening and looking area.

Television Sets and VCRs. These can be purchased as separate units or as combined machines. Children's classic literature is available on cassettes priced from about $35 and up. Local video rental stores and public libraries stock a variety of titles.

Commercial Sources for Audiovisuals

AA Records, 250 W. Fiftyseventh Street, New York, NY 10019

ABC School Supply, 437 Armour Circle N.E., Box 13048, Atlanta, GA 30324

A. B. LeCrone Company, 819 N.W. Ninetysecond Street, Oklahoma City, OK 73114

Argosy Music Corporation, Motivation Records, 101 Harbor Road, Westport, CT 06880

Bilingual Educational Services, 816 South Fair Oaks, South Pasadena, CA 91030

Bowmar, P.O. Box 3623, Glendale, CA 91201

Capitol Records, Inc., 1750 N. Vine Street, Hollywood, CA 90028

Childcraft Education Corp., 20 Kilmer Road, Edison, NJ 08817

Childrens Record Guild (CRG), 225 Park Avenue South, New York, NY 10003

David C. Cook Publishing Co., 850 N. Grove Avenue, Elgin, IL 60120

Decca Records, 445 Park Avenue, New York, NY 10022

Disneyland Records, 800 Sonora Avenue, Glendale, CA 91201

Encyclopedia Britannica Education Corp., 425 N. Michigan Avenue, Chicago, IL 60611

Educational Activities, Inc., P.O. Box 392, Freeport, NY 11520

Folkway Records, 43 W. Sixtyfirst Street, New York, NY 10023

Golden Records, 250 W. Fiftyseventh Street, New York, NY 10019

Happy Time Records, 8016 43rd Avenue, Long Island City, NY 10001

Kaplan School Supply, 1310 Lewisville-Clemmons Road, Lewisville, NC 27023

Kimbo Educational, P.O. Box 246, Deal, NJ 07723

KTAV Publishing House, Inc., 120 E. Broadway, New York, NY 10022

Learning Arts, P.O. Box 179, Wichita, KS 67201

Mercury Record Productions, Phonogram, Inc., One IBM Plaza, Chicago, IL 60611

MGM Record Corporation, 7165 W. Sunset Boulevard, Los Angeles, CA 90046

Miller-Brody Productions, Inc., 342 Madison Avenue, New York, NY 10017

Peter Pan Industries, 88 St. Francis Street, Newark, NJ 07105

Pickwick Records, 135 Crossways Park Drive, Woodbury, NY 11797

RCA Records, 1133 Avenue of the Americas, New York, NY 10036

Rhythms Productions, P.O. Box 34485, Los Angeles, CA 90034

Scholastic Book Services, Audiovisual Dept., 904 Sylvan Avenue, Englewood Cliffs, NJ 07632

W. Schwann, Inc., 137 Newbury Street, Boston, MA 02116

Scott, Foresman and Company, 1900 E. Lake Avenue, Glenview, IL 60025

Singer Society for Visual Education, Inc., 1345 Diversey Parkway, Chicago, IL 60614

Tikva Records, 22 E. Seventeenth Street, New York, NY 10003

UNICEF, U.S. Committee for UNICEF, 331 E. Thirty-eighth Street, New York, NY 10016

United Synagogue Book Service, 155 Fifth Avenue, New York, NY 10010

Record, Cassette, and Picture-Book Combinations

Bantam Books, 666 Fifth Avenue, New York, NY 10103

Children's Press, 1224 W. Van Buren Street, Chicago, IL 60607

Scholastic Book Services, Audiovisual Dept., 904 Sylvan Avenue, Englewood Cliffs, NJ 07632

Viking Penguin Audiovisual Catalog, Charles Wieser Assoc., P.O. Box 538, El Toro, CA 92630

Children's Book Publishers

(Many publishers also supply audiovisual materials.)

Abingdon Press, 201 Eighth Avenue, Box 801, Nashville, TN 37202

Atheneum Publishers, 115 Fifth Avenue, New York, NY 10017

The Bobbs-Merrill Co. Inc., 4300 W. Sixtysecond Street, Indianapolis, IN 46206

Bradbury Press, 866 Third Avenue, New York, NY 10022

Thomas Y. Crowell Company, 201 Park Avenue South, New York, NY 10003

The John Day Company, Inc., 62 W. Fortyfifth Street, New York, NY 10036

Dial Books, 2 Park Avenue, New York, NY 10016

Doubleday & Company, Inc., 245 Park Avenue, New York, NY 10067

E. P. Dutton & Co. Inc., 2 Park Avenue, New York, NY 10067

Elephant Walk, 2544 N. Monticello, Chicago, IL 60647

Farrar, Straus & Giroux, Inc., 19 Union Square West, New York, NY 10003

Gryphon House, Inc., 3706 Otis Street, Box 275, Mt. Ranier, MD 20712

Harper & Row Publishers, 10 E. Fiftythird Street, New York, NY 10022

Holiday House Inc., 18 E. Fiftysixth Street, New York, NY 10022

Houghton Mifflin Co., 2 Park Street, Boston, MA 02108

Alfred A. Knopf, Inc., 201 E. Fiftieth Street, New York, NY 10022

Lothrop, Lee & Shepard Co., Inc., 105 Madison Avenue, New York, NY 10016

Margaret K. McElderry Books, 115 Fifth Avenue, New York, NY 10003

McGraw-Hill Book Co., 1221 Avenue of the Americas, New York, NY 10020

The Macmillan Co., 866 Third Avenue, New York, NY 10022

Morrow Junior Books, 105 Madison Avenue, New York, NY 10016

Thomas Nelson Publishers, Nelson Place at Elm Hill Pike, Nashville, TN 37214

Oak Tree Publications, Inc., 9601 Aero Drive, Suite 202, San Diego, CA 92123

Pantheon Press, 201 E. Fiftieth Street, New York, NY 10022

Philomel Books, 51 Madison Avenue, New York, NY 10010

Prentice-Hall, Inc., Englewood Cliffs, NJ 07632

G. P. Putnam's Sons, 200 Madison Avenue, New York, NY 10022

Raintree Publishers, Inc., 330 E. Kilbourn Avenue, Milwaukee, WI 53202

Scott, Foresman & Co., 1900 East Lake Avenue, Glenview, IL 60024

Charles Scribner's Sons, 115 Fifth Avenue, New York, NY 10003

Three Trees Press, 2 Silver Avenue, Toronto, Ontario M6R 3A2 Canada

Film Distributors

Association Films, 600 Grand Avenue, Ridgefield, NJ 07657

Avis Films, P.O. Box 643, Burbank, CA 91503

Bailey Films, Inc., 6509 DeLongpre Avenue, Los Angeles, CA 90028

Charles Cahill & Assoc., Inc., 5746 Sunset Boulevard, Los Angeles, CA 90028

Churchill Films, 662 N. Robertson Boulevard, Los Angeles, CA 90069

Coronet Films, 65 E. South Water Street, Chicago, IL 60601

Walt Disney Productions, 350 S. Buena Vista Avenue, Burbank, CA 91503

Encyclopedia Britannica Educational Corporation, 425 N. Michigan Avenue, Chicago, IL 60611

Film Associate of California, 11559 Santa Monica Boulevard, Los Angeles, CA 90025

Indiana University Audiovisual Center, Indiana University, Bloomington, IN 47405

Sterling Films, 241 E. Thirtyfourth Street, New York, NY 10016

Filmstrip Suppliers

Stanley Bowmar Co., Inc., 12 Cleveland Street, Valhalla, NY 10595

Eye Gate House, Inc., 146-01 Archer Avenue, Jamaica, NY 11435

The Jam Handy Organization, 2821 East Grand Boulevard, Detroit, MI 48211

Society for Visual Ed., Inc., 1345 Diversey Parkway, Chicago, IL 60614

PLANNING LANGUAGE CENTERS AND COMPUTER CENTERS

Once rooms or areas are designated as language centers, staff members classify materials into "looking and listening" or "working with" categories. Display, storage, working space, and looking and listening areas are determined. Activities that require concentration are screened off when possible. Many different arrangements of materials and equipment within a language arts center are possible. Most centers rearrange furnishings until the most functional arrangement is found. For sample arrangements with different functions, refer to figure 22-10.

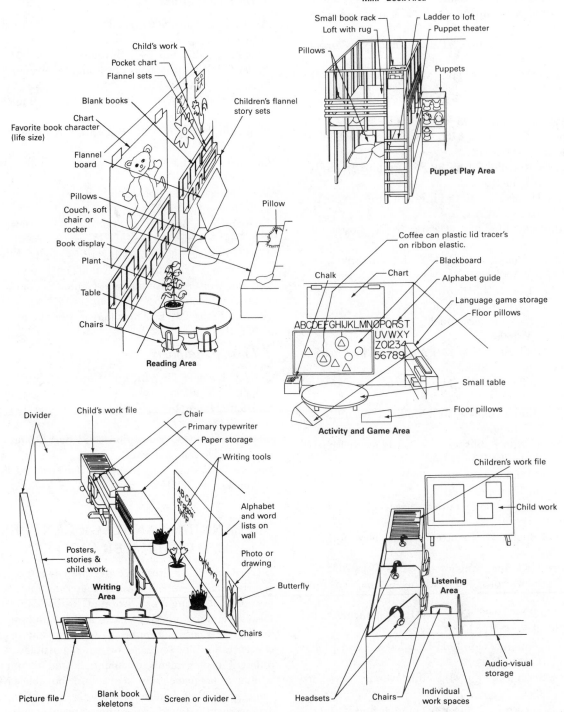

"Mini" Book Area

Small book rack — / Ladder to loft
Loft with rug — / Puppet theater
Pillows —
Puppets

Puppet Play Area

Child's work —
Pocket chart —
Flannel sets —
Blank books —
Chart —
Favorite book character (life size) —
Children's flannel story sets
Flannel board —
Pillows —
Couch, soft chair or rocker —
Book display —
Plant —
Table —
Chairs —
Pillow

Reading Area

Coffee can plastic lid tracer's on ribbon elastic.
Chalk — / Chart
Blackboard
Alphabet guide
Language game storage
Floor pillows
ABCDEFGHIJKLMNOPQRST
UVWXY
ZOI234
56789
Small table
Floor pillows

Activity and Game Area

Divider
Child's work file — / Chair
Primary typewriter
Paper storage
Writing tools
Alphabet and word lists on wall
Photo or drawing
Posters, stories & child work.
Butterfly
Writing Area
Chairs
Picture file — / Blank book skeletons / Screen or divider

Children's work file
Child work
Listening Area
Audio-visual storage
Headsets — / Chairs / Individual work spaces

FIGURE 22-10 Language arts center

Many children like to escape noise with a favorite book or puppet. Most centers provide these quiet retreats within a language arts center. School staffs have found creative ways of providing private space. Old footed bathtubs with soft pillows, packing crates and barrels, pillow-lined closets with doors removed, tepees, tents, screened off couch and arm chairs have been found workable in some classroom language arts areas.

Computer centers are a new addition to many classrooms. Many are open only when an adult computer adviser is present. Setting up the physical space requirements in an easily monitored and supervised quiet area away from active play and art materials may call for staff ingenuity (figure 22-11). Some schools place computers and computer-related equipment in adjacent rooms or room areas separated by doors or move computers in and out of classrooms on rolling carts. Ideally a computer would be placed within the language arts center because of its use as a word processor. Davidson (1988) suggests the following:

1. Set up the center near the library or listening area. These areas are usually quiet and will enable children to concentrate while playing on the computer. Like any other classroom area, you need to set rules and limits about the number of children allowed in the area, and how long individuals or small groups of children can play there.
2. Place the computer table or desk against a wall to minimize the chances of a child knocking the components on the floor. Make sure the computer table is at the children's eye level. If it's too high, the children will have difficulty reaching the keyboard and removing the printouts from the printer. In their efforts to reach things, they may knock the keyboard or printer on the floor.
3. Tape down exposed power cords with duct tape or electrical tape. This will keep children from tripping over them.
4. Label each switch with a number to indicate the sequence in which to turn on each part of the system. This will remind the children of the correct steps that are needed to turn on the computer. Simple picture directions on disk covers help children differentiate between programs and remind children how to use each program. You and the children might try coming up with these picture "codes" together.
5. To protect disks from dust, food, playdough, and sources of magnetism, store them upright in their jackets in boxes. It is also a good idea to keep the computer protected with a dust cover when it is not in use.

A computer area needs chairs that children can move so that more than one child can sit in front of the screen. The added expense of a printer is considered worth the investment. With a printer available, a teacher can print out children's work adding to their experience and knowledge of print and reading connections.

Summary

When there is a language arts center within an early childhood playroom, language development materials are arranged in one central room location. Children follow their own interests, according to their preferences, which increases the children's interaction with materials and expands language skills (figure 22-12).

A language center's material can include a wide range of teacher-made and commercially purchased items. Activities in listening, speaking, writing, and reading (or combinations of these) are side by side, promoting the child's ability to see relationships among them.

Audiovisual materials and equipment are useful language center devices. Costs sometimes limit their availability. Training in the use and care of audiovisual machines is necessary for efficient operation.

FIGURE 22-11 Finding space in a classroom for a computer may take staff ingenuity.

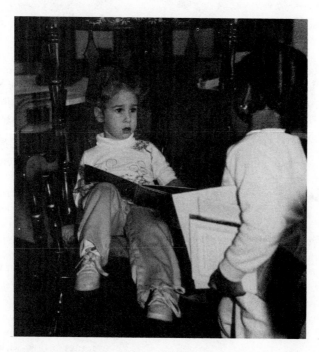

FIGURE 22-12 A large rocking chair can accommodate a child's desire to look at books on his or her own.

Student Activities

- Observe an early childhood program. Describe the use and storage of language development materials.

- Listen to three story records. Judge and compare the quality of the recordings.

- Invite an audiovisual company's sales representative to the class to demonstrate the company's product.

- Develop a price list for five pieces of audiovisual equipment found in this unit.

- Interview two early childhood teachers on their use of audiovisuals in their language arts curriculum. Report the findings to the group.

- Sketch a language arts center to promote dramatizing favorite stories. Label each item and furnishing.

- Plan and conduct an activity for a group of preschoolers using a tape recorder.

- Find a school where child computer access is commonplace. Observe and interview staff and children. Report your findings.

- Borrow audiovisuals appropriate for preschoolers, and evaluate three with classmates. (Try your local library.)

Unit Review

A. List the advantages of an early childhood language arts center. What are the disadvantages?

B. List the teacher's duties in a well-functioning classroom language arts center (for example, supervision).

C. Describe or draw a picture of an imaginary language arts center that has a crawl-into bunk or loft area. It should be a place where a child could be alone to enjoy a book.

D. List seven useful machines mentioned in this unit for classroom language arts centers.

References

Davidson, Jane. "Computers For Preschoolers?" *Pre-K Today* 2.5 (Feb. 1988): 32–41.
———. *Computers in Early Childhood Education*. Albany: Delmar, 1989.
Ditlow, Timothy. "Making a Book Into A Successful Cassette." *CBC Features* 41.3 (May–Dec. 1988): 4–6.
Gaffney, Maureen. "A Film On Its Own: Looking At Media Based On Literature." *CBC Features* 41.3 (May–Dec. 1988): 8–10.
MacDonald, Mary F. "Don't Overlook Your Overhead!" *Instructor* 98.5 (Jan. 1989): 88–92.
Miller, Karen. "Room Arrangement." *Pre-K Today* 2.1 (Aug./Sept. 1987): 28–33.

Section 8

Settings Promoting Literacy

Home and School

What's in a well-planned early childhood language arts' room center? The supplies, equipment, materials, and tools that should be included in the center to help children complete their own projects and promote play are described in this section. Pictorial representations are included of suggested room areas that can make language arts centers inviting to children.

Parents, who are children's most important and influential teachers, join with professional teachers to reinforce the school program with home activities in language arts. Teacher-parent interactions are discussed, and parent resources are mentioned in Unit 24.

READY...SET...ROLE: PARENTS' ROLE IN EARLY READING

by Amy Wahl

Parents do not need to focus on specific reading skills to perform their role as reading teachers, but they can provide informal learning experiences which can foster an interest in and love for reading.

ABCs of early reading for parents

Assortment of books

Have an assortment of picture books, ABC books, poetry books, nursery rhymes, and fairy tale collections within your child's reach throughout the entire house. Book ownership is important for promoting the reading habit.

Bookmaking

Assist your child in creating his/her own books. You can purchase blank books or create your own homemade ones. Your child can dictate stories to you and illustrate them. Help your child keep a diary or write special events on a calendar. Bookmaking helps the child to see talk being written down, and it is fun for children to read their own stories.

Cooking

Cooking is a daily activity in which you can include your child. S/he can help read the recipes, add the ingredients, recognize food names and name brands, and become familiar with abbreviations. Kitchen experiences provoke questions and enable your child to experiment with new words.

Discussions

Your child's vocabulary can be extended through participation in discussions with you and others. It is important to be a good listener and let your child know that what s/he says is important.

Errands

Taking your children on errands exposes them to the print in their world. You can read and point out signs for fast food restaurants, gas stations, movie theaters, and stores as you do your errands. Don't forget to read billboards, stop signs, license plates, and street signs. It is important for children to become aware of environmental print.

Free play
Play is the child's work, and it is through play that s/he learns about other people and their world. Encourage free play and provide your child with opportunities to interact with other children. You can provide props for playing house, hospital, grocery store, and office. Puppets are excellent props for retelling stories. Other good investments include a sand box, magnetic letters, blocks, and picture dominoes.

Grocery shopping
Your child can be an active participant in grocery shopping. Invite children to write and read grocery lists, sort coupons, read grocery ads, discover labels on the food packages, and read the signs in the grocery store. Grocery shopping experiences enable your child to see the importance of reading in an ordinary, everyday situation.

Habits
Habits are formed early in life. Help your children develop the library habit by taking them to the library regularly. Young children enjoy having their own library cards and being able to check out the books they select. The library offers a variety of media materials, story hours, and other programs.

Informal learning
Informal learning experiences can start during infancy. You can turn daily routines into hands-on, concrete experiences. These experiences can help prepare your child for the formal learning experiences at school.

Junk treasures
Your child can participate in opening the mail — opening junk mail can be a treat. You also can read letters and other mail to your child. Children can help pay bills, answer letters, and write letters to friends and relatives. Children enjoy sending and receiving mail. With your assistance, they can create birthday cards and write thank you notes for gifts.

Kidwatching
Yetta Goodman coined the term "kidwatching" to describe an important job of parents (Lamme,

1985). Kidwatching involves observing your child to become familiar with what s/he knows and doesn't know as well as what s/he can and cannot say (Lamme, 1985). You can learn a lot about your child through observing in different settings.

Lap technique
The lap technique of reading aloud to your child provides a sense of security as you hold the child close and share books. Booksharing can create a special bond as you learn about each other and the world of books. The lap technique can help your child associate reading with a pleasant, nonthreatening situation.

Magazines
A subscription to a children's magazine is a worthwhile investment.

Nursery rhymes
It is fun to share the nursery rhymes from your own childhood with your children. It is through repetition that they will learn the nursery rhymes and begin to recite them on their own. You also can share your favorite songs and fingerplays.

Opportunities for booksharing
Booksharing opportunities should become part of the daily routine before your child's first birthday. It is helpful to establish a certain time for reading to your child each day, and no interruptions should disturb this valuable experience. Booksharing can develop a sense of curiosity and enthusiasm for books in just 15 minutes a day.

Patience
The parents' role in reading requires patience. You need to create a supportive environment and encourage your child to experiment with language. Including your child in errands, cooking experiences, and other daily routines requires time and energy, but the benefits are many. Be patient as your child learns about the world.

Questions
Children ask many questions about things new to them. Be sensitive to these questions and take the time to explain the answers. In booksharing, you can provide time for questions before and after the book is read. Remember to ask a variety of questions which require your child to think critically

about the story, and try to avoid focusing on factual questions which test your child on the story content.

Read aloud sessions

Reading aloud to your child requires some practice, and you need to consider the atmosphere around you. There should be good lighting, minimal noise distractions, and comfortable seating. Choose books that relate to your child's experiences as well as those that introduce new people, places, and experiences. Read aloud sessions can involve more than reading a book and talking about it — you can extend them through extra activities, such as baking gingerbread cookies after reading a version of *The Gingerbread Man*.

Sensory experiences

Your child needs to become aware of the 5 senses. It is not difficult to provide stimulating sensory activities. An example is a walk in the woods where the child can touch trees, hear birds, smell flowers, and see the leaves.

Television time

You can help your children develop good television habits and help them monitor their TV time. You need to select worthwhile programs and watch and discuss them with your children. Discussions make TV time a less passive activity.

Unpressured learning

You do not need to put extra pressure on your children to read words, but you can encourage them to read their world as they experience it. Be understanding and supportive.

Value of reading

Become a reading role model. Your child should see you getting into books, magazines, and newspapers. It is important for her/him to see the different purposes for reading, such as reading for information, pleasure, and survival in a world saturated with print. Reading should be valued in your home.

Writing experiences

Writing is an essential in the reading process. Writing materials like pens, pencils, crayons, markers, and an assortment of paper should be available for experimenting. You might even want to have a special writing spot. Writing experiences include letter writing, making labels for photo albums or other household items, journal writing, story writing, and making words for wordless picture books.

eXtra attention

Your role in early reading requires you do devote extra attention to your children's needs and help with their first encounters with print.

Your literate home

Create a nurturing and literate environment for your young child to learn and grow in. The experiences in your home can make a difference in your child's reading development.

Zoo trips

Zoo trips, museums, amusement parks, and community parks are places that you can visit with your child. Visits to these special places engage your child in new experiences to learn from and talk about. These experiences can be extended by using children's literature before and after the visits.

References

Lamme, Linda Leonard, *Growing Up Reading*. Washington, DC: Acropolis Books, 1985.

Simmons, Barbara, and Paula Smith Lawrence. "Beginning Reading: Welcoming Parents." *Childhood Education*, vol. 57 (January–February 1981), pp. 156–59.

Resource list for parents

Butler, Dorothy, and Marie Clay. *Reading Begins at Home*. Exeter, NH: Heinemann, 1982.

Goodman, Ken. *What's Whole in Whole Language?* Portsmouth, NH: Heinemann, 1986.

Larrick, Nancy. *A Parent's Guide to Children's Reading*. New York, NY: Bantam Books, 1982.

Schickendanz, Judith A. *More Than ABCs: The Early Stages of Reading and Writing*. Washington, DC: National Association for the Education of Young Children, 1986 (1834 Connecticut Avenue NW, Washington, DC 20009).

Taylor, Denny, and Dorothy Strickland. "Family Literacy: Myths and Magic." In *The Pursuit of Literacy*, edited by Michael Sampson. Dubuque, IA: Kendall/Hunt, 1986.

Trelease, Jim. *The Read-Aloud Handbook*. Fairfield, PA: Penguin Books, 1982.

UNIT 23

Classroom Language Arts Centers

An inviting, comfortable language arts center can become a child's favorite place at school. Language materials within easy reach and soft textures to lean or lie on in a quiet semi-secluded area offer different pleasures and enjoyments from active and vigorous play areas.

ADVANTAGES

Language activities are always available for children when a language arts center is part of an early childhood classroom. Materials placed at children's eye level motivate the children to explore and offer the opportunity for them to follow individual interests. Well-stocked, well-supervised language centers encourage the development and integration of language arts skills. Listening, speaking, reading, and writing activities are all available. Individual and group work areas plus quiet play spots are provided.

- They provide the reality behind words and ideas.
- Exploration using the sense organs increases children's knowledge of relationships and identifying properties.
- Materials capture attention, motivate play, and build communication skills.

- Familiar and favorite materials can be enjoyed over and over, with the child deciding how much time to devote to self-chosen tasks.
- Many materials isolate one language and perceptual skill so that it can be practiced and accomplished.
- Materials can help motivate creative expression.

TYPES OF MATERIALS

Materials described here are objects or items used by either teachers or children. Materials may be made by teachers or commercially produced. A partial listing of commercial suppliers for early childhood materials is included in the Appendix. Additional addresses may be found in early childhood professional magazines.

Some materials are made for teachers' use only. Other materials are used by both teachers and children. Still others are made solely for children's use (figure 23-1).

Staff-Made Materials

Every center has budget limitations. Staff-made items can increase the variety of materials available for language development activities (figure 23-2).

FIGURE 23-1 Some materials are designed for children to use without a teacher's help.

FIGURE 23-2 Children playing with a teacher-made card game

Many materials are creatively designed for special language teaching purposes. Some have been made from ideas obtained from other centers, other teachers, commercially manufactured items, resource magazines, or teacher workshops.

Staff-made materials are based on the interests and development levels of each group of children. They can be devised and designed to motivate and stimulate. This is part of the challenge of teaching — to keep a program continually inviting, expanding, and interesting to a unique group of individual children.

The Teacher's Role

The teacher's role in providing staff-made materials includes:

- Designing and creating appropriate materials that minimize competition and emphasize task completion.
- Constructing and preparing materials.
- Using materials with children.
- Caring for, storing, and replacing existing materials.

Appropriateness, cost, and sturdiness must be considered in the design and construction of materials. Most teacher-made materials are appreciated and wel-

comed by the entire staff and enjoyed by the children (figure 23-3).

Commercially Developed Materials

There is a wide variety of commercially manufactured materials for early childhood language development. They are available from teachers' supply stores and from educational media and equipment companies. Pictures, books, puppets, games, toys, audiovisual items, and idea resource books for early childhood teachers are just a few of the many items manufactured.

Teachers' magazines are a good source for addresses of companies that will send free catalogs on request.

Language-Development Kits and Sets

In addition to single items, special kits and sets are made to promote language development. These kits and sets may include various combinations of pictures, objects, games, charts, puppets, and audiovisual aids, such as records and filmstrips.

Most large kits include a teacher's manual with daily, planned activities for a language-development program. The goals of each activity are explained in detail along with suggestions for teachers and specific directions on what the teacher is to say during the activity. Most of the kits are based on sound educa-

FIGURE 23-3 Teacher-made materials are welcomed by teachers and children.

tional principles and have been designed by early childhood educators. Many of the kits are developmental, starting with basic language arts skills and progressing to more mature levels. Some sets are designed for use with children who have special language needs. Objectives cited in kits and sets include the following:

- Child's vocabulary development.
- Development of child's thought processes and problem-solving techniques.
- Practice with basic sentence patterns of standard English.
- Child's use of existing syntax and promotion of new syntax patterns.
- Child's expression of feelings and points of view.
- Child's use of creative language.
- Promotion of child's enjoyment and the development of positive attitudes through suggested activities.
- Development of child's self-concept.
- Use of techniques and methods that teach standard English as a second language.

The Teacher's Role

Teachers have different opinions on the use of language-development kits. Some prefer one kit over another; others prefer to plan their own programs; still others combine their own ideas with kit activities.

Teachers have expressed concern that a language kit might become the total program. They maintain that if this should happen, language arts might be offered only one way and at only one time of the day. They also point out that activities should be planned with regard for a particular group's current interests and past experiences. Kits that are based on the life experiences of children who live in only large cities may lack reality for rural children; kits based on the familiar experiences of the middle-class child may not be appropriate for children in other settings.

Care, proper storage, repair, and replacement of commercial language-development materials are part of the teacher's duties. Some kits are rather expensive, making teacher use, storage, and care even more important.

Figure 23-4 provides a listing of a few commercial kits and programs.

Alpha Time. New York: Arista Publishing.
Amazing Life Games. Boston: Houghton Mifflin.
Bilingual Early Childhood Program. Texas: Southwest Education Development.
Beginning Readiness. New York: Scribner-Laidlaw.
Focus on Meaning. London: George, Allen and Unwin, 1973. (Published in the United States as *Talking, Thinking, Growing.* New York: Schocken Books.)
Developing Oral Language with Young Children. Cambridge: Educator's Publishing Service.
Peabody Language Development Kit. Level P, Circle Pines: American Guidance Service.
SELF. Self, Morristown, NJ: Silver Burdett.
Special A. New York: Arista Publishing.
SWRL. Communication Skills Program: Expressive Language, Blocks 1 and 2. Lexington: Ginn.
The Children's Language Program. Menlo Park, CA: Addison-Wesley.
The Bank Street Early Childhood Explorer Series. Menlo Park, CA: Addison-Wesley.

FIGURE 23-4 Commercial language-development programs and kits

RESOURCES FOR TEACHER-MADE MATERIALS

Materials used in the construction of teaching aids can be obtained from a variety of community resources. Some materials are free or inexpensive; others are higher in cost. Some local resources that can provide materials include the following.

Local Businesses. Often displays and advertising material can be adapted. Boxes, containers, and packaging material are also available for the asking.

Thrift or Second-Hand Shops. Besides flea markets, garage sales, and so forth, these shops offer various kinds of resources.

Home Discards. Food packaging and mail advertising materials are plentiful. Items that are no longer useful, such as children's games with missing parts, can be restored and adapted to preschool playroom use.

Elementary School Discards. Old workbooks can be a good source for patterns and pictures.

School Supply Stores, Stationery Stores, Variety Stores, Five-and-Dime Stores. Dice, small plastic items, game spinners, colorful decals, decorative stamp packs, plastic and clear contact paper, construction paper and chartboard, binding tape, and so forth, are available.

Out-of-Town Companies and Public Agencies. Many national companies send teachers educational and promotional materials involving their products.

Printed Resource Guides to Free and Inexpensive Materials. Some examples include:

> *Free and Inexpensive Learning Materials.* George Peabody College for Teachers, Nashville: Division of Surveys and Field Services. (product company resources)
>
> Garlitz, Edward. *Resource Guide to Free and Inexpensive Materials.* NEA Center, Washington, D.C.: American Association of Elementary Kindergarten-Nursery Education. (public resources)

Construction Tips

The extra time devoted to adding protective coverings and sturdy storage containers for teacher-made items adds extra life to these items (figure 23-5). Clear

FIGURE 23-5 These sturdy, teacher-made puzzles are covered with clear plastic adhesive and made from coloring book pages mounted on cardboard. *(Colored by elementary school children.)*

contact paper, strapping tape, and plastic book-binding tape are often used to seal edges and protect surfaces. A lamination process is available at some centers. Material that is compact and can be folded is a must when storage space is limited.

Volunteer help and parents' talents and efforts are often used to construct classroom materials. Simple directions for construction prepared in advance minimizes the need for teachers' directions. One or more parent meetings a year is often devoted to construction of useful child language materials.

Teacher-Made Language-Development Materials

Pictures and Picture-File Collections. Magazine ads, calendar art, photographs, coloring-book pages, or drawings mounted on construction paper and filed in categories can be used in a variety of child activities and displays. Butterfly wall clips at the children's eye level add another display possibility.

Suggestions:

- Use pictures in a conversational way. The children can select pictures of their choice to talk about.
- Children can make their own picture books or picture dictionaries.
- A series of pictures can motivate children to tell stories.
- Pictures, drawings, or photos can be pasted to heavy paper or cardboard and easily cut into puzzles. Puzzles can be stored in flat boxes or flapped envelopes.

Patterns and Silhouettes. Seasonal shapes, animal and object shapes, and so forth, can be used in many interesting ways to create

- games in which children match or classify items
- tracing activities (figure 23-6)
- charts, murals, and display visuals
- shadow stories and overhead projector stories
- blank book-cover shapes
- flannel-board activity shapes

Storage:
Categorized patterns stored in see-through envelopes help teachers find shapes quickly. Small patterns can be enlarged using projectors.

Resources:

- Barnhart, Duane, et al. *The All Purpose Pattern Book.* Minneapolis, MN: T. S. Denison, 1982.

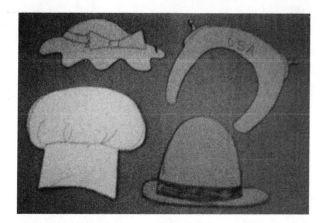

FIGURE 23-6 Children can choose a cardboard hat pattern to trace and then draw a face below it if they wish.

- *Jumbo Pattern Pads.* St. Louis: Milliken, 1986.
- *Animals to Color.* Racine: A Whitman Book, Western Publishing, 1979.

Activity Books. Commercial materials for children's activities and play books offer teachers a variety of ideas. Activities can be packaged separately for storage of games, patterns, and language activities.

Resources:

- *Play Book 1 and 2*, 1975. Available in local children's toy stores. Loughborough, Leicester, England: Ladybird Books Ltd.
- *Sticker Fun and Stamp Books.* Wayne: Western Publishing Co., Inc., Education Division, 1982.

Tracing Tablets. Materials needed include acetate (or X-ray film or heavy plastic see-through paper), cardboard, masking or cloth mending tape.

Construction:
Tape acetate and cardboard together, leaving three sides open (for younger children, leave only one side open).

LANGUAGE GAMES

Language games are defined as games in which children use communication skills. Played inside or outside, there are many game possibilities. The following concentrates on language arts games involving indoor teacher-made materials that emphasize skills in reading, speaking, and writing. The games are noncompetitive; each child finishes the task at his or her own rate of speed.

Children often make up their own games with their own rules. The games that follow usually need some direction and demonstration by the teacher before children proceed on their own.

Teachers' supervisory tasks during games include:

- eliminating undue competition
- monitoring, maintaining, and repairing games
- assisting children, when necessary (figure 23-7)
- responding positively, noting children's completion of tasks and proper handling of materials

Tips in constructing games include the following:

- Make child safety your first concern.
- Be sure the games are sturdy. Flimsy parts or

FIGURE 23-7 Teachers sometimes need to demonstrate a game.

frustrating tasks should be avoided. Reinforce edges and folds.

- Package each game as a complete unit in an attractive container.
- Make games that are colorful and attractive.
- Experiment with clear contact covering.
- Base games on observed child interests. If Yogi the Bear is an often-talked-about character, perhaps a game with a bear theme would immediately motivate the children.
- Include children's names, teachers' names, familiar school and community names and settings.
- Monitor children's game playing. Be watchful for instances in which a child needs teacher assistance.
- Be open to children's ideas; for example, find new ways to play a game or devise new rules. If games are changed, be sure the revised game makes good use of materials, so that materials are not lost or broken.
- Discover bookbinding, plastic, and strapping tape; book pockets; tongue depressors; and brads.
- Obtain inexpensive plastic and metal spinners from school suppliers.
- Design games using materials such as seeds, leaves, or wood.
- Design flat and freestanding types of games.

- Common preschool games often use the following materials:

  tongs and tweezers
  dice and spinners
  marbles, small balls, bean bags
  interesting textures and coverings
  small toys, such as metal cars and airplanes, small dolls, animal figures, and so forth
  rubber bands, nails, and pegs
  shoestrings and colored pipe cleaners
  commercial stamp sets
  hooks, clothespins, snaps
  small, colored blocks and rods
  magnets, paper clips
  discarded playing cards (figure 23-8)
  doweling or wood scraps

Resources:

Game Component Collection
Creative Publications, Inc.
Box 10382
Palo Alto, CA 94303

(Components include blank game boards, blank playing cards, wooden pawns, dice, spinners, shape and number pressure-sensitive stickers, felt game mats, and brightly colored storage boxes for the games created.)

Reading Readiness
Early Childhood Education Gameboards #2032
Communications Skill Building, Inc.
817 E. Broadway
P.O. Box 6081-E
Tucson, AZ 85733

GAMES

Matching Clothesline Game

Materials:

two lengths of clothesline rope, colorful clothespins, storage box, and a collection of paired, matching items (such as alphabet letters, felt shapes, pictures)

Procedure:

One child (or teacher) pins one of the pair of picture cards on the first line. Another child matches the cards in sequence on a second line.

FIGURE 23-8 A teacher supervises while children enjoy a tabletop activity with cards.

Lotto

Sets can be made to be difficult or easy, depending on the matches and the complexity of card figures.

Materials:

cardboard or tagboard sheets, ruler, pictures, pen, clear contact paper, scissors, small box for storing set, colorful contact paper for storage box (paper cutter optional)

Construction:

Make enough small cards to cover each square on each large Lotto card.

Procedure:

The game is played until all cards are drawn.

Word and Picture Dominoes

Materials:

oblong divided cards, small stamps or pictures, felt pen, ruler, scissors, paste, clear contact paper, tape (optional), playing board (optional), storage box

Procedure:

Cards are dealt face down. The second child to play matches one side of the first-played card or passes.

Classification Game

Materials:

two boxes, cards with fruit and fish pictures (many other categories are possible — birds, people, cars, farm, jungle, food), knife, scissors, paint (or scenes can be made from construction paper), glue, and felt pen

Construction:

Cut a door in the back of the box so cards can be retrieved. Make cards with pictures in two categories.

Procedure:

The child slips a card into the correct box (figure 23-9).

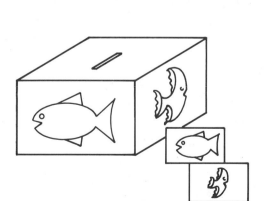
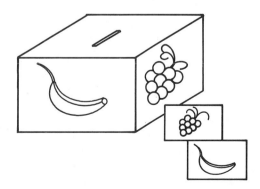

FIGURE 23-9 Classifying cards in correct box

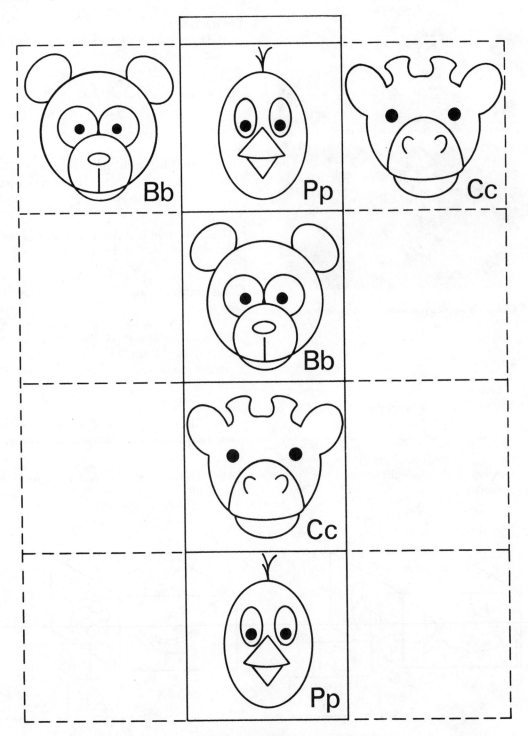

FIGURE 23-10 Dice patterns

Dice Games

Board and matching games that use dice are popular for language activities. Figure 23-10 shows a pattern for a large die. Games using one, two, or more dice are possible.

Matching Wheel Games

Pictures, spots, alphabet letters, and so forth, are matched (figure 23-11).

Large-Snake Floor Alphabet Puzzle

Draw a large snake on newsprint to be used as a pattern. Make segments large enough to printscript the alphabet in lowercase and uppercase. Cut segments; trace pieces on cardboard. Cut out. Print the alphabet. Cover with clear contact paper. Store in a large box.

Matching Tongue Depressors

A design is made in pairs on the tongue depressors. Bright paint is preferred. Children match the designs.

Spinner and Board Games

There are many possible game ideas. Old game boards or new game boards are easily designed (figure 23-12).

Card Games

Simple games made with commercial card sets save construction time. Pictures are colorful and card sets are available on many themes — cars, flowers, fish, animals, and so forth.

Resource:
EDU-CARDS, Binney and Smith, Easton, PA 18024

What Comes First?

Materials:

file cards, prepasted or instant-stick stickers, one large flapped manila envelope, a long piece of ribbon or strip of fabric, stapler

Construction:

Make two sets of sequence cards. Add sticker(s) to first card in set. Each sequence card contains an additional or new feature (figure 23-13). Then make an answer strip by stapling one card set in correct sequence on fabric or ribbon.

Procedure:

The child places cards in row from left to right, choosing the card that comes first, next, and so forth. The child checks the answer envelope to see whether his or her sequence matches the answer strip sequence. The strip is then placed under the child's row of cards.

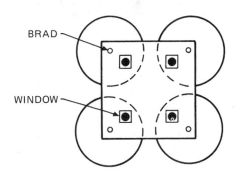

FIGURE 23-11 Wheel games

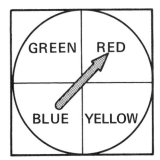 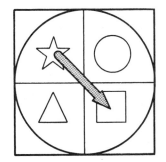 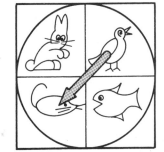

FIGURE 23-12 Spinners for game boards

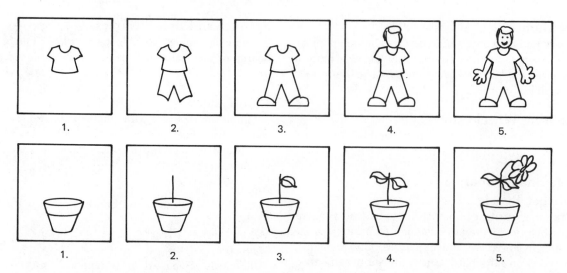

FIGURE 23-13 What comes first?

Puzzle with Words

Teachers can add word labels to large cardboard puzzle pieces. This helps increase children's awareness of written words. An example of a commercially prepared puzzle is the Magic Cottage Popout Puzzle, produced by Bank St. College of Education and published by Intelicor Products and Services, Inc., New York, NY 10018. (This puzzle is available at toy stores and school supply stores.)

Body-Part Matching Game

Materials:

cardboard (or tagboard), scissors, felt pens, pencil, clear contact paper

Construction:

Trace a child's foot and hand. Draw a large ear and eye pattern. Cut out the patterns. Trace the patterns on tagboard and cut matching pairs. Each set of two is different (change color or details).

Procedure:

The child picks out matching pairs from the collection.

SKILLS INCORPORATED IN GAMES

Table games often are designed to develop the following skills and abilities:

- small-muscle manipulation
- sorting ability — color, size, weight, shape, symbols
- visual matching of objects, symbols, patterns, colors, and categories (figure 23-14)
- sequence and ordering skills
- following game patterns and directions
- noticing likenesses and differences
- verbal and vocabulary development and labeling skill
- noting relationships
- visual memory
- tactile discrimination
- predicting outcomes

A game can be played until everyone finishes, and two or more turns can be given to speed this process and to avoid waiting time in group games. Many games are solitary pursuits or joint efforts with a friend or two.

When a new game is introduced, the teacher can make a statement like: "We play until everyone gets his or her marker on the pot of honey," or "If you've finished, others may need an extra turn to catch up," or "Everyone finishes this game. You keep taking turns spinning until you reach the end." Help reinforce this concept of noncompetitive play (figure 23-15).

Resources for Game Ideas

The following references contain additional ideas for early childhood language games.

Barrata-Lorton, Mary. *Workjobs.* Menlo Park, CA: Addison-Wesley, 1972.

FIGURE 23-14 This child is sorting by color.

Belton, Sandra, and Christine Terborgh. *Sparks.* Washington, D.C.: Human Service Press, 1972.

Day, Barbara. *Open Learning in Early Childhood.* New York: MacMillan, 1975.

Kaplan, Sandra, et al. *Change for Children.* Pacific Palisades: Goodyear Publishing Company, 1973.

Kay, Evelyn. *Games That Teach for Children Three Through Six.* Minneapolis: T. S. Denison.

McCord, Andy, and Shirley Ross. *Animal Rhythms.* San Jose: Personal Learning Association, 1973.

Playbooks. Loughborough, Leicester, England: Ladybird Books Ltd., 1979. (Available in many local toy stores).

Sesame Street Magazine, 1 Lincoln Plaza, New York, NY 10023.

FIGURE 23-15 Playing, rather than winning, is emphasized.

COMPUTERS — THE NEW AUDIOVISUAL

Preschool educators taking a serious look at microcomputer use by preschool children are hard put to find features that don't mesh well with their professional educational philosophy and practice. Many educators are as enthusiastic as the children who are lucky enough to experience them. Computers will neither replace nor displace the teacher or the teacher's planned activities. Instead, computers will add immeasurably to children's first-hand learning opportunities.

An increasing number of software programs developed for three- and four-year-olds and that run on a wide variety of microcomputers are being designed and manufactured. Stechert (1984) estimates that between 1984 and 1985 children's educational software increased from 5% of the software market to 20%. Prices vary but are no more expensive than other preschool play equipment. The computer itself is a large investment. Programs designed by knowledgeable early childhood educators are highly participatory, sensitive to the child's self-esteem, and aesthetically pleasing, as well as novel and fun. The child may listen, talk, create, express, make decisions, actively explore, build and destroy, and solve problems, all while feeling a sense of power. Van Nuy (1985) believes that children have an enviable attitude toward computers. Unlike adults, children aren't afraid of or awed by computers, and they go at the keyboard with an enthusiasm that can make adults cringe.

Research studies have made the following generalities concerning young children (in group programs) and microcomputers.

- Most four- and five-year-olds are interested.
- Waiting lists for computer use are usually necessary because of the popularity of computers.
- A knowledgeable, clear demonstration on operation and care is necessary.
- Children tend to work and discuss in small groups. Van Nuy (1985) feels that teachers will find that computers actually encourage social interaction among preschool children.
- After becoming proficient, some children prefer working alone.
- Time spent at the computer averages about 20 minutes a seating.
- Children adopt computer terms quickly (disk, boot, save, and so forth).
- Graphic programs that allow children to draw capture their fancy.
- Children learn to use joysticks, paddles, and hand controls after a brief introduction.
- A standard keyboard doesn't intimidate children.
- There is equal interest in computers by girls and boys.
- Children seem rewarded and don't seek or need outside teacher reinforcement.
- Both color and sound usually add to experiences.

From the evidence, it seems that microcomputers will take their place among the various children's games, toys, and activities. A computer can do what educators planning other experiences for children hope for — capture interest and make children feel competent. Computers are here to stay. How quickly they become standard preschool equipment depends on staff and school budget. Early childhood teachers are increasingly facing parents' questions regarding computer use and will be opening more and more computer centers in their classrooms.

The Teacher's Task in Computer Instruction

Where should a preschool teacher start? You'll need hands-on experiences; many county and city education offices already have computer education centers for teachers that are equipped with advisors and children's computer programs. Local computer stores gladly provide demonstrations. Local computer clubs abound with experts, or perhaps a parent can serve as a school resource.

Many language arts, reading, and writing skills are already part of existing preschool-level software programs. Software programs need serious previewing by preschool teachers before being included in the curriculum. The programs should advance a school's goals rather than serve as a gimmick to increase enrollment. Teachers, as mentioned before, will have to master using software programs in order to become effective coexplorers and resourceful guides (figure 23-16). Fortunately, this is not a difficult task although it is time-consuming.

Screening software programs for preschool use requires attention to the following:

Graphics. Are colors bright with high resolution? Is there on-screen clutter? Are animation and sound clear and pleasing?

FIGURE 23-16 Teachers can enthusiastically explore computers with children.

Manual dexterity. What degree of dexterity is required? Is it appropriate for preschoolers?

Quality. Is the program fun and easy? Does it have child identifiable content? Is it appealing? Is problem solving involved? Do problems have more than one right answer? Are errors handled without put-downs? Does the pacing allow for child reflection? Is inputting simple rather than complicated?

Values. Does the program represent or reflect appropriate values?

Computer Instruction Resources

Buckleitner, W. *1987 Survey of Early Childhood Software.* Ypsilanti, MI: High/Scope Press, 1987.

Davidson, Jane. *Computers in Early Childhood Education.* Albany: Delmar Publishers Inc., 1989.

Key Notes Newsletter, Ypsilanti, MI: High/Scope Press.

MicroNotes on Children & Computers, ERIC/EECE, College of Education, Univ. of Illinois, Urbana, IL 61801.

A listing of recommended computer programs appropriate for preschool and older children follows.

Alf in the Color Caves (Spinnaker Software)
Brilliant color and music and cause and effect relationships.
Color Me (Mindscape, Inc.)
A drawing program.
Delta Drawing (Spinnaker)
A drawing program for all ages. Creative and open-ended.
Ducks Ahoy (J. Hakanson Associates)
Delightful program that encourages prediction and planning with wit and charm.
Explore-a-Story Series (D. C. Heath & Co.)
Can be used to create and print child stories.
Getting Ready to Read (Sunburst Communications)
Sound-reinforced reward to matching games. Adult help required.
Kinder Comp (Spinnaker Software)
Child drawing and uppercase and lowercase letters plus pattern recognition.
The Learning Line (Eric Software)
Fun in matching a variety of textures and objects.

Learning With Leeper (Sierra On-Line)
Games that increase self-esteem on completion; letter matching.
Sea Horse Hide 'N Seek (CBS Software)
Game with color and music in which child estimates size, anticipates, and plans different strategies.
Stickybear ABC (Xerox Weekly Reader Family Software)
A bright and lively introduction to the alphabet.

Summary

A variety of materials and media is used to promote language development in early childhood centers. Materials can:

- motivate and stimulate
- promote play and interaction
- introduce new learnings
- keep children interested
- provide variety
- offer opportunities to manipulate and explore

Materials can be made by staff members or can be purchased. Staff-made items help provide a variety of activities. The needs, motivations, and interests of each particular group of children serve as the basis for the design of sturdy and inexpensive materials.

Commercial language-development kits and sets are also available. They differ in goals, activity plans, and types of items included. Most of the kits are sequential, starting with the simple and moving toward higher and broader levels of development. Teacher manuals should be studied closely before using the kits with children.

There are many teacher-made language game ideas in which skills are learned through game participation. Inexpensive materials for staff-made games are available from a variety of sources.

Microcomputers may take their place alongside traditional preschool materials as new software programs for young children are developed. Selecting programs in line with a school's goals may be the responsibility of an early childhood teacher, as well as serving as a resource person for both children and parents. Use of well-designed classroom computer centers may contribute to young children's educational opportunities.

Student Activities

- Visit an early childhood center; list and describe staff-made materials for language development.

- In small groups, compare language-development materials found in catalogs. Make comparisons between companies. Find 5 to 10 items that your group feels would be valuable for a center's language-development program.

- Visit a local stationery and supply store. Describe five items used in developing staff-made materials, or describe five commercially manufactured language-development materials or media.

- List and describe language-development kits used in local programs.

- Obtain a language kit. Read the teacher's manual and outline the goals of the program. Present an activity in class, with other students playing the role of the children.

- Design a dice game that uses a language arts skill. Draw a sketch and list the materials needed.

- Design a language-developing spinner and board game. Draw a sketch and list the materials needed.

- Invite an early childhood teacher to describe to the class the use of teacher-made and commercially made materials.

- Invite a manufacturer's representative of an early childhood language kit to describe the company's products to the class.

- Visit a computer center and preview a preschooler's software program.

- With a group of fellow students, discuss your feelings about the use of micro-computers for young children. Record your ideas and share them with the group.

Unit Review

A. Briefly discuss the following statements.
1. Many different types of media and materials are used to promote language arts for young children.
2. A teacher can add to a center's program by being aware of commercial materials for use in the language arts.
3. In designing and constructing materials for young children, there are several important considerations.
4. One of the duties of the teacher is proper maintenance of materials.

B. Match each item in Column I with the statement that best suits it from Column II.

Column I	Column II
1. games	a. free on request
2. local business	b. categorized collection
3. picture file	c. usually less expensive
4. staff-made items	d. a construction concern
5. sturdiness	e. storage, proper use, and replacement
6. care	f. resource for materials
7. catalogs	g. a collection of teaching materials
8. kit or set	h. every child wins
9. goals	i. from simple to complex
10. a sequence	j. objectives

C. Discuss the positive and negative features in the use of commercial language-development kits or sets.

D. Select the best answer.
  1. A large quantity of language materials
     a. makes a center interesting to young children.
     b. may not make a center interesting unless materials are also appropriate.
     c. assures language arts will be enjoyed.
     d. assures appropriateness of materials.
  2. Teachers can obtain valuable ideas for materials from
     a. catalogs
     b. school supply stores.
     c. resource books.
     d. visiting preschools.
     e. All the above.
  3. Materials can be purchased
     a. as single items or in groups.
     b. directly from manufacturers.
     c. at teachers' supply stores.
     d. All the above.
  4. A teacher who notices that a child is becoming frustrated with a language game should
     a. distract the child and suggest another activity.
     b. tell the child that he or she has chosen a game that is too difficult.
     c. subtly help the child by asking problem-solving questions or completing parts for the child.
     d. make sure the game is withheld from the classroom for a few months until the child is ready for it.

5. Language-development kits should be used
   a. without question because they are usually designed by expert educators.
   b. as the total language program.
   c. when the staff wants a sequential program.
   d. when staff members clearly understand goals and methods.
6. The main goal of teacher-made language games is
   a. enjoyable skill development for all players.
   b. to help winners gain self-esteem.
   c. reducing budget expenditures.
   d. teacher-child interaction.

E. Complete and discuss the following: "A preschool teacher's role in offering microcomputer programs is _____."

References

Piestrup, Ann M. "Young Children Use Computer Graphics." *Harvard Computer Graphics Weekly* 16.4. Boston: Harvard University Press. 1982. 18–25.

Stechert, Kathryn. "How Much Can A Preschooler Learn From A Computer?" *Better Homes and Gardens* 51.6 (Sept. 1984): 72–74.

Swigger, Kathleen M. "Is One Better?" *Educational Computer* 31.1 (Nov.–Dec. 1983): 102–109.

Van Nuys, Ute Elisabeth. "Overview of Preschool Computing." *MicroTimes* 2.9 (Sept. 1985): 49–57.

Watt, Molly. "Electronic Thinker Toys." *Popular Computing* 10.14 (June 1983): 22–31.

UNIT 24

The Parent-Center Partnership

OBJECTIVES

After studying this unit, you should be able to

- describe the parent-teacher partnership that affects language arts programs.
- list types of parent-school communications.
- identify ways in which parents can strengthen a child's language growth.

Although parents and teachers are partners in a child's education, parents are always the child's foremost teachers and models, and the home is the child's first and most influential school (figure 24-1). Parents are usually informed of the school's language and literacy curriculum during enrollment interviews. Most parents are eager to find out how teachers interact with their children on a daily basis to realize their instructional goals. Many educators believe that some parents have a great need to be told what to do in terms of their children's education and are vulnerable as a result. It is suggested that anxious parents need reassurance and can be encouraged to trust their instincts.

Child literacy at home and school is influenced by three important factors: (1) setting, (2) models, (3) planned and unplanned events. The setting involves what the home or school provides or makes available, including furnishings, space, materials and supplies, toys, books, and so forth. Access to additional settings outside the home is also considered (figure 24-2). Time allowed or spent in community settings can increase or decrease literacy. Family economics may determine the opportunities and materials that

FIGURE 24-1 A parent and child talking about discoveries.

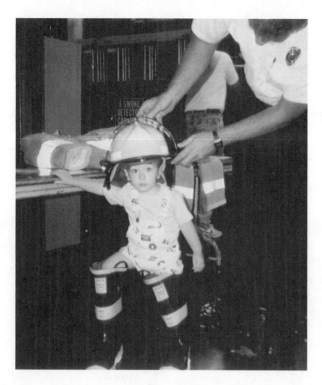

FIGURE 24-2 A trip to a fire station can include trying on a helmet and boots.

FIGURE 24-3 Parents sometimes need information about quality books.

are available, and family ingenuity may overcome a lack of monetary resources. The usefulness of speaking, writing, and reading can be emphasized in any home. Children's literature may be borrowed from public libraries and other sources in almost all communities (figure 24-3).

Adults and older children in a family who are literate and who model reading and writing can instill attitudes that these pursuits are worthwhile. Children will learn the speech they hear; children learn best by example, and the home model is more powerful than the school model.

Family interactions during activities involve both the quality and quantity of communication. The supportive assistance given at home, the atmosphere of the home, parent-child conversations, and joint ventures can greatly affect the child's literacy development.

PARENT GUIDELINES FOR LITERACY AND LANGUAGE DEVELOPMENT

The techniques or actions recommended to help children's language and literacy development apply to both teachers and parents. Parents have different and more varied opportunities to use these techniques. The following guidelines have been gathered from a variety of sources dealing primarily with parent-child relations and some have been mentioned previously in this text.

General hints for promotion of literacy

- Keep in mind that children's early experiences with print, writing tools, alphabet letters, and books can be puzzling. When children ask questions, they should readily be given assistance and answers, while they are focused. Parents are interrupted frequently, and children's questions may seem endless, but parents get used to slipping quickly in and out of children's play. This type of on-the-move teaching is natural and different from sit-down structured teaching to which the child tunes out as interest wanes.

- Offer what is just a little beyond what the child already knows in a supportive, enthusiastic, discovery setting. Interactions between parents and children should be shared and enjoyable.
- Turning conversations into commands aimed at teaching language arts turns children away.
- Arrange things so that children have many opportunities to see operations from beginning to end. For example, make butter from whipping cream or applesauce from picked apples. Make cloth from yarn (knitted, crocheted). Make peanut butter. Grow pumpkins, and make pumpkin pie or pumpkin bread, as well as jack-o'-lanterns. Children often are not aware of the origins of the things we take for granted (Hutinger, 1978).
- Encourage each success or honest effort with a smile of approval or loving words.
- Be available as a resource person. When children ask questions that you can't answer, don't hesitate to seek help from others (A Guide for Parents of Young Children, 1982).
- Help children to feel secure and successful. Your interactions can build feelings of self-worth if children's ideas and opinions are valued, or feelings of worthlessness if their ideas and opinions are negated or ignored (News for Parents from the International Reading Council, 1980).

Stimulating speaking abilities

- Talk to children lovingly, taking care to speak naturally and clearly. Listen when children want to tell you something; don't nag or interrupt children when they are speaking (but do make an effort to correct speech errors casually, that is, without drawing attention to the error). Read stories, poems, jingles, and riddles to children; don't regard incorrect speech as "cute" or encourage baby talk (but don't expect perfect speech from

the preschooler, either). Encourage play with puppets, bendable family dolls, dress-up clothes, play stores, doctor kits, and play telephones, letting the children act out various events and practice the language patterns we use in our daily lives. Encourage children to tell you stories (Rogers, 1980).

- Increase your attempts to build vocabulary by including new and descriptive words in your vocabulary.
- Give attention; listen for intent rather than correctness. Show children that what they say is important. Communicate with children at their eye level, when possible. Expand and tactfully extend children's comments; talk on the children's chosen subjects.
- Use your best speech model — standard English, if it comes naturally. If you speak a language other than English, provide a good model of that language.
- Become a skilled questioner by asking questions that promote thinking, predicting, and a number of possible answers based on the children's viewpoints.
- Encourage children to talk about whatever they are making, but don't keep asking them, "What is it?" (Hutinger, 1978).
- Talk frequently; give objects names; describe the things you do; speak distinctly and be specific; use full sentences; encourage children to ask questions; and include children in mealtime conversations (News for Parents from the International Reading Council, 1980).

Building print awareness and skill

- Provide literature and a language-rich setting in the home.
- Write down the things children tell you about their pictures. Make books of each child's work and photographs, and talk about the books (Hutinger, 1978).
- Read family letters and mail to children along with circulars, junk mail, restaurant menus, wrappers and packaging, signs, labels, building identifications, catalogs, brand names, and calendars.

- Provide scrap paper and writing tools, and reserve an area in the home as a writing center for children's use.
- Make or buy alphabet letter toys or word books.
- Ask teachers for copies of the alphabet your children will use in kindergarten.
- Encourage scribbling and doodling.
- Write messages to children or make signs for their play, such as "Mark's boat."
- Talk about what you are writing and its use to you.
- Read signs when driving or walking, especially safety signs.
- Point out print on home equipment and products.
- Encourage interest in paper and crayon activities by showing children their names in print. Give attention to their attempts to copy their names or write them from memory (A Guide For Parents of Young Children, 1982).

Providing experiences outside the home

- Take trips to interesting places: bowling alley, shoe-repair shop, bakery, zoo, farm, airport, different kinds of stores, and train and bus trips. When you get back, make drawings related to the trip. Talk about it. Recreate it in creative dramatics. Effective trips can be quite simple but need careful planning. Visit community events such as 4-H fairs, craft shows, antique-auto shows, new-car shows, farm-equipment displays (Hutinger, 1978).
- Having children accompany you to the store, bank, post office, zoo, or park can turn the trip into an educational excursion. A home has many advantages that a school cannot duplicate (Rogers, 1980).

Promoting listening

- Try teaching children to listen and identify sounds, such as the whine of car tires, bird calls, insect noises, and sounds of different kinds of doors in the house closing. Records, television, and storybooks also stimulate interest in listening (Rogers, 1980).
- Be a good listener — pause before answering, and wait patiently for children to formulate answers or speech.

Promoting an interest in reading

- Reading is dependent on facility with oral language. Children who talk easily, handle words skillfully, asks questions, and look for answers usually become good readers. Parents have an easy job compared with teachers who have groups of children to help. Parents should talk to their infants, chant nursery rhymes, and sing old folk songs and lullabies. This is the beginning of conversation, which is basic to reading (Larrick, 1980).
- Stop reading to a child who has lost concentration. Search for enthralling books.
- Read to children every day. Be sure to read quality stories that are written for the appropriate age level. Ask librarians for help (Hutinger, 1978). See figure 24-4 for a listing of books with an element of predictability that usually increases enjoyment and self-esteem.
- Get children actively involved, participating in reading by chanting lines, pointing, speaking in different voices for each character, or whatever is natural and logical for the book's text or format.
- Give reading status and importance; read recipes and directions; emphasize the functional uses of reading.
- A child's age will determine, in part, what he or she will find interesting in a book. The preschooler is interested in rhyming words, repetitions, characters the child's own age, bright colors, and fun things to feel. The more a child is exposed to pleasurable reading activities, the greater will be his or her interest in reading. Read aloud and provide books for browsing and a special place to keep the collection. Enjoy reading and encourage children to read a wide variety of materials. Go to the library. Arrange a time to read with children. You may read your own materials separately or read the same story together. Provide reading-related activities. Encourage children to write stories. Try story telling without a book (Ransbury, 1980).
- Children will become readers only if their emotions are engaged and their imaginations are stretched and stirred by what they find on the printed page. The truly literate are not those who know how to read, but those who read fluently, responsively, critically, and because they want to (Sloan, 1980).

Author	Title	Publisher
Arno, Ed	The Gingerbread Man	Crowell
Baum, Arline and Joseph	One Bright Monday Morning	Random House
Bonne, Rose, and Mills, Alan.	I Know an Old Lady	Rand McNally
Brandenberg, Franz	I Once Knew a Man	Macmillan
Brown, Marcia	The Three Billy Goats Gruff	Harcourt
Burmingham, John	Mr. Grumpy's Outing	Holt
Charlip, Remy	What Good Luck! What Bad Luck!	Scholastic
Charlip, Remy, and Supree, Burton	Mother Mother I feel Sick Send for the Doctor Quick Quick Quick	Scholastic
Chwast, Seymour	The House That Jack Built	Random House
Emberly, Barbara and Ed	One Wide River to Cross	Prentice-Hall
Flack, Marjorie	Ask Mr. Bear	Macmillan
Galdone, Paul	The Three Billy Goats Gruff	Seabury
Graham, John	I Love You, Mouse	Harcourt
Hogrogian, Nonny	One Fine Day	Macmillan
Hutchins, Pat	The Surprise Party	Collier
	Rosie's Walk	Macmillan
Kraus, Ruth	Bears	Scholastic
Langstaff, John	Oh, A-Hunting We Will Go	Atheneum
	Soldier, Soldier, Won't You Marry Me?	Doubleday
Leodhas, Sorche Nic	All in the Morning Early	Holt
Martin, Bill, Jr.	Brown Bear, Brown Bear, What Do You See?	Holt
	A Ghost Story	Holt
	The Haunted House	Holt
	Tatty Mae and Catty Mae	Holt
	Ten Little Squirrels	Holt
	Welcome Home, Henry	Holt
	When It Rains . . . It Rains	Holt
Merriam, Eve	Do You Want To See Something?	Scholastic
Sendak, Maurice	Chicken Soup with Rice	Scholastic
Shaw, Charles B.	It Looked Like Spilt Milk	Harper
Shulevitz, Uri	One Monday Morning	Scribner's
Slobodkina, Esphyr	Caps for Sale	Scholastic
Spier, Peter	The Fox Went Out on a Chilly Night	Doubleday
Stover, JoAnn	If Everybody Did	McKay
Viorst, Judith	Alexander and the Terrible, Horrible, No Good, Very Bad Day	Atheneum
Zolotow, Charlotte	If It Weren't for You	Harper

FIGURE 24-4 Books with predictable features help children gain confidence. *(From* A Primer on Teaching Reading, *by George Mason. Permission to reprint from F. E. Peacock Publishers, Inc., © 1981.)*

- It is wise to select from among the best books for even the youngest children. The best are well-designed with uncluttered pages, interesting print, and colorful pictures that stimulate young imaginations. If children are introduced to excellence from the beginning, they will gradually develop a taste for the finest (Sloan, 1980).

- Parents often think that children learn about

reading in school. The truth of the matter is that many children already know a lot about reading when they enter kindergarten, because parents have been teaching their children about reading since they were born. Methods that parents use to teach differ from those used by school teachers. Parents help children every day — when they take them to the grocery store or point out street signs. Experience with print gives a broad and meaningful introduction to reading. Reading really cannot be learned very well if it is first taught only with lessons on isolated letters and sounds. If reading is to make sense to children, they must see how it is used in life (Schickedanz, 1983).

- When children select books, show a genuine interest; don't criticize children's selection.
- When children ask for the pronunciation of words, tell them the words; don't analyze the words or sound them out.
- Discuss authors and illustrations at times.
- Enjoy humor or fun in books. Relate book happenings to the children's real life experiences.
- Parents have a much better chance to help children form good attitudes about books than do teachers, because of the close, personal relationship between parent and child. Intimate discussions and warm, relaxed, unpressured readings are typical in home experiences. Parents also can best match the books to their children's interests.
- Subscribe to children's magazines or borrow copies from libraries.

Parents who may wish to rate themselves using figure 24-5 may discover they are already promoting child language and literacy in a number of ways.

Home Reading Centers

Home reading centers are a lot like school reading areas. A comfortable, warm, private, well-lighted place free of distraction works best. Adjacent shelving and a chair for parent comfort is important to book-sharing times. Window seats and room dividers make cozy corners. Parents can get creative in selecting and furnishing reading centers. A good parent resource is "A Home Reading Corner," by Sister St. John Delaney (*Pre-K Today* 2.4, Jan. 1988, 34).

Family book collections build children's attitudes concerning books as personal possessions and give books status. Homes model appropriate storage and care.

Library Services

Parents are sometimes unaware of the development of children's library services. Children's librarians are great sources of information and often offer children a wide-ranging program of literary events and activities. They are good at finding books that match a particular child's interest. Teachers who are in touch with a preschool child's emerging interests can alert parents.

Television Viewing and Young Children's Language Development

Parents often ask teachers about the value of television and their children's viewing habits. The average child entering first grade has spent nearly 5,000 hours watching television (Finn, 1980). Rosemond (1988) estimates that the average preschooler has 30 hours of television viewing per week. Researchers indicate that over half of the children in the U.S. watch Sesame Street regularly (Lesser, 1974). This figure has increased due to expanded home use of video cassettes.

Most educators suggest that parents limit and guide children's viewing. Screening programs and video cassettes is a wise move because of varying quality and values presented. Conversational follow-up after watching programs together gives parents their best opportunity for promoting language development. As Honig (1983) points out, children learn best from educational television shows if adults who watch television with them explain difficult words and ideas and build on the concepts that were introduced. Parents can talk about what has happened, what could have happened, and what may happen.

Teachers alert parents to consider how to use television in positive ways. Recognized benefits of some children's programs include relaxation and entertainment, exposure to new experiences and ideas, vocabulary enlargement, introduction to classic children's literature, and educational information. Criscuolo (1982) suggests that parents should:

- Limit in some way the amount of television a child watches, leaving time for reading and other more active pursuits.

Use the following ratings: O = often, S = sometimes, I = infrequently, D = doesn't apply.

Parent attempts to:

	1. Initiate family discussions at mealtimes.

_____ 1. Initiate family discussions at mealtimes.

_____ 2. Give full attention to child's comments.

_____ 3. Purposeful addition of descriptive or new words in conversation.

_____ 4. Take child to library.

_____ 5. Take time at post office to discuss letters and postage.

_____ 6. Discuss children's books.

_____ 7. Read to child daily.

_____ 8. Point out print around the house.

_____ 9. Accept child's opinions.

_____ 10. Use dictionary with child.

_____ 11. Talk on the child's chosen subject.

_____ 12. Ask questions that promote child's descriptions or predictions.

_____ 13. Listen patiently.

_____ 14. Discuss TV programs.

_____ 15. Plan community outings.

_____ 16. Invite interesting people to home and promote interactions with child.

_____ 17. Correct child's speech casually with little attention to errors.

_____ 18. Encourage child hobbies.

_____ 19. Answer questions readily.

_____ 20. Discuss care and storage of books.

_____ 21. Play word games or rhyme words playfully.

_____ 22. Talk about how print is used in daily life.

_____ 23. Find books on subjects of interest to child.

_____ 24. Consult with child's teacher.

_____ 25. Give attention and notice accomplishments.

_____ 26. Take dictation from child.

_____ 27. Try not to interrupt child's speech frequently.

_____ 28. Initiate family reading times and family discussions of classics.

_____ 29. Establish a book center in the home.

_____ 30. Create child writing or art center in the home.

_____ 31. Give books as gifts.

_____ 32. Provide different writing tools and scrap paper.

_____ 33. Provide alphabet toys in the home.

FIGURE 24-5 Parent self-rating.

- Serve as an example by limiting the amount of television parents watch and scheduling times when the set is switched off and the entire family reads something.
- Ask children to describe favorite TV characters, using a variety of different words that stimulate the use of a rich vocabulary. This makes parents aware of the types of qualities children admire.
- Encourage children to watch programs like Sesame Street.

Other suggestions include:

- Finding local PBS (public broadcasting) listings of appropriate programs.
- Purchasing or borrowing follow-up materials, such as *Sesame Street Magazine*, puppets, toys, and books.

HOME-SCHOOL COMMUNICATION

Schools differ widely both in the amounts of written home-school communication and time spent talking or meeting with parents. Most preschool teachers desire more time and more conversations and additional written communication with parents. This suits some parents who seem to be seeking supportive assistance in child rearing. Each parent group and center is unique, and consequently tremendous differences exist in the degree to which preschools and parents work together. Most centers try to provide some type of parent assistance. Parents who receive help and support feel more open to contribute to the school's activities (Wardle, 1987).

Parent-school contacts usually take place in at least four ways:

1. daily conversations
2. written communications (figure 24-6).
3. planned parent meetings, workshops, and social events
4. individual conferences

On the Fly

Teachers have a good chance to share children's interests and favorite school activities with the parent at the end of the day, when parents arrive to take their children home from the center: books, play objects, and child-created or constructed work can be mentioned. Children spend time with and talk about what excites them; the observant teacher is aware of attending children's at-school play and work. Parents are usually interested in what their children have shared about their homes and out-of-school activities.

Bulletin Boards

Many schools use "parent" bulletin boards as a communicative device. Schools receive more announcements of literary happenings in their communities than do parents. Language-developing local events and activities can be advertised to parents. Short magazine and newspaper articles of interest can be posted at eye-catching levels.

Planned Meetings

Planned meetings include individual and group gatherings.

Conferences

Parents need to know how the school plans for their children's individual interests and growth. When children have interests in alphabet letters, dramatizing, or special-topic books, parents and teachers can discuss related school and home activities.

Issue 2, Vol. 1   **Child Development Center**   **November, 1988**

FIGURE 24-6 A newsletter letterhead that encourages the home-school partnership *(Courtesy of Katherine Blanton, San Jose City College Child Development Center, San Jose City College, San Jose, CA 1988.)*

Goal Identification Meetings

Meetings with parents and staff identify language arts planning areas and parents' wishes and concerns. A center's language arts goals reflect the ideas of both parents and staff. Parents, as well as teachers, value the development of young children's listening, speaking, writing, and reading skills. Teachers contribute ideas and play an integral role in the home-school partnership.

Method-and-Material Review Meetings

A meeting can be planned to take a closer look at the preschool's planned language program, materials, and language arts center. Parents get a first-hand look and an opportunity to explore. Teachers conduct sample activities and demonstrate material and equipment use. Parents may ask questions about their children's use of or interest in a center's planned opportunities.

Parent-Teacher Study Meetings

Some possible themes of study meetings include (1) the effects of television viewing on children's language development, (2) bilingualism, or (3) free and inexpensive home toys that promote language. The center's staff, parents, outside experts, or films can present ideas to be studied and discussed. This type of meeting helps inform all who are present. Differing views clarify everyone's thinking.

It's a good idea to analyze what's really important to communicate to parents concerning children's language arts development. The following items are the author's high-priority topics:

1. So many parents show concern over their children's articulation and vocabulary. It is helpful to assure parents that the school's staff monitors fluency and to share typical child speech characteristics. Such discussions often relax parents and dispel their fears. Hints concerning simple modeling of correct forms is well-received by most parents.

2. Sharing information on school interaction techniques that the staff uses to increase children's speech by listening, following children's leads, and expanding interest in daily conversation is very important.

3. Parents need to know how influential they are in modeling an interest in and positive attitudes toward reading, writing, and speaking. Their ability to listen closely to ideas rather than judging correctness of grammar or ideas should be discussed.

4. Another topic to discuss with parents is the warm, unpressured social environments that promote conversations about pleasurable happenings.

5. Reading picture books and sharing stories with the family at home will stimulate children's desire for more. Discussing quality books and "advertising" books to children can perhaps combat a television dominance in the home. Two resources that teachers can recommend to parents are "Activities to Strengthen Reading at Home (Ages 4–6), Part 2, by Dorothy Rich, *Instructor* 98.2 (Oct. 1988): 52–60, and "For Love of Reading — a Parent's Guide to Encouraging Young Readers From Infancy Through Age 5," by Masha Rudman, New York: Consumer Reports Books, 1987.

6. The child's home access to creative materials, such as drawing and marking tools, is important.

7. Parents have many questions about early reading and writing of alphabet letters. Both reading and writing acquisition is aided by a widely enriching home and preschool curriculum that preserves children's feelings of competence by offering that which is slightly above their level and related closely to their present interests.

DAILY CONTACTS

Greeting both parents and children as they arrive starts a warm, comfortable atmosphere, encourages talking, and sets the tone for conversation. Short, personal comments build parent-school partnership feelings, and help children enter the school discussing the morning's happenings. Children are offered choices of possible activities through certain statements such as "We've put red playdough on the table by the door for you," or "The matching game you told me you liked yesterday is waiting for you on the shelf near the bird cage."

Parent mailboxes can hold daily teacher messages. Important milestones, such as the child's first interest or attempt at printing alphabet letters or his or her name, or first created stories, should be shared. A short note from the teacher about a child's special events is appreciated by most parents. Special daily happenings such as "I think Toni would like to tell you about the worm she found in the garden," or "Saul has been asking many questions about airplanes," keep parents aware of their children's expanding interests.

WRITTEN COMMUNICATION

Often centers prepare informal letters or newsletters that describe school happenings or daily themes. Fig-

ures 24-7 and 24-8 are two examples of this type of teacher-parent communication.

A written communication may concern the following:

- Local library addresses or a description of services or programs such as story hours or puppet shows.
- Local children's theater or drama productions.
- Children's book stores.
- Film presentations of interest to the young child.
- Special community events.
- Adult programs, workshops, meetings, and so forth, that include topics concerned with the development of children's language arts.

BIG, BIGGER, BIGGEST

Dear Parents,

At school we are learning to talk about the size of things. Sometimes we compare the size of two things. Sometimes we compare more than two.

We listen for the sounds at the end of the size words, especially for *-er* and *-est*. When we compare two objects or people, we hear and say the *-er* form. (Example: Alonzo is *bigger* than Antonio.) When we compare more than two, we hear and say the *-est* form. (Example: Alonzo is the *biggest* boy in the class.)

Here are some suggestions you can use at home to help your child learn to talk about the size of things:

1. Place some objects such as boxes, small containers, buttons, or cards, in a box or on the floor. Let your child arrange them according to size:

   smallest to largest
   largest to smallest
   same sizes together.

   During the arranging, talk about which are bigger, which are smaller, and which is biggest or smallest of all.

2. Play games of "smaller but larger."
   - Find something smaller than your hand, but larger than your finger.
   - Find something smaller than the clock but bigger than a penny.
   - Find something smaller than an orange but larger than a pea.

3. Play size games while walking around. Say, "I see something tall. It is a telephone pole. Can you find something taller? Or shorter?" Keep playing until no one can find anything taller or shorter, wider or narrower, etc.

   Use many words that tell the size of things.

   Sincerely,

FIGURE 24-7 An informal teacher letter describing a concept the child is learning in school *(From Language Experiences in Early Childhood, by Roach Van Allen and Claryce Allen. Chicago: Encyclopedia Britannica Ed. Corporation, 1969.)*

- Requests for "junk" materials useful in language arts games or activities.

Monthly Newsletters

If a school is trying to help parents expand their children's experiences, newsletters can suggest family outings and excursions to local community events and low-cost and free entertainment. Dates, times, costs, telephone numbers, and simple maps can be included. Wardle (1987) describes newsletter production as a team project.

Dear Parents:

This week we've talked about many means of transportation — of how we use animals and machines to take us from one place to another.

We built things, painted things and learned songs and heard stories about different vehicles such as bikes, cars, trucks, buses, boats, trains, airplanes, horses and wagons, etc., and even took a bus ride.

Here are some suggested home activities to reinforce school learnings:

- Talk about places you go together in your car.
- Save large cardboard boxes — line them up, and pretend they're railroad cars.
- Save old magazines. Let your child find "Vehicles that move things from place to place." They may want to find, cut and paste pictures.
- Take a walk, and find all the moving vehicles you can.
- Sing a train song, "I've been Working on the Railroad," or any other.
- Plan a ride on or in a vehicle that's new to the child.

As you enjoy life together you may want to point out and talk about transportation.

Sincerely,

P.S. Here's a rebus poem to share.

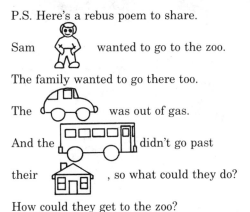

Sam   wanted to go to the zoo.

The family wanted to go there too.

The   was out of gas.

And the   didn't go past

their   , so what could they do?

How could they get to the zoo?

FIGURE 24-8 A partnership letter

A newsletter is a team project. The size of your staff will determine the number of people available to work on it. One person should be responsible to pull it together while other staff members work on specific pages. Childen can illustrate pages after they've been typed — drawing in margins only!

Completed newsletters can be handed out to parents at pick-up or drop-off time. Try to keep the newsletter upbeat and fun with jokes, quotes, and anecdotes scattered throughout the pages.

PARENT RESOURCES

Centers sometimes provide informational articles, magazines, and books that may be borrowed for short periods or available at the school's office. Photocopied magazine articles in manila folders that have been advertised on the school's parent bulletin board are a good resource for busy parents.

Descriptions of home activities aiding children's language development can be either created by the teacher or commercially prepared. One such commercial kit is *Learning Language at Home*, by Merle B. Karnes, published by the Council for Exceptional Children, 1920 Association Dr., Reston, VA 22091 (about $35.00). It offers parents 1,000 ideas for home activities.

Information on children's books and reading can be obtained from:

American Library Association, 50 E. Huron St., Chicago, IL 60611.

Butler, Dorothy. *Babies Need Books*. New York: Atheneum, 1985.

Children's Book Council, Inc., P.O. Box 706, Irving Place, New York, NY 10276.

Copperman, Paul. *Taking Books to Heart*. Menlo Park, CA: Addison-Wesley, 1986.

International Reading Association, 800 Barksdale Road, P.O. Box 8139, Newark, DE 19714.

Larrick, Nancy. *A Parent's Guide to Children's Reading*. New York: Bantam, 1975.

Kimmel, Mary Margaret, and Elizabeth Segal. *For Reading Out Loud!: A Guide to Sharing Books With Children*. New York: Delacorte Press, 1984.

Oppenheim, Joanne, Barbara Brenner, and Betty Boegehold. *Choosing Books for Kids*. New York: Ballantine Books, 1986.

Trelease, Jim. *The Read-Aloud Handbook*. New York: Penguin Books, 1982.

PARENTS AS PROGRAM VOLUNTEERS

Most parent groups include willing volunteers who donate their time, talents, skills, and abilities or share hobby collections with the children (figure 24-9). The following are some of the ways parents can contribute:

- Celebrating "book week"
- Explaining occupations. Encourage parents to be guest speakers, discussing their occupations. Ask them to bring in items used in their occupations and to wear the clothing associated with their jobs.
- Demonstrating special skills and hobbies. From yoga to weaving, parents' simple demonstrations interest children.
- Providing cooking demonstrations. Cooking demonstrations by parents can add to children's language knowledge.
- Organizing field trips. Parents may volunteer their time or suggest places to go.
- Organizing fund-raisers.

FIGURE 24-9 Parent volunteers are a welcomed resource.

In addition to volunteering their time, parents can be good resources for providing materials (figure 24-10). Many parents often work in businesses where useful language arts materials are discarded, such as scrap paper, cardboard, and so forth. The parent is usually more than willing to obtain these previously discarded materials, especially if they are unable to volunteer their time to the center.

Many parent volunteers enjoy making language-developing games and visuals. Parent creativity and ability can astonish teachers. Art, photography, sewing, and carpentry talent lends itself to creating and constructing many classroom materials. Repairing a school's books, flannel board sets, and puppet collections can be an ongoing task. Directing the efforts of volunteers and preparing for them takes time but saves much more time in the long run. Most schools survey parents for unique skills, hobbies, and abilities by sending home questionnaires. Even the busiest parents seem to find time to share their expertise as visiting guest speakers. Through the joint efforts of home and school, centers are able to provide a wider range of language-developing experiences for attending children.

FIGURE 24-10 A parent discarded these placemats, which are used for art activities.

Summary

Schools differ in both the amount and types of interactions between families and the center. School personnel need to clarify priorities that they wish to communicate to parents concerning children's language development. By teachers and parents working together, children's learning experiences can be reinforced and expanded.

Contact with parents takes place in a variety of ways, both planned and unplanned, including daily conversations, written notes and letters, and scheduled conferences. Centers are interested in promoting the reading of quality books in the home and alerting parents to community opportunities. Parent volunteers can aid goal realization in the language arts by sharing their talents, hobbies, labor, time, and energy. Together, home and school can work toward children's language growth and competence.

Student Activities

- Photocopy the following, and cut the sections into cards. Rate each card before joining a group of classmates to discuss ratings.

Rating Scale

1	2	3
teacher used good judgment	uncertain about teacher's behavior	teacher used poor judgment

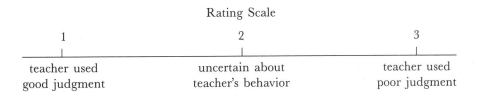

A field trip is in progress. Mrs. Winkler, a parent, is acting as a volunteer supervisor. A teacher overhears Mrs. Winkler tell her group to be quiet and listen to her explanation of what is happening at the shoe factory. The teacher tactfully suggests to Mrs. Winkler that the children may wish to ask questions.

During a study meeting, two parents are having a heated discussion concerning television's value. A teacher offers her views. Her views happen to support one side of the argument.

Mr. Sousa is a violinist. He is also Tami's father. Tami's teacher sends a special note to Mr. Sousa, inviting him to share his talents with the class. The note mentions that he will be allowed to play the violin for a five-minute period.

Mr. Thomas, a teacher, knows about a book sale at a local children's book store. He includes the item in the school's newsletter to parents.

Sending written messages to parents is not personal, Ms. Garcia (a teacher) feels. She telephones parents in the evenings with news of milestones their children have accomplished in the school's language arts program.

Parent bulletin-board posting is part of Miss Alexian's duties. She feels parents rarely read posted materials. At a staff meeting, she asks others for helpful ideas for displays that would grab parents' attention.

Mr. Washington, a teacher, greets the children by waving from across the room or saying "Hi, Mark, I'm glad you're here."

"Oh, that's not the right way to ask a child about his or her artwork," Mrs. Yesmin, a teacher, says to Patsy's father.

"You're her teacher. Why ask me what she does at home? It's what goes on at school I'm interested in!" says Mrs. McVey, Pam's mother. "Knowing how Pam spends her time at home helps me plan school activities," explains Mrs. Lerner, Pam's teacher.

"Do you read to your child?" Miss Hernandez asks Mike's mother. "Of course, didn't you think I did?" the child's mother answers.

"There's an article on the parent bulletin board about children's use of slang words that you might want to look over, Mrs. Chung," says Mr. Benjamin (a teacher) to one of the parents.

During a parent-teacher meeting, Mrs. Texciera says, "Jill's work is always so messy." Miss Flint, the teacher, answers, "With time, it will improve. She's working with small puzzles and painting. This will give her more practice and control."

- Plan a parent newsletter for a local preschool center with helpful information concerning children's language development.

- Invite a school's director to discuss parent involvement in a school's language arts goals.

- Identify three books that might help parents understand children's language development or that might provide home activity ideas. Cite the title, author, and copyright date.

- Find three magazine articles that might be useful in a discussion concerning home television viewing.

- Interview a few parents of preschoolers. Ask, "What three communication skills do you feel are important for your child's success in elementary school (which he or she will attend after preschool)?"

- Discuss the following statement with a classmate: "Many parents are so busy and tired after work that parent meetings are just an added burden."

Unit Review

A. In a short paragraph, describe parent involvement in an early childhood center's language arts program.

B. List the teacher's duties and responsibilities in school-home communications.

C. What is the meaning of the following statement? "Early childhood centers reinforce home learnings just as homes can reinforce center learnings."

References

"Choosing a Child's Book." New York: Children's Book Council, 1986.

Copperman, Paul. *Taking Books To Heart.* Menlo Park, CA: Addison-Wesley, 1986.

Criscuolo, Nicholas P. "You Can Use Television To Stimulate Your Child's Reading Habits." Newark, Delaware: International Reading Association, 1982. 5–6.

Delaney, Sister St. John. "A Home Reading Corner." *Pre-K Today* 2.4. Jan. 1988. 34.

Finn, Peter. "Developing Critical Television Viewing Skills." *Educational Forum* 44.2 (May 1980): 41–48.

Friedrich, Otto, "What Do Babies Know?" In H. E. Fitzgerald and M. G. Walraven (Eds.). *Human Development 85/86.* Guilford, CT: The Duskin Publishing Group, 1985.

Honig, Alice Sterling. "Television and Young Children." *Young Children* 38.2 (May 1983): 67–74.

"How Does Your Child Grow and Learn?" *A Guide for Parents of Young Children.* Jefferson City: Missouri Department of Elementary Ed. and Secondary Ed., 1982.

Hutinger, Patricia L. "Language Development: It's Much More Than a Kit." *Day Care and Early Education* 5.2 (Spring 1978): 44–47.

Jewell, Margaret Greer, and Miles V. Zintz. *Learning To Read Naturally.* Dubuque, IA: Kendall/Hunt, 1986.

Kaye, Evelyn. *The Family Guide to Children's Television.* New York: Pantheon Books, 1974.

Kimmel, Mary Margaret, and Elizabeth Segal. *For Reading Out Loud!: A Guide to Sharing Books With Children.* New York: Delacorte Press, 1986.

Larrick, Nancy. *A Parent's Guide to Children's Reading.* New York: Bantam Books, 1975.

————. "Parents And Teachers — Partners in Children's Reading." An interview. *Education Update #7,* Fall 1980.

"News for Parents." Newark, Delaware. International Reading Association. Sept. 1980. 2–5.

Ransbury, Molly Kayes. You Can Encourage Your Child to Read. Newark: International Reading Association, 1986.

Rich, Dorothy. "Activities To Strengthen Reading At Home." Part 2 *Instructor* 98.2 (Oct. 1988): 89–96.

Rogers, Norma. Your Home Is Your Child's First School. Newark: International Reading Association, 1986.

Rosemond, John. Taming the TV Monster. *Better Homes and Gardens* 66.9 (Sept. 1988): 26.

Schickedanz, Judith A. Helping Children Learn About Reading. Washington, D.C.: NAEYC, 1983.

Sloan, Glenna Davis. Good Books Make Reading Fun For Your Child. Newark: International Reading Association, 1985.

Trelease, Jim. *The Read-Aloud Handbook.* New York: Penguin Books, 1982.

Wardle, Francis. "Getting Parents Involved!" *Pre-K Today* 2.3 (Nov.–Dec. 1987): 71–75.

Appendix

NONFICTION BOOK LIST

Basic Science Education Series. Primary level. New York: Harper and Row.
Encyclopaedia Britannica True-to-Life Books. Chicago: Encyclopaedia Britannica, Inc.
Golden Library of Knowledge Series. New York: Golden Press.
Golden Nature Guide Series. New York: Simon and Schuster.
How and Why Wonder Books. New York: Grosset & Dunlap.
"Learn About" Series. Racine: Whitman Publishing Company.
Let's-Read-and-Find-Out Science Books. New York: Thomas Y. Crowell Co.
Question and Answer Series. New York: Golden Press.
Webster Beginner Science Series. New York: McGraw-Hill Book Company.

ADDITIONAL STORIES (UNIT 10)

THE LITTLE ELF WHO LISTENS
— Author Unknown

Do you know what an elf is? No one ever saw an elf, but we can pretend it is a little boy about the size of a squirrel. This elf I'm going to tell you about lived at the edge of a big woods.

He played with chattering chipmunks, with bushy-tailed squirrels, and with hopping rabbits. They were his best friends.

Now, this little elf had something very special. His fairy godmother had given him *three pairs* of listening ears! That would be *six* ears, wouldn't it?

There was a *big* pair of ears, a *middle-sized* pair of ears, and a *tiny* pair of ears.

When the little elf wore his *big* ears, he could hear the faintest (smallest) sounds in the woods — leaves falling from the trees, the wind whispering to the flowers, the water rippling over stones in the little stream. He could hear the dogs barking far, far away. The little elf always told his friends, the squirrels, the chipmunks, and the rabbits, about the dogs, so they could run and hide. They were very thankful.

The little elf wore his *tiny* ears when the storms came and the wind blew loud and fierce, and when the thunder roared and crashed. The little animals, who had only one pair of ears apiece, were frightened by the loud noises, but their friend, the elf, told them that the wind and the thunder were important. After them would come the rain, and the rain was needed to help the food to grow.

Most of the time the little elf wore his *middle-sized* ears. He liked them best of all. He listened to all the middle-sized sounds with them, not the very loud and not the very soft sounds.

One morning some children came to the woods to pick flowers. "What shall we do with our pretty flowers?" a little girl asked.

A boy called Billy said, "Let's take them to school." "Let's!" the little girl agreed. "We can show them to the other children."

The little elf listened, and he wished that he could go to school. He wanted to see and hear what the children did at school.

He told his friends, the squirrels, the chipmunks and the rabbits, about it, but they said, "No, an elf can't go to school. School is just for children."

The little elf decided he would go to school anyway. So the next morning he crept out of his warm bed of leaves under the toadstool and skippety-skipped down the road toward the school.

Soon he came to a big building. Girls and boys were playing out on the playground. There was a red, white, and blue flag flying high on a pole, so the little elf knew this was really the school.

Just then a bell rang, and the children all went inside. The little elf quietly slipped inside too.

You were the girls and boys playing outside. You are the children that the little elf followed.

Which pair of ears do you think he will have to use?

— His *big* ears because you talk too low, as if you were afraid of your own voice?

— His *tiny* ears because you talk so loud that you sound like a thunderstorm?

— Or his *middle-sized* ears because you are talking just right — loud enough so everyone in the room can hear, but not so loud that you seem to be shouting? Remember, the little elf likes his *middle-sized* ears best!

Suggestion: It's a good idea to show tiny, middle-sized, and big ears drawn on the chalkboard or on paper or on the flannel board.

(A follow-up to this story could be sorting objects into three groups by size.)

LITTLE DUCK

A good group-participation story. Children imitate the actions with teacher (Scott, 1968).

Run	=	Slap thighs quickly.
Walk	=	Slap thighs slowly.
Big Steps	=	Thump fists on chest.
Swim	=	Rub palms of hands together rapidly.
Bang	=	Clap hands once.

Little Duck was scolded for eating too many bugs, so he said to his mother, "I am going to run away. Then I can eat anything I like."

So Little Duck left the barnyard and his own dear mother who loved him. He walked down the road on his little flat feet. (Action)

Little Duck met a cow who was munching hay.

"Have some," offered the cow.

Hay was much too rough for Little Duck to eat because he had no teeth to chew it. He thanked the cow for her thoughtfulness and walked on. (Action) Suddenly, he heard a big BANG. (Clap) Little Duck trembled with fright.

"Oh, oh, that must be a hunter with a gun," he cried.

Little Duck ran away from there fast. (Action) Then Little Duck heard some BIG LOUD steps coming toward him. (Action) He hid in some bushes until the big steps went by.

"Why, that was only a HORSE," said Little Duck happily.

Little Duck met a dog with a bone.

"Have some," said the dog.

"No, thank you," said Little Duck as he walked on. (Action)

Little Duck came to a pond. He jumped into the water and swam across the pond. (Action) He climbed out of the water and walked on. (Action)

Suddenly Little Duck heard a fierce sound, "Grrrrrowl, Rrrrrruff."

Right in front of Little Duck sat a fox!

"Yum, yum," said the fox, smacking his lips. "Duck for dinner!"

"Oh, oh!" cried Little Duck as he began to run. (Action)

He ran and ran faster and faster. (Action) He came to the pond and swam across. (Action) The fox was right behind him.

Suddenly there was a loud BANG. (Action) When the fox heard the big noise, he turned and ran away. (Action)

Little Duck felt safer now, but he kept right on running. (Action)

He passed the horse — and the cow — and the dog with a bone. Soon he was back in the barnyard with his own dear mother who loved him.

He said:

"I'm a little duck as you can see,

And this barnyard is the best place for me."

Little Duck knew that being scolded was for his own good, and he never ate too many bugs again. He never ran away again, either.

I'M GOING TO CATCH A LION FOR THE ZOO

I'll get up in the morning (yawn and stretch)

I'll put on my clothes (go through motions)

I'll take a long piece of rope down from the wall (reach up)

I'll carry it over my shoulder (push up arm to shoulder)

Open the door (pretend to turn door handle)

And close the door (clasp hands)

I'm going on a lion hunt, and I'm not afraid (slap hands on knees)

Whoops — comin' to a hill (climbing with hands)

Now I'm crossing a bridge (pound closed fists on chest)

And I'm crossing a river (motion as though swimming)

Now I'm going through tall grass (rub hands together)

Whoops — I'm walking in mud (poke air-filled cheeks)

I'm going on a lion hunt, and I'm not afraid (slap hands on knees)

Comin' to a lion territory — want to catch a lion

With green stripes and pink polka dots

Have to go tippy-toe (finger tips on knees)

I'm climbing up a tree (climb up and look all around)

No lion!

Going in a dark cave (cup hands around eyes and look around)

Oh, a lion!

(The trip back home is exactly the same, only in reverse and faster. *The cave* is first and *slam the door* is last)

Home at last. I'm not going on any more lion hunts. I've found a lion, and I'm afraid.

(This story is full of child participation and action. It takes teacher practice, but is well worth the effort.)

Note: This is a variation of "Bear Hunt" found in Unit 16.

HOW SAMMY SNAKE GETS A NEW SKIN

by Pauline C. Peck (1968)

"My skin is too small,"
  said Sammy Snake.
"I need a new skin."
  Sammy met Toby Turtle.
"I need a new skin,"
  said Sammy.
"Where can I get one?"
"I don't know," said Toby,
"I never need a new skin."
  Sammy met Katy Caterpillar.
"I need a new skin,"
  said Sammy.
"Where can I get one?"
"I know," said Katy.
"Spin a cocoon, the way I do."
"I can't do that," said Sammy.
  And he slid away.
  Sammy met Grampa Snake.
"I need a new skin,"
  said Sammy.
"Where can I get one?"
"I know," said Grampa.
"You just wiggle and wiggle."
Sammy wiggled and wiggled.
He wiggled his old skin right off!
And do you know what?
Underneath his old skin
there was a shiny new skin
that was JUST RIGHT!

HALLOWEEN HOUSE

(For this story, a large sheet of orange construction paper and a pair of scissors are needed.)

Hugo, the bear, and his friend, Bitsy, the mouse, wanted to give a Halloween party for all of the forest animals, but they didn't have a house, just a small den and a hole.

They thought about the fun they'd all have wearing scary costumes and telling ghost stories. Hugo wanted to make honey cookies, and Bitsy knew how to make a delicious mouse candy from maple sugar and pine nuts.

But, alas, they had no house.

One day while walking through the forest together, Hugo found a large piece of orange paper. Running as fast as he could, carrying the paper in one hand and Bitsy in the other, Hugo went straight to his den.

"Watch this," he said, putting Bitsy down. Hugo folded the paper and cut a round house shape with a big door.

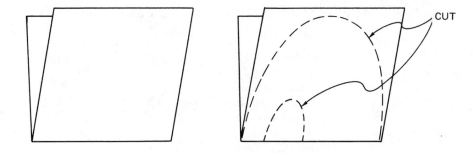

"You need a window," said Bitsy. So, Hugo cut a window.

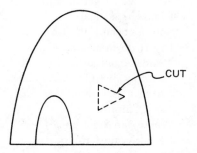

"But, I need a small door, too," Bitsy said. Hugo cut a small door.

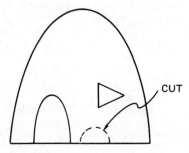

"Now we can invite all our friends to a Halloween party, whoopee!" said Hugo.
"Wait a minute. Just wait a minute," said Bitsy. "We need a jack-o-lantern!"
"We already have one!" Hugo said.
(Unfold the house.)

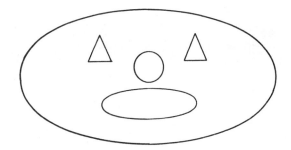

THE CROOKED-MOUTH FAMILY

There are many versions of this action story. This one, however, appeals to young children and never fails to bring laughter and requests to have it repeated. Before beginning the story, quietly light a candle — preferably a dripless one.

Once there was a family called The Crooked-Mouth Family.
The father had a mouth like this.
  (Twist mouth to the right.)
The mother had a mouth like this.
  (Twist mouth to the left.)
The Big Brother had a mouth like this.
  (Bring lower lip over upper lip.)
The Big Sister had a mouth like this.
  (Bring upper lip over lower lip.)
But the Baby Sister had a pretty mouth just like yours.
  (Smile naturally.)

(Repeat mouth positions as each character speaks.)

One night they forgot to blow the candle out when they went upstairs to bed.
The father said, "I'd better go downstairs and blow that candle out."
  (With mouth still twisted to the right, blow at the flame being careful not to blow it out.)
"What's the matter with this candle? It won't go out."
  (Repeat blowing several times.)
"I guess I'd better call Mother. Mother! Please come down and blow the candle out."
Mother said, "Why can't you blow the candle out? Anybody can blow a candle out. You just go like this."
  (She blows at the flame, mouth still twisted to the left.)
"I can't blow it out either. We'd better call Big Brother."
  (Change to father's mouth.)
"Brother! Please come down and blow the candle out."
Big Brother said, "That's easy. All you have to do is blow hard."
  (With lower lip over upper, hold the candle low and blow.)
Father said, "See. You can't blow it out either. We'll have to call Big Sister. Sister! Please come down and
    blow the candle out!"
Big Sister said, "I can blow it out. Watch me."
  (With upper lip over lower, candle held high, blow several times.)
Father said, "That's a funny candle. I told you I couldn't blow it out."

Mother said, "I couldn't blow it out, either."

Big Brother said, "Neither could I."

Big Sister said, "I tried and tried, and I couldn't blow it out."

Father said, "I guess we'll have to call Baby Sister. Baby! Please come down and blow the candle out."

Baby Sister came downstairs, rubbing her eyes because she had been asleep. She asked, "What's the matter?"

Father said, "I can't blow the candle out."

Mother said, "I can't blow it out either."

Big Brother said, "Neither can I."

Big Sister said, "I can't either."

Baby Sister said, "Anybody can blow a candle out. That's easy." And she did.

Author Unknown

THE BIG-MOUTHED FROG

A small big-mouthed frog decided to leave home and see the world. The first creature the frog met went "Quack, quack." "Hi, I'm a big-mouthed frog, and I eat bugs. Who are you and what do you eat?" "I'm a duck, and I eat seeds and grain," said the duck. "So long Mr. Duck, I'm off to discover the world!" "Meow, meow." "Hi, I'm a big-mouthed frog! I eat bugs. Who are you and what do you eat?" "Silly child, I'm a cat, and cream is what I prefer — purr purr," said Ms. Cat. "Goodbye Ms. Cat. I'm off to discover the world and all that's in it!" "Bow wow. Bow wow." "Hi there, I'm a big-mouthed frog, and I eat bugs. Who are you, and what do you eat?" "I'm Bowser the Beagle and I chew on bones." "You're a bowser?" "Nope, I'm a dog!" "See you later, I'm off to discover the world and all that's in it." "Moo, moo." "Hi up there," yelled the big-mouthed frog. "I'm a big-mouthed frog, I eat bugs. Who are you, and what do you eat?" "I'm a cow, and I eat grass — watch out, move aside, I might step on you." "Goodbye cow I'm off to see the world." "Hiss Hiss." "Hi there I'm a big-mouthed frog and I eat bugs. Who are you, and what do you eat?" "I'm a SNAKE, AND I EAT BIG-MOUTHED FROGS!!!!" "Ooooo oooo you don't say," said the frog. (This last line is said with the mouth compressed in a small circle!)

Courtesy of Katherine Blanton

FOOLISH FRED

(Traditional)

"Fred, Fred, we are so very poor! You will have to go to work," mother said. "Yes, mother, I will see if the farmer will give me a job," Fred said.

"Be sure to put your pay in your pocket," said Fred's mother.

The next day Fred worked cleaning the barn for the farmer. "Thank you for your work, Fred," said the farmer. "I have no money, but here is some milk for your day's work." "Thank you," said Fred. I will do just as mother told me, and put my pay in my pocket Fred thought. He poured the milk into his pant's pocket, and walked home.

"Where is your pay?" said his mother.

"I put it in my pocket just as you said, but now it's not there!" "Foolish Fred! You should have carried it in your hands carefully," said his mother. "OK. I'll do that next time."

The next day Fred got a job with the baker at the bakery. He frosted all the cakes, and put colored sprinkles on the cookies. "I have no money," said the baker at the end of the day, "but take this cat as pay; he's a very good cat for catching mice." "Thank you," said Fred.

Fred carried the cat in his hands just as his mother said, but the cat went "Pssssst! Pssssst!" and scratched his hands. "Ouch, ouch," Fred said as he dropped the cat.

"Where is your pay?" his mother said. "It was a big cat, and it bit me and ran away," Fred told his mother.

"You should have tied it with a string and pulled it home," said mother. "Yes, that's a good idea. I'll do that next time," answered Fred.

The next day Fred worked for the butcher. "Here Fred, I have no money, but here is some very good meat for your pay," said the butcher. "My mother will like that," said Fred. "Thank you."

Fred tied the meat with a string and pulled it all the way home.

"Foolish Fred, we can't eat this meat. It's too dirty!" his mother said. "You should have carried it on your back!" "I will next time, mother," he said.

The next day, Fred got a job with a man who was an animal doctor. He fed and gave water to all the animals the doctor was taking care of. At the end of the day the animal doctor said, "I have no money but take this donkey." "Thank you," Fred replied, putting the donkey that was almost as big as Fred on his back. Slowly, Fred walked home with the great weight on his back weaving and staggering on the street.

"Ha..ha, you look so funny. They will like you in my circus. Will you come and work for me and travel with the circus?" said the man. "Can my mother come, too?" asked Fred. "Oh yes" said the circus man. "You can bring her on the donkey's back." "Thank you! Please stay here. I will be right back," said Fred as he walked off with the donkey still on his back. The man sat down to wait and laughed again as Fred walked toward home.

"Ah, here they come, and look — there's Fred's mother on the donkey and the donkey is on Fred's back." He held his sides laughing at the sight. Foolish Fred.

Now Foolish Fred and his mother live happily with the circus, and they are not poor.

References

Peck, Pauline C., Special permission granted by *My Weekly Reader I*, published by Xerox Education Publications, Xerox Corporation, 1968.

Scott, Louise Binder, *Learning Time with Language Experiences for Young Children*, New York: McGraw-Hill, 1968.

ADDITIONAL FLANNEL BOARD STORIES AND PATTERNS
(UNIT 12)

Note: Patterns in this section have been reduced to fit the page size. It is suggested that students enlarge these patterns for child activities on the flannel board. This can be done by using an overhead opaque projector, and then cutting pieces with enlarged patterns. Consult your instructor.

THE PUMPKIN THAT GREW

Pieces: green leaves for vine (five or six)
large vine
finished pumpkin
(green stem, orange face)

pumpkins in three different sizes:
small (dark green)
medium (light green)
large (yellow)

Action: See story in Unit 12.

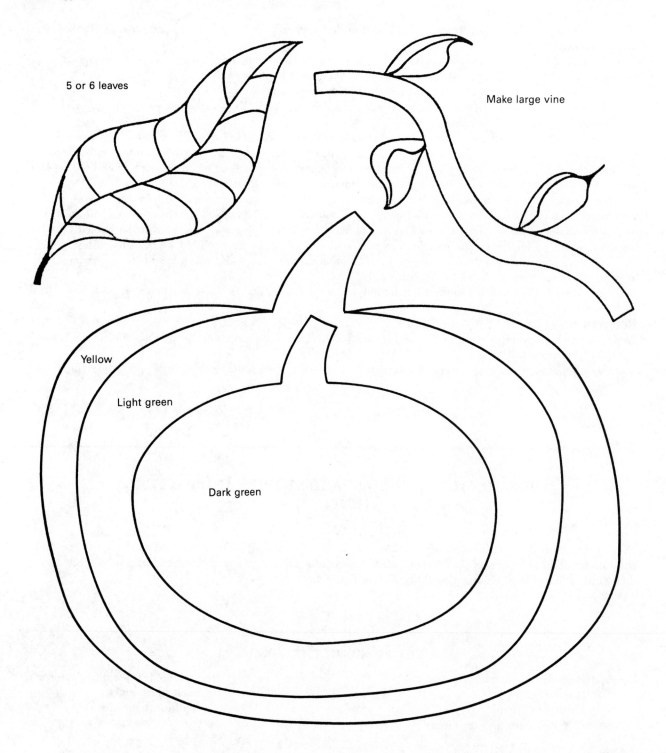

5 or 6 leaves

Make large vine

Yellow

Light green

Dark green

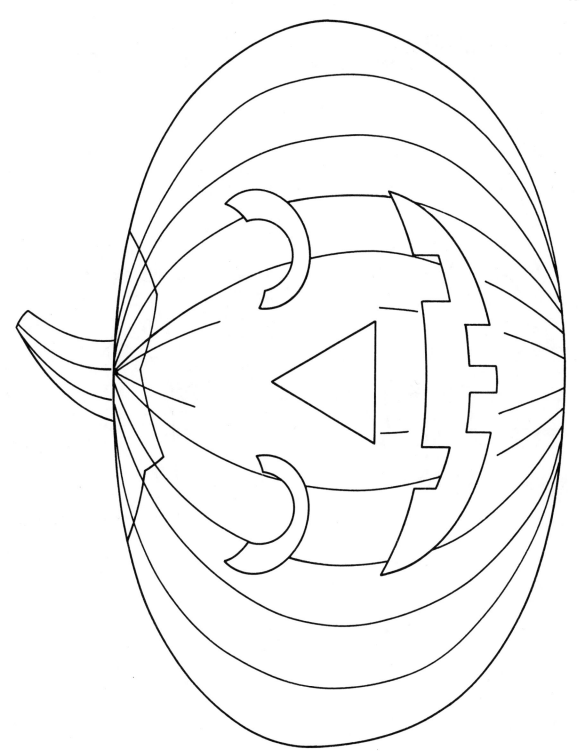

THE SEED

Pieces:	small roots and shoot	seed	beaver
	deer	bird	large tree
	Mr. Man	small trunk with leaves	apples (5 or 6)

Action: See story in Unit 12.

Cut as one piece.

Cut as one piece.

JUST LIKE DADDY

Pieces: little brown bear
little bear's blue vest
flower
brown father bear
red boots for father bear
yellow coat for father bear
purple vest for mother bear

green fish (large)
green fish (small)
brown mother bear
red boots for little bear
blue vest for father bear
yellow coat for little bear

Action: See story in Unit 12.

Little bear's
Blue vest (cut 1)

Little brown bear (cut 1)

Flower (cut 1)

Brown father bear (cut 1)

Green fish (cut 2)

Small green fish (cut 1)

Brown mother bear (cut 1)

Red boots
for father bear
(cut 2)

Red boots
for little bear
(cut 2)

Yellow coat
for father bear
(cut 1)

Blue vest
for father bear
(cut 1)

Yellow coat
for little bear
(cut 1)

Purple vest
for mother bear
(cut 1)

THE TREE IN THE WOODS

Pieces: grass   bird's nest
tree   bird's egg
tree trunk   bird
tree limb   wing
tree branch   feather

Action: See story in Unit 12.

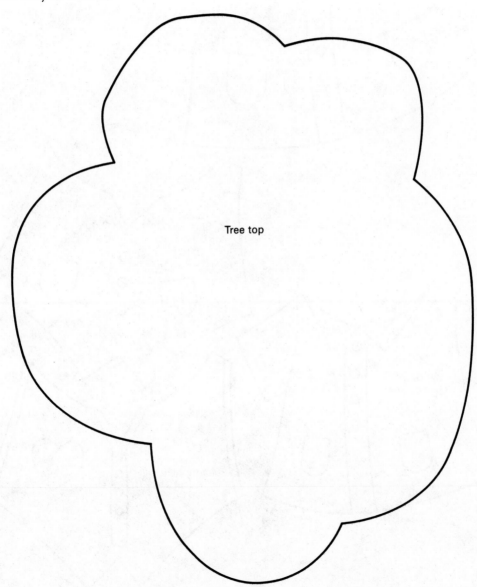

Tree top

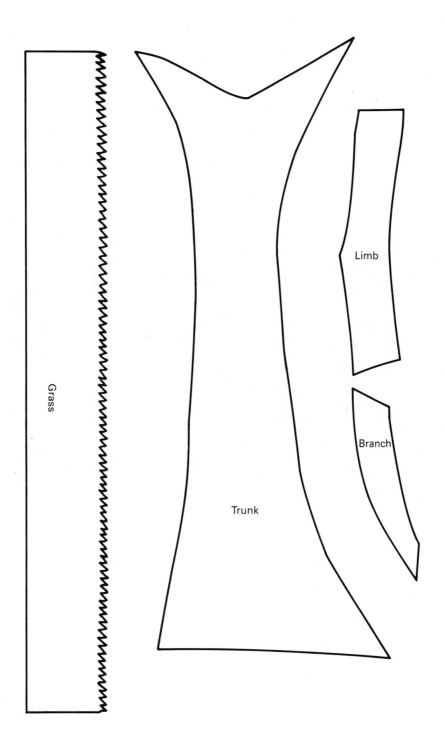

Board assemblage — for tree in the woods

Tree top

Grass

THE LION AND THE MOUSE

Pieces: lion awake   tree   mouse
         lion sleeping   rope   two hunters

Action: See story in Unit 12.

Patterns from *Adventures in Felt* by Jeanne M. Machado, © 1972.

← Cut line

FORTUNATELY/UNFORTUNATELY

Pieces: boy
         plane
         parachute
         snake

haystack
pitchfork
water and shark fin
birthday cake

tiger
cave

Action: See story in Unit 12.

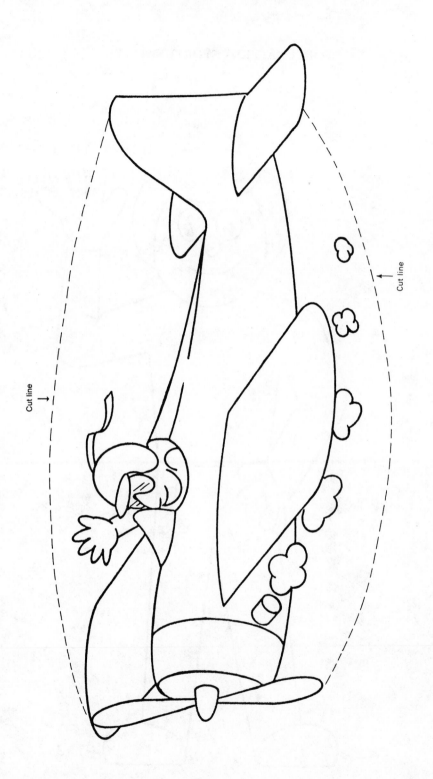

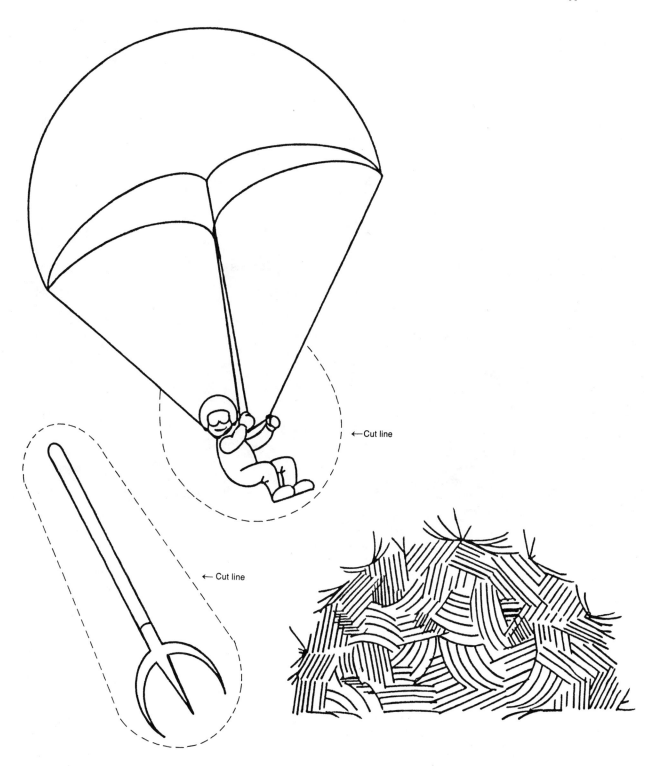

← Cut line

← Cut line

Cut line →

APPLE AND WORM

Pieces: apple, worm

Action: Move the worm to fit the following positional words:

in	on	front	side	bottom	behind
out	off	back	top	under	

THE HARE AND THE TORTOISE
Adapted from Aesop

Pieces: rabbit   dog   rabbit running   finish line flag
         turtle   hen   rabbit sleeping   tree

One day the rabbit was talking to some of the other animals. "I am the fastest runner in the forest," he said. "I can beat anyone! Do you want to race?"

"Not I," said the dog.

"Not I," said the hen.

"I will race with you," said the turtle.

"That's a good joke," said the rabbit. "I could dance around you all the way and still win."

Put on turtle, dog, hen, rabbit at left edge of board.

"Still bragging about how fast you are," answered the turtle. "Come on, let's race. Do you see that flag over there? That will be the finish line. Hen, would you stand by the flag so that you can tell who wins the race?"

"Dog, will you say the starting words — get on your mark, get ready, get set, go!"

Add finishing line flag on right edge of board. Move hen by flag.

"Stand there," said the dog. "Get on your mark, get ready, get set, go!"

The rabbit ran very fast. He looked over his shoulder and saw how slowly the turtle was running on his short little legs. Just then he saw a shady spot under a tree. He thought to himself — that turtle is so slow I have time to rest here under this tree. So he sat down on the cool grass, and before he knew it, he was fast asleep.

Put on running rabbit. Remove standing rabbit.

While he slept, the turtle was running. (Clump, Clump — Clump, Clump) He was not running very fast, but he kept on running. (Clump, Clump — Clump, Clump) Pretty soon the turtle came to the tree where the rabbit was sleeping. He went past and kept on running. (Clump, Clump — Clump, Clump)

Add sleeping rabbit while removing running rabbit.

The turtle was almost to the finish line. The hen saw the turtle coming and said, "Turtle, keep on running. You've almost won the race."

When the hen spoke, the rabbit awoke. He looked down by the finish line and saw the turtle was almost there. As fast as he could, the rabbit started running again. Just then he heard the hen say, "The turtle is the winner!"

Change sleeping rabbit to running rabbit.

"But I'm the fastest," said the rabbit.

"Not this time," said the hen. "Sometimes slow and steady wins the race."

FIVE YELLOW DUCKLINGS
(A Flannel-Board Poem)

Pieces: five yellow ducklings   1 mother duck   1 pond (large enough for five ducklings)

Special permission granted by *Adventures in Felt* © 1972 by Jeanne M. Machado.

Cut pond
as separate
piece.

Cut as
separate
piece.

Five yellow ducklings went swimming one day,
Across the pond and far away.
Old mother duck said, "Quack, Quack, Quack,"
Four yellow ducklings came swimming back.

Place pond, mother duck and five ducklings on flannel board.
Remove one duckling.

Four yellow ducklings went swimming one day,
Across the pond and far away.
Old mother duck said, "Quack, Quack, Quack,"
Three yellow ducklings came swimming back.

Remove one duckling.

Three yellow ducklings went swimming one day,
Across the pond and far away.
Old mother duck said, "Quack, Quack, Quack,"
Two yellow ducklings came swimming back.

Remove one duckling.

Two yellow ducklings went swimming one day,
Across the pond and far away.
Old mother duck said, "Quack, Quack, Quack,"
One little duckling came swimming back.

Remove one duckling.

One yellow duckling went swimming one day,
Across the pond and far away.
Old mother duck said, "Quack, Quack, Quack,"
No little ducklings came swimming back.
Old mother duck said, "Quack, Quack, Quack," (very loudly)
Five yellow ducklings came swimming back.

Remove last duckling.

Add five ducklings.

Suggestions:

Have children listen and participate when mother duck says "Quack, Quack, Quack." The last "Quack, Quack, Quack" should be louder than the first five. This is a good poem for children to dramatize. Outline a pond area with chalk, tape, or use an old blue blanket. Decide which child (duckling) will not return in the order of the poem. Teacher reads poem as five ducklings swim across pond. Teacher can demonstrate how ducklings waddle, and how hands can be used for ducks' beak. This poem leads well into discussions about loud and soft or "inside and outside" voices.

THE BIG, BIG TURNIP

(Traditional)

Pieces: farmer   turnip   daughter   cat

farmer's wife   large piece of ground   dog   mouse

Cut line →

← Cut line

A farmer once planted a turnip seed. And it grew, and it grew, and it grew. The farmer saw it was time to pull the turnip out of the ground. So he took hold of it and began to pull.

Place farmer on board. Cover turnip so that only top is showing with ground piece, and place on board.

He pulled, and he pulled, and he pulled, and he pulled. But the turnip wouldn't come up.

So the farmer called to his wife who was getting dinner.

Fe, fi, fo, fum.

I pulled the turnip,

But it wouldn't come up.

And the wife came running, and she took hold of the farmer, and they pulled, and they pulled, and they pulled, and they pulled. But the turnip wouldn't come up.

Move farmer next to turnip with hands on turnip top. Place wife behind farmer.

So the wife called to the daughter who was feeding the chickens nearby.

Fe, fi, fo, fum.

We pulled the turnip,

But it wouldn't come up.

And the daughter came running. The daughter took hold of the wife. The wife took hold of the farmer. The farmer took hold of the turnip. And they pulled, and they pulled, and they pulled, and they pulled. But the turnip wouldn't come up.

Place daughter behind farmer's wife.

So the daughter called to the dog who was chewing a bone.

Fe, fi, fo, fum.

We pulled the turnip,

But it wouldn't come up.

And the dog came running. The dog took hold of the daughter. The daughter took hold of the wife. The wife took hold of the farmer. And the farmer took hold of the turnip. And they pulled, and they pulled, and they pulled. But the turnip wouldn't come up.

Place dog behind daughter.

The dog called to the cat who was chasing her tail.

Fe, fi, fo, fum.

We pulled the turnip,

But it wouldn't come up.

And the cat came running. The cat took hold of the dog. The dog took hold of the daughter. The daughter took hold of the wife. The wife took hold of the farmer. The farmer took hold of the turnip. And they pulled, and they pulled, and they pulled. But the turnip wouldn't come up.

Place cat behind dog.

So the cat called the mouse who was nibbling spinach nearby.

Fe, fi, fo, fum.

We pulled the turnip,

But it wouldn't come up.

And the mouse came running.

"That little mouse can't help," said the dog. "He's too little." "Phooey," squeaked the mouse. "I could pull that turnip up myself, but since you have all been pulling, I'll let you help too."

So the mouse took hold of the cat. The cat took hold of the

Place mouse behind cat.

dog. The dog took hold of the daughter. The daughter took hold of the wife. The wife took hold of the farmer. The farmer took hold of the turnip. And they pulled, and they pulled, and they pulled. And up came the turnip.

And the mouse squeaked, "I told you so!"

Remove ground.

THE LITTLE RED HEN

Pieces: cottage   sticks   fox

            little red hen   fire   sack

            mouse   pot   two large rocks

            rooster   table

It was morning. In the cottage where the little red hen and the rooster and the mouse lived, little red hen was happily setting the table for breakfast.

"Who will get some sticks for the fire?" said little red hen.

"I won't," grumbled the rooster.

"I won't," squeaked the mouse.

"Then I'll do it myself," said the little red hen, and off she went to gather them.

When she returned with the sticks and had started the fire, she asked, "Who will get water from the spring to fill the pot?"

"I won't," grumbled the rooster.

"I won't," squeaked the mouse.

"Then I'll do it myself," she said and ran off to fill the pot.

"Who will cook the breakfast?" said the hen.

"I won't," grumbled the rooster.

"I won't," squeaked the mouse.

"Then I'll do it myself," said the hen, and she did.

When breakfast was ready, the hen, the mouse, and the rooster ate together but the rooster spilled the milk, and the mouse scattered crumbs on the floor.

"Who will clear the table?" said the hen.

"I won't," grumbled the rooster.

"I won't," squeaked the mouse.

"Then I'll do it myself," said the hen. So she cleared everything and swept the floor.

The lazy rooster and mouse by this time had moved closer to the fire, and had fallen fast asleep.

"Knock, knock, knock," the noise at the door awakened them. "Who's that?" said the rooster. "Oh it might be the mail carrier with

Place cottage, table, and hen on board.
Add rooster.
Add mouse.

Remove hen.

Replace with hen and sticks. Place fire over sticks.

Place pot over fire.

Move hen, mouse, and rooster near table.

Move rooster and mouse near the fire.

a letter for me," so the mouse went to the door and opened it without looking out the window first to see who was there.

It was a fox. "Help," said the mouse, but the fast old fox, quick as a wink, caught not only the mouse, but also the rooster and the little red hen. Quickly he popped them all into his sack and headed off toward home, thinking about the fine dinner he was bringing to his family.

The bag was heavy, and home was a long way, so the fox decided to put it down and rest.

"Snore, Snore, Snore," went the fox.

Little red hen said to the rooster and mouse, "Now we have a chance to escape. I have a pair of scissors and a needle and thread in my apron pocket. I've cut a hole in the bag. Hurry and jump out, find a rock, the biggest one you can carry, and bring it back quickly. "Snore, Snore, Snore," went the fox. Soon the mouse and the rooster returned with large rocks. They pushed them into the sack, and the hen sewed the hole up. Off they ran to their home. They closed the door and locked it, and they bolted the windows. They were safe now.

The fox didn't know he'd been fooled until he got home and opened his sack.

The mouse and the rooster were so happy to be home that they didn't grumble and fight anymore; they even helped to cook the dinner with smiles on their faces.

Place fox and sack on board. Hide fox, mouse, and hen behind sack. Remove cottage.

Put fox in horizontal position.

Add rocks.
Move rocks behind sack.

Remove fox and sack.

Place cottage, hen, rooster, and mouse beside it on board.

← Cut line

Cut line →

↑
Cut line

HUSH, LITTLE BABY
Flannel-Board Song

Pieces: mother   billy goat
          sleeping baby   cart
          crying baby   bull
          mocking bird   dog
          ring   horse
          looking glass

Courtesy of *Adventures in Felt* © Copyright 1972

Hush, little baby, don't say a word, Mama's going to buy you a mockingbird.	*Place mother and crying baby on her lap.*
If that mockingbird won't sing, Mama's going to buy you a diamond ring.	*Add ring.*
If that diamond ring turns to brass, Mama's going to buy you a looking glass.	*Add looking glass.*
If that looking glass gets broke, Mama's going to buy you a billy goat.	*Add billy goat.*
If that billy goat won't pull, Mama's going to buy you a cart and bull.	*Add cart and bull.*
If that cart and bull turn over, Mama's going to buy you a dog named Rover.	*Add dog.*
If that dog named Rover won't bark, Mama's going to buy you a horse and cart.	*Add horse and move cart from bull.*
If that horse and cart break down, YOU'LL be the sweetest little baby in town.	
Lullaby, baby sweet of mine, you'll be asleep by half past nine.	*Replace crying baby with sleeping baby.*

← Cut line

ONE, TWO, BUCKLE MY SHOE

Pieces: numerals 0–9   sticks
shoe   straight sticks
door   hen

Cut line →

Cut two.

THIS OLD MAN

Pieces: old man   shoe   hive   gate
         dog   tree   sticks   vine
         bones   door   heaven (clouds)   hen
         thumb

(Note: Use numerals, shoe, tree, sticks, and hen patterns found in other sets in this Appendix.)

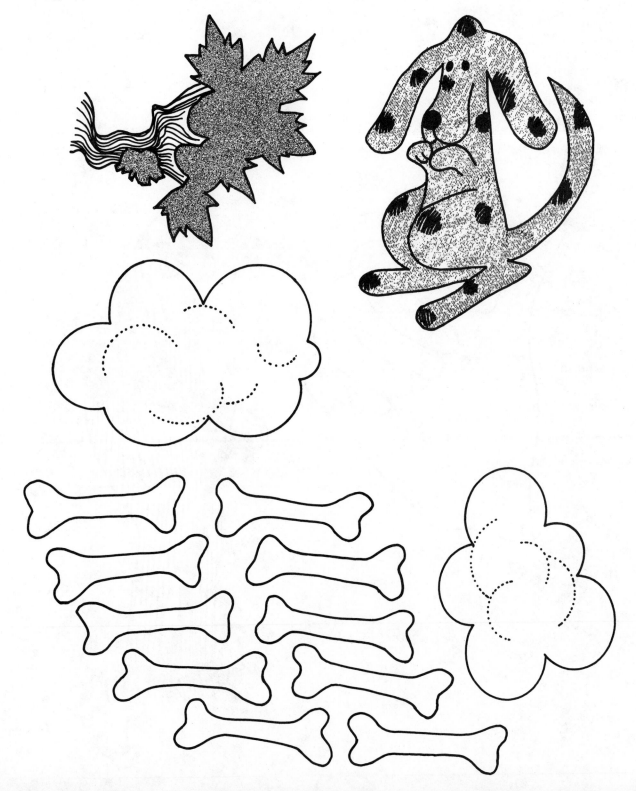

ADDITIONAL PUPPETRY IDEAS AND PATTERNS (UNIT 16)

Paper Bag Puppets

Construction: Draw a face on the upper part of bag; color. Stuff with cotton or newspaper. Put neck cylinder into head and tie string around neck. (Neck cylinder is made by rolling a piece of tag board and taping together. The roll should fit around the first finger.)

If the puppet needs hair, paste on. Add other distinguishing characteristics. Cut hole in paper or cloth and stick neck cylinder through the hole. Paste, sew, or otherwise fasten. Add hands or paws cut from tag board.

Materials: 5″ × 8″ paper bag   paste
string   crepe paper or cloth for dress
crayons or paint   scissors
newspapers or cotton

Movement: Holding forefinger in neck tube.

Potato or Tennis Ball Puppets

Construction: Cut a hole the size of your forefinger in the bottom of a fairly smooth, evenly shaped potato. Insert neck tube. Paint face. Add hair. It may be fastened with pins stuck into the potato. Sew dress to neck tube. Add tag board hands and feet.

Same procedure for the tennis ball.

Materials: potato or tennis ball   cloth for dress
scissors or paring knife to cut hole   material for hair
tag board

Stuffed Cloth Puppet

Construction: Draw head pattern and cut around it on a fold of cloth (white, tan, or pink). Sew around front and back, turn inside out, and stuff with cotton or rags. Insert neck tube and tie. Paint on face. Cut dress and sew to neck tube. Add hands and feet.

Materials:
cloth (for head and dress)
scissors
needle and thread

tag board for hands and feet
material for hair (cotton, yarn, and so forth)

Stuffed Paper Puppet

Construction: Have the child draw himself or herself or any character the child chooses on a piece of butcher paper. Then trace and cut second figure for the back.

Paper Bag Puppet Face — Lamb

Basic Puppet Body

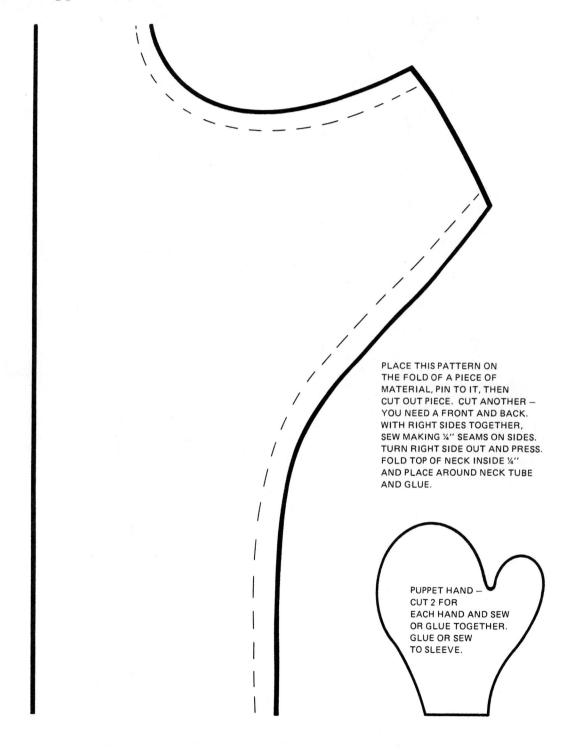

PLACE THIS PATTERN ON
THE FOLD OF A PIECE OF
MATERIAL, PIN TO IT, THEN
CUT OUT PIECE. CUT ANOTHER —
YOU NEED A FRONT AND BACK.
WITH RIGHT SIDES TOGETHER,
SEW MAKING ¼" SEAMS ON SIDES.
TURN RIGHT SIDE OUT AND PRESS.
FOLD TOP OF NECK INSIDE ¼"
AND PLACE AROUND NECK TUBE
AND GLUE.

PUPPET HAND —
CUT 2 FOR
EACH HAND AND SEW
OR GLUE TOGETHER.
GLUE OR SEW
TO SLEEVE.

Frog and Bird Puppet Patterns

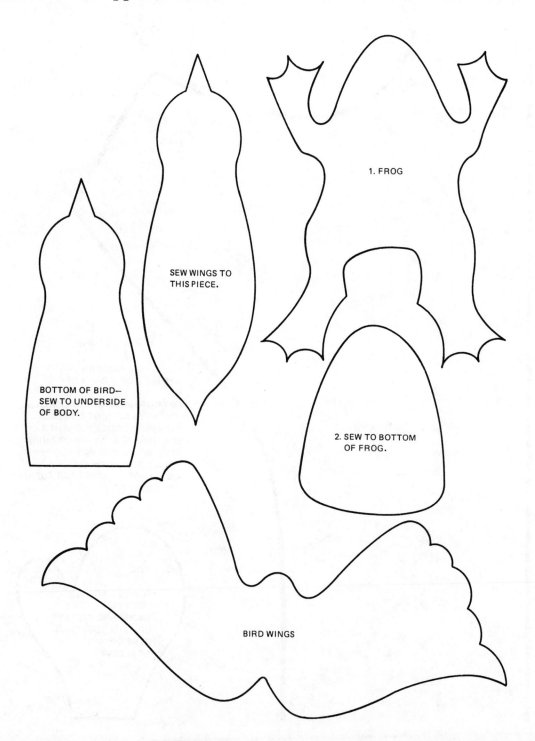

SEW WINGS TO
THIS PIECE.

1. FROG

BOTTOM OF BIRD—
SEW TO UNDERSIDE
OF BODY.

2. SEW TO BOTTOM
OF FROG.

BIRD WINGS

Large Cloth Hand-Puppet Pattern

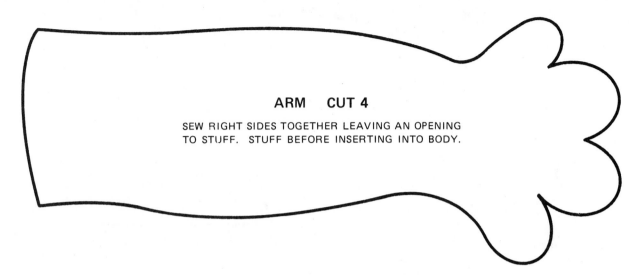

ARM   CUT 4

SEW RIGHT SIDES TOGETHER LEAVING AN OPENING
TO STUFF. STUFF BEFORE INSERTING INTO BODY.

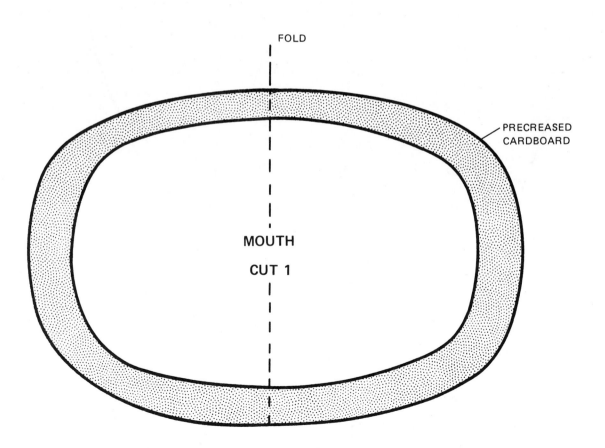

FOLD

PRECREASED
CARDBOARD

MOUTH

CUT 1

Large Cloth Puppet Pattern

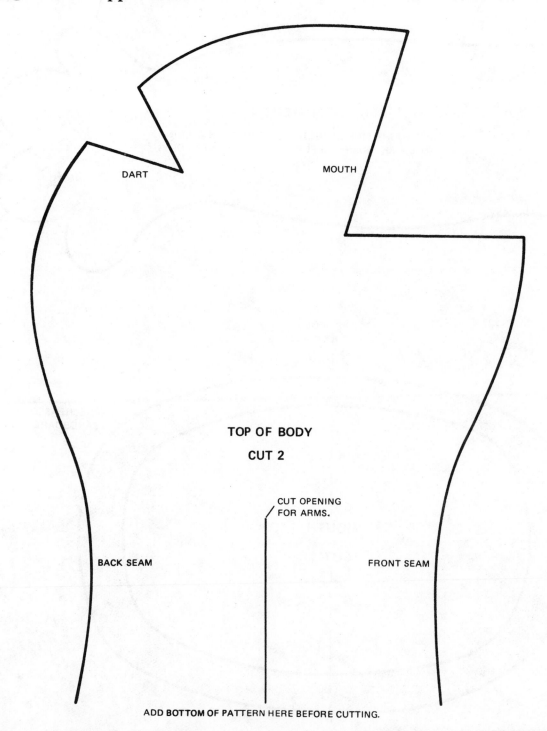

DART

MOUTH

TOP OF BODY

CUT 2

CUT OPENING
FOR ARMS.

BACK SEAM

FRONT SEAM

ADD **BOTTOM OF PATTERN** HERE BEFORE CUTTING.

BOTTOM OF BODY

CUT 2

There Was an Old Woman Who Swallowed a Fly

Materials Needed: two large pieces of white poster board
18″ × 36″ piece of plywood
one skein black rug yarn
one clear plastic drop cloth or ½ yd. clear plastic
½ yd. material (any color or pattern)
marking pens
fishing line (about 18 inches)
two black pipe cleaners
two wiggly eyes
colored feathers
craft glue
woodworking glue
clothespins
thumbtacks and a hammer, or a staplegun

Instructions:

Old Woman

Step 1:   Trace the pattern of the old woman onto the poster board and onto the plywood.

Step 2:   Transfer all of the details onto the poster board old woman. Cut out, including the inner square for the stomach.

Step 3:   Use an electric jigsaw and cut out the plywood old woman — including the inner square for the stomach.

Step 4:   Using the woodworking glue, spread a thin layer over the entire plywood old woman. Lay the poster board old woman on top and clip with clothespins around the outer and inner edges. Let dry thoroughly before removing the clothespins. If necessary, sand the outer and inner edges to make them smooth.

Step 5:   Spread a thin layer of the craft glue on the bottom half of the poster board, up to the neckline.

Step 6:   Lay the piece of material wrong side down on top of the glue. Let dry thoroughly.

Step 7:   Cut off the excess material from the outer edges and inner stomach.

Step 8:   Starting at the outer edges of the hairline, use craft glue to glue the rug yarn onto the poster board. Glue the yarn around and around, filling in the whole area. Glue small pieces of yarn on for the eyes and eyebrows. Let the hair dry thoroughly.

Step 9:   Turn the old woman over to the backside.

Step 10:   Cut a piece of 18″ × 72″ clear plastic. Fold the plastic in half widthwise to form two 18″ × 36″ pieces with a fold at the bottom.

Step 11:   Place the plastic on the back of the old woman, with the fold down at the bottom of the stomach hole.

Step 12:   Open the plastic, leaving the bottom layer in place on the old woman.

Step 13:   Using tacks or a staplegun, attach the bottom layer of plastic around the outer edge of the old woman's body, mouth, and head, making sure the plastic is smooth and tight.

Step 14:   Bring the second layer of plastic back up and tack or staple it at the very bottom of the stomach hole. Push the top layer of plastic in from the edge of the bottom piece, forming a loose bag or pocket. Tack the second layer in place up to the neckline in the side with the mouth. NOTE: Do not tack the mouth shut! Leave that portion of the plastic open for putting in the animals. Continue tacking at the top of the head and tack the rest of the plastic, continuing to push the plastic in to form a pocket. Trim the excess plastic from around the edges.

Animals

Step 1: Trace each animal onto the poster board. Color each one appropriately and cut out.

Step 2: Glue two wiggly eyes onto the spider.

Step 3: Cut each pipe cleaner into fourths and glue four on each side of the spider for legs.

Step 4: Tie one end of the fishing line to the top of the spider's head. Attach the other end to one of the tacks at the top of the old woman's head (wind the line around the tack or tie a loop).

Step 5: Place the spider inside the bag so that it extends down into the old woman's stomach. The spider is a permanent part of the old woman and should be left as it is.

Step 6: Another addition you can make is to add colored feathers to the bird's tail.

Use: Place the old woman against a wall or in front of you. Remove the spider and hold onto it until time to place it back inside the plastic stomach. As you sing or chant place the appropriate animal in the mouth, letting it drop down into the stomach. The spider can be wiggled and jiggled on each verse by holding the fishing line and bouncing it up and down.

from Magic Moments
P.O. Box 53635
San Jose, CA. 95135

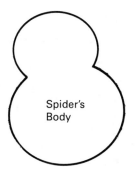

Spider's Body

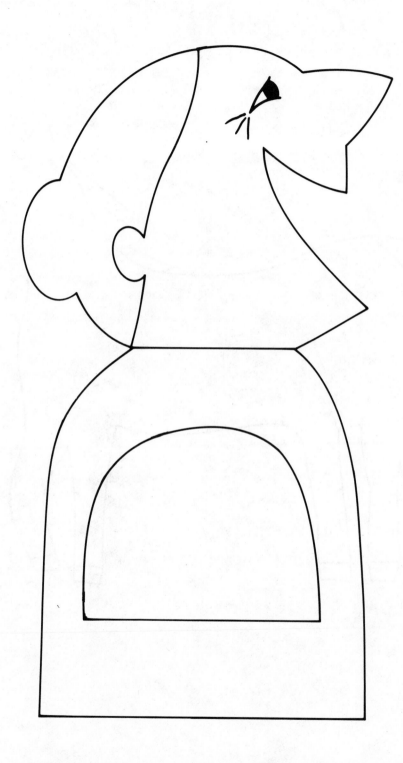

Little Miss Muffet

Materials Needed: one large piece white posterboard
four black pipe cleaners
12″ × 12″ piece black velour
two large wiggly eyes
craft glue
felt pens
black rug yarn
black marker
clothes pins
one tongue depressor

Instructions:

Miss Muffet

Step 1:   Trace the Miss Muffet pattern onto the poster board. Add the details with the black marker. Use the felt markers to color in the hair and face. Cut out.

Step 2:   Glue the tongue depressor onto the back of Miss Muffet. Let dry.

Spider

Step 1:   Trace the spider pattern onto the poster board twice. Cut out.

Step 2:   Glue one of the spiders onto the wrong side of the black velour. Let dry. Cut off the excess material from around the poster board.

Step 3:   Cut each pipe cleaner in half for the legs. On the wrong side of the poster board, position four legs on each side of the body so that two-thirds of each pipe cleaner is extending out. Glue down and let dry.

Step 4:   Put a generous amount of glue all over the wrong side of the spider, being sure to put glue over the legs. Place the second spider on top of the glue and secure all the way around the clothespins. Let dry.

Step 5:   Glue the two wiggly eyes onto the black velour side of the spider.

Step 6:   Punch a hole into the top of the spider's head. Cut a piece of black rug yarn about 24 inches long. Tie the yarn securely through the hole and tie a loop at the top end of the yarn for a handle.

Use: You will need two children to participate in this dramatic play activity. Have Little Miss Muffet sit on a small stool or on the floor. As you and the other students recite the poem, the child holding the spider will walk over to Miss Muffet, and Miss Muffet will run away.

from Magic Moments
P.O. Box 53635
San Jose, CA. 95135

Miss Muffet

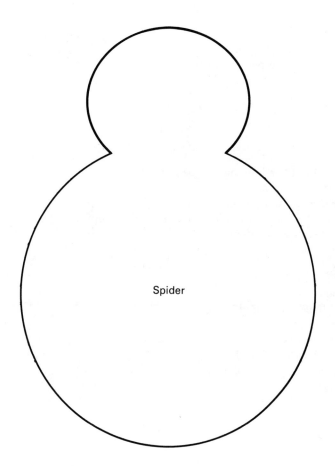

Spider

CHECKLIST FOR THE DEVELOPMENT OF READING BEHAVIORS

1 YEAR
_____ Handles books without necessarily verbalizing.
_____ Crumples, tears, and chews books.
_____ Ignores print.

15 MONTHS
_____ Turns book pages in random order.
_____ Verbalizes while pointing to pictures in books.
_____ Points to pictures of known objects when objects are named.
_____ Pats pictures of things liked.
_____ Points to round things (circles, balls, the letter *O*).

18 MONTHS
_____ Orients pictures to line of vision.
_____ Asks for pictured objects and animals to be named.
_____ Demonstrates pictured action.
_____ Tells a "story" related to pictures on pages.
_____ Answers questions about story that has been read aloud several times.
_____ Shows concern for book's condition.
_____ Guesses outcomes when hearing new story.

2 YEARS
_____ Has a favorite book.
_____ Pretends to read (holds book and talks).
_____ Turns pages right-to-left.
_____ Asks for stories to be read aloud.
_____ Remains attentive as story is read.
_____ Remembers names of picture book characters.
_____ Recalls plots of stories read aloud.
_____ Asks what the printed words say.

30 MONTHS
_____ Can turn to the front of a book when asked.
_____ Can turn to the back of a book when asked.
_____ Can point to the top of a page when asked.
_____ Can point to the bottom of a page when asked.
_____ Pretends to pick up objects pictured on pages.
_____ Enjoys looking through picture books.
_____ Likes hearing and repeating nursery rhymes.
_____ Completes oral sentence by saying the last word omitted by an adult.
_____ Talks to book characters (slaps, kisses, and so forth).
_____ Reacts emotionally to story content.
_____ Repeats sentence verbatim.
_____ Asks for a book about a particular topic to be read aloud.

_____ Rejects changed oral version of a familiar story.
_____ Tells purpose of coloring book.
_____ Can tell what common adjectives are not (wet is not dry).
_____ Notices capital letters in color.

3 YEARS

_____ Remains attentive as story is read aloud, even when pictures are not visible.
_____ Can choose two pictures as being the same when given three to choose from.
_____ Can draw a cross (+ or ×) after being shown one.
_____ Can relate activities in the order in which they occurred.
_____ Can name some of the capital letters in own name.
_____ Asks to see pictures when listening to someone read aloud.

4 YEARS

_____ Can rearrange a set of pictures in an order appropriate for a story.
_____ Can name six or more capital letters.
_____ Points to printed area of page as the place to look when you read.
_____ Chooses a set of letters when given letters and numbers and asked to point to a word.
_____ Copies letters, reversing only a few.
_____ Can retell the plot of a short story after hearing it only once.

5 YEARS

_____ Can spell three or more words orally.
_____ Asks what letter sequences spell.
_____ Recognizes letters comprising own name.
_____ Recognizes words from signs, food containers, and television commercials.
_____ Can select and order letters to form own name.
_____ Can point to capital (or "big") letters on a page of print.
_____ Copies letters from books on separate paper.
_____ Tells story appropriate to newspaper comic strip.

From Mason, George E., *A Primer on Teaching Reading*, F. E. Peacock Publishers, 1981, Copyright © 1981. Permission To Reprint from F. E. Peacock Publishers, Inc.

ALPHABET PRONUNCIATION GUIDE (UNIT 21)

Symbols	Sounds as in the Words	Symbols	Sounds as in the Words
a	fat, apple, asks	g	rag, go, gem
$\bar{a}$	ate, name	h	hat, how, high
b	rib, big	i	it, individual, pin
c	traffic, cat, certain	$\underline{i}$	piece, niece
d	lid, end, feed	$\bar{i}$	ice, while
e	end, wet, pen	j	jump, jeep
$\bar{e}$	me, Elaine, eat	k	lick, kiss, milk
f	if, leaf, full	l	will, late, little

m	him, me, custom		u	up, rug, custom
n	sun, not, even		ū	useful, unite
o	ox, on, not		v	give, have, very
ō	go, open, home		w	we, win, watch
p	sip, pat		x	box
r	ran, rip, very		y	yea, you
s	kiss, so, last, sugar		ȳ	my, cry
t	hit, top		z	zoo, fuzz

Vowel Digraph Sounds

ai . . .	snail	ey . . .	key
ay . . .	say	ey . . .	they
ea . . .	lead	oa . . .	float
ea . . .	tea		
ee . . .	sheep	oe . . .	hoe
ei . . .	receive	ow . . .	grow
ie . . .	believe	ou . . .	though

Vowel Diphthongs

oa . . .	foal		
oi . . .	toil	ue . . .	sue
ou . . .	though	ew . . .	new
oy . . .	soy		

SOURCES FOR LEARNING MATERIALS (UNIT 22)

ABC School Supply Inc., 437 Armour Circle N.E., Box 13084, Atlanta, Georgia 30324
Afro-Am Publishing Co., Inc., 1727 S. Indiana Avenue, Chicago, Illinois 60616
Angeles Nursery Toys, 4105 N. Fairfax Drive, Arlington, Virginia 22203
Ashland Co., 22221 Drury Lane, Shawnee Mission, Kansas 66208
Bailey Films, Inc., 6509 DeLongpre Avenue, Hollywood, California 90028
Beckley-Cardy, 1900 N. Narragansett Avenue, Chicago, Illinois 60639
Binney and Smith, Inc., 380 Madison Avenue, New York, New York 10017
Bowmar, P.O. Box 3623, Glendale, California 91201
Childcraft Education Corporation, 20 Kilmer Road, Edison, New Jersey 08817
Child Guidance, Questor Education Products Co., 200 Fifth Avenue, New York, New York 10010
Childhood Resources, 5307 Lee Highway, Arlington, Virginia 22207
Community Playthings, Rifton, New York 12471
Constructive Playthings, 1040 E. Eightyfifth Street, Kansas City, Missouri 64131
Creative Playthings, A Division of CBS Inc., Princeton, New Jersey 08540
Creative Publications, P.O. Box 10328, Palo Alto, California 94303
David C. Cook Publishing Co., 850 N. Grove Avenue, Elgin, Illinois 60120
Dennison Manufacturing Co., 67 Ford Avenue, Framingham, Massachusetts 01701
Developmental Learning Materials (DLM), 7440 Natchez Avenue, Niles, Illinois 60648

Ed-U-Card/Ed-U-Card Corporations, Subsidiaries of Binney & Smith, 60 Austin Boulevard, Commack, New York 11725

Educational Performance Associates, 563 Westview Avenue, Ridgefield, New Jersey 07657

Educational Teaching Aids Division (ETA), A. Daigger & Co., Inc., 159 W. Kinzie Street, Chicago, Illinois 60610

Eureka Resale Products, Dunmore, Pennsylvania 18512

Fisher Price Toys, A Division of Quaker Oats Co., East Aurora, New York 14052

GAF Corporation, Consumer Photo Products/ViewMaster, 140 West Fiftyfirst Street, New York, New York 10020

Growing Child Playthings, 22 North Second Street, P.O. Box 101, Lafayette, Indiana 47902

Gryphon House, 1333 Connecticut Avenue, N.W., Washington, D.C. 20036

Hayes School Publishing Co., Inc., 321 Pennwood Avenue, Wilkinsburg, Pennsylvania 15221

Holcomb's, 3000 Quigley Road, Cleveland, Ohio 44113

Ideal School Supply, 11000 S. Lavergne Avenue, Oak Lawn, Illinois 60453

Information Center on Children's Cultures, Administrative Offices, 331 East Thirtyeighth Street, New York, New York 10016

Instructo Corporation, Subsidiary of McGraw-Hill Inc., Cedar Hollow and Mathews Roads, Paoli, Pennsylvania 19301

Judy Instructional Aids, The Judy Company, Sales Office, 250 James Street, Morristown, New Jersey 07960

Lakeshore Equipment Company, P.O. Box 2116, 1144 Montague Avenue, San Leandro, California 94577

Lauri Enterprises, Phillips-Avon, Maine 04966

Learning Products, Inc., 11632 Fairgrove Industrial Boulevard, St. Louis, Missouri 63043

Lego Systems, Inc., P.O. Box 2273, Enfield, Connecticut 06082

Mab-Graphic Products Inc., 310 Marconi Boulevard, Copiague, New York 11726

Mead Educational Services, B & T Learning, 5315-A Tulane Drive, Atlanta, Georgia 30336

Milton Bradley Company, Springfield, Massachusetts 01100

National Dairy Council, 111 N. Canal Street, Chicago, Illinois 60606

National Geographic Society, Seventeenth and M Streets N.W., Washington, D.C. 20036

National Wildlife Federation, 1412 Sixteenth Street, N.W., Washington, D.C. 20036

Parker Brothers Inc., Division of General Mills, Fun Group Inc., Salem, Massachusetts 01970

Playskool Incorporated, Milton Bradley Company, Springfield, Massachusetts 01100

Practical Drawing Company, P.O. Box 5388, Dallas, Texas 75222

Romper Room Toys, Hasbro Industries, Inc., Pawtucket, Rhode Island 02861

Scholastic Early Childhood Center, 904 Sylvan Avenue, Englewood Cliffs, New Jersey 07632

Scott Foresman and Co., 1900 E. Lake Avenue, Glenview, Illinois 60025

Scripture Press, Victor Books, 1825 College Avenue, Wheaton, Illinois 60187

Shindana Toys, Division of Operation Bootstrap, Inc., 6107 S. Central Avenue, Los Angeles, California 90001

Standard Publishing Co., 8121 Hamilton Avenue, Cincinnati, Ohio 45231

Trend Enterprises, P.O. Box 3073, St. Paul, Minnesota 55165

Uniworld Toys, P.O. Box 61, West Hempstead, New York 11552

Glossary

Accent — a distinctive, perhaps unique, manner of oral expression that is highly characteristic of an individual or a group possessing typical speech habits associated with a geographic region or location. The speaker with an accent may or may not be speaking standard English.

Acquisition — to gain possession by one's own endeavor (such as acquiring a skill) or by purchasing something (such as acquiring a piece of equipment).

Acuity — how well or clearly one uses senses — the degree of perceptual sharpness.

Articulation — the adjustments and movements of the muscles of the mouth and jaw involved in producing clear oral communication.

Assimilation — the process that allows new experiences to merge with previously stored mental structures.

Associative play — a type of social play in which children talk and play together, but each has his or her own goals.

Auditory — relating to or experienced through hearing.

Auditory discrimination — the act of perceiving different sounds, such as the differences of sounds within words.

Black English — a language usually spoken in some economically depressed black homes. A dialect of nonstandard English having its own rules and patterns.

Bonding — the formation of an affectionate attachment between caregiver and infant. An enduring love-play dialogue.

Categorize — to place items, events, ideas, and so forth, in the correct class, group, or division.

Classify — the act of systematically grouping things according to identifiable common characteristics; for example, size.

Cognitive behavior — thinking process behavior. Also, the act or process of knowing, including both awareness and judgement.

Cognitive structure — a system of organized and integrated perceptions.

Cognitive style — the way an individual conceptualizes or approaches tasks; a distinctive way of perceiving, feeling, and solving problems that is part of an individual's personality.

Communication — the giving (sending) and receiving of information, signals, or messages.

Concept — a commonly recognized element (or elements) that identifies groups or classes, usually has a given name.

Conceptual tempo — a term associated with Jerome Kagan's theory of different individual pacing in perceptual exploration of objects.

Configuration — the figure, shape, contour, or pattern produced by the relative arrangement of parts.

Convergent thinking — moving toward a single, acceptable, conventional solution to a problem.

Cooing — an early stage during the prelinguistic period in which vowel sounds are repeated, particularly the u-u-u sound.

Curriculum — an overall plan for the content of instruction to be offered in a program.

Decoding — the process by which the individual is able to translate written language forms into their oral counterparts. Strategies used in this process range from grapheme/phoneme relationships and letter-pattern/sound-pattern generalizations to structural analysis.

Deprivation — being kept from acquiring, using, or enjoying.

Dialect — a variety of spoken language unique to a geographical area or social group. Variations in dialect may include phonological or sound variations, syntactical variations, and lexical or vocabulary variations.

Directionality — the ability to understand right, left, up, down, north, south; directional orientation.

Discrimination; auditory — ability to detect differences in sounds.

Discrimination; visual — ability to detect differences in objects seen.

Divergent thinking — differing lines of thinking and possible searching for a new idea(s).

Dramatic play — acting out experiences or creating drama episodes during play.

Echolalia — a characteristic of the babbling period. The child repeats (echoes) the same sounds over and over.

English language — a structure of arbitrary systems relating sounds and meanings and the rules combining sounds and meanings to form sentences — in the language of the people of England, the U.S., and many areas that were or currently are under British control.

Expressive jargon — a term describing a child's first attempts at combining words into narration that results in a mimic of adult speech.

Equilibrium — a balance attained with consistent care and satisfaction of needs that leads to a sense of security and lessens anxiety.

Fluency — a ready flow of ideas, possibilities, consequences, and objects.

Gaze coupling — infant-mother extended eye contacts.

Grammar — the word order and knowledge of "marker" word meanings necessary to send communications to (and receive them from) another in the same language.

Handedness — preference for use of the right or left hand either in tasks requiring the use of one hand or in the coordination of hands.

Holophrases — the expression of a whole idea in a single word. They are characteristic of the child's language from about 12–18 months.

Identity — personal individuality. The collective aspect of a set of characteristics by which a person is recognized or known.

Impulsivity — a quick answer or reaction to either a simple or complex situation or problem.

Infer — draw a conclusion.

Inflections — the grammatical "markers" such as plurals. Also, a change in pitch or loudness of the voice.

Inner speech — mentioned in Vygotsky's theory as private speech that becomes internalized and is useful in organizing ideas.

Intonation — varying the tone, pitch, or inflection of the voice in speaking.

Intonational patterns — variations in voicing, such as in tone (loud or soft) and pitch, that help convey meaning.

Language — the means by which a person communicates ideas or feelings to another in such a way that the meaning is mutually understood.

Language-experience reading — an approach that uses the oral and written expressions of children as the medium of instruction, rather than teacher-made or commercially prepared materials.

Large motor skill — ability to make one's large muscles perform in a coordinated way.

Linguistics — the study of human speech in its various aspects.

Markers (language markers) — the two types in the English language are function words (such as a, an, the, with) and suffixes (such as -s, -ing). Markers often identify classes (such as nouns), specify relations, or signal meanings (such as -ing, an ongoing activity, or -s indicating plurality).

Moderation level — an individual preferred state of arousal between bored and excited when learning and pleasure peak.

Modifier — giving special characteristic to a noun (for example, a *large* ball).

Morpheme — the smallest unit in a language that by itself has a recognizable meaning.

Morphology — the study of the units of meaning in a language.

Neonate — newborn baby.

Nonstandard English — a dialect that deviates from standard English in pronunciation, vocabulary, or grammar.

Objectives — purposes to be realized through activities, sometimes stated in behaviors.

Otitis media — inflammation and/or infection of the middle ear.

Overregularization — the tendency on the part of children to make the language regular, such as using past tenses like -ed on verb endings.

Perception — mental awareness of objects and other data gathered through the five senses.

Phonation — exhaled air passes the larynx's vibrating folds and produces "voice."

Phoneme — one of the smallest units of speech that distinguishes one utterance from another.

Phonetic — pertaining to representing the sounds of speech with a set of distinct symbols, each denoting a single sound.

Phonology — the sound system of a language and how it is represented with an alphabetic code.

Rate — speed with which sounds, syllables, or words are spoken.

Reflection — taking time to weigh aspects or alternatives in a given situation.

Resonation — amplification of laryngeal sounds using cavities of the mouth, nose, sinuses, and pharynx.

Rhythm — uniform or patterned recurrence of a beat, accent, or melody in speech.

Semantics — the study of meanings, of how the sounds of language are related to the real world and our own experiences.

Sensory motor development — the control and use of sense organs and the body's muscle structure.

Signing — infant and toddler signals that include vocalizations, gestures, postures, or body actions, or combinations of these, communicating needs, wishes, and desires.

Small motor skill — ability to make one's small muscles perform in a coordinated way (such as holding a pencil and writing or playing the piano).

Standard English — substantially uniform formal and informal speech and writing of educated people that is widely recognized as acceptable wherever English is spoken and understood.

Stress — emphasis in the form of prominent loudness of a syllable, word, or between compound words and noncompound words and phrases.

Subculture — an ethnic, regional, economic, or social group exhibiting characteristic patterns of behavior sufficient to distinguish it from others within an embracing culture or society.

Syllable — a part word (or whole word) pronounced with a single uninterrupted sounding of the voice, usually blending vowel and consonant sounds.

Symbol — something standing for or suggesting (such as pictures, models, word symbols, and so forth).

Symbolization — using symbols to convey a message or meaning.

Syntax — the arrangement of words as elements in a sentence to show their relationship.

Tactile — perceptible to the sense of touch.

Telegraphic speech — a characteristic of early child sentences in which everything but the crucial word(s) is omitted, as if for a telegram.

Whole language — a philosophy and reading-instruction approach integrating oral and written language. Advocates believe that when children are given literature-abundant and print-rich environments they will follow their natural curiosity and learn to read as they learned to speak. A thematic focus is used. Teachers seize opportunities to connect and interrelate language arts areas.

Zone of proximal development — a theory attributed to Vygotsky (1978) that concludes that an area exists between what a child can solve on his or her own and what the same child can solve with adult help.

Answers to Review Questions

Unit 1 Beginnings of Communication

A. Answers will differ.

B. Be responsive and attentive to each infant.
Be sensitive, alert and loving.
Read infant's nonverbal and vocalized cues.
Be physically warm; touching and holding often.
Note individualness.
Hold firmly yet gently.
Interact playfully.
Imitate child sound.
Talk to infants about what's happening to them.
Speak clearly.
Engage in word play.
Plan first-hand experiences.

C. Phonation. Exhaled air that passes the larynx and produces voice.
Resonation. The amplification of sounds by the mouth area.
Echolalia. A characteristic of the babbling period when the child repeats or echoes.
Bonding. The formation of an attachment or affectionate bond, especially in the period immediately following birth. A combination of love and play. A wordless dialogue.
Moderation level. An individual preferred state of arousal when new information is easily absorbed, between too excited or overly bored.
Infant signing. Infant signals that include vocalizations, gestures, postures, or body actions (or combinations of these), communicating needs, wishes, or desires.
Babbling. The infants preverbal vocalizations.
Articulation. The adjustments and movements of the mouth and jaw involved in producing clear oral communication. A modification of the breath stream.
Larynx. The upper part of the respiratory tract containing the vocal cords.

D. Understand the reciprocal nature of adult-infant conversations and are responsive, attentive, and at times playful.

E. 1. Heredity and environment.
2. By satisfying infant needs consistently, responding to infant's nonverbal and verbal messages, providing learning opportunities, respecting infant individuality, providing pleasurable social interaction, showing love and attention, and providing speech for the child to hear.
3. Possible speech mechanism exercise or self-entertainment, although the purpose of babbling is not clearly understood.
4. Language requires mutual understanding and infers a reciprocal circumstance for at least two individuals.

5. Ears, eyes, skin surfaces, mouth, and throat area.

6. Perceptions.

F . 1. b   2. c   3. b.   4. a   5. c

G . Communication is defined as sending and receiving information, signals, or messages. Language is defined as communicating ideas, feelings, and so forth, in such a way that the meaning is mutually understood.

H . 1. k   4. c   6. e   8. j   10. l   12. d
    2. a   5. h   7. i   9. b   11. m   13. f
    3. g

Unit 2 The Tasks of the Toddler

A . 1. f   2. e   3. c   4. b   5. a   6. d   7. g

B . Answers will differ.

C . Van — four wheels, larger than a car, double doors in side or rear, boxlike look, uses gasoline
    Rain — drops of water from the sky, outdoors, makes noise on glass, roof, or umbrella, darkened sky, feels wet
    Needle — thin, sharp, used with thread, used in sewing, pointed
    Giraffe — four legs, spots, long neck, eats leaves, found in zoos

D . Answers will differ.

E . Period of fastest language growth; child starts using sentences he or she creates; vocabulary increases dramatically; time of active language sending; child has tremendous learning capacity

F . See Glossary in text, or refer to a dictionary.

G . 1. a   2. c   3. c   4. c   5. d

H . Supplying words; tying words to sensory experiences; being active listeners; answering child speech in a positive way; being accepting of child's ability; being warm, responsive companions

Unit 3 Preschool Years

A . *Younger Preschoolers (age 2–3)*
    telegram sentences
    repetitions
    substitutions
    omissions of letter sounds
    nonverbal communication
    talking about what one is doing
    stuttering
    talking through an adult

Older Preschoolers (age 4–5)
    75% perfect articulation
    "Look, I'm jumping."
    name-calling
    adultlike speech
    2,000- to 2,500-word vocabulary
    role-playing
    planning play with others
    rhyming and nonsense words
    bathroom words
    arguing

B . 1. a, c   3. b, c, d   5. a, b, c   7. a, b, c   9. b   11. a, b
    2. a, b, d   4. a, b, c   6. a, b, d   8. a, b, c, d   10. a, b, c, d   12. a, c, d

Unit 4 Growth Systems Affecting Early Language Ability

A. See unit material for definition.

B. See unit material.

C.
1. b	4. b	7. c	10. a or b	13. a
2. c	5. b	8. b	11. b	14. b
3. a	6. c	9. a	12. c	15. c

D. 1, 3, 4, 5, 6, 7, 9

E. Vision is in the 20/45–20/30 range, and hearing is essentially mature at ages 4 and 5.

F. It's important for a teacher to respect and understand individual differences.

G. 1. a   2. c   3. d   4. a   5. d   6. c

Unit 5 Achieving Language and Literacy Goals Through Programming

A. Listening, speaking, writing, and reading

B. Answers will differ.

C. Answers will differ.

D.
1. a, b, d	3. a, b, d	5. a, b, c, d	7. b, c, d	9. c
2. b, c, d	4. a, b, c, d	6. a, d	8. b, d	10. a, b, c, d

Unit 6 Promoting Language and Literacy

A. Modeling speech behavior and attitudes; providing opportunities for language growth; interacting with the children

B.
Models	*Provides*	*Interacts*
speech	opportunities	focusing attention
intonation	activities	asking questions
pitch	equipment	motivating
articulation	materials	planning repetitions
attitudes	words	giving feedback
actions	information	reinforcing
grammar	the necessity to speak	taking advantage of unplanned events
sentence patterns	group situations	listening
standard English	listening	wonders out loud
courtesy words	an accepting classroom atmosphere	notices children's interest
listening	physical contact	affirms children's statements
pronunciation	variety	links new learnings to old
enthusiasm		daily personal conversation
care and concern		
problem solving		
curiosity		

C. *Appropriate*
attempts to focus attention on the activity
use of "please"
full sentences
clear, concise speech
use of standard English

Inappropriate
negative reinforcement of child's desire to speak
denies child's perceptions
not answering
not listening
fails to ask clarifying questions
fails to supply words
doesn't pursue conversation about child's interest
makes speaking a task instead of a pleasure
omits any positive reinforcement of child's speaking

D. The child's developmental level and individual needs

E. 1. a, b   2. a, e   3. a, b, c, d   4. a, b, d   5. a, c   6. a, b, c

F. Realize he/she has room for improvement, but may possess insights into attending children's culture and language usage.

F. Answers will differ.

G. *First Mother:*   Explains in specific terms; encourages child in task.
Second Mother: Tells child in general terms in commanding way; criteria for classifying by color is not verbalized.

H. Adult adds words but does not increase the child's interest or discovery.

Unit 7 *Developing Listening Skills*

A. 1. creative listening   3. appreciative listening   5. purposeful listening
2. critical listening   4. discriminative listening

B. Sustain attention span
Follow directions or commands
Listening to details
Identify and associate sounds
Discriminate by tempo, pitch, or intensity between sounds
Use auditory memory

C. 1. b, d   2. b, c   3. a, b, c, d   4. a, b   5. a, b, c

D. Intensity. An extreme degree of strength, force, or energy.
Pitch. The highness or lowness of sound.
Tempo. The rate of speed.

E. Answers will differ.

Unit 8 *Listening Activities*

A. Answers will differ.

B. Using a sound signal or visual signal.

Unit 9 Children and Books

A. 2, 3, 12, 15, 16

B. 1. It may be inappropriate for young children. A teacher should be familiar with the content, so that the book can be presented enthusiastically. The teacher is better prepared for discussions that promote goals.
   2. Model this behavior with statements and actions.
   3. The teacher can make the experience successful in relation to reading goals and assessing children's interest.

C. 1. e   3. a   5. c   7. f   9. j   11. l
   2. g   4. b   6. d   8. h   10. i   12. k

D. Answers will differ.

E. 1. b, c, d   2. a, b, c, d, e   3. none   4. b, d   5. c, e

Unit 10 Story Telling

A. 1. f   2. c   3. a   4. b   5. e   6. d

B. 1. It involves close personal contact between teachers and children while using language.
      It promotes children's story telling.
      Teachers model speech usage and gestures.
      It is one way teachers can share their own experiences and attitudes with children.
      Children can create their own mental pictures as stories are told.
      School or life problems can be dealt with in story-telling experiences.
      New vocabulary can be introduced.
      Listening is promoted.
      It establishes enjoyment and familiarity with oral literature.
      It enables children to form initial ideas concerning story structure.
      It is a vehicle for children's creativity.
   2. Books, children's magazines, movies, other teachers, stories created by the teachers
   3. They present one generalized type when many varieties exist. Example: People with glasses are studious and shy.

C. 1. a, b, c, d   2. a, d   3. b, c   4. b, d   5. a, b, c, d

D. Answers should include acceptance, showing appreciation and interest, taking dictation of story if the child wishes, promoting the child's telling his or her story to others, discussion of enjoyed parts, extending his or her interest in creating stories, suggesting child records his or her creation, providing additional story-telling experiences.

Unit 11 Poetry

A. 1. Poetry promotes literacy and language development.
   2. Children enjoy poetry's rhythm, fast action, and imaginative aspects.
   3. Children can learn new words and concepts.
   4. It is easy to learn and remember for many children; therefore, it builds children's self-confidence.
   5. It is a language arts form that promotes children's speaking.
   6. Many poems add humor to the language arts program.
   7. Poems are an important part of young children's literary heritage.

B . 1. j   4. f   7. g   10. k   13. o
     2. e   5. d   8. i   11. m   14. a
     3. c   6. b   9. h   12. n   15. l

C . 5, 6, 7, 8, 10

D . rhyme, sound, stress, accented and unaccented syllables, format, visual images, figurative language, cadence, subject matter.

Unit 12 Flannel Boards and Activity Sets

A . Wood, heavy cardboard, composition board, foam for base, flannel, felt, tape, glue, tacks, staplers, paddings, metallic inserts for base covering.

B . Pellon, felt, flannel, paper with any backing that sticks (such as sandpaper or fuzzy velour paper)

C . Answers will differ.

D . Focuses attention; adds a visual representation for words used during activities

E . 3, 4, 2, 5, 7, 6, 10, 1, 8, 9

F . Answers will differ.

G . 1. Pieces stick better on board
     2. It is good for storage, carrying, changing locations
     3. "This is a teacher's set. We'll find a set for you in the language center right after story time."
     4. They stick better when flat
     5. Weight, low cost, can be used with pins
     6. It is breakable

Unit 13 Realizing Speaking Goals

A . 1. Activities that teachers have planned and prepared during which they actively lead and direct the participation
     2. Words that show ownership
     3. Words implying a denial or refusal; saying "no"
     4. A relational word that connects a noun, pronoun, or noun phrase to another part of a sentence (such as: in, by, for, with, to)
     5. A word that compares one thing with something else, or examines in order to observe or discover similarities or differences (examples: more, less, equal, big, bigger, biggest)

B . 1. Planned activities, daily staff-child interaction, use of equipment and materials
     2. Be interested and focus attention on details.
     3. Children's eye level

C . 1. c   2. a, b, c, d   3. a, c   4. a, d   5. c

D . 1. Plan many activities where children have speaking successes.
     2. Listen and respond to their speaking.
     3. Appreciate their communication efforts.
     4. Reward their speaking with smiles and answers.
     5. Do not make verbal comparisons of children's speaking abilities.

E . 1. e   2. d   3. a   4. b   5. c   6. f

F . 1. divergent   3. recall   5. recall   7. divergent or convergent
     2. convergent   4. evaluative   6. divergent or convergent   8. convergent

Unit 14 Speech in Play and Routines

A . Child's play in which children act out past experiences and creatively improvise new ones

B . 1, 2, 3, 5, 6, 8, 9, 11, 12, 13, 14

C . 1. A collection of items, clothing, or other props that would stimulate children's activity and play; centered around one theme such as fire fighter, nurse, and so forth
    2. Children feel pressured to speak; children become restless and bored

D . 2, 3, 4, 5, 9

E . Answers will differ.

F . Bonnie, you didn't say it. You were playing with your hair ribbon.
Say it now, Bonnie.
Speak louder, Susie, we can't hear you.
Not "I'm present," Brett. Say "I'm here, Mrs. Brown."
David, you must answer when I call your name!
No, Andy, say "I'm here Mrs. Brown" not "I'm here" and that's all.
I don't know what's the matter with all of you; you did it right yesterday.
We're going to stay here until we all do it right.
I can't understand what you said, Dana; say it again.
No, it's not time to talk to Ronnie now; it's time to speak up.
I give up, you'll never learn.

The teacher's manner and attitude seem focused on her own importance and authoritarian control. Children's speech development and self-concept are probably low or absent teacher priorities.

Unit 15 Group Times

A . 1. It allows for a smooth dispersal
    2. Building group spirit and identity; teaching customs and values
    3. Active, enthusiastic, prepared, accepting, appropriate, clearly stated concepts, familiar, novel, relaxed, sharing

B . Children learn finger plays easily, and the plays involve body motion. The children experience "groupness" and a sense of belonging. They can exhibit a learned skill to others. Once learned, they produce a feeling of security and competency. Children enjoy rhyming and word play.

C . 3, 2, 6, 5, 8, 4, 1, 7

D . Bell, flicking light switch, finger play, short song, teacher statement

E . Actively participate, encourage, and monitor child attention; move closer to a child when the child is distracted

F . 1. G   3. G   5. P   7. P   9. P
    2. P   4. G   6. P   8. P   10. G

Unit 16 *Puppetry and Beginning Drama Experiences*

A. Puppets increase speech usage, help children coordinate speech and actions, build vocabulary, and build audience skill. A puppet is a useful teacher technique for holding and focusing attention, helping children develop auditory memory skills, promoting creative imagination.

B. 1. –   2. +   3. +   4. +   5. –

C. 1. a   2. c   3. b   4. e   5. c   6. a

Unit 17 *Understanding Differences*

A. 1. A teacher can learn about the cultural background of the child by visiting the home and observing the neighborhoods and communities in which the particular children reside. Parents are valuable resources in giving teachers more insights into understanding the lives and customs of the home.
   2. The teacher accepts and values them as individuals just as they are, not "as they could be."

B. 1. The teacher did not continue the conversation with a comment that would motivate or stimulate the child's speaking further in greater detail.
   2. The teacher was admonishing and making a moral evaluation of the child's behavior. A better answer could have been "It hurts when someone hits us. Ask Johnny for a turn with the truck when you want to play with it."
   3. The teacher has already received three verbal responses from the child without rewarding his request. The child simply gives up, and does not want to play a verbal game where he must ask for things in exactly the right way.
   4. The teacher could have shown interest and discussed with the child where the bug was found, how it was caught, the bug's color or other distinguishing characteristics, with questions that would have promoted the child's putting his or her ideas into words.
   5. In this case, the child is speaking words, not sentences. To define "fellow" is probably offering too much. A better response would have been "Here's the yellow one, Lindy," for the child's words were spoken as a question.

C. Refer to text glossary or dictionary.

D. 1. "You are playing with the ball. Throw the ball up like this." (Demonstrate)
   2. "Oh, you went to get the crayon. What are you going to do with it?"
   3. "Does it have a name?"
   4. "I like chicken soup, too. Do you like the chicken pieces or the noodles best?"
   5. "That's right, we don't run into the street. We walk after looking both ways for cars."
   6. "If you don't want to play with them, what are you going to choose to play with in our playroom?"

E. 1. a, b, c   2. b, c, d   3. a, b, c, d   4. b, c, d   5. b, c, d   6. a, b, c, d

Unit 18 *Print — Early Knowledge and Emerging Interest*

A. 1. b, d   2. a, b, c   3. b   4. a, b, c, d

B. 1. b, a, c   2. b, c, a   3. b, c, a   4. b, a, c   5. a, b, c

C. 1. They have had access to writing tools. They have seen others writing. Parents have shown interest in alphabet letters or numbers. They have had experiences with picture books.
   2. Crayons; small manipulative toys; chalk; puzzles; string beads; any toy that involves small finger, hand, or arm muscle use

3. It is correct for their geographical area, large enough for young children to see, written in a left-to-right fashion, a good model for children.
4. Children do not come to school with the same home experiences or with the same maturity or interests as other children.
5. Other factors include a child's interest, motivation, mental readiness, and past experiences with symbols.
6. Say, "Yes, that is the alphabet letter named *m.*"
7. Wait for the child's lead and plan a stimulating environment with lots of interesting things to do.
8. Say, "It's an alphabet letter just like *f* but it's called a *b.*" Plan interesting activities that name *b* and involve tracing the outline of the letter.

Unit 19 Developing Print Awareness and Skill

A. 1. Recognize the child's effort with positive comments.
  2. Use the situation to direct them to a printed alphabet in the room where, with the teacher's help, the argument could be settled and become a learning situation for both.
  3. During roll taking; labeling possessions or objects; making signs that fit into children's play situations; writing children's names on artwork; preparing bulletin boards or charts

B. In accordance with local printscript of elementary schools

C. 1. Printed Bob's name in correct form
  2. Printed Chris's name over his shoulder
  3. Asked Chris's permission to write his name on his paper
  4. Answered Bob with more interest, positive reinforcement, and enthusiasm
  5. Answered Sue; printed her name and encouraged her to trace and then write it for herself

D. 1. c, d   2. b, d   3. a, c

E. Student prints name and address in printscript

F. 1. The teacher has noticed the child's interest in printing and alphabet letters.
  2. The teacher would like the parent to have a copy of the forms the child should learn. (The printscript alphabet obtained from a local elementary school.)
  3. Children's early attempts are often upside down or backward, but this is nothing to worry about.
  4. Whether the child writes or not at this age is not very important; a child's interests change.
  5. The preschool will supply activities and materials in the area of printing as long as the child has continued interest in these activities.

G. Answers will differ.

Unit 20 Activities with Printscript

A. Circles, squares, triangles, rectangles, stars, dots, moon shapes, or any other commonly recognized shapes, geometric or other

B. It helps each child know the limits of his or her drawing area.

C. Answers will differ.

D. Answers will differ.

E. Answers will differ.

Unit 21 *Reading and Preschoolers*

A. 1. The teacher should listen approvingly whether the child is really reading or has just memorized the story, or is retelling the story in his or her own words. A positive comment by the teacher is helpful, such as "Thank you for sharing your favorite book with me."
   2. Since the child has demonstrated both his or her ability and interest, the teacher should plan activities to expand the child's beginning skill.
   3. Teachers suggest that the family provide for the child's interest by borrowing library books and spending time with the child in reading activities. It is helpful for parents to know that supplying words when the child asks and offering to read words found naturally in home environments will increase the child's beginning attempts.

B. Make every effort to interrelate or combine activities, stressing how they fit together in the communication process.

C. Reading. To understand the meaning of a symbol or group of symbols by interpreting its characters or signs; to utter or repeat aloud words of written or printed material.
   Readiness. A state that allows one to proceed without hesitation, delay, or difficulty.
   Method. A regular, orderly, definite procedure or way of teaching.
   Phonics. The use of elementary speech sounds in teaching beginners to read.
   Configuration. Outline or shape of a word.
   Incongruities. Lack of fitness or appropriateness; not corresponding to what is right, proper, or reasonable.

D. 1. b   2. c   3. d   4. a   5. c

E. Answers will differ.

Unit 22 *Language-Development Materials*

A. Advantages
   1. Supplies and equipment are centrally located.
   2. Inviting language arts activities promote center use.
   3. There are spaces for individual exploration.
   4. There is comfortable seating.
   5. Like materials are grouped and accessible.
   6. Resources, such as alphabet strips or charts, can be immediately available.

   Disadvantages
   1. The space used may not serve other play and learning activities.
   2. Supervision of audiovisuals may require additional staff.

B. 1. supervising children's activity
   2. maintaining supplies and equipment
   3. periodic changing of display areas
   4. providing new activities and materials
   5. taking child dictation
   6. listening to child conversation
   7. serving as a resource in finding or securing materials

C. Students draw their own ideas of a language arts crawl-into area

D. Computer, printer, filmstrip projector, tape recorder, television set, video cassette recorder, record player, Language Master, super 8 and 16mm film projector, opaque projector, slide projector.

Unit 23 Classroom Language Arts Centers

A. 1. Almost all real objects (with the exception of those that are dangerous or too large to explore) can be used to promote firsthand exploration and language development. Pictures and drawings are also useful.
   2. Most programs use visuals and materials that are both commercially manufactured and teacher made. By continually reviewing new materials, programs improve and remain interesting to the children.
   3. Sturdiness, teaching goals, children's individual or group interests, the maturity level of the group or child using them
   4. Periodic checking of materials, repairing worn parts or replacing them is part of the teacher's responsibility. Creating and constructing materials for individual and group interests is another.

B. 1. h   3. b   5. d   7. a   9. j
   2. f   4. c   6. e   8. g   10. i

C. There are many possible answers. These are a few.

Positive	Negative
Most have sequentially planned experiences.	A set or kit could become the total language arts program.
Activities are included with teacher instructions.	Set or kit goals could differ from a particular program's goals.
Most have been designed by experts in language development.	The set or kit may not take into consideration the needs of individual children.
Kits and sets include commercially made visuals and teaching materials	Some commercial materials may not hold up under heavy use.

D. 1. b   2. e   3. d   4. c   5. d   6. a

E. Answers will differ.

Unit 24 The Parent–Center Partnership

A. Paragraph could include:

- Parent understanding of school's language- and literacy-developing program and materials.
- Parental input through discussion of school's goals.
- Parents as staff and program resources.
- Parent awareness of school activities that can be reinforced by home activities and discussions.
- Parents as fund-raisers and providers of materials.
- Centers as sources of information concerning child communication and local community happenings and resources.
- Teacher-parent discussions that build home-school partnership bonds.
- Individual conferencing.

B. Answers will differ.

C. Working together, parents and teachers can aid language and emerging literacy through joint recognition of developmentally appropriate activities and experiences.

Index